thomson.com

changing the way the world learns℠

To get extra value from this book for no additional cost, go to:

http://www.thomson.com/wadsworth.html

thomson.com is the World Wide Web site for Wadsworth/ITP
and is your direct source to dozens of on-line resources.
thomson.com helps you find out about supplements,
experiment with demonstration software, search for a job,
and send e-mail to many of our authors. You can even
preview new publications and exciting new technologies.

thomson.com: *It's where you'll find us in the future.*

ETHICS

Theory and Contemporary Issues

Second Edition

Barbara MacKinnon

The University of San Francisco

Wadsworth Publishing Company
I(T)P® **An International Thomson Publishing Company**

Belmont • Albany • Bonn • Boston • Cincinnati • Detroit • Johannesburg • London • Madrid • Melbourne
Mexico City • New York • Paris • San Francisco • Singapore • Tokyo • Toronto • Washington

Philosophy Editor: Peter Adams
Assistant Editors: Clay Glad and Kerri Abdinoor
Editorial Assistants: Greg Brueck and Kelly Bush
Marketing Manager: Dave Garrison
Production, Composition, & Illustration: Summerlight Creative
Copy Editing: S.M. Summerlight
Print Buyer: Stacey Weinberger
Permissions Editor: Robert Kauser
Text and Cover Designer: Harry Voigt
Printer: Maple-Vail, Binghampton, New York
Cover Art: Klee, Paul. *Castle and Sun*. 1928. Private Collection, London, Great Britain. Giraudon/Art Resource, NY.

Printed in the United States of America
3 4 5 6 7 8 9 10

For more information, contact Wadsworth Publishing Company, 10 Davis Drive, Belmont, CA 94002, or electronically at
http://www.thomson.com/wadsworth.html

International Thomson Publishing Europe
Berkshire House 168-173
High Holborn
London, WC1V 7AA, England

International Thomson Editores
Campos Eliseos 385, Piso 7
Col. Polanco
11560 México D.F. México

Thomas Nelson Australia
102 Dodds Street
South Melbourne 3205
Victoria, Australia

International Thomson Publishing Asia
221 Henderson Road
#05-10 Henderson Building
Singapore 0315

Nelson Canada
1120 Birchmount Road
Scarborough, Ontario
Canada M1K 5G4

International Thomson Publishing Japan
Hirakawacho Kyowa Building, 3F
2-2-1 Hirakawacho
Chiyoda-ku, Tokyo 102, Japan

International Thomson Publishing GmbH
Königswinterer Strasse 418
53227 Bonn, Germany

International Thomson Publishing Southern Africa
Building 18, Constantia Park
240 Old Pretoria Road
Halfway House, 1685 South Africa

Library of Congress Cataloging-in-Publication Data
MacKinnon, Barbara
    Ethics : theory and contemporary issues / Barbara MacKinnon. —
2nd ed.
      p.   cm.
    Includes bibliographical references and index.
    ISBN 0-534-52504-0 (alk. paper)
    1. Ethics. 2. Ethics, Modern—20th century. I. Title.
BJ1012.M3281997
170—dc21   97-12685

This book is printed on acid-free recycled paper.

For Edward,
Jennifer,
and Kathleen

Brief Contents

Contents

READINGS

Appendix

How to Write an Ethics Paper   457

Preface

This second edition of *Ethics: Theory and Contemporary Issues* retains the basic elements of the first edition, but also makes significant changes. It retains the basic two-part structure of both ethical theory in Part I and contemporary practical issues in Part II. It also continues the combination of text and readings. In this it not only remains a comprehensive introduction to ethics, but also continues to emphasize pedagogy with examples that interest students and various study guides that help them.

Although these elements remain basically the same, this edition also makes the following additions and changes:

- A new chapter on feminist thought and the ethics of care.

- A new chapter on ethical issues in science and technology.

- Separate chapters on environmental ethics and animal rights.

- New readings by Locke and Hobbes in the theory section.

- Reorganization of the chapter on naturalistic ethical theories, including Aristotelian virtue ethics, natural law theory, and natural rights.

- A variety of new readings in the contemporary issues section; these address the issues of feminist ethics, multiculturalism, sexual morality, deep ecology, computer ethics, and military intervention.

- Updated empirical data and news items in the introductions to the contemporary issues chapters.

Many of these and other changes throughout the text, both in content and readings, have been suggested by the reviewers for this new edition. The idea for a new chapter on ethical issues in science and technology was the idea of philosophy editor Peter Adams. I am very grateful for all of these suggestions. Other revisions have come from my own continuing use of the text, and from both the student response and my own rethinking. The focus of the changes has been primarily on content. The pedagogical aids listed here remain basically the same, except for the question sections titled "For Further Thought," which have been moved from the end of each chapter to the instructor's manual. The following are again key elements of this edition.

Text
Each chapter in both the theory and issues parts of the text contains an extended introduction. These are somewhat more detailed than what is usually found in a reader.

The theory chapters present moderately detailed summaries of the theories and major issues, positions, and arguments. The contemporary issues chapters present several different things, including overviews or summaries of:

- the social situation and recent events that will interest the student in the topic;
- conceptual issues such as how to define pornography or legal punishment; and
- arguments and suggested ways to organize ethical thoughts on the particular topic.

The presentations often ask questions of the reader. These are usually followed by answers that might be or have been given. The aim is to present a neutral or unbiased overview that allows students to decide for themselves what position they will take and which allows instructors to put whatever emphases they wish on the material.

Where possible, the relation of ethical theory to the practical issues is indicated. For example, one pervasive distinction used throughout is that between consequentialist and nonconsequentialist considerations and arguments. The idea is that if students are able to situate or categorize a kind of reason or argument, then they will be better able to evaluate it critically.

Pedagogical Aids

This text is designed to be "user-friendly." To aid both instructor and student, the following pedagogical aids are provided.

- clear organization of material in the textual sections by means of diagrams, subheadings, definitions, and word emphases;
- a real-life event or hypothetical dialogue at the beginning of each chapter to capture students' interest;
- study guide questions for each reading selection;
- review exercises at the end of each chapter that can actually be used as test or exam questions;
- opportunities for class or group discussions in the discussion cases that follow each chapter;
- topics and resources for written assignments in the discussion cases and the selected bibliography at the end of each chapter; and

- the appendix on how to write an ethics paper, which gives students who need it helpful advice and some sample examples of ethics papers.

An instructor's manual is available from the publisher on request. For each chapter it includes:

- suggestions for how to introduce the chapter;
- a list of key words;
- answers to the review exercises;
- questions to stimulate further thought; and further test questions and answers.

Feminist Concerns

Although this is primarily a general ethics text, it does make an extra attempt to include writings of female authors in the reading selections for each chapter as well as in the bibliographies. Moreover, in addition to the new chapter on feminist ethics, feminist issues are also treated throughout the text. These include questions of sex equality and sexual harassment, abortion, pornography, ecofeminism, and gender discrimination in Third World development programs.

Global Ethical Issues

The last chapter is particularly significant. Although it covers a wide range of topics, it is meant primarily to direct students to consider the ways in which ethics also applies in this broader context. Thus, issues of development, the rich and the poor, environmental problems, terrorism, and war and peace are the primary topics treated here. The new edition also includes more examples of contemporary international problems such as religious fundamentalism, uprisings, proliferation of nuclear weapons, and civil strife.

In Summary

Ethics: Theory and Contemporary Issues continues to be the most comprehensive ethics text available. It combines theory and issues, text, and readings.

It is flexible in that instructors can emphasize the theory or issues or the textual material or readings as they choose.

It is user-friendly while at the same time philosophically accurate. This book is not "pop ethics." You cannot do that and at the same time be philosophically accurate and adequate. On the other hand, it uses many pedagogical aids both throughout and at the end of chapters. This text often provides examples and up-to-date newsworthy events. I ask stimulating questions throughout the textual presentations. I give diagrams wherever I think that it will help. I provide helpful headings.

It is current not only on the day-to-day developments in the news and in scientific data, but also on the issues as they are discussed by philosophers.

It is pedagogically helpful, including a number of teaching aids. These amplify its teachability.

It has a balanced collection of readings, from both the three ethical theories included and contemporary sources on the issues.

Acknowledgments

I wish to thank the many reviewers of this text: Susan Armstrong, Humboldt State University; Samantha Brennan, University of Western Ontario; Wendy Lee-Lampshire, Bloomsburg University of Pennsylvania; Andrew McLaughlin, City University of New York; and Anita Superson, University of Kentucky. I also wish to thank my colleague at the University of San Francisco, Eduardo Mendieta, for his helpful comments and suggestions.

I wish also to thank the many professional people from Wadsworth Publishing Company who have contributed greatly to this book, especially Peter Adams, philosophy editor, and Steven Summerlight of Summerlight Creative.

Finally, I greatly appreciate the support given me by my husband and fellow philosopher, Edward MacKinnon. To him and to our two wonderful daughters, Jennifer and Kathleen, this edition is dedicated.

Barbara MacKinnon
University of San Francisco

Part I

Ethical Theory

❧ 1 ❧

Ethics and Ethical Reasoning

Why Study Ethics?

A few years ago, the *New York Times* reported on the morally controversial case of James McElveen.[1] In July 1990 he fell from a thirty-foot cliff while on an outing with friends in Tennessee. He was unconscious and bleeding heavily as his friends drove him forty-three miles to the nearest hospital. One of them, Benny Milligan, knew that James needed to go to the emergency room but had no insurance. However, he had read about cases in which uninsured emergency room patients in his state were reportedly not given the best care. He thus was worried whether his friend would receive adequate treatment. In a panic Mr. Milligan checked his friend into the hospital with his own medical insurance card. Mr. McElveen received not only excellent emergency aid, but also first-class ongoing treatment. His total bill of more than $41,000 was sent to the federal government because Mr. Milligan's medical insurance coverage was from a government space-shuttle project on which he had been working. In September 1992 the deception was discovered, and both Mr. Milligan and Mr. McElveen were convicted of fraud and conspiracy to defraud the government. They were ordered to repay the $41,000 and were given prison terms. There was no question that they had lied. However, they argued that the health care system was unfair and that they had feared for Mr. McElveen's life. Was their action justified?

Most of us usually condemn dishonesty. But was it wrong in this case? On the one hand, we tend to agree that some behaviors and attitudes are simply wrong. We criticize the lack of standards of honesty in public campaigning, for example. We condemn excessive greed by the financially powerful. We abhor vicious street crime and its wanton disregard for human life. And many of us bemoan the general lack of concern for the plight of the homeless and the disadvantaged. The fact that such behaviors and attitudes exist, we say, does not make them right.

On the other hand, we disagree about many moral issues. Is the death penalty a barbarous and inhumane practice or just recompense? Is abortion unjustified killing or—at least sometimes—a morally permissible choice? Is lying always wrong or is it sometimes justifiable?—the question raised by the case of Mr. Milligan. Even sincere people who try to decide what is right in such matters have difficulty doing so.

Moreover, we often face difficult choices of a more personal type. Financially strapped students agonize over whether to take a heavier schedule of classes, knowing that the overload will prevent them from doing their best work.

Parents worry about whether they are being too strict or too lenient with their children. Employees wonder whether they should inform supervisors of another worker's drug problems. We may wonder whether these are actually moral problems, but they are: Because they are choices about what is good and bad, or better and worse, or even right and wrong.

How do we know what is the right or better thing to do? An in-depth study of matters of good and bad, and right and wrong, should be of some help.

What Is Ethics?

I once asked students on the first day of an ethics class to write one-paragraph answers to each of two questions: "What is ethics?" and "Can it be taught?" How would you answer? There were significant differences of opinion among these students on both issues. Ethics is a very personal thing, some wrote, a set of moral beliefs that develop over the years. Although the values may initially come from one's family upbringing, they later result from one's own choices. Others thought that ethics is a set of social principles, the codes of one's society or particular groups within it, such as medical or legal organizations. One student wrote that many people get their ethical beliefs from their religion.

On the question of whether ethics can be taught, the students again gave a variety of answers. "If it can't be taught, why are we taking this class?" one person wondered. "Look at public immorality; these people haven't been taught properly," another commented. Still another disagreed. Although certain ideas or types of knowledge can be taught, ethical behavior cannot—it is a matter of individual choice.

One general conclusion can be drawn from these students' comments: We tend to think of ethics as the set of values or principles held by individuals or groups. I have my ethics and you have yours, and groups also have sets of values with which they tend to identify. We can think of ethics as a study of the various sets of values

that people do have. This could be done historically and comparatively, for example, or with a psychological interest in determining how people form their values and when they tend to act on them. We can also think of ethics as a critical enterprise. We would then ask whether any particular set of values or beliefs is better than any other. Are there good reasons for holding them? Ethics, as we will pursue it in this text, is this latter type of study. We will examine various ethical views and types of reasoning from a critical or evaluative standpoint. This examination will also help us come to a better understanding of our own and our society's values.

Ethics is a branch of *philosophy*. It is also called *moral philosophy*. Although not everyone agrees on what philosophy is, let's think of it as a discipline or study in which we ask (and attempt to answer) basic questions about key areas or subject matters of human life and about pervasive and significant aspects of experience. Some philosophers, such as Plato and Kant, have tried to do this systematically by interrelating their philosophical views in many areas. According to Alfred North Whitehead, "Philosophy is the endeavor to frame a coherent, logical, necessary system of general ideas in terms of which every element of our experience can be interpreted."[2] Others believe that philosophers today must work at problems piecemeal, focusing on one particular issue at a time. For instance, some might analyze the meaning of the phrase "to know," while others might work on the morality of lying. Furthermore, some philosophers are optimistic about our ability to answer these questions, while others are more skeptical because they think that the way we analyze the issues and the conclusions we draw will always be colored by our background, culture, and ways of thinking. Most agree, however, that the questions are worth wondering and caring about.

We can ask philosophical questions about many subjects. In aesthetics, or the philosophy of art, philosophers ask questions not about how to interpret a certain novel or painting, but about basic or foundational questions such as, What kinds of things do or should count as art (rocks arranged in a certain way, for example)? Is what makes something an object of aesthetic interest its emotional expressiveness, or its peculiar formal nature, or its ability to show us certain truths that cannot be described? In philosophy of science, philosophers ask not about the structure or composition of some chemical or biological material, but about such matters as whether scientific knowledge gives us a picture of reality as it is, whether progress exists in science, and the nature of the scientific method. Philosophers of law seek to understand the nature of law itself, the source of its authority, the nature of legal interpretation, and the basis of legal responsibility. In the philosophy of knowledge, called epistemology, we try to answer questions about what we can know of ourselves and our world and what it even is to know something rather than just believe it. In each area, philosophers ask basic questions about the particular subject matter. This is also true of moral philosophy.

Ethics, or moral philosophy, asks basic questions about the good life, about what is better and worse, about whether there is any objective right and wrong, and how we know it if there is.

This definition of ethics assumes that its primary objective is to help us decide what is good or bad, better or worse, either in some general way or regarding particular ethical issues. This is generally called *normative ethics*. Ethics, however, can be done in another way. From the mid-1930s until recently, this type of ethics predominated in English-speaking universities. It is called *metaethics*. In doing metaethics we would analyze the meaning of ethical language. Instead of asking whether the death penalty is morally justified, we would ask what we meant in calling something "morally justified" or "good" or "right." We would analyze ethical language, ethical terms, and ethical statements to determine what they mean. In doing this we would be functioning at a level removed from that implied by our definition. It is for this

reason that this other type of ethics is called metaethics, *meta* meaning "beyond." Some of the discussions in this chapter are metaethical discussions—for example, the analysis of various senses of "good." As you can see, much can be learned from such discussions. The various chapters of Part II of this text do normative ethics, for they are concerned with particular concrete issues and how to evaluate or judge them.

Ethics and Reasons

Ethics does ask the most general questions about the nature of the good life. But it also aims to help us determine what is the right or better thing to do in particular situations. Thus, it should help us determine whether Mr. Milligan was justified in lying in order to get medical help for his friend. If I said that it was wrong for him to lie, then I would be expected to give *reasons* for this position. I may argue that the ability to trust other peoples' word is so important for our social life that people ought to always tell the truth even if it means that we cannot do the good that we might otherwise be able to do. Alternatively, I might *reason* that although honesty is desirable, in this case my friend's life would take precedence. I could be challenged on my conclusion, and then I would have to give further reasons. In another example, suppose I said that affirmative action is unjustified. I should give reasons for this conclusion; it will not be acceptable for me to respond that this is just the way I feel. If I have some intuitive negative response to preferential treatment forms of affirmative action, then I will be expected to delve deeper to determine if there are some reasons for this attitude. Perhaps I have experienced the bad results of such programs. Or I may believe that giving preference in hiring or school admissions on the basis of race or sex is unfair. In either case, I will also be expected to push the matter further and explain *why* it is unfair, or even what constitutes fairness and unfairness.

To be required to give reasons and make arguments to justify one's moral conclusions is essential to the moral enterprise and to doing ethics. However, this does not mean that making ethical judgments is and must be purely *rational*. We might be tempted to think that good moral judgments require us to be objective and not let our *feelings*, or *emotions*, enter into our decision making. Yet this assumes that feelings always get in the way of making good judgments. Sometimes this is surely true, as when we are overcome by anger, jealousy, or fear and cannot think clearly. Bias and prejudice may stem from such strong feelings. We think prejudice is wrong because it prevents us from judging rightly. But emotions can often aid good decision making. We may, for example, simply feel the injustice of a certain situation or the wrongness of someone's suffering. Furthermore, our caring about some issue or person may, in fact, direct us to think about the ethical issues involved. However, some explanation of why we hold a certain moral position is required. Not to give an explanation, but simply to say "x is just wrong," or simply to have strong feelings or convictions about "x," is not sufficient.

Ethical and Other Types of Evaluation

"That's great!" "Now, this is what I call a delicious meal!" "That play was wonderful!" All of these statements express approval of something. They do not tell us much about the meal or the play. However, they do imply that the speaker thought they were good. These are *evaluative* statements. Ethical statements or judgments are also evaluative. They tell us what the speaker believes is good or bad. They do not simply describe what the object of the judgment is like—for example, that it occurred at a certain time or affected people in a certain way. They go further and express a positive or negative regard for the object of their judgment. However, factual matters are often relevant to our moral evaluations. For example, factual judgments about whether capital punishment has a deterrent effect might be quite relevant to our moral judgments about it. Because ethical judgments often rely on such

empirical or experientially based information, ethics is often indebted to other disciplines such as sociology or psychology. Thus, we can distinguish between empirical or *descriptive judgments,* by which we state certain factual beliefs, and *evaluative judgments,* by which we make judgments about these matters. Evaluative judgments are also called *normative judgments.* Thus,

- Descriptive (empirical) judgment: Capital punishment acts (or does not act) as a deterrent.
- Normative (moral) judgment: Capital punishment is justifiable (or unjustifiable).

Moral judgments are evaluative because they "place a value," negative or positive, on some action or practice such as capital punishment. Because these evaluations also rely on beliefs in general about what is good or right—in other words, on *norms* or *standards* of good and bad or right and wrong—they are also *normative.* For example, the judgment that people ought to give their informed consent to participate as research subjects may rely on beliefs about the value of human autonomy. In this case, autonomy functions as a norm by which we judge the practice of using persons as subjects of research. Thus, ethics of this sort is called *normative ethics,* both because it is evaluative and not simply descriptive and because it grounds its judgments in certain norms or values.[3]

"That is a good knife" is an evaluative or normative statement. However, it does not mean that the knife is morally good. In making ethical judgments, we use terms such as *good, bad, right, wrong, obligatory,* and *permissible.* We talk about what we ought or ought not to do. These are evaluative terms. *But not all evaluations are moral in nature.* We speak of a good knife without attributing moral goodness to it. In so describing the knife, we are probably referring to its practical usefulness for cutting or impressing others. People tell us that we ought to pay this amount in taxes or stop at that corner before crossing because that is what the law requires. We read that two styles ought not to be worn or

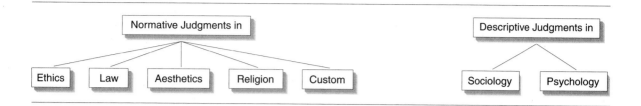

placed together because such a combination is distasteful. Here someone is making an aesthetic judgment. Religious leaders tell members of their communities what they ought to do because it is required by their religious beliefs. We may say that in some countries people ought to bow before the elders or use eating utensils in a certain way. This is a matter of custom. These normative or evaluative judgments appeal to practical, legal, aesthetic, religious, or customary norms for their justification.

Thus, we can distinguish the various types of *normative* or evaluative judgments (and areas in which such judgments are made) from *descriptive* judgments about factual matters (and areas or disciplines that are in this sense descriptive).

How do other types of normative judgments differ from moral judgments? Some philosophers believe that it is a characteristic of moral "oughts" in particular that they override other "oughts" such as aesthetic ones. In other words, if we must choose between what is aesthetically pleasing and what is morally good, then we ought to do what is morally right. In this way morality may also take precedence over the law and custom. The doctrine of civil disobedience relies on this belief, because it holds that we may disobey certain laws for moral reasons. Although moral evaluations are different from other normative evaluations, this is not to say that there is no relation between them. For example, moral reasons often form the basis for certain laws. Furthermore, the fit or harmony between forms and colors grounding some aesthetic judgments may be similar to the rightness or moral fit between certain actions and certain situations or beings. Moreover, in some ethical systems, actions are judged morally by their practical usefulness for

producing valued ends. For now, however, note that ethics is not the only area in which we make normative judgments.

Can Ethics Be Taught?

It would be interesting to know just why some college and university programs require their students to take a course in ethics. Does this requirement rely on a belief that ethics or moral philosophy is designed to make people good and is capable of doing that? When asked about this, some of the students mentioned earlier said that ethics could be taught but that some people do not learn the lessons well. Others believed that it could not be taught because one's ethical views are a matter of personal choice.

The ancient Greek philosopher Plato thought that ethics *could* be taught. He wrote, "All evil is ignorance." In other words, the only reason we do what is wrong is because we do not know or believe it is wrong. If we come to believe that something is right, however, it should then follow that we will necessarily do it. Now, we are free to disagree with Plato by appealing to our own experience. If I know that I should not have that second piece of pie, does this mean that I will not eat the second piece? Never? Plato might attempt to convince us that he is right by examining or clarifying what he means by the phrase "to know." If we were really convinced with our whole heart and mind, so to speak, that something is wrong, then we might be very likely (if not determined) not to do it. However, whether ethics courses should attempt to convince students of such things is surely debatable.

Most, if not all, moral philosophers think that ethics, or a course on ethics, should do several other things. It should help students understand the nature of an ethical problem. It should help them think critically about ethical matters by providing certain conceptual tools and skills. It should enable them to form and critically analyze ethical arguments. It is up to the individual, however, to use these skills to reason about ethical matters. A study of ethics should also lead students to be respectful of opposing views, because it requires them to analyze carefully the arguments that support views contrary to their own. It also provides opportunities to consider the reasonableness of at least some viewpoints that they previously may not have considered.

Ethical Theory and Reasoning

In this text you will study several ethical theories. We would do well first to consider what an ethical theory is. An *ethical theory* is a systematic exposition of a particular view about what is the nature and basis of good or right. The theory provides reasons or norms for judging acts to be right or wrong and attempts to give a justification for these norms. It provides ethical principles or guidelines that embody certain values. These can be used to decide in particular cases what action should be chosen and carried out. We can diagram the relationship between ethical theories and moral decision making as shown in the following diagram. We can think of the diagram as a ladder. In practice we can start at the ladder's top or bottom. At the top, at the level of theory, we can start by clarifying for ourselves what we think are basic ethical values. We then move downward to the level of principles generated from the theory. Moving next to conclusions about moral values in general, the bottom level, we use these principles to make concrete ethical judgments. Or we can start at the bottom of the ladder, facing a particular ethical choice or dilemma. We do not know what is best or what we ought to do. We work our way up the ladder by trying to think through our own values. Would it be better to realize this or that value, and why? Ultimately and ideally, we come to a

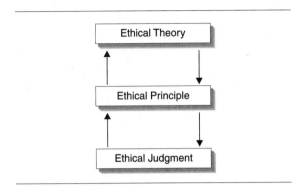

basic justification, or the elements of what would be an ethical theory. If we look at the actual practice of thinking people as they develop their ethical views over time, the movement is probably in both directions. We use concrete cases to reform our basic ethical views, and we use the basic ethical views to throw light on concrete cases.

An example of this movement in both directions would be if we started with the belief that pleasure is the ultimate value, and then found that in practice applying this value would lead us to do things that are contrary to common moral sense or that are repugnant to us and others. We may then be forced to look again and possibly alter our views about the moral significance of pleasure. Or we may change our views about the rightness or wrongness of some particular act or practice on the basis of our theoretical reflections. Obviously, this sketch of moral reasoning is quite simplified. Moreover, this model of ethical reasoning has been criticized by feminists and others, partly because it shows ethics to be governed by general principles that are supposedly applicable to all ethical situations. Does this form of reasoning give due consideration to the particularities of individual, concrete cases? Can we really make a general judgment about the value of truthfulness or courage that will help us know what to do in particular cases in which these issues play a role? See Chapter 7 for further discussion of this problem.

Types of Ethical Theory

In Part I of this text we will consider four types of moral theory. These theories exemplify different approaches to doing ethics. Some differ in terms of what they say we should look at in making moral judgments about actions or practices. For example, does it matter morally that I tried to do the right thing, that I had a good motive? Surely it must make some moral difference, we think. But suppose that in acting sincerely I violate someone's rights. Does this make the action a bad action? We would probably be inclined to say yes. Suppose, however, that in violating someone's rights I am able to bring about a great good. Does this justify the violation of rights? Some theories judge actions in terms of their *motive*, some in terms of the character or nature of *the act itself*, and others in terms of the *consequences* of the actions or practices.

We often appeal to one or the other type of reason. Take a situation in which I strike a person, Jim. We can make the following judgments about this action. Note the different types of reasons given for the judgments.

- That was good because you intended to do Jim good by awakening him or bad because you meant to do him harm. (Motive)

- That was bad because it violated the bodily integrity of another, Jim, or good because it was an act of generosity. (Act)

- That was bad because of the great suffering it caused Jim or good because it helped form a sense of community. (Consequences)

While we generally think that a person's *motive* is relevant to the overall moral judgment about his or her action, we tend to think that it reflects primarily on the moral evaluation of the person. We also have good reasons to think that the results of actions matter morally. Those theories that base moral judgments on consequences are called *consequentialist* or sometimes *teleological* moral theories (from the Greek root *telos*, meaning "goal" or "end"). We also may think that what we actually do or how we act also counts

morally. Those theories that hold that actions can be right or wrong regardless of their consequences are called *nonconsequentialist* or *deontological* theories (from the Greek root *deon*, meaning "duty"). One of the moral theories that we will examine is utilitarianism. It provides us with an example of a consequentialist moral theory in which we judge whether an action is better than alternatives by its actual or expected results or consequences; actions are classically judged in terms of the promotion of human happiness. Kant's moral theory, which we will also examine, provides us with an example of a nonconsequentialist theory according to which acts are judged right or wrong independently of their consequences; in particular, acts are judged by whether they conform to requirements of rationality and human dignity. The Naturalistic ethical theories that we will examine stress human nature as the source of what is right and wrong. Some elements of these theories are deontological and some teleological. Feminist theories of care provide yet another way of determining what one ought to do. In Part II of this text we will examine several concrete ethical issues. As we do so, we will note how these ethical theories analyze the problems from different perspectives and sometimes give different conclusions about what is right and wrong, better and worse morally.

In this opening chapter we have questioned the value of ethics and learned something about what ethics is and how it is different from other disciplines. We have examined briefly the nature of ethical theories and principles and the role they play in ethical reasoning. We have classified theories according to four different types. We will examine these theories more carefully in the chapters to come, and we will see how and whether they might help us analyze and come to conclusions about particular ethical issues.

Notes

1. *New York Times,* Jan. 8, 1993, A7.
2. Alfred North Whitehead, *Process and Reality* (New York: Macmillan, 1929), 4.
3. Notice that one can have an opinion about a matter of good and bad as well as an opinion about what is the case. For example, I might indicate that my opinion about whether random drug testing is a good thing is only an opinion because I do not feel adequately informed about the matter. This is an opinion about a moral matter. I can also have an opinion about the connection between passive smoking (inhaling of others' tobacco smoke) and lung cancer. This would be an opinion about a factual matter. Because I can have an opinion about both values and matters of fact, I should not use this criterion as a basis for distinguishing values and facts. To do so would imply that moral matters were always matters of opinion and factual matters were never such.

Review Exercises

1. Tell whether the following statements about the nature of ethics are true or false. Explain your answers.
   a. Ethics is the study of why people act in certain ways.
   b. To say that moral philosophy is foundational means that it asks questions about such things as the meaning of right and wrong and how we know what is good and bad.
   c. The statement "Most people believe that cheating is wrong" is an ethical evaluation of cheating.
2. Label the following statements as either normative (N) or descriptive (D). If normative, label each as ethics (E), aesthetics (A), law (L), religion (R), or custom (C).
   a. One ought to respect one's elders because it is one of God's commandments.
   b. Twice as many people today, as compared to ten years ago, believe that the death penalty is morally justified in some cases.
   c. It would be wrong to put an antique chair in a modern room.
   d. People do not always do what they believe to be right.
   e. I ought not to turn left here because the sign says "No Left Turn."
   f. We ought to adopt a universal health insurance policy because everyone has a right to health care.
3. As they occur in the following statements, label the reasons for the conclusion as appeals to motive (M), the act (A), or the consequences (C).
   a. Although you intended well, what you did was bad because it caused more harm than good.
   b. We ought always to tell the truth to others because they have a right to know the truth.
   c. Although it did turn out badly, you did not want that, and thus you should not be judged harshly for what you caused.

Selected Bibliography

Antony, Louise, and Charlotte Witt (Eds.). *A Mind of One's Own: Feminist Essays on Reason and Objectivity.* Boulder, CO: Westview, 1992.

Art, Brad. *What Is the Best Life? An Introduction to Ethics.* Belmont, CA: Wadsworth, 1993.

Becker, Lawrence, with Charlotte B. Becker. *A History of Western Ethics.* Hamden, CT: Garland, 1991.

Bishop, Sharon, and Marjorie Weinzweig. *Philosophy and Women.* Belmont, CA: Wadsworth, 1993.

Bostock, Stephen St. C. *Zoos and Animal Rights.* New York: Routledge, 1993.

Brandt, Richard. *Ethical Theory: The Problems of Normative and Critical Ethics.* New York: Prentice-Hall, 1973.

DeGrazia, David. *Taking Animals Seriously: Mental Life and Moral Status.* New York: Cambridge University Press, 1996.

Donagan, Alan. *The Theory of Morality.* Chicago: University of Chicago Press, 1977.

Frankena, William K. *Ethics,* 2d ed. Englewood Cliffs, NJ: Prentice-Hall, 1987.

Gert, Bernard. *Morality: A New Justification of the Moral Rules,* 2d ed. New York: Oxford University Press, 1988.

Kourany, Janet, James Sterba, and Rosemarie Tong. *Feminist Frameworks.* Englewood Cliffs, NJ: Prentice-Hall, 1992.

MacIntyre, Alasdair. *A Short History of Ethics.* New York: Macmillan, 1966.

Noddings, Nel. *Caring: A Feminine Approach to Ethics and Moral Education.* Berkeley: University of California Press, 1984.

Nussbaum, Martha. *The Fragility of Goodness.* New York: Cambridge University Press, 1993.

Pearsall, Marilyn. *Women and Values: Readings in Recent Feminist Philosophy,* 2d ed. Belmont, CA: Wadsworth, 1993.

Rachels, James. *The Elements of Moral Philosophy.* New York: Random House, 1986.

Rollin, Bernard E. *The Frankenstein Syndrome: Ethical and Social Issues in the Genetic Engineering of Animals.* New York: Cambridge University Press, 1995.

Taylor, Paul. *Principles of Ethics.* Encino, CA: Dickenson, 1975.

Thomson, Judith Jarvis. *The Realm of Rights.* Cambridge, MA: Harvard University Press, 1990.

Warnock, G. J. *The Object of Morality.* New York: Methuen, 1971.

Williams, Bernard. *Ethics and the Limits of Philosophy.* Cambridge, MA: Harvard University Press, 1985.

2

Ethical Relativism

For decades anthropologists and sociologists have collected information on the diverse mores of different cultures. Some societies hold bribery to be morally acceptable, but other societies condemn it. Views on appropriate sexual behavior and practices vary widely. Some societies believe that cannibalism—the eating of human flesh—is good because it ensures tribal fertility or increases manliness. Some Inuit groups, the native peoples of northern Canada and Alaska, believed that it was appropriate to abandon their elderly when they could no longer travel with the group, while other groups once practiced ritual strangulation of the old by their children. Ruth Benedict has documented the case of a North-west Indian group that believed it was justified in killing an innocent person for each member of the group who had died. This was not a matter of revenge but a way of fighting death. In place of bereavement, they felt relieved by the second killing.[1]

Before we begin to examine some ethical theories, we ought to consider whether the very idea of applying ethical theories is misguided. We commonly hear people say, "What is right for one person is not necessarily right for another," and "What is right in some circumstances is not right in other circumstances." If this were true, then it seems to imply that we cannot make any general or objective moral assessments. "When in Rome," should we not, then, "do as the Romans do"? In other words, would not morality be either entirely a personal matter or a function of cultural values? These are the kinds of questions raised by the topic of ethical relativism. In this chapter we will take an overview of ethical relativism and its two basic forms and then present reasons for and against it. The last sections—"Moral Realism" and "Moral Pluralism"—are more technical and not necessary for a basic understanding of ethical relativism. However, they do introduce two key issues of relativism addressed by philosophers today.

What Is Ethical Relativism?

Although there are different types of ethical relativism (see the following descriptions of the two basic forms), in general we can say that ethical relativism is the view that ethical values and beliefs are relative to the various individuals or societies that hold them. In saying that they are relative to individuals or societies, we mean that they are a function of, or dependent on, what those individuals or societies do, in fact, believe. *According to ethical relativism, there is no objective right and wrong.* The opposite point of view—that there is an objective right and wrong—is often called *objectivism*, or sometimes *non-relativism*.

We can understand more about ethical relativism by comparing our views of the status of ethics and ethical matters with our ordinary beliefs about science. Most people believe that the natural sciences (biology, chemistry, physics, geology, and their modern variants) tell us things about the natural world. Throughout the centuries, and in modern times in particular, science seems to have made great progress in uncovering the nature and structure of our world. Moreover, science seems to have a universal validity. No matter what a person's individual temperament, background, or culture, the same natural world seems accessible to all who sincerely and openly investigate it. Modern science is thought to be governed by a generally accepted method and seems to produce a gradually evolving common body of knowledge. Although this is the popular view of science, philosophers hold that the situation regarding science is much more complex. Nevertheless, it is useful to compare this ordinary view of science with common understandings of morality.

Morality, in contrast to science, does not seem so objective. The few examples of diversity of moral beliefs noted earlier could be multiplied many times over. Not only is there no general agreement about what is right and wrong, but also we often doubt that this is the kind of matter about which we can agree. We tend, then, to think of morality as a matter of subjective opinion. This is basically the conclusion of ethical relativism. According to ethical relativism, morality is simply a function of the moral beliefs that people have. There is nothing beyond this. Specifically, no realm of objective moral truth or reality exists that is comparable to that which we seem to find in the world of nature, which is investigated by science.

Two Forms of Ethical Relativism

In further exploring the nature of ethical relativism, we should note that it has two basic and different forms.[2] According to one version, called *personal* or *individual ethical relativism*, ethical judgments and beliefs are the expressions of the moral outlook and attitudes of individual persons. I have my ethical views, and you have yours; neither my views nor yours are better or more correct. I may believe that a particular war was unjust, and you may believe it was just. Someone else may believe that all war is wrong. According to this form of relativism, because no objective right or wrong exists, that particular war or all wars cannot be said to be really just or unjust, right or wrong. We each have our individual histories that explain how we have come to hold our particular views or attitudes. But they are just that: our own individual views and attitudes. We cannot say that they are correct or incorrect, because to do so would assume some objective standard of right and wrong against which we could judge their correctness. Such a standard does not exist, according to ethical relativism.[3]

The second version of ethical relativism, called *social* or *cultural ethical relativism*, holds that ethical values vary from society to society and that the basis for moral judgments lies in these social or cultural views. For an individual to decide and do what is right, he or she must look to the norms of the society. People in a society may, in fact, believe that their views are the correct moral views. However, cultural ethical relativism holds that no society's views are better than any other in a transcultural sense. Some may be different from others, and some may not be the views generally accepted by a wider group of societies, but that does not make these views worse, more backward, or incorrect in an objective sense.

Reasons Supporting Ethical Relativism

There are many reasons for believing that what ethical relativism holds is true. We will first summarize three of the reasons most commonly given, and then we will evaluate these arguments.[4]

The Diversity of Moral Views

One reason most often given to support relativism is the existence of moral diversity among people and cultures. In fields such as science and history, investigation tends to result in general agreement despite this diversity. But we have come to no such agreement in ethics. Philosophers have been investigating questions about the basis of morality since ancient times. With sincere and capable thinkers pursuing a topic over centuries, one would think that some agreement would have been reached. But this seems not to be the case. It is not only on particular issues such as abortion that sincere people disagree, but also on basic moral values or principles.

Moral Uncertainty

A second reason to believe that what relativism holds is true is the great difficulty we often have in knowing what is the morally right thing to believe or do. We don't know what is morally most important. For example, we do not know whether it is better to help one's friend or do the honest thing in a case in which we cannot do both. Perhaps helping the friend is best in some circumstances, but being honest is the best in others. We are not sure which is best in a particular case. Furthermore, we cannot know for sure what will happen down the line if we choose one course over another. Each of us is also aware of our personal limitations and the subjective glance that we bring to moral judging. Thus, we distrust our own judgments. We then generalize and conclude that all moral judgments are simply personal and subjective viewpoints.

Situational Differences

Finally, people and situations, cultures and times, differ in significant ways. The situations and life world of different people vary so much that it is difficult to believe that the same things that would be right for one would be right for another. In some places overpopulation or drought is a problem; other places have too few people or too much water. In some places people barely have access to the basic necessities of life; in other places food is plentiful and the standard of living is high. How can the same things be right and wrong under such different circumstances? It seems unlikely, then, that any moral theory or judgment can apply in a general or universal manner. We thus tend to conclude that they must be relative to the particular situation and circumstance and that no objective or universally valid moral good exists.

Are These Reasons Convincing?

Let us consider possible responses by a nonrelativist or objectivist to the preceding three points.

The Diversity of Moral Views

We can consider the matter of diversity of moral views from two different perspectives. First, we can ask, how widespread and deep is the disagreement? Second, we may ask, what does the fact of disagreement prove?

How Widespread and Deep Is the Disagreement? If two people disagree about a moral matter, does this always amount to a moral disagreement? For example, Bill says that we ought to cut down dramatically on carbon dioxide emissions, while Jane says that we do not have a moral obligation to do this. This looks like a basic moral disagreement, but it actually may result from differences in their factual beliefs. Bill may believe that the current rate of such emissions will result in dramatic and serious harmful global climate effects in the next decades, the so-called greenhouse effect. Jane may believe no such harmful consequences are likely, because she believes that the assessments and predictions are in error. If they did agree on the factual issues, Bill and Jane would agree on the moral conclusion. They both agree on the basic moral obligation to do what we can to improve the current human condition and prevent serious harm to existing and future generations. In other words, they agree about basic moral matters.

Basic Moral Agreement	Factual Disagreement	Different Moral Conclusions
We ought not to harm.	CO_2 emissions harm.	We ought to reduce emissions.
We ought not to harm.	CO_2 emissions do not harm.	We need not reduce emissions.

It is an open question how many of our seeming moral disagreements are not basic moral disagreements at all but disagreements about factual or other beliefs. But suppose that at least some of them are about moral matters. Suppose that we do disagree about the relative value, for example, of health and peace, honesty and generosity, or about what rights people do and do not have. It is this type of disagreement that the moral relativist would need to make his or her point.

What Would Disagreement About Basic Moral Matters Prove? I have asked students in my ethics class to tell me in what year George Washington died. A few brave souls venture a guess: 1801, or at least after 1790? No one is sure. Does this disagreement or lack of certitude prove that he did not die or that he died on no particular date? Belief that he did die and on a particular date is consistent with differences of opinion and with uncertainty. So also in ethics: People can disagree about what constitutes the right thing to do and yet believe that there *is* a right thing to do. "Is it not because of this belief that we try to decide what is right and worry that we might miss it?" the nonrelativist would ask.

Or consider the supposed contrast between ethics and science. Although there is a body of knowledge about which those working in the physical sciences agree, those working at the forefront of these sciences often profoundly disagree. Does the fact that scientists working on these issues disagree prove that no objectivity exists in such matters? If people disagree about whether the universe began with a "big bang" or about what happened in the first millisecond, does this prove that no answer is to be found, even in principle, about the universe's beginning? Not necessarily.

Moral Uncertainty

Let us examine the point that moral matters are complex and difficult to determine. Because of this we are often uncertain about what the best thing is to do morally. For example, those who "blow the whistle" on companies for which they work must find it difficult to know whether they are doing the right thing when they consider the possible cost of doing so to themselves and others around them. However, what is described here is not strictly relativism but *skepticism*. Skepticism is the view that it is difficult, if not impossible, to know something. However, does the fact that we are uncertain about the answer to some question, even a moral question, prove that it lacks an answer? The nonrelativist could argue that in our very dissatisfaction with not knowing and in our seeking to know what we ought to do, we behave as though we believe that a better choice can be made.

In contrast, matters of science and history often eventually get clarified and settled. We can now look up the date of George Washington's death, and scientists gradually improve our knowledge in various fields. "Why is there no similar progress in ethical matters?" relativists might respond.

Situational Differences

Does the fact that people's life situations differ so dramatically make it unlikely or impossible for them to have any common morality? A nonrelativist might suggest the following. Suppose, for example, that health is taken as an objective value. Is it not the case that what contributes to the health of some is different than what contributes to the health of others? Insulin is good for the diabetic but not the nondiabetic. Or assume that justice is an objective moral value and that

Objective Value	Situational Differences	Different Moral Conclusions
Health	Diabetic	Insulin injections are good.
Health	Nondiabetic	Insulin injections are not good
Justice	Works hard.	Deserves reward.
Justice	Does not work hard.	Does not deserve the reward.

it involves "giving to each his or her due." Would what is due people in justice be the same? Those who work might well deserve something different from those who do not, and the guilty deserve punishment that the innocent do not.

One reason why situational differences may lead us to think that no objective moral value is possible is that we may be equating objectivism with what is sometimes called absolutism. *Absolutism* may be described as the view that moral rules or principles have no exceptions and are context-independent. One example of such a rule is "Stealing is always wrong." According to absolutism, situational differences such as whether or not a person is starving would make no difference to moral conclusions about whether they are justified in stealing food, if stealing is wrong (see below).

sion of relativism is not necessarily so. Consider this statement: "What is right for one person is not necessarily right for another." If the term *for* means "in the view of," then the statement simply states the fact that people do disagree. It states that "What is right in the view of one person is not what is right in the view of the other." However, this is not yet relativism. If *for* is used in the sense "Insulin is good for some people but not (necessarily) for others," then the original statement is also not necessarily relativistic. It could, in fact, imply that health is a true or objective good and that what leads to it is good and what diminishes it is bad. For ethical relativism, on the other hand, there is no such objective good.

Absolute Value	Situational Differences	Same Moral Conclusions
Stealing is always wrong.	Person is starving.	Do not steal.
Stealing is always wrong.	Person is not starving.	Do not steal.

However, an objectivist who is not an absolutist holds that although there is some objective good, what is good in a concrete case may vary from person to person and circumstance to circumstance. She or he could hold that stealing might be justified in some circumstances because it is necessary for life, an objective good, and a greater good than property. Opposing absolutism does not necessarily commit one to a similar opposition to objectivism.

One result of this clarification should be the realization that what is often taken as an expres-

Further Considerations

The previous discussion should provide a basis for both critically evaluating and understanding ethical relativism. Each type of relativism and its opposite, nonrelativism, must overcome additional problems, however.

One problem for the social or cultural relativist who holds that moral values are simply a reflection of society's views is to identify that society. With which group should my moral views coincide—my country, my state, my family, or myself and my peers? Different groups to which

I belong have different moral views. Moreover, if a society changes its views, does this mean that morality changes? If at one time 52 percent of its people supported some war and later only 48 percent did so, does this mean that earlier the war was just and it became unjust when the people changed their minds about it?

One problem that the individual relativist faces is whether that view accords with personal experience. According to individual relativism, it seems that I should turn within and consult my moral feelings in order to solve a personal moral problem. This is often just the source of the difficulty, however, for when I look within I find conflicting feelings. I want to know not how I *do* feel but how I *ought* to feel and what I *ought* to believe. But to hold that there is something I possibly ought to believe would not be relativism.

A problem for both types of relativist lies in the implied belief that relativism is a more tolerant position than objectivism. However, the cultural relativist can hold that people in a society should be tolerant only if tolerance is one of the dominant values of their society. He or she cannot hold that all people should be tolerant, because tolerance cannot be an objective or transcultural value, according to relativism. We can also question whether there is any reason for an individual relativist to be tolerant, especially if being tolerant means not just putting up with others who disagree with us, but also listening to their positions and arguments. Why should I listen to another who disagrees with me? If ethical relativism is true, it cannot be because the other person's moral views may be better than mine in an objective sense, for there is no objectively better position. Objectivists might insist that their position provides a better basis for both believing that tolerance is an objective and transcultural good and that we ought to be open to others' views because they may be closer to the truth than ours are.

Relativism, or expressions that seem to be relativistic, may sometimes manifest a kind of intellectual laziness or a lack of moral courage. Rather than attempt to give reasons or arguments for my own position, I may hide behind some statement like, "What is good for some is not necessarily good for others." I may say this simply to excuse myself from having to think or be critical of various ethical positions. Those who hold that there is an objective right and wrong may also do so uncritically. They may simply adopt the views of their parents or peers without evaluating them themselves. However, the major difficulty with an objectivist position is the problem it has in providing an alternative to the relativist position. The objectivist should give us reason to believe that there *is* an objective good. To pursue this problem in a little more detail, we will examine briefly two issues discussed by contemporary moral philosophers. One is the issue of the reality of moral values— moral realism; and the other is the issue of whether the good is one or many—moral pluralism.

Moral Realism

If there is an objective morality beyond the morality of cultures or individuals, what would it be like? Earlier in this chapter you were asked to compare science and ethics. I suggested that natural science is generally regarded as the study of a reality independent of scientists—namely, nature. This view of the relation of science and nature can be called *realism*. Realism is the view that there exists a reality independent of those who know it. Most people are probably realists in this sense.

Now compare this to the situation regarding ethics. If I say that John's act of saving the drowning child was good, what is the object of my moral judgment? Is there some real existing fact of goodness that I can somehow sense in this action? I can observe the actions of John to save the child, the characteristics of the child, John, the lake, and so forth. But in what sense, if any, do I observe the goodness itself? The British philosopher G. E. Moore held that goodness is a specific quality that attaches to people or acts.[5] Although we cannot observe it (we cannot hear, touch, taste, or see it), we intuit its presence.

Philosophers such as Moore have had difficulty explaining both the nature of the quality and the particular intuitive or moral sense by which we are supposed to perceive it.

Some moral philosophers who want to hold something of a realist view of morality try to argue, for example, that moral properties such as goodness are *supervenient,* or based on or flowing from other qualities such as courage or generosity or honesty. Obviously, the exact relation between the moral and other qualities would need further explanation. Others also attempt to explain moral reality as a relational matter: perhaps as a certain fit between actions and situations or actions and our innate sensibilities.[6] For example, because of innate human sensibilities, some say, we just would not be able to approve of torturing the innocent. The problems here are complex. However, the question is an important one. Are moral rights and wrongs, goods and bads, something independent of particular people or cultures and their beliefs about what is right and wrong or good and bad? Or are they, as relativism holds, a reflection or expression of individuals or cultures?

Moral Pluralism

Another problem that nonrelativists or objectivists face is the issue of whether the good is one or many. According to some theories, there is one primary moral principle by which we can judge all actions. However, suppose this were not the case. Suppose a variety of equally valid moral principles or equal moral values existed. For example, suppose that autonomy, justice, well-being, authenticity, and peace were all equally valuable. This would present a problem if we were ever forced to choose between the more just resolution and that which promoted the well-being of more people. For example, we may be able to do more good overall with our health care resources if we spend them on diseases that affect more people. However, there is some element of unfairness in this proposal because people who have rare diseases did not choose to have them. In cases of such a conflict of values we may be forced simply to choose one or the other for no reason or on the basis of something other than reason. Whether some rational and nonarbitrary way exists to make such decisions is an open question. Whether ultimate choices are thus subjective or can be grounded in an assessment of what is objectively best is not only a question about how we do behave but also about what is possible in matters of moral judgment.

The issue of moral relativism is not one easily digested or decided. The belief that guides this text, however, is that better and worse choices can be made, and that morality is not simply a matter of what we believe to be morally right or wrong. If this were not the case, then there would not seem much point in studying ethics. The purpose of studying ethics, as noted in Chapter 1, is to improve one's ability to make good ethical judgments. If ethical relativism were true, then this purpose could not be achieved.

The two major ethical theories that we will examine, utilitarianism and Kant's moral theory, are both objectivist or nonrelativist moral theories. Naturalist theories also tend to be objective because they have as their basis human nature and what perfects it. The feminist ethics of care may be more open to allegations of relativism; you can judge that for yourself as you examine that view. As you learn more about them, consider what their reasons are for holding that the objective good that they specify really exists.

Notes

1. Ruth Benedict, "Anthropology and the Abnormal," *Journal of General Psychology* 10 (1934): 60–70.
2. We could also think of many forms of ethical relativism from the most individual or personal to the more universal. Thus, we could think of individual relativism, or that based on family values, or local community or state or cultural values. The most universal, however, in which moral values are the same for all human beings, would probably no longer be a form of relativism.

3. According to some versions of individual ethical relativism, moral judgments are similar to expressions of taste. We each have our own individual tastes. I like certain styles or foods, and you like others. Just as no taste can be said to be correct or incorrect, so also no ethical view can be valued as better than any other. My saying that this war or all wars are unjust is, in effect, my expression of my dislike of or aversion toward war. An entire tradition in ethics, sometimes called "emotivism," holds this view. For an example, see Charles Stevenson, *Ethics and Language* (New Haven, CT: Yale University Press, 1944).

4. These are not necessarily complete and coherent arguments for relativism. Rather, they are more popular versions of why people generally are inclined toward what they believe is relativism.

5. G. E. Moore, *Principia Ethica* (Cambridge: Cambridge University Press, 1903).

6. Bruce W. Brower, "Dispositional Ethical Realism," *Ethics* 103, no. 2 (Jan. 1993): 221–249.

Review Exercises

1. Explain the definition of ethical relativism given in the text, "the view that ethical values and beliefs are relative to the various individuals or societies that hold them."

2. What is the difference between individual and social or cultural relativism?

3. What is the difference between the theory that people do differ in their moral beliefs and what the theory of ethical relativism holds?

4. What are the differences between the three reasons for supporting ethical relativism given in this chapter? In particular, what is the basic difference between the first and second? Between the first and third?

5. How would you know whether a moral disagreement was based on a basic difference in moral values or facts? As an example, use differences about the moral justifiability of capital punishment.

6. What is moral realism, and how does it differ from scientific realism? Is it in any way similar to scientific realism?

Selected Bibliography

Bambrough, Renford. *Moral Skepticism and Moral Knowledge*. New York: Routledge & Kegan Paul, 1979.

Benedict, Ruth. *Patterns of Culture*. New York: Pelican, 1946.

Brink, David. *Moral Realism and the Foundation of Ethics*. Cambridge: Cambridge University Press, 1989.

Fishkin, James. *Beyond Subjective Morality*. New Haven, CT: Yale University Press, 1984.

Herskovits, Melville. *Cultural Relativism*. New York: Random House, 1972.

Kluckhorn, Clyde. "Ethical Relativity: Sic et Non," *Journal of Philosophy* 52 (1955): 663–666.

Krausz, Michael (Ed.). *Relativism: Interpretation and Confrontation*. Notre Dame, IN: Notre Dame University Press, 1989.

Ladd, John (Ed.). *Ethical Relativism*. Belmont, CA: Wadsworth, 1973.

Summer, W. G. *Folkways*. Lexington, MA: Ginn, 1906.

Taylor, Paul W. "Four Types of Ethical Relativism," *Philosophical Review* 62 (1954): 500–516.

Westermarck, Edward. *Ethical Relativity*. Atlantic Highlands, NJ: Humanities Press, 1960.

Wong, David. *Moral Relativity*. Berkeley: University of California Press, 1984.

❦ 3 ❦

Egoism

In this chapter we will give thought to the issues raised by the following dialogue. Because the issues concern egoism and its opposite, altruism, our speakers are Edna Egoist and Alan Altruist.

Edna: I think that people are basically selfish. Everyone primarily looks out for number one.

Alan: That's not so. At least some people sometimes act unselfishly. Our parents made sacrifices for us. Look at Mother Theresa. She has given her whole life to helping the poor of Calcutta.

Edna: But isn't she really doing what she wants? I'm sure she gets personal satisfaction from her work.

Alan: I don't believe that is why she does what she does. But wouldn't it be disappointing if that were true? And wouldn't it be an awful world if everyone just looked out for themselves? For one thing, there would be no cooperation. Conflicts and wars would be everywhere.

Edna: I don't agree. Even if people are basically selfish, we do live together and we would need some rules. Otherwise individuals would have no way to plan and get what they want.

Alan: If you were completely self-centered, you would not be likely to have many friends.

Edna: I would want to have the satisfaction of having friends. I would help them when they were in need, because I would want help in return when I needed it. Isn't that what friends are for?

Alan: I don't think so. Rather, I think what John Kennedy said is right. "Ask not what your country can do for you but what you can do for your country." We do want too much from others, including the government, without giving of ourselves. And that is not right.

Edna: But if people did not take care of themselves first, then they would have nothing to give to others. I think people should think of themselves first.

Notice in this dialogue that Edna and Alan first argue about whether people are basically self-centered or selfish. Then they move to talk about the implications or consequences of one or the other type of behavior. Finally, they differ about whether such behavior would be a good or a bad thing. Notice that Edna and Alan disagree about two distinctly different issues. One is whether people are basically selfish; the second is whether being selfish is good or bad. These two issues illustrate two different versions or meanings of egoism. One is *descriptive*. According to this version, egoism is a theory that describes what people are like. Simply put, this theory holds that people are basically self-centered or selfish. It is a view about how people behave or why they do what they do. It is often referred to as *psychological egoism*. The other version of egoism is *normative*. It is a theory about how people ought to behave. Thus, it is an ethical theory and is called *ethical egoism*. We will examine each of these theories in turn. We will first attempt to understand each theory, what it holds, and then try to evaluate it, asking whether it is reasonable or true. The final sections—"The Moral Point of View" and "Why Be Moral?"— are more technical. One can understand the basic philosophical concerns about egoism apart from these treatments. However, the issues are interesting, and the treatments of them do summarize key ideas from contemporary debates about egoism.

Another type of moral theory has a long history in Western philosophy and can be exemplified by Thomas Hobbes (1588–1679), from whose writings this chapter's reading is taken. That theory is sometimes called *contractarianism*. In some ways it can be considered a form of egoism in that it is rooted in individual self-interested choice. According to this theory, the best social rules are those that we would accept if we chose rationally: The context in which we choose is society, so each person must make his or her choices depending on what others will do and in cooperation with them.¹ To the extent that this rational choice is a form of self-interested choice, this tradition in ethics may also belong in a chapter discussion of egoism. In the interests of simplicity, however, we will omit further discussion of it here. John Rawls's theory of justice exemplifies aspects of this tradition, and thus some discussion of it can be found in the summary of his theory and the reading from his work in Chapter 12.

Psychological Egoism

What Is Psychological Egoism?

In general, psychological egoism is a theory about what people are like, but we can under-

stand what it asserts in several ways. One way to understand it is to say that people are basically selfish. This is what Edna says in the dialogue. The implication of this version is that people usually or always act for their own narrow and short-range self-interest. However, another formulation of this theory asserts that while people do act for their own self-interest, this self-interest is to be understood more broadly and more long-term. Thus, we might distinguish between acting selfishly and acting in our own interest.

On the broader view, many things are in a person's interest: good health, satisfaction in a career or work, prestige, self-respect, family, and friends. Moreover, if we really wanted to attain these things, we would need to avoid being shortsighted. For example, we would have to be self-disciplined in diet and lifestyle in order to be healthy. We would need to plan long-term for a career. And we would need to be concerned about others and not overbearing if we wanted to make and retain friends.

However, as some have pointed out, we would not actually need to be concerned about others but only to appear to be concerned. Doing good to others, as Edna suggested, would be not for their sake but to enable one to call on those friends when they were needed. This would be helping a friend not for the friend's sake but for one's own sake.

Putting the matter in this way also raises another question about *how* to formulate this theory. Is psychological egoism a theory according to which people always do act in their own best interest? Or does it hold that people are always motivated by the desire to attain their own best interest? The first version would be easily refuted; we notice that people do not always do what is best for them. They eat too much, choose the wrong careers, waste time, and so forth. This may be because they do not have sufficient knowledge to be good judges of what is in their best interest. It may be because of a phenomenon known as "weakness of will." For example, I may want to lose weight or get an A in a course, but may not quite get myself to do what I have to do to achieve my goal. Philosophers have puzzled over how this can be so, and how to explain it. It is a complex issue; to treat it adequately would take us beyond what we can do here.[2] On the other hand, it might well be true that people always do what they *think* is the best thing for them. This version of psychological egoism, which we will address next, asserts that human beings act for the sake of their own best interests. In this version, the idea is not that people sometimes or always act in their own interests, but that this is the only thing that ultimately does motivate people. If they sometimes act for others, it is only because they think that it is in their own best interests to do so. This is what Edna Egoist said in the dialogue about Mother Theresa.[3]

Is Psychological Egoism True?

Not long ago, a study was done in which people were asked whether they believed in or supported the jury system; that is, should people be proven innocent or guilty by a group of peers? Most responded that they did. However, when asked whether they would serve on a jury if called, significantly fewer responded positively.[4] Those who answered the two questions differently might have wanted justice for themselves but were not willing to give it to others. Or consider the story about Abraham Lincoln.[5] It was reported that one day as he was riding in a coach over a bridge he heard a mother pig squealing. Her piglets had slipped into the water and she could not get them out. Lincoln supposedly asked the coachman to stop, got out, and rescued the piglets. When his companion cited this as an example of unselfishness, Lincoln responded that it was not for the sake of the pigs that he acted as he did. Rather, it was because he would have no peace later when he recalled the incident if he did not do something about it now. In other words, although it seemed unselfish, his action was quite self-centered.

Is the tendency to be self-oriented something that is innate to all of us, perhaps part of our survival instinct? Or are these traits learned? Developmental psychologists tell us about how children develop egoistic and altruistic tendencies. Are female children, for example, expected to be altruistic and caring while male children are taught to be independent and self-motivated? (See the discussion of gender differences in these psychological traits in Chapter 7.) In the dialogue above you may have noticed that these expectations have been turned around: Edna was the egoist and Alan the altruist. While psychologists describe the incidence and development of these characteristics, philosophers speculate about how a person comes to be able to sympathize with another and take the other's point of view. These philosophical speculations and empirical descriptions attempt to tell us what the case is about human development and motivation. Do they also make the case for or against psychological egoism?

How are we to evaluate the claims of psychological egoism? Note again that the view we will examine is a theory about human motivation. As such a theory, however, we will find it difficult, if not impossible, to prove. Suppose, for example, that Edna and Alan are trying to assess the motivation of particular people, say, their parents or Mother Theresa. How are they to know what motivates these people? They cannot just assume that their parents or Mother Theresa are acting for the sake of the satisfaction they receive from what they do. Nor can we ask them, for people themselves are not always the best judge of what motivates them. We commonly hear or say to ourselves, "I don't know why I did that!"

Moreover, suppose that their parents and Mother Theresa do, in fact, get satisfaction from helping others. This is not the same thing as acting for the purpose of getting that satisfaction. What psychological egoism needs to show is not that people do get satisfaction from what they do, but that it is the achieving of satisfaction that is their aim. Now we can find at least some examples in our own actions to test this theory. Do we read the book to get satisfaction or to learn something? Do we pursue that career opportunity because of the satisfaction that we think it will bring or because of the nature of the opportunity? In addition, directly aiming at satisfaction may not be the best way to achieve it. We probably have a better chance of being happy if we do not aim at happiness itself but rather at the things that we enjoy doing.

Thus, we have seen that the most reasonable or common form of psychological egoism, a theory about human motivation, is especially difficult to prove. Even if it were shown that we *often* act for the sake of our own interest, this is not enough to prove that psychological egoism is true. According to this theory, we must show that people *always* act to promote their own interests. We need next to consider whether this has any relevance to the normative question of *how* we ought to act.

Ethical Egoism

What Is Ethical Egoism?

Ethical egoism is a normative theory. It is a theory about what we ought to do, how we ought to act. As with psychological egoism, we can formulate the normative theory called ethical egoism in different ways. One version is *individual ethical egoism.* According to this version, I ought to look out only for my own interests. I ought to be concerned about others only to the extent that this also contributes to my own interests. In the dialogue, Edna first said only that she would do what was in her own best interest. Her final comment also implied that she believed that others also ought to do what is in their own best interests. According to this formulation of ethical egoism, sometimes called *universal ethical egoism,* everyone ought to look out for and seek only their own best interests. As in the individual form, in this second version people ought to help others only when and to the extent that it is in their own best interests.

Is Ethical Egoism True?

We can evaluate ethical egoism in several ways. We will consider four: its grounding in psychological egoism, its consistency or coherence, its derivation from economic theory, and its conformity to commonsense moral views.

Grounding in Psychological Egoism Let us consider first whether psychological egoism, if true, would provide a good basis for ethical egoism. If people were always motivated by their own interests, would this be a good reason to hold that they ought to be so moved? On the one hand, it seems superfluous to tell people that they ought to do what they always do anyway or will do no matter what. One would think that at least sometimes one of the functions of moral language is to try to motivate ourselves or others to do what we are not inclined to do. For example, I might tell myself that even though I could benefit by cheating on a test, it is wrong, and so I should not do it.[6]

On the other hand, the fact that we do behave in a certain way seems a poor reason for believing that we ought to do so. If people cheated or lied, we ask, would that in itself make these acts right? Thus, although it may at first seem reasonable to rely on a belief about people's basic selfishness to prove that people ought to look out for themselves alone, this seems far from convincing.

Consistency or Coherence Universal ethical egoism in particular is possibly inconsistent or incoherent. According to this version of ethical egoism, everyone ought to seek their own best interests. However, could anyone consistently support such a view? Wouldn't this mean that we would want our own best interests served and at the same time be willing to allow that others serve their interests, even to our own detriment? If food were scarce, I would want enough for myself, and yet at the same time would have to say that I should not have it for myself when another needs it to survive. This view seems to have an internal inconsistency. It may be possible to compare it to playing a game in which I can say that the other player ought to block my move, even though at the same time I hope that she or he does not do so. These arguments are complex and difficult to fully evaluate. Philosophers disagree about whether universal ethical egoism is inconsistent on the grounds that no one can will it as a universal practice.[7]

Derivation from Economic Theory One argument for ethical egoism is taken from economic theory, such as that proposed by Adam Smith. He and other proponents of laissez-faire or government-hands-off capitalism believe that self-interest provides the best economic motivation. Where the profit motive or individual incentives are absent, people will either not work or not as well. If it is my land or my business, then I will be more likely to take care of it than if the profits go to others or the government. In addition, Smith believed that in a system in which each person looks out for his or her own economic interests the general outcome will be best, as though an "invisible hand" was guiding things.[8]

Although this is not the place to go into an extended discussion of economic theory, it is enough to point out that not everyone agrees on the merits of laissez-faire capitalism. Much can be said for the competition that it supports, but it does raise questions about those who are unable to compete or unable to do so without help. Is care for these people a community responsibility? Recent community-oriented theories of social morality stress just this notion of responsibility and oppose laissez-faire capitalism's excessive emphasis on individual rights.[9] In any case, a more basic question can be asked about the relevance of economics to morality. Even if an economic system worked well, would this prove that morality ought to be modeled on it? Is not the moral life broader than the economic life? For example, are all human relations economic relations?

Furthermore, the argument that everyone ought to seek his or her own best interest because this contributes to general well-being is not ethical egoism at all. As we will come to see more clearly when we examine it, this is a form of utilitarianism. Thus, we can evaluate it in our discussion of utilitarianism in the next chapter.

Conformity to Commonsense Morality Finally, is ethical egoism supported by commonsense mo-

rality? On the one hand, some elements of ethical egoism are contrary to commonsense morality. For example, doesn't it assume that anything is all right as long as it serves an individual's best interests? Torturing human beings or animals would be permitted so long as this served one's interests. When not useful to one's interests, traditional virtues of honesty, fidelity, and loyalty would have no value. Ethical egoists could argue on empirical or factual grounds that the torturing of others is never in one's best interests because this would make one less sensitive, and being sensitive is generally useful to people. Also, they might argue that the development of traditional virtues is often in one's own best interest because these traits are valued by the society. For example, my possessing these traits may enable me to get what I want more readily. Whether this is a good enough reason to value these virtues or condemn torture is something you must judge for yourself.

On the other hand, the argument that people ought to take better care of themselves has some validity. By having a high regard for ourselves, we increase our self-esteem. We then depend less on others and more on ourselves. We might also be stronger and happier. These are surely desirable traits. The altruist, moreover, might be too self-effacing. He might be said to lack a proper regard for himself. There is also some truth in the view that unless one takes care of oneself, one is not of as much use to others. This view is not ethical egoism, but again a form of utilitarianism.

The Moral Point of View

Finally, we will consider briefly two issues related to that of ethical egoism that have puzzled philosophers in recent times. One is whether one must take a particular point of view to see things morally and whether this is incompatible with egoism. The other, treated in the following section, is whether there are self-interested reasons to be moral.

Suppose that a person cares for no one but herself. Would you consider that person to be a *moral* person? This is not to ask whether the person is a morally *good* person, but rather whether one can think of that person as even operating in the moral realm, so to speak. In other words, the question concerns not whether the person's morality is a good one but whether she has any morals at all.

To take an example from W. D. Falk, suppose we want to know whether a person has been given a moral education.[10] Someone might answer that she had because she had been taught not to lie, to treat others kindly, not to drink to excess, and to work hard. When asked what reasons she had been given for behaving thus, suppose she responded that she was taught not to lie because others would not trust her if she did. She was taught to treat others well because then they would treat her well in return. She was taught to work hard because of the satisfaction this would bring her or because she would be better able then to support herself. Would you consider her to have been given a moral education?

Falk thinks not. He suggests that she was given counsels of prudence, not morality. She was told what she probably should do to succeed in certain ways in life. She was taught the means that prudence would suggest she use to secure her own self-interest. According to Falk, only if she had been taught not to lie because it was wrong to do so, or because others had a right to know the truth, would she have been given a moral instruction. Only if she had been taught to treat others well because they deserved to be so treated, or that it would be wrong to do otherwise, would the counsel be a moral one. Similarly with working hard, if she had been told that she ought not to waste her talents or that she ought to contribute to society because it was the right thing to do, the teaching would have been a moral one. In summary, the education would not have been a moral one if it had been egoistically oriented. Do you agree?

Taking the moral point of view on this interpretation would then involve being able to see beyond ourselves and our own interests. It may also mean that we attempt to see things from another's point of view, or to be impartial. Morality would then be thought of as providing rules for social living—ways, for example, of settling conflicts. The rules would apply equally to all, or one would have to give reasons why some persons would be treated differently than others. One reason might be that some persons had worked harder than others, or their role demanded differential treatment.

In contrast, we do not think that we have to justify treating those close to us differently and more favorably than others. If we care more for our own children or our own friends than others, does this mean that we are not operating in the moral domain? Questions can be raised about the extent to which impartiality colors the moral domain. Some feminists, for example, would rather define it in terms of sympathy and caring. See the treatment of this issue in Chapter 7.

Why Be Moral?

Assume that morality does involve being able at least sometimes to take the other's point of view and at some level to treat people equally or impartially. Why should anyone do that, especially when it is not in her or his best interest? In other words, can we give any reasons to show why one should be moral? One reason might be that doing what one ought to do is just what being moral means. One could not then ask why one ought to do what one ought to do! However, this response may not be totally satisfactory.

Notice, further, that this is a question about why I as an individual ought to be moral. This is not the same as asking why everyone ought to be moral. We could argue that it is generally better for people to have and follow moral rules. Without such rules our social life would be pretty wretched. As Alan Altruist noted in the dialogue, our life together would be one of constant conflict and wars. However, this does not answer the question concerning why I should be moral when it is not in my best interest to do so.

If you were trying to convince someone why he should be moral, how would you do it? You might appeal to his fear of reprisal if he did not generally follow moral rules. If one is not honest, he will not be trusted. If he steals, he risks being punished. In *The Republic,* one of Plato's characters, Glaucon, tells the story of a shepherd named Gyges. Gyges comes into possession of a ring that he finds makes him invisible when he turns it around on his finger. He proceeds to take advantage of his invisibility and take what he wants from others. Glaucon then asks whether we all would not do the same if we, like Gyges, could get away with it. He believes we would. But is he right? Is the only reason why people are just or do the right thing to avoid being punished for not doing so?

There are other more positive but still self-interested reasons you might offer someone to convince her that she ought to be moral. You might tell her that, as in Falk's moral education example, being virtuous is to one's own advantage. You might recall some of the advice from Benjamin Franklin's *Poor Richard's Almanac.*[11] "A stitch in time saves nine." "Observe all men, thyself most." "Spare and have is better than spend and crave." These are the self-interested counsels of a practical morality. Contemporary philosophers such as Philippa Foot also believe that most of the traditional virtues are in our own best interest.[12] You might go even further and make the point that being moral is ennobling. Even when it involves sacrifice for a cause, being a moral person gives one a certain dignity, integrity, and self-respect. Only humans are capable of being moral, you might say, and human beings cannot flourish without being moral. Nevertheless, one can point to many examples in which people who break the moral rules seem to get away with it and fare better than those who keep them. "Nice guys [and gals?] finish last," as baseball great Leo Durocher put it.

We can think of being moral as something that contributes to or detracts from the good life. This depends on how one envisions the good life. If being moral seems too demanding, then some say this is too bad for morality. We ought to have a good life, even if it means sacrificing

something of morality. On another view, if being moral involves sacrificing something of the personally fulfilling life, then this is what must be done. No one ever said being moral was going to be easy![13]

Notes

1. See David Gauthier, *Morals by Agreement* (New York: Oxford University Press, 1986) and *Paradoxes of Rationality and Cooperation: Prisoner's Dilemma and Newcomb's Problem,* Richmond Campbell and Lanning Snowden (Eds.) (Calgary: University of British Columbia Press, 1985).

2. For a discussion of "weakness of will," see Gwynneth Matthews, "Moral Weakness," *Mind,* 299 (July 1966), 405–419; Donald Davidson, "How Is Weakness of the Will Possible?" in *Moral Concepts,* Joel Feinberg (Ed.) (New York: Oxford University Press, 1970), 93–113.

3. A stronger version of psychological egoism asserts that people cannot do otherwise. According to this stronger version, people are such that they cannot but act for the sake of their own interest. But how would we know this? We know how people do act, but how could we show that they cannot act otherwise? Perhaps we could appeal to certain views about human nature. We could argue that we always seek our own best interests because we are depraved by nature or perhaps by a religious "fall" such as the one described in the biblical "Book of Genesis."

4. Amitai Etzioni, a presentation at the University of San Francisco, December 1, 1992.

5. From the *Springfield Monitor* (ca. 1928), cited in Louis Pojman, *Ethics* (Belmont, CA: Wadsworth, 1990), p. 41.

6. However, we might by nature always act in our short-term interest. Morality might require, rather, that we act in our long-term interest. In this case, another problem arises. How could we be commanded by morality to do what we are not able to do? As we shall see in Chapter 5, according to Kant, "an ought implies a can."

7. We will return to this argument in looking at discussions on egoism by Kant. Other discussions of it can be found, for example, in James Sterba, "Justifying Morality: The Right and the Wrong Ways," *Synthese* 72 (1987): 45–69; James Rachels, "Egoism and Moral Skepticism," in *A New Introduction to Philosophy,* Steven M. Cahn (Ed.) (New York: Harper & Row, 1971).

8. See Adam Smith, *The Wealth of Nations* (New York: Edwin Cannan, 1904).

9. See the communitarian views in Robert Bellah, *Habits of the Heart* (Berkeley: University of California Press, 1985), and Amitai Etzioni, *The Spirit of Community: Rights, Responsibilities, and the Communitarian Agenda* (New York: Crown, 1993).

10. W. D. Falk, "Morality, Self and Others," in *Morality and the Language of Conduct,* Hector-Neri Castaneda and George Nakhnikian, 25–67 (Eds.) (Detroit: Wayne State University Press, 1963).

11. Benjamin Franklin, "Poor Richard's Almanac," in *American Philosophy: A Historical Anthology,* Barbara MacKinnon (Ed.), 46–47 (New York: State University of New York Press, 1985).

12. However, Foot has some problems fitting the virtue of justice into this generalization. Furthermore, she thinks of our best interest broadly—that is, as a kind of human flourishing. More discussion of this view can be found in Chapter 6.

13. See Thomas Nagel's discussion of these different possibilities of the relation between the good life and the moral life in "Living Right and Living Well," in *The View from Nowhere,* 189–207 (New York: Oxford University Press, 1986). Also see David Gauthier, "Morality and Advantage," *The Philosophical Review* (1967): 460–475.

Self Love*

Thomas Hobbes

Study Questions

1. What are the two sorts of motion of the body of which animals including humans are capable, according to Hobbes?

2. What kinds of motions are appetite and aversion? How are these related to love and hate?

3. How are good and evil related to these bodily motions, according to Hobbes?

4. In what ways are people equal and unequal? Which is more significant?

5. What happens when they desire the same thing? How does one solve this problem for oneself, according to Hobbes?

6. Should power or dominion over others be allowed, according to Hobbes?

7. According to Hobbes, what are the three principal causes of our quarrels with others?

8. How does Hobbes describe the state in which we live, then, if we do not have some power over us to keep order?

9. According to Hobbes, why do we establish societies with authorities and rules? How do fear and self-protection play a role in this?

10. What does Hobbes mean when he says that nature has given everyone a right to all? What is the result of this?

11. Outside of society and its rules, is there any right or wrong, or just or unjust, according to Hobbes?

There be in animals, two sorts of *motions* peculiar to them: one called *vital*; begun in generation, and continued without interruption through their whole life; such as are the *course* of the *blood,* the *pulse,* the *breathing,* the *concoction, nutrition, excretion,* etc. to which motions there needs no help of imagination: the other is *animal motion,* otherwise called *voluntary motion*; as to *go,* to *speak,* to *move* any of our limbs, in such manner as is first fancied in our minds. That sense is motion in the organs and interior parts of man's body, caused by the action of the things we see, hear, etc.; and that fancy is but the relics of the same motion, remaining after sense. . . . And because *going, speaking,* and the like voluntary motions, depend always upon a precedent thought of *whither, which way,* and *what*; it is evident, that the imagination is

Thomas Hobbes, "Leviathan," in *The English Works of Thomas Hobbes,* Vol. II, Sir William Molesworth (Ed.) (London: John Bohn, 1839), pp. 38–41, 85, 110–116.

*Title supplied by the editor.

the first internal beginning of all voluntary motion. And although unstudied men do not conceive any motion at all to be there, where the thing moved is invisible; or the space it is moved in is, for the shortness of it, insensible; yet that doth not hinder, but that such motions are. For let a space be never so little, that which is moved over a greater space, whereof that little one is part, must first be moved over that. These small beginnings of motion, within the body of man, before they appear in walking, speaking, striking, and other visible actions, are commonly called ENDEAVOR.

This endeavor, when it is toward something which causes it, is called APPETITE, or DESIRE; the latter, being the general name; and the other oftentimes restrained to signify the desire of food, namely *hunger* and *thirst*. And when the endeavor is fromward something, it is generally called AVERSION. These words, *appetite* and *aversion,* we have from the Latins; and they both of them signify the motions, one of approaching, the other of retiring. . . . For nature itself does often press upon men those truths, which afterwards, when they look for somewhat beyond nature, they stumble at. For the schools find in mere appetite to go, or move, no actual motion at all: but because some motion they must acknowledge, they call it metaphorical motion; which is but an absurd speech: for though words may be called metaphorical; bodies and motions cannot.

That which men desire, they are also said to LOVE: and to HATE those things for which they have aversion. So that desire and love are the same thing; save that by desire, we always signify the absence of the object; by love, most commonly the presence of the same. So also by aversion, we signify the absence; and by hate, the presence of the object.

Of appetites and aversions, some are born with men; as appetite of food, appetite of excretion, and exoneration, which may also and more properly be called aversions, from somewhat they feel in their bodies; and some other appetites, not many. The rest, which are appetites of particular things, proceed from experience, and trial of their effects upon themselves or other men. For of things we know not at all, or believe not to be, we can have no further desire, than to taste and try. But aversion we have for things, not only which we know have hurt us, but also that we do not know whether they will hurt us, or not.

Those things which we neither desire, nor hate, we are said to *contemn;* CONTEMPT being nothing else but an immobility, or contumacy of the heart, in resisting the action of certain things; and proceeding from that the heart is already moved otherwise, by other more potent objects; or from want of experience of them.

And because the constitution of a man's body is in continual mutation, it is impossible that all the same things should always cause in him the same appetites, and aversions: much less can all men consent, in the desire of almost any one and the same object.

But whatsoever is the object of any man's appetite or desire, that is it which he for his part calleth *good:* and the object of his hate and aversion, *evil;* and of his contempt, *vile* and *inconsiderable.* For these words of good, evil, and contemptible, are ever used with relation to the person that useth them: there being nothing simply and absolutely so; nor any common rule of good and evil, to be taken from the nature of the objects themselves. . . .

Felicity of this life consisteth not in the repose of a mind satisfied. For there is no such *finis ultimus,* utmost aim, nor *summum bonum,* greatest good, as is spoken of in the books of the old moral philosophers. Nor can a man any more live, whose desires are at an end, than he, whose senses and imaginations are at a stand. Felicity is a continual progress of the desire, from one object to another; the attaining of the former, being still but the way to the latter. The cause whereof is, that the object of man's desire, is not to enjoy once only, and for one instant of time; but to assure for ever, the way of his future desire. . . .

So that in the first place, I put for a general inclination of all mankind, a perpetual and restless desire of power after power, that ceaseth only in death. And the cause of this, is . . . that a man . . . cannot assure the power and means to live well, which he hath present, without the acquisition of more. . . .

Nature hath made men so equal, in the faculties of the body, and mind; as that though there be found one man sometimes manifestly stronger in body, or of quicker mind than another; yet when all is reckoned together, the difference between man, and man, is not so considerable, as that one man can thereupon claim to himself any benefit, to which another may not pretend, as well as he. For as to the strength of body, the weakest has strength enough to kill the strongest, either by secret machination, or by confederacy with others, that are in the same danger with himself.

And as to the faculties of the mind, setting aside the arts grounded upon words, and especially that skill of proceeding upon general, and infallible rules, called science; which very few have, and but in few things; as being not native faculty, born with us; nor attained, as prudence, while we look after somewhat else, I find yet a greater equality amongst men, than that of strength. For prudence, is but experience; which equal time, equally bestows on all men, in those things they equally apply themselves unto. That which may perhaps make such equality incredible, is but a vain conceit of one's own wisdom, which almost all men think they have in a greater degree, than the vulgar; that is, than all men but themselves, and a few others, whom by fame, or for concurring with themselves, they approve. For such is the nature of men, that howsoever they may acknowledge many others to be more witty, or more eloquent, or more learned; yet they will hardly believe there be many so wise as themselves; for they see their own wit at hand, and other men's at a distance. But this proveth rather that men are in that point equal, than unequal. For there is not ordinarily a greater sign of the equal distribution of any thing, than that every man is contented with his share.

From this equality of ability, ariseth equality of hope in the attaining of our ends. And therefore if any two men desire the same thing, which nevertheless they cannot both enjoy, they become enemies; and in the way to their end, which is principally their own conservation, and sometimes their delectation only, endeavor to destroy, or subdue one another. And from hence it comes to pass, that where an invader hath no more to fear, than another man's single power; if one plant, sow, build, or possess a convenient seat, others may probably be expected to come prepared with forces united, to dispossess, and deprive him, not only of the fruit of his labor, but also of his life, or liberty. And the invader again is in the like danger of another.

And from this diffidence of one another, there is no way for any man to secure himself, so reasonable, as anticipation; that is, by force, or wiles, to master the persons of all men he can, so long, till he see no other power great enough to endanger him: and this is no more than his own conservation requireth, and is generally allowed. Also because there be some, that taking pleasure in contemplating their own power in the acts of conquest, which they pursue farther than their security requires; if others, that otherwise would be glad to be at ease within modest bounds, should not by invasion increase their power, they would not be able, long time, by standing only on their defense, to subsist. And by consequence, such augmentation

of dominion over men being necessary to a man's conservation, it ought to be allowed him.

Again, men have no pleasure, but on the contrary a great deal of grief, in keeping company, where there is no power able to overawe them all. For every man looketh that his companion should value him, at the same rate he sets upon himself: and upon all signs of contempt, or undervaluing, naturally endeavors, as far as he dares, (which amongst them that have no common power to keep them in quiet, is far enough to make them destroy each other), to extort a greater value from his contemners, by damage; and from others, by the example. . . .

So that in the nature of man, we find three principal causes of quarrel. First, competition; secondly, diffidence; thirdly, glory.

The first, maketh men invade for gain; the second, for safety; and the third, for reputation. The first use violence, to make themselves masters of other men's persons, wives, children, and cattle; the second, to defend them; the third, for trifles, as a word, a smile, a different opinion, and any other sign of undervalue, either direct in their persons, or by reflection in their kindred, their friends, their nation, their profession, or their name.

Hereby it is manifest, that during the time men live without a common power to keep them all in awe, they are in that condition which is called war; and such a war, as is of every man, against every man. For WAR, consisteth not in battle only, or the act of fighting; but in a tract of time, wherein the will to contend by battle is sufficiently known: and therefore the notion of *time*, is to be considered in the nature of war; as it is in the nature of weather. For as the nature of foul weather, lieth not in a shower or two of rain; but in an inclination thereto of many days together: so the nature of war, consisteth not in actual fighting; but in the known disposition thereto, during all the time there is no assurance to the contrary. All other time is PEACE.

Whatsoever therefore is consequent to a time of war, where every man is enemy to every man; the same is consequent to the time, wherein men live without security, than what their own strength, and their own invention shall furnish them withal. In such condition, there is no place for industry; because the fruit thereof is uncertain: and consequently no culture of the earth; no navigation, nor use of the commodities that may be imported by sea; no commodious building; no instruments of moving, and removing, such things as require much force; no knowledge of the face of the earth; no account of time; no arts; no letters; no society; and which is worst of all, continual fear, and danger of violent death; and the life of man, solitary, poor, nasty, brutish, and short. . . .

It may peradventure be thought, there was never such a time, nor condition of war as this; and I believe it was never generally so, over all the world: but there are many places, where they live so now. For the savage people in many places of America, except the government of small families, the concord whereof dependeth on natural lust, have no government at all; and live at this day in that brutish manner, as I said before. Howsoever, it may be perceived what manner of life there would be, where there were no common power to fear, by the manner of life, which men that have formerly lived under a peaceful government, use to degenerate into, in a civil war.

But though there had never been any time, wherein particular men were in a condition of war one against another; yet in all times, kings, and persons of sovereign authority, because of their independency, are in continual jealousies, and in the state and posture of gladiators; having their weapons pointing, and their eyes fixed on one another; that is, their forts, garrisons, and guns upon the frontiers of their kingdoms; and continual spies upon their neighbors; which is a posture of war. But because they uphold thereby, the industry of their subjects; there does not follow from it, that misery, which accompanies the liberty of particular men.

All society therefore is either for gain, or for glory; that is, not so much for love of our fellows, as for the love of ourselves. But no society can be great or lasting, which begins from vain glory. Because that glory is like honor; if all men have it no man hath it, for they consist in comparison and precellence. Neither doth the society of others advance any whit the cause of my glorying in myself; for every man must account himself, such as he can make himself without the help of others. But though the benefits of this life may be much furthered by mutual help; since yet those may be better attained to by dominion than by the society of others, I hope no body will doubt, but that men would much more greedily be carried by nature, if all fear were removed, to obtain dominion, than to gain society. We must therefore resolve, that the original of all great and lasting societies consisted not in the mutual goodwill men had towards each other, but in the mutual fear they had of each other.

The cause of mutual fear consists partly in the natural equality of men, partly in their mutual will of hurting: whence it comes to pass, that we can neither expect from others, nor promise to ourselves the least security. For if we look on men full grown, and consider how brittle the frame of our human body is, which perishing, all its strength, vigor, and wisdom itself perisheth with it; and how easy a matter it is, even for the weakest man to kill the strongest: there is no reason why any man, trusting to his own strength, should conceive himself made by nature above others. They are equals, who can do equal things one against the other; but they who can do the greatest things, namely, kill, can do equal things. All men therefore among themselves are by nature equal; the inequality we now discern, hath its spring from the civil law. . . .

Among so many dangers therefore, as the natural lusts of men do daily threaten each other withal, to have a care of one's self is so far from being a matter scornfully to be looked upon, that one has neither the power nor wish to have done otherwise. For every man is desirous of what is good for him, and shuns what is evil, but chiefly the chiefest of natural evils, which is death; and this he doth by a certain impulsion of nature, no less than that whereby a stone moves downward. It is therefore neither absurd nor reprehensible, neither against the dictates of true reason, for a man to use all his endeavors to preserve and defend his body and the members thereof from death and sorrows. But that which is not contrary to right reason, that all men account to be done justly, and with right. Neither by the word *right* is anything else signified, than that liberty which every man hath to make use of his natural faculties according to right reason. Therefore the first foundation of natural right is this, that *every man as much as in him lies endeavor to protect his life and members.*

But because it is in vain for a man to have a right to the end, if the right to the necessary means be denied him, it follows, that since every man hath a right to preserve himself, he must also be allowed a right *to use all the means, and do all the actions, without which he cannot preserve himself.*

Now whether the means which he is about to use, and the action he is performing, be necessary to the preservation of his life and members or not, he himself, by the right of nature, must be judge. For if it be contrary to right reason that I should judge of mine own peril, say that another man is judge. Why now, because he judgeth of what concerns me, by the same reason, because we are equal by nature, will I judge also of things which do belong to him. Therefore it agrees with right reason, that is, it is the right of nature that I judge of his opinion, that is, whether it conduce to my preservation or not.

Nature hath given to *everyone a right to all*; that is, it was lawful for every man, in the bare state of nature, or before such time as men had engaged themselves by any covenants or bonds, to do what he would, and against whom he thought fit, and to possess, use, and enjoy all what he would, or could get. Now because whatsoever a man would, it therefore seems good to him because he wills it, and either it really doth, or at least seems to him to contribute towards his preservation, (but we have already allowed him to be judge, in the foregoing article, whether it doth or not, insomuch as we are to hold all for necessary whatsoever he shall esteem so), and . . . it appears that by the right of nature those things may be done, and must be had, which necessarily conduce to the protection of life and members, it follows, that in the state of nature, to have all, and do all, is lawful for all. And this is that which is meant by that common saying, *nature hath given all to all*. From whence we understand likewise, that in the state of nature profit is the measure of right.

But is was the least benefit for men thus to have a common right to all things. For the effects of this right are the same, almost, as if there had been no right at all. For although any man might say of every thing, *this is mine,* yet could he not enjoy it, by reason of his neighbor, who having equal right and equal power, would pretend the same thing to be his.

If now to this natural proclivity of men, to hurt each other, which they derive from their passions, but chiefly from a vain esteem of themselves, you add, the right of all to all, wherewith one by right invades, the other by right resists, and whence arise perpetual jealousies and suspicions on all hands, and how hard a thing it is to provide against an enemy invading us with an intention to oppress and ruin, though he come with a small number, and no great provision; it cannot be denied but that the natural state of men, before they entered into society, was a mere war, and that not simply, but a war of all men against all men. For what is WAR, but that same time in which the will of contesting by force is fully declared, either by words or deeds?

Review Exercises

1. Explain the basic difference between psychological egoism and ethical egoism.
2. Give two different formulations or versions of each.
3. To prove that the motivational version of psychological egoism is true, what must be shown?
4. How does the argument for ethical egoism differ from psychological egoism? What is one problem with this argument?
5. Summarize the arguments regarding the consistency or inconsistency of ethical egoism.
6. In what sense does the argument for ethical egoism based on economics support not egoism but utilitarianism, in other words, the view that we ought to do what is in the best interest of all or the greatest number?
7. What is meant by taking the "moral point of view"?
8. How does the example of the "Ring of Gyges" illustrate the question "Why be moral?"

Selected Bibliography

Baier, Kurt. *The Moral Point of View.* Ithaca, NY: Cornell University Press, 1958.

Campbell, Richmond. "A Short Refutation of Ethical Egoism," *Canadian Journal of Philosophy* 2 (1972): 249–254.

Feinberg, Joel. "Psychological Egoism" in *Reason and Responsibility.* Belmont, CA: Wadsworth, 1985.

Gauthier, David (Ed.). *Morality and Rational Self-Interest.* Englewood Cliffs, NJ: Prentice-Hall, 1970.

MacIntyre, Alasdair. "Egoism and Altruism," in *The Encyclopedia of Philosophy,* vol. 2, pp. 462–466, Paul Edwards (Ed.). New York: Macmillan, 1967.

Milo, Ronald D. (Ed.). *Egoism and Altruism.* Belmont, CA: Wadsworth, 1973.

Nagel, Thomas. *The Possibility of Altruism.* Oxford, England: Clarendon, 1970.

Olson, Robert G. *The Morality of Self-Interest.* New York: Harcourt Brace Jovanovich, 1965.

Rand, Ayn. *The Virtue of Selfishness.* New York: New American Library, 1964.

❧ 4 ❧

Utilitarianism

On January 29, 1993, a horrible chain of events occurred. Steven Page, the manager of a horticulture nursery, threw his three-year-old daughter, Kellie, from the Golden Gate Bridge in San Francisco and then jumped to his own death. Earlier that day, he had shot and killed his thirty-seven-year-old ex-wife, Nancy. Local police were mystified about his motive, and neighbors were shocked. In addition to the personal tragedy and its mysterious circumstances, the issue of erecting a suicide barrier on the bridge was again put before the public.

From 1937, the year the bridge was built, until March 1995, 987 people had jumped from the bridge to their deaths; more than 100 of these had taken place since 1990.[1] It is possible that many of these people's lives might have been spared if it had not been relatively easy to jump from the bridge. The barrier would consist of eight-foot-high vertical metal bars placed along the current railing. Those people arguing against the barrier cited the cost, which would now far exceed the 1975 estimate of $3 million. Others doubted that it would have much effect on the incidence of suicide, claiming that people intent on killing themselves would find some other way to do so. Still others objected to the barrier because of its negative aesthetic effect. People

can now use a sidewalk on the bridge to cross it and thus easily and clearly take in the beautiful views as they stroll.

Should such a barrier be erected? In a call-in poll conducted by the *San Francisco Examiner,* 46 percent said there should be a barrier on the bridge, but 54 percent said there should not.[2] Typical of the reasons given by those voting for the barrier is that it would save lives and "serve as a message that society cares, that we don't want you to kill yourself." Those voting against the barrier said that it would not prevent suicides anyway, and we should not do everything possible to prevent people from hurting themselves. Another asked, "Why punish millions who want to enjoy a breathtakingly beautiful view as we walk or drive across the bridge?"[3]

How should such a matter be decided? One way is to compare the benefits and costs of each alternative. Whichever has the greater net benefit is the best alternative. This method of cost-benefit analysis uses a contemporary version of utilitarianism. We begin with this moral theory because in some ways it is the easiest to understand and the closest to common sense. Put simply, this moral theory asserts that we ought to produce the most happiness or pleasure that we can and reduce suffering and unhappiness.

Historical Background: Jeremy Bentham and John Stuart Mill

The classical formulation of utilitarian moral theory is found in the writings of Jeremy Bentham (1748–1832) and John Stuart Mill (1806–1873). Jeremy Bentham was an English-born student of law and the leader of a radical movement for social and legal reform based on utilitarian principles. His primary published work was *Introduction to the Principles of Morals and Legislation* (1789). The title itself indicates his aim—namely, to take the same principles that provide the basis for morals as a guide for the formation and revision of law. He believed that there is not one set of principles for personal morality and another for social morality.

James Mill, the father of John Stuart Mill, was an associate of Bentham's and a supporter of his views. John Stuart was the eldest of his nine children. He was educated in the classics and history at home. By the time he was twenty, he had read Bentham and had became a devoted follower of his philosophy. According to one writer, John Stuart Mill "is generally held to be one of the most profound and effective spokesmen for the liberal view of man and society."[4] The basic ideas of utilitarian moral theory are summarized in his short work, *Utilitarianism.* In it he sought to dispel misconceptions that morality had nothing to do with usefulness or utility or that it was opposed to pleasure. He was also a strong supporter of personal liberty, and in his pamphlet *On Liberty* he argued that the only reason for society to interfere in a person's life to force that person to behave in certain ways was to prevent him or her from doing harm to others. People might choose wrongly, but he believed that allowing this was better than government coercion. Liberty to speak one's own opinion, he believed, would benefit all. However, it is not clear that utility is always served by promoting liberty. Nor is it clear what Mill would say in cases where liberty must be restricted to promote the general good. Thus, in his work *On the Subjection of Women,* Mill criticized those social treatments of women that did not allow them to develop their talents and contribute to society. He supported the right of women to vote. Later in life he married his longtime companion and fellow liberal, Harriet Taylor. He also served in the British Parliament from 1865 to 1868.

The original utilitarians were democratic in the sense that they believed that social policy ought to work for the good of all persons, not just the upper class. However, they also believed that when interests of various persons conflicted, the best choice was that which promoted the interests of the greater number. The utilitarians were progressive in that they questioned the status quo. If the contemporary punishment system was not working well, for example, then they believed that it ought to be changed. Social programs should be judged by their usefulness in promoting what was deemed to be good. Observation would determine whether a project or practice promoted this good. Thus, utilitarianism is part of the empiricist tradition in philosophy, for we only know what is good by observation or by appeal to experience. Bentham and Mill were also optimists. They believed that human wisdom and science would improve the lot of humanity. Mill wrote in *Utilitarianism,* "All the grand sources of human suffering are in a great degree, many of them almost entirely, conquerable by human care and effort."[5]

In this chapter you will learn about the basic principle of utilitarianism and how it is used to make moral judgments in individual cases. You will also learn something about different forms of utilitarianism. You can examine a few criticisms of the theory so as to judge for yourself whether it is a reasonable theory. Again, you will have the substance of utilitarianism in these sections. More detail about the theory can be found in the sections on act and rule utilitarianism, on Mill's proof of the theory, and on contemporary versions of utilitarianism.

The Principle of Utility

The basic moral principle of utilitarianism is called "The Principle of Utility" or "The Greatest

Happiness Principle." This principle has several formulations in Bentham and Mill as well as in utilitarianism since them. Here are two simplified formulations, one correlated with each title.

The morally best (or better) alternative is that which produces the greatest (or greater) net utility, where utility is defined in terms of happiness or pleasure.

We ought to do that which produces the greatest amount of happiness for the greatest number of people.

Notice that if we ask which of two actions is better, then our answer will be given in terms of the happiness or pleasure produced by each. If we ask which act is best overall, however, then we must consider not only the alternatives before us but also other possible choices. The right action will be the best possible action. The practical meaning of this distinction may be that we should not be satisfied with the most obvious alternative choices that we have before us, but that we ought to look further for better alternatives. However, this is getting a little ahead of ourselves in coming to understand utilitarianism. To understand the meaning of utilitarianism and its basic moral principle, you must examine several of its essential characteristics.

A Consequentialist Principle

First, utilitarianism is *teleological* in orientation. In other words, it stresses the end or goal of actions. Second, it is also a *consequentialist* moral theory. Consider the diagram used to classify moral theories given in Chapter 1.

According to utilitarian moral theory, to evaluate human acts or practices we do not consider the nature of the acts or practices nor the motive for which people do what they do. For example, building a suicide barrier on a bridge in itself is neither good nor bad. Nor is it sufficient that people supporting the building of such a barrier be well-intentioned. As Mill put it, "He who saves a fellow creature from drowning does what is morally right, whether his motive be duty or the hope of being paid for his trouble."[6] It is the result of one's action—that a life is saved—that matters morally. According to utilitarianism, we ought to decide which action or practice is best by considering the likely or actual consequences of each alternative. If erecting a suicide barrier on the Golden Gate Bridge is likely to have overall better consequences than not doing so, then that is what should be done. If one version of the barrier will save more lives than another at lesser or equal cost, then that is preferable. If the status quo has a greater balance of good over bad, then that is best. Nevertheless, this is not so simple to understand or to calculate. Thus, we will need to consider the theory and its method in more detail.

The Intrinsic Good: Pleasure or Happiness

It is not sufficient to say we ought to do that which has the best results or consequences because this in itself does not tell us which type of consequences are good. Classical utilitarianism is a *pleasure* or *happiness* theory. It was not the first such theory to appear in the history of philosophy. Aristotle's ethics, as we shall see in Chapter 6, is a happiness theory although different from utilitarianism. Closer to utilitarianism is the classical theory that has come to be known as *hedonism* (from *hedon*, the Greek word for pleasure) or *Epicureanism* (named after Epicurus, 341 B.C.–270 B.C.). Epicurus held that the good life was the pleasant life. For him this meant avoiding distress and desires for things beyond one's basic needs. Bodily pleasure and mental delight and peace were the goods to be sought in life.

Utilitarians also believed that pleasure or happiness is the good to be produced. As Bentham put it, "Nature has placed mankind under the governance of two sovereign masters, *pain* and *pleasure*. It is for them alone to point out what we ought to do, as well as to determine what we shall do."[7] Things such as fame, fortune, education, and freedom may be good, but only to the extent that they produce pleasure or happiness. In philosophical terms, they are *instrumental goods* because they are useful for attaining the goals of happiness and pleasure. Happiness and pleasure are the only *intrinsic goods*—that is, the only things good in themselves.

In this explanation of utilitarianism you may have noticed the seeming identification of pleasure and happiness. In classical utilitarianism there is no difference between pleasure and happiness. Both terms refer to a kind of psychic state of satisfaction. However, there are different types of pleasure of which humans are capable. According to Mill, we experience a range of pleasures or satisfactions from the physical satisfaction of hunger to the personal satisfaction of a job well done. Aesthetic pleasures, such as the pleasure of watching a beautiful sunset, are yet another type of pleasure. We also can experience intellectual pleasures such as the peculiar pleasure of making sense out of something. We express this satisfaction in phrases such as, "Ah, so that's it!" or "Now I see!" If this wider sense of pleasure is accepted, then it is easier to identify it with happiness.

We should consider the range of types of pleasure in our attempts to decide what the best action is. We also ought to consider other aspects of the pleasurable or happy experience. According to the greatest happiness or utility principle, we must measure, count, and compare the pleasurable experiences likely to be produced by various alternative actions in order to know which is best.

Calculating the Greatest Amount of Happiness

Utilitarianism is not an egoistic theory. As we noted in the previous chapter's presentation on egoism, those versions of egoism that say we ought to take care of ourselves because this works out better for all in the long run are actually versions of utilitarianism, not egoism. Some have called utilitarianism universalistic because it is the happiness or pleasure of all who are affected by an action or practice that is to be considered. We are not just to consider our own good, as in egoism, nor just the good of others, as in altruism. Sacrifice may be good, but not in itself. As Mill puts it, "A sacrifice which does not increase or tend to increase the sum total of happiness, [utilitarianism] considers as wasted."[8] Everyone affected by some action is to be counted equally. We ourselves hold no privileged place, so our own happiness counts no more than that of others. I may be required to do what displeases me but pleases others. Thus, in the following scenario, Act B is a better choice than Act A:

Act A makes me happy
and 2 other people happy.

Act B makes me unhappy
but 5 others happy.

In addition to counting each person equally, these five elements are used to calculate the greatest amount of happiness: the net amount of pleasure or happiness, its intensity, its duration, its fruitfulness, and the likelihood of any act to produce it.[9]

Pleasure Minus Pain Almost every alternative that we choose produces unhappiness or pain as well as happiness or pleasure for ourselves, if not for others. Pain is intrinsically bad and pleasure is intrinsically good. Something that produces pain may be accepted, but only if it causes more pleasure overall. For instance, if the painfulness of a punishment deters an unwanted behavior, then we ought to punish but no more than is necessary or useful. When an act produces both pleasure or happiness and pain or unhappiness, we can think of each moment of unhappiness as canceling out a moment of happiness, so that what is left to evaluate is the remaining or *net* happiness or unhappiness. We are also to think of pleasure and pain as coming in bits or moments. We can then calculate this net amount by adding and subtracting units of pleasure and displeasure. This is a device for calculating the greatest amount of happiness even if we cannot make mathematically exact calculations. The following simplified equation indicates how the net utility for two acts, A and B, might be determined. Think of the units as either happy persons or days of happiness:

Act A produces 12 units of happiness
and 6 of unhappiness
(12 – 6 = 6 units of happiness)

Act B produces 10 units of happiness
and 1 of unhappiness
(10 – 1 = 9 units of happiness)

In this case, Act B is preferable because it produces a greater net amount of happiness, namely, nine units compared to six for Act A.

Intensity   Moments of happiness or pleasure are not all alike. Some are more intense than others. The thrill of some exciting adventure—say, running the rapids—may produce a more intense pleasure than the serenity we feel in view of one of nature's wonders. All else being equal, the more intense the pleasure the better. All other factors being equal, if I have an apple to give away and am deciding which of two friends to give it to, I ought to give it to the friend who will enjoy it most. In calculations involving intensity of pleasure, a scale is sometimes useful. For example, we could use a positive scale of 1 to 10 degrees, from the least pleasurable to the most pleasurable. In the following scenario, then, Act B is better (all other things being equal) than Act A even though Act A gives pleasure to more people; this result is due to the greater intensity of pleasure produced by Act B:

Act A gives 40 people
each mild pleasure
(40 × 2 = 80 degrees of pleasure)

Act B gives 10 people
each intense pleasure
(10 × 10 = 100 degrees of pleasure)[10]

Duration   This is not all that matters regarding pleasure. The more serene pleasure may last longer. This also must be factored in our calculation. The longer lasting the pleasure the better, all else being equal. Thus, in the following scenario Act A is better than Act B because it gives more total days of pleasure or happiness, even though it affects fewer people:

Act A gives 3 people each
8 days of happiness
(3 × 8 = 24 days of happiness)

Act B gives 6 people each
2 days of happiness
(6 × 2 = 12 days of happiness)

Fruitfulness   A more serene nature pleasure may or may not be more fruitful than an exciting rapids-running pleasure. The fruitfulness of experiencing pleasure depends on whether it makes us more capable of experiencing similar or other pleasures. For example, the relaxing event may make one person more capable of experiencing other pleasures of friendship or understanding, while the thrilling event may do the same for another. The fruitfulness depends not only on the immediate pleasure, but also on the long-term results. Indulging in immediate pleasure may bring pain later on, as we know only too well! So also the pain today may be the only way to prevent more pain tomorrow. The dentist's work on our teeth may be painful today, but it makes us feel better in the long run by providing us with pain-free meals and undistracted, enjoyable meal conversations.

Likelihood   If we are attempting to decide between two available alternative actions, we must estimate the likely results of each before we compare their net utility. If one is considering whether to go out for some competition, one should consider the chances of doing well. One might have greater hope of success trying something else. It may turn out that we ought to choose an act with lesser rather than greater beneficial results if the chances of coming to be are better. It is not only the chances that would count but also the size of the prize. In the following equation, A is preferable to B. In this case, "A bird in the hand is worth two in the bush," as the old saying goes:

Act A has a 90% chance of giving
8 people each 5 days of pleasure
(40 days @ .90 = 36 days of pleasure)

Act B has a 40% chance of giving
10 people each 7 days of pleasure
(70 days @ .40 = 28 days of pleasure)

Quantity and Quality of Pleasure

Bentham and Mill are in agreement that the more pleasure or happiness the better. However, there is one significant difference between them. According to Bentham, we ought to consider only the *quantity* of pleasure or happiness brought about by various acts: how much pleasure, to how many people, how intense it is, how long-lasting, how fruitful, and how likely the desired outcome will occur. Consider Bentham's own comment on this point: The "quantity of pleasure being equal, pushpin [a game] is as good as poetry."[11] The aesthetic or intellectual pleasure that one might derive from reading and understanding a poem is no better in itself than the simple pleasures gained from playing a mindless game (which we suppose pushpin to be).

While Mill agreed with Bentham that the greater amount of pleasure and happiness the better, he believed that the *quality* of the pleasure should also count. In his autobiography, Mill describes his experience of a mental crisis in which he realized that he had not found sufficient place in his life for aesthetic experiences; he realized that this side of the human personality also needed developing and that these pleasures were significantly different from others.

This experience and his thoughts about it may have led him to focus on the quality of pleasures. Some are intrinsically better than others. Intellectual pleasures are more valuable in themselves than purely sensual pleasures. Although he does not tell us how much more valuable they are (twice as valuable?), he clearly believed this ought to be factored into our calculation of the "greatest amount of happiness." While I may not always be required to choose a book over food (for example, I may now need the food more than the book), the intellectual pleasures that might be derived from reading the book are better in themselves than the pleasures gained from eating. Bentham, in contrast, would have asked how such pleasures can be more valuable except as they give us a greater amount of pleasure.

Mill attempts to prove or show that intellectual pleasures are better than sensual ones. We are to ask persons who have experienced a range of pleasures whether they would prefer to live a life of a human, in spite of all its disappointments and pains, or the life of an animal, which is full of pleasures but only sensual pleasures. He believes that people generally would choose the former. They would prefer, as he puts it, "to be a human being dissatisfied than a pig satisfied; better to be Socrates dissatisfied than a fool satisfied."[12] Socrates, as you may know, was often frustrated in his attempt to know certain things. He did not know what was true beauty or justice. Because human beings have greater possibilities for knowledge and achievement, they also have greater potential for failure, pain, and frustration. The point of the argument is that the only reason why we would prefer a life of fewer net pleasures (the dissatisfactions subtracted from the total satisfactions of human life) to a life of a greater total amount of pleasures (the life of the pig) is that we value something other than the *amount* of pleasures; we value the *kind* of pleasures as well.[13] When considering this argument, you might ask yourself two questions. First, would people generally prefer to be Socrates rather than the pig? Second, if Mill is correct on his factual assessment, then what does this fact prove? If people do want a certain type of life with certain pleasures, does this fact make it a better life and the pleasures better pleasures? For that matter, this argument may introduce another independent criterion for what is good and perhaps create a quite different type of moral theory than utilitarianism.

When we consider all of the variables concerning pleasure and happiness that are to be counted when trying to estimate the "greatest amount of pleasure or happiness," the task of doing so looks extremely difficult. We must consider how many people will be affected by alternative actions, whether they will be pleased or pained by them, how pleased or pained they will be and for how long, and the likelihood that what we estimate will happen will, in fact, come to be. In addition, if we want to follow Mill, rather than Bentham, we must consider whether the pleasures will be the more lowly sensual pleasures, the higher types of more intellectual pleasures, or something in between. However, in reality we may at any one time only have to consider a couple of these variables because only they may be relevant. Where it does get complex, utilitarians would tell us that the more we are able to factor these variables into our decision making the better our judgments and choices.

Evaluating Utilitarianism

The following considerations are just some of the many that have been raised by those who wish to determine whether utilitarianism is a valid moral theory.

Application of the Principle

One reaction to calculating the greatest amount of happiness that students often have is that this theory is too complex. No one can consider all of the variables that it requires us to consider: the probable consequences of our action to all affected in terms of duration, intensity, fruitfulness, likelihood, and type or quality of pleasure.[14] However, a utilitarian could respond that, although given this complexity no one is a perfect judge, we do make better judgments the bet-

ter we are able to consider these variables. No moral theory is simple in its application. A more difficult problem in how to apply the principle of utility comes from Mill's own statements of it. It may well be that in some cases, at least, one cannot both maximize happiness and make the greatest number of people happy. Thus, one choice may produce 200 units of happiness—but for just one person. The other alternative might produce 150 units of happiness, 50 for each of three people. If the maximization overall is taken as primary, then we should go with the first choice, while if the number of people is to take precedence we should go with the second choice. The best reading of Mill, however, seems to give preference to the maximization overall. In that case, how the happiness was distributed (to one or three) would not in effect count; that is one of the problems some people have with this theory.

Consistency with Other Moral Beliefs

A more substantive criticism of utilitarianism concerns its universalist and maximizing nature, that we should always do that which maximizes overall happiness. For one thing, this theory does not seem to allow us to consider our own happiness in some privileged place, nor the happiness of those closer to us when to do so does not maximize happiness. I can give no more weight to my own projects or my own children in determining what to do than other peoples' similar projects or others' children. For some philosophers, that I must treat all persons equally is contrary to common sense. Utilitarians might respond that we should probably give more attention to our own projects and our own children, but only because this is likely to have better results overall. We know better how to promote our own projects and have more motivation to do so. Thus, giving preference to ourselves will probably be more effective. The objection remains that not to give some preference to ourselves is an affront to our personal integrity.[15] The idea is that utilitarianism seems to imply that I am not important from my own point of view. However, a utilitarian might respond that it is important that people regard themselves as unique and give due consideration for their own interests because this will probably have better consequences for both the society and themselves. An ethics that stresses caring for individuals would object to the impersonalism of this aspect of utilitarianism. (See Chapter 7.)

A second criticism concerns utilitarianism's consequentialist nature. You may have heard the phrase, "The end justifies the means." People often refer to this phrase with a certain amount of disdain. Utilitarianism, as a consequentialist moral theory, holds that it is the consequences or ends of our actions that determine whether particular means to them are justified. This seems to lead to conclusions that are contrary to commonsense morality. For example, wouldn't it justify punishing an innocent person, a "scapegoat," in order to prevent a great evil or promote a great good? Or could we not justify on utilitarian grounds the killing of some for the sake of the good of a greater number? Or could I not make an exception for myself from obeying a law, alleging it is for some greater long-term good? Utilitarians might respond by noting that such actions or practices will probably do more harm than good, especially if we take a long-range view. In particular, they might point out that practices that allow the punishment of those known to be innocent are not likely to deter as well as those that punish only the guilty or proven guilty.

Act and Rule Utilitarianism

One criticism that is brought against utilitarianism as so far described is that it justifies any action just so long as it has better consequences than other available actions. Therefore, cheating, stealing, lying, and breaking promises may all seem to be justified, depending on whether they maximize happiness in some particular case. Whether as a response to this type of criticism or for other reasons, a slightly different version of utilitarianism has been developed in the decades since Mill. Some people find evidence for it in Mill's own writings.[16] This second version is usually called *rule utilitarianism*, and it is contrasted with what we have so far described, which is called *act utilitarianism*.

Both are forms of utilitarianism. They are alike in requiring us to produce the greatest amount of happiness or pleasure (in all the senses described) for the greatest number of people. They differ in what they believe we ought to consider in estimating the consequences. Act utilitarianism states that we ought to consider the consequences of *each act* separately. Rule utilitarianism states that we ought to consider the consequences of the act performed as a *general practice*.[17]

Take the following example. Sue is considering whether to keep or break her promise to go out with Ken. She believes that if she breaks this promise in order to do something else with some other friends, Ken will be unhappy, but she and the other friends will be happier. According to act utilitarianism, if the consequences of her breaking the promise are better than keeping it, then that is what she ought to do. She may use handy "rules of thumb" to help her determine whether keeping the promise or breaking it is more likely to result in the better consequences. Mill called these "direction points along the way" that one can use.[18] "Honesty is the best policy" is one such guide. It is still the consequences of the act under consideration that determine what Sue ought to do.

Act utilitarianism: Consider the consequences of this act of promise keeping or promise breaking.

A rule utilitarian would tell Sue to consider what the results would be if everyone broke promises or broke promises in similar situations. The question "What if everyone did that?" is familiar to us.[19] She should ask what the results would be if this were a general practice or a general rule that people followed. It is likely that trust in promises would be weakened. This would be bad, she might think, because if we could not trust one another to keep our promises, then we would generally be less capable of making plans and relating to one another, two sources of human happiness. So, even if there would be no breakdown in that trust from just this one case of breaking a promise, Sue should still probably keep her promise according to rule utilitarian thinking.

Rule utilitarianism: Consider the consequences of the practice of promise keeping or promise breaking.

Another way to consider the method of reasoning used by the rule utilitarian is the following. I should ask what would be the best practice. For example, regarding promises, what rule would have the better results when people followed that rule? Would it be the rule or practice "Never break a promise made"? At the other extreme end of the spectrum would be a practice of keeping promises only if the results of doing so would be better than breaking them. (This actually amounts to act utilitarian reasoning.) However, there might be a better rule yet such as "Always keep your promise unless to do so would have very serious harmful consequences." If this rule were followed, people would generally have the benefits of being able to say, "I promise," and have people generally believe and trust them. The fact that the promise would not be kept in some limited circumstances would probably not do great harm to the practice of making promises.

Some philosophers go further and ask us to think about sets of rules. It is not only the practice of truthfulness but also of promise keeping and bravery and care for children that we must evaluate. Moreover, we should think of these rules as forming a system in which there are rules for priority and stringency. These rules would tell us which practices were more important and how important they were compared to the others. We should then do what the best system of moral rules would dictate, where best is still defined in terms of the maximization of happiness.[20]

Which form of utilitarianism is better is a matter of dispute. Act utilitarians can claim that we ought to consider only what will or is likely to happen if we act in certain ways, not what *would* happen if we acted in certain ways but is not going to happen because we are not going to so act. Rule utilitarians can claim that acts are similar to one another and so can be thought of as practices. My lying in one case to get myself out of a difficulty is similar to others' lying in other cases to get themselves out of difficulties. Because we should make the same judgments about similar cases (for consistency's sake), we should judge this act by comparing it with the results of the actions of everyone in similar circumstances. We can thus evaluate the general practice of "lying to get oneself out of a difficulty."

"Proof" of the Theory

One of the best ways to evaluate a moral theory is to examine carefully the reasons that are given to support it. Being an empiricist theory, utilitarianism must draw its evidence from experience. This is what Mill does in his attempt to prove that the principle of utility is the correct moral principle. (Note, however, that Mill himself believes that the notion of "proof" is different for moral theory than perhaps for science.) His argument is as follows: Just as the only way in which we know that something is visible is its being seen, and the only way we can show that something is audible is if it can be heard, so also the only proof that we have that something is desirable is its being desired. Because we desire happiness, we thus know it is desirable or good. In fact, Mill holds that happiness is the only thing we desire for its own sake. All else we desire because we believe it will lead to happiness. Thus, happiness or pleasure is the only thing good in itself or the only intrinsic good. All other goods are instrumental goods; in other words, they are good in so far as they lead to happiness. For example, reading is not good in itself but only in so far as it brings us pleasure or understanding (which is either pleasurable in itself or leads to pleasure).

Critics have pointed out that Mill's analogy between what is visible, audible, and desirable does not hold up under analysis. In all three words, the suffix means "able to be," but in the case of "desirable" Mill needs to prove not only that we can desire happiness (it is able to be desired), but also that it is *worth* being desired. Furthermore, just because we do desire something does not necessarily mean that we ought to desire it or that it is good. The moral philosopher David Hume put it succinctly: You cannot derive an "ought" from an "is."[21] However, Mill himself recognizes the difficulty of proving matters in ethics, and that the proofs here will be indirect rather than direct. He does add a further comment to bolster his case about happiness, in particular, as an object of desire. He asserts that this desire for happiness is universal and that we are so constructed that we can desire nothing except what appears to us to be or to bring happiness. You may want to consider whether these latter assertions are consistent with his empiricism. Does he know these things from experience? In addition, Mill may be simply pointing to what we already know, rather than giving a proof of the principle. You can find out what people believe is good by noticing what they do desire. In this case, they desire to be happy.[22]

Contemporary Versions

In this chapter we have described what is known as the classical form of utilitarianism. It is a happiness or pleasure maximization theory. Note that other forms of utilitarian thinking exist that would be derived from taking other goods as the end to be promoted. One could hold that knowledge, peace, freedom, education, beauty, or power were the goods to be maximized. Depending on what was on the list of intrinsic goods, different forms of utilitarianism or consequentialism could be developed. Details similar to those in the classical formulation would then need to be worked out. Since Mill's writings, other forms of utilitarianism also have been developed. Two of these forms are *preference utilitarianism* and *cost-benefit analysis*.

Preference Utilitarianism

Those people of a more behaviorist orientation who are skeptical of being able to measure and compare human feelings of happiness or pleasure have turned to considerations of preference satisfaction. They have developed what has been called *preference utilitarianism*. According to this version, the action that is best is the one that satisfies the most preferences, either in themselves or according to their strength or their order of importance. Theories that attempt to do this can become quite complex. Democracy is just such a system in which we count the preferences. However, in voting we do not take into consideration the strength of people's preferences or support or what they would choose in the second or third place, for example.

One method of identifying people's preferences is looking at what they say they want or prefer. People express their preferences in a variety of ways, such as through polls. In the Golden Gate Bridge suicide barrier poll, results showed that 54 percent of those polled opposed the barrier. The best choice, then, would be to satisfy the majority of preferences and not build the barrier. Critics, of course, may want to know how informed the choices were and whether the poll was scientific or valid.

Another method of knowing what people want or value is *implied* from their behavior. If we want to know whether people appreciate the national parks, we ought to consider the numbers of people who visit them. If we want to know whether people prefer fancy sports cars or four-wheel drives, we ask, "Which cars do they buy?" Although making such calculations has practical problems, there are also more substantive difficulties with this form of utilitarianism. One of these more substantive problems is that any preference seems to count equally with any other, no matter if it is for hurting or helping others. Some philosophers have attempted to get around this objection by considering only self-regarding preferences. Thus, our preferences for others, whether to benefit them or harm them, will not be considered. Do you think that this revision of preference utilitarianism satisfies this objection to it?

Cost-Benefit Analysis

A version of utilitarianism used widely today is *cost-benefit analysis*. One policy is better than another if it is the least costly compared to the benefits expected. Often the measure is money. Cost-benefit analysis is a measure of efficiency. One problem with this method of evaluation is that it is difficult, if not impossible, to put a dollar value on things such as freedom or a life— so-called intangibles. Nevertheless, there are many times in which we explicitly or implicitly do make such dollar assignments. Insurance and court settlements for loss of life or limb, and decisions about how much to pay to reduce risk to human life, as in safety regulations, are but two of these. According to one method of valuing human life, we ought to consider what people are willing to pay to reduce their risk of death by a certain amount. Or we can calculate what increase in compensation people would accept to do a job in which the risk to their lives is correspondingly increased. From these calculations economists can figure a dollar amount that is equivalent to the value that people seem to place on their own lives.[23] (See Chapter 16 for further discussion of this method.)

Now consider how this version might be used to determine whether to build a suicide-prevention barrier for the Golden Gate Bridge. One would have to estimate the number of lives likely to be saved by this barrier, and then give some monetary value to each life. Then one would have to estimate the likely negative consequences of building the barrier, such as the estimate of financial cost. In addition, one would have to determine the negative aesthetic effect, not only by counting the number of lost aesthetic experiences but also by calculating their value. While we tend to think that putting a dollar value either on lives or on aesthetic experiences is not something we can or ought to do, that is what is done in many instances in policy. For example, although we could make our buildings and highways safer by spending more, we implicitly believe that we need not spend more than a certain amount.

Another example of the use of cost-benefit analysis is the debate over the U.S. federal deficit. One issue that arises in this debate is how to value the cost of social programs that benefit the poor or the elderly. Ought their value be judged by their contributions to society or the number of years of life they are expected to live, or ought every life be valued equally? A further problem is added when we consider the effect of this spending on future generations. For example, if the spending increases the federal deficit, would this have a negative effect on future people? Are these people, who do not yet exist, also to be valued for the purposes of cost-benefit calculations?[24]

Utilitarianism is a highly influential moral theory that also has had significant influence on a wide variety of policy assessment methods. It can be quite useful for evaluating alternative health care systems, for example. Whichever system brings the most benefit to the most people with the least cost is the system that we probably ought to support. While Mill was quite optimistic about the ability and willingness of people to increase human happiness and reduce suffering, there is no doubt that the ideal is a good one. Nevertheless, utilitarianism has some difficulties, some of which we have discussed here. You will have a better view of this theory when you can compare it with those treated in the following chapters.

Notes

1. *San Francisco Chronicle,* Jan. 30, 1993, and the *San Francisco Examiner,* Jan. 31, 1993. Also see the March 26, 1995, issue of the *San Francisco Chronicle,* p. A3.
2. *San Francisco Examiner,* Feb. 2, 1993, A4.
3. Ibid.
4. J. B. Schneewind in the *Encyclopedia of Philosophy,* Paul Edwards (Ed.), vol. 5, p. 314 (New York: Macmillan, 1967).
5. *Utilitarianism,* Oskar Priest (Ed.) (Indianapolis, IN: Bobbs-Merrill, 1957), 20.
6. Ibid., 24.

7. Jeremy Bentham, *An Introduction to the Principles of Morals and Legislation* (New York: Oxford University Press, 1789).

8. *Utilitarianism,* 22.

9. These elements for calculation of the greatest amount of happiness are from Bentham's *Principles of Morals and Legislation.*

10. You may have noticed some ambiguity in the formulation of the "greatest happiness" principle version just described and used so far in our explanation. In this example, Act A makes more people happy than Act B, but the overall amount of happiness when considering degrees is greater in Act B. Thus, it is the greater amount of happiness that we have counted as more important than the greater number of people. One must choose whether we shall count the greatest amount of happiness or the greatest number of people, for we cannot always have both.

11. Bentham, *Principles of Morals and Legislation.*

12. *Utilitarianism,* 14.

13. This is an empiricist argument: It is based on an appeal to purported facts. People's actual preferences for intellectual pleasures (if true) are the only source we have for believing them to be more valuable.

14. It also requires us to have a common unit of measurement of pleasure. Elementary units called *hedons* have been suggested. We must think of pleasures of all kinds, then, as variations on one basic type. Obviously, this is problematic.

15. J.J.C. Smart and Bernard Williams, *Utilitarianism: For and Against* (Cambridge: Cambridge University Press, 1973). Also see Samuel Scheffler, *The Rejection of Consequentialism* (Oxford, England: Clarendon, 1982). Shelley Kagan distinguishes the universalist element of utilitarianism, *its demand that I treat all equally,* from the maximizing element, *that I must bring about the most good possible.* The first element makes utilitarianism too demanding, while the second allows us to do anything as long as it maximizes

16. One comment from *Utilitarianism* has a decidedly rule utilitarian ring: "In the case of abstinences indeed—of things which people forbear to do from moral considerations, though the consequences in the particular case might be beneficial—it would be unworthy of an intelligent agent not to be consciously aware that the action is of a class which, if practiced generally, would be generally injurious, and that this is the ground of the obligation to abstain from it" (p. 25). Other such examples can be found in the final chapter.

17. See, for example, the explanation of this difference in J.J.C. Smart, "Extreme and Restricted Utilitarianism," *Philosophical Quarterly* IV (1956).

18. Ibid., 31.

19. Just how to formulate the "that," the practice or rule whose consequences we are to consider, is a significant problem for rule utilitarians, but one that we will not develop here. Suffice it to note that it must have some degree of generality and not be something that applies to just me: "What if everyone named John Doe did that?" It would be more like, "What if everyone broke their promise in order to get themselves out of a difficulty?"

20. Richard Brandt, "Some Merits of One Form of Rule Utilitarianism," in *Morality and the Language of Conduct,* H. N. Castaneda and George Nakhnikian (Eds.) (Detroit: Wayne State University Press, 1970), 282–307.

21. David Hume, *Treatise on Human Nature* (London, 1739–1740).

22. This explanation is given by Mary Warnock in her introduction to the Fontana edition of Mill's *Utilitarianism,* 25–26.

23. See Barbara MacKinnon, "Pricing Human Life," *Science, Technology & Human Values,* 11, no. 2 (Spring 1986): 29–39.

24. This example was provided by one of the reviewers.

happiness overall. In *The Limits of Morality* (New York: Oxford University Press, 1989).

Utilitarianism

John Stuart Mill

Study Questions

1. How does Mill describe the basic moral standard of utilitarianism?

2. How does he defend himself against those who say that this is a crass pleasure theory?

3. What is the basis for knowing that some pleasures are better in quality than others? Which pleasures are these? How does he answer those who might say that people would not always prefer the life of a human being over the life of a fully satisfied animal such as a pig?

4. Whose happiness or pleasure, then, should we promote? Are animals included?

5. According to Mill, how are we to know whether anything is desirable or good?

6. How do we know that happiness is a good in itself or as an end?

7. How does he respond to the assertion that there are things other than happiness that people seem to desire for their own sakes?

What Utilitarianism Is

The creed which accepts as the foundation of morals "utility" or the "greatest happiness principle" holds that actions are right in proportion as they tend to promote happiness; wrong as they tend to produce the reverse of happiness. By happiness is intended pleasure and the absence of pain; by unhappiness, pain and the privation of pleasure. To give a clear view of the moral standard set up by the theory, much more requires to be said; in particular, what things it includes in the ideas of pain and pleasure, and to what extent this is left an open question. But these supplementary explanations do not affect the theory of life on which this theory of morality is grounded—namely, that pleasure and freedom from pain are the only things desirable as ends; and that all desirable

Selections from *Utilitarianism,* Chapters 2 and 4 (London, 1863).

things (which are as numerous in the utilitarian as in any other scheme) are desirable either for pleasure inherent in themselves or as means to the promotion of pleasure and the prevention of pain.

Now such a theory of life excites in many minds, and among them in some of the most estimable in feeling and purpose, inveterate dislike. To suppose that life has (as they express it) no higher end than pleasure—no better and nobler object of desire and pursuit—they designate as utterly mean and groveling, as a doctrine worthy only of swine, to whom the followers of Epicurus were, at a very early period, contemptuously likened; and modern holders of the doctrine are occasionally made the subject of equally polite comparisons by its German, French, and English assailants.

When thus attacked, the Epicureans have always answered that it is not they, but their accusers, who represent human nature in a degrading light, since the accusation supposes human beings to be capable of no pleasures except those of which swine are capable. If this supposition were true, the charge could not be gainsaid, but would then be no longer an imputation; for if the sources of pleasure were precisely the same to human beings and to swine, the rule of life which is good enough for the one would be good enough for the other. The comparison of the Epicurean life to that of beasts is felt as degrading, precisely because a beast's pleasures do not satisfy a human being's conceptions of happiness. Human beings have faculties more elevated than the animal appetites and, when once made conscious of them, do not regard anything as happiness which does not include their gratification. I do not, indeed, consider the Epicureans to have been by any means faultless in drawing out their scheme of consequences from the utilitarian principle. To do this in any sufficient manner, many Stoic, as well as Christian, elements require to be included. But there is no known Epicurean theory of life which does not assign to the pleasures of the intellect, of the feelings and imagination, and of the moral sentiments a much higher value as pleasures than to those of mere sensation. It must be admitted, however, that utilitarian writers in general have placed the superiority of mental over bodily pleasures chiefly in the greater permanency, safety, uncostliness, etc., of the former—that is, in their circumstantial advantages rather than in their intrinsic nature. And on all these points utilitarians have fully proved their case; but they might have taken the other and, as it may be called, higher ground with entire consistency. It is quite compatible with the principle of utility to recognize the fact that some kinds of pleasure are more desirable and more valuable than others. It would be absurd that, while in estimating all other things quality is considered as well as quantity, the estimation of pleasure should be supposed to depend on quantity alone.

Some Pleasures Are Better than Others*

If I am asked what I mean by difference of quality in pleasures, or what makes one pleasure more valuable than another, merely as a pleasure, except its being greater in amount, there is but one possible answer. Of two pleasures, if there be one to which all or almost all who have experience of both give a decided preference, irrespective of any feeling of moral obligation to prefer it, that is the more desirable pleasure. If one of the two is, by those who are competently acquainted with both, placed so far above the other that they prefer it, even though knowing it to be attended with a greater amount of discontent, and would not resign it for any quantity of the other pleasure which their nature is capable of, we are justified in ascribing to the preferred enjoyment a superiority in quality so far outweighing quantity as to render it, in comparison, of small account.

Now it is an unquestionable fact that those who are equally acquainted with and equally capable of appreciating and enjoying both do give a most marked preference to the manner of existence which employs their higher faculties. Few human creatures would consent to be changed into any of the lower animals for a promise of the fullest allowance of a beast's pleasures; no intelligent human being would consent to be a fool, no instructed person would be an ignoramus, no person of feeling and conscience would be selfish and base, even though they should be persuaded that the fool, the dunce, or the rascal is better satisfied with his lot than they are with theirs. They would not resign what they possess more than he for the most complete satisfaction of all the desires which they have in common with him. If they ever fancy they would, it is only in cases of unhappiness so extreme that to escape from it they would exchange their lot for almost any other, however undesirable in their own eyes. A being of higher faculties requires more to make him happy, is capable probably of more acute suffering, and certainly accessible to it at more points, than one of an inferior type; but in spite of these liabilities, he can never really wish to sink into what he feels to be a lower grade of existence. We may give what explanation we please of this unwillingness; we may attribute it to pride, a name which is given indiscriminately to some of the most and to some of the least estimable feelings of which mankind are capable; we may refer it to the love of liberty and personal independence, an appeal to which was with the Stoics one of the most effective means for the inculcation of it; to the love of power or to the love of excitement, both of which do really enter into and contribute to it; but its most appropriate appellation is a sense of dignity, which all human beings possess in one form or other, and in some, though by no means in exact, proportion to their higher faculties, and which is so essential a part of the happiness of those in whom it is strong that nothing which conflicts with it could be otherwise than momentarily an object of desire to them. Whoever supposes that this preference takes place at a sacrifice of happiness—that the superior being, in anything like equal circumstances, is not happier than the inferior—confounds the two very different ideas of happiness and content. It is indisputable that the being whose capacities of enjoyment are low has the greatest chance of having them fully satisfied; and a highly endowed being will always feel that any happiness which he can look for, as the world is constituted, is imperfect. But he can learn to bear its imperfections, if they are at all bearable; and they will not make him envy the being who is indeed unconscious of the imperfections, but only because he feels not at all the good which those imperfections qualify. It is better to be a human being dissatisfied than a pig satisfied; better to be Socrates dissatisfied than a fool satisfied. And if the fool, or the pig, are of a different opinion, it is because they only know their own side of the question. The other party to the comparison knows both sides.

---

*Headings added by the editor—ED.

It may be objected that many who are capable of the higher pleasures occasionally, under the influence of temptation, postpone them to the lower. But this is quite compatible with a full appreciation of the intrinsic superiority of the higher. Men often, from infirmity of character, make their election for the nearer good, though they know it to be the less valuable; and this no less when the choice is between two bodily pleasures than when it is between bodily and mental. They pursue sensual indulgences to the injury of health, though perfectly aware that health is the greater good. It may be further objected that many who begin with youthful enthusiasm for everything noble, as they advance in years, sink into indolence and selfishness. But I do not believe that those who undergo this very common change voluntarily choose the lower description of pleasures in preference to the higher. I believe that, before they devote themselves exclusively to the one, they have already become incapable of the other. Capacity for the nobler feelings is in most natures a very tender plant, easily killed, not only by hostile influences, but by mere want of sustenance; and in the majority of young persons it speedily dies away if the occupations to which their position in life has devoted them, and the society into which it has thrown them, are not favorable to keeping that higher capacity in exercise. Men lose their high aspirations as they lose their intellectual tastes, because they have not time or opportunity for indulging them; and they addict themselves to inferior pleasures, not because they deliberately prefer them, but because they are either the only ones to which they have access or the only ones which they are any longer capable of enjoying. It may be questioned whether anyone who has remained equally susceptible to both classes of pleasures ever knowingly and calmly preferred the lower, though many, in all ages, have broken down in an ineffectual attempt to combine both.

From this verdict of the only competent judges, I apprehend there can be no appeal. On a question which is the best worth having of two pleasures, or which of two modes of existence is the most grateful to the feelings, apart from its moral attributes and from its consequences, the judgment of those who are qualified by knowledge of both, or, if they differ, that of the majority among them, must be admitted as final. And there needs be the less hesitation to accept this judgment respecting the quality of pleasures, since there is no other tribunal to be referred to even

on the question of quantity. What means are there of determining which is the acutest of two pains, or the intenser of two pleasurable sensations, except the general suffrage of those who are familiar with both? Neither pains nor pleasures are homogeneous, and pain is always heterogeneous with pleasure. What is there to decide whether a particular pleasure is worth purchasing at the cost of a particular pain, except the feelings and judgment of the experienced? When, therefore, those feelings and judgment declare the pleasures derived from the higher faculties to be preferable in kind, apart from the question of intensity, to those of which the animal nature, disjoined from the higher faculties, is susceptible, they are entitled on this subject to the same regard.

The Moral Standard

I have dwelt on this point as being a necessary part of a perfectly just conception of utility or happiness considered as the directive rule of human conduct. But it is by no means an indispensable condition to the acceptance of the utilitarian standard; for that standard is not the agent's own greatest happiness, but the greatest amount of happiness altogether; and if it may possibly be doubted whether a noble character is always the happier for its nobleness, there can be no doubt that it makes other people happier, and that the world in general is immensely a gainer by it. Utilitarianism, therefore, could only attain its end by the general cultivation of nobleness of character, even if each individual were only benefited by the nobleness of others, and his own, so far as happiness is concerned, were a sheer deduction from the benefit. But the bare enunciation of such an absurdity as this last renders refutation superfluous.

According to the greatest happiness principle, as above explained, the ultimate end, with reference to and for the sake of which all other things are desirable—whether we are considering our own good or that of other people—is an existence exempt as far as possible from pain, and as rich as possible in enjoyments, both in point of quantity and quality; the test of quality and the rule for measuring it against quantity being the preference felt by those who, in their opportunities of experience, to which must be added their habits of self-consciousness and self-observation, are best furnished with the means of comparison. This, being according to the utilitarian opinion the end of human action, is necessarily also the standard of morality, which may accordingly be defined "the rules and precepts for human conduct," by the observance of which an existence such as has been described might be, to the greatest extent possible, secured to all mankind; and not to them only, but, so far as the nature of things admits, to the whole sentient creation. . . .

Of What Sort of Proof the Principle of Utility Is Susceptible

It has already been remarked that questions of ultimate ends do not admit of proof, in the ordinary acceptation of the term. To be incapable of proof by reasoning is common to all first principles, to the first premises of our knowledge, as well as to those of our conduct. But the former, being matters of fact, may be the subject of a direct appeal to the faculties which judge of fact—namely, our senses and our internal consciousness. Can an appeal be made to the same faculties on questions of practical ends? Or by what other faculty is cognizance taken of them?

Questions about ends are, in other words, questions [about] what things are desirable. The utilitarian doctrine is that happiness is desirable, and the only thing desirable, as an end; all other things being only desirable as means to that end. What ought to be required of this doctrine, what conditions is it requisite that the doctrine should fulfill—to make good its claim to be believed?

The only proof capable of being given that an object is visible is that people actually see it. The only proof that a sound is audible is that people hear it; and so of the other sources of our experience. In like manner, I apprehend, the sole evidence it is possible to produce that anything is desirable is that people do actually desire it. If the end which the utilitarian doctrine proposes to itself were not, in theory and in practice, acknowledged to be an end, nothing could ever convince any person that it was so. No reason can be given why the general happiness is desirable, except that each person, so far as he believes it to be attainable, desires his own happiness. This, however, being a fact, we have not only all the proof which the case admits of, but all which it is possible to require, that happiness is a good, that each person's happiness is a good to that person, and the general happiness, therefore, a good to the aggregate of all persons. Happiness has made out its title as one of the ends of conduct and, consequently, one of the criteria of morality.

But it has not, by this alone, proved itself to be the sole criterion. To do that, it would seem, by the same rule, necessary to show, not only that people desire happiness, but that they never desire anything else. Now it is palpable that they do desire things which, in common language, are decidedly distinguished from happiness. They desire, for example, virtue and the absence of vice no less really than pleasure and the absence of pain. The desire of virtue is not as universal, but it is as authentic a fact as the desire of happiness. And hence the opponents of the utilitarian standard deem that they have a right to infer that there are other ends of human action besides happiness, and that happiness is not the standard of approbation and disapprobation.

Happiness and Virtue

But does the utilitarian doctrine deny that people desire virtue, or maintain that virtue is not a thing to be desired? The very reverse. It maintains not only that virtue is to be desired, but that it is to be desired disinterestedly, for itself. Whatever may be the opinion of utilitarian moralists as to the original conditions by which virtue is made virtue, however they may believe (as they do) that actions and dispositions are only virtuous because they promote another end than virtue, yet this being granted, and it having been decided, from considerations of this description, what is virtuous, they not only place virtue at the very head of the things which are good as means to the ultimate end, but they also recognize as a psychological fact the possibility of its being, to the individual, a good in itself, without looking to any end beyond it; and hold that the mind is not in a right state, not in a state conformable to utility, not in the state most conducive to the general happiness, unless it does love virtue in this manner—as a thing desirable in itself, even although, in the individual instance, it should not produce those other desirable consequences which it tends to produce, and on account of which it is held to be virtue. This opinion is not, in the smallest degree, a departure from the happiness principle. The ingredients of happiness are very various, and each of them is desirable in itself, and not merely when considered as swelling an aggregate. The principle of utility does not mean that any given pleasure, as music, for instance, or any given exemption from pain, as for example health, is to be looked upon as means to a collective something termed happiness, and to be desired on that account. They are desired and desirable in and for themselves; besides being means, they are a part of the end. Virtue, according to the utilitarian doctrine, is not naturally and originally part of the end, but it is capable of becoming so; and in those who live it disinterestedly it has become so, and is desired and cherished, not as a means to happiness, but as a part of their happiness.

To illustrate this further, we may remember that virtue is not the only thing originally a means, and which if it were not a means to anything else would be and remain indifferent, but which by association with what it is a means to comes to be desired for itself, and that too with the utmost intensity. What, for example, shall we say of the love of money? There is nothing originally more desirable about money than about any heap of glittering pebbles. Its worth is solely that of the things which it will buy; the desires for other things than itself, which it is a means of gratifying. Yet the love of money is not only one of the strongest moving forces of human life, but money is, in many cases, desired in and for itself; the desire to possess it is often stronger than the desire to use it, and goes on increasing when all the desires which point to ends beyond it, to be compassed by it, are falling off. It may, then, be said truly that money is desired not for the sake of an end, but as part of the end. From being a means to happiness, it has come to be itself a principal ingredient of the individual's conception of happiness. The same may be said of the majority of the great objects of human life: power, for example, or fame, except that to each of these there is a certain amount of immediate pleasure annexed, which has at least the semblance of being naturally inherent in them—a thing which cannot be said of money. Still, however, the strongest natural attraction, both of power and of fame, is the immense aid they give to the attainment of our other wishes; and it is the strong association thus generated between them and all our objects of desire which gives to the direct desire of them the intensity it often assumes, so as in some characters to surpass in strength all other desires. In these cases the means have become a part of the end, and a more important part of it than any of the things which they are means to. What was once desired as an instrument for the attainment of happiness has come to be desired for its own sake. In being desired for its own sake it is, however, desired as part of happiness. The person is made, or thinks he would be made, happy by its mere possession; and

is made unhappy by failure to obtain it. The desire of it is not a different thing from the desire of happiness any more than the love of music or the desire of health. They are included in happiness. They are some of the elements of which the desire of happiness is made up. Happiness is not an abstract idea but a concrete whole; and these are some of its parts. And the utilitarian standard sanctions and approves their being so. Life would be a poor thing, very ill provided with sources of happiness, if there were not this provision of nature by which things originally indifferent, but conducive to, or otherwise associated with, the satisfaction of our primitive desires, become in themselves sources of pleasure more valuable than the primitive pleasures, both in permanency, in the space of human existence that they are capable of covering, and even in intensity.

Virtue, according to the utilitarian conception, is a good of this description. There was no original desire of it, or motive to it, save its conduciveness to pleasure, and especially to protection from pain. But through the association thus formed it may be felt a good in itself, and desired as such with as great intensity as any other good; and with this difference between it and the love of money, of power, or of fame—that all of these may, and often do, render the individual noxious to the other members of the society to which he belongs, whereas there is nothing which makes him so much a blessing to them as the cultivation of the disinterested love of virtue. And consequently, the utilitarian standard, while it tolerates and approves those other acquired desires, up to the point beyond which they would be more injurious to the general happiness than promotive of it, enjoins and requires the cultivation of the love of virtue up to the greatest strength possible, as being above all things important to the general happiness.

Happiness the Only Intrinsic Good

It results from the preceding considerations that there is in reality nothing desired except happiness. Whatever is desired otherwise than as a means to some end beyond itself, and ultimately to happiness, is desired as itself a part of happiness, and is not desired for itself until it has become so. Those who desire virtue for its own sake desire it either because the consciousness of it is a pleasure, or because the consciousness of being without it is a pain, or for both reasons united; as in truth the pleasure and pain seldom exist separately, but almost always together—the same person feeling pleasure in the degree of virtue attained, and pain in not having attained more. If one of these gave him no pleasure, and the other no pain, he would not love or desire virtue, or would desire it only for the other benefits which it might produce to himself or to persons whom he cared for.

We have now, then, an answer to the question, of what sort of proof the principle of utility is susceptible. If the opinion which I have now stated is psychologically true—if human nature is so constituted as to desire nothing which is not either a part of happiness or a means of happiness—we can have no other proof, and we require no other, that these are the only things desirable. If so, happiness is the sole end of human action, and the promotion of it the test by which to judge all of human conduct; from whence it necessarily follows that it must be the criterion of morality, since a part is included in the whole.

Review Exercises

1. Give and explain the basic idea of the "principle of utility" or "the greatest happiness principle."

2. What does it mean to speak of utilitarianism as a consequentialist moral theory? As a teleological moral theory?

3. What is the difference between intrinsic and instrumental good? Give examples of each.

4. Which of the following as stated are consequentialist reasonings? Can all of them be given consequentialist interpretations if expanded? Explain your answers.

   a. Honesty is the best policy.

   b. Sue has the right to know the truth.

   c. What good is going to come from giving money to a homeless person on the street?

   d. There is a symbolic value present in personally giving something to another person in need.

   e. It is only fair that you give him a chance to compete for the position.

   f. If I do not study for my ethics exam, it will hurt my GPA.

   g. If you are not honest with others, you cannot expect them to be honest with you.

5. Is utilitarianism a hedonist moral theory? Why or why not?

6. Using utilitarian calculation, which choice in each of the following pairs is better, X or Y?

   a. X makes 4 people happy and me unhappy.
   Y makes me and 1 other happy and 3 people unhappy.

   b. X makes 20 people happy and 5 unhappy.
   Y makes 10 people happy and no one unhappy.

   c. X will give 5 people each 2 hours of pleasure.
   Y will give 3 people each 4 hours of pleasure.

   d. X will make 5 people very happy and 3 people mildly unhappy.
   Y will make 6 people moderately happy and 2 people very unhappy.

7. What is Mill's argument for the difference in value between intellectual and sensual pleasures?

8. Which of the following is an example of act utilitarian reasoning and which rule utilitarian reasoning? Explain your answers.

   a. If I do not go to the meeting, then others will not go either. If that happens, then there would not be a quorum for the important vote, which would be bad. Thus, I ought to go to the meeting.

   b. If doctors generally lied to their patients about their diagnosis, then patients would lose trust in their doctors. Because that would be bad, I should tell this patient the truth.

   c. We ought to keep our promises because it is a valuable practice.

   d. If I cheat here, I will be more likely to cheat elsewhere. No one would trust me then. So I should not cheat on this test.

Selected Bibliography

Ayer, A. J. "The Principle of Utility," in *Philosophical Essays*. London: Macmillan, 1954.

Bayles, Michael D. (Ed.). *Contemporary Utilitarianism*. Garden City, NY: Doubleday, 1968.

Bentham, Jeremy. *Introduction to the Principles of Morals and Legislation* (1789), W. Harrison (Ed.). Oxford, England: Hafner, 1948.

Brandt, Richard B. "In Search of a Credible form of Rule-Utilitarianism," in H. N. Castaneda and George Nakhnikian (Eds.), *Morality and the Language of Conduct*. Detroit: Wayne State University Press, 1953.

Cooper, Wesley E., Kai Nielsen, and Steven C. Patten (Eds.). "New Essays on John Stuart Mill and Utilitarianism." *Canadian Journal of Philosophy*, supplementary vol. 5 (1979).

Feinberg, Joel. "The Forms and Limits of Utilitarianism," *Philosophical Review* 76 (1967), 368–381.

Frey, R. G. (Ed.). *Utility and Rights*. Minneapolis: University of Minnesota Press, 1984.

Gorovitz, Samuel (Ed.). *Mill: Utilitarianism, with Critical Essays*. New York: Bobbs-Merrill, 1971.

Hare, Richard M. *Freedom and Reason*. Oxford, England: Clarendon, 1963.

Lyons, David. *Forms and Limits of Utilitarianism*. Oxford, England: Clarendon, 1965.

Mill, John Stuart. *On Liberty*. London: J. W. Parker, 1859.

———. *Utilitarianism*. London: Longmans, Green, 1863.

Ryan, Alan. *Utilitarianism and Other Essays*. New York: Penguin, 1987.

Scheffler, Samuel (Ed.). *Consequentialism and Its Critics*. New York: Oxford University Press, 1988.

Scheffler, Samuel. *The Rejection of Consequentialism*. Oxford, England: Clarendon, 1982.

Sen, Amartya, and Bernard Williams (Eds.). *Utilitarianism and Beyond*. Cambridge, England: Cambridge University Press, 1982.

Smart, J.J.C., and Bernard Williams. *Utilitarianism: For and Against*. Cambridge, England: Cambridge University Press, 1973.

Smith, James M., and Ernest Sosa (Eds.). *Mill's Utilitarianism: Text and Criticism*. Belmont, CA: Wadsworth, 1969.

Kant's Moral Theory

Two decades ago, a Yale University professor designed and conducted an experiment to determine whether ordinary people would follow the directions of an authority figure even when the directions required them to act against commonly held moral beliefs.[1] He asked for volunteers for a "learning experiment." The volunteers or "teachers" were told to ask questions of learners who were in an adjoining room but who could not be seen. The teachers were to administer an electric shock to the learners when they gave the wrong answer. As the experiment proceeded, the volunteers were instructed by a researcher in a white coat to increase the shock dosage. The learners were actually part of the experiment and were not really being shocked. Even though a learner in the next room would cry out in pain after the shocks, and at one point was seemingly reduced to unconsciousness, many of the teachers continued to do what the researcher told them to do. They were later informed that they themselves had been the subjects of the research and that it was an experiment about people's obedience to authorities, not about learning. Not surprisingly, many subjects were quite upset when they learned this. They were angry both at being lied to and on realizing what they had done or had been willing to do. Supporters of this experiment argued that it was justifiable because their subjects had not been coerced but had volun-teered and because useful information had been gained from the experiment. Critics objected that the volunteers were not informed and that, in fact, they had been used by the researchers for an experiment for which they had not, strictly speaking, consented.

According to utilitarian thinking, this experiment may well have been quite justifiable. If the psychological harm done to the participants was minimal and the study had no other negative effects, and if the knowledge gained about obedience to authority was valuable, then the study would be justified.[2] It would have done more good than harm, and that is the basis for judging it to be morally praiseworthy. However, since the post–World War II trials of Nazi war criminals held in Nuremberg, Germany, other standards for treatment of human research subjects have become widely accepted. One of the most basic principles of the Nuremberg Code is, "The voluntary consent of the human subject is absolutely essential."[3] Implied in this principle is the belief that persons are autonomous, and this autonomy ought to be respected and protected even if this means that we cannot do certain types of research and cannot thereby find out valuable information. This view of the significance of personal autonomy is also a central tenet of the moral philosophy of Immanuel Kant, which we will now examine.

Historical Background: Immanuel Kant

Immanuel Kant (1724–1804) was a German philosophy professor who taught at the University of Königsberg in what is now the city of Kaliningrad in the westernmost part of Russia. He was such a popular lecturer that students at the university who wanted a seat had to arrive at his classroom at six in the morning, one hour before Kant was due to begin his lecture![4] After many years of financial and professional insecurity, he finally was appointed to a chair in philosophy. The writings that followed made him renowned even in his own time. Kant is now regarded as a central figure in the history of modern philosophy. Modern philosophy itself is sometimes divided into pre-Kantian and post-Kantian periods. In fact, some people regard him as the greatest modern philosopher. Although he is renowned for his philosophy, he wrote on a variety of matters including science, geography, beauty, and war and peace. He was a firm believer in Enlightenment ideas, especially reason and freedom, and he also supported the American Revolution.

The three main questions that Kant believed philosophy should address were: "What can I know? What ought I do? (and) What May I Hope?"[5] In answering the first question he thought he was creating a new Copernican revolution. Just as the astronomer Copernicus had argued in 1543 that we should no longer consider the earth as the center of the solar system with heavenly bodies revolving around it, Kant asserted that we should no longer think of the human knower as revolving around objects known. Knowledge, he believed, was not the passive perception of things just as they are. Rather, he argued, the very nature of human perception and understanding determines the basic character of the world as we experience it. There are forms within the mind that determine the spatial and temporal nature of our world and give to experience its basic structure. In his moral philosophy Kant addressed the second question, "What ought I do?" His answers can be found for the most part in two works. One is the *Fundamental Principles* (or *Foundations*) *of the Metaphysics of Morals* (1785), which one commentator described as "one of the most important ethical treatises ever written."[6] The other is the *Critique of Practical Reason* (1788). Selections from the first work are included in this text.

You will be able to understand the basic elements of Kant's moral philosophy from the following sections on the basis of morality and the categorical imperative. You should benefit in your own reflections on this theory from the section on evaluating Kant's moral theory. The final sections on perfect and imperfect duties and contemporary versions of Kantian moral theory add further detail to this basic treatment.

What Gives an Act Moral Worth?

One way to begin understanding Kant's moral theory is to think about how he would answer the question, What gives an act *moral* worth? It is not the consequences of the act, according to Kant. Suppose, for example, that I try to do what is right by complimenting someone on her achievements. Through no fault of my own, my action ends up hurting that person because she misunderstands my efforts. According to Kant, because I intended and tried to do what I thought was right, I ought not to be blamed for things having turned out badly. The idea is that we generally ought not to be blamed or praised for what is not in our control. The consequences of our acts are not always in our control and things do not always turn out as we want. However, Kant believed that our motives are in our control. We are responsible for our motive to do good or bad, and thus it is for this that we are held morally accountable.

Kant also objected to basing morality on the consequences of our actions for another reason. To make morality a matter of producing certain states of affairs, such as happy experiences, puts matters backwards, he might say. On such a view we could be thought of as having *use value*. We would be valued to the extent that we were instrumental in bringing about what itself was of greater value, namely, happy states or experiences. However, on Kant's view, we should not be used in this way for we are rational beings or persons. Persons have intrinsic value, according to Kant, not simply instrumental value. The belief that *people ought not to be used,* but ought to be regarded as having the highest intrinsic value, is central to Kant's ethics, as is the importance of a *motive to do what is right.* As we shall see in the next two sections, Kant uses this second idea to answer the question, What gives an act moral worth?

What Is the Right Motive?

Kant believed that an act has specifically moral worth only if it is done with a right intention or motive.[7] He referred to this as a "good will." In his famous first lines of the first section of *Foundations,* Kant writes that only such a will is good unconditionally. Everything else needs a good will to make it good. Without a right intention, such things as intelligence, wit, and control of emotions can be bad and used for evil purposes.[8] Having a right intention is to do what is right (or what one believes to be right) just because it is right. In Kant's words, it is to act "out of duty," out of a concern and respect for the moral law. Kant was not a relativist. He believed there was a right and a wrong thing to do, whether or not we knew or agreed about it. This was the moral law.

To explain his views on the importance of a right motive or intention, Kant provides the example of a shopkeeper who does the right thing, who charges the customers a fair price and charges the same to all. But what is her motive? There are three possible motives that Kant discusses. (1) The shopkeeper's motive or reason for acting might be because it is a good business practice to charge the same to all. It is in her own best interest that she do this. This motive is not praiseworthy. (2) The shopkeeper might charge a fair and equal price because she is sympathetic toward her customers and is naturally inclined to do them good. Kant said that this motive is also not the highest. We do not have high moral esteem or praise for persons who simply do what they feel like doing, even if we believe they are doing the right thing. (3) However, if

the shopkeeper did the right thing just because she believed it was right, then this act would have the highest motive. We do have a special respect, or even a moral reverence, for persons who act out of a will to do the right thing, especially when this is at great cost to themselves. Only when an act is motivated by this concern for morality, or for the moral law as Kant would say, does it have moral worth.

Now we do not always *know* when our acts are motivated by self-interest, inclination, or pure respect for morality. Also, we often act from mixed motives. We are more certain that the motive is pure, however, when we do what is right even when it is not in our best interest (when it costs us dearly) and when we do not feel like doing the right thing. In these cases, we can know that we are motivated by concern to do the right thing because the other two motives are missing. Moreover, this ability to act for moral reasons and resist the pushes and pulls of nature or natural inclination is one indication of and reason why Kant believes that persons have a unique value and dignity. The person who says to himself, "I feel like being lazy (or mean or selfish), but I am going to try not to because it would not be right," is operating out of the motive of respect for the very nature of morality. This ability to act for moral reasons or motives, Kant believes, is one part of what makes people possess particularly high and unique value.

What Is the Right Thing to Do?

For our action to have moral worth, according to Kant, we must not only act out of a right motivation but also do the right thing. Consider again the diagram that we used in the first chapter.

As noted earlier, Kant does not believe that morality is a function of producing good consequences. We may do what has good results, but if we do so for the wrong motive, then that act has no moral worth. However, it is not only the motive that counts for Kant. We must also do what is right. The act itself must be morally right. Both the act and the motive are morally relevant. In Kant's terms, we must not only act "out of duty" (have the right motive) but also "according to duty" or "as duty requires" (do what is right). How then are we to know what is the right thing to do? Once we know this, we can try to do it just because it is right.

To understand Kant's reasoning on this matter, we need to examine the difference between what he calls a *hypothetical imperative* and a *categorical imperative*. First of all, an imperative is simply a form of statement that tells us to do something, for example, "Stand up straight" and "Close the door" and also "You ought to close the door." Some, but only some, imperatives are moral imperatives. Other imperatives are hypothetical. For example, the statement "If I want to get there on time, I ought to leave early" does not embody a moral "ought" or imperative. What I ought to do in that case is a function of what I happen to want—to get there on time—and of the means necessary to achieve this—leave early. Moreover, I can avoid the obligation to leave early by changing my goals. I can decide that I do not need or want to get there on time. Then I need not leave early. These ends may be good or bad. Thus, the statement "If I want to harm someone, then I ought to use effective means" also expresses a hypothetical "ought." These "oughts" are avoidable, or, as Kant would say, contingent. They are contingent or dependent on what I happen to want or the desires I happen to have, such as to please others, to harm someone, to gain power, or to be punctual.

These "oughts" are also quite individualized. What I ought to do is contingent or dependent on my own individual goals or plans. These actions serve as means to whatever goals I happen to have. Other people ought to do different things than I because they have different goals and plans. For example, I ought to take introduction to sociology because I want to be a sociology major, while you ought to take a course on the philosophy of Kant because you want to be a philosophy major. These are obligations only for those who have these goals or desires. Think of them in this form: "If (or because) I want X, then I ought to do Y." Whether I ought to do Y is totally contingent or dependent on my wanting X.

Moral obligation, on the other hand, is quite different in nature. Kant believed that we experience moral obligation as something quite demanding. If there is something I morally ought to do, I ought to do it no matter what—whether or not I want to, and whether or not it fulfills my desires and goals or is approved by my society. Moral obligation is not contingent on what I or anyone happens to want or approve. Moral "oughts" are thus, in Kant's terminology, unconditional or necessary. Moreover, while hypothetical "oughts" relate to goals we each have as individuals, moral "oughts" stem from the ways in which we are alike as persons, for only persons are subject to morality. This is because persons are rational beings and only persons can act from a reason or from principles. These "oughts" are thus not individualized but universal as they apply to all persons. Kant calls moral "oughts" categorical imperatives because they tell us what we ought to do no matter what, under all conditions, or categorically.

It is from the very nature of categorical or moral imperatives, their being unconditional and universally binding, that Kant derives his views about what it is that we ought to do. In fact, he calls the statement of his basic moral principle by which we determine what we ought and ought not to do simply the "categorical imperative."

The Categorical Imperative

The categorical imperative, Kant's basic moral principle, is comparable in importance for his moral philosophy to the principle of utility for utilitarians. It is Kant's test for right and wrong. Just as there are different ways of formulating the principle of utility, so also Kant had different formulations for his principle. Although at least four of them may be found in the writings of

Kant, we will concentrate on just two and call them the first and second forms of the categorical imperative. The others, however, do add different elements to our understanding of his basic moral principle and will be mentioned briefly.

The First Form

Recall that moral obligation is categorical; that is, it is unconditional and applies to all persons as persons rather than to persons as individuals. It is in this sense universal. Moreover, because morality is not a matter of producing good consequences of any sort (be it happiness or knowledge or peace), the basic moral principle will be formal, without content. It will not include reference to any particular good. Knowing this, we are on the way to understanding the first form of the categorical imperative, which simply requires that we only do what we can accept or will that everyone do. Kant's own statement of it is basically the following:

Act only on that maxim that you can will as a universal law.

In other words, whatever I consider doing, it must be something that I can will or accept that all do. A law by its very nature has a degree of universality. By "maxim" Kant means a description of the action that I will put to the test. For example, I might want to know whether "being late for class" or "giving all my money to the homeless" describe morally permissible actions. I need to ask whether I could will that all follow these maxims. How do I know what I can and cannot will as a universal practice? As a rational being I can only will what is noncontradictory. What do we think of a person who says that it is both raining and not raining here now? It can be raining here and not there or now and not earlier. But it is either raining here or it is not. It cannot be both. So also we say that a person who wants to "have his cake and eat it, too" is not being rational. "Make up your mind," we say. "If you eat it, it is gone."

Again, how do I know if I can rationally, without contradiction, will something for all? This can best be explained by using one of Kant's own examples. He asks us to consider whether it is morally permissible for me to "make a lying or false promise in order to extricate myself from some difficulty." To know whether this would be morally acceptable, it must pass the test of the categorical imperative. If I were to use this test, I would ask whether I could will that sort of thing for all. I must ask whether I could will a general practice in which people who made promises, for example, to pay back some money, made the promises without intending to keep them. If people who generally made such promises did so falsely, others would know this and would not believe the promises. Consider whether you would lend money to a person if she said she would pay you back but you knew she was lying. If I tried to will a general practice of false promise making, I would find that I could not do it because by willing that the promises could be false I would also will a situation in which it would be impossible to make a lying promise. No one could then make a promise, let alone a false promise, because no one would believe him or her. Part of being able to make a promise is to have it believed. This universal practice itself could not even exist. It is a self-destructive practice. If everyone made such lying promises, no one could!

Now consider the example at the beginning of this chapter, the obedience experiment using people without their full knowing consent. Using Kant's categorical imperative to test this, one would see that if it were a general practice for researchers to lie to their subjects in order to get them into their experiments, they would not be able to get people to participate. They could not even lie because no one would believe them. The only way a particular researcher could lie would be if other researchers told the truth. Only then could she get her prospective subjects to believe her. But this would be to make herself an exception to the universal rule. Because a universal practice in which researchers lied to their prospective subjects could not even exist, it is a morally impermissible action.[9]

The Second Form

In the second form of Kant's categorical imperative, we are asked to consider what constitutes proper treatment of persons as persons. According to Kant, one key characteristic of persons is their ability to set their own goals. Persons are autonomous. They are literally self-ruled or at least capable of being self-ruled (from *auto,* meaning "self," and *nomos,* meaning "rule" or "law"). As persons we choose our own life plans, what we want to be, our friends, our college courses, and so forth. We have our own reasons for doing so. We believe that while we are influenced in these choices and reasons by our situation and by others, these are at least sometimes our own choices.[10] In this way persons are different from things. Things cannot choose what they wish to do. We decide how we shall use things. We impose our own goals on things, using the wood to build the house and the pen or computer to write our words and express our ideas. It is appropriate in this scheme of things to use things for our ends, but it is not appropriate to use persons as though they were things purely at our own disposal and without a will of their own. Kant's statement of this second form of the categorical imperative is as follows:

Always treat humanity, whether in your own person or that of another, never simply as a means but always at the same time as an end.

This formulation tells us several things. First, it tells us how we ought to treat ourselves as well as others. Second, it tells us to treat ourselves and others as ends rather than merely as means. Kant believes that we should treat persons as having intrinsic value and not just as having instrumental value. People are valuable in themselves, regardless of whether they are useful or loved or valued by others. However, this form also specifies that we should not simply use oth-

ers or let ourselves be used. Although I may in some sense use someone—for example, to paint my house—I may not simply use them. The goal of getting my house painted must also be the goal of the painter, who is also a person and not just an object to be used by me for my own ends. She must know what is involved in the project. I cannot lie to her to get her to do something to which she otherwise would not agree. And she must agree to paint the house voluntarily rather than be coerced into doing it. This is to treat the person as an end rather than as a means to my ends or goals.

We can use this second form to evaluate the examples considered for the first form of the categorical imperative. The moral conclusions should be the same whether we use the first or second form. Kant believes that in lying to another—for example, saying that we will pay back the money when we have no intention of doing so—we would be attempting to get that other to do what we want but which she or he presumably does not want to do, namely, just give us the money. This would violate the requirement not to use persons. So also in the experiment described at the beginning of this chapter, the researcher would be using deception to get people to "volunteer" for the study. One difficulty this type of study presents, however, is that if the participants were to know the truth, it would undermine the study. Some people have argued that in such studies we can presume the voluntary consent of the subjects, judging that they would approve if they knew what was going on in the study. Do you think that presuming consent in this or similar cases would be sufficient?

We noted above that Kant had more than these two formulations of his categorical imperative. In one of these other formulations, Kant relies on his views about nature as a system of everything that we experience as it is organized according to laws. Thus, he says that we ought always to ask whether some action we are contemplating could become a universal law of nature. The effect of this version is to stress the universality and rationality of morality, for nature necessarily operates according to coherent laws. Other formulations of the categorical imperative stress autonomy. We are to ask whether we could consider ourselves as the author of the moral practice that we are about to accept. We are both subject to the moral law and its author because it flows from our own nature as a rational being. Another formulation amplifies what we have here called the second form of the categorical imperative. This formulation points out that we are all alike persons and together form a community of persons. He calls the community of rational persons a "kingdom of ends," that is, a kingdom in which all persons are authors as well as subjects of the moral law. Thus, we ask whether the action we are contemplating would be fitting for and further or promote such a community. These forms of the categorical imperative involve other interesting elements of Kant's philosophy, but they also involve more than we can explore further here.

Evaluating Kant's Moral Theory

There is much that is appealing in Kant's moral philosophy, particularly its central aspects—fairness, consistency, and treating persons as autonomous and morally equal beings. They are also key elements of a particular tradition in morality. It is a quite different tradition than that exemplified by utilitarianism with its emphasis on the maximization of happiness and the production of good consequences. To more fully evaluate Kant's theory, consider the following aspects of his thought.

The Nature of Moral Obligation

One of the bases on which Kant's moral philosophy rests is his view about the nature of moral obligation. He believes that moral obligation is real and strictly binding. According to Kant, this is how we generally think of moral obligation. If there is anything that we morally ought to do, we simply ought to do it. Thus, this type of obligation is unlike that which flows from what we ought to do because of the particular goals that

we each have as individuals. To evaluate this aspect of Kant's moral philosophy, you must ask yourself if this is also what you think about the nature of moral obligation. This is important for Kant's moral philosophy because acting out of respect for the moral law is required for an action to have moral worth. Furthermore, being able to act out of such a regard for morality is also the source of human dignity.

The Application of the Categorical Imperative

Critics have argued that when using the first form of the categorical imperative there are many things that I could will as universal practices that would hardly seem to be moral obligations. I could will that everyone write their name on the top of their test papers. If everyone did that, it would not prevent anyone from doing so. There would be no contradiction involved if this were a universal practice. Nevertheless, this would not mean that people have a moral obligation to write their names on their test papers. A Kantian might explain that to write your name on your test paper is an example of a hypothetical, not a categorical, imperative. I write my name on my paper because I want to be given credit for it. If I can will it as a universal practice, I then know it is a morally permissible action. If I cannot will it universally, then it is impermissible or wrong. Thus, the categorical imperative is actually a negative test, in other words, a test for what we should not do, more than a test for what we ought to do. Whether or not this is a satisfactory response, you should know that this is just one of several problems associated with Kant's universalizing test.

Note especially that while both Kantians and rule utilitarians must universalize, how their reasoning proceeds from there is not identical. Rule utilitarians, on the one hand, require that we consider what the results would be if some act we are contemplating were to be a universal practice. We must ask what would be the results or consequences of some general practice, such as making false promises, or whether one practice would have better results than another. Kantians, on the other hand, must ask whether there would be anything contradictory in willing the practice as a universal law. Because we are rational beings, we must not will contradictory things.

The second form of the categorical imperative also has problems of application. In the concrete, it is not always easy to determine what is coercion and what is simply influence, or what is deception and what is not. When I try to talk a friend into doing something for me, how do I know whether I am simply providing input for the person's own decision making or whether I am crossing the line and becoming coercive? Moreover, if I do not tell the whole truth or withhold information from another, should this count as deception on my part? Although these are real problems for anyone who tries to apply Kant's views about deceit and coercion, they are not unique to his moral philosophy. Theories vary in the ease of their use or application. But as Kant puts it, "Ease of use and apparent adequacy of a principle are not any sure proof of its correctness."[11] The fact that a theory has a certain amount of ambiguity should not necessarily disqualify it. Difficulty of application is a problem for most, if not all, reasonable moral philosophies.

Duty

Some of the language and terminology found in Kant's moral theory can sound harsh to modern ears. Duty, obligation, law, and universality may not be the moral terms most commonly heard today. Yet if one considers what Kant meant by *duty,* the idea may not be so strange to us. He did not mean any particular moral code or set of duties that is held by any society or group. Rather, duty is whatever is the right thing to do. However, Kant might respond that there is a streak of absolutism in his philosophy. *Absolutism* usually refers to a morality that consists in a set of exceptionless rules. Kant does, at times, seem to favor such rules. He provides examples in which it seems clear that he believes that it is always wrong to make a false promise or to lie deliberately. There is even one example in which Kant

himself suggests that if a killer comes to the door asking for a friend of yours inside whom he intends to kill, you must tell the truth. But Kant's philosophy has only one exceptionless rule and that is given in the categorical imperative. We are never permitted to do what we cannot will as a universal law or what violates the requirement to treat persons as persons. Even with these tests in hand, it is not always clear just how they always apply. Furthermore, they may not give adequate help in deciding what to do when they seem to give us contradictory duties, as in the example, both to tell the truth and preserve life. Kant believed that he was only setting basic principles of morality and establishing it on a firm basis. Nevertheless, it is reasonable to expect that a moral theory should go further.

Moral Equality and Impartiality

One positive feature of Kant's moral theory is its emphasis on the moral equality of all persons, which is implied in his view about the nature of moral obligation as universally binding. We should not make exceptions for ourselves but only do what we can will for all. Moral obligation and morality itself flow from our nature as persons, as rational and autonomous. Morality is grounded in the ways in which we are alike as persons rather than the ways in which we are different as individuals. These views might provide a source for those who want to argue for moral equality and equal moral rights.

Another feature of Kant's moral philosophy is its spirit of impartiality. For an action to be morally permissible, we should be able to will it for all. However, persons do differ in significant ways. Among these are differences in gender, race, age, and talents. In what way does morality require that all persons be treated equally and in what way does it perhaps require that different persons be treated differently? Further discussion of this issue can be found in Chapter 11 on equality and discrimination. See also the criticism of Kantian theories of justice in the treatment of gender and justice in the article by Susan Okin in Chapter 12.[12]

Others have wondered about Kant's stress on the nature of persons as rational beings. Some believe it is too male-oriented in its focus on reason rather than emotion. In Chapter 7 we will examine feminist ethical theories. For example, the ethics of care criticizes the universalizing aspects of Kantian types of morality and stresses the emotional and personal ties that we have to particular individuals. Kant might reply that we often have no control over how we feel and thus it should not be the key element of our moral lives. He might also point out that it is the common aspects of our existence as persons, and not the ways in which we are different and unique, that give us dignity and are the basis for the moral equality that we possess.

Perfect and Imperfect Duties

In his attempt to explain his views, Kant provides us with several examples. We have already considered one of these, making a false promise. His conclusion is that we should not make a false or lying promise, both because we could not consistently will it for all and because it violates our obligation to treat persons as persons and not to use them only for our own purposes. Kant calls such duties *perfect* or *necessary duties*. As the terms suggest, perfect duties are absolute. We can and should absolutely refrain from making false or lying promises. From the perspective of the first form of the categorical imperative, we have a perfect duty not to do those things that could not even exist and are inconceivable as universal practices. Using the second form of the categorical imperative, we have a perfect duty not to do what violates the requirement to treat persons as persons.

However, some duties are more flexible. Kant calls these duties *imperfect* or *meritorious duties*. Consider another example he provides us, egoism. Ethical egoism, you will recall, is the view that we may rightly seek only our own interest and help others only to the extent that this also benefits us. Is this a morally acceptable philosophy of life? Using the first form of Kant's cate-

gorical imperative to test the morality of this practice, we must ask whether we could will that everyone was an egoist. If I try to do this, I would need to will that I was an egoist as well as others, even in those situations when I needed others' help. In those situations, I must allow that they not help me when it is not in their own best interest. But being an egoist myself, I would also want them to help me. In effect, I would be willing contradictories: that they help me (I being an egoist) and that they not help me (they being egoists). Although a society of egoists could indeed exist, Kant admits, no rational person could will it, for a rational person does not will contradictories. We have an imperfect or meritorious duty, then, not to be egoists, but to help people for their own good and not just for ours. However, just when to help others and how much is a matter of some choice. There is a certain flexibility here. One implication of this view is that there is no absolute duty to give one's whole life to helping others. We, too, are persons and thus have moral rights and also can at least sometimes act for our own interests.

The same conclusion regarding the wrongness of egoism results from the application of the second form of the categorical imperative. If I were an egoist and concerned only about myself, then no one could accuse me of using other people. I would simply leave them alone. According to Kant, such an attitude and practice would be inconsistent with the duty to treat others as persons. As persons, they also have interests and plans, and to recognize this I must at least sometimes and in some ways seek to promote their ends and goals.

Variations on Kantian Moral Theory

Just as there are contemporary versions of and developments within the utilitarian tradition, so also we can find many contemporary versions of Kantian moral philosophies. One is found in the moral philosophy of W. D. Ross (1877–1971), who held that there are things that we ought and ought not do regardless of the consequences.[13]

We not only have duties of beneficence, but also have duties to keep promises, pay our debts, and be good friends and parents and children. Contrary to Kant, Ross believed that we can know through moral intuition in any instance what we ought to do. Sometimes we are faced with a conflict of moral duties. It seems intuitively that we ought to be both loyal and honest but we cannot do both. We have *prima facie* or conditional duties of loyalty and honesty. Ross is the source of this phrase, which is often used in ethical arguments. (See our use of it in Chapter 14.) In such cases, according to Ross, we have to consider which duty is the stronger—that is, which has the greater balance of rightness over wrongness. In choosing honesty in some situation, however, one does not negate or forget that one also has a duty to be loyal. Obvious problems arise for such a theory. For example, how does one go about determining the amount of rightness or wrongness involved in some action? Don't people have different intuitions about the rightness or wrongness? This is a problem for anyone who holds that intuition is the basis for morality.

One of the most noted contemporary versions of Kant's moral philosophy is found in the political philosophy of John Rawls. In *A Theory of Justice*, Rawls applies Kantian principles to issues of social justice. According to Rawls, justice is fairness.[14] To know what is fair, we must put ourselves imaginatively in the position of a group of free and equal rational beings who are choosing principles of justice for their society. In thinking of persons as free and equal rational beings in order to develop principles of justice, Rawls is securely in the Kantian tradition of moral philosophy. Kant has also stressed autonomy. It is this aspect of our nature that gives us our dignity as persons. Kant's categorical imperative also involved universalization. We must do only those things that we could will that everyone do. It is only a short move from these notions of autonomy and universalization to the Rawlsian requirement to choose those principles of justice that we could accept no matter whose position we were in. For details about the principles, see Chapter 13 on economic justice. Just as utilitarian moral theory is still being debated today and has many followers, so also Kantian types of philosophy continue to intrigue and interest moral thinkers.

Notes

1. Stanley Milgram, *Obedience to Authority: An Experimental View* (New York: Harper & Row, 1974), and "Issues in the Study of Obedience: A Reply to Baumrind," *American Psychologist* 19 (1964): 848–852.

2. At least this might be true from an act utilitarian point of view. A rule utilitarian might want to know whether the results of the general practice of not fully informing research participants would be such that the good achieved would not be worth it.

3. From *The Trials of War Criminals Before the Nuremberg Military Tribunals Under Control Council Law No. 10*, vol. 2, 181–182. Washington, DC: U.S. Government Printing Office, 1949.

4. Reported by the philosopher J. G. Hammann and noted in Roger Scruton's *Kant* (Oxford: Oxford University Press, 1982), 3–4.

5. Immanuel Kant, *Critique of Pure Reason*, Norman Kemp Smith (Trans.) (New York: St. Martin's, 1965), p. 635.

6. Lewis White Beck, introduction to his translation of Kant's *Foundations of the Metaphysic of Morals* (New York: Bobbs-Merrill, 1959), vii. The title is also sometimes translated as *Fundamental Principles of the Metaphysics of Morals*.

7. We will not distinguish here motive and intention, although the former usually signifies that out of which we act (a pusher) and the latter that for which we act (an aim).

8. Kant, *Foundations*, 9.

9. In some ways Kant's basic moral principle, the categorical imperative, is a principle of fairness. I cannot do what I am not able to will that everyone do. In the example, for me to make a lying promise, others must generally make truthful promises so that my lie will be believed. This would be to treat myself as an exception. But this is not fair. In some ways the principle is similar to the so-called golden rule, which requires us only to do unto others what we would be willing for them to do unto us. However, it is not quite the same, for Kant's principle requires our not willing self-defeating or self-canceling, contradictory practices, whereas the golden rule requires that we appeal in the final analysis to what we would or would not like to have done to us.

10. Kant does treat the whole issue of determinism versus freedom, but it is difficult to follow and to at-

tempt to explain it would involve us deeply in his metaphysics. Although it is a serious issue, we will assume for purposes of understanding Kant that sometimes, at least, human choice is free.

11. Kant, *Foundations*, 8.

12. See also Marilyn Friedman, "The Social Self and the Partiality Debates," in *Feminist Ethics*, Claudia Card (Ed.) (Lawrence: University of Kansas Press, 1991).

13. W. D. Ross, *The Right and the Good* (Oxford: Oxford University Press, 1930).

14. John Rawls, *A Theory of Justice* (Cambridge, MA: Harvard University Press, 1971).

Fundamental Principles of the Metaphysic of Morals

Immanuel Kant

Study Questions

1. What is meant by a "good will," and why is it the only thing good "without qualification"?

2. Out of what motives other than duty do people act?

3. If we do the right thing, such as not overcharging customers or preserving our life, do these actions always have full moral worth, according to Kant?

4. What does he mean when he says that some kinds of love cannot be commanded?

5. What does duty have to do with having respect for morality?

6. How does Kant state his basic moral principle?

7. What is the difference between how one would reason about whether it is prudent to make a false or lying promise and how one should determine whether it is the right thing to do?

8. How does Kant describe what it means to be under obligation or subject to an "ought"?

9. What is the difference between a rule of skill, a counsel of prudence, and a command of morality?

10. Explain how Kant uses the categorical imperative in his four examples.

11. What does Kant mean by an "end"? How does this notion relate to the second form of the moral imperative?

12. Explain how Kant uses the second formulation in the same four examples.

The Good Will*

Nothing can possibly be conceived in the world, or even out of it, which can be called good without qualification, except a Good Will. Intelligence, wit, judgment, and the other *talents* of the mind, however they may be named, or courage, resolution, perseverance, as qualities of temperament, are undoubtedly good and desirable in many respects; but these gifts of nature may also become extremely bad and mischievous if the will which is to make use of them, and which, therefore, constitutes what is called *character*, is not good. It is the same with the *gifts of fortune*. Power, riches, honour, even health, and the general well-being and contentment with one's condition which is called *happiness*, inspire pride, and often presumption, if there is not a good will to correct the influence of these on the mind, and with this also to rectify the whole principle of acting and adapt it to its end. The sight of a being who is not adorned with a single feature of a pure and good will, enjoying unbroken prosperity, can never give pleasure to an

---

Selections from Abbott translation, first and second sections (1879).

*Headings added by the editor.—ED.

impartial rational spectator. Thus a good will appears to constitute the indispensable condition even of being worthy of happiness.

There are even some qualities which are of service to this good will itself, and may facilitate its action, yet which have no intrinsic unconditional value, but always presuppose a good will, and this qualifies the esteem that we justly have for them, and does not permit us to regard them as absolutely good. Moderation in the affections and passions, self-control and calm deliberation are not only good in many respects, but even seem to constitute part of the intrinsic worth of the person; but they are far from deserving to be called good without qualification, although they have been so unconditionally praised by the ancients. For without the principles of a good will, they may become extremely bad, and the coolness of a villain not only makes him far more dangerous, but also immediately makes him more abominable in our eyes than he would have been without it.

A good will is good not because of what it performs or effects, not by its aptness for the attainment of some proposed end, but simply by virtue of the volition, that is, it is good in itself, and considered by itself is to be esteemed much higher than all that can be brought about by it in favour of any inclination, nay even of the sum total of all inclinations. Even if it should happen that, owing to special disfavour of fortune, or the niggardly provision of a step-motherly nature, this will should wholly lack power to accomplish its purpose, if with its greatest efforts it should yet achieve nothing, and there should remain only the good will (not, to be sure, a mere wish, but the summoning of all means in our power), then, like a jewel, it would still shine by its own light, as a thing which has its whole value in itself. Its usefulness or fruitlessness can neither add nor take away anything from this value. It would be, as it were, only the setting to enable us to handle it the more conveniently in common commerce, or to attract to it the attention of those who are not yet connoisseurs, but not to recommend it to true connoisseurs, or to determine its value. . . .

Acting from Duty

We have then to develop the notion of a will which deserves to be highly esteemed for itself, and is good without a view to anything further, a notion which exists already in the sound natural understanding, requiring rather to be cleared up than to be taught, and which in estimating the value of our actions always takes the first place, and constitutes the condition of all the rest. In order to do this we will take the notion of duty, which includes that of a good will, although implying certain subjective restrictions and hindrances. These, however, far from concealing it, or rendering it unrecognizable, rather bring it out by contrast, and make it shine forth so much the brighter.

I omit here all actions which are already recognized as inconsistent with duty, although they may be useful for this or that purpose, for with these the question whether they are done *from duty* cannot arise at all, since they even conflict with it. I also set aside those actions which really conform to duty, but to which men have no direct inclination, performing them because they are impelled thereto by some other inclination. For in this case we can readily distinguish whether the action which agrees with duty is done *from duty*, or from a selfish view. It is much harder to make this distinction when the action accords with duty, and the subject has besides a *direct* inclination to it. For example, it is always a matter of duty that a dealer should not overcharge an inexperienced purchaser, and wherever there is much commerce the prudent tradesman does not overcharge, but keeps a fixed price for every one, so that a child buys of him as well as any other. Men are thus *honestly* served; but this is not enough to make us believe that the tradesman has so acted from duty and from principles of honesty: his own advantage required it; it is out of the question in this case to suppose that he might besides have a direct inclination in favour of the buyers, so that, as it were, from love he should give no advantage to one over another. Accordingly the action was done neither from duty nor from direct inclination, but merely with a selfish view.

On the other hand, it is a duty to maintain one's life; and, in addition, every one has also a direct inclination to do so. But on this account the often anxious care which most men take for it has no intrinsic worth, and their maxim has no moral import. They preserve their life *as duty requires*, no doubt, but not *because duty requires*. On the other hand, if adversity and hopeless sorrow have completely taken away the relish for life; if the unfortunate one, strong in mind, indignant at his fate rather than desponding or dejected, wishes for death, and yet preserves his life without loving it—not from inclination or fear, but from duty—then his maxim has a moral worth.

To be beneficent when we can is a duty; and besides this, there are many minds so sympathetically constituted that without any other motive of vanity or self-interest, they find a pleasure in spreading joy around them, and can take delight in the satisfaction of others so far as it is their own work. But I maintain that in such a case an action of this kind, however proper, however amiable it may be, has nevertheless no true moral worth, but is on a level with other inclinations, e.g., the inclination to honour, which, if it is happily directed to that which is in fact of public utility and accordant with duty, and consequently honourable, deserves praise and encouragement, but not esteem. For the maxim wants the moral import, namely, that such actions be done *from duty*, not from inclination. Put the case that the mind of that philanthropist were clouded by sorrow of his own, extinguishing all sympathy with the lot of others, and that while he still has the power to benefit others in distress he is not touched by their trouble because he is absorbed with his own; and now suppose that he tears himself out of this dead insensibility, and performs the action without any inclination to it, but simply from duty, then first has his action its genuine moral worth. Further still; if nature has put little sympathy in the heart of this or that man; if he, supposed to be an upright man, is by temperament cold and indifferent to the sufferings of others, perhaps because in respect of his own he is provided with the special gift of patience and fortitude, and supposes, or even requires, that others should have the same—and such a man would certainly not be the meanest product of nature—but if nature had not specially framed him for a philanthropist, would he not still find in himself a source from whence to give himself a far higher worth than that of a good-natured temperament could be? Unquestionably. It is just in this that the moral worth of the character is brought out which is incomparably the highest of all, namely, that he is beneficent, not from inclination, but from duty.

To secure one's own happiness is a duty, at least indirectly; for discontent with one's condition under a pressure of many anxieties and amidst unsatisfied wants might easily become a great temptation to *transgression of duty.* . . .

It is in this manner, undoubtedly, that we are to understand those passages of Scripture also in which we are commanded to love our neighbour, even our enemy. For love, as an affection, cannot be commanded, but beneficence for duty's sake; even though we are not impelled to it by any inclination, nay, are even repelled by a natural and unconquerable aversion. This is *practical* love, and not *pathological,* a love which is seated in the will, and not in the propensions of sense, in principles of action and not of tender sympathy; and it is this love alone which can be commanded.

The second proposition[1] is: That an action done from duty derives its moral worth, *not from the purpose* which is to be attained by it, but from the maxim by which it is determined, and therefore does not depend on the realization of the object of the action, but merely on the *principle of volition* by which the action has taken place, without regard to any object of desire. It is clear from what precedes that the purposes which we may have in view in our actions, or their effects regarded as ends and springs of the will, cannot give to actions any unconditional or moral worth. In what then can their worth lie, if it is not to consist in the will and in reference to its expected effect? It cannot lie anywhere but in the *principle of the will* without regard to the ends which can be attained by the action. For the will stands between its *a priori* principle which is formal, and its *a posteriori* spring which is material, as between two roads, and as it must be determined by something, it follows that it must be determined by the formal principle of volition when an action is done from duty, in which case every material principle has been withdrawn from it.

Respect for the Moral Law

The third proposition, which is a consequence of the two preceding, I would express thus: *Duty is the necessity of acting from respect for the law.* I may have *inclination* for an object as the effect of my proposed action, but I cannot have respect for it, just for this reason, that it is an effect and not an energy of will. Similarly, I cannot have respect for inclination, whether my own or another's; I can at most if my own, approve it; if another's, sometimes even love it; i.e., look on it as favorable to my own interest. It is only what is connected with my will as a principle, by no means as an effect—what does not subserve my inclination, but overpowers it, or at least in case of choice excludes it from its calculation—in other words, simply the law of itself, which can be an object of respect, and hence a command. Now an action done from duty must wholly exclude the influence of inclination, and with it every object of the will, so that nothing remains which can determine the will except objectively the *law,* and subjectively *pure respect* for this practical law, and consequently the maxim[2] to follow this law even to the thwarting of all my inclinations.

Thus the moral worth of an action does not lie in the effect expected from it, nor in any principle of action which requires to borrow its motive from this expected effect. For all these effects—agreeableness of one's condition, and even the promotion of the happiness of others—could have been also brought about by other causes, so that for this there would have been no need of the will of a rational being; it is in this, however, alone that the supreme and unconditional good can be found. The preeminent good which we call moral can therefore consist in nothing else than *the conception of law* in itself, *which certainly is only possible in a rational being,* in so far as this conception, and not the expected effect, determines the will. This is a good which is already present in the person who acts accordingly, and we have not to wait for it to appear first in the result.[3]

The Categorical Imperative

But what sort of law can that be, the conception of which must determine the will, even without paying any regard to the effect expected from it, in order that this will may be called good absolutely and without qualification? As I have deprived the will of every impulse which could arise to it from obedience to any law, there remains nothing but the universal conformity of its actions to law in general, which alone is to serve the will as a principle, i.e., *I am never to act otherwise than so that I could also will that my maxim should become a universal law.* Here now, it is the simple conformity to law in general, without assuming any particular law applicable to certain actions, that serves the will as its principle, and must so serve it, if duty is not to be a vain delusion and a chimerical notion. The common reason of men in its practical judgments perfectly coincides with this, and always has in view the principle here suggested. Let the question be, for example: May I when in distress make a promise with the intention not to keep it? I readily distinguish here between the two significations which the question may have: Whether it is prudent, or whether it is right, to make a false promise. The former may undoubtedly often be the case. I see clearly indeed that it is not enough to extricate myself from a present difficulty by means of this subterfuge, but it must be well considered whether there may not hereafter spring from this lie much greater inconvenience than that form which I now free myself, and as, with all my supposed *cunning,* the consequences cannot be so easily foreseen but that credit once lost may be much more injurious to me than any mischief which I seek to avoid at present, it should be considered whether it would not be more *prudent* to act herein according to a universal maxim, and to make it a habit to promise nothing except with the intention of keeping it. But it is soon clear to me that such a maxim will still only be based on the fear of consequences. Now it is a wholly different thing to be truthful from duty, and to be so from apprehension of injurious consequences. In the first case, the very notion of the action already implies a law for me; in the second case, I must first look about elsewhere to see what results may be combined with it which would affect myself. For to deviate from the principle of duty is beyond all doubt wicked; but to be unfaithful to my maxim of prudence may often be very advantageous to me, although to abide by it is certainly safer. The shortest way, however, and an unerring one, to discover the answer to this question whether a lying promise is consistent with duty, is to ask myself, Should I be content that my maxim (to extricate myself from difficulty by a false promise) should hold good as a universal law, for myself as well as for others? and should I be able to say to myself, 'Every one may make a deceitful promise when he finds himself in a difficulty from which he cannot otherwise extricate himself'? Then I presently become aware that while I can will the lie, I can by no means will that lying should be a universal law. For with such a law there would be no promises at all, since it would be in vain to allege my intention in regard to my future actions to those who would not believe this allegation, or if they over hastily did so would pay me back in my own coin. Hence my maxim, as soon as it should be made a universal law, would necessarily destroy itself.

I do not therefore need any far-reaching penetration to discern what I have to do in order that my will may be morally good. Inexperienced in the course of the world, incapable of being prepared for all its contingencies, I only ask myself: Canst thou also will that thy maxim should be a universal law? If not, then it must be rejected, and that not because of a disadvantage accruing from it to myself or even to others, but because it cannot enter as a principle into a possible universal legislation, and reason extorts from me immediate respect for such legislation. I do not indeed as yet discern on what this respect is based (this the philosopher may inquire), but at least I understand this, that it is an estimation of the worth which far outweighs all worth of what is recommended by inclination, and that the necessity of acting from pure respect for the practical law is what constitutes duty, to which every other motive must give place, because it is the condition of a will being good in itself, and the worth of such a will is above everything.

Thus then, without quitting the moral knowledge of common human reason, we have arrived at its principle. And although no doubt common men do not conceive it in such an abstract and universal form, yet they always have it really before their eyes, and use it as the standard of their decision. . . .

Moral and Nonmoral Imperatives

Everything in nature works according to laws. Rational beings alone have the faculty of acting according *to the conception of laws*, that is according to principles, i.e., have a will. Since the deduction of actions from principles requires *reason*, the will is nothing but practical reason. If reason infallibly determines the will, then the actions of such a being which are recognised as objectively necessary are subjectively necessary also; i.e., the will is a faculty to choose *that only* which reason independent on inclination recognises as practically necessary, i.e., as good. But if reason of itself does not sufficiently determine the will, if the latter is subject also to subjective conditions (particular impulses) which do not always coincide with the objective conditions; in a word, if the will does not in itself completely accord with reason (which is actually the case with men), then the actions which objectively are recognised as necessary are subjectively contingent, and the determination of such a will according to objective laws is obligation, that is to say, the relation of the objective laws to a will that is not thoroughly good, is conceived as the determination of the will of a rational being by principles of reason, but which the will from its nature does not of necessity follow.

The conception of an objective principle, in so far as it is obligatory for a will, is called a command (of reason), and the formula of the command is called an Imperative.

All imperatives are expressed by the word *ought* [or *shall*], and thereby indicate the relation of an objective law of reason to a will, which from its subjective constitution is not necessarily determined by it (an obligation). They say that something would be good to do or to forbear, but they say it to a will which does not always do a thing because it is conceived to be good to do it. That is practically *good,* however, which determines the will by means of the conceptions of reason, and consequently not from subjective causes, but objectively, that is, on principles which are valid for every rational being as such. It is distinguished from the *pleasant,* as that which influences the will only by means of sensation from merely subjective causes, valid only for the sense of this or that one, and not as a principle of reason, which holds for every one.[4]

A perfectly good will would therefore be equally subject to objective laws (viz., of good), but could not be conceived as *obliged* thereby to act lawfully, because of itself from its subjective constitution it can only be determined by the conception of good. Therefore no imperatives hold for the Divine will, or in general for a *holy* will; *ought* is here out of place, because the volition is already of itself necessarily in unison with the law. Therefore imperatives are only formulae to express the relation of objective laws of all volition to the subjective imperfection of the will of this or that rational being, e.g., the human will.

Now all imperatives command either *hypothetically* or *categorically*. The former represent the practical necessity of a possible action as means to something else that is willed (or at least which one might possibly will). The categorical imperative would be that which represented an action as necessary of itself without reference to another end, that is, as objectively necessary.

Since every practical law represents a possible action as good, and on this account, for a subject who is practically determinable by reason as necessary, all imperatives are formulae determining an action which is necessary according to the principle of a will good in some respects. If now the action is good only as a *means to something else,* then the imperative is *hypothetical;* if it is conceived as good in itself and consequently as being necessarily the principle of a will which of itself conforms to reason, then it is *categorical.*

Thus the imperative declares what action possible by me would be good, and presents the practical rule in relation to a will which does not forthwith perform an action simply because it is good, whether because the subject does not always know that it is good, or because, even if it know this, yet its maxims might be opposed to the objective principles of practical reason.

Accordingly the hypothetical imperative only says that the action is good for some purpose, *possible* or *actual*. In the first case it is a *problematical*, in the second an *assertorial* practical principle. The categorical imperative which declares an action to be objectively necessary in itself without reference to any purpose, that is, without any other end, is valid as an *apodictic* (practical) principle.

Whatever is possible only by the power of some rational being may also be conceived as a possible purpose of some will; and therefore the principles of action as regards the means necessary to attain some possible purpose are in fact infinitely numerous. All sciences have a practical part consisting of problems expressing that some end is possible for us, and of imperatives directing how it may be attained. These may, therefore, be called in general imperatives of skill. Here there is no question whether the end is rational and good, but only what one must do in order to attain it. The precepts for the physician to make his patient thoroughly healthy, and for a poisoner to ensure certain death, are of equal value in this respect, that each serves to effect its purpose perfectly. Since in early youth it cannot be known what ends are likely to occur to us in the course of life, parents seek to have their children taught a *great many things*, and provide for their skill in the use of means for all sorts of arbitrary ends, of none of which can they determine whether it may not perhaps hereafter be an object to their pupil, but which it is at all events possible that he might aim at; and this anxiety is so great that they commonly neglect to form and correct their judgment on the value of the things which may be chosen as ends.

There is *one* end, however, which may be assumed to be actually such to all rational beings (so far as imperatives apply to them, viz., as dependent beings), and, therefore, one purpose which they not merely may have, but which we may with certainty assume that they all actually have by a natural necessity, and this is *happiness*. The hypothetical imperative which expresses the practical necessity of an action as means to the advancement of happiness is *assertorical*. We are not to present it as necessary for an uncertain and merely possible purpose, but for a purpose which we may presuppose with certainty and a priori in every man, because it belongs to his being. Now skill in the choice of means to his own greatest well-being may be called *prudence*,[5] in the narrowest sense. And thus the imperative which refers to the choice of means to one's own happiness, that is, the precept of prudence, is still always *hypothetical*; the action is not commanded absolutely, but only as means to another purpose.

Finally, there is an imperative which commands a certain conduct immediately, without having as its condition any other purpose to be attained by it. This imperative is *categorical*. It concerns not the matter of the action, or its intended result, but its form and the principle of which it is itself a result; and what is essentially good in it consists in the mental disposition, let the consequence be what it may. This imperative may be called that of *morality*.

There is a marked distinction also between the volitions on these three sorts of principles in the dissimilarity of the obligation of the will. In order to mark this difference more clearly, I think they would be most suitably named in their order if we said they are either *rules* of skill, or *counsels* of prudence, or *commands* (laws) of morality. For it is law only that involves the conception of an unconditional and objective necessity, which is consequently universally valid; and commands are laws which must be obeyed, that is, must be followed, even in opposition to inclination. Counsels, indeed, involve necessity, but one which can only hold under a contingent subjective condition, viz., they depend on whether this or that man reckons this or that as part of his happiness; the categorical imperative, on the contrary, is not limited by any condition, and as being absolutely, although practically, necessary may be quite properly called a command. We might also call the first kind of imperatives *technical* (belonging to art), the second *pragmatic*[6] (belonging to welfare), the third *moral* (belonging to free conduct generally, that is, to morals).

Now arises the question, how are all these imperatives possible? This question does not seek to know how we can conceive the accomplishment of the action which the imperative ordains, but merely how we can conceive the obligation of the will which the imperative expresses. No special explanation is needed to show how an imperative of skill is possible. Whoever wills the end wills also (so far as reason decides his conduct) the means in his power which are indispensably necessary thereto. . . .

We shall therefore have to investigate *a priori* the possibility of a categorical imperative, as we have not in this case the advantage of its reality being given in experience, so that [the elucidation of] its possibility should be requisite only for its explanation, not for its establishment. In the meantime it may be discerned beforehand that the categorical imperative alone has the purport of a practical law; all the rest may indeed be called principles of the will but not laws, since whatever is only necessary for the attainment of some arbitrary purpose may be considered as in itself contingent, and we can at any time be free from the precept if we give up the purpose; on the contrary, the unconditional command leaves the will no liberty to choose the opposite, consequently it alone carries with it that necessity which we require in a law. . . .

In this problem we will first inquire whether the mere conception of a categorical imperative may not perhaps supply us also with the formula of it, containing the proposition which alone can be a categorical imperative; for even if we know the tenor of such an absolute command, yet how it is possible will require further special and laborious study; which we postpone to the last section.

When I conceive a hypothetical imperative in general, I do not know before hand what it will contain, until I am given the condition. But when I conceive a categorical imperative I know at once what it contains. For as the imperative contains, besides the law, only the necessity of the maxim[7] conforming to this law, while the law contains no condition restricting it, there remains nothing but the general statement that the maxim of the action should conform to a universal law, and it is this conformity alone that the imperative properly represents as necessary.

There is therefore but one categorical imperative, namely this: *Act only on that maxim whereby thou canst at the same time will that it should become a universal law.*

Now if all imperatives of duty can be deduced from this one imperative as from their principle, then although it should remain undecided whether what is called duty is not merely a vain notion, yet at least we shall be able to show what we understand by it and what this notion means.

Applying the Categorical Imperative

Since the universality of the law according to which effects are produced constitutes what is properly called *nature* in the most general sense (as to form), that is the existence of things so far as it is determined by general laws, the imperative of duty may be expressed thus: *Act as if the maxim of thy action were to become by thy will a Universal Law of Nature.*

We will now enumerate a few duties, adopting the usual division of them into duties to ourselves and to others, and into perfect and imperfect duties.[8]

1. A man reduced to despair by a series of misfortunes feels wearied of life, but is still so far in possession of his reason that he can ask himself whether it would not be contrary to his duty to himself to take his own life. Now he inquires whether the maxim of his action could become a universal law of nature. His maxim is: From self-love I adopt it as a principle to shorten my life when its longer duration is likely to bring more evil than satisfaction. It is asked then simply whether this principle of self-love can become a universal law of nature? Now we see at once that a system of nature of which it should be a law to destroy life by the very feeling which is designed to impel to the maintenance of life would contradict itself, and therefore could not exist as a system of nature; hence that maxim cannot possibly exist as a universal law of nature and consequently would be wholly inconsistent with the supreme principle of all duty.

2. Another finds himself forced by necessity to borrow money. He knows that he will not be able to repay it, but sees also that nothing will be lent to him, unless he promises stoutly to repay it in a definite time. He desires to make this promise, but he has still so much conscience as to ask himself: Is it not unlawful and inconsistent with duty to get out of a difficulty in this way? Suppose however that he resolves to do so: then the maxim of his action would be expressed thus: When I think myself in want of money, I will borrow money and promise to repay it, although I know that I never can do so. Now this principle of self-love or of one's own advantage may perhaps be consistent with my whole future welfare; but the question now is, Is it right? I change then the suggestion of self-love into a universal law, and state the question thus: How would it be if my maxim were a universal law? Then I see at once that it could never hold as a universal law of nature, but would necessarily contradict itself. For supposing it to be a universal law that every one when he thinks himself in a difficulty should be able to promise whatever he pleases, with the purpose of not keeping his promise, the promise itself would become impossible, as well as the end that one might have in view in it, since no one would consider that anything was promised to him, and would ridicule all such statements as vain pretences.

3. A third finds in himself a talent which with the help of some culture might make him a useful man

in many respects. But he finds himself in comfortable circumstances, and prefers to indulge in pleasure rather than to take pains in enlarging and improving his happy natural capacities. He asks, however, whether his maxim of neglect of his natural gifts, besides agreeing with his inclination to indulgence, agrees also with what is called duty? He sees then that a system of nature could indeed subsist with such a universal law, though men (like the South Sea islanders) should let their talents rust, and resolve to devote their lives merely to idleness, amusement, and propagation of their species, in a word to enjoyment; but he cannot possibly will that this should be a universal law of nature, or be implanted in us as such by a natural instinct. For, as a rational being, he necessarily wills that his faculties be developed, since they serve him for all sorts of possible purposes, and have been given him for this.

4. A fourth, who is in prosperity, while he sees that others have to contend with great wretchedness and that he could help them, thinks: What concern is it of mine? Let every one be as happy as heaven pleases or as he can make himself; I will take nothing from him nor even envy him, only I do not wish to contribute anything either to his welfare or to his assistance in distress! Now no doubt if such a mode of thinking were a universal law, the human race might very well subsist, and doubtless even better than in a state in which every one talks of sympathy and good will, or even takes care occasionally to put it into practice, but on the other side, also cheats when he can, betrays the rights of men or otherwise violates them. But although it is possible that a universal law of nature might exist in accordance with that maxim, it is impossible to will that such a principle should have the universal validity of a law of nature. For a will which resolved this would contradict itself, inasmuch as many cases might occur in which one would have need of the love and sympathy of others, and in which by such a law of nature, sprung from his own will, he would deprive himself of all hope of the aid he desires.

These are a few of the many actual duties, or at least what we regard as such, which obviously fall into two classes on the one principle that we have laid down. We must be *able to will* that a maxim of our action should be a universal law. This is the canon of the moral appreciation of the action generally. Some actions are of such a character, that their maxim cannot without contradiction be even *conceived* as a universal law of nature, far from it being possible that

we should *will* that it should be so. In others this intrinsic impossibility is not found, but still it is impossible to *will* that their maxim should be raised to the universality of a law of nature, since such a will would contradict itself. It is easily seen that the former violate strict or rigorous (inflexible) duty; the latter only laxer (meritorious) duty. Thus it has been completely shown how all duties depend as regards the nature of the obligation (not the object of the action) on the same principle.

If now we attend to ourselves on occasion of any transgression of duty, we shall find that we in fact do not will that our maxim should be a universal law, for that it is impossible for us; on the contrary we will that the opposite should remain a universal law, only we assume the liberty of making an *exception* in our own favour or (just for this time only) in favour of our inclination. . . .

The will is conceived as a faculty of determining oneself to action *in accordance with the conception of certain laws.* And such a faculty can be found only in rational beings. Now that which serves the will as the objective ground of its self-determination is the *end*, and if this is assigned by reason alone, it must hold for all rational beings. On the other hand, that which merely contains the ground of possibility of the action of which the effect is the end, this is called the *means.* The subjective ground of the desire is the spring, the objective ground of the volition is the *motive*; hence the distinction between subjective ends which rest on springs, and objective ends which depend on motives that hold for every rational being. Practical principles are *formal* when they abstract from all subjective ends, they are *material* when they assume these, and therefore particular springs of action. The ends which a rational being proposes to himself at pleasure as *effect*s of his actions (material ends) are all only relative, for it is only their relation to the particular desires of the subject that gives them their worth, which therefore cannot furnish principles universal and necessary for all rational beings and for every volition, that is to say practical laws. Hence all these relative ends can give rise only to hypothetical imperatives.

Persons as Ends

Supposing, however, that there were something *whose existence has in itself* an absolute worth, something which being *an end in itself,* could be a source of definite laws, then in this and this alone would lie the source of a possible categorical imperative, i.e., a practical law. Now I say: man and generally any rational being exists as an end in himself, *not merely as a means* to be arbitrarily used by this or that will, but in all his actions, whether they concern himself or other rational beings, must always be regarded at the same time as an end. All objects of the inclinations have only a conditional worth, for if the inclinations and the wants founded on them did not exist, then their object would be without value. But the inclinations themselves being sources of want, are so far from having an absolute worth for which they should be desired, that on the contrary it must be the universal wish of every rational being to be wholly free from them. Thus the worth of any object which is *to be acquired* by our action is always conditional. Beings whose existence depends not on our will but on nature's, have nevertheless, if they are irrational beings, only a relative value as means, and are therefore called *things*; rational beings on the contrary, are called *persons*, because their very nature points them out as ends in themselves, that is as something which must not be used merely as means, and so far therefore restricts freedom of action (and is an object of respect). These, therefore, are not merely subjective ends whose existence has a worth for us as an effect of our action, but *objective ends,* that is things whose existence is an end in itself; an end moreover for which no other can be substituted, which they should subserve merely as means, for otherwise nothing whatever would possess *absolute worth*; but if all worth were conditioned and therefore contingent, then there would be no supreme practical principle of reason whatever.

If then there is a supreme practical principle or, in respect of the human will, a categorical imperative, it must be one which, drawn from the conception of that which is necessarily an end for every one because it is *an end in itself*, constitutes an objective principle of will, and can therefore serve as a universal practical law. The foundation of this principle is: *rational nature exists as an end in itself.* Man necessarily conceives his own existence as being so; so far then, this is a *subjective* principle of human actions. But every other rational being regards its existence similarly, just on the same rational principle that holds for me:[9] so that it is at the same time an objective principle, from which as a supreme practical law all laws of the will must be capable of being deduced. Accordingly the practical imperative will be as follows: *So act as to treat humanity, whether in thine own person or in that of any other, in every case as an end withal, never as a means only. . . .*

We will now inquire whether this can be practically carried out.

To abide by the previous examples:

First, under the head of necessary duty to oneself: He who contemplates suicide should ask himself whether his action can be consistent with the idea of humanity *as an end in itself*. If he destroys himself in order to escape from painful circumstances, he uses a person merely as a *means* to maintain a tolerable condition up to the end of life. But a man is not a thing, that is to say, something which can be used merely as means, but must in all his actions be always considered as an end in himself. I cannot, therefore, dispose in any way of a man in my own person so as to mutilate him, to damage or kill him. (It belongs to ethics proper to define this principle more precisely, so as to avoid all misunderstanding, for example, as to the amputation of the limbs in order to preserve myself; as to exposing my life to danger with a view to preserve it, etc. This question is therefore omitted here.)

Secondly, as regards necessary duties, or those of strict obligation, towards others: He who is thinking of making a lying promise to others will see at once that he would be using another man *merely as a means,* without the latter containing at the same time the end in himself. For he whom I propose by such a promise to use for my own purposes cannot possibly assent to my mode of acting towards him, and therefore cannot himself contain the end of this action. This violation of the principle of humanity in other men is more obvious if we take in examples of attacks on the freedom and property of others. For then it is clear that he who transgresses the rights of men intends to use the person of others merely as means, without considering that as rational beings they ought always to be esteemed also as ends, that is, as beings who must be capable of containing in themselves the end of the very same action.[10]

Thirdly, as regards contingent (meritorious) duties to oneself: It is not enough that the action does not violate humanity in our own person as an end in itself, it must also *harmonize with it.* . . . Now there are in humanity capacities of greater perfection which belong to the end that nature has in view in regard to humanity in ourselves as the subject; to neglect these might perhaps be consistent with the *maintenance* of humanity as an end in itself, but not with the *advancement* of this end.

Fourthly, as regards meritorious duties towards others: The natural end which all men have is their own happiness. Now humanity might indeed subsist although no one should contribute anything to the happiness of others, provided he did not intentionally withdraw anything from it; but after all, this would only harmonize negatively, not positively, with *humanity as an end in itself,* if everyone does not also endeavor, as far as in him lies, to forward the ends of others. For the ends of any subject which is an end in himself ought as far as possible to be *my* ends also, if that conception is to have its *full* effect with me.

Notes*

1. [The first proposition was that to have moral worth an action must be done from duty.]

2. A *maxim* is the subjective principle of volition. The objective principle (*i.e.,* that which would also serve subjectively as a practical principle to all rational beings in reason had full power over the faculty of desire) is the practical *law.*

3. It might here be objected to me that I take refuge behind the word *respect* in an obscure feeling instead of giving a distinct solution of the question by a concept of the reason. But although respect is a feeling, it is not a feeling *received* through influence, but is *self-wrought* by a rational concept, and, therefore, is specially distinct from all feelings of the former kind, which may be referred either to inclination or fear. What I recognise immediately as a law for me, I recognise with respect. This merely signifies the consciousness that my will is *subordinate* to a law, without the intervention of other influences on my sense. The immediate determination of the will by the law, and the consciousness of this is called *respect,* so that this is regarded as an *effect* of the law on the subject, and not as the *cause* of it. Respect is properly the conception of a work which thwarts my self-love. Accordingly it is something which is considered neither as an object of inclination nor of fear, although it has something analogous to both. The *object* of respect is the law only, and that, the law which we impose on *ourselves,* and yet recognise as necessary in itself. As a law, we are subjected to it without consulting self-love; as imposed by us on ourselves, it is a result of our will. In the former respect it has an analogy to fear, in the latter to inclination. Respect for a person is properly only respect for the law (of honesty, & c.,) of which he gives us an example. . . .

4. The dependence of the desires on sensations is called *inclination,* and this accordingly always indicates a *want.* The dependence of a contingently determinable will on principles of reason is called an *interest.* This, therefore, is found only in the case of a dependent will which does not always of itself conform to reason; in the Divine will we cannot conceive any interest. But the human will can also *take an interest* in a thing without therefore acting *from interest.* The former signifies the *practical* interest in the action, the latter the *pathological* in the object of the action. The former indicates only dependence of the will on principles of reason in themselves; the second, dependence on principles of reason for the sake of inclination, reason supplying only the practical rules how the requirement of the inclination may be satisfied. In the first case the action interests me; in the second the object of the action (because it is pleasant to me). We have seen in the first section that in an action done from duty we must look not to the interest in the object, but only to that in the action itself, and in its rational principle (viz., the law).

5. The word *prudence* is taken in two senses: in the one it may bear the name of knowledge of the world, in the other that of private prudence. The former is a man's ability to influence others so as to use them for his own purposes. The latter is the sagacity to combine all these purposes for his own lasting benefit. This latter is properly that to which the value even of the former is reduced, and when a man is prudent in the former sense, but not in the latter, we might better say of him that he is clever and cunning, but, on the whole, imprudent.

6. It seems to me that the proper signification of the word *pragmatic* may be most accurately defined in this way. For *sanctions* . . . are called pragmatic which flow properly, not from the law of the states as necessary enactments, but from *precaution* for the general welfare. A history is composed pragmatically when it teaches *prudence,* that is, instructs the world how it can provide for its interests better, or at least as well as the men of former time.

7. A MAXIM is a subjective principle of action . . . the principle on which the subject *acts;* but the law is the objective principle valid for every rational being, and is the principle on which it *ought to act* that is an imperative.

8. It must be noted here that I reserve the division of duties for a *future metaphysic of morals;* so that I give it here only as an arbitrary one (in order to arrange my examples). For the rest, I understand by a perfect duty, one that admits no exception in favour of inclination, and then I have not merely external but also internal perfect duties.

---

*Some notes have been deleted and the remaining ones renumbered.—ED.

9. This proposition is here stated as a postulate. The ground of it will be found in the concluding section.

10. Let it not be thought that the common: *quod tibi non vis fieri, etc.*, could serve here as the rule or principle. For it is only a deduction from the former, though with several limitations; it cannot be a universal law, for it does not contain the principle of duties to oneself, nor of the duties of benevolence to others (for many a one would gladly consent that others should not benefit him, provided only that he might be excused from showing benevolence to them), nor finally that of duties of strict obligation to one another, for on this principle the criminal might argue against the judge who punishes him, and so on.

Review Exercises

1. Give one of Kant's reasons for opposing locating the moral worth of an action in its consequences.

2. Does Kant mean by "a good will" or "good intention" wishing others well? Explain.

3. What does Kant mean by "acting out of duty"? How does the shopkeeper exemplify this?

4. What is the basic difference between a categorical and a hypothetical imperative? In the following examples, which are hypothetical and which categorical imperatives? Explain your answers.

   a. If you want others to be honest with you, then you ought to be honest with them.

   b. Whether or not you want to pay your share, you ought to do so.

   c. Because everyone wants to be happy, we ought to consider everyone's interests equally.

   d. I ought not to cheat on this test if I do not want to get caught.

5. How does the character of moral obligation lead to Kant's basic moral principle, the categorical imperative?

6. Explain Kant's use of the first form of the categorical imperative to argue that it is wrong to make a false promise. (Note that you do not appeal to the bad consequences as the basis of judging it wrong.)

7. According to the second form of Kant's categorical imperative, would it be morally permissible for me to agree to be someone's slave? Explain.

8. What is the practical difference between a perfect and an imperfect duty?

Selected Bibliography

Acton, Harry. *Kant's Moral Philosophy.* New York: Macmillan, 1970.

Annas, George J., and Michael A. Grodin (Eds.). *The Nazi Doctors and the Nuremberg Code.* New York: Oxford University Press, 1992.

Aune, Bruce. *Kant's Theory of Morals.* Princeton, NJ: Princeton University Press, 1979.

Beck, Lewis White. *A Commentary on Kant's Critique of Practical Reason.* Chicago: University of Chicago Press, 1960.

Gulyga, Arsenij. *Immanuel Kant: His Life and Thought.* Marijan Despalotovic (Trans.). Boston: Birkhauser, 1987.

Harrison, Jonathan. "Kant's Examples of the First Formulation of the Categorical Imperative," *Philosophical Quarterly* 7 (1957), 50–62.

Hill, Thomas E., Jr. "Kantian Constructivism in Ethics," *Ethics* 99 (1989).

Kant, Immanuel. *Critique of Practical Reason.* Lewis White Beck (Trans.). Indianapolis, IN: Bobbs-Merrill, 1956.

———. *Foundations of the Metaphysics of Morals.* J.H.J. Paton (Trans.). New York: Harper & Row, 1957.

Korner, Stephen. *Kant.* New Haven, CT: Yale University Press, 1982.

Korsgaard, Christine M. "Kant's Formula of Universal Law," *Pacific Philosophical Quarterly* 66 (1985), 24–47.

Nell, Onora. *Acting on Principle: An Essay on Kantian Ethics.* New York: Columbia University Press, 1975.

Paton, Herbert J. *The Categorical Imperative: A Study in Kant's Moral Philosophy.* Chicago: University of Chicago Press, 1948.

Ross, Sir William David. *Kant's Ethical Theory.* New York: Oxford University Press, 1954.

Scruton, Roger. *Kant.* New York: Oxford University Press, 1982.

Sullivan, Roger J. *An Introduction to Kant's Ethics.* New York: Cambridge University Press, 1994.

Walker, Ralph. C. *Kant.* New York: Methuen, 1982.

Wolff, Robert P. *The Autonomy of Reason: A Commentary on Kant's "Groundwork of the Metaphysics of Morals."* New York: Harper & Row, 1973.

❀ 6 ❀

Naturalism and Virtue Ethics

In 1776 Thomas Jefferson wrote, "We hold these truths to be self evident, that all men are created equal and that they are endowed by their creator with certain inalienable rights, among which are life, liberty, and the pursuit of happiness."[1] Jefferson had read the work of philosopher John Locke (1632–1704), who in his *Second Treatise on Government* had written that all human beings were of the same species, born with the same basic capacities.[2] Thus, Locke argued, because all humans had the same basic nature, they should be treated equally. The idea that morality is based on human nature is a form of what we will refer to here as "naturalism in ethics."

Philosophers sometimes use the term *naturalism* in ethics to apply to any kind of ethics that holds that what is good is a function in some way of the way things are. For example, pleasure is said to be good because of the way things are, namely, that people do seek pleasure. Another example is to call something good for us because of the fact that it fits or fulfills human nature. One version of this type of naturalism in ethics is *natural law theory,* the view that the moral law is based on human nature. A second example of naturalism in this broad sense is a *natural rights theory,* the view that human rights are those things that we can validly claim because they are essential for our functioning as human beings. A third example can be found in some types of *vir-*

tue ethics. Here virtues are thought to be good habits, and good habits are those habits that enable us to function well as human beings. In this chapter we will give a brief account of all three types of what can be called naturalism in ethics.

Virtue Ethics

Let us begin with the notion of virtue. Although we probably do not use the term *virtuous* as commonly today as in times past, we still understand the essence of its meaning. A virtuous person is a morally good person, and virtues are good traits. Loyalty is a virtue, and so is honesty. The opposite of virtue is vice. Stinginess is a vice. A moral philosophy that concentrates on the notion of virtue is called a *virtue ethics*. All of the moral theories that we have analyzed so far have been theories that attempt to tell us what we ought to *do.* For virtue ethics, on the contrary, the moral life is rather about developing good *character.* Morality ought to address the question "What should I *be?*" rather than "What should I *do?*" The moral life ought to be about determining what are the ideals for human life and trying to embody these ideals in one's life. The virtues are then ways in which we embody these ideals. If we consider honesty to be such an ideal, for example, then we ought to try to become honest persons. We can learn more about the notion of virtue and virtue ethics from an examination of one of the first discussions of it in the history of Western philosophy, namely, in the writings of the philosopher Aristotle.

Historical Background: Aristotle

The general tradition of natural law theory had its primary source in the moral philosophy of Aristotle, who was born in 384 B.C. in Stagira, in northern Greece. His father was a physician for King Philip of Macedonia. At about age seventeen, he went to study at Plato's Academy in Athens. Historians of philosophy have traced the influence of Plato's philosophy on Aristotle, but they have also noted significant differences between the two philosophers. Putting one difference somewhat simply, Plato's philosophy stresses the reality of the general and abstract, this reality being his famous forms or ideas that exist apart from the things that imitate them or in which they participate. Aristotle was more interested in the individual and the concrete manifestations of the forms. After Plato's death, Aristotle traveled for several years and then for two or three years was the tutor to the young son of King Philip, Alexander, later known as Alexander the Great. In 335 B.C. Aristotle returned to Athens and organized his own school called the Lyceum. There he taught and wrote almost until his death thirteen years later in 322 B.C.[3] Aristotle is known not only for his moral theory but also for writings in logic, biology, physics, metaphysics, art, and politics. The basic notions of his moral theory can be found in his *Nicomachean Ethics,* named after his son Nicomachus.[4]

The Nature and Kinds of Virtue

For Aristotle, virtue was an excellence of some sort. Originally, our word *virtue* meant "strength" (from the Latin *vir*) and referred to manliness.[5] In Aristotle's ethics, the term used for what we translate as virtue was *arete.* It referred to excellences of various types. According to Aristotle, there are two basic types of excellence or virtues: intellectual virtues and moral virtues. Intellectual virtues are excellences of

mind, such as the ability to understand and reason and judge well. Aristotle said these traits are learned from teachers. Moral virtues dispose us to act well. These virtues are learned not by being taught but by repetition. For instance, by practicing courage or honesty, we become more courageous and honest. Just as repetition in playing a musical instrument makes playing easier, so also repeated acts of honesty make it easier to be honest. The person who has the virtue of honesty finds it easier to be honest than the person who does not have the virtue. It has become second nature to him or her. The same thing applies to the opposite of virtue, namely, vice. The person who lies and lies again finds that lying is easier and telling the truth more difficult. One can have bad moral habits (vices) as well as good ones (virtues). Just like other bad habits, bad moral habits are difficult to change or break.

Philosophers have listed and classified virtues and vices differently. Aristotle's list of virtues includes courage, temperance, justice, pride, and magnanimity. However, Aristotle is probably most well known for his position that virtue is a mean between extremes. Thus, the virtue of courage is to be understood as a mean or middle between the two extremes of deficiency and excess. Too little courage is cowardice, and too much is foolhardiness. We should have neither too much fear when facing danger or challenges, which makes us unable to act; nor too little fear, which makes us throw all caution to the wind, as we say. Courage is having just the right amount of fear, depending on what is appropriate for us as individuals and for the circumstances we face. So, also, the other virtues are means between extremes. Consider the examples above from Aristotle's list, and see if you could add any.

Our own list today might differ from this. For example, we might include loyalty and honesty in our list. If loyalty is a virtue, can there be such a thing as too little or too much loyalty? What about honesty? Too much honesty might be seen as undisciplined openness, and too little as deceitfulness. Would the right amount of hon-

	Deficit (Too Little)	Virtue (the Mean)	Excess (Too Much)
Fear	Cowardice	Courage	Foolhardiness
Giving	Illiberality	Liberality	Prodigality
Self-Regard	Humility	Pride	Vanity
Pleasures	[No Name Given]	Temperance	Profligacy

esty be forthrightness? In other words, not all virtues may be rightly thought of as a mean between extremes. If justice is a virtue, could there be such a thing as being too just or too little just? We could exemplify this view with the childhood story of Goldilocks. When she entered the bears' house, she ate the porridge that was not too hot and not too cold, but "just right"![6]

Contemporary Virtue Ethics

Various contemporary philosophers have been concerned about virtue.[7] Philippa Foot has developed a type of neonaturalistic virtue ethics. She believes that we all would probably agree that the virtues are "in some general way, beneficial. Human beings do not get on well without them."[8] According to Foot, it is both ourselves and our community that benefit from our having certain virtues, just as having certain vices harms both ourselves and our communities. Think of courage, temperance, and wisdom, for example, and ask yourself how persons having these virtues might benefit themselves and others. Some virtues such as charity, however, seem to benefit mostly others. She also wonders how we should determine which beneficial traits are to be thought of as moral virtues and which are not. Wit or powers of concentration benefit us, but we would probably not consider them to be *moral* virtues. Foot also asks whether the virtue is in the intention or the action. Think of generosity. Does the person who intends to be generous but cannot seem to do what helps others really possess the virtue of generosity? Or rather is it the person who actually does help who has the virtue? She believes that possessing the virtue of generosity must be more than simply having a naturally outgoing personality. Following Aris-

totle, Foot also agrees that the virtues are corrective.[9] They help us be and do things that are difficult for us. Courage, for example, helps us overcome natural fear. Temperance helps us control our desires. People differ in their natural inclinations and thus would also differ in what virtues would be most helpful for them to develop. This is just one example of how the notion of virtue continues to be discussed by moral philosophers.

Evaluating Virtue Ethics

One question that has been raised for virtue ethics concerns how we ought to decide which traits are virtues. Are there any universally valuable traits, for example? We might think that Aristotle's own list reflected what were considered civic virtues of his day. Our own list would reflect our own times. Contemporary moral philosopher Alasdair MacIntyre believes that virtues depend at least partly on the practices that constitute a culture or society. A warlike society will value heroic virtues, while a peaceful and prosperous society might think of generosity as a particularly important virtue.[10] However, these must be virtues specific to human beings as humans, for otherwise one could not speak of "human excellences." But this is just the problem. What is it to live a full human life? Can one specify this apart from what it is to live such a life in a particular society? Furthermore, are there certain virtues for males and others for females? Are there certain masculine virtues such as courage and perseverance that are more proper to men and other feminine virtues such as sensitivity and compassion that are more proper to women? (This issue is addressed in the following chapter on feminist ethics.) The problem here is not only how we know what excellences are human excellences, but also whether there are any such traits that are ideal for all persons.

A problem about virtue is raised by Philippa Foot herself. Who manifests the virtue of courage most, the person "who wants to run away but does not or the one who does not even want to run away?"[11] One reason why this question is difficult to answer is that we generally believe that we ought to be rewarded for our moral efforts and thus the person who wants to run away but does not seems the more courageous. On the other hand, if one has the virtue of courage, it is supposed to make it easier to be brave. Her own answer to this dilemma has to do with the distinction between those fears for which we are in some way responsible and those that we cannot help. Thus, the person who feels like running away because he or she has contributed by their choices to being fearsome is not the more virtuous person.

We can also ask whether virtue ethics is really a distinct type of ethics. Consider the other theories we have treated, utilitarianism and Kantianism. The concept of virtue is not foreign to Mill or Kant. However, for both of them it is secondary. Their moral theories tell us how we ought to decide what to *do*. Doing the right thing, and with Kant for the right reason, is primary. However, if the development of certain habits of action or tendencies to act in a certain way will enable us to do good more easily, then they would surely be recognized by these philosophers as good. Utilitarians would encourage the development of those virtues that would be conducive to the maximization of happiness. If temperance in eating and drinking will help us avoid the suffering that can come from illness and drunkenness, then this virtue ought to be encouraged and developed in the young. So also with other virtues. According to a Kantian, it would be well to develop in ourselves and others habits that would make it more likely that we would be fair and treat people as ends rather than simply as means.

In virtue ethics, however, the primary goal is to be a good person. Now, some argue that *being*

good is only a function of being more inclined to *do* good. For every virtue, there is a corresponding good to be achieved or done. The just person acts justly and does what increases justice, for example. Is virtue then simply one aspect of these otherwise action-oriented moral philosophies? Perhaps so. However, virtue ethics still has a different emphasis. It is an ethics whose goal is to determine what is essential to be a well-functioning or flourishing human being or person. It stresses the ideal for humans or persons. As an ethics of ideals or excellences, it is an optimist and positive type of ethics. One problem that it may face is what to say about those of us who do not meet the ideal. If we fall short of the ideal, does this make us bad? As with all moral theories, many questions concerning virtue remain to engage and puzzle us.

Natural Law Theory

Natural law theory is another example of a moral theory that holds that morality is based on human nature. According to this tradition, to know what morality requires we need only look to nature—human nature—and ask what it requires. Thus, John Locke argued that because people are as a matter of fact all equally human, they ought to be treated equally. Morality is not found in some esoteric realm but rather relies on what can be determined from a close scrutiny of human nature by our own mental faculties. The moral law is thus accessible to human reason. Both ideas, that morality is grounded in human nature and that it is accessible to human reason, are exemplified in the arguments of the Nuremberg trials. These trials also exemplify a third characteristic of natural law, its universality. It applies universally to all human beings and endures through time. It also is thought to transcend the individual laws and practices of particular societies, including the laws of the German Third Reich.

The Nuremberg trials were trials of Nazi war criminals held in Nuremberg, Germany, from 1945 to 1949. There were thirteen trials in all. In the first trial, Nazi leaders were found guilty of violating international law by starting an aggressive war. Nine of them, including Hermann Goering and Rudolf Hess, were sentenced to death. In other trials, defendants were accused of committing atrocities against civilians. Nazi doctors who had conducted medical experiments on those imprisoned in the death camps were among those tried. Their experiments maimed and killed many people, all of whom were unwilling subjects. For example, experiments for the German air force were conducted to determine how fast people would die in very thin air. Other experiments tested the effects of freezing water on the human body. The defense contended that the military personnel, judges, and doctors were only following orders. However, the prosecution argued successfully that even if the experimentation did not violate the defendants' own laws, they were still "crimes against humanity." The idea was that there is a law more basic than civil laws—a moral law—and these doctors and others should have known what this basic moral law required.

What Kind of Law Is Natural Law?

Let us consider what type of law it is, how it is grounded in human nature, and what it requires. The natural law, as this term is used in discussions of natural law theory, should not be confused with those other "laws of nature" that are the generalizations of natural science. The laws of natural science are descriptive laws. They tell us how scientists believe nature behaves. Gases, for example, expand with their containers and when heat is applied. Boyle's Law about the behavior of gases does not tell gases how they *ought* to behave. In fact, if gases were found to behave differently from what we had so far observed, then the laws would be changed to match this new information. Simply put, scientific laws are descriptive generalizations of fact.

Moral laws, on the other hand, are prescriptive laws. They tell us how we ought to behave. The natural law is the moral law. However, natural law is not unrelated to nature, for what we

ought to do according to natural law theory is determined by considering some aspects of nature—in particular, our nature as human beings. We look to certain aspects of our nature to know what is our good and what we ought to do.

Civil law is also prescriptive. As the moral law, however, natural law is supposed to be more basic or higher than the laws of any particular society. Although laws of particular societies vary and change over time, the natural law is universal and stable. In the ancient Greek tragedy of Sophocles, Antigone disobeyed the king and buried her brother. She did so because she believed that she must follow a higher law that required her to do this. In the story, she lost her life for obeying this law. In the Nuremberg trials, prosecutors had also argued that there was a higher law that all humans should recognize and that takes precedence over state laws. People today sometimes appeal to the moral law in order to argue which civil laws ought to be instituted or changed.[12]

On What Is Natural Law Based?

Natural law theory is part of a long tradition that also can be said to have its origins in Aristotle's writings. Aristotle was a close observer of nature. In fact, in his writings he mentions some 500 different kinds of animals.[13] He noticed that seeds of the same sort always grew to the same mature form. He opened developing eggs of various species and noticed that these organisms manifested a pattern in their development even before birth. Tadpoles, he might have said, always follow the same path and become frogs, not turtles. So also with other living things. Acorns always become oak trees, not elms. He concluded that an order existed in nature. It was as if natural beings such as plants and animals had a principle of order within them that directed them toward their goal, their mature final form. This view can be called a *teleological* view from the Greek word for goal, *telos,* because of its emphasis on a goal embedded in natural things. It was from this that he developed his notion of the good.

According to Aristotle, "the good is that at which all things aim."[14] We are to look at the purpose or end or goal of some activity or being to see what is its good. Thus, the good of the shipbuilder is to build ships. The good of the lyre player is to play well. Aristotle asks whether there is anything that is the good of the human being—not as shipbuilder or lyre player, but simply as human. To answer this question, we must first think about what it is to be human. According to Aristotle, natural beings come in kinds or species. From their species flow their essential characteristics and certain key tendencies or capacities. A squirrel, for example, is a kind of animal that is first of all a living being, an animal. It develops from a young form to a mature form. It is a mammal and has other characteristics of mammals. It is bushy-tailed, can run along telephone wires, and gathers and stores nuts for its food. From the characteristics that define a squirrel, we also can know what a *good* squirrel is. A good specimen of a squirrel is one that is effective, successful, and functions well. It follows the pattern of development and growth it has by nature. It does, in fact, have a bushy tail and good balance, and knows how to find and store its food. It would be a bad example of a squirrel or a poor one that had no balance, couldn't find its food, or had no fur and was sickly. It would have been better for the squirrel if its inherent natural tendencies to grow and develop and live as a healthy squirrel had been realized.

According to the natural law tradition from Aristotle on, human beings are also thought to be natural beings with a specific human nature. They have certain specific characteristics and abilities that they share as humans. Unlike squirrels and acorns, human beings can choose to do what is their good or act against it. Just what is their good? Aristotle recognized that a good eye is a healthy eye that sees well. A good horse is a well functioning horse, one that is healthy and able to run and do what horses do. What about human beings? Was there something comparable for the human being as human? Was there some good for humans as humans?

Human Nature and the Human Good

Just as we can tell what the good squirrel is from its own characteristics and abilities as a squirrel, according to natural law theory, the same should be true for the human being. For human beings to function well or flourish, they should perfect their human capacities. If they do this, they will be functioning well as human beings. They will also be happy, for a being is happy to the extent that it is functioning well. Aristotle believed that the ultimate good of humans is happiness, blessedness, or prosperity: Eudaimonia. But in what does happiness consist? To know what happiness is, we need to know what is the function of the human being.

Human beings have much in common with lower forms of beings. We are living just as plants are, for example. Thus, we take in material from outside us for nourishment, and grow from an immature to a mature form. We have senses of sight and hearing and so forth as do the higher animals. But is there anything unique to humans? Aristotle believed that it was our "rational element" that was peculiar to us. The good for humans, then, should consist in their functioning in a way consistent with and guided by this rational element. Our rational element has two different functions: One is to know, and the other is to guide choice and action. We must develop our ability to know the world and the truth. We must also choose wisely. In doing this we will be functioning well specifically as humans. Yet what is it to choose wisely? In partial answer to this, Aristotle develops ideas about prudential choice and suggests that we choose as a prudent person would choose.

One of the most well-known interpreters of Aristotle's philosophy was Thomas Aquinas (1224–1274). Aquinas was a Dominican friar who taught at the University of Paris. He was also a theologian who held that the natural law was part of the divine law or plan for the universe. The record of much of what he taught can be found in his work, the *Summa Theologica*.[15] Following Aristotle, Aquinas held that the moral good consists in following the innate tendencies of our nature. We are by nature biological beings. Because we tend by nature to grow and mature, we ought to preserve our being and our health by avoiding undue risks and doing what will make us healthy. Furthermore, like sentient animals, we can know our world through physical sense capacities. We ought to use our senses of touch, taste, hearing, and sight; we ought to develop and make use of these senses for appreciating those aspects of existence that they reveal to us. We ought not to do, or do deliberately, what injures these senses. Like many animals we reproduce our kind not asexually but sexually and heterosexually. This is what nature means for us to do.

Unique to persons are the specific capacities of knowing and choosing freely. Thus, we ought to treat ourselves and others as beings capable of understanding and free choice. Those things that help us pursue the truth, such as education and freedom of public expression, are good. Those things that hinder pursuit of the truth are bad. Deceit and lack of access to the sources of knowledge are morally objectionable simply because they prevent us from fulfilling our innate natural drive or orientation to know the way things are.[16] Moreover, whatever enhances our ability to choose freely is good. A certain amount of self-discipline, options from which to choose, and reflection on what we ought to choose are among the things that enhance freedom. To coerce people, or limit their possibilities of choosing freely, are examples of what is inherently bad or wrong. We also ought to find ways to live well together, for this is a theory according to which "no man—or woman—is an island." We are social creatures by nature. Thus, the essence of natural law theory is that we ought to further the inherent ends of human nature and not do what frustrates human fulfillment or flourishing.

Evaluating Natural Law Theory

Natural law theory has many appealing characteristics, among them a belief in the objectivity of moral values and the notion of the good as human flourishing. Criticisms of the theory have also been advanced, including the following two.

First, according to natural law theory, we are to determine what we ought to do from deciphering the moral law as it is written into nature—specifically, human nature. One problem that natural law theory must address concerns our ability to read nature. The moral law is supposedly knowable by natural human reason. However, throughout the history of philosophy various thinkers have read nature differently. Even Aristotle, for example, thought that slavery could be justified in that it was in accord with nature.[17] Today people argue against slavery on just such natural law grounds.[18] Philosopher Thomas Hobbes defended the absolutist rule of despots and John Locke criticized it, both doing so on natural law grounds. Moreover, traditional natural law theory has picked out highly positive traits: the desire to know the truth, to choose the good, and to develop as healthy mature beings. Not all views of the essential characteristics of human nature have been so positive, however. Some philosophers have depicted human nature as deceitful, evil, and uncontrolled. This is why Hobbes argued that we need a strong government. Without it, he wrote, life in a state of nature would be "nasty, brutish, and short."[19]

Moreover, if nature is taken in the broader sense, meaning all of nature, and if a natural law as a moral law were based on this, the general approach might even cover such theories as Social Darwinism. This view holds that because the most fit organisms in nature are the ones that survive, so also the most fit should endure in human society and the weaker ought to perish. When combined with a belief in capitalism, this led to notions such as that it was only right and according to nature that wealthy industrialists at the end of the nineteenth century were rich and powerful. It also implied that the poor were so by the designs of nature and we ought not interfere with this situation.

A second question raised for natural law theory is the following. Can the way things are by nature provide the basis for knowing how they ought to be? On the face of it, this may not seem right. Just because something exists in a certain way does not necessarily mean that it is good. Floods, famine, and disease all exist, but that does not make them good. According to David Hume, as noted in our discussion of Mill's proof of the principle of utility in Chapter 4, you cannot derive an "ought" from an "is."[20] Factual matters are entirely disconnected from evaluations. Other moral philosophers have agreed. When we know something to be a fact, it still remains an open question whether it is good. However, the natural law assumes that nature is teleological, that it has a certain directedness. In Aristotle's terms, it moves toward its natural goal, its final purpose. Yet from the time of the scientific revolution of the seventeenth century, such final purposes have become suspect. One could not always observe nature's directedness, and it came to be associated with other nonobservable spirits. If natural law theory does depend on there being purposes in nature, it must be able to explain how this can be so.

Consider one possible explanation of the source of whatever purposes there might be in nature. The medieval Christians, among others, believed that nature manifested God's plan for the universe. For Aristotle, however, the universe was eternal; it always existed and was not created by God. His concept of God was that of a most perfect being toward which the universe was in some way directed. According to Aristotle, there is an order in nature, but it did not come from the mind of God. For Thomas Aquinas, however, the reason why nature had the order that it did was because God, so to speak, had put it there. Because the universe was created after a divine plan, nature was not only intelligible, but also existed for a purpose that was built into it. Some natural law theorists follow Thomas Aquinas on this, while others either follow Aristotle or abstain from judgments about the source of the order (telos) in nature. But can we conceive of an order in nature without an orderer? This depends on what we mean by order in nature. If it is taken in the sense of a plan, then this does give reason to believe that it has an author. However, natural beings may simply

develop in certain ways as if they were directed there by some plan, but there is no plan. This may just be our way of reading or speaking about nature.[21]

Evolutionary theory also may present a challenge to natural law theory. If the way that things have come to be is the result of many chance variations, how can this resulting form be other than arbitrary? Theists generally interpret evolution itself as part of a divine plan. Chance, then, would not mean without direction. Even a nontheist such as mid-nineteenth-century American philosopher Chauncey Wright had an explanation of Darwin's assertion that chance evolutionary variations accounted for the fact that some species were better suited to survive than others. Wright said that "chance" did not mean "uncaused"; it meant only that the causes were unknown to us.[22]

Natural Rights

A third way in which moral requirements may be grounded in human nature is the theory of natural rights. Thomas Jefferson provides a good example of it in the Declaration of Independence, as noted at the beginning of this chapter. However, there is a long tradition of natural rights in Western philosophy. For example, we find a variant of the natural rights tradition in the writings of the first- and second-century A.D. Stoics. Their key moral principle was to "follow nature." For them this meant we should follow reason rather than human emotion. They also believed that there were laws to which all people were subject no matter what their local customs or conventions. Early Roman jurists believed that a common element existed in the codes of various peoples, a *Jus Gentium*. For example, the jurist Grotius held that the moral law was determined by right reason. These views can be considered variations on natural law theory because of their reliance on human nature and human reason to ground a basic moral law that is common to all peoples.[23]

Throughout the eighteenth century philosophers of various persuasions often referred to the laws of nature. For example, Voltaire wrote that morality had a universal source. It was the "natural law . . . which nature teaches all men" what we should do.[24] The Declaration of Independence was influenced by the writings of jurists and philosophers who believed that a moral law was built into nature. Thus, in the first section it reads that the colonists were called on "to assume, among the powers of the earth, the separate and equal station, to which the laws of nature and of nature's God entitle them."[25]

Today various international codes of human rights, such as the United Nations' "Declaration of Human Rights" and the Geneva Conventions principles for the conduct of war, contain elements of a natural rights tradition. These attempt to specify rights that all people have simply as a virtue of their being human beings, regardless of their country of origin, race, or religion.

Evaluating Natural Rights Theory

One problem for a natural rights theory is that not everyone agrees on what human nature requires or what human natural rights are central. In the 1948 U.N. "Declaration of Human Rights," the list of rights includes welfare rights and rights to food, clothing, shelter, and basic security. Just what kinds of things can we validly claim as human rights? Freedom of speech? Freedom of assembly? Housing? Clean air? Friends? Work? Income? Many of these are listed in various documents that nations have signed that provide lists of human rights. However, more is needed than lists. A rationale for what is to be included in those lists of human rights is called for. This is also something that a natural rights theory should provide. Some contemporary philosophers argue that the basic rights which society ought to protect are not welfare rights such as rights to food, clothing, and shelter, but liberty rights, such as the right not to be interfered with in our daily life.[26] How are such differences to be settled? Moreover, women historically have not been given equal rights with men. In the United States, for example, they were not all granted the right to vote until 1920 on grounds

that they were by nature not fully rational or closer in nature to animals than males! How is it possible that such different rights exist if the morality they involve is supposed to be knowable by natural human reason?

A second challenge for a natural rights theory concerns what it must prove to justify its holdings. First, it must show that human nature as it is ought to be furthered and that certain things ought to be granted to us to further our nature. These things we then speak of as rights. Basic to this demonstration would be to show why human beings are so valuable that what is essential for their full function can be claimed as a right. For example, do human beings have a value higher than other beings and if so why? Is a reference to something beyond this world—a creator God, for example—necessary to give value to humans or is there something about their nature itself that is the reason why they have such a high value? Second, a natural rights theorist has the job of detailing just what things are essential for the good functioning of human nature.

Finally, not all discussions of human rights have been of the sort described here. For example, one Norman Daniels claims that the reason why people have a right to basic health care is because of the demands of justice; that is, justice demands that there be equal opportunity to life's goods and whether people have equal opportunity depends, among other things, on their health. Another example is found in the writings of Walter Lippmann, a political commentator half a century ago. He held that we ought to agree that there are certain rights because these provide the basis for a democratic society, and it is the society that works best. It is not that we can prove that such rights as freedom of speech or assembly exist, we simply accept them for pragmatic reasons because they provide the basis for democracy.[27]

The notion of rights can be and has been discussed in many different contexts. Among those treated in this book are issues of animal rights (Chapter 15), economic rights (Chapter 12), fetal and women's rights (Chapter 9), and equal rights and discrimination (Chapter 11), among other discussions.

The selections here from Aristotle and John Locke discuss virtue and the grounding of morality and rights in human nature.

Notes

1. Thomas Jefferson, "The Declaration of Independence," *Basic Writings of Thomas Jefferson,* Philip S. Foner (Ed.) (New York: Wiley, 1944), 551.
2. John Locke, *Two Treatises of Government* (London, 1690), Peter Laslett (Ed.) (Cambridge: Cambridge University Press, 1960).
3. W. T. Jones, *A History of Western Philosophy: The Classical Mind,* 2d ed. (New York: Harcourt, Brace, & World, 1969), 214–216.
4. This was asserted by the neo-Platonist Porphyry (ca. A.D. 232). However, others believe that the work got its name because it was edited by Nicomachus. See Alasdair MacIntyre, *After Virtue* (Notre Dame, IN: Notre Dame University Press, 1984), 147.
5. Milton Gonsalves, *Fagothy's Right and Reason,* 9th ed. (Columbus, OH: Merrill, 1989), 201.
6. I thank one of my reviewers, Robert P. Tucker of Florida Southern College, for this example.
7. See, for example, the collection of articles in Christina Hoff Sommers, *Vice and Virtue in Everyday Life* (New York: Harcourt Brace Jovanovich, 1985).
8. Philippa Foot, *Virtues and Vices* (Berkeley: University of California Press, 1978).
9. Ibid.
10. Alasdair MacIntyre, "The Virtue in Heroic Societies" and "The Virtues at Athens," in *After Virtue* (Notre Dame, IN: Notre Dame University Press, 1984), 121–145.
11. Ibid.
12. This is the basic idea behind the theory of civil disobedience as outlined and practiced by Henry David Thoreau, Mahatma Gandhi, and Martin Luther King, Jr. When Thoreau was imprisoned for not paying taxes that he thought were used for unjust purposes, he wrote his famous essay, "Civil Disobedience." In it he writes, "Must the citizen ever for a moment, or in the least degree, resign his conscience to the legislator? Why has every man a conscience, then? I think that we should be men first, and subjects afterward. It is not desirable to cultivate a respect for the law, so much as for the right." Henry David Thoreau, "Civil Disobedience, " in *Miscellanies* (Boston: Houghton Mifflin, 1983), 136–137.
13. W. T. Jones, op. cit., p. 233.
14. See the selection in this chapter from the *Nicomachean Ethics.*
15. Thomas Aquinas, "Summa Theologica," in *Basic Writings of Saint Thomas Aquinas,* Anton Pegis (Ed.) (New York: Random House, 1948).
16. This is obviously an incomplete presentation of the moral philosophy of Thomas Aquinas. We should at least note that he was as much a theologian as a philosopher, if not more so. True and complete happiness, he believed, would be achieved only in knowledge or contemplation of God.
17. Aristotle, *Politics,* Chap. V, VI.
18. An example of this type of natural law argument was given by Clarence Thomas in the 1991 Senate hearings for his appointment as justice of the U.S. Supreme Court.
19. Thomas Hobbes, *Leviathan,* Michael Oakeshott (Ed.) (New York: Oxford University Press, 1962).
20. David Hume, *Treatise on Human Nature* (London, 1739–1740).
21. Such a view can be found in Kant's work, *The Critique of Judgment.*
22. See Chauncey Wright, "Evolution by Natural Selection," *The North American Review* (July 1872): 6–7.
23. See Roscoe Pound, *Jurisprudence* (St. Paul, MN: West, 1959).
24. Voltaire, *Ouvres,* XXV, 39; XI, 443.
25. Thomas Jefferson, Declaration of Independence.
26. On negative or liberty rights see, for example, the work of Robert Nozick, *State, Anarchy and Utopia* (New York: Basic Books, 1974). See further discussion on welfare and liberty rights in Chapter 13, "Economic Justice."
27. The term *pragmatic* concerns what "works." Thus, to accept something on pragmatic grounds means to accept it because it works for us in some way. For Walter Lippmann's views, see *Essays in the Public Philosophy* (Boston: Little, Brown, 1955).

The Nicomachean Ethics

Aristotle

Study Questions

1. According to Aristotle, what is meant by the "good"?
2. What is the function of a person?
3. What is virtue and how do we acquire it?
4. How is virtue a mean? Explain by using some of Aristotle's examples.
5. Why is it so difficult to be virtuous?

The Nature of the Good*

Every art and every scientific inquiry, and similarly every action and purpose, may be said to aim at some good. Hence the good has been well defined as that at which all things aim. But it is clear that there is a difference in the ends; for the ends are sometimes activities, and sometimes results beyond the mere activities. Also, where there are certain ends beyond the actions, the results are naturally superior to the activities.

As there are various actions, arts, and sciences, it follows that the ends are also various. Thus health is the end of medicine, a vessel of shipbuilding, victory of strategy, and wealth of domestic economy. It often happens that there are a number of such arts or sciences which fall under a single faculty, as the art of making bridles, and all such other arts as make the instruments of horsemanship, under horsemanship, and this again as well as every military action under strategy, and in the same way other arts or sciences under other faculties. But in all these cases the ends of the architectonic arts or sciences, whatever they may be, are more desirable than those of the subordinate arts or sciences, as it is for the sake of the former that the latter are themselves sought after. It makes no difference to the argument whether the activities themselves are the ends of the actions, or something else beyond the activities as in the above mentioned sciences.

If it is true that in the sphere of action there is an end which we wish for its own sake, and for the sake of which we wish everything else, and that we do not desire all things for the sake of something else (for, if that is so, the process will go on ad infinitum, and our desire will be idle and futile) it is clear that this will be the good or the supreme good. Does it not follow then that the knowledge of this supreme good is of great importance for the conduct of life, and that, if we know it, we shall be like archers who have a mark at which to aim, we shall have a better chance of attaining what we want? But, if this is the case, we must endeavour to comprehend, at least in outline, its nature, and the science or faculty to which it belongs. . . .

Happiness: Living and Doing Well

As every knowledge and moral purpose aspires to some good, what is in our view the good at which the political science aims, and what is the highest of all practical goods? As to its name there is, I may say, a general agreement. The masses and the cultured classes agree in calling it happiness, and conceive that "to live well" or "to do well" is the same thing as "to be happy." But as to the nature of happiness they do not agree, nor do the masses give the same account of it as the philosophers. The former define it as something visible and palpable, e.g. pleasure, wealth, or honour; different people give different definitions of it, and often the same person gives different definitions at different times; for when a person has been ill, it is health, when he is poor, it is wealth, and, if he is conscious of his own ignorance, he envies people who use grand language above his own comprehension. Some *philosophers*[1] on the other hand have held that, besides these various goods, there is an absolute good which is the cause of goodness in them all. . . .

Selections from *The Nicomachean Ethics*, Books 1 and 2.
Translated by J.E.C. Welldon (London: Macmillan, 1892).

*Headings added by the editor.—ED.

The Function of a Person

Perhaps, however, it seems a truth which is generally admitted, that happiness is the supreme good; what is wanted is to define its nature a little more clearly. The best way of arriving at such a definition will probably be to ascertain the function of Man. For, as with a flute-player, a statuary, or any artisan, or in fact anybody who has a definite function and action, his goodness, or excellence seems to lie in his function, so it would seem to be with Man, if indeed he has a definite function. Can it be said then that, while a carpenter and a cobbler have definite functions and actions, Man, unlike them, is naturally functionless? The reasonable view is that, as the eye, the hand, the foot, and similarly each several part of the body has a definite function, so Man may be regarded as having a definite function apart from all these. What then, can this function be? It is not life; for life is apparently something which man shares with the plants; and it is something peculiar to him that we are looking for. We must exclude therefore the life of nutrition and increase. There is next what may be called the life of sensation. But this too, is apparently shared by Man with horses, cattle, and all other animals. There remains what I may call the practical life of the rational part of Man's being. But the rational part is twofold; it is rational partly in the sense of being obedient to reason, and partly in the sense of possessing reason and intelligence. The practical life too may be conceived of in two ways,[2] viz., either as a moral state, or as a moral activity: but we must understand by it the life of activity, as this seems to be the truer form of the conception.

The function of Man then is an activity of soul in accordance with reason, or not independently of reason. Again the functions of a person of a certain kind, and of such a person who is good of his kind e.g. of a harpist and a good harpist, are in our view generically the same, and this view is true of people of all kinds without exception, the superior excellence being only an addition to the function; for it is the function of a harpist to play the harp, and of a good harpist to play the harp well. This being so, if we define the function of Man as a kind of life, and this life as an activity of soul, or a course of action in conformity with reason, if the function of a good man is such activity or action of a good and noble kind, and if everything is successfully performed when it is performed in accordance with its proper excellence, it follows that the good of Man is an activity of soul in accordance with virtue or, if there are more virtues than one, in accordance with the best and most complete virtue. But it is necessary to add the words "in a complete life." For as one swallow or one day does not make a spring, so one day or a short time does not make a fortunate or happy man. . . .

Virtue

Virtue or excellence being twofold, partly intellectual and partly moral, intellectual virtue is both originated and fostered mainly by teaching; it therefore demands experience and time. Moral[3] virtue on the other hand is the outcome of habit. . . . From this fact it is clear that no moral virtue is implanted in us by nature; a law of nature cannot be altered by habituation. Thus a stone naturally tends to fall downwards, and it cannot be habituated or trained to rise upwards, even if we were to habituate it by throwing it upwards ten thousand times; not again can fire be trained to sink downwards, nor anything else that follows one natural law be habituated or trained to follow another. It is neither by nature then nor in defiance of nature that virtues are implanted in us. Nature gives us the capacity of receiving them, and that capacity is perfected by habit.

Again, if we take the various natural powers which belong to us, we first acquire the proper faculties and afterwards display the activities. It is clearly so with the senses. It was not by seeing frequently or hearing frequently that we acquired the senses of seeing or hearing; on the contrary it was because we possessed the senses that we made use of them, not by making use of them that we obtained them. But the virtues we acquire by first exercising them, as is the case with all the arts, for it is by doing what we ought to do when we have learnt the arts that we learn the arts themselves; we become e.g. builders by building and harpists by playing the harp. Similarly it is by doing just acts that we become just, by doing temperate acts that we become temperate, by doing courageous acts that we become courageous. The experience of states is a witness to this truth, for it is by training the habits that legislators make the citizens good. This is the object which all legislators have at heart; if a legislator does not succeed in it, he fails of his purpose, and it constitutes the distinction between a good polity and a bad one.

Again, the causes and means by which any virtue is produced and by which it is destroyed are the same; and it is equally so with any art; for it is by playing the harp that both good and bad harpists are produced and the case of builders and all other *artisans* is similar, as it is by building well that they will be good builders and by building badly that they will be bad builders. If it were not so, there would be no need of anybody to teach them; they would all be born good or bad *in their several trades*. The case of the virtues is the same. It is by acting in such transactions as take place between man and man that we become either just or unjust. It is by acting in the face of danger and by habituating ourselves to fear or courage that we become either cowardly or courageous. It is much the same with our desires and angry passions. Some people become temperate and gentle, others become licentious and passionate, according as they conduct themselves in one way or another way in particular circumstances. In a word moral states are the results of activities corresponding to the moral states themselves. It is our duty therefore to give a certain character to the activities, as the moral states depend upon the differences of the activities. Accordingly the difference between one training of the habits and another from early days is not a light matter, but is serious or rather all-important. . . .

Deficiency and Excess

The first point to be observed then is that in such matters as we are considering deficiency and excess are equally fatal. It is so, as we observe, in regard to health and strength; for we must judge of what we cannot see by the evidence of what we do see. Excess or deficiency of gymnastic exercise is fatal to strength. Similarly an excess or deficiency of meat and drink is fatal to health, whereas a suitable amount produces, augments and sustains it. It is the same then with temperance, courage, and the other virtues. A person who avoids and is afraid of everything and faces nothing becomes a coward; a person who is not afraid of anything but is ready to face everything becomes foolhardy. Similarly he who enjoys every pleasure and never abstains from any pleasure is licentious; he who eschews all pleasures like a boor is an insensible sort of person. For temperance and courage are destroyed by excess and deficiency but preserved by the mean state.

Again, not only are the causes and the agencies of production, increase and destruction in the moral states the same, but the sphere of their activity will be proved to be the same also. It is so in other instances which are more conspicuous, e.g. in strength; for

strength is produced by taking a great deal of food and undergoing a great deal of labour, and it is the strong man who is able to take most food and to undergo most labour. The same is the case with the virtues. It is by abstinence from pleasures that we become temperate, and, when we have become temperate, we are best able to abstain from them. So too with courage; it is by habituating ourselves to despise and face alarms that we become courageous, and, when we have become courageous, we shall be best able to face them. . . .

The Nature of Virtue

We have next to consider the nature of virtue.

Now, as the qualities of the soul are three, viz. emotions, faculties and moral states, it follows that virtue must be one of the three. By the emotions I mean desire, anger, fear, courage, envy, joy, love, hatred, regret, emulation, pity, in a word whatever is attended by pleasure or pain. I call those faculties in respect of which we are said to be capable of experiencing these emotions, e.g. capable of getting angry or being pained or feeling pity. And I call those moral states in respect of which we are well or ill-disposed towards the emotions, ill-disposed e.g. towards the passion of anger, if our anger be too violent or too feeble, and well-disposed, if it be duly moderated, and similarly towards the other emotions.

Now neither the virtues nor the vices are emotions; for we are not called good or evil in respect of our emotions but in respect of our virtues or vices. Again, we are not praised or blamed in respect of our emotions; a person is not praised for being afraid or being angry, nor blamed for being angry in an absolute sense, but only for being angry in a certain way; but we are praised or blamed in respect of our virtues or vices. Again, whereas we are angry or afraid without deliberate purpose, the virtues are in some sense deliberate purposes, or do not exist in the absence of deliberate purpose. It may be added that while we are said to be moved in respect of our emotions, in respect of our virtues or vices we are not said to be moved but to have a certain disposition.

These reasons also prove that the virtues are not faculties. For we are not called either good or bad, nor are we praised or blamed, as having an abstract capacity for emotion. Also while Nature gives us our faculties, it is not Nature that makes us good or bad, but this is a point which we have already discussed. If then the virtues are neither emotions nor faculties, it remains that they must be moral states.

The nature of virtue has been now generically described. But it is not enough to state merely that virtue is a moral state, we must also describe the character of that moral state.

It must be laid down then that every virtue or excellence has the effect of producing a good condition of that of which it is a virtue or excellence, and of enabling it to perform its function well. Thus the excellence of the eye makes the eye good and its function good, as it is by the excellence of the eye that we see well. Similarly, the excellence of the horse makes a horse excellent and good at racing, at carrying its rider and at facing the enemy.

If then this is universally true, the virtue or excellence of man will be such a moral state as makes a man good and able to perform his proper function well. We have already explained how this will be the case, but another way of making it clear will be to study the nature or character of this virtue.

Virtue as a Mean

Now in everything, whether it be continuous or discrete,[4] it is possible to take a greater, a smaller, or an equal amount, and this either absolutely or in relation to ourselves, the equal being a mean between excess and deficiency. By the mean in respect of the thing itself, or the absolute mean, I understand that which is equally distinct from both extremes; and this is one and the same thing for everybody. By the mean considered relatively to ourselves I understand that which is neither too much nor too little; but this is not one thing, nor is it the same for everybody. Thus if 10 be too much and 2 too little we take 6 as a mean in respect of the thing itself; for 6 is as much greater than 2 as it is less than 10, and this is a mean in arithmetical proportion. But the mean considered relatively to ourselves must not be ascertained in this way. It does not follow that if 10 pounds of meat be too much and 2 be too little for a man to eat, a trainer will order him 6 pounds, as this may itself be too much or too little for the person who is to take it; it will be too little e.g. for Milo,[5] but too much for a beginner in gymnastics. It will be the same with running and wrestling; the right amount will vary with the individual. This being so, everybody who understands his business avoids alike excess and deficiency; he seeks and chooses the mean, not the absolute mean, but the mean considered relatively to ourselves.

Every science then performs its function well, if it regards the mean and refers the works which it produces to the mean. This is the reason why it is usually said of successful works that it is impossible to take anything from them or to add anything to them, which implies that excess or deficiency is fatal to excellence but that the mean state ensures it. Good . . . artists too, as we say, have an eye to the mean in their works. But virtue, like Nature herself, is more accurate and better than any art; virtue therefore will aim at the mean;—I speak of moral virtue, as it is moral virtue which is concerned with emotions and actions, and it is these which admit of excess and deficiency and the mean. Thus it is possible to go too far, or not to go far enough, in respect of fear, courage, desire, anger, pity, and pleasure and pain generally, and the excess and the deficiency are alike wrong; but to experience these emotions at the right times and on the right occasions and towards the right persons and for the right causes and in the right manner is the mean or the supreme good, which is characteristic of virtue. Similarly there may be excess, deficiency, or the mean, in regard to actions. But virtue is concerned with emotions and actions, and here excess is an error and deficiency a fault, whereas the mean is successful and laudable, and success and merit are both characteristics of virtue.

It appears then that virtue is a mean state, so far at least as it aims at the mean.

Again, there are many different ways of going wrong; for evil is in its nature infinite, to use the Pythagorean[6] figure, but good is finite. But there is only one possible way of going right. Accordingly the former is easy and the latter difficult; it is easy to miss the mark but difficult to hit it. This again is a reason why excess and deficiency are characteristics of vice and the mean state a characteristic of virtue.

"For good is simple, evil manifold."[7]

Virtue then is a state of deliberate moral purpose consisting in a mean that is relative to ourselves, the mean being determined . . . by reason, or as a prudent man would determine it.

It is a mean state *firstly as lying* between two vices, the vice of excess on the one hand, and the vice of deficiency on the other, and secondly because, whereas the vices either fall short of or go beyond what is proper in the emotions and actions, virtue not only discovers but embraces that mean.

Accordingly, virtue, if regarded in its essence or theoretical conception, is a mean state, but, if regarded from the point of view of the highest good, or of excellence, it is an extreme.

But it is not every action or every emotion that admits of a mean state. There are some whose very name implies wickedness, as e.g. malice, shameless-ness, and envy, among emotions, or adultery, theft, and murder, among actions. All these, and others like them, are censured as being intrinsically wicked, not merely the excesses or deficiencies of them. It is never possible then to be right in respect of them; they are always sinful. Right or wrong in such actions as adultery does not depend on our committing them with the right person, at the right time or in the right manner; on the contrary it is sinful to do anything of the kind at all. It would be equally wrong then to suppose that there can be a mean state or an excess or deficiency in unjust, cowardly, or licentious con-duct; for, if it were so, there would be a mean state of an excess or of a deficiency, an excess of an excess and a deficiency of a deficiency. But as in temperance and courage there can be no excess or deficiency because the mean is, in a sense, an extreme, so too in these cases there cannot be a mean or an excess or defi-ciency, but, however the acts may be done, they are wrong. For it is a general rule that an excess or deficiency does not admit of a mean state, nor a mean state of an excess or deficiency.

But it is not enough to lay down this as a general rule; it is necessary to apply it to particular cases, as in reasonings upon actions general statements, al-though they are broader . . . , are less exact than particular statements. For all action refers to particu-lars, and it is essential that our theories should har-monize with the particular cases to which they apply.

Some Virtues

We must take particular virtues then from the cata-logue of *virtues*.[8]

In regard to feelings of fear and confidence, cour-age is a mean state. On the side of excess, he whose fearlessness is excessive has no name, as often hap-pens, but he whose confidence is excessive is fool-hardy, while he whose timidity is excessive and whose confidence is deficient is a coward.

In respect of pleasures and pains, although not indeed of all pleasures and pains, and to a less extent in respect of pains than of pleasures, the mean state is temperance . . . , the excess is licentiousness. We never find people who are deficient in regard to pleasures; accordingly such people again have not received a name, but we may call them insensible.

As regards the giving and taking of money, the mean state is liberality, the excess and deficiency are

prodigality and illiberality. Here the excess and defi-ciency take opposite forms; for while the prodigal man is excessive in spending and deficient in taking, the illiberal man is excessive in taking and deficient in spending. (For the present we are giving only a rough and summary account *of the virtues*, and that is sufficient for our purpose; we will hereafter deter-mine their character more exactly.[9])

In respect of money there are other dispositions as well. There is the mean state which is magnificence; for the magnificent man, as having to do with large sums of money, differs from the liberal man who has to do only with small sums; and the excess *corre-sponding to it* is bad taste or vulgarity, the deficiency is meanness. These are different from the excess and deficiency of liberality; what the difference is will be explained hereafter.

In respect of honour and dishonour the mean state is highmindedness, the excess is what is called vanity, the deficiency littlemindedness. Corresponding to liberality, which, as we said, differs from magnificence as having to do *not with great but* with small sums of money, there is a moral state which has to do with petty honour and is related to highmindedness which has to do with great honour; for it is possible to aspire to honour in the right way, or in a way which is excessive or insufficient, and if a person's aspirations are excessive, he is called ambitious, if they are defi-cient, he is called unambitious, while if they are be-tween the two, he has no name. The dispositions too are nameless, except that the disposition of the ambi-tious person is called ambition. The consequence is that the extremes lay claim to the mean or intermedi-ate place. We ourselves speak of one who observes the mean sometimes as ambitious, and at other times as unambitious; we sometimes praise an ambitious, and at other times an unambitious person. The reason for our doing so will be stated in due course, but let us now discuss the other virtues in accordance with the method which we have followed hitherto.

Anger, like other emotions, has its excess, its defi-ciency, and its mean state. It may be said that they have no names, but as we call one who observes the mean gentle, we will call the mean state gentleness. Among the extremes, if a person errs on the side of excess, he may be called passionate and his vice passionateness, if on that of deficiency, he may be called impassive and his deficiency impassivity.

There are also three other mean states with a certain resemblance to each other, and yet with a difference.

For while they are all concerned with intercourse in speech and action, they are different in that one of them is concerned with truth in such intercourse, and the others with pleasantness, one with pleasantness in amusement and the other with pleasantness in the various circumstances of life. We must therefore discuss these states in order to make it clear that in all cases it is the mean state which is an object of praise, and the extremes are neither right nor laudable but censurable. It is true that these mean and extreme states are generally nameless, but we must do our best here as elsewhere to give them a name, so that our argument may be clear and easy to follow. . . .

Why It Is So Difficult to Be Virtuous

That is the reason why it is so hard to be virtuous; for it is always hard work to find the mean in anything, e.g. it is not everybody, but only a man of science, who can find the mean or centre[10] of a circle. So too anybody can get angry—that is an easy matter—and anybody can give or spend money, but to give it to the right persons, to give the right amount of it and to give it at the right time and for the right cause and in the right way, this is not what anybody can do, nor is it easy. That is the reason why it is rare and laudable and noble to do well. Accordingly one who aims at the mean must begin by departing from that extreme which is the more contrary to the mean; he must act in the spirit of Calypso's[11] advice,

> "Far from this smoke and swell keep thou thy bark,"

for of the two extremes one is more sinful than the other. As it is difficult then to hit the mean exactly, we must take the second best course,[12] as the saying is, and choose the lesser of two evils, and this we shall best do in the way that we have described, i.e. *by steering clear of the evil which is further from the mean.* We must also observe the things to which we are ourselves particularly prone, as different natures have different inclinations, and we may ascertain what these are by a consideration of our feelings of pleasure and pain. And then we must drag ourselves in the direction opposite to them; for it is by removing ourselves as far as possible from what is wrong that we shall arrive at the mean, as we do when we pull a crooked stick straight.

But in all cases we must especially be on our guard against what is pleasant and against pleasure, as we are not impartial judges of pleasure. Hence our attitude towards pleasure must be like that of the elders of the people in the *Iliad* towards Helen, and we must never be afraid of applying the words they use; for if we dismiss pleasure as they dismissed Helen, we shall be less likely to go wrong. It is by action of this kind, to put it summarily, that we shall best succeed in hitting the mean.

Notes*

1. Aristotle is thinking of the Platonic "ideas."
2. In other words life may be taken to mean either the mere possession of certain faculties or their active exercise.
3. The student of Aristotle must familiarize himself with the conception of intellectual as well as of moral virtues, although it is not the rule in modern philosophy to speak of the "virtues" of the intellect.
4. In Aristotelian language, as Mr. Peters says, a straight line is a "continuous quantity" but a rouleau of sovereigns a "discrete quantity."
5. The famous Crotoniate wrestler.
6. The Pythagoreans, starting from the mystical significance of number, took the opposite principles of "the finite" . . . and "the infinite" . . . to represent good and evil.
7. A line—perhaps Pythagorean—of unknown authorship.
8. It would seem that a catalogue of virtues . . . must have been recognized in the Aristotelian school. Cp. *Eud. Eth.* ii. ch. 3.
9. I have placed this sentence in a parenthesis, as it interrupts the argument respecting the right use of money.
10. Aristotle does not seem to be aware that the centre . . . of a circle is not really comparable to the mean . . . between the vices.
11. *Odyssey,* xii. 219, 200; but it is Odysseus who speaks there, and the advice has been given him not by Calypso but by Circe (ibid. 101–110).
12. The Greek proverb means properly "we must take to the oars, if sailing is impossible."

---

*Some notes have been deleted and the remaining ones renumbered.—ED.

Second Treatise on Civil Government

John Locke

Study Questions

1. What two things characterize human beings in their natural state, according to Locke?

2. On the second characteristic, why does Locke hold that human beings are equal?

3. Why is the natural state of human liberty not a state of license, according to Locke? What does he mean by that?

4. How does the "state of nature" provide a basis for a "law of nature," according to Locke?

5. According to Locke, how is it that some members of a society may have power over others in meting out punishment and taking reparations from them?

6. Why, according to Locke, do we need civil government?

7. According to Locke, was there ever a really existing state of nature as he describes it?

Book II

Chapter II
Of the State of Nature

4. To understand political power aright, and derive it from its original, we must consider what estate all men are naturally in, and that is, a state of perfect freedom to order their actions, and dispose of their possessions and persons as they think fit, within the bounds of the law of Nature, without asking leave or depending upon the will of any other man.

A state also of equality, wherein all the power and jurisdiction is reciprocal, no one having more than another, there being nothing more evident than that creatures of the same species and rank, promiscuously born to all the same advantages of Nature, and the use of the same faculties, should also be equal one

amongst another, without subordination or subjection, unless the lord and master of them all should, by a manifest declaration of his will, set one above another, and confer on him, by an evident and clear appointment, an undoubted right to dominion and sovereignty. . . .

6. But though this be a state of liberty, yet it is not a state of license; though man in that state have an uncontrollable liberty to dispose of his person or possessions, yet he has not liberty to destroy himself, or so much as any creature in his possession, but where some nobler use than its bare preservation calls for it. The state of Nature has a law of Nature to govern it, which obliges every one, and reason, which is that law, teaches all mankind who will but consult it, that being all equal and independent, no one ought to harm another in his life, health, liberty or possessions; for men being all the workmanship of one omnipotent and infinitely wise Maker; all the servants of one sovereign Master, sent into the world by His order and about His business; they are His property, whose workmanship they are made to last during His, not one another's pleasure. And, being furnished with like faculties, sharing all in one community of Nature, there cannot be supposed any such subordination among us that may authorize us to destroy one another, as if we were made for one another's uses, as the inferior ranks of creatures are for ours. Every one as he is bound to preserve himself, and not to quit his station wilfully, so by the like reason, when his own preservation comes not in competition, ought he as much as he can to preserve the rest of mankind, and not unless it be to do justice on an offender, take away, or impair the life, or what tends to the preservation of the life, the liberty, health, limb, or goods of another.

7. And that all men may be restrained from invading other's rights, and from doing hurt to one another, and the law of Nature be observed, which willeth the peace and preservation of all mankind, the execution of the law of Nature is in that state put into every man's hands, whereby every one has a right to punish the transgressors of that law to such a degree as may

Selection from John Locke, *Second Treatise on Civil Government* (London: Routledge and Sons, 1887).

hinder its violation. For the law of Nature would, as all other laws that concern men in this world, be in vain if there were nobody that in the state of Nature had a power to execute that law, and thereby preserve the innocent and restrain offenders; and if any one in the state of Nature may punish another for any evil he has done, every one may do so. For in that state of perfect equality, where naturally there is no superiority or jurisdiction of one over another, what any may do in prosecution of that law, every one must needs have a right to do.

8. And thus, in the state of Nature, one man comes by a power over another, but yet no absolute or arbitrary power to use a criminal when he has got him in his hands, according to the passionate heats, or boundless extravagancy of his own will, but only to retribute to him so far as calm reason and conscience dictate, what is proportionate to his transgression, which is so much as may serve for reparation and restraint. For these two are the only reasons why one man may lawfully do harm to another, which is that we call punishment. In transgressing the law of Nature, the offender declares himself to live by another rule than that of reason and common equity, which is that measure God has set to the actions of men for their mutual security, and so he becomes dangerous to mankind; the tie which is to secure them from injury and violence being slighted and broken by him, which being a trespass against the whole species, and the peace and safety of it, provided for by the law of Nature, every man upon this score, by the right he hath to preserve mankind in general, may restrain, or where it is necessary, destroy things noxious to them, and so may bring such evil on any one who hath transgressed that law, as may make him repent the doing of it, and thereby deter him, and, by his example, others from doing the like mischief. And in this case, and upon this ground, every man hath a right to punish the offender, and be executioner of the law of Nature. . . .

11. From these two distinct rights (the one of punishing the crime, for restraint and preventing the like offence, which right of punishing is in everybody, the other of taking reparation, which belongs only to the injured party) comes it to pass that the magistrate, who by being magistrate hath the common right of punishing put into his hands, can often, where the public good demands not the execution of the law, remit the punishment of criminal offences by his own authority, but yet cannot remit the satisfaction due to any private man for the damage he has received. That he who hath suffered the damage has a right to demand in his own name, and he alone can remit. The damnified person has this power of appropriating to himself the goods or service of the offender by right of self-preservation, as every man has a power to punish the crime to prevent its being committed again, by the right he has of preserving all mankind, and doing all reasonable things he can in order to that end. And thus it is that every man in the state of Nature has a power to kill a murderer, both to deter others from doing the like injury (which no reparation can compensate) by the example of the punishment that attends it from everybody, and also to secure men from the attempts of a criminal who, having renounced reason, the common rule and measure God hath given to mankind, hath, by the unjust violence and slaughter he hath committed upon one, declared war against all mankind, and therefore may be destroyed as a lion or a tiger, one of those wild savage beasts with whom men can have no society nor security. And upon this is grounded that great law of Nature, "Whoso sheddeth man's blood by man shall his blood be shed." And Cain was so fully convinced that every one had a right to destroy such a criminal, that, after the murder of his brother, he cries out, "Every one that findeth me shall slay me," so plain was it writ in the hearts of all mankind.

12. By the same reason may a man in the state of Nature punish the lesser breaches of that law, it will, perhaps, be demanded, with death? I answer: Each transgression may be punished to that degree, and with so much severity, as will suffice to make it an ill bargain to the offender, give him cause to repent, and terrify others from doing the like. Every offence that can be committed in the state of Nature may, in the state of Nature, be also punished equally, and as far forth, as it may, in a commonwealth. For though it would be beside my present purpose to enter here into the particulars of the law of Nature, or its measures of punishment; yet it is certain there is such a law, and that too as intelligible and plain to a rational creature and a studier of that law as the positive laws of commonwealths, nay, possibly plainer; as much as reason is easier to be understood than the fancies and intricate contrivances of men, following contrary and hidden interests put into words; for truly so are apart of the municipal laws of countries, which are only so far right as they are founded on the law of Nature, by which they are to be regulated and interpreted.

13. To this strange doctrine—viz., That in the state of Nature every one has the executive power of the law of Nature, I doubt not but it will be objected that it is unreasonable for men to be judges in their own cases, that self-love will make men partial to themselves and their friends; and, on the other side, ill-nature, passion, and revenge will carry them too far in punishing others, and hence nothing but confusion and disorder will follow, and that therefore God hath certainly appointed government to restrain the partiality and violence of men. I easily grant that civil government is the proper remedy for the inconveniencies of the state of Nature, which must certainly be great where men may be judges in their own case, since it is easy to be imagined that he who was so unjust as to do his brother an injury will scarce be so just as to condemn himself for it. But I shall desire those who make this objection to remember that absolute monarchs are but men; and if government is to be the remedy of those evils which necessarily follow from men being judges in their own cases, and the state of Nature is therefore not to be endured, I desire to know what kind of government that is, and how much better it is than the state of Nature, where one man commanding a multitude has the liberty to be judge in his own case, and may do to all his subjects whatever he pleases without the least question or control of those who execute his pleasure? and in whatsoever he doth, whether led by reason, mistake, or passion, must be submitted to? which men in the state of Nature are not bound to do one to another. And if he that judges, judges amiss in his own or any other case, he is answerable for it to the rest of mankind.

14. It is often asked as a might objection, where are, or ever were, there any men in such a state of Nature? To which it may suffice as an answer at present, that since all princes and rulers of "independent" governments all through the world are in a state of Nature, it is plain the world never was, nor never will be, without numbers of men in that state. I have named all governors of "independent" communities, whether they are, or are not, in league with others; for it is not every compact that puts an end to the state of Nature between men, but only this one of agreeing together mutually to enter into one community, and make one body politic; other promises and compacts men may make one with another, and yet still be in the state of Nature. The promises and bargains for truck, &c., between the two men in

Soldania, or between a Swiss and an Indian, in the woods of America, are binding to them, though they are perfectly in a state of Nature in reference to one another for truth, and keeping of faith belongs to men as men, and not as members of society. . . .

Review Exercises

1. What is the basic difference between a virtue ethics and other types of ethics we have studied?
2. What is the difference according to Aristotle between intellectual and moral virtues?
3. In what sense are virtues habits?
4. Give a list of some traits that have been thought to be virtues, according to Aristotle and other virtue theorists.
5. According to Aristotle, how is virtue a mean between extremes? Give some examples.
6. Give a basic definition of natural law theory.
7. What is the difference between the scientific laws of nature and the natural law?
8. In what way is natural law theory teleological?
9. What specific natural or human species capacities are singled out by natural law theorists? How do these determine what we ought to do, according to the theory?
10. What is the difference between Aristotle and Aquinas on the theistic basis of natural law?
11. Explain one area of concern or criticism of natural law theory.
12. Describe the basis of rights according to natural rights theorists.
13. Give examples of a natural rights tradition.
14. Explain one of the things that a natural rights theorist must show to prove that we can ground rights in human nature.

Selected Bibliography
Virtue Ethics
Aquinas, St. Thomas. *Treatise on the Virtues*. John A. Oesterle (Trans.). Notre Dame, IN: Notre Dame University Press, 1984.

Baron, Marcia. "Varieties of Ethics of Virtue," *American Philosophical Quarterly* 22 (1985): 47–53.

Foot, Philippa. *Virtues and Vices*. London: Blackwell, 1978.

Geach, Peter. *The Virtues*. Cambridge: Cambridge University Press, 1977.

Hardie, W.F.R. *Aristotle's Ethical Theory*. Oxford, England: Clarendon, 1968.

Hooks, Bell. *Feminist Theory: From Margin to Center.* Boston: South End, 1984.

Kruschwitz, Robert B., and Robert C. Roberts (Eds.). *The Virtues: Contemporary Ethics and Moral Character.* Belmont, CA: Wadsworth, 1987.

MacIntyre, Alasdair. *After Virtue*. Notre Dame, IN: Notre Dame University Press, 1981.

Noddings, Nel. *Caring: A Feminine Approach to Ethics and Moral Education*. Berkeley: University of California Press, 1984.

Pence, Gregory. "Recent Work on Virtues," *American Philosophical Quarterly* 24 (1984).

Sherman, Nancy. *The Fabric of Character: Aristotle's Theory of Virtue*. Oxford, England: Clarendon, 1989.

Slote, Michael. *Goods and Virtues*. Oxford, England: Clarendon, 1983.

———. *From Morality to Virtue*. New York: Oxford University Press, 1992.

Wallace, James. *Virtues and Vices*. Ithaca, NY: Cornell University Press, 1978.

Natural Law

Ackrill, J. L. *Aristotle's Ethics*. New York: Humanities Press, 1980.

Aquinas, St. Thomas. *Summa Theologica,* I–II, QQ. 90–108.

Aristotle. *Nicomachean Ethics*. J.E.C. Welldon (Trans.), 1897. New York: Prometheus Books, 1987.

———. *Aristotle's Eudemian Ethics*. Oxford, England: Clarendon, 1982.

Cooper, John M. *Reason and the Human Good in Aristotle*. Cambridge, MA: Harvard University Press, 1975.

Engberg-Pedersen, Troels. *Aristotle's Theory of Moral Insight*. Oxford, England: Clarendon, 1983.

George, Robert P. (Ed.). *Natural Law Theory: Contemporary Essays*. Oxford, England: Clarendon, 1992.

Haakonssen, Knud. *Natural Law and Moral Philosophy*. New York: Cambridge University Press, 1996.

Kraut, Richard. *Aristotle on the Human Good*. Princeton, NJ: Princeton University Press, 1991.

Rorty, Amelie (Ed.). *Essays on Aristotle's Ethics*. Berkeley: University of California Press, 1980.

Urmson, J. O. *Aristotle's Ethics*. Oxford, England: Clarendon, 1988.

Williams, B.A.O. "Aristotle on the Good," *Philosophical Quarterly* 12 (1962): 289–296.

Natural Rights

Brownlie, Ian (Ed.). *Basic Documents on Human Rights*. Oxford, England: Clarendon, 1971.

Cicero. *De Republica*. Bk. III, xxii, 33. New York: Putnam's, 1928.

Feinberg, Joel. *Rights, Justice and the Bounds of Liberty*. Princeton, NJ: Princeton University Press, 1980.

Finnis, John. *Natural Law and Natural Rights*. New York: Oxford University Press, 1980.

Hannum, Hurst (Ed.). *Guide to International Human Rights Practice*. Philadelphia: University of Pennsylvania Press, 1984.

Harris, Ian. *The Mind of John Locke*. New York: Cambridge University Press, 1994.

Locke, John. *Second Treatise on Civil Government*. Peter Laslett (Ed.). Cambridge, England: Cambridge University Press, 1960.

Luytgaarden, Eric van de. *Introduction to the Theory of Human Rights*. Utrecht: Utrecht University, 1993.

Machan, Tibor R. *Individuals and Their Rights*. LaSalle, IL: Open Court, 1989.

Nino, Carlos Santiago. *The Ethics of Human Rights*. New York: Oxford University Press, 1991.

Selby, David. *Human Rights*. New York: Cambridge University Press, 1987.

Shue, Henry. *Basic Rights*. Princeton, NJ: Princeton University Press, 1980.

Simmons, A. John. *The Lockean Theory of Rights*. Princeton, NJ: Princeton University Press, 1994.

Thomson, Judith. *Rights, Restitution and Risk*. William Parent (Ed.). Cambridge, MA: Harvard University Press, 1990.

Wellman, Carl. *Real Rights*. New York: Oxford University Press, 1995.

7

Feminist Thought and the Ethics of Care

Not long ago, a moral question about the following hypothetical situation was posed to two eleven-year-old children, Jake and Amy.[1] A man's wife was extremely ill and in danger of dying. A certain drug might save her life, but the man could not afford it, in part because the druggist had set an unreasonably high price for it. The question was whether the man should steal the drug. Jake answered by trying to figure out the relative value of the woman's life and the druggist's right to his property. He concluded that the man should steal the drug because he calculated that the woman's life was worth more. Amy was not so sure. She wondered what would happen to both the man and his wife if he stole the drug. "If he stole the drug, he might save his wife then, but if he did, he might have to go to jail, and then his wife might get sicker again." She said that if the husband and wife talked about this they might be able to think of some other way out of the dilemma.

One interesting thing about this case is the very different ways in which the two children tried to determine the right thing to do. The boy used a rational calculation in which he weighed and compared values from a neutral standpoint. The girl spoke about the possible effects of the proposed action on the two individuals and their relationship. Her method did not give the kind of definitive answer apparent in the boy's

method. Perhaps the difference in their moral reasoning is the result of their sex or gender.[2]

Another example also seems to show a gender difference in moral reasoning.[3] In explaining how they would respond to a moral dilemma about maintaining one's moral principles in the light of peer or family pressure, two teens responded quite differently. The case was one in which the religious views of the teens differed from their parents. The male said that he had a right to his own opinions, though he respected his parents' views. The female said that she was concerned about how her parents would react to her views. "I understand their fear of my new religious ideas." However, she added, "they really ought to listen to me and try to understand my beliefs."[4] Although their conclusions were similar, their reasoning was not. They seemed to have two decidedly different orientations or perspectives. The male spoke in terms of an individual's right to his own opinions, while the female talked of the need for the particular people involved to talk and to come to understand one another. These two cases raise questions about whether a gender difference actually exists in the way people reason about moral matters.

An Ethics of Care
Debate about sex or gender differences in moral perspectives and moral reasoning has been

sparked by the work of psychologist Carol Gilligan.[5] She interviewed both male and female subjects about various moral dilemmas and found that the women she interviewed had a different view than the men of what was morally required of them. They used a different moral language to explain themselves and their reasoning involved a different moral logic. They talked in terms of hurting and benefiting others, and they reasoned that they ought to do that which helped the people involved in a particular case at hand. She concluded that males and females had a different kind of ethics. Since then others have noted a variety of qualities that characterize male and female ethics. The debate that has followed has focused on whether there is a specifically feminine morality, an ethics of caring or care. First, we will examine the supposed characteristics of feminine morality. Then we will summarize various explanations that have been given for it. Finally, we will suggest some things to consider in evaluating the theory that a feminine ethics of care does indeed exist.

Several contrasting pairs of terms are associated with or can be used to describe the two types of ethical perspective. These are listed in the following table.

Female Ethical Perspective	Male Ethical Perspective
Personal	Impersonal
Partial	Impartial
Private	Public
Natural	Contractual
Feeling	Reason
Compassionate	Fair
Concrete	Universal
Responsibility	Rights
Relationship	Individual
Solidarity	Autonomy

The various characteristics or notions in this list may need some explanation. First, consider the supposed typical *female moral perspective.* The context for women's moral decision making is said to be one of relatedness. Women think about particular people and their relations and how they will be affected by some action. Women's morality is highly personal. They are partial to their particular loved ones and think that one's moral responsibility is first of all to these persons. It is the private and personal natural relations of family and friends that are the model for other relations. Women stress the concrete experiences of this or that event and are concerned about the real harm that might befall a particular person or persons. The primary moral obligation is to prevent harm and to help people. Women are able to empathize with others and are concerned about how they might feel if certain things were to happen to them. They believe that moral problems can be solved by talking about them and by trying to understand the perspectives of others. Caring and compassion are key virtues. The primary moral obligation is not to turn away from those in need. Nel Noddings's work *Caring: A Feminine Approach to Ethics and Moral Education* provides a good example and further description of the ethics of care.[6]

The supposed typical *male moral perspective* contrasts with a feminine ethics of care. Supposedly, men take a more universal and more impartial standpoint in reasoning about what is morally good and bad. Men are more inclined to talk in terms of fairness and justice and rights. They ask about the overall effects of some action and whether the good effects, when all are considered, outweigh the bad. It is as though they think moral decisions ought to be made impersonally or from some unbiased and detached point of view. The moral realm would then in many ways be similar to the public domain of law and contract. The law must not be biased and must treat everyone equally. Moral thinking involves a type of universalism, recognizing the equal moral worth of all as persons both in themselves and before the law. People ought to keep their promises because this is the just thing to do and helps create a reliable social order. Morality is a matter of doing one's duty, of keeping one's agreements and respecting another person's rights. Impartiality and respectfulness are key virtues. The primary obligation is not to act unfairly.

What are we to make of the view that two very different sets of characteristics describe male and female morality? In suggesting a difference between men's and women's morality, Carol Gilligan was taking aim at one of the dominant points of view about moral development—namely, that of Lawrence Kohlberg.[7] According to Kohlberg, the highest stage of moral development was supposed to be the stage in which an adult can be governed not by social pressure but by personal moral principles and a sense of justice. The principles treated people as moral equals. They manifested an impartial and universal perspective. In his own research, Kohlberg found that women did not often reach this stage of development. He thus judged them to be morally underdeveloped or morally deficient. Of course, his conclusions were not totally surprising because he had used an all-male sample in working out his theory.[8] After deriving his principles from male subjects, he then used them to judge both male and female moral development.

Gilligan and Kohlberg were not the first psychologists to believe that there was a difference between men's and women's morality. Freud had also held that women "show less sense of justice than men, that they are less ready to submit to the great exigencies of life, that they are more often influenced in their judgments by feelings of affection or hostility. . . ."[9] According to Freud, women were morally inferior to men. Instead of being able to establish themselves as separate persons living in society and adapting to its rules, girls remained in the home attached to their mothers. Thus, they developed a capacity for personal relations and intimacy while their male counterparts developed a sense of separateness and personal autonomy. The idea was that women base their morality on concerns about personal relations while men base their morality on rules that can reconcile the separate competing individuals in society.[10] Believing that a focus on personal relations rather than a sense of justice was a lesser form of morality, Freud

and others thought that women were inferior to men morally.

Three questions ought to be asked about the theory that women and men exhibit a different type of moral perspective and moral reasoning. First, is this true? Is it an empirical fact that men and women do manifest a different type of moral thinking? Second, if it is a fact, then how are we to explain it? What may be the source or cause of this difference? Third, if there is a difference, is one type of moral thinking higher or more developed or better than the other?

Is There a Gender Difference in Morality?

To determine whether there is, in fact, a difference between the moral language and logic of males and females we need to rely on empirical surveys and studies. What do people find who have examined this supposed phenomena? We have already described some of the earlier findings of Carol Gilligan. In more recent studies, her findings have varied somewhat.[11] For example, she now has found some variation in moral reasoning among both men and women. According to her latest findings, although both men and women sometimes think in terms of a justice perspective, few men think in terms of a care perspective. Being able to take one perspective rather than the other, she wrote, is much like being able to see the well-known line drawing figure as a rabbit or as a duck. The perspective that one has affects how one sees the figure. If one has a justice perspective, one will see that "the *self* as moral agent stands as the figure against a ground of social relationships, judging the conflicting claims of self and others against a standard of equality or equal respect." If one has a care perspective, one will see that "the *relationship* becomes the figure, defining self and others. Within the context of relationship, the self as a moral agent perceives and responds to the perception of need."[12] In these recent studies Gilligan used "educationally advantaged North American adolescents and adults" and found that two-thirds had one or the other orientation as their primary focus. Still she found sex differences in the focus. "With one exception, all of the men who focused, focused on justice. The women divided, with roughly one-third focusing on justice and one-third on care."[13] In this study, women did not always take the care perspective, but without the women in the study the care focus would have been almost absent.

Others are not so sure about what the data show. For example, Catherine Greeno and Eleanor Maccoby believe that any difference between men's and women's morality can be accounted for by their social status and experience rather than their gender. Using other studies, they point out that in many cases those who exhibit so-called feminine morality have been housewives and women who were less well educated. They found that career women showed types of moral reasoning similar to men.[14] The question of whether women do exhibit a unique type of moral language and logic will need to be decided by those who study the empirical data. And, of course, you can examine your own experience to see whether the males and females you know seem to talk differently when discussing moral issues.

The Source of Feminine Morality

At least three distinct types of explanation address a possible difference between male and female morality. One proposes differences in the psychosexual development of the two sexes. A second points to biological differences. A third gives a social, cultural, or educational explanation.

We have already described something of the Freudian account of the effects of psychosexual development on male and female moral thinking. A few more points may be added. Males and females have different concepts of the self and their gender identity; this is influenced by their development in relation to their mothers and fathers. As they grow up, females develop a sense of being connected with their mothers, whereas males find themselves being different from their mothers. According to Nancy Chodorow, who amplifies Freud's theory, development of the self

and one's sense of individuality depends on being able to separate oneself from others. Thus males, who tend to separate themselves from their mothers, come to have a sense of self as independent, whereas females do not develop the sense of separate selves and rather see themselves as attached or connected to others. From this developmental situation males and females supposedly develop different senses of morality: males a morality associated with separation and autonomy, and females a morality with relationships and interdependence. According to a traditional view, mature moral thinking involves being able to be detached and see things from some impartial perspective. Judging from a care perspective means that one cannot judge dispassionately or without bias, as was noted above, and this was judged to be a moral defect. However, we will consider the opposite position about the value of these perspectives shortly.

A second account of the source of the difference, exemplified by the writings of Caroline Whitbeck, locates it at least in part in women's and men's biology—that is, in the difference in their reproductive capacities and experiences. In pregnancy, labor, and childbirth, women experience certain feelings of dependency and contingency.[15] They do not have full control of their bodies. They experience weakness and pain. They feel themselves participating in species life at its very primitive level. Because of their own feelings during this time, they can sympathize more readily with the infant's or child's feelings of helplessness and dependency. Caring and nurturing are said to spring naturally from the intimate and sympathetic relation to the child.

Other people believe that mothering is not only a biological phenomenon but also a social and cultural one. Although women bear children, it is not necessary that they rear them. Still, because they do give birth to and nurse infants, women have generally come to be the first child rearers. It is from the elements of so-called maternal practice that women's morality arises, according to this third view.[16] To Sara Ruddick, for example, maternal practice results in "maternal thinking," which is the "vocabulary and logic of connections" that arises from "acting in response to demands of their children."[17] She believes that maternal thinking is not simply a kind of feeling that comes naturally to women, but a way of thinking and acting. It involves finding ways to preserve and develop and promote one's children. Infants are extremely vulnerable and will not survive if they do not have the basics of food, clothing, and shelter. Children must be safeguarded from the many dangers of life. They need help in growing physically, socially, and morally. Particular virtues are needed for a mother to be able to satisfy the needs of her children. Among those described by Ruddick are humility (for one cannot do everything), cheerfulness combined with realism, and love and affection. Mothers also need to guard against certain negative traits and feelings—for example, feelings of hopelessness and possessivism. According to this view, it is because they spend much of their lives mothering that women develop a morality consistent with this experience. This morality stresses relationships and the virtues that are necessary for mothering. One does not necessarily have to be a biological mother, however, both to engage in mothering and develop maternal ethics, according to this viewpoint. Just because men and some women do not give birth does not mean that they cannot be parents and develop the outlook required for this practice. Until now, it has been a social phenomenon that maternal practice has been principally women's work.

Feminine Versus Masculine Morality

Many questions remain concerning these three hypotheses. Some are factual or *empirical questions*, for they ask whether something is or is not the case. Do women in fact think thus and so? Are they more likely to do so than men? Does giving birth or rearing children cause those involved in these practices to think in a certain way and to have a certain moral perspective? Much of what we say here is quite speculative in that we are making guesses that cannot strictly

be proven to be true. Nevertheless, there is a great deal of appeal and suggestiveness in the theory of the ethics of care. In particular, we should compare this type of morality with more traditional theories such as utilitarianism and Kantianism to see how different the perspectives are as exemplified by the theories.

Whether one way of judging morally is *better* than the other is also an open question. As we have seen, there has been a tradition of thought that says that the so-called feminine morality, an ethics of care and relations and particularity and partiality, is a lower level morality. When we consider the sources of this tradition, we find many reasons to criticize it. Perhaps, on the contrary, it is the ethics of care that provides a better moral orientation. For example, instead of judging war in terms of whether the overall benefits outweigh the costs, we may do well to think about the particular people involved—that every soldier, for example, is someone's daughter or son or sister or brother or mother or father. Or perhaps the two orientations are complementary. Perhaps a justice orientation is the minimum that morality requires. We could then build on this minimum and, for example, temper justice with care and mercy. On the other hand, the care orientation may be the more basic one, and justice concerns could then be brought in to determine how best to care.

If specific female and male virtues parallel these orientations, then another question arises. Would it not be possible and good for both men and women to develop both sets of virtues? If these virtues are described in a positive way—say, caring and not subservience—would they not be traits that all should strive to possess? These traits might be simply different aspects of the human personality, rather than the male or female personality. They would then be human virtues and human perspectives rather than male or female virtues and perspectives. On this view an ethics of fidelity and care and sympathy would be just as important for human flourishing as an ethics of duty and justice and acting on principle. While there would be certain moral virtues that all persons should develop, other psychological traits could also vary according to temperament and choice. Individuals would be free to choose to manifest, according to their own personality, any combination of characteristics. These sets of characteristics and virtues would be various forms of *androgyny*, or the manifestation of both stereotypical masculine and feminine traits.[18]

Feminist Thought

Not all feminist writers support some version of an ethics of care. While most would agree that one can describe a particular type of morality exhibiting the characteristics said to belong to an ethics of care, they question whether all aspects of such an ethics of care are good. For example, the ethics seems to be based on relations between unequals. The mother-child relation is such a relation. The dependency in the relation goes only one way. One does all (or most of) the giving and the other all (or most of) the receiving. This may tend to reinforce or promote a one-sided morality of self-sacrifice and subjugation. It may reinforce the view that women ought to be the ones who sacrifice and help and support others, chiefly children and men. Feminist writers, as we have described the orientation here, would have us rather focus on the social status of women. One of their main ethical concerns is the historical and present-day continuing oppression of women: their status in many cases and ways as second-class citizens.

According to Seyla Benhabib, there are two "premises" of feminist thinking:

> First, for feminist theory, the gender-sex system is not a contingent but an essential way in which social reality is organized, symbolically divided, and experienced. By the "gender-sex" system, I mean the social-historical, symbolic constitution, and interpretation of the differences of the sexes. The gender-sex system is the context in which the self develops an *embodied* identity. . . .

Benhabib here points out how powerful and pervasive are the ways in which we are perceived and exist as males and females. It is not just a biological difference, but a difference resulting from behavioral and social expectations. One might conclude from this picture of the situation of females (and males) that there are these two different types of gender-based morality. However, Benhabib describes another premise of feminist thinking.

Second, the historically known gender-sex systems have contributed to the oppression and exploitation of women, and it is the duty of feminist critical theory to contribute to overcoming such oppression and exploitation.[19] Women need not be thought of as the opposite of men, as not autonomous or independent, not competitive, not public.[20] They can define their own position and identity.

These feminist views are only some of the most recent examples of what has been one of the goals of the so-called women's movement, which began in earnest in the West in the late nineteenth century. The history of the women's movement includes both those women primarily concerned with promoting women's equality with men and those who wanted to raise the value of women's unique characteristics. However, the most well-known writers and activists of this movement have been those who have stressed women's rights. Among the earliest examples is Mary Wollstonecraft's *A Vindication of the Rights of Women* (1792).[21] She wrote that women were not by nature weak and emotional, but that their social situation had in many ways made them so. It is society that teaches women negative moral traits such as cunning and vanity, she insisted. The suffragettes who sought political equality and the right to vote for women followed in her footsteps. Many years later Simone de Beauvoir's work *The Second Sex* (1949) became a classic text for what has been called a "second wave" of feminists (the "first wave" being the nineteenth-century women's rights advocates).[22] According to de Beauvoir, women were a second sex because they were regarded always in terms of being an "other" to the primary male sex. In an existentialist vein, she stressed the need for women to be independent selves and free to establish their own goals and projects. Various other writers in the history of the women's movement stressed the importance of raising women's consciousness, of helping women be aware of their second-class status and the various ways in which they were subject to oppression and subordination in their lives. The movement's aim was not only to raise consciousness, but also to act politically to bring about the equality of women. Thus, for example, they sought the passage of the Equal Rights Amendment to the U.S. Constitution.

Today feminist moral thought is sometimes simply called *feminist ethics* and is distinguished from an ethics of care that is called *feminine ethics*.[23] Writers who explore what has been called feminist ethics focus on bringing out the causes of women's subordination and oppression and suggesting ways to eliminate these causes and their results. They also have a political orientation. (See, for example, the selection by Catharine MacKinnon in Chapter 10.) Among the causes of women's oppression has been philosophy itself.

Traditional moral philosophy has not been favorable to women. It has tended to support the view that women should develop women's virtues, and these are often to her detriment. For example, Aristotle seems to have held that women were inferior to men not only because of certain biological phenomena having to do with heat in the body, but also because they lacked certain elements in their rationality. According to Aristotle, free adult males could rule over not only slaves but also women and children because of the weakness in their "deliberative" faculty. In the case of woman, while she has such a faculty, he said, it is "without authority."[24] Rousseau, in his work on the education of the young, described a quite different type of ideal education for Emile than for Sophie. Because morality is different for men and women, the young of each sex ought to be trained in different virtues, ac-

cording to Rousseau. Emile is to be trained in virtues such as justice and fortitude, while Sophie is to be taught to be docile and patient.[25]

Even contemporary moral philosophers have not given women and women's concerns their due, according to many feminist writers. They have not been interested in matters of the home and domesticity. They have tended to ignore issues such as the "feminization of poverty," the use of reproductive technologies, sexual harassment, and violence against and sexual abuse of women. It is mainly with women writing on these topics in contemporary ethics that they have gained some respectability as topics of genuine philosophical interest. So also have the issues of female domination and oppression and subordination become topics of a wider philosophical interest. Lesbian feminists in particular have written about patriarchal practices that prevent women from flourishing. They believe that other feminist treatments sometimes do not go far enough, because they continue to see women in terms of their relation to men. Instead, they exhort women to become independent creative beings in their own right.[26]

Evaluation of Feminist Thought and the Ethics of Care

We have already pointed out some questions that have been raised about the ethics of care. There are others as well. First, some point out that mothering does not always come naturally to women, and not all women are good mothers or caring and nurturing. However, supporters of the ethics of care may reply that this is not the issue, but that there exists an ethics of care as a viable and valuable alternative morality. Second, critics contend that to promote the view that women should manifest these feminine traits may not be of benefit to women, for doing this can be used to continue women's subservient position in society, especially if the virtues that it includes are obedience, self-sacrifice, silence, and service. Supporters might respond that it is not these virtues that define an ethics of care.

Rather, such an ethics tells us from what perspective we are to judge morally—namely, from the perspective of concrete persons in relation to one another who can individually be harmed and benefited in particular ways. However, can an ethics of care free itself from the more negative aspects that these critics point out? Can feminist ethicians support an ethics of care while also seeking to promote women's equality? It is clear at least that women cannot be restricted to the role of those who serve others if they are to be treated equally and fairly in both the public social realm and in the realm of the home and family.

What these discussions have also suggested is that we can no longer maintain that one ethics exists for the home and the private realm (an ethics of care and relationships) and another ethics for work or the public realm (an ethics of justice and fairness and impartiality). "Neither the realm of domestic, personal life, nor that of non-domestic, economic and political life, can be understood or interpreted in isolation from the other."[27] These two realms not only overlap and interpenetrate each other, but also each should exemplify the values and virtues of the other. Elements of altruism and concern for particular concrete individuals have a place in the political as well as the domestic realm. Furthermore, when feminists say that "the personal is political" they mean that "what happens in the personal life, particularly in relations between the sexes, is not immune from the dynamic *of power,* which has typically been seen as a distinguishing feature of the political."[28] These relations should thus also be restrained by considerations of fairness and justice. (See the selection by Susan Okin in Chapter 12.)

One further question arises about the ethics of care. While it describes an ideal context for ethical decision making, it does not tell us how we are to determine what will help and harm particular individuals. It does not in itself say what constitutes benefit and harm. It gives no rules for what we are to do in cases of conflict of interest even among those to whom we are partial or what to do when we cannot benefit all. It seems to give little definite help for knowing what to do in cases where we must harm some to benefit others. Supporters may respond that it is in setting the context for decision making that it already has done something valuable, for it thus provides a balance for the otherwise one-sided traditional ethics of the impersonal and universal. Perhaps this is a valuable minimum. Or, even further, it may be that today we are more than ever in need of something such as this ethic, which promotes the connectedness of humans. As Gilligan notes:

> By rendering a care perspective more coherent and making its terms explicit, moral theory may facilitate women's ability to speak about their experiences and perceptions and may foster the ability of others to listen and to understand. At the same time, the evidence of care focus in women's moral thinking suggests that the study of women's development may provide a natural history of moral development in which care is ascendant, revealing the ways in which creating and sustaining responsive connection with others becomes or remains a central moral concern. The promise in joining women and moral theory lies in the fact that human survival, in the late twentieth century, may depend less on formal agreement than on human connection.[29]

If it is true for the late twentieth century, then it may even be more true for the early twenty-first century. Further thoughts on how these various perspectives might be reconciled can be found in this chapter's readings by Virginia Held and Annette Baier. Other discussions of women's issues also occur throughout this text.

Notes

1. This is a summary of a question that was posed by researchers for Lawrence Kohlberg. In Carol Gilligan, *In a Different Voice* (Cambridge, MA: Harvard University Press, 1982), 28, 173.
2. We use the term *sex* to refer to the biological male or female. The term *gender* includes psychological feminine and masculine traits as well as social roles that are assigned to the two sexes.
3. From Carol Gilligan, "Moral Orientation and Moral Development," in *Women and Moral Theory,* Eva Kit-

tay and Diana Meyers (Eds.) (Totowa, NJ: Rowman & Littlefield, 1987), 23.

4. Ibid.

5. Carol Gilligan, "Concepts of the Self and of Morality," *Harvard Educational Review* (Nov. 1977), 481–517.

6. Nel Noddings, *Caring: A Feminine Approach to Ethics and Moral Education* (Berkeley: University of California Press, 1984).

7. Lawrence Kohlberg, *The Psychology of Moral Development* (San Francisco: Harper & Row, 1984).

8. Gilligan, "Moral Orientation and Moral Development," 22.

9. Cited in Gilligan, op. cit.

10. See also Nancy Chodorow, *The Reproduction of Mothering* (Berkeley: University of California Press, 1978).

11. See, for example, Gilligan, "Adolescent Development Reconsidered," in *Mapping the Moral Domain,* Carol Gilligan, Janie Victoria Ward, and Jill McLean Taylor (Eds.) (Cambridge, MA: Harvard University Press, 1988).

12. Gilligan, "Moral Orientation and Moral Development," 22–23. Emphasis added.

13. Ibid., 25.

14. Catherine G. Greeno and Eleanor E. Maccoby, "How Different Is the Different Voice?" in "On *In a Different Voice:* An Interdisciplinary Forum," *Signs: Journal of Women in Culture and Society* 11, no. 2 (Winter 1986), 211–220.

15. See, for example, Caroline Whitbeck, "The Maternal Instinct," in *Mothering: Essays in Feminist Theory,* Joyce Treblicot (Ed.) (Totowa, NJ: Rowman & Allanheld, 1984).

16. See, for example, Sara Ruddick, *Maternal Thinking: Toward a Politics of Peace* (Boston: Beacon, 1989).

17. Ibid., 214.

18. See Joyce Treblicot, "Two Forms of Androgynism," in *Journal of Social Philosophy,* vol. VIII, no. 1 (Jan. 1977), 4–8.

19. Seyla Benhabib, "The Generalized and the Concrete Other," in *Women and Moral Theory,* 156–157.

20. Ibid., 162.

21. Mary Wollstonecraft, *A Vindication of the Rights of Women,* Miriam Brody (Ed.) (London: Penguin, 1988).

22. Simone de Beauvoir, *The Second Sex,* H. M. Parshley (Trans.) (New York: Knopf, 1953).

23. This terminology is from Rosemary Tong's *Feminine and Feminist Ethics* (Belmont, CA: Wadsworth, 1993). As a source of this terminology, Tong also cites Betty A. Sichel, "Different Strains and Strands: Feminist Contributions to Ethical Theory," *Newsletter on Feminism* 90, no. 2 (Winter 1991), 90; and Susan Sherwin, *No Longer Patient: Feminist Ethics and Health Care* (Philadelphia: Temple University Press, 1992), 42.

24. Aristotle, *Politics,* as quoted in "Theories of Sex Difference," by Caroline Whitbeck in *Women and Moral Theory,* 35.

25. Jean-Jacques Rousseau, *Emile,* Allan Bloom (Trans.) (New York: Basic Books, 1979). Also see Nancy Tuana, *Woman and the History of Philosophy* (New York: Paragon House, 1992).

26. See, for example, Sarah Lucia Hoagland, *Lesbian Ethics* (Palo Alto, CA: Institute of Lesbian Studies, 1989).

27. Susan Moller Okin, "Gender, the Public and the Private," in *Political Theory Today,* David Held (Ed.) (Stanford, CA: Stanford University Press, 1991), 77.

28. Ibid.

29. Gilligan, "Moral Orientation and Moral Development," 32.

Feminism and Moral Theory

Virginia Held

Study Questions

1. What does the author mean by saying that there may be different moral approaches for different domains of human activity? What is meant by the "private" and the "public" domains?

2. With what domain has Western philosophical thought been associated since its Greek origins, according to Held?

3. With what is a person's moral experience concerned? How does this make a difference in men's and women's moral experience? Is either moral experience more valid than the other, according to the author?

4. What two reasons does Held give for why we need a feminist moral theory?

5. According to the author, what is the most fundamental social relationship? Why?

6. How is human birth and mothering different from that of other animals? Why is this important when developing a morality or a moral theory?

7. How is this relationship different from that on which social contract theory is based? Which is the more important for moral theory, according to Held?

8. What would morality look like if the relationship between mother and child was taken as primary or paradigmatic?

9. How would taking this relationship as primary influence the way we understand the traditional moral problem of reconciling the interests of the self with those of society?

10. Does Held agree with those who say that we ought to dispense with an ethics of principles? Why or why not? In what way does she agree with those who attack an ethics of principles?

11. According to Held, is the activity of mothering restricted to women? How is her answer both a "yes" and a "no"?

12. What experiences affect our valuation of children, by mothers in particular, according to Held? How might this play a role in questions about why we ought to value human beings?

13. How would this basis for valuing people differ from that of those moral philosophers who take pleasure as the basis for morality?

The tasks of moral inquiry and moral practice are such that different moral approaches may be appropriate for different domains of human activity. I have argued in a recent book that we need a division of moral labor.[1] In *Rights and Goods,* I suggest that we ought to try to develop moral inquiries that will be as satisfactory as possible for the actual contexts in which we live and in which our experience is located. Such a division of moral labor can be expected to

yield different moral theories for different contexts of human activity, at least for the foreseeable future. In my view, the moral approaches most suitable for the courtroom are not those most suitable for political bargaining; the moral approaches suitable for economic activity are not those suitable for relations within the family, and so on. The task of achieving a unified moral field theory covering all domains is one we may do well to postpone, while we do our best to devise and to "test" various moral theories in actual contexts and in light of our actual moral experience.

What are the implications of such a view for women? Traditionally, the experience of women has been located to a large extent in the context of the family. In recent centuries, the family has been thought of as a "private" domain distinct not only from that of the "public" domain of the polis, but also from the domain of production and of the marketplace. Women (and men) certainly need to develop moral inquiries appropriate to the context of mothering and of family relations, rather than accepting the application to this context of theories developed for the marketplace or the polis. We can certainly show that the moral guidelines appropriate to mothering are different from those that now seem suitable for various other domains of activity as presently constituted. But we need to do more as well: we need to consider whether distinctively feminist moral theories, suitable for the contexts in which the experience of women has or will continue to be located, are better moral theories than those already available, and better for other domains as well.

The Experience of Women

We need a theory about how to count the experience of women. It is not obvious that it should count equally in the construction or validation of moral theory. To merely survey the moral views of women will not necessarily lead to better moral theories. In the Greek thought that developed into the Western philosophical tradition,[2] reason was associated with the public domain from which women were largely excluded. If the development of adequate moral theory is best based on experience in the public domain, the experience of women so far is less relevant. But that the public domain is the appropriate locus for the development of moral theory is among the tacit assumptions of existing moral theory being effectively challenged by feminist scholars. We cannot escape the need for theory in confronting these issues.

*Virginia Held, "Feminism and Moral Theory," in *Women and Moral Theory,* Eva Feder and Diana T. Meyers (Eds.) (Savage, MD: Rowman & Littlefield, 1987). ©1987 by Rowman & Littlefield Publishers. Reprinted with permission.

We need to take a stand on what moral experience is. As I see it, moral experience is "the experience of consciously choosing, of voluntarily accepting or rejecting, of willingly approving or disapproving, of living with these choices, and above all of acting and of living with these actions and their outcomes. . . . Action is as much a part of experience as is perception."[3] Then we need to take a stand on whether the moral experience of women is as valid a source or test of moral theory as is the experience of men, or on whether it is more valid.

Certainly, engaging in the process of moral inquiry is as open to women as it is to men, although the domains in which the process has occurred has been open to men and women in different ways. Women have had fewer occasions to experience for themselves the moral problems of governing, leading, exercising power over others (except children), and engaging in physically violent conflict. Men, on the other hand, have had fewer occasions to experience the moral problems of family life and the relations between adults and children. Although vast amounts of moral experience are open to all human beings who make the effort to become conscientious moral inquirers, the contexts in which experience is obtained may make a difference. It is essential that we avoid taking a given moral theory, such as a Kantian one, and deciding that those who fail to develop toward it are deficient, for this procedure imposes a theory on experience, rather than letting experience determine the fate of theories, moral and otherwise.

We can assert that as long as women and men experience different problems, moral theory ought to reflect the experience of women as fully as it reflects the experience of men. The insights and judgments and decisions of women as they engage in the process of moral inquiry should be presumed to be as valid as those of men. In the development of moral theory, men ought to have no privileged position to have their experience count for more. If anything, their privileged position in society should make their experience more suspect rather than more worthy of being counted, for they have good reasons to rationalize their privileged positions by moral arguments that will obscure or purport to justify these privileges.[4]

If the differences between men and women in confronting moral problems are due to biological factors that will continue to provide women and men with different experiences, the experience of women should still count for at least as much as the experience of men. There is no justification for discounting the experience of women as deficient or underdeveloped on biological grounds. Biological "moral inferiority" makes no sense.

The empirical question of whether and to what extent women think differently from men about moral problems is being investigated.[5] If, in fact, women approach moral problems in characteristic ways, these approaches should be reflected in moral theories as fully as are those of men. If the differing approaches to morality that seem to be displayed by women and by men are the result of historical conditions and not biological ones, we could assume that in nonsexist societies, the differences would disappear, and the experience of either gender might adequately substitute for the experience of the other.[6] Then feminist moral theory might be the same as moral theory of any kind. But since we can hardly imagine what a nonsexist society would be like, and surely should not wait for one before evaluating the experience of women, we can say that we need feminist moral theory to deal with the differences of which we are now aware and to contribute to the development of the nonsexist society that might make the need for a distinctively feminist moral theory obsolete. Specifically, we need feminist moral theory to deal with the regions of experience that have been central to women's experience and neglected by traditional moral theory. If the resulting moral theory would be suitable for all humans in all contexts, and thus could be thought of as a human moral theory or a universal moral theory, it would be a feminist moral theory as well if it adequately reflected the experience and standpoint of women.

That the available empirical evidence for differences between men and women with respect to morality is tentative and often based on reportage and interpretation, rather than on something more "scientific,"[7] is no problem at all for the claim that we need feminist moral theory. If such differences turn out to be further substantiated, we will need theory to evaluate their implications, and we should be prepared now for this possibility (or, as many think, probability). If the differences turn out to be insignificant, we still need feminist moral theory to make the moral claim that the experience of women is of equal worth to the experience of men, and even more important, that women themselves are of equal worth as human beings. If it is true that the only differences between women and men are anatomical, it still does not follow that women are the moral equals of men. Moral equality has to be based on moral claims. Since the devaluation of women is a constant in human society as so far developed, and has been accepted by those holding a wide variety of traditional moral theories, it is apparent that feminist moral theory is needed to provide the basis for women's claims to equality.

We should never forget the horrors that have resulted from acceptance of the idea that women think differently from men, or that men are rational beings, women emotional ones. We should be constantly on guard for misuses of such ideas, as in social roles that determine that women belong in the home or in educational programs that discourage women from becoming, for example, mathematicians. Yet, excessive fear of such misuses should not stifle exploration of the ways in which such claims may, in some measure, be true. As philosophers, we can be careful not to conclude that whatever tendencies exist ought to be reinforced. And if we succeed in making social scientists more alert to the naturalistic fallacy than they would otherwise be, that would be a side benefit to the development of feminist moral theory.

Mothering and Markets

When we bring women's experience fully into the domain of moral consciousness, we can see how questionable it is to imagine contractual relationships as central or fundamental to society and morality. They seem, instead, the relationships of only very particular regions of human activity.[8]

The most central and fundamental social relationship seems to be that between mother or mothering person and child. It is this relationship that creates and recreates society. It is the activity of mothering which transforms biological entities into human social beings. Mothers and mothering persons produce children and empower them with language and symbolic representations. Mothers and mothering persons thus produce and create human culture.

Despite its implausibility, the assumption is often made that human mothering is like the mothering of other animals rather than being distinctively human. In accordance with the traditional distinction between the family and the polis, and the assumption that what occurs in the public sphere of the polis is distinctively human, it is assumed that what human mothers do within the family belongs to the "natural" rather than to the "distinctively human" domain. Or, if it is recognized that the activities of human mothers do not resemble the activities of the mothers of other mammals, it is assumed that, at least, the difference is far narrower than the difference between what animals do and what humans who take part in government and industry and art do. But, in fact, mothering is among the most human of human activities.

Consider the reality. A human birth is thoroughly different from the birth of other animals, because a human mother can choose not to give birth. However extreme the alternative, even when abortion is not a possibility, a woman can choose suicide early enough in her pregnancy to consciously prevent the birth. A human mother comprehends that she brings about the birth of another human being. A human mother is then responsible, at least in an existentialist sense, for the creation of a new human life. The event is essentially different from what is possible for other animals.

Human mothering is utterly different from the mothering of animals without language. The human mother or nurturing person constructs with and for the child a human social reality. The child's understanding of language and of symbols, and of all that they create and make real, occurs in interactions between child and caretakers. Nothing seems more distinctively human than this. In comparison, government can be thought to resemble the governing of ant colonies, industrial production to be similar to the building of beaver dams, a market exchange to be like the relation between a large fish that protects and a small fish that grooms, and the conquest by force of arms that characterizes so much of human history to be like the aggression of packs of animals. But the imparting of language and the creation within and for each individual of a human social reality, and often a new human social reality, seems utterly human.

An argument is often made that art and industry and government create new human reality, while mothering merely "reproduces" human beings, their cultures, and social structures. But consider a more accurate view: in bringing up children, those who mother create new human *persons*. They change persons, the culture, and the social structures that depend on them, by creating the kinds of persons who can continue to transform themselves and their surroundings. Creating new and better persons is surely as "creative" as creating new and better objects or institutions. It is not only bodies that do not spring into being unaided and fully formed; neither do imaginations, personalities, and minds.

Perhaps morality should make room first for the human experience reflected in the social bond between mothering person and child, and for the human projects of nurturing and of growth apparent for both persons in the relationship. In comparison, the transactions of the marketplace seem peripheral; the authority of weapons and the laws they uphold, beside the point.

The relation between buyer and seller has often been taken as the model of all human interactions.[9] Most of the social contract tradition has seen this relation of contractual exchange as fundamental to law and political authority as well as to economic activity. And some contemporary moral philosophers see the contractual relation as the relation on which even morality itself should be based. The marketplace, as a model for relationships, has become so firmly entrenched in our normative theories that it is rarely questioned as a proper foundation for recommendations extending beyond the marketplace. Consequently, much moral thinking is built on the concept of rational economic man. Relationships between human beings are seen as arising, and as justified, when they serve the interests of individual rational contractors.

In the society imagined in the model based on assumptions about rational economic man, connections between people become no more than instrumental. Nancy Hartsock effectively characterizes the worldview of these assumptions, and shows how misguided it is to suppose that the relationship between buyer and seller can serve as a model for all human relations: "the paradigmatic connections between people [on this view of the social world] are instrumental or extrinsic and conflictual, and in a world populated by these isolated individuals, relations of competition and domination come to be substitutes for a more substantial and encompassing community."[10]

Whether the relationship between nurturing person (who need not be a biological mother) and child should be taken as itself paradigmatic, in place of the contractual paradigm, or whether it should be seen only as an obviously important relationship that does not fit into the contractual framework and should not be overlooked, remains to be seen. It is certainly instructive to consider it, at least tentatively, as paradigmatic. If this were done, the competition and desire for domination thought of as acceptable for

rational economic man might appear as a very particular and limited human connection, suitable perhaps, if at all, only for a restricted marketplace. Such a relation of conflict and competition can be seen to be unacceptable for establishing the social trust on which public institutions must rest,[11] or for upholding the bonds on which caring, regard, friendship, or love must be based.[12]

The social map would be fundamentally altered by adoption of the point of view here suggested. Possibly, the relationship between "mother" and child would be recognized as a much more promising source of trust and concern than any other, for reasons to be explored later. In addition, social relations would be seen as dynamic rather than as fixed-point exchanges. And assumptions that human beings are equally capable of entering or not entering into the contractual relations taken to characterize social relations generally would be seen for the distortions they are. Although human mothers could do other than give birth, their choices to do so or not are usually highly constrained. And children, even human children, cannot choose at all whether to be born.

It may be that no human relationship should be thought of as paradigmatic for all the others. Relations between mothering persons and children can become oppressive for both, and relations between equals who can decide whether to enter into agreements may seem attractive in contrast. But no mapping of the social and moral landscape can possibly be satisfactory if it does not adequately take into account and provide appropriate guidance for relationships between mothering persons and children.

Between the Self and the Universal

Perhaps the most important legacy of the new insights will be the recognition that more attention must be paid to the domain *between* the self—the ego, the self-interested individual—on the one hand, and the universal—everyone, others in general—on the other hand. Ethics traditionally has dealt with these poles, trying to reconcile their conflicting claims. It has called for impartiality against the partiality of the egoistic self, or it has defended the claims of egoism against such demands for a universal perspective.

In seeing the problems of ethics as problems of reconciling the interests of the self with what would be right or best for everyone, moral theory has neglected the intermediate region of family relations and relations of friendship, and has neglected the sympathy and concern people actually feel for particular others. As Larry Blum has shown, "contemporary moral philosophy in the Anglo-American tradition has paid little attention to [the] morally significant phenomena" of sympathy, compassion, human concern, and friendship.[13]

Standard moral philosophy has construed personal relationships as aspects of the self-interested feelings of individuals, as when a person might favor those he loves over those distant because it satisfies his own desires to do so. Or it has let those close others stand in for the universal "other," as when an analysis might be offered of how the conflict between self and others is to be resolved in something like "enlightened self-interest" or "acting out of respect for the moral law," and seeing this as what should guide us in our relations with those close, particular others with whom we interact.

Owen Flanagan and Jonathan Adler provide useful criticism of what they see as Kohlberg's "adequacy thesis"—the assumption that the more formal the moral reasoning, the better.[14] But they themselves continue to construe the tension in ethics as that between the particular self and the universal. What feminist moral theory will emphasize, in contrast, will be the domain of particular others in relations with one another.

The region of "particular others" is a distinct domain, where it can be seen that what becomes artificial and problematic are the very "self" and "all others" of standard moral theory. In the domain of particular others, the self is already closely entwined in relations with others, and the relation may be much more real, salient, and important than the interests of any individual self in isolation. But the "others" in the picture are not "all others," or "everyone," or what a universal point of view could provide. They are particular flesh and blood others for whom we have actual feelings in our insides and in our skin, not the others of rational constructs and universal principles.

Relationships can be characterized as trusting or mistrustful, mutually considerate or selfish, and so forth. Where trust and consideration are appropriate, we can find ways to foster them. But doing so will depend on aspects of what can be understood only if we look at relations between persons. To focus on either self-interested individuals or the totality of all persons is to miss the qualities of actual relations between actual human beings.

Moral theories must pay attention to the neglected realm of particular others in actual contexts. In doing so, problems of egoism vs. the universal moral point of view appear very different, and may recede to the region of background insolubility or relative unimportance. The important problems may then be seen to be how we ought to guide or maintain or reshape the relationships, both close and more distant, that we have or might have with actual human beings.

Particular others can, I think, be actual starving children in Africa with whom one feels empathy or even the anticipated children of future generations, not just those we are close to in any traditional context of family, neighbors, or friends. But particular others are still not "all rational beings" or "the greatest number."

In recognizing the component of feeling and relatedness between self and particular others, motivation is addressed as an inherent part of moral inquiry. Caring between parent and child is a good example.[15] We should not glamorize parental care. Many mothers and fathers dominate their children in harmful or inappropriate ways, or fail to care adequately for them. But when the relationship between "mother" and child is as it should be, the caretaker does not care for the child (nor the child for the caretaker) because of universal moral rules. The love and concern one feels for the child already motivate much of what one does. This is not to say that morality is irrelevant. One must still decide what one ought to do. But the process of addressing the moral questions in mothering and of trying to arrive at answers one can find acceptable involves motivated acting, not just thinking. And neither egoism nor a morality of universal rules will be of much help.

Mothering is, of course, not the only context in which the salient moral problems concern relations between particular others rather than conflicts between egoistic self and universal moral laws; all actual human contexts may be more like this than like those depicted by Hobbes or Kant. But mothering may be one of the best contexts in which to make explicit why familiar moral theories are so deficient in offering guidance for action. And the variety of contexts within mothering, with the different excellences appropriate for dealing with infants, young children, or adolescents, provide rich sources of insight for moral inquiry.

The feelings characteristic of mothering—that there are too many demands on us, that we cannot do everything that we ought to do—are highly instructive. They give rise to problems different from those of universal rule vs. self-interest. They require us to weigh the claims of one self-other relationship against the claims of other self-other relationships, to try to bring about some harmony between them, to see the issues in an actual temporal context, and to act rather than merely reflect.

For instance, we have limited resources for caring. We cannot care for everyone or do everything a caring approach suggests. We need moral guidelines for ordering our priorities. The hunger of our own children comes before the hunger of children we do not know. But the hunger of children in Africa ought to come before some of the expensive amusements we may wish to provide for our own children. These are moral problems calling to some extent for principled answers. But we have to figure out what we ought to do when actually buying groceries, cooking meals, refusing the requests of our children for the latest toy they have seen advertised, and sending money to UNICEF. The context is one of real action, not of ideal thought.

Principles and Particulars

When we take the context of mothering as central, rather than peripheral, for moral theory, we run the risk of excessively discounting other contexts. It is a commendable risk, given the enormously more prevalent one of excessively discounting mothering. But I think that the attack on principles has sometimes been carried too far by critics of traditional moral theory.

Noddings, for instance, writes that "To say, 'It is wrong to cause pain needlessly,' contributes nothing by way of knowledge and can hardly be thought likely to change the attitude or behavior of one who might ask, 'Why is it wrong?' . . . Ethical caring . . . depends not upon rule or principle" but upon the development of a self "in congruence with one's best remembrance of caring and being cared for."[16]

We should not forget that an absence of principles can be an invitation to capriciousness. Caring may be a weak defense against arbitrary decisions, and the person cared for may find the relation more satisfactory if both persons, but especially the person caring, are guided, to some extent, by principles concerning obligations and rights. To argue that no two cases are ever alike is to invite moral chaos. Furthermore, for one person to be in a position of caretaker means that that person has the power to withhold care, to leave the other without it. The person cared for is usually

in a position of vulnerability. The moral significance of this needs to be addressed along with other aspects of the caring relationship. Principles may remind a giver of care to avoid being capricious or domineering. While most of the moral problems involved in mothering contexts may deal with issues above and beyond the moral minimums that can be covered by principles concerning rights and obligations, that does not mean that these minimums can be dispensed with.

Noddings's discussion is unsatisfactory also in dealing with certain types of questions, for instance those of economic justice. Such issues cry out for relevant principles. Although caring may be needed to motivate us to act on such principles, the principles are not dispensable. Noddings questions the concern people may have for starving persons in distant countries, because she sees universal love and universal justice as masculine illusions. She refrains from judging that the rich deserve less or the poor more, because caring for individuals cannot yield such judgments. But this may amount to taking a given economic stratification as given, rather than as the appropriate object of critical scrutiny that it should be. It may lead to accepting that the rich will care for the rich and the poor for the poor, with the gap between them, however unjustifiably wide, remaining what it is. Some important moral issues seem beyond the reach of an ethic of caring, once caring leads us, perhaps through empathy, to be concerned with them.

On ethical views that renounce principles as excessively abstract, we might have few arguments to uphold the equality of women. After all, as parents can care for children recognized as weaker, less knowledgeable, less capable, and with appropriately restricted rights, so men could care for women deemed inferior in every way. On a view that ethics could satisfactorily be founded on caring alone, men could care for women considered undeserving of equal rights in all the significant areas in which women have been struggling to have their equality recognized. So an ethic of care, essential as a component of morality, seems deficient if taken as an exclusive preoccupation.

That aspect of the attack on principles which seems entirely correct is the view that not all ethical problems can be solved by appeal to one or a very few simple principles. It is often argued that all more particular moral rules or principles can be derived from such underlying ones as the Categorical Imperative or the Principle of Utility, and that these can be applied to all moral problems. The call for an ethic of care may be a call, which I share, for a more pluralistic view of ethics, recognizing that we need a division of moral labor employing different moral approaches for different domains, at least for the time being.[17] Satisfactory intermediate principles for areas such as those of international affairs, or family relations, cannot be derived from simple universal principles, but must be arrived at in conjunction with experience within the domains in question.

Attention to particular others will always require that we respect the particularity of the context, and arrive at solutions to moral problems that will not give moral principles more weight than their due. But their due may remain considerable. And we will need principles concerning relationships, not only concerning the actions of individuals, as we will need evaluations of kinds of relationships, not only of the character traits of individuals.

Birth and Valuing

To a large extent, the activity of mothering is potentially open to men as well as to women. Fathers can conceivably come to be as emotionally close, or as close through caretaking, to children as are mothers. The experience of relatedness, of responsibility for the growth and empowerment of new life, and of responsiveness to particular others, ought to be incorporated into moral theory, and will have to be so incorporated for moral theory to be adequate. At present, in this domain, it is primarily the experience of women (and of children) that has not been sufficiently reflected in moral theory and that ought to be so reflected. But this is not to say that it must remain experience available only to women. If men came to share fully and equitably in the care of all persons who need care—especially children, the sick, the old—the moral values that now arise for women in the context of caring might arise as fully for men.

There are some experiences, however, that are open only to women: menstruating, having an abortion, giving birth, suckling. We need to consider their possible significance or lack of significance for moral experience and theory. I will consider here only one kind of experience not open to men but of obviously great importance to women: the experience of giving birth or of deciding not to. Does the very experience of giving birth, or of deciding not to exercise the capacity to do so, make a significant difference for moral experience and moral theory? I think the answer must be: perhaps.

Of course birthing is a social as well as a personal or biological event. It takes place in a social context structured by attitudes and arrangements that deeply affect how women experience it: whether it will be accepted as "natural," whether it will be welcomed and celebrated, or whether it will be fraught with fear or shame. But I wish to focus briefly on the conscious awareness women can have of what they are doing in giving birth, and on the specifically personal and biological aspects of human birthing.

It is women who give birth to other persons. Women are responsible for the existence of new persons in ways far more fundamental than are men. It is not bizarre to recognize that women can, through abortion or suicide, choose not to give birth. A woman can be aware of the possibility that she can act to prevent a new person from existing, and can be aware that if this new person exists, it is because of what she has done and made possible.

In the past we have called attention to the extent to which women do not control their capacity to give birth. They are under extreme economic and social pressure to engage in intercourse, to marry, and to have children. Legal permission to undergo abortion is a recent, restricted, and threatened capacity. When the choice not to give birth requires grave risk to life, health, or well-being, or requires suicide, we should be careful not to misrepresent the situation when we speak of a woman's "choice" to become a mother, or of how she "could have done other" than have a child, or that "since she chose to become a mother, she is responsible for her child." It does not follow that because women are responsible for creating human beings, they should be held responsible by society for caring for them, either alone, primarily, or even at all. These two kinds of responsibility should not be confused, and I am speaking here only of the first. As conscious human beings, women can do other than give birth, and if they do give birth, they are responsible for the creation of other human beings. Though it may be very difficult for women to avoid giving birth, the very familiarity of the literary image of the woman who drowns herself or throws herself from a cliff rather than bear an illegitimate child should remind us that such eventualities are not altogether remote from consciousness.

Women have every reason to be justifiably angry with men who refuse to take responsibility for their share of the events of pregnancy and birth, or for the care children require. Because, for so long, we have wanted to increase the extent to which men would recognize their responsibilities for causing pregnancy, and would share in the long years of care needed to bring a child to independence, we have tended to emphasize the ways in which the responsibilities for creating a new human being are equal between women and men.[18] But in fact, men produce sperm and women produce babies, and the difference is enormous. Excellent arguments can be made that boys and men suffer "womb envy"; indeed, men lack a wondrous capacity that women possess.[19]

Of all the human capacities, it is probably the capacity to create new human beings that is most worth celebrating. We can expect that a woman will care about and feel concern for a child she has created as the child grows and develops, and that she feels responsible for having given the child life. But her concern is more than something to be expected. It is, perhaps, justifiable in certain ways unique to women.

Children are born into actual situations. A mother cannot escape ultimate responsibility for having given birth to this particular child in these particular circumstances. She can be aware that she could have avoided intercourse, or used more effective contraception, or waited to get pregnant until her circumstances were different; that she could have aborted this child and had another later; or that she could have killed herself and prevented this child from facing the suffering or hardship of this particular life. The momentousness of all these decisions about giving or not giving life can hardly fail to affect what she experiences in relation to the child.

Perhaps it might be thought that many of these issues arise in connection with infanticide, and that if one refrains from killing an infant, one is responsible for giving the infant life. Infanticide is as open to men as to women. But to kill or refrain from killing a child, once the child is capable of life with caretakers different from the person who is responsible for having given birth to the child, is a quite different matter from creating or not creating this possibility, and I am concerned in this discussion with the moral significance of giving birth.

It might also be thought that those, including the father, who refrain from killing the mother, or from forcing her to have an abortion, are also responsible for not preventing the birth of the child.[20] But unless the distinction between suicide and murder, and between having an abortion and forcing a woman to have an abortion against her will, are collapsed completely, the issues would be very different. To refrain from murdering someone else is not the same as deciding not to kill oneself. And to decide not to force someone else to have an abortion is different from deciding not to have an abortion when one could. The person capable of giving birth who decides not to prevent the birth is the person responsible, in the sense of "responsible" I am discussing, for creating another human being. To create a new human being is not the same as to refrain from ending the life of a human being who already exists.

Perhaps there is a tendency to want to approve of or to justify what one has decided with respect to giving life. In deciding to give birth, perhaps a woman has a natural tendency to approve of the birth, to believe that the child ought to have been born. Perhaps this inclines her to believe whatever may follow from this: that the child is entitled to care, and that feelings of love for the child are appropriate and justified. The conscious decision to create a new human being may provide women with an inclination to value the child and to have hope for the child's future. Since, in her view, the child ought to have been born, a woman may feel that the world ought to be hospitable to the child. And if the child ought to have been born, the child ought to grow into an admirable human adult. The child's life has, and should continue to have, value that is recognized.

Consider next the phenomenon of sacrifice. In giving birth, women suffer severe pain for the sake of new life. Having suffered for the child in giving the child life, women may have a natural tendency to value what they have endured pain for. There is a tendency, often noted in connection with war, for people to feel that because sacrifices have been made, the sacrifice should have been "worth it," and if necessary, other things ought to be done so that the sacrifice "shall not have been in vain." There may be a similar tendency for those who have suffered to give birth to assure themselves that the pain was for the good reason of creating a new life that is valuable and that will be valued.

Certainly, this is not to say that there is anything good or noble about suffering, or that merely because people want to believe that what they suffered for was worthwhile, it was. A vast amount of human suffering has been in vain, and could and should have been avoided. The point is that once suffering has already occurred and the "price," if we resort to such calculations, has already been paid, it will be worse if the result is a further cost, and better if the result is a clear benefit that can make the price, when it is necessary for the result, validly "worth it."

The suffering of the mother who has given birth will more easily have been worthwhile if the child's life has value. The chance that the suffering will be outweighed by future happiness is much greater if the child is valued by the society and the family into which the child is born. If the mother's suffering yields nothing but further suffering and a being deemed to be of no value, her suffering may truly have been in vain. Anyone can have reasons to value children. But the person who has already undergone the suffering needed to create one has a special reason to recognize that the child is valuable and to want the child to be valued so that the suffering she has already borne will have been, truly, worthwhile.

These arguments can be repeated for the burdens of work and anxiety normally expended in bringing up a child. Those who have already borne these burdens have special reasons for wanting to see the grown human being for whom they have cared as valuable and valued. Traditionally, women have not only borne the burdens of childbirth, but, with little help, the much greater burdens of child rearing. Of course, the burdens of child rearing could be shared fully by men, as they have been partially shared by women other than natural mothers. Although the concerns involved in bringing up a child may greatly outweigh the suffering of childbirth itself, this does not mean that giving birth is incidental.

The decision not to have children is often influenced by a comparable tendency to value the potential child.[21] Knowing how much care the child would deserve and how highly, as a mother, she would value the child, a woman who gives up the prospect of motherhood can recognize how much she is losing. For such reasons, a woman may feel overwhelming ambivalence concerning the choice.

Consider, finally, how biology can affect our ways of valuing children. Although men and women may share a desire or an instinctive tendency to wish to reproduce, and although these feelings may be equally strong for both men and women, such feelings might affect their attitudes toward a given child very differently. In terms of biological capacity, a mother has a relatively greater stake in a child to which she has given birth. This child is about one-twentieth or one twenty-fifth of all the children she could possibly have, whereas a man could potentially have hundreds or thousands of other children. In giving birth, a woman has already contributed a large amount of energy and effort toward the production of this particular child, while a man has, biologically, contributed only a few minutes. To the extent that such biological facts may influence attitudes, the attitudes of the mother and father toward the "worth" or "value" of a particular child may be different. The father might consider the child more easily replaceable in the sense that the father's biological contribution can so easily and so painlessly be repeated on another occasion or with another woman; for the mother to repeat her biological contribution would be highly exhausting and painful. The mother, having already contributed so much more to the creation of this particular child than the father, might value the result of her effort in proportion. And her pride at what she has accomplished in giving birth can be appropriately that much greater. She has indeed "accomplished" far more than has the father.

So even if instincts or desires to reproduce oneself or one's genes, or to create another human being, are equally powerful among men and women, a given child is, from the father's biological standpoint, much more incidental and interchangeable: any child out of the potential thousands he might sire would do. For the mother, on the other hand, if this particular child does not survive and grow, her chances for biological reproduction are reduced to a much greater degree. To suggest that men may think of their children as replaceable is offensive to many men, and women. Whether such biological facts as those I have mentioned have any significant effect on parental attitudes is not known. But arguments from biological facts to social attitudes, and even to moral norms, have a very long history and are still highly popular; we should be willing to examine the sorts of unfamiliar arguments I have suggested that can be drawn from biological facts. *If* anatomy is destiny, men may be "naturally" more indifferent toward particular children than has been thought.

Since men, then, do not give birth, and do not experience the responsibility, the pain, and momentousness of childbirth, they lack the particular motives to value the child that may spring from this capacity and this fact. Of course, many other reasons for valuing a child are felt by both parents, by care-takers of either gender, and by those who are not parents, but the motives discussed, and others arising from giving birth, may be morally significant. The long years of child care may provide stronger motives for valuing a child than do the relatively short months of pregnancy and hours of childbirth. The decisions and sacrifices involved in bringing up a child can be more affecting than those normally experienced in giving birth to a child. So the possibility for men to acquire such motives through child care may out-weigh any long-term differences in motivation be-tween women and men. But it might yet remain that the person responsible for giving birth would con-tinue to have a greater sense of responsibility for how the child develops, and stronger feelings of care and concern for the child.

That adoptive parents can feel as great concern for and attachment to their children as can biological parents may indicate that the biological components in valuing children are relatively modest in impor-tance. However, to the extent that biological compo-nents are significant, they would seem to affect men and women in different ways.

Morality and Human Tendencies

So far, I have been describing possible feelings rather than attaching any moral value to them. That children are valued does not mean that they are valuable, and if mothers have a natural tendency to value their children, it does not follow that they ought to. But if feelings are taken to be relevant to moral theory, the feelings of valuing the child, like the feelings of empathy for other persons in pain, may be of moral significance.

To the extent that a moral theory takes natural male tendencies into account, it would at least be reasonable to take natural female tendencies into account. Traditional moral theories often suppose it is legitimate for individuals to maximize self-interest, or satisfy their preferences, within certain constraints based on the equal rights of others. If it can be shown that the tendency to want to pursue individual self-interest is a stronger tendency among men than among women, this would certainly be relevant to an evaluation of such theory. And if it could be shown that a tendency to value children and a desire to foster the developing capabilities of the particular others for whom we care is a stronger tendency among women

than among men, this too would be relevant in evalu-ating moral theories.

The assertion that women have a tendency to value children is still different from the assertion that they ought to. Noddings speaks often of the "natural" caring of mothers for children.[22] I do not intend to deal here with the disputed empirical question of whether human mothers do or do not have a strong natural tendency to love their children. And I am certainly not claiming that natural mothers have greater skills or excellences in raising children than have others, including, perhaps, men. I am trying, rather, to explore possible "reasons" for mothers to value children, reasons that might be different for mothers and potential mothers than they would be for anyone else asking the question: why should we value human beings? And it does seem that certain possible reasons for valuing living human beings are present for mothers in ways that are different from what they would be for others. The reason, if it is one, that the child should be valued because I have suf-fered to give the child life is different from the reason, if it is one, that the child should be valued because someone unlike me suffered to give the child life. And both of these reasons are different from the reason, if it is one, that the child should be valued because the continued existence of the child satisfies a preference of a parent, or because the child is a bearer of univer-sal rights, or has the capacity to experience pleasure.

Many moral theories, and fields dependent on them such as economics, employ the assumption that to increase the utility of individuals is a good thing to do. But if asked *why* it is a good thing to increase utility, or satisfy desire, or produce pleasure, or *why* doing so counts as a good reason for something, it is very difficult to answer. The claim is taken as a kind of starting assumption for which no *further* reason can be given. It seems to rest on a view that people seek pleasure, or that we can recognize pleasure as having intrinsic value. But if women recognize quite different assumptions as more likely to be valid, that would certainly be of importance to ethics. We might then take it as one of our starting assumptions that creating good relations of care and concern and trust between ourselves and our children, and creating social arrangements in which children will be valued and well cared for, are more important than maximiz-ing individual utilities. And the moral theories that might be compatible with such assumptions might be very different from those with which we are familiar.

A number of feminists have independently declared their rejection of the Abraham myth.[23] We do not approve the sacrifice of children out of religious duty. Perhaps, for those capable of giving birth, reasons to value the actual life of the born will, in general, seem to be better than reasons justifying the sacrifice of such life.[24] This may reflect an accordance of priority to caring for particular others over abstract principle. From the perspectives of Rousseau, of Kant, of Hegel, and of Kohlberg, this is a deficiency of women. But from a perspective of what is needed for late twentieth century survival, it may suggest a superior morality. Only feminist moral theory can offer a satisfactory evaluation of such suggestions, because only feminist moral theory can adequately understand the alternatives to traditional moral theory that the experience of women requires.

Notes

1. See Virginia Held, *Rights and Goods: Justifying Social Action* (New York: Free Press, Macmillan, 1984).
2. See Genevieve Lloyd, *The Man of Reason: "Male" and "Female" in Western Philosophy* (Minneapolis: University of Minnesota Press, 1984).
3. Virginia Held, *Rights and Goods,* 272. See also V. Held, "The Political 'Testing' of Moral Theories," *Midwest Studies in Philosophy* 7 (1982): 343–363.
4. For discussion, see especially Nancy Hartsock, *Money, Sex, and Power* (New York: Longman, 1983), chaps. 10, 11.
5. Lawrence Kohlberg's studies of what he claimed to be developmental stages in moral reasoning suggested that girls progress less well and less far than boys through these stages. See his *The Philosophy of Moral Development* (San Francisco: Harper & Row, 1981); and L. Kohlberg and R. Kramer, "Continuities and Discontinuities in Child and Adult Moral Development," *Human Development* 12 (1969): 93–120. James R. Rest, on the other hand, claims in his study of adolescents in 1972 and 1974 that "none of the male-female differences on the Defining Issues Test . . . and on the Comprehension or Attitudes tests were significant." See his "Longitudinal Study of the Defining Issues Test of Moral Judgment: A Strategy for Analyzing Developmental Change," *Developmental Psychology* (Nov. 1975): 738–748; quotation at 741. Carol Gilligan's *In a Different Voice* (Cambridge: Harvard University Press, 1982) suggests that girls and women tend to organize their thinking about moral problems somewhat differently from boys and men; her subsequent work supports the view that whether people tend to construe moral problems in terms of rules of justice or in terms of caring relationships is at present somewhat associated with gender (Carol Gilligan, address at Conference on Women and Moral Thought, SUNY Stony Brook, March 21, 1985). Other studies have shown that females are significantly more inclined than males to cite compassion and sympathy as reasons for their moral positions; see Constance Boucher Holstein, "Irreversible, Stepwise Sequence in the Development of Moral Judgment: A Longitudinal Study of Males and Females," *Child Development* 47, no. 1 (March 1976): 51–61.
6. For suggestions on how Gilligan's stages, like Kohlberg's, might be thought to be historically and culturally, rather than more universally, based, see Linda Nicholson, "Women, Morality, and History," *Social Research* 50, no. 3 (Autumn 1983): 514–536.
7. See, e.g., Debra Nails, "Social-Scientific Sexism: Gilligan's Mismeasure of Man," *Social Research* 50, no. 3 (Autumn 1983): 643–664.
8. I have discussed this in a paper that has gone through several major revisions and changes of title, from its presentation at a conference at Loyola University on April 18, 1983, to its discussion at Dartmouth College, April 2, 1984. I will refer to it as "Non-Contractual Society: A Feminist Interpretation." See also Carole Pateman, "The Fraternal Social Contract: Some Observations on Patriarchy," paper presented at American Political Science Association meeting, Aug. 30–Sept. 2, 1984, and "The Shame of the Marriage Contract," in *Women's Views of the Political World of Men*, edited by Judith Hicks Stiehm (Dobbs Ferry, NY: Transnational Publishers, 1984).
9. For discussion, see especially Nancy Hartsock, *Money, Sex, and Power*.
10. Ibid., 39.
11. See Held, *Rights and Goods*, chap. 5.
12. Ibid., chap. 11.
13. Lawrence A. Blum, *Friendship, Altruism and Morality* (London: Routledge & Kegan Paul, 1980), 1.
14. Owen J. Flanagan, Jr., and Jonathan E. Adler, "Impartiality and Particularity," *Social Research* 50, no. 3 (Autumn 1983): 576–596.
15. See, e.g., Nel Noddings, *Caring: A Feminine Approach to Ethics and Moral Education* (Berkeley: University of California Press, 1984), 91–94.
16. Ibid., 91–94.
17. Participants in the conference on Women and Moral Theory offered the helpful term "domain relativism" for the version of this view that I defended.
18. See, e.g., Virginia Held, "The Obligations of Mothers and Fathers," reprinted in *Mothering: Essays in Feminist Theory,* edited by Joyce Trebilcot (Totowa, NJ: Rowman & Allanheld, 1984).

19. See Eva Kittay, "Womb Envy: An Explanatory Concept," in *Mothering,* edited by Joyce Trebilcot. To overcome the pernicious aspects of the "womb envy" she skillfully identifies and describes, Kittay argues that boys should be taught that their "procreative contribution is of equal significance" (p. 123). While boys should certainly be told the truth, the truth may remain that, as she states elsewhere, "there is the . . . awesome quality of creation itself—the transmutation performed by the parturient woman" (p. 99).

20. This point was made by Marcia Baron in correspondence with me.

21. In exploring the values involved in birth and mothering, we need to develop views that include women who do not give birth. As Margaret Simons writes, "we must define a feminist maternal ethic that supports a woman's right not to have children." See Margaret A. Simons, "Motherhood, Feminism and Identity," *Hypatia, Women's Studies International Forum* 7, 5 (1984): 353.

22. E.g., Noddings, *Caring,* 31, 43, 49.

23. See Gilligan, *In a Different Voice,* 104; Held, "Non-Contractual Society: A Feminist Interpretation"; and Noddings, *Caring,* 43.

24. That some women enthusiastically send their sons off to war may be indicative of a greater than usual acceptance of male myths rather than evidence against this claim, since the enthusiasm seems most frequent in societies where women have the least influence in the formation of prevailing religious and other beliefs.

The Need for More than Justice

Annette Baier

Study Questions

1. Who are the challengers to the supremacy of justice as a social virtue, and why does Baier suggest that this is surprising?

2. What kind of ethic or perspective (influenced by the work of Carol Gilligan) is contrasted with the ethics of justice?

3. According to Gilligan, what two evils of childhood parallel the two dimensions of moral development she describes?

4. What is the tradition contrasted with Gilligan's position, according to Baier? How do Kohlberg, Piaget, and Kant exemplify this tradition?

5. From her interview studies, what did Gilligan find about women's moral experience and moral maturity?

6. Why do some believe that it will not do to say that an ethic of care is an option that only some might choose?

7. How has the tradition of rights worked both against and for women?

8. According to Baier, what is wrong with the view that stresses relationships of equality?

9. What also does Baier believe is wrong with the stress this tradition places on free choice?

10. What is the fourth feature of the Gilligan challenge to liberal orthodoxy?

11. What, then, does Gilligan think is the best moral theory?

Annette Baier, "The Need for More than Justice," *Canadian Journal of Philosophy,* supplementary vol. 13., Marshal Hanen and Kai Nielsen (Eds.) (Calgary: University of Calgary Press, 1988), 41–56. Reprinted with permission of the author and publisher.

In recent decades in North American social and moral philosophy, alongside the development and discussion of widely influential theories of justice, taken as Rawls takes it as the "first virtue of social institutions,"[1] there has been a counter-movement gathering strength, one coming from some interesting sources. For some of the most outspoken of the diverse group who have in a variety of ways been challenging the assumed supremacy of justice among the moral and social virtues are members of those sections of society whom one might have expected to be especially aware of the supreme importance of justice, namely blacks and women. Those who have only recently won recognition of their equal rights, who have only recently seen the correction or partial correction of long-standing racist and sexist injustices to their race and sex, are among the philosophers now suggesting that justice is only one virtue among many, and one that may need the presence of the others in order to deliver its own undenied value. Among these philosophers of the philosophical counterculture, as it were—but an increasingly large counterculture—I include Alasdair MacIntyre,[2] Michael Stocker,[3] Lawrence Blum,[4] Michael Slote,[5] Laurence Thomas,[6] Claudia Card,[7] Alison Jaggar,[8] Susan Wolf[9] and a whole group of men and women, myself included, who have been influenced by the writings of Harvard educational psychologist Carol Gilligan, whose book *In a Different Voice* (Harvard 1982; hereafter D.V.) caused a considerable stir both in the popular press and, more slowly, in the philosophical journals.[10]

Let me say quite clearly at this early point that there is little disagreement that justice is *a* social value of very great importance, and injustice an evil. Nor would those who have worked on theories of justice want to deny that other things matter besides justice. Rawls, for example, incorporates the value of freedom into his account of justice, so that denial of basic freedoms counts as injustice. Rawls also leaves room for a wider theory of right, of which the theory of justice is just a part. Still, he does claim that justice is the "first" virtue of social institutions, and it is only that claim about priority that I think has been challenged. It is easy to exaggerate the differences of view that exist, and I want to avoid that. The differences are as much in emphasis as in substance, or we can say that they are differences in tone of voice. But these differences do tend to make a difference in approaches to a wide range of topics not just in moral theory but in areas like medical ethics, where the discussion used to be conducted in terms of patients' rights, of informed consent, and so on, but now tends to get conducted in an enlarged moral vocabulary, which draws on what Gilligan calls the ethics of *care* as well as that of *justice*.

For "care" is the new buzz-word. It is not, as Shakespeare's Portia demanded, mercy that is to season justice, but a less authoritarian humanitarian supplement, a felt concern for the good of others and for community with them. The "cold jealous virtue of justice" (Hume) is found to be too cold, and it is "warmer" more communitarian virtues and social

ideals that are being called in to supplement it. One might say that liberty and equality are being found inadequate without fraternity, except that "fraternity" will be quite the wrong word, if as Gilligan initially suggested, it is *women* who perceive this value most easily. ("Sorority" will do no better, since it is too exclusive, and English has no gender-neuter word for the mutual concern of siblings.) She has since modified this claim, allowing that there are two perspectives on moral and social issues that we all tend to alternate between, and which are not always easy to combine, one of them what she called the justice perspective, the other the care perspective. It is increasingly obvious that there are many male philosophical spokespersons for the care perspective (Laurence Thomas, Lawrence Blum, Michael Stocker) so that it cannot be the prerogative of women. Nevertheless Gilligan still wants to claim that women are most unlikely to take only the justice perspective, as some men are claimed to, at least until some mid-life crisis jolts them into "bifocal" moral vision (see D.V., ch. 6).

Gilligan in her book did not offer any explanatory theory of why there should be any difference between female and male moral outlook, but she did tend to link the naturalness to women of the care perspective with their role as primary caretakers of young children, that is with their parental and specifically maternal role. . . . Later, both in "The Conquistador and the Dark Continent: Reflections on the Nature of Love" (*Daedalus* Summer 1984), and "The Origins of Morality in Early Childhood" (in press), she develops this explanation. She postulates two evils that any infant may become aware of, the evil of detachment or isolation from others whose love one needs, and the evil of relative powerlessness and weakness. Two dimensions of moral development are thereby set—one aimed at achieving satisfying community with others, the other aiming at autonomy or equality of power. The relative predominance of one over the other development will depend both upon the relative salience of the two evils in early childhood, and on early and later reinforcement or discouragement in attempts made to guard against these two evils. This provides the germs of a theory about *why,* given current customs of childrearing, it should be mainly women who are not content with only the moral outlook that she calls the justice perspective, necessary though that was and is seen by them to have been to their hard won liberation from sexist oppression. They, like the blacks, used the language of rights and justice to change their own social position, but nevertheless see limitations in that language, according to Gilligan's findings as a moral psychologist. She reports their discontent with the individualist more or less Kantian moral framework that dominates Western moral theory and which influenced moral psychologists such as Lawrence Kohlberg,[11] to whose conception of moral maturity she seeks an alternative. Since the target of Gilligan's criticism is the dominant Kantian tradition, and since that has been the target also of moral philosophers as diverse in their own views as Bernard Williams,[12] Alasdair MacIntyre, Philippa Foot,[13] Susan Wolf, Claudia Card, her book is of interest as much for its attempt to articulate an alternative to the Kantian justice perspective as for its implicit raising of the question of male bias in Western moral theory, especially liberal democratic theory. For whether the supposed blind spots of that outlook are due to male bias, or to non-parental bias, or to early traumas of powerlessness or to early resignation to "detachment" from others, we need first to be persuaded that they *are* blind spots before we will have any interest in their cause and cure. Is justice blind to important social values, or at least only one-eyed? What is it that comes into view from the "care perspective" that is not seen from the "justice perspective"?

Gilligan's position here is most easily described by contrasting it with that of Kohlberg, against which she developed it. Kohlberg, influenced by Piaget and the Kantian philosophical tradition as developed by John Rawls, developed a theory about typical moral development which saw it to progress from a pre-conventional level, where what is seen to matter is pleasing or not offending parental authority-figures, through a conventional level in which the child tries to fit in with a group, such as a school community, and conform to its standards and rules, to a post-conventional critical level, in which such conventional rules are subjected to tests, and where those tests are of a utilitarian, or, eventually, a Kantian sort—namely ones that require respect for each person's individual rational will, or autonomy, and conformity to any implicit social contract such wills are deemed to have made, or to any hypothetical ones they would make if thinking clearly. What was found when Kohlberg's questionnaires (mostly by verbal response to verbally sketched moral dilemmas) were applied to female as well as male subjects, Gilligan reports, is that the girls and women not only scored generally lower than the boys and men, but tended to *revert* to the lower stage of the conventional level even after briefly (usually in adolescence) attaining the post-conventional level. Piaget's finding that girls were deficient in "the legal sense" was confirmed.

These results led Gilligan to wonder if there might not be a quite different pattern of development to be discerned, at least in female subjects. She therefore conducted interviews designed to elicit not just how far advanced the subjects were towards an appreciation of the nature and importance of Kantian autonomy, but also to find out what the subjects themselves saw as progress or lack of it, what conceptions of moral maturity they came to possess by the time they were adults. She found that although the Kohlberg version of moral maturity as respect for fellow persons, and for their rights as equals (rights including that of free association), did seem shared by many young men, the women tended to speak in a different voice about morality itself and about moral maturity. To quote Gilligan, "Since the reality of interconnexion is experienced by women as given rather than freely contracted, they arrive at an understanding of life that reflects the limits of autonomy and control. As a result, women's development delineates the path not only to a less violent life but also to a maturity realized by interdependence and taking care" (D.V., 172). She writes that there is evidence that "women perceive and construe social reality differently from men, and that these differences center around experiences of attachment and separation . . . because women's sense of integrity appears to be intertwined with an ethics of care, so that to see themselves as women is to see themselves in a relationship of connexion, the major changes in women's lives would seem to involve changes in the understanding and activities of care" (D.V., 171). She contrasts this progressive understanding of care, from merely pleasing others to helping and nurturing, with the sort of progression that is involved in Kohlberg's stages, a progression in the understanding, not of mutual care, but of mutual *respect,* where this has its Kantian overtones of distance, even of some fear for the respected, and where personal autonomy and *independence,* rather than more satisfactory interdependence, are the paramount values.

This contrast, one cannot but feel, is one which Gilligan might have used the Marxist language of alienation to make. For the main complaint about the Kantian version of a society with its first virtue justice, construed as respect for equal rights to formal goods such as having contracts kept, due process, equal opportunity including opportunity to participate in political activities leading to policy and law-making, to basic liberties of speech, free association and assembly, religious worship, is that none of these goods do much to ensure that the people who have and mutually respect such rights will have any other relationships to one another than the minimal relationship needed to keep such a "civil society" going. They may well be lonely, driven to suicide, apathetic about their work and about participation in political processes, find their lives meaningless and have no wish to leave offspring to face the same meaningless existence. Their rights, and respect for rights, are quite compatible with very great misery, and misery whose causes are not just individual misfortunes and psychic sickness, but social and moral impoverishment. . . .

Let me try to summarize the main differences, as I see them, between on the one hand Gilligan's version of moral maturity and the sort of social structures that would encourage, express and protect it, and on the other the orthodoxy she sees herself to be challenging. I shall from now on be giving my own interpretation of the significance of her challenges, not merely reporting them.[14] The most obvious point is the challenge to the individualism of the Western tradition, to the fairly entrenched belief in the possibility and desirability of each person pursuing his own good in his own way, constrained only by a minimal formal common good, namely a working legal apparatus that enforces contracts and protects individuals from undue interference by others. Gilligan reminds us that noninterference can, especially for the relatively powerless, such as the very young, amount to neglect, and even between equals can be isolating and alienating. On her less individualist version of individuality, it becomes defined by responses to dependency and to patterns of interconnexion, both chosen and unchosen. It is not something a person *has,* and which she then chooses relationships to suit, but something that develops out of a series of dependencies and interdependencies, and responses to them. This conception of individuality is not flatly at odds with, say, Rawls' Kantian one, but there is at least a difference of tone of voice between speaking as Rawls does of each of us having our own rational life plan, which a just society's moral traffic rules will allow us to follow, and which may or may not include close

association with other persons, and speaking as Gilligan does of a satisfactory life as involving "progress of affiliative relationship" (D.V., 170) where "the concept of identity expands to include the experience of interconnexion" (D.V., 173). Rawls can allow that progress to Gilligan-style moral maturity may be *a* rational life plan, but not a moral constraint on every life-pattern. The trouble is that it will not do just to say "let this version of morality be an optional extra. Let us agree on the essential minimum, that is on justice and rights, and let whoever wants to go further and cultivate this more demanding ideal of responsibility and care." For, first, it cannot be satisfactorily cultivated without closer cooperation from others than respect for rights and justice will ensure, and, second, the encouragement of some to cultivate it while others do not could easily lead to exploitation of those who do. It obviously *has* suited some in most societies well enough that others take on the responsibilities of care (for the sick, the helpless, the young) leaving them free to pursue their own less altruistic goods. Volunteer forces of those who accept an ethic of care, operating within a society where the power is exercised and the institutions designed, redesigned, or maintained by those who accept a less communal ethic of minimally constrained self-advancement, will not be the solution. The liberal individualists may be able to "tolerate" the more communally minded, if they keep the liberals' rules, but it is not so clear that the more communally minded can be content with just those rules, not be content to be tolerated and possibly exploited.

For the moral tradition which developed the concept of rights, autonomy and justice is the same tradition that provided "justifications" of the oppression of those whom the primary right-holders depended on to do the sort of work they themselves preferred not to do. The domestic work was left to women and slaves, and the liberal morality for right-holders was surreptitiously supplemented by a different set of demands made on domestic workers. As long as women could be got to assume responsibility for the care of home and children, and to train their children to continue the sexist system, the liberal morality could continue to be the official morality, by turning its eyes away from the contribution made by those it excluded. The long unnoticed moral proletariat were the domestic workers, mostly female. Rights have usually been for the privileged. Talking about laws, and the rights those laws recognize and protect, does not in itself ensure that the group of legislators and rights-holders will not be restricted to some elite. Bills of rights have usually been proclamations of the rights of some in-group, barons, landowners, males, whites, non-foreigners. The "justice perspective," and the legal sense that goes with it, are shadowed by their patriarchal past. What did Kant, the great prophet of autonomy, say in his moral theory about women? He said they were incapable of legislation, not fit to vote, that they needed the guidance of more "rational" males.[15] Autonomy was not for them, only for first class, really rational, persons. It is ironic that Gilligan's original findings in a way confirm Kant's views—it seems that autonomy really may not be for women. Many of them reject that ideal (D.V., 48), and have been found not as good at making rules as are men. But where Kant concludes—"so much the worse for women," we can conclude—"so much the worse for the male fixation on the special skill of drafting legislation, for the bureaucratic mentality of rule worship, and for the male exaggeration of the importance of independence over mutual interdependence."

It is however also true that the moral theories that made the concept of a person's rights central were not just the instruments for excluding some persons, but also the instruments used by those who demanded that more and more persons be included in the favored group. Abolitionists, reformers, women, used the language of rights to assert their claims to inclusion in the group of full members of a community. The tradition of liberal moral theory has in fact developed so as to include the women it had for so long excluded, to include the poor as well as rich, blacks and whites, and so on. Women like Mary Wollstonecraft used the male moral theories to good purpose. So we should not be wholly ungrateful for those male moral theories, for all their objectionable earlier content. They were undoubtedly patriarchal, but they also contained the seeds of the challenge, or antidote, to this patriarchal poison.

But when we transcend the values of the Kantians, we should not forget the facts of history—that those values were the values of the oppressors of women. The Christian church, whose version of the moral law Aquinas codified, in his very legalistic moral theory, still insists on the maleness of the God it worships, and jealously reserves for males all the most powerful positions in its hierarchy. Its patriarchical prejudice is open and avowed. In the secular moral theories of men, the sexist patriarchal prejudice is today often less open, not as blatant as it is in Aquinas, in the later natural law tradition, and in Kant . . . , but is often still there. No moral theorist today would say that women are unfit to vote, to make laws, or to rule a nation without powerful male advisors (as most queens had), but the old doctrines die hard. . . . Traces of the old patriarchal poison still remain in even the best contemporary moral theorizing. Few may actually say that women's place is in the home, but there is much muttering, when unemployment figures rise, about how the relatively recent flood of women into the work force complicates the problem, as if it would be a good thing if women just went back home whenever unemployment rises, to leave the available jobs for the men. We still do not really have a wide acceptance of the equal right of women to employment outside the home. Nor do we have wide acceptance of the equal duty of men to perform those domestic tasks which in no way depend on special female anatomy, namely cooking, cleaning, and the care of weaned children. All sorts of stories (maybe true stories), about children's need for one "primary" parent, who must be the mother if the mother breast feeds the child, shore up the unequal division of domestic responsibility between mothers and fathers, wives and husbands. If we are really to transvalue the values of our patriarchal past, we need to rethink all of those assumptions, really test those psychological theories. And how will men ever develop an understanding of the "ethics of care" if they continue to be shielded or kept from that experience of caring for a dependent child, which complements the experience we all have had of being cared for as dependent children? These experiences form the natural background for the development of moral maturity as Gilligan's women.

Exploitation aside, why would women, once liberated, not be content to have their version of morality merely tolerated? Why should they not see themselves as voluntarily, for their own reasons, taking on *more* than the liberal rules demand, while having no quarrel with the content of those rules themselves, nor with their remaining the only ones that are expected to be generally obeyed? To see why, we need to move on to three more differences between the Kantian liberals (usually contractarians) and their critics. These concern the relative weight put on relationships between equals, and the relative weight put on freedom of choice, and on the authority of intellect over emotions. It is a typical feature of the dominant moral theories and traditions . . . that relationships between equals or those who are deemed equal in some important sense, have been the relations that morality is concerned primarily to regulate. Relationships between those who are clearly unequal in power, such as parents and children, earlier and later generations in relation to one another, states and citizens, doctors and patients, the well and the ill, large states and small states, have had to be shunted to the bottom of the agenda, and then dealt with by some sort of "promotion" of the weaker so that an appearance of virtual equality is achieved. Citizens collectively become equal to states, children are treated as adults-to-be, the ill and dying are treated as continuers of their earlier more potent selves, so that their "rights" could be seen as the rights of equals. This pretense of an equality that is in fact absent may often lead to desirable protection of the weaker, or more dependent. But it somewhat masks the question of what our moral relationships *are* to those who are our superiors or our inferiors in power. A more realistic acceptance of the fact that we begin as helpless children, that at almost every point of our lives we deal with both the more and the less helpless, that equality of power and interdependency, between two persons or groups, is rare and hard to recognize when it does occur, might lead us to a more direct approach to questions concerning the design of institutions structuring these relationships between unequals (families, schools, hospitals, armies) and of the morality of our dealings with the more and the less powerful. . . .

The recognition of the importance for all parties of relations between those who are and cannot but be unequal, both of these relations in themselves and for their effect on personality formation and so on other relationships, goes along with a recognition of the plain fact that not all morally important relationships can or should be freely chosen. So far I have discussed three reasons women have not to be content to pursue their own values within the framework of the liberal morality. The first was its dubious record. The second was its inattention to relations of inequality or its pretense of equality. The third reason is its exaggeration of the scope of choice, or its inattention to unchosen relations. Showing up the partial myth of equality among actual members of a community, and of the undesirability of trying to pretend that we are treating all of them as equals, tends to go along with

an exposure of the companion myth that moral obligations arise from freely *chosen* associations between such equals. Vulnerable future generations do not choose their dependence on earlier generations. The unequal infant does not choose its place in a family or nation, nor is it treated as free to do as it likes until some association is freely entered into. Nor do its parents always choose their parental role, or freely assume their parental responsibilities any more than we choose our power to affect the conditions in which later generations will live. Gilligan's attention to the version of morality and moral maturity found in women, many of whom had faced a choice of whether or not to have an abortion, and who had at some point become mothers, is attention to the perceived inadequacy of the language of rights to help in such choices or to guide them in their parental role. It would not be much of an exaggeration to call the Gilligan "different voice" the voice of the potential parents. The emphasis on care goes with a recognition of the often unchosen nature of the responsibilities of those who give care, both of children who care for their aged or infirm parents, and of parents who care for the children they in fact have. Contract soon ceases to seem the paradigm source of moral obligation once we attend to parental responsibility, and justice as a virtue of social institutions will come to seem at best only first equal with the virtue, whatever its name, that ensures that each new generation is made appropriately welcome and prepared for their adult lives.

. . . The fourth feature of the Gilligan challenge to liberal orthodoxy is a challenge to its typical *rationalism*, or intellectualism, to its assumption that we need not worry what passions persons have, as long as their rational wills can control them. This Kantian picture of a controlling reason dictating to possibly unruly passions also tends to seem less useful when we are led to consider what sort of person we need to fill the role of parent, or indeed want in any close relationship. It might be important for father figures to have rational control over their violent urges to beat to death the children whose screams enrage them, but more than control of such nasty passions seems needed in the mother or primary parent, or parent-substitute, by most psychological theories. They need to love their children, not just to control their irritation. So the emphasis in Kantian theories on rational control of emotions, rather than on cultivating desirable forms of emotion, is challenged by Gilligan, along with the challenge to the assumption of the centrality of autonomy, or relations between equals, and of freely chosen relations. . . .

It is clear, I think, that the best moral theory has to be a cooperative product of women and men, has to harmonize justice and care. The morality it theorizes about is after all for all persons, for men and for women, and will need their combined insights. As Gilligan said (D.V., 174), what we need now is a "marriage" of the old male and the newly articulated female insights. If she is right about the special moral aptitudes of women, it will most likely be the women who propose the marriage, since they are the ones with more natural empathy, with the better diplomatic skills, the ones more likely to shoulder responsibility and take moral initiative, and the ones who find it easiest to empathize and care about how the other party feels. Then, once there is this union of male and female moral wisdom, we maybe can teach each other the moral skills each gender currently lacks, so that the gender difference in moral outlook that Gilligan found will slowly become less marked.

Notes

1. John Rawls, *A Theory of Justice* (Harvard University Press).
2. Alasdair MacIntyre, *After Virtue* (Notre Dame: Notre Dame University Press).
3. Michael Stocker, "The Schizophrenia of Modern Ethical Theories," *Journal of Philosophy* 73, 14, 453–466; and "Agent and Other: Against Ethical Universalism," *Australasian Journal of Philosophy* 54, 206–220.
4. Lawrence Blum, *Friendship, Altruism and Morality* (London: Routledge & Kegan Paul, 1980).
5. Michael Slote, *Goods and Virtues* (Oxford: Oxford University Press, 1983).
6. Laurence Thomas, "Love and Morality," in *Epistemology and Sociobiology,* James Fetzer (Ed.) (1985); and "Justice, Happiness and Self Knowledge," *Canadian Journal of Philosophy* (March 1986). Also "Beliefs and the Motivation to be Just," *American Philosophical Quarterly* 22 (4), 347–352.
7. Claudia Card, "Mercy," *Philosophical Review* 81, 1; and "Gender and Moral Luck," forthcoming.
8. Alison Jaggar, *Feminist Politics and Human Nature* (London: Rowman & Allenheld, 1983).
9. Susan Wolf, "Moral Saints," *Journal of Philosophy* 79 (August 1982), 419–439.
10. For a helpful survey article see Owen Flanagan and Kathryn Jackson, "Justice, Care & Gender: The Kohlberg-Gilligan Debate Revisited," *Ethics.*
11. Lawrence Kohlberg, *Essays in Moral Development,* vols. I & II (New York: Harper & Row, 1981, 1984).
12. Bernard Williams, *Ethics and the Limits of Philosophy* (Cambridge: Cambridge University Press, 1985).
13. Philippa Foot, *Virtues and Vices* (Berkeley: University of California Press, 1978).
14. I have previously written about the significance of her findings for moral philosophy in "What Do Women Want in a Moral Theory?" *Nous* 19 (March 1985); "Trust and Antitrust," *Ethics* 96 (1986); and in "Hume the Women's Moral Theorist?" in *Women and Moral Theory,* Kittay and Meyers (Eds.), forthcoming.
15. Immanuel Kant, *Metaphysics of Morals,* sec. 46.

Review Exercises

1. How do the two examples given of male and female reasoning exemplify the various supposed characteristics of female and male ethical perspectives?
2. Contrast the research findings of Carol Gilligan and Lawrence Kohlberg on male and female moral development.
3. According to Freud, why were women supposed to be morally deficient?
4. What three types of explanation for the male–female difference in morality have been given?
5. How does Gilligan's duck and rabbit example help explain the difference between the two moral perspectives?
6. Describe the psychosexual development explanation of female and male morality.
7. Summarize Caroline Whitbeck's biological explanation of the difference.
8. How has the difference been explained in terms of "maternal thinking"?
9. Describe the basic issues involved in trying to decide if one type of morality is better than another.
10. Describe some of the history and characteristics of feminist thought.

Selected Bibliography

Antony, Louise, and Charlotte Witt (Eds.). *A Mind of One's Own: Feminist Essays on Reason and Objectivity.* Boulder, CO: Westview, 1992.

Bartkey, Sandra Lee. *Femininity and Domination: Studies in the Phenomenology of Oppression.* New York: Routledge, 1990.

Benhabib, Seyla. *Situating the Self*. New York: Routledge, Chapman & Hall, 1992.

Bishop, Sharon, and Marjorie Weinzweig. *Philosophy and Women*. Belmont, CA: Wadsworth, 1993.

Card, Claudia (Ed.). *Feminist Ethics*. Lawrence: University of Kansas Press, 1991.

Chodorow, Nancy. *The Reproduction of Mothering: Psychoanalysis and the Sociology of Gender.* Los Angeles: University of California Press, 1978.

Code, Lorraine, Sheila Mullett, and Christine Overall (Eds.). *Feminist Perspectives*. Toronto: University of Toronto Press, 1989.

Cole, Eve Browning, and Susan Coultrap-McQuin (Eds.). *Exploration in Feminist Ethics*. Bloomington: Indiana University Press, 1992.

De Beauvoir, Simone. *The Second Sex*. H. M. Parshley (Trans.). New York: Knopf, 1953.

Dinnerstein, Dorothy. *The Mermaid and the Minotaur.* New York: Harper Colophon, 1976.

Dworkin, Andrea. *Pornography: Men Possessing Women*. New York: Perigree, 1981.

Eisenstein, Zillah. *The Radical Future of Liberal Feminism*. New York: Longman, 1981.

Elshtain, Jean Bethke. *Public Man, Private Woman*. Princeton, NJ: Princeton University Press, 1981.

Fisher, Dexter (Ed.). *The Third Woman: Minority Women Writers of the United States*. Boston: Houghton Mifflin, 1980.

Friedan, Betty. *The Feminine Mystique*. New York: Norton, 1963.

Frye, Marilyn. *The Politics of Reality*. Trumansburg, NY: Crossing, 1983.

Garry, Ann, and Marilyn Pearsall (Eds.). *Women, Knowledge, and Reality: Explorations in Feminist Philosophy*. Boston: Unwin Hyman, 1989.

Gilligan, Carol, Janie Victoria Ward, and Jill McLean Taylor (Eds.). *Mapping the Moral Domain*. Cambridge, MA: Harvard University Press, 1988.

Gilligan, Carol. *In a Different Voice*. Cambridge, MA: Harvard University Press, 1982.

Griffin, Susan. *Woman and Nature: The Roaring Inside Her.* New York: Harper & Row, 1978.

Grimshaw, Jean. *Philosophy and Feminist Thinking*. Minneapolis: University of Minnesota Press, 1986.

Hanen, Marsha, and Kai Nielsen (Eds.). *Science, Morality and Feminist Theory*. Calgary: University of Calgary Press, 1987.

Hill, S., and M. Weinzweig (Eds.). *Philosophy and Women*. Belmont, CA: Wadsworth, 1978.

Hoagland, Sarah Lucia. *Lesbian Ethics*. Palo Alto, CA: Institute of Lesbian Studies, 1989.

Hooks, Bell. *Feminist Theory: From Margin to Center.* Boston: South End Press, 1984.

Irigaray, Luce. *Speculum of the Other Woman*. Gillian C. Gill (Trans.). Ithaca, NY: Cornell University Press, 1985.

Jaggar, Alison M. *Feminist Politics and Human Nature*. Totowa, NJ: Rowman & Allanheld, 1983.

Kittay, Eva Feder, and Diana T. Meyers. *Women and Moral Theory*. Totowa, NJ: Rowman & Littlefield, 1987.

Kohlberg, Lawrence, Charles Levine, and Alexandra Hewer. *Moral Stages: A Current Reformulation and Response to Critics*. Basel, Switzerland: Karger, 1983.

Kohlberg, Lawrence. *Essays in Moral Development*. San Francisco: Harper & Row, 1981.

Kourany, Janet, James Sterba, and Rosemarie Tong. *Feminist Frameworks*. Englewood Cliffs, NJ: Prentice-Hall, 1992.

Larrabee, Mary Jeanne (Ed.). *An Ethic of Care*. New York: Routledge, Chapman & Hall, 1993.

Maccoby, Eleanor, and Carol Jacklin. *The Psychology of Sex Differences*. Stanford, CA: Stanford University Press, 1974.

MacKinnon, Catharine. *Toward a Feminist Theory of the State*. Cambridge, MA: Harvard University Press, 1989.

May, Larry, and Robert A. Strikwerda. *Rethinking Masculinity*. Lanham, MD: Rowman & Littlefield, 1992.

Mill, John Stuart. *On the Subjection of Women*. New York: Frederick A. Stokes, 1911.

Mitchell, Juliet. *Psychoanalysis and Feminism*. New York: Vintage, 1975.

Noddings, Nel. *Caring: A Feminine Approach to Ethics and Moral Education*. Berkeley: University of California Press, 1984.

————. *Women and Evil*. Berkeley: University of California Press, 1989.

Okin, Susan Moller. *Women in Western Political Thought*. Princeton, NJ: Princeton University Press, 1979.

Pearsall, Marilyn. *Women and Values: Readings in Recent Feminist Philosophy,* 2nd ed. Belmont, CA: Wadsworth, 1993.

Raymond, Janice G. *A Passion for Friends: Toward a Philosophy of Female Affection*. Boston: Beacon, 1986.

Rich, Adrienne. *Of Woman Born*. New York: Norton, 1979.

Ruddick, Sara. *Maternal Thinking: Toward a Politics of Peace*. Boston: Beacon, 1989.

Sherwin, Susan. *No Longer Patient: Feminist Ethics and Health Care*. Philadelphia: Temple University Press, 1992.

Tong, Rosemarie. *Feminine and Feminist Ethics*. Belmont, CA: Wadsworth, 1993.

————. *Feminist Thought: A Comprehensive Introduction*. Boulder, CO: Westview, 1989.

Treblicot, Joyce (Ed.). *Mothering: Essays in Feminist Theory*. Totowa, NJ: Rowman & Allanheld, 1984.

Tuana, Nancy. *Woman and the History of Philosophy*. New York: Paragon House, 1992.

Part II

Ethical Issues

❧ 8 ❧

Euthanasia

Twenty years ago, a *New York Times* article reported the case of a judge before whom a disputed medical situation had been brought. The dispute concerned whether or not a woman's respirator could be disconnected. The judge was reported to have said, "This lady is dead, and has been dead, and they are keeping her alive artificially."[1] Did the judge believe that the woman was alive or dead? Presumably, she could not be both at the same time—at least not in the way we commonly regard life and death. I note this item to make the point that people, even judges, confuse questions about whether someone is dead or ought to be considered dead with other questions about whether it is permissible to do things that might hasten the person's death.

This confusion also has practical upshots. The judge's comment seems to imply that the woman's respirator could be disconnected because she was dead. However, we need not believe an individual to be dead to think it justifiable to disconnect her from a respirator and let her die. And only if someone is not dead can we then ask whether we may let him die. It seems useful here to think briefly about how we do determine whether someone is dead so as to distinguish this issue from other questions that are properly euthanasia questions.

Throughout history people have used various means to determine whether someone is dead,

and those means were a function of what they believed to be essential aspects of life. For example, if spirit was thought to be essential and was equated with a kind of thin air or breath, then to know if a person was living one would check for the presence or absence of this life breath. When heart function was regarded as the key element of life, and the heart was thought to be like a furnace, then people would feel the body to see if it was warm in order to know if the person was still living. Even today, with our better understanding of the function of the heart and other organs and organ systems, we have great difficulty with this issue. One reason for this is that we can artificially maintain certain body functions such as respiration (oxygenation of the blood) and blood circulation. Apart from such intervention and aids, the three major life systems—circulatory, respiratory, and nervous (including the brain)—fail together. If one ceases, the others also cease shortly thereafter.

Brain Death

Being able to give precise conditions and tests for determining whether or when an individual is dead was particularly problematic just two to three decades ago. It was problematic not only because of the arrival of new medical technologies, but also because surgeons had just begun doing human heart transplants. One could not take a heart for transplant from someone considered living, but only from someone declared dead. Was an individual whose heart function was being maintained artificially, but who had lost all brain function, considered living or dead? We still wonder about this today. In one odd case a man accused of murder pleaded guilty to a lesser charge of assault and battery claiming that even though the victim had lost all brain function his heart was still beating after the assault. The defendant argued that it was the doctor at Stanford Medical Center who had removed the heart for transplant and had killed this individual![2]

In 1968 an ad hoc committee of the Harvard Medical School was set up to establish criteria for determining when someone is dead. This committee determined that someone should be considered dead if she or he has permanently lost all detectable brain function. This means that if there was some nonconscious brain function, for example, or if the condition is temporary, then the individual would not be considered dead. Thus, various tests of reflexes and responsiveness were required to determine whether an individual had sustained a permanent and total loss of all brain function.[3] This condition is now known as *whole brain death* and is the primary criterion used for legal determination of death. This is true even when secondary criteria or tests such as loss of pulse are used, for it is assumed that lack of blood circulation for more than five to ten minutes results in brain cell death.

Whole brain death is distinguished from other conditions such as *persistent vegetative state* (PVS). In PVS, the individual has lost all cerebral cortex function but has retained good brain stem function. Many nonconscious functions that are based in that area of the brain—respiration and heart beat, facial reflexes and muscle control, and gag and swallowing reflexes—continue. Yet the individual in a permanent or persistent vegetative state has lost all conscious function. One reason for this condition is that the rate of oxygen use by the cerebral cortex is much higher than that by the brain stem, so if deprived of oxygen for some time these cells die much more quickly than those of the brain stem. The result is that the individual in this state will never regain consciousness but can often breathe naturally and needs no artificial aids for maintaining circulation. Such an individual does not feel pain because he or she cannot interpret it as such. Because the gag reflex is good, individuals in this condition can clear their airways and thus may live for many years. They go through wake and sleep cycles in which they have their eyes open and then closed. They are unconscious but "awake." In contrast, someone who is not totally brain dead but who is in a coma is unconscious but "asleep." Their brain stem functions poorly, and thus they do not live as long as someone in a persistent vegetative state.[4]

If we focus on the question of whether such individuals are dead or living, we can conclude two things. First, if someone is dead, euthanasia is not the question that needs to be addressed. In these cases disconnecting so-called life-sustaining equipment is not any kind of euthanasia. Second, if someone is not dead, we or that person may still judge that certain death-hastening actions or inactions are permissible. In thinking about euthanasia, we should discuss only those cases in which someone is not dead. Only then can questions arise about what we may rightly do or refrain from doing that may then result in their death.

Meaning and Types of Euthanasia

The term *euthanasia* has Greek roots and literally means "good death." While the term itself implies that there can be a good death, in itself it does not tell us when or under what conditions death is good. Is a good death one that comes suddenly or after some time to think about and prepare for it? Is it one that takes place at home and in familiar surroundings or one that occurs in a medical facility? Is it one that we know is coming and over which we have control or one that comes upon us without notice? We usually think of life as a good, so the more of it the better. But we also know that in some conditions life is very difficult and that some people have judged it too painful to continue. In these conditions, could we think of death as good or as the lesser of two evils?

Active and Passive Euthanasia

If you were approached by a pollster who asked whether you supported euthanasia, you would do well first to ask what she meant and to what kind of euthanasia she was referring. Some people limit the use of the term to cases called *active euthanasia*. In the past this was often called "mercy killing." These are cases in which we bring about death by our actions and instruments. This can be by the use of drugs or other death-causing devices.

In recent years, many doctors, as many as 96 percent, have withdrawn or withheld life-prolonging treatment for their patients. In some cases they have done this unilaterally, either without consulting patients or their family or even against their wishes.[5] The reasons given were that such treatment would not extend the patient's life for very long or that the patient's life during this time would be of little value; this is especially the case when the patient would be unconscious before death. On the other hand, only a limited number of people have acted to deliberately bring about someone's death. Among those who have publicly assisted patients by providing them with the means to die and helping them to use these means is retired pathologist Dr. Jack Kevorkian.

Kevorkian is probably quite well known because his recent activities in assisting suicides have been much publicized. For several years he has helped people who have come to him to die; he has provided them with the means to kill themselves. His first method was a "suicide machine" that consisted of a metal pole to which bottles of three solutions were attached. First, a simple saline solution flowed through an intravenous needle that had been inserted into the person's vein. The patient then flipped a switch that started a flow of an anesthetic, thiopental, which caused the person to become unconscious. After sixty seconds, a solution of potassium chloride followed and caused death within minutes by heart seizure. In a later version of the machine, carbon monoxide was used. When a person pushed a control switch, carbon monoxide flowed through a tube to a bag placed over his or her head.[6] Between 1990 and 1996, Kevorkian assisted more than forty-five suicides, and the number was still growing. Almost all of his assisted suicides took place in Michigan. To prevent these incidents from taking place in their state, in 1993 Michigan legislators passed a law against assisted suicide. However, the law was struck down in the courts. Kevorkian was brought to trial in three cases, but the juries found him not guilty in each case.

The families of people whom Kevorkian has helped to die speak highly of him. In the videotapes that he has made before each death, the individuals who died were seen pleading to be allowed to die. His critics have a different view, however. They say that at least some of the people who wanted to die might not have done so if they had been helped—if their pain were adequately treated, for example. Some of the people were not terminally ill. One was in the early stages of Alzheimer's disease, and another had multiple sclerosis. The primary physician of another who claimed to have multiple sclerosis found no evidence of this disease or any other; the patient had a history of depression, however. Another was determined by the medical examiner to have no trace of an earlier diagnosed cancer.[7] In one case a woman had what has come to be called "chronic fatigue syndrome" and a history of abuse by her husband. Kevorkian's "patients" have been predominantly women who may have been worried about the impact of their disease on others as much as about the difficulty of the disease itself or its prospects for them. In fact, three times as many women as men attempt suicide, though men succeed more often than women.[8] Some people suggest that women's attempts are more of a cry for help. Death may also appear different to women. "If it is given a human face by a soothing physician/assister there is all the more reason why the super-altruistic woman with a life spent serving others would want to put down her burdens, and succumb."[9]

While the American Medical Association continues to oppose doctor-assisted suicide, federal appeals courts for the states of Washington and New York have recently upheld the practice as constitutionally protected, one on grounds of privacy and the other on the assertion that physician-assisted suicide was the same as turning off a respirator.[10] In one analysis, the reason for the difference between the court and physicians may be that "members of the legal profession have a higher opinion of their colleagues in medicine than the doctors do of themselves. Or perhaps physicians simply have a better understanding of the pressures of contemporary medical practice than do judges."[11]

What of the other type of euthanasia, *passive euthanasia*? In this type, we allow a person to die by not providing him with certain life-prolonging treatment. Turning off a respirator would be a case of passive euthanasia. A person may be dying, and measures to cure him or improve his health may have been ineffective. The patient or others may decide not to use these measures or treatments either because the chances of the treatment helping the person are regarded as slim or because the kind of life they would provide if they did work would be too burdensome. At this point, we want simply to distinguish these two kinds of euthanasia. Thus, the difference between active and passive euthanasia may be defined as follows:

Active euthanasia: Doing something, such as administering a lethal drug or using other means that cause a person's death.

Passive euthanasia: Stopping (or not starting) some treatment, which allows a person to die. The person's condition causes his or her death.

One type of action that is liable to be confused with active euthanasia but which ought to be distinguished from it is the giving of pain medication to critically ill and dying patients. Physicians are often hesitant to give sufficient pain medication to such patients because they fear that the medication will actually cause their deaths. They fear that this would be considered comparable to mercy killing (active euthanasia), which is legally impermissible. Some philosophers believe that the *principle of double effect* may be of some help here.[12] According to this principle, it is one thing to intend and do something bad as a means to an end, and it is another to do something morally permissible for the purpose of achieving some good while knowing that it may also have a bad secondary effect.

The following diagram may help you understand the essence of this principle. It shows a morally permissible act with two effects: one intended effect and one an unintended side effect. According to the principle of double effect, it may be morally permissible to administer a drug intending to relieve pain (a good effect) even though we know or foresee that our action may also have a bad effect (weakening the person and risking his or her death). Certain conditions must be met, however, for this to be permissible. *First,* the act must be morally permissible. One cannot do what is wrong to bring about a good end. *Second,* the person acting must intend to bring about the good end rather than the harmful result. *Third,* the good results must outweigh the bad ones.

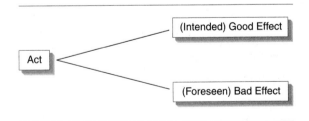

The idea behind the double effect principle is that there is a moral difference between intending to kill someone and intending to relieve pain. There is a moral difference between intending that someone die by means of one's actions (giving a drug overdose) and foreseeing that he or she will die because of one's actions (giving medication to relieve pain). Doing the latter is not, strictly speaking, active euthanasia. Active euthanasia would be the intentional giving of a drug with the purpose of bringing about a person's death. The difference is seen in the case of the dentist who foresees that she might pain her patient and the dentist who aims at paining her patient. The principle of double effect, nevertheless, continues to be the object of debate.[13]

In actual practice, it may be difficult to know what is going on—whether, for example, in giving a drug a person intends to just relieve the pain or actually bring about the death. People may also have mixed or hidden motives for their actions. Yet it would seem helpful to use this principle so that doctors are permitted to give their patients sufficient pain medication without fear of being prosecuted for homicide. The fact that they might cause addiction in their patients is another reason why some doctors hesitate to give narcotics for pain relief. This seems hardly a reasonable objection, however, especially if the patient is dying!

Ordinary and Extraordinary Measures

Philosophers have sometimes labeled those measures that are ineffective or excessively burdensome *extraordinary*. They are often called "heroic" in the medical setting. Thus, a person's hospital medical chart might have the phrase "no heroics" on it, indicating that no such measures are to be used. There are other cases in which what is refused would actually be effective for curing or ameliorating a life-threatening condition. And yet decisions are made not to use these measures and to let the person die. These measures are called *ordinary*—not because they are common, but because they promise reasonable hope of benefit. With ordinary measures, the chances that the treatment will help are good, and the expected results are also good.

One difficulty with determining whether a treatment would be considered ordinary or extraordinary is making an objective evaluation of the benefit and burden. It would be easier to do this if there were such a thing as a range for a normal life. Any measure that would not restore a life to that norm could then be considered extraordinary. However, if we were to set this standard very high, using it might also wrongly imply that the lives of disabled persons are of little or no benefit to them.

What would be considered an ordinary measure in the case of one person may be considered extraordinary in the case of another; a measure may effectively treat one person's condition, but another person will die shortly even if the measure were used (a blood transfusion, for example). Furthermore, the terminology can be misleading because many of the things that used to be experimental and risky are now common and quite beneficial. Drugs such as antibiotics and technologies such as respirators, which were once experimental and with questionable benefit, are now more effective and less expensive. In many cases they would now be considered ordinary, whereas they once could have been considered extraordinary. It is their proven benefit in a time period and for particular individuals that makes them ordinary in our sense of the term, however, and not their commonness. Thus, the basic difference between ordinary and extraordinary measures of life support is as follows:

Ordinary measures: Measures or treatments with reasonable hope of benefit, or the benefits outweigh the burdens.

Extraordinary measures: Measures or treatments with no reasonable hope of benefit, or the burdens outweigh the benefits.

Voluntary and Nonvoluntary Euthanasia

Before moving on to consider the arguments regarding the morality of euthanasia, one more distinction needs to be made between what can be called voluntary and nonvoluntary euthanasia. In many cases, it is the person whose life is at issue who makes the decision about what is to be done. This is *voluntary euthanasia.* In other cases, persons other than the one whose life is at issue decide what is to be done. These are cases of *nonvoluntary euthanasia.*[14] Nonvoluntary simply means not *through* the will of the individual. It does not mean *against* their will. Sometimes others must make the decision because the person or patient is incapable of doing so. This is true of infants and small children and of persons who are in a coma or permanent vegetative state. This is also true of persons who are only minimally competent, as in cases of senility or certain psychiatric disorders. Although in many cases deciding who is sufficiently competent to make decisions for themselves is clear, this is not always the case. What should we say, for example, of the mental competence of the eighty-year-old man who refuses an effective surgery that would save his life and at the same time says he does not want to die? Is such a person being rational? The difference between voluntary and nonvoluntary cases can be specified as follows:

Voluntary euthanasia: The person whose life is at issue knowingly and freely decides what shall be done.

Nonvoluntary euthanasia: Persons other than the one whose life is at issue decide what shall be done.

Advance Directives   In some cases, when a patient is not able to express his or her wishes, we can attempt to imagine what the person would want. We can rely, for example, on past personality or statements made by the person. Perhaps the person made comments to friends or relatives as to what he or she would want if such and such a situation occurred. In other cases, a person might have left a written expression of his or her wishes in the form of a "living will." Living wills, or *advance directives,* have become more common in the last decades. In such a di-

rective a person can specify that she wants no extraordinary measures used to prolong her life if she is dying and unable to communicate this desire. In another advance directive, a "durable power of attorney," a person can appoint someone (who need not be a lawyer) as her legal representative to make medical decisions for her in the event she is incapacitated. The form for durable power of attorney also provides for individualized expressions in writing about what a person would or would not want done under certain conditions. At the very least, these directives have moral force. They also have legal force in those states that have recognized them.[15] However, even then these directives are often not followed by physicians, especially if the patient is a woman. These measures can, if enforced or strengthened, give people some added control over what happens to them in their last days. To further ensure this, in December 1991, the Patient Self-Determination Act, passed by the U.S. Congress, went into effect. This act requires that health care institutions that participate in Medicare or Medicaid have written policies for providing individuals in their care with information about and access to advance directives such as living wills.

Combining the Types of Euthanasia

We have noted the differences between various types of euthanasia: voluntary and nonvoluntary, active and passive, and (if passive) the withholding of ordinary and extraordinary measures. Combining the types of euthanasia gives six forms, as illustrated above.

There are three types of voluntary euthanasia.

1. Voluntary active euthanasia: The person who is dying says, "Give me the fatal dose."

2. Voluntary passive euthanasia, withholding ordinary measures: The person says, "Don't use lifesaving or life-prolonging medical measures even though the likely results of using them would be good and the costs or burdens minimal, because I want to die."

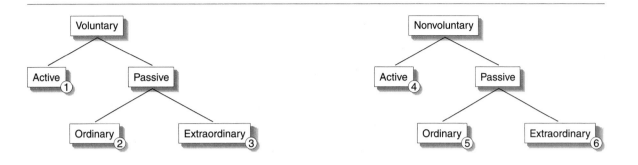

3. Voluntary passive euthanasia, withholding extraordinary measures: The person says, "Don't use those medical measures because the chances of benefit in terms of lifesaving or life extension would be small, the burdens too great, or both."

Likewise, there are three types of nonvoluntary euthanasia.

4. Nonvoluntary active euthanasia: Others decide to give the person the fatal drug overdose.
5. Nonvoluntary passive euthanasia, withholding ordinary measures: Others decide not to use lifesaving or life-prolonging medical measures even though the likely results of using them would be good and the costs or burdens minimal.
6. Nonvoluntary passive euthanasia, withholding extraordinary measures: Others decide not to use those medical measures for the chances of benefit in terms of lifesaving or life extension are small, the burdens too great, or both.

So far, we have been attempting only to classify types of euthanasia. The purpose of this classification has been to clarify the various possible types so that we will also be able to make appropriate distinctions in our moral judgments about these cases.

Morality and the Law

Before considering the moral arguments about euthanasia, we should first distinguish moral judgments about euthanasia from assertions about what the law should or should not be on this matter. Although we may sometimes have moral reasons for what we say the law should or should not do, *the two areas are distinct.* There are many things that are moral matters that ought not to be legislated or made subject to law and legal punishment. *Not everything that is immoral ought to be illegal.* For example, lying, while arguably a moral issue, is only sometimes subject to the law. In our thinking about euthanasia, it would be well to keep this distinction in mind. On the one hand, in some case we might say that a person acted badly, though understandably, in giving up too easily on life. Yet we also may believe that the law should not force some action here if the person knows what he or she is doing, and the person's action does not seriously harm others. On the other hand, a person's request to end his or her life might be reasonable given his circumstances, but there might also be social reasons why the law should not permit it. These reasons might be related to the possible harmful effects of some practice on other persons or on the practice of medicine. *Just because some action (for example, euthanasia) might be morally permissible, does not necessarily mean that it ought to be legally permissible.*

In many cases over the past three decades, people have sought to change the laws regarding euthanasia. In general, we recognize a basis in the law that allows people to refuse treatment, even lifesaving treatment for themselves, if they are judged to be mentally and legally competent to do so. Otherwise, to treat them without their consent could be judged a form of impermissible touching or battery. Other issues about the law and euthanasia have been crystallized by certain well-publicized cases. The noted cases of Karen Quinlan in 1975 and Nancy Cruzan in 1990 are good examples.[16] In Quinlan's landmark case, the issue was whether a respirator that was keeping her alive could be disconnected. For some still unknown reason (some say it was a combination of barbiturates and alcohol), she had gone into a coma from which doctors judged she would not recover. When they were assured of this, her parents sought permission to retain legal guardianship (because by then she was twenty-one years old) and have her respirator disconnected. After several court hearings and final approval by the supreme court of the state of New Jersey, they were finally permitted to disconnect her respirator. Although they expected she would die shortly after her respirator was removed, she continued to live in this comatose state for ten more years. One basic reason given by this court for its opinion in this case was that Karen did not lose her right of privacy by becoming incompetent and that she could thus refuse unwanted and useless interventions by others to keep her alive. None of the various state interests or social concerns that might override this right were found to be relevant in her case.

Nancy Cruzan was twenty-five years old at the time of an accident in 1983 that left her in a permanent vegetative state until her death eight years later. In her case, the issue brought to the courts was whether a feeding tube providing her with food and water could be withdrawn. This case eventually reached the U.S. Supreme Court, which ruled that such lifesaving procedures could be withdrawn or withheld, but only if there was "clear and convincing evidence" that that is what Nancy herself would have wanted. Eventually, such evidence was brought forward. By that time, those who had been protesting her case had withdrawn, and her feeding tube was removed and she was allowed to die.

Despite such cases of passive euthanasia, no state in this country permits active euthanasia or

mercy killing. Active euthanasia is practiced somewhat openly in the Netherlands, even though it is officially against the law. It is estimated that some five thousand or more incidences occur there each year. Legislation to officially legalize it had been proposed but not passed. However, only token sentences were given for violations of the law. In early 1993, the Dutch parliament approved rules according to which doctors would not be prosecuted if they notified the appropriate government agency and followed these guidelines: The person requesting to be put to death must be competent at the time of the request, and the request must be consistent and repeated. The person's suffering must be intolerable, and euthanasia must be performed only by a physician after consultation with another physician.[17] In 1990, a California proposition to legalize active euthanasia for those with a terminal illness who request it either at the time of illness or who have done so earlier through an advance directive failed to obtain the necessary signatures for a ballot measure. In the state of Washington in 1991, a similar ballot measure also failed. Since then, Oregon voters approved a euthanasia measure, but this was appealed and is still in the courts. Polls through the years have shown a modest support for some change in the law regarding active euthanasia. The reasons for the support and the opposition are varied. In the summary that follows we will focus on some of the moral arguments about euthanasia. These moral arguments may have a bearing on what the law should be, but other considerations also are relevant to laws in this area.

The Moral Significance of Voluntariness

Today an individual's rights over his or her own life are highly valued. And yet the commonsense moral view is that there are limits to this right. It is limited, for example, when it conflicts with the interests or rights of others. Under what conditions and for what reasons should a person's own wishes prevail in euthanasia matters? How important is voluntary consent?

Consequentialist Considerations

From your study of utilitarianism, you know that one major method of deciding moral right and wrong appeals to the consequences of our actions (act utilitarianism) or practices (rule utilitarianism). From this perspective, voluntariness matters morally only to the extent that it affects human happiness and welfare. Respecting people's own choices about how they will die surely would have some beneficial consequences. For example, when people know that they will be allowed to make decisions about their own lives and not be forced into things against their will, they may gain a certain peace of mind. Moreover, knowing themselves better than others, they also may be the ones best able to make good decisions in situations that primarily affect them. These are good consequentialist reasons to respect a person's wishes in euthanasia cases. But it is not just the person who is dying who will be affected by the decision. Thus it also can be argued that the effects on others, on their feelings, for example, are also relevant to the moral decision making.

However, individual decisions are not always wise and do not always work for the greatest benefit of the person making them or others. For example, critics of euthanasia worry that people who are ill or disabled would refuse certain life-saving treatment because they lack or do not know about services, support, and money that are available to them. In a recent decision, the Nevada Supreme Court ruled that people must receive information about care alternatives before they may refuse lifesaving treatment.[18] On consequentialist grounds, we should do that which, in fact, is most likely to bring about the greatest happiness, not only to ourselves but also to all those affected by our actions. It does not in itself matter who makes the judgment. But it does matter insofar as one person rather than another is more likely to make a better judgment, one that would have better consequences overall, including consequences to the individual.

Moreover, from the perspective of rule utilitarian thinking, we ought to consider which policy would maximize happiness. (It is here that morality comes closer to concerns about what the law should be.) Would a policy that universally follows individual requests about dying be most likely to maximize happiness? Or would a policy that gives no special weight to individual desires, but directs us to do whatever some panel decides, be more likely to have the best outcome? Or would some moderate policy be best, such as one that gives special weight to what a person wants but does not give absolute weight to those desires? An example of such a policy might be one in which the burden of proof not to do what a person wishes is placed on those who would refuse. In other words, they must show some serious reason not to go along with what the person wanted.

Nonconsequentialist Considerations

To appeal to the value of personal autonomy in euthanasia decisions is to appeal to a nonconsequentialist reason or moral norm. The idea is that autonomy is a good in itself and therefore carries heavy moral weight. We like to think of ourselves, at least ideally, as masters of our own fate. A world peopled by robots would probably be a lesser world than one peopled by persons who make their own decisions even when those decisions are unwise. In fact, according to Kant, only in such a world is morality itself possible. His famous phrase, "an ought implies a can," indicates that if and only if we can or are *free* to act in certain ways can we be *commanded* to do so. According to a Kantian deontological position, persons are unique in being able to choose freely, and this ought to be respected.

However, in many euthanasia cases a person's mental competence and thus autonomy is compromised by fear and lack of understanding. Illness also makes a person more subject to undue influence or coercion. How, in such instances, do we know what the person really wants? These are practical problems that arise when attempting to respect autonomy. In addition, the issue raises theoretical problems. Autonomy literally means self-rule. But how often are we fully clear about who we are and what we want to be? Is the self whose decisions are to be respected the present self or one's ideal or authentic self? These issues of selfhood and personal identity are important but go beyond ethics.

Note also here that while we have concentrated on pointing out the kinds of things that would be morally relevant from both consequentialist and nonconsequentialist points of view, the issues may also be analyzed from the perspective of an ethics of care. One would suppose that from this perspective both matters relating to benefits and harms and those relating to a person's autonomy would be relevant.

Active Versus Passive Euthanasia

The distinction between active and passive euthanasia is a conceptual distinction, a matter of classification. Giving a patient a lethal drug to end her life is classified as active euthanasia. Stopping or not starting some life-lengthening treatment knowing that a patient will die is classified as passive euthanasia. For example, either not starting a respirator or disconnecting it is generally considered passive euthanasia because it is a matter of not providing life-prolonging aid for the person. In this case, the person's illness or weakness is the cause of his death if he dies. This does not mean that it is either justified or unjustified.

Let us pose the *moral* question about active and passive euthanasia as follows: Is there any moral difference between them? This prompts the following questions: Is active euthanasia more morally problematic than passive euthanasia? Or are they on a moral par such that if passive euthanasia is morally permissible in some cases, so is active euthanasia? Is physician-assisted suicide (in which a physician only provides the means of death to the person) any more or less problematic than cases in which the physician actually administers the drug or other means to bring about death?

Consequentialist Concerns

Again, if we take the perspective of the consequentialist or act utilitarian, for example, we should only be concerned about our actions in terms of their consequences. The means by which the results come about do not matter in themselves. They matter only if they make a difference in the result. Generally, then, if a person's death is the *best outcome* in a difficult situation, it would not matter whether it came about through the administration of a lethal drug dose or from the discontinuance of some lifesaving treatment. Now, if one or the other means did make a difference in a person's experience (as when a person is relieved or pained more by one method than another), then this would count in favor of or against that method.

If we take the perspective of a rule utilitarian, we would be concerned about the consequences of this or that practice or policy. We would want to know which of the various alternative practices or policies would have the best results overall. Which would be the best policy: one that allowed those involved to choose active euthanasia, one that required active euthanasia in certain cases, one that permitted it only in rare cases, or one that prohibited it and attached legal penalties to it? Which policy would make more people happy and fewer people unhappy? One that prohibited active euthanasia would frustrate those who wished to use it, but it would prevent some abuses that might follow if it were permitted. Essential to this perspective are predictions about how a policy would work. Some are concerned in particular about the effects of physician participation in the practice of euthanasia. It may have the positive results of being under the control of a profession known for its ethical concerns. Or it may have negative effects such as the lessening of patient trust in physicians.

One of the biggest concerns is whether the practice would be open to abuse. The argument that there would be abuse has been given various names, depending on the particular metaphor of choice: the "domino effect," "slippery slope," "wedge," or "camel's nose" argument. The idea is that if we permit active euthanasia in a few reasonable cases, we would slide and approve it in more and more cases until we were approving it in cases that were clearly unreasonable. In other words, if we permit euthanasia when a person is dying shortly, is in unrelievable pain, and has requested that his life be ended, we would permit it when a person is not dying or has not requested to be killed. The questions to ask are: Would we slide down the slope? Is there something about us that would cause us to slide? Would we be so weak of mind that we could not see the difference between these cases? Would we be weak of will, not wanting to care for people whose care is costly and burdensome? This is an empirical and predictive matter. To know the force of the argument, we would need to show evidence for one or the other position about the likelihood of sliding.[19]

Nonconsequentialist Concerns

Many arguments and concerns about active and passive euthanasia are not based on appeals to good or bad results or consequences. Arguments about the right to die or to make one's own decisions about dying are nonconsequentialist arguments. On the one hand, some people argue that respecting personal autonomy is so important that it should override any concerns about bad results. Thus, we might conclude that people ought to be allowed to end their lives when they choose as an expression of their autonomy, and that this choice should be respected regardless of the consequences to others or even mistakes about their own cases.

On the other hand, some people believe that there is a significant moral difference between killing a person and letting a person die. Killing people except in self-defense is morally wrong, according to this view. Just why it is thought wrong is another matter. Some rely on reasons like those of natural law theorists, citing the innate drive toward living as a good in itself, however compromised—a good that should not be suppressed. Kant used reasoning similar to this. He argued that using the concern for life that usually promotes it to make a case for ending life was inherently contradictory and a violation of the categorical imperative.[20] Some people use religious reasons such as the belief that life and death decisions are for God and not ourselves to make. Some people use reasons that rely on concerns about the gravity of ending a life directly and intentionally, that in doing so we ally ourselves with what is at best a necessary evil.

We each need to consider what role consequentialist and nonconsequentialist reasons play in our own views about the morality of active and passive euthanasia. If consequentialist arguments have primacy, then one's argument for or against active euthanasia will depend on empirical judgments about the predicted consequences. If nonconsequentialist reasons have primacy, then these reasons must be evaluated. Are the nonconsequentialist reasons about autonomy, for example, stronger than the nonconsequentialist arguments about the morality of killing? This text does not intend to answer these questions for the student, but it does assume that a good start can be made in answering them if one is able to know whether an argument is based on consequentialist or nonconsequentialist considerations.

Ordinary Versus Extraordinary Measures

There is considerable disagreement about the usefulness of the distinction between ordinary and extraordinary measures of life support. People disagree first of all about the definitions of the terms.[21] If the terms are defined primarily in terms of commonness and uncommonness, then surely it is difficult to see that this should make a moral difference. It would amount to saying that we ought to use those things that we commonly use and not use those we usually do not use. However, if the terms are defined in relation to benefit and burden, they are by their nature morally relevant because these are value terms. The primary difficulty with using this distinction is that it is difficult to measure and compare benefits and burdens (as noted earlier). For instance, should financial cost to a family or society be part of the calculation? One danger with including the effect on others in the calculation, and not just the benefits and burdens to the patient herself, is that we might be inclined to say that some people should die because the burdens of caring for them are just too great.

If we could determine what are ordinary and extraordinary measures in a particular case, we would be on the way to deciding whether or not there is at least some good reason to provide the measures. If we judge them ordinary, they probably ought to be provided. If we judge them extraordinary, they probably need not be provided.

Infant Euthanasia

Today at least half of live-born infants weighing less than 1,000 grams (2.2 pounds) survive, compared with less than 10 percent just twenty years ago.[22] Survival rates for those born with congenital defects have also shown marked improvements.[23] However, some seriously ill newborns do not fare well. Some have low birth weight or severe defects and cannot survive for long, while others have serious impairments. Thus, improvements in medicine that have enabled us to save the lives of newborns have also given us new life-and-death decisions.

Every few years a case of disputed life-and-death decisions regarding an infant seems to appear in the news. They are called Baby Doe cases in order to protect the families' privacy. Those that have drawn the most criticism are cases like the one in which an infant born with Down's syndrome was left untreated and died. Down's syndrome is a genetic anomaly that causes mental retardation and sometimes physical problems as well. In this case, the child had a repairable but life-threatening blockage between the stomach and the small intestines. The parents refused permission for the surgery to repair the problem, and the doctors followed their wishes and let the infant die. Critics of this case protested that this surgery was simple and effective, and the infant, though retarded, could lead a happy life.

Not to treat in such cases has been interpreted as not using what would be considered ordinary means of life support—*ordinary* because the

benefits to the patient would outweigh any burdens. Such cases have been criticized for their "buck-passing"—shifting responsibility for the death to nature, as though in this situation but not elsewhere in medicine we should "let nature take its course."[24] Because the infant is not able to express his wishes, these will always be cases of nonvoluntary euthanasia. Although strong arguments can be made for treatment in such cases, in other cases knowing what is best is not so simple. Sometimes it is difficult to tell whether treatment is always in the baby's best interest. Moreover, some cases raise again the issue of determining when an individual is dead. In cases in Florida and California, for example, parents of a newborn with anencephaly, or no upper brain, wanted their child declared brain dead so that its organs could be used for transplant. However, such infants are not brain dead according to statutes in these states.

Two different types of moral questions can be raised about such cases. One is the question, who would be the best to decide whether to provide or deny certain treatments? The other is, what are the reasons to provide or deny care? Some people insist that the primary decision makers should be the parents because they not only are most likely to have the infant's best interests at heart, but also will be the ones to provide care for the child. Needless to say, we can imagine situations in which the parents would not be the most objective judges. They might be fearful, disappointed at the child's birth, or simply disagree about what is best to do. A presidential commission established to review medical ethical problems concluded that parents ought to make decisions for their seriously ill newborns, except in cases of decision-making incapacity, an unresolvable difference between them, or a choice that is clearly not in the infant's best interests. According to this commission, if a treatment is futile it is not advised. However, in other cases the infant's best interests are said to be primary.

Permanent handicaps justify a decision not to provide life-sustaining treatment only when they are so severe that continued existence would not be a net benefit to the infant. Though inevitably somewhat subjective and imprecise in actual application, the concept of "benefit" excludes honoring idiosyncratic views that might be allowed if a person were deciding about his or her own treatment. Rather, net benefit is absent only if the burdens imposed on the patient by the disability or its treatment would lead a competent decision maker to choose to forego the treatment. As in all surrogate decision making, the surrogate is obligated to try to evaluate benefits and burdens from the infant's own perspective.[25]

A society has an interest in protecting and providing for its children and is therefore obligated to intervene in cases of parental neglect or abuse. However, just what constitutes neglect or abuse and what is reasonable parental decision making is far from clear. In addition, there are practical legal difficulties involved in treatment decisions for children. What would be the best policy regarding ill newborns? Should the federal government require state child-abuse agencies to monitor treatment of newborns and withhold funds if states do not comply? Critics of such a policy believe that this would be an unwarranted state interference in legitimate medical decision making. Obviously, more than medical decisions about diagnosis and prognosis are involved in such cases. These are judgments about what is best to do—they are value or moral judgments. Finding the best balance between the need to protect children and to support parents in difficult and painful decision making remains a continuing problem.

In the readings in this chapter, J. Gay-Williams and James Rachels address the issue of whether there is any moral difference between active and passive euthanasia. The selection from the President's Commission report presents an overview of some of the problems faced by those who must make life-and-death decisions.

Notes

1. *New York Times,* Dec. 5, 1976.

2. The case occurred in Oakland, California. The jury in the case found the defendant guilty even though California did not at that time have a "brain death" statute. See the *San Francisco Examiner* for May 1972.

3. Ad Hoc Committee of the Harvard Medical School to Examine the Definition of Brain Death, "A Definition of Irreversible Coma," *Journal of the American Medical Association* 205 (1968): 377.

4. Two types of cases are to be distinguished from both persistent vegetative state and coma. One is called "locked-in syndrome" in which a person may be conscious but not able to respond. The other is "dementia" or senility in which the content of consciousness is impaired, as in Alzheimer's disease. Neither the person in a persistent vegetative state or coma nor the person with locked-in syndrome or dementia is considered dead by whole brain death criteria. We may say their life has a diminished value, but they are not legally dead. However, some people argue that because the ability to think is what makes us persons, when someone loses this ability, as in the case of a persistent vegetative state, we ought to consider the person dead. Newborns with little or no upper brain or brain function could also for the same reason then be considered dead. However, these are living, breathing beings and it would be difficult to think of them as dead in the sense that we would bury them as they are. Rather than declare them dead, as some have argued, others believe that it would be more practical and reasonable to judge these cases in terms of the kind of life they are living and to ask whether it would be morally permissible to bring about their deaths or allow them to die.

5. *San Francisco Chronicle* (Feb. 2, 1995), p. A4.

6. The *New York Times,* Dec. 4, 1990, describes the first publicized case in which Dr. Kevorkian's "suicide machine" was used; the other two cases can be found, for example, in the *San Francisco Chronicle,* Oct. 29, 1991.

7. Stephanie Gutmann, "Death and the Maiden," *The New Republic* (June 24, 1996), 20–28.

8. Ibid.

9. Ibid.

10. *New York Times* (July 15, 1996), p. A11. For a good analysis of these two court opinions, see "What Right to Die?" by Jeffrey Rosen in *The New Republic* (July 24, 1996), 28–31.

11. Ibid.

12. This principle was developed by the theologians of Salmance, in particular by John of St. Thomas in *De Bonitate et Malitia Actuum Humanorum.* See Antony Kenny, "The History of Intention in Ethics," in *Anatomy of the Soul* (London: Basil Blackwell, 1973), 140 ff.

13. See, for example, Warren S. Quinn, "Actions, Intentions, and Consequences: The Doctrine of Double Effect," *Philosophy and Public Affairs,* vol. 18, no. 4 (Fall 1989), 334–351.

14. Some writers on this topic also list involuntary as a type of euthanasia. Because it is a conceptual distinction rather than a moral one that is at issue here, I believe that the two-type classification system is preferable.

15. However, what is requested in these documents may or may not be followed depending on the circumstances and on what is requested. Medical staff may decide not to stop lifesaving treatments for a person who is not otherwise dying, even if she has stated this in writing. They also may decide not to do certain things that they consider not medically appropriate or not legally permissible, even though these things have been requested in writing.

16. See *In re Quinlan,* 70 N.J. 10, 335 A. 2d 647 (1976), and *Cruzan v. Director, Missouri Department of Health,* United States Supreme Court, 110 S.Ct. 2841 (1990).

17. See final report of the Netherlands State Commission on Euthanasia: An English Summary. *Bioethics* 1 (1987): 163–174.

18. Reported in *Medical Ethics Advisor,* vol. 7, no. 4 (April 1991): 50–54.

19. In an interesting version of this consequentialist argument, Susan Wolff writes that we ought to maintain a sharp dividing line between active and passive euthanasia, which allows a wide range of permissible cases of passive euthanasia but prohibits active euthanasia. The reason she gives is that if we do not have such a line and attempt to allow active euthanasia even only in a limited number of cases, this will cause concern about the whole area of euthanasia and in the end work to limit acceptance of passive euthanasia as well. To retain freedom for passive euthanasia, she argues, we need to maintain the prohibition against active euthanasia. Again, this is an argument that relies on predictions of what would be likely to occur, and we would need some reason to believe that this would be so. Presentation at the University of California at San Francisco Medical Center, Conference on "The Ethics and Economics of Death," November 1989.

20. Immanuel Kant, *Foundations of the Metaphysics of Morals,* second section, no. 422.

21. Comments about the history of the distinction and the debate over its usefulness can be found in the President's Commission report, "Deciding to Forego Life Sustaining Treatment" (March 1983): 82–89.

22. Ibid.

23. Ibid.

24. From a comment made by a reviewer of this text, Robert P. Tucker of Florida Southern College, who had had some hospital experience in this regard.

25. The President's Commission report, op. cit.

The Wrongfulness of Euthanasia

J. Gay-Williams

Study Questions

1. What is Gay-Williams's definition of euthanasia? Why does he believe that it is misleading to speak of "passive euthanasia"?

2. How does he believe that euthanasia acts against our nature?

3. In what ways does he believe that euthanasia is not in our best interest?

4. How could euthanasia have a corrupting influence and lead to a "slippery slope"?

My impression is that euthanasia—the idea, if not the practice—is slowly gaining acceptance within our society. Cynics might attribute this to an increasing tendency to devalue human life, but I do not believe this is the major factor. The acceptance is much more likely to be the result of unthinking

From Ronald Munson, *Intervention and Reflection: Basic Issues in Medical Ethics,* 5th ed. Belmont, CA: Wadsworth, 1995. © 1979 by Ronald Munson. Reprinted with permission.

sympathy and benevolence. Well-publicized, tragic stories like that of Karen Quinlan elicit from us deep feelings of compassion. We think to ourselves, "She and her family would be better off if she were dead." It is an easy step from this very human response to the view that if someone (and others) would be better off dead, then it must be all right to kill that person.[1] Although I respect the compassion that leads to this conclusion, I believe the conclusion is wrong. I want to show that euthanasia is wrong. It is inherently wrong, but it is also wrong judged from the standpoints of self-interest and of practical effects.

Before presenting my arguments to support this claim, it would be well to define "euthanasia." An essential aspect of euthanasia is that it involves taking a human life, either one's own or that of another. Also, the person whose life is taken must be someone who is believed to be suffering from some disease or injury from which recovery cannot reasonably be expected. Finally, the action must be deliberate and intentional. Thus, euthanasia is intentionally taking the life of a presumably hopeless person. Whether the life is one's own or that of another, the taking of it is still euthanasia.

It is important to be clear about the deliberate and intentional aspect of the killing. If a hopeless person is given an injection of the wrong drug by mistake and this causes his death, this is wrongful killing but not euthanasia. The killing cannot be the result of accident. Furthermore, if the person is given an injection of a drug that is believed to be necessary to treat his disease or better his condition and the person dies as a result, then this is neither wrongful killing nor euthanasia. The intention was to make the patient well, not kill him. Similarly, when a patient's condition is such that it is not reasonable to hope that any medical procedures or treatments will save his life, a failure to implement the procedures or treatments is not euthanasia. If the person dies, this will be as a result of his injuries or disease and not because of his failure to receive treatment.

The failure to continue treatment after it has been realized that the patient has little chance of benefitting from it has been characterized by some as "passive euthanasia." This phrase is misleading and mistaken.[2] In such cases, the person involved is not killed (the first essential aspect of euthanasia), nor is the death of the person intended by the withholding of additional treatment (the third essential aspect of euthanasia). The aim may be to spare the person additional and unjustifiable pain, to save him from the indignities of hopeless manipulations, and to avoid increasing the financial and emotional burden on his family. When I buy a pencil it is so that I can use it to write, not to contribute to an increase in the gross national product. This may be the unintended consequence of my action, but it is not the aim of my action. So it is with failing to continue the treatment of a dying person. I intend his death no more than I intend to reduce the GNP by not using medical supplies. His is an unintended dying, and so-called "passive euthanasia" is not euthanasia at all.

1. The Argument from Nature

Every human being has a natural inclination to continue living. Our reflexes and responses fit us to fight attackers, flee wild animals, and dodge out of the way of trucks. In our daily lives we exercise the caution and care necessary to protect ourselves. Our bodies are similarly structured for survival right down to the molecular level. When we are cut, our capillaries seal shut, our blood clots, and fibrogen is produced to start the process of healing the wound. When we are invaded by bacteria, antibodies are produced to fight against the alien organisms, and their remains are swept out of the body by special cells designed for clean-up work.

Euthanasia does violence to this natural goal of survival. It is literally acting against nature because all the processes of nature are bent towards the end of bodily survival. Euthanasia defeats these subtle mechanisms in a way that, in a particular case, disease and injury might not.

It is possible, but not necessary, to make an appeal to revealed religion in this connection.[3] Man as trustee of his body acts against God, its rightful possessor, when he takes his own life. He also violates the commandment to hold life sacred and never to take it without just and compelling cause. But since this appeal will persuade only those who are prepared to accept that religion has access to revealed truths, I shall not employ this line of argument.

It is enough, I believe, to recognize that the organization of the human body and our patterns of behavioral responses make the continuation of life a natural goal. By reason alone, then, we can recognize that euthanasia sets us against our own nature.[4] Furthermore, in doing so, euthanasia does violence to our dignity. Our dignity comes from seeking our ends.

When one of our goals is survival, and actions are taken that eliminate that goal, then our natural dignity suffers. Unlike animals, we are conscious through reason of our nature and our ends. Euthanasia involves acting as if this dual nature—inclination towards survival and awareness of this as an end—did not exist. Thus, euthanasia denies our basic human character and requires that we regard ourselves or others as something less than fully human.

2. The Argument from Self-Interest

The above arguments are, I believe, sufficient to show that euthanasia is inherently wrong. But there are reasons for considering it wrong when judged by standards other than reason. Because death is final and irreversible, euthanasia contains within it the possibility that we will work against our own interest if we practice it or allow it to be practiced on us.

Contemporary medicine has high standards of excellence and a proven record of accomplishment, but it does not possess perfect and complete knowledge. A mistaken diagnosis is possible, and so is a mistaken prognosis. Consequently, we may believe that we are dying of a disease when, as a matter of fact, we may not be. We may think that we have no hope of recovery when, as a matter of fact, our chances are quite good. In such circumstances, if euthanasia were permitted, we would die needlessly. Death is final and the chance of error too great to approve the practice of euthanasia.

Also, there is always the possibility that an experimental procedure or a hitherto untried technique will pull us through. We should at least keep this option open, but euthanasia closes it off. Furthermore, spontaneous remission does occur in many cases. For no apparent reason, a patient simply recovers when those all around him, including his physicians, expected him to die. Euthanasia would just guarantee their expectations and leave no room for the "miraculous" recoveries that frequently occur.

Finally, knowing that we can take our life at any time (or ask another to take it) might well incline us to give up too easily. The will to live is strong in all of us, but it can be weakened by pain and suffering and feelings of hopelessness. If during a bad time we allow ourselves to be killed, we never have a chance to reconsider. Recovery from a serious illness requires that we fight for it, and anything that weakens our determination by suggesting that there is an easy way

out is ultimately against our own interest. Also, we may be inclined towards euthanasia because of our concern for others. If we see our sickness and suffering as an emotional and financial burden on our family, we may feel that to leave our life is to make their lives easier.[5] The very presence of the possibility of euthanasia may keep us from surviving when we might.

3. The Argument from Practical Effects

Doctors and nurses are, for the most part, totally committed to saving lives. A life lost is, for them, almost a personal failure, an insult to their skills and knowledge. Euthanasia as a practice might well alter this. It could have a corrupting influence so that in any case that is severe doctors and nurses might not try hard enough to save the patient. They might decide that the patient would simply be "better off dead" and take the steps necessary to make that come about. This attitude could then carry over to their dealings with patients less seriously ill. The result would be an overall decline in the quality of medical care.

Finally, euthanasia as a policy is a slippery slope. A person apparently hopelessly ill may be allowed to take his own life. Then he may be permitted to deputize others to do it for him should he no longer be able to act. The judgment of others then becomes the ruling factor. Already at this point euthanasia is not personal and voluntary, for others are acting "on behalf of" the patient as they see fit. This may well incline them to act on behalf of other patients who have not authorized them to exercise their judgment. It is only a short step, then, from voluntary euthanasia (self-inflicted or authorized), to directed euthanasia administered to a patient who has given no authorization, to involuntary euthanasia conducted as part of a social policy.[6] Recently many psychiatrists and sociologists have argued that we define as "mental illness" those forms of behavior that we disapprove of.[7] This gives us license then to lock up those who display the behavior. The category of the "hopelessly ill" provides the possibility of even worse abuse.

Embedded in a social policy, it would give society or its representatives the authority to eliminate all those who might be considered too "ill" to function normally any longer. The dangers of euthanasia are too great to all to run the risk of approving it in any form. The first slippery step may well lead to a serious and harmful fall.

I hope that I have succeeded in showing why the benevolence that inclines us to give approval of euthanasia is misplaced. Euthanasia is inherently wrong because it violates the nature and dignity of human beings. But even those who are not convinced by this must be persuaded that the potential personal and social dangers inherent in euthanasia are sufficient to forbid our approving it either as a personal practice or as a public policy.

Suffering is surely a terrible thing, and we have a clear duty to comfort those in need and to ease their suffering when we can. But suffering is also a natural part of life with values for the individual and for others that we should not overlook. We may legitimately seek for others and for ourselves an easeful death, as Arthur Dyck has pointed out.[8] Euthanasia, however, is not just an easeful death. It is a wrongful death. Euthanasia is not just dying. It is killing.

Notes

1. For a sophisticated defense of this position see Philippa Foot, "Euthanasia," *Philosophy and Public Affairs*, vol. 6 (1977), pp. 85–112. Foot does not endorse the radical conclusion that euthanasia, voluntary and involuntary, is always right.
2. James Rachels rejects the distinction between active and passive euthanasia as morally irrelevant in his "Active and Passive Euthanasia," *New England Journal of Medicine*, vol. 292, pp. 78–80. But see the criticism by Foot, pp. 100–103.
3. For a defense of this view see J. V. Sullivan, "The Immorality of Euthanasia," in *Beneficent Euthanasia*, ed. Marvin Kohl (Buffalo, NY: Prometheus Books, 1975), pp. 34–44.
4. This point is made by Ray V. McIntyre in "Voluntary Euthanasia: The Ultimate Perversion," *Medical Counterpoint*, vol. 2, 26–29.
5. See McIntyre, p. 28.
6. See Sullivan, "Immorality of Euthanasia," pp. 34–44, for a fuller argument in support of this view.
7. See, for example, Thomas S. Szasz, *The Myth of Mental Illness*, rev. ed. (New York: Harper & Row, 1974).
8. Arthur Dyck, "Beneficent Euthanasia and Benemortasia," in Kohl, op. cit., pp. 117–129.

Active and Passive Euthanasia

James Rachels

Study Questions

1. What is the position of the American Medical Association on euthanasia as stated in its 1973 set of principles?
2. Why does Rachels believe that sometimes letting a person die is worse than bringing about their death, such as through a lethal injection?
3. Why does he believe that maintaining a moral distinction between active and passive euthanasia allows us to make life and death decisions on irrelevant grounds?
4. What is the example of Smith and Jones and their nephew supposed to show?
5. Does Rachels believe that an intentional cessation of treatment in which a patient dies can be equivalent to killing the patient?
6. Why does he believe that we usually think that killing is worse than letting die?
7. Does the doctor who lets a patient die do nothing?
8. What is Rachels's final conclusion?

The distinction between active and passive euthanasia is thought to be crucial for medical ethics. The idea is that it is permissible, at least in some cases, to withhold treatment and allow a patient to die, but it is never permissible to take any direct action designed to kill the patient. This doctrine seems to be accepted by most doctors, and it is endorsed in a

From the *New England Journal of Medicine*, vol. 292, no. 2 (January 9, 1975): 78–80. Reprinted by permission. © 1975 Massachusetts Medical Society.

statement adopted by the House of Delegates of the American Medical Association on December 4, 1973:

> The intentional termination of the life of one human being by another—mercy killing—is contrary to that for which the medical profession stands and is contrary to the policy of the American Medical Association.
>
> The cessation of the employment of extraordinary means to prolong the life of the body when there is irrefutable evidence that biological death is imminent is the decision of the patient and/or his immediate family. The advice and judgment of the physician should be freely available to the patient and/or his immediate family.

However, a strong case can be made against this doctrine. In what follows I will set out some of the relevant arguments, and urge doctors to reconsider their views on this matter.

To begin with a familiar type of situation, a patient who is dying of incurable cancer of the throat is in terrible pain, which can no longer be satisfactorily alleviated. He is certain to die within a few days, even if present treatment is continued, but he does not want to go on living for those days since the pain is unbearable. So he asks the doctor for an end to it, and his family joins in the request.

Suppose the doctor agrees to withhold treatment, as the conventional doctrine says he may. The justification for his doing so is that the patient is in terrible agony, and since he is going to die anyway, it would be wrong to prolong his suffering needlessly. But now notice this. If one simply withholds treatment, it may take the patient longer to die, and so he may suffer more than he would if more direct action were taken and a lethal injection given. This fact provides strong reason for thinking that, once the initial decision not to prolong his agony has been made, active euthanasia is actually preferable to passive euthanasia, rather than the reverse. To say otherwise is to endorse the option that leads to more suffering rather than less, and is contrary to the humanitarian impulse that prompts the decision not to prolong his life in the first place.

Part of my point is that the process of being "allowed to die" can be relatively slow and painful, whereas being given a lethal injection is relatively quick and painless. Let me give a different sort of example. In the United States about one in 600 babies is born with Down's syndrome. Most of these babies are otherwise healthy—that is, with only the usual

pediatric care, they will proceed to an otherwise normal infancy. Some, however, are born with congenital defects such as intestinal obstructions that require operations if they are to live. Sometimes, the parents and the doctor will decide not to operate, and let the infant die. Anthony Shaw describes what happens then:

> . . . When surgery is denied [the doctor] must try to keep the infant from suffering while natural forces sap the baby's life away. As a surgeon whose natural inclination is to use the scalpel to fight off death, standing by and watching a salvageable baby die is the most emotionally exhausting experience I know. It is easy at a conference, in a theoretical discussion, to decide that such infants should be allowed to die. It is altogether different to stand in the nursery and watch as dehydration and infection wither a tiny being over hours and days. This is a terrible ordeal for me and the hospital staff—much more so than for the parents who never set foot in the nursery.[1]

I can understand why some people are opposed to all euthanasia, and insist that such infants must be allowed to live. I think I can also understand why other people favor destroying these babies quickly and painlessly. But why should anyone favor letting "dehydration and infection wither a tiny being over hours and days"? The doctrine that says that a baby may be allowed to dehydrate and wither, but may not be given an injection that would end its life without suffering, seems so patently cruel as to require no further refutation. The strong language is not intended to offend, but only to put the point in the clearest possible way.

My second argument is that the conventional doctrine leads to decisions concerning life and death made on irrelevant grounds.

Consider again the case of the infants with Down's syndrome who need operations for congenital defects unrelated to the syndrome to live. Sometimes, there is no operation, and the baby dies, but when there is no such defect, the baby lives on. Now, an operation such as that to remove an intestinal obstruction is not prohibitively difficult. The reason why such operations are not performed in these cases is, clearly, that the child has Down's syndrome and the parents and doctor judge that because of that fact it is better for the child to die.

But notice that this situation is absurd, no matter what view one takes of the lives and potentials of such babies. If the life of such an infant is worth preserving, what does it matter if it needs a simple operation? Or, if one thinks it better that such a baby should not live on, what difference does it make that it happens to have an unobstructed intestinal tract? In either case, the matter of life and death is being decided on irrelevant grounds. It is the Down's syndrome, and not the intestines, that is the issue. The matter should be decided, if at all, on that basis, and not be allowed to depend on the essentially irrelevant question of whether the intestinal tract is blocked.

What makes this situation possible, of course, is the idea that when there is an intestinal blockage, one can "let the baby die," but when there is no such defect there is nothing that can be done, for one must not "kill" it. The fact that this idea leads to such results as deciding life or death on irrelevant grounds is another good reason why the doctrine should be rejected.

One reason why so many people think that there is an important moral difference between active and passive euthanasia is that they think killing someone is morally worse than letting someone die. But is it? Is killing, in itself, worse that letting die? To investigate this issue, two cases may be considered that are exactly alike except that one involves killing whereas the other involves letting someone die. Then, it can be asked whether this difference makes any difference to the moral assessments. It is important that the cases be exactly alike, except for this one difference, since otherwise one cannot be confident that it is this difference and not some other that accounts for any variation in the assessments of the two cases. So, let us consider this pair of cases:

In the first, Smith stands to gain a large inheritance if anything should happen to his six-year-old cousin. One evening while the child is taking his bath, Smith sneaks into the bathroom and drowns the child, and then arranges things so that it will look like an accident.

In the second, Jones also stands to gain if anything should happen to his six-year-old cousin. Like Smith, Jones sneaks in planning to drown the child in his bath. However, just as he enters the bathroom Jones sees the child slip and hit his head, and fall face down in the water. Jones is delighted; he stands by, ready to push the child's head back under if it is necessary, but it is not necessary. With only a little thrashing about, the child drowns all by himself, "accidentally," as Jones watches and does nothing.

Now Smith killed the child, whereas Jones "merely" let the child die. That is the only difference between them. Did either man behave better, from a moral point of view? If the difference between killing and letting die were in itself a morally important matter, one should say that Jones's behavior was less reprehensible than Smith's. But does one really want to say that? I think not. In the first place, both men acted from the same motive, personal gain, and both had exactly the same end in view when they acted. It may be inferred from Smith's conduct that he is a bad man, although that judgment may be withdrawn or modified if certain further facts are learned about him—for example, that he is mentally deranged. But would not the very same thing be inferred about Jones from his conduct? And would not the same further considerations also be relevant to any modification of this judgment? Moreover, suppose Jones pleaded, in his own defense, "After all, I didn't do anything except stand there and watch the child drown. I didn't kill him; I only let him die." Again, if letting die were in itself less bad than killing, this defense should have at least some weight. But it does not. Such a "defense" can only be regarded as a grotesque perversion of moral reasoning. Morally speaking, it is no defense at all.

Now, it may be pointed out, quite properly, that the cases of euthanasia with which doctors are concerned are not like this at all. They do not involve personal gain or the destruction of normal healthy children. Doctors are concerned only with cases in which the patient's life is of no further use to him, or in which the patient's life has become or will soon become a terrible burden. However, the point is the same in these cases: the bare difference between killing and letting die does not, in itself, make a moral difference. If a doctor lets a patient die, for humane reasons, he is in the same moral position as if he had given the patient a lethal injection for humane reasons. If his decision was wrong—if, for example, the patient's illness was in fact curable—the decision would be equally regrettable no matter which method was used to carry it out. And if the doctor's decision was the right one, the method used is not in itself important.

The AMA policy statement isolates the crucial issue very well; the crucial issue is "the intentional termination of the life of one human being by another." But after identifying this issue, and forbidding "mercy killing," the statement goes on to deny that the cessation of treatment is the intentional termination of a life. This is where the mistake comes in, for what is the cessation of treatment, in these circumstances, if it is not "the intentional termination of the life of one human being by another"? Of course it is exactly that, and if it were not, there would be no point to it.

Many people will find this judgment hard to accept. One reason, I think, is that it is very easy to conflate the question of whether killing is, in itself, worse than letting die, with the very different question of whether most actual cases of killing are more reprehensible than most actual cases of letting die. Most actual cases of killing are clearly terrible (think, for example, of all the murders reported in the newspapers), and one hears of such cases every day. On the other hand, one hardly ever hears of a case of letting die, except for the actions of doctors who are motivated by humanitarian reasons. So one learns to think of killing in a much worse light than of letting die. But this does not mean that there is something about killing that makes it in itself worse than letting die, for it is not the bare difference between killing and letting die that makes the difference in these cases. Rather, the other factors —the murder's motive of personal gain, for example, contrasted with the doctor's humanitarian motivation—account for different reactions to the different cases.

I have argued that killing is not in itself any worse than letting die; if my contention is right, it follows that active euthanasia is not any worse than passive euthanasia. What arguments can be given on the other side? The most common, I believe, is the following:

"The important difference between active and passive euthanasia is that, in passive euthanasia, the doctor does not do anything to bring about the patient's death. The doctor does nothing, and the patient dies of whatever ills already afflict him. In active euthanasia, however, the doctor does something to bring about the patient's death: he kills him. The doctor who gives the patient with cancer a lethal injection has himself caused his patient's death; whereas if he merely ceases treatment, the cancer is the cause of the death."

A number of points need to be made here. The first is that it is not exactly correct to say that in passive euthanasia the doctor does nothing, for he does do one thing that is very important: he lets the patient die. "Letting someone die" is certainly different, in some respects, from other types of action—mainly in

that it is a kind of action that one may perform by way of not performing certain other actions. For example, one may let a patient die by way of not giving medication, just as one may insult someone by way of not shaking his hand. But for any purpose of moral assessment, it is a type of action nonetheless. The decision to let a patient die is subject to moral appraisal in the same way that a decision to kill him would be subject to moral appraisal: it may be assessed as wise or unwise, compassionate or sadistic, right or wrong. If a doctor deliberately let a patient die who was suffering from a routinely curable illness, the doctor would certainly be to blame for what he had done, just as he would be to blame if he had needlessly killed the patient. Charges against him would then be appropriate. If so, it would be no defense at all for him to insist that he didn't "do anything." He would have done something very serious indeed, for he let his patient die.

Fixing the cause of death may be very important from a legal point of view, for it may determine whether criminal charges are brought against the doctor. But I do not think that this notion can be used to show a moral difference between active and passive euthanasia. The reason why it is considered bad to be the cause of someone's death is that death is regarded as a great evil—and so it is. However, if it has been decided that euthanasia—even passive euthanasia—is desirable in a given case, it has also been decided that in this instance death is no greater an evil than the patient's continued existence. And if this is true, the usual reason for not wanting to be the cause of someone's death simply does not apply.

Finally, doctors may think that all of this is only of academic interest—the sort of thing that philosophers may worry about but that has no practical bearing on their own work. After all, doctors must be concerned about the legal consequences of what they do, and active euthanasia is clearly forbidden by the law. But even so, doctors should also be concerned with the fact that the law is forcing upon them a moral doctrine that may well be indefensible, and has a considerable effect on their practices. Of course, most doctors are not now in the position of being coerced in this matter, for they do not regard themselves as merely going along with what the law requires. Rather, in statements such as the AMA policy statement that I have quoted, they are endorsing this doctrine as a central point of medical ethics. In that statement, active euthanasia is condemned not merely as illegal but as "contrary to that for which the medical profession stands," whereas passive euthanasia is approved. However, the preceding considerations suggest that there is really no moral difference between the two, considered in themselves (there may be important moral differences in some cases in their consequences, but, as I pointed out, these differences may make active euthanasia, and not passive euthanasia, the morally preferable option). So, whereas doctors may have to discriminate between active and passive euthanasia to satisfy the law, they should not do any more than that. In particular, they should not give the distinction any added authority and weight by writing it into official statements of medical ethics.

Note

1. A. Shaw, "Doctor, Do We Have a Choice?" *The New York Times Magazine,* January 30, 1972, p. 54.

Deciding to Forego Life-Sustaining Treatment

President's Commission for the Study of Ethical Problems in Medicine and Biomedical and Behavioral Research

Study Questions

1. How does the commission describe the situation of most seriously ill or dying patients today?

2. How does this contrast with dying in times past?

3. What new concerns, uncertainties, and fears about dying do patients have today?

4. What different views of death does the commission describe?

5. The commission suggests that we find the "golden mean" regarding our control of dying. What did it mean by this?

6. What particular phrases does the commission think are often a matter of empty rhetoric?

7. Why are the ideas intended by these phrases problematic?

8. What three underlying values does the commission believe ought to direct our decisions and public policy regarding medicine and death? Explain each.

9. What is the issue the commission points out regarding general rules and specific cases?

From the *President's Commission for the Study of Ethical Problems in Medicine and Biomedical and Behavioral Research.* 83-600503. Washington, DC: U.S. Government Printing Office, March 1983.

The Origins of Public Concern

Death comes to everyone. To a few, it comes suddenly and completely unexpectedly, but to most, it follows an opportunity for leave-taking and for directing to some extent the mode and timing of death.[1] Virtually all people who die in this country will have been under treatment by health care professionals who have, especially in the last four decades, developed powerful means to forestall death. This power is so dramatic that sometimes it seems that medicine aims first and foremost to conquer death. Physicians realize, of course, that the mission of vanquishing death is finally futile, but often they and their patients are quite determined to do all that is possible to postpone the event. Sometimes this objective so dominates care that patients undergo therapies whose effects do not actually advance their own goals and values. Specifically, the drive to sustain life can conflict with another fundamental (and arguably more venerable) objective of medicine—the relief of suffering.[2] Physicians and others who establish health care policies and practices have come to recognize that the attempt to postpone death should at times yield to other, more important goals of patients.

Recent Changes in How and Where People Die

Until this century decisions about medical interventions to prolong life probably appeared more straightforward, for doctors had few effective therapies from which to choose.[3] For most patients, diagnosis of serious illness no longer connotes sure, fairly swift death, requiring of the physician "philosophy and sympathy, not science."[4] Between 1900 and the present, the causes of death have changed dramatically: communicable diseases have declined sharply while chronic, degenerative diseases have become more prominent. At the turn of the century, influenza and pneumonia were the leading causes of death, followed by tuberculosis and "gastritis."[5] By 1976, these had been supplanted by heart disease, cancer, and cerebrovascular disease[6]—illnesses that occur later in life and that are ordinarily progressive for some years before death. Consequently, those facing death today are more likely to be aged and to be suffering from one or more ailments for which at least some potentially therapeutic interventions exist. "In this age of surgical derring-do and widespread use of drugs, almost no disease can be said any longer to have a 'natural history'."[7]

Just as recent years have seen alterations in the underlying causes of death, the places where people die have also changed. For most of recorded history, deaths (of natural causes) usually occurred in the home.

> Everyone knew about death at first hand; there was nothing unfamiliar or even queer about the phenomenon. People seem to have known a lot more about the process itself than is the case today. The "deathbed" was a real place, and the dying person usually knew where he was and when it was time to assemble the family and call for the priest.[8]

Even when people did get admitted to a medical care institution, those whose conditions proved incurable were discharged to the care of their families. This was not only because the health care system could no longer be helpful, but also because alcohol and opiates (the only drugs available to ease pain and suffering) were available without a prescription.[9] Institutional care was reserved for the poor or those without family support; hospitals often aimed more at saving patients' souls than at providing medical care.[10]

As medicine has been able to do more for dying patients, their care has increasingly been delivered in institutional settings. By 1949, institutions were the sites of 50% of all deaths; by 1958, the figure was 61%; and by 1977, over 70%.[11] Perhaps 80% of the deaths in the United States now occur in hospitals and long-term care institutions, such as nursing homes.[12] The change in where very ill patients are treated permits health care professionals to marshall the instruments of scientific medicine more effectively. But people who are dying may well find such a setting alienating and unsupportive.

> Patients who are known to be dying are segregated as much as possible from all the others, and . . . doctors spend as little time in attendance as they can manage. . . . When [doctors] avert their eyes it is not that they have lost interest, or find their attendance burdensome because wasteful of their talents; it is surely not because of occupational callousness. Although they are familiar with the business, seeing more of it at first hand than anyone else in our kind of society, they never become used to it. Death is shocking, dismaying, even terrifying. A dying patient is a kind of freak. It is the most unacceptable of all abnormalities, an offense against nature itself.[13]

Meeting Patients' Needs

With the process of dying prolonged and increasingly institutionalized, new concerns have arisen from and on behalf of dying patients. As in all areas of medicine, care of these patients is shaped by the varying degrees of uncertainty regarding diagnosis and prognosis. On the one hand, for most patients death is not unanticipated. One study, for example, found that half the population dies of an illness diagnosed at least 29 months earlier[14]; chronic conditions were the cause of 87% of all deaths in 1978.[15] On the other hand, dying follows no regular path.[16] The varied and somewhat unpredictable nature of the physical course of a dying patient is often a major source of anxiety to the patient, family, and care givers.

Patients frequently are afraid of symptoms and conditions, especially pain,[17] that may accompany the dying process. With appropriate medical management, many of these fears can be allayed. Patients who fear pain do so most often when it is out of control, overwhelming, or chronic, when it comes from an unknown source, or when it warns of devastating injury or death.[18] Each of these sources of fear can be treated. People at the forefront of the hospice movement, for example, have demonstrated that presently available drugs and other techniques can reduce even overwhelming pain to acceptable levels.[19] Some physicians may previously have withheld drugs to control pain out of a fear of addiction,[20] a concern that is unwarranted for dying patients.[21] Moreover, other uncomfortable or dangerous side effects of adequate pain medication can often be mitigated by careful attention to drug schedule, the strength of the medication, or a combination of these.[22] Symptoms such as nausea, anxiety, constipation, insomnia, and shortness of breath can also usually be ameliorated.[23] Simple attention to details such as skin care, oral hygiene, and proper positioning can greatly improve the lives of patients who are dying.

In the past several decades, the emotional and psychic course of dying patients has also received increasing attention.[24] The concern of the public as well as health care professionals has been evidenced by conferences, courses and training seminars, and publications such as *On Death and Dying*, a landmark book by Dr. Elisabeth Kübler-Ross published in 1969.[25] Critics of her work point out that dying patients do not all pass in lock-step fashion through the five psychological stages (denial and isolation, anger, bargaining, depression, and acceptance) that Dr. Kübler-Ross observed during counseling sessions, and that her theory has yet to be confirmed by systematic research. Although Dr. Kübler-Ross emphasized that patients in all stages continue to evidence hope, the very notion of "stages" is potentially misleading since they are not independent, in the sense of a patient being "in" one stage or another. Perhaps most important, experience shows that acceptance is not always possible or appropriate for a patient.[26] Eschewing the theory of stages of death, one thanatologist sees instead "a complicated clustering of intellectual and affective states, some fleeting, lasting for a moment or a day or a week, set not unexpectedly against a backdrop of that person's total personality, 'his philosophy of life.'"[27]

Views of Death

Dying patients often are not entirely averse to the prospect of death,[28] which may be seen as preferable to prolonging an inexorable process of suffering or as less important than other concerns (personal salvation, the welfare of loved ones, and so forth). People's perceptions of the nature and meaning of death, especially in this pluralistic society, are quite diverse. For some, life is infinitely important and death is always to be opposed:

> The value of human life is infinite and beyond measure, so that a hundred years and a single second are equally precious.[29]

For some, life is the norm and death an oddity or annoyance:

> To make matters worse, the process of dying cannot even be treated as a tragedy since our Doing and mastery-over-Nature values make it seem more like technical failure. Tragedy, in our society, is something that should have been avoided rather than something to be appreciated. The implication is that someone slipped up or that research simply has not yet got around to solving this kind of thing. Thus dying is covered over with optimistic or reassuring statements and the dying person is scarcely given the opportunity to make the most of his position.[30]
>
> All men must die: but for every man his death is an accident and, even if he knows it and consents to it, an unjustifiable violation.[31]

Some have noted that the inevitability of death is what gives life meaning and purpose:

> Protect me
> From a body without death. Such indignity
> Would be outcast, like a rock in the sea.
> But with death, it can hold
> More than time gives it, or the earth shows it.[32]
>
> Death forces us to shore up, personally and aggregatively, the conviction of life; that we persist and survive, as at least minimally rational creatures, confirms the pragmatic adequacy of our beliefs.[33]

For some, death is the release of the soul from its body:

> The soul which is pure at departing . . . departs to the invisible world—to the devine and immortal and rational: Hither arriving, she is secure of bliss and is released from the error and folly of men, their fears and wild passions and all other human ills, and forever dwells, as they say of the initiated, in the company with the gods.[34]

The perspectives on death are as numerous as the philosophies and religions that give them birth. And for each perspective there is a complementary set of values and priorities in the medical care of dying patients. Someone who holds that every second of life under any circumstances is worth living, for example, will make very different decisions than a person who is accepting of death.[35]

The view that there is no one way to die that is right for all persons has ancient roots:

> Just as I choose a ship to sail in or a house to live in, so I choose a death for my passage from life. . . .

Nowhere should we indulge the soul more than in dying. . . . A man's life should satisfy other people as well, his death only himself, and whatever sort he likes best.[36]

Under modern conditions, to achieve some harmony between an individual's death and personal values throughout life will probably entail not only awareness of personal values but also the sensitivity and compassion of others and the tolerance of a society willing to allow a fair range of choice—both for people to find and create meaning in living while dying, and for survivors to incorporate and interpret their loss.

Achieving this harmony is made more complex because of an apparently unavoidable tension that accompanies the medical care of dying patients. It is a tension that persists even when both the general society and health care professionals agree that avoiding death should not always be the preeminent goal of therapy and that assisting each patient to achieve a personally appropriate death is among the professionals' obligations. Once someone realizes that the time and manner of death are substantially under the control of medical science, he or she wants to be protected against decisions that make death too easy and quick as well as from those that make it too agonizing and prolonged. Yet such a "golden mean" defies ready definition, both in theory and often in practical application in individual cases.[37] Each case is different, both objectively and in the subjective experience of the patient, so definitions of "too quick" and "too long" vary widely. This does not, however, preclude setting forth some general guidelines and policy tools.

Considerations in Framing Social Policy

The Commission uses the term public policy in its broadest sense, which includes all the various rules, norms, laws, and practices that a society employs in a given area. Regulations may be formal, such as statutes enforced according to specified procedures, or informal, as in the expectations regarding acceptable professional behavior that health care professionals absorb while learning other things.[38] A public policy also exists when society chooses not to intervene in private actions. Indeed, a major issue in establishing wise public policies on life-sustaining treatment is the degree to which the community and its agents should be involved in medical decision making.

Public policy is mediated through a variety of societal practices and institutions: governmental bodies (both legislative and regulatory), health care professionals and institutions (individually and collectively), organized religions, and other social groups. Yet the people who must implement such policies are often the directly affected patients and their families.

The Disservice Done by Empty Rhetoric

Discussions of life-sustaining treatment have often been confused by the use of slogans and code words. As a general matter, the issues can be understood much better if the exact meaning of these rhetorical devices is spelled out. Phrases like "right to die," "right to life," "death with dignity," "quality of life," and "euthanasia" have been used in such conflicting ways that their meanings, if they ever were clear, have become hopelessly blurred.

In recent years, for example, many have commented on the claim that patients have a "right to die with dignity."[39] Much can and should be done to ensure that patients are treated with respect and concern throughout life. Insofar as "death with dignity" means that the wishes of dying patients are solicited and respected, it is a concept the Commission endorses.[40] Many who use the phrase seem to go well beyond this, however, to a vision in which everyone is guaranteed a peaceful and aesthetically appealing death. This is clearly beyond reach; a fair proportion of dying patients are confused, nauseated, vomiting, delirious, bleeding, or breathless. Avoiding these distressing symptoms is not always possible; likewise, naturalness may have to be sacrificed since mechanical assistance is sometimes required to ensure comfort at the end of life.[41] Thus, the apparent appeal of the slogan "dignified death" often disappears before the reality of patients' needs and desires. Comparable problems arise with other slogans that are frequently heard in discussions on life-sustaining treatment.[42]

Other phrases—though useful as general descriptions—are similarly unacceptable when an unambiguous definition is required. For example, attempts—such as those in several statutes[43]—to make the obligations of patients and providers different when a patient is "terminally ill" are dubious for several reasons. First, although a decision to undertake a life-sustaining treatment will frequently depend on whether the patient believes the treatment is likely to extend life substantially enough to be worth its burdens, patients with similar prognoses evaluate relevant facts very differently. The closeness of death may be strongly felt by someone who has only a remote chance of dying soon, while for another person it may not seem imminent until his or her organs have nearly ceased to function. Moreover, prognostication near the end of life is notoriously uncertain.[44] At best, confidence in predicting death is possible only in the final few hours. Patients with the same stage of a disease but with different family settings, personalities, and "things to live for" actually do live for strikingly varied periods of time.[45] It seems difficult to devise or to justify policies that restrict people's discretion to make appropriate decisions by allowing some choices only to "terminally ill" patients or by denying them other choices.

Although the Commission has attempted to avoid rhetorical slogans so as to escape the ambiguities and misunderstandings that often accompany them, it uses "dying" and "terminally ill" as descriptive terms for certain patients, not as ironclad categories. There seem to be no other terms to use for a patient whose illness is likely to cause death within what is to that person a very short time. Of course, the word "dying" is in some ways an unilluminating modifier for a "patient"— since life is always a "terminal" condition—and further refinements, such as "imminently," do little to clarify the situation. . . .

Underlying Values

In its work on the ethical issues in health care the Commission discussed the importance of three basic values: self-determination, well-being, and equity. The concepts are not all-encompassing; nor was any attempt made to relate them in a hierarchical fashion. In *Making Health Care Decisions,* the Commission focused almost entirely upon the values of self-determination and well-being[46]; in *Securing Access to Health Care,* principally upon considerations of equity.[47] . . .

The primary goal of health care in general is to maximize each patient's well-being. However, merely acting in a patient's best interests without recognizing the individual as the pivotal decision maker would fail to respect each person's interest in self-determination—the capacity to form, revise, and pursue his or her own plans for life. Self-determination has both an instrumental value in achieving subjectively defined well-being and an intrinsic value as an element of personal worth and integrity.

Given the special importance of health care in promoting individuals' well-being and opportunities, the Commission also concluded that society has a moral obligation to ensure that everyone has access to an adequate level of care and is able to obtain such care without excessive burdens (in terms of financial or time expenditures). Since differences in health status are largely determined by natural and social contingencies beyond an individual's control and are so unevenly distributed that some people are unable through their own efforts to obtain adequate care, the moral obligation to ensure equitable access rests with society as a whole. This obligation is particularly acute when health care is needed to sustain life itself.

Though a given decision will often serve all relevant values, sometimes conflict occurs. When the conflicts that arise between a competent patient's self-determination and his or her apparent well-being remain unresolved after adequate deliberation, a competent patient's self-determination is and usually should be given greater weight than other people's views on that individual's well-being. Similarly, while a competent patient's choice about treatment is usually more compelling than claims based on resource allocations, considerations of equitable access to health care in society will in fact partially determine the availability of options for a particular patient. Fair treatment of individuals necessitates basing decisions about availability and funding on defensible principles, and then implementing decisions through general rules and institutional policies that are insulated from the subjectivity of ad hoc decisions.

General Rules and Specific Cases

Although good public policy should reflect morally sound treatment of the individual cases that the policy concerns, the many distinctions among different cases that might be made in a careful, complete moral analysis cannot usually be included in a manageable public policy. Yet general rules are adopted to govern the behavior of many people with diverse values and goals in a manner that is morally acceptable in the vast majority of cases and that tends to permit only the most acceptable errors. But the weight of certain ethical considerations is changed when they are applied to matters of general public policy instead of merely to the private concerns of individuals. Consequently, policies that are predominantly procedural rather than substantive are often favored as a means of attempting to allocate responsibility in a way that allows decision makers to take account of the full range and subtlety of each case's morally relevant features.

As in so many other areas, there is tension between substance and procedures in making policies about foregoing life-sustaining treatment. Decisions are commonly made under adverse conditions; the individuals who make them have varying capacities for judgment and their disinterest and goodwill are sometimes imperfect. Caution is warranted, then, in considering procedural policies that fail to place some substantive constraints on the decision makers. For the same reasons, however, policies that *do* contain substantive criteria for decisions may be subject to misuse and abuse. To limit the potential for both well-intentioned misapplication and ill-intentioned abuse, justifiable social and legal policies in this area (as elsewhere) may forbid certain classes of actions that include cases in which the forbidden act would actually be morally justified, while at the same time allowing other classes that include cases in which the permitted act would be morally wrong. The problem, then, is determining which guidelines and procedures are most likely to produce optimal decisions—in this case, the best balance between overuse and underuse of life-sustaining treatment.

Consistent with this goal, the conflict between the careful assessments of the concerned parties in a particular case and the demands of public policy should be minimized. Otherwise patients, providers, and families will continually be acting contrary either to generally accepted, and often legally enforced, public policy or to their own responsible assessment of a situation.

Notes

1. Approximately 2 million people die each year in the United States. The illnesses causing mortality most often are heart disease (34%), malignancies (22%), and cerebrovascular disease (7%). Traumatic death—including accidents, homicide and suicide—account for 13% of all deaths. Dept. of Health, Education and Welfare, *Facts of Life and Death* (Washington, DC: U.S. Government Printing Office, 1978), pp. 31–33. Only the relatively few who die very suddenly from accident, heart attack, or stroke are likely to have been without medical attention.

2. Physicians may not have recognized a duty to prolong life until fairly recently: "The treatise entitled *The Art* in the Hippocratic Corpus defines medicine as having three roles: doing away with the sufferings of the sick, lessening the violence of their diseases, and refusing to treat those who are overmastered by their diseases, realizing that in such cases, medicine is powerless." Darrell W. Admundsen, "The Physicians' Obligation to Prolong Life: A Medical Duty Without Classical Roots," *Hastings Center Report,* 8 (Aug. 1978): 23, 24; Warren T. Reich, "The 'Duty' to Preserve Life," *Hastings Center Report,* 5 (April 1975): 14.

    One modern formulation of the physician's role toward the terminally ill is found in this statement from the American Medical Association. "The social commitment of the physician is to prolong life and relieve suffering. Where the observance of one conflicts with the other, the physician, patient, and/or family of the patient have the discretion to resolve the conflict." Judicial Council, *Current Opinions of the Judicial Council of the American Medical Association.* (Chicago: AMA, 1982), p. 9.

3. Ivan L. Bennett, Jr., "Technology as a Shaping Force," in John H. Knowles (Ed.), *Doing Better and Feeling Worse: Health in the United States* (New York: W.W. Norton, 1977), pp. 128–129.

4. Louis Lasagna, "The Prognosis of Death," in Orville G. Brim, Jr., et al. (Eds.), *The Dying Patient* (New York: Russell Sage Foundation, 1970), pp. 67, 76.

5. Monroe Lerner, "When, Why and Where People Die," in Brim, note 4, p. 5. See also Thomas M. Perry, "The New and Old Diseases: A Study of Mortality Trends in the United States, 1900–1969," *American Journal of Clinical Pathology,* 63 (1975): 453.

6. *Facts of Life and Death.*

7. Lasagna, p. 68.

8. Lewis Thomas, "Dying as Failure," *American Academy of Political & Social Science,* 447 (1980): 1, 3.

9. The Harrison Act of 1914 restricted access to narcotics, making them available only through a physician's prescription. Harrison Act, 38 Stat. 785 (1914), as amended 26 U.S.C.; Alfred R. Lindesmith, *The Addict and the Law* (New York: Random House, 1965), pp. 3–8. At the turn of the century many of the widely available elixirs and patent medicines contained substantial quantities of narcotics. Nicholas N. Kittrie, *The Right to Be Different* (Baltimore: Johns Hopkins University Press, 1971), pp. 216–217; James Harvey Young, *The Toadstool Millionaires* (Princeton, NJ: Princeton University Press, 1961). See also David E. Kyvig, *Repealing National Prohibition* (Chicago: University of Chicago Press, 1979), p. 33 (describing physicians' reactions to restrictions on medicinal use of alcohol during prohibition).

10. "The first hospitals for the sick . . . remained, of course, the least preferred setting for medical treatment, and people with sufficient funds received care at home. But by the end of the colonial period, the almshouse had become a hospital for the poor." David J. Rothman, *The Discovery of the Asylum: Social Order and Disorder in the New Republic* (Boston: Little, Brown, 1971), pp. 43–45.

John W. Knowles, "The Hospital," in *Life and Death and Medicine* (San Francisco: W.H. Freeman, 1973), p. 91.

11. Lerner, p. 22; Jack M. Zimmerman, "Experience with a Hospice-Care Program for the Terminally Ill," *Annals of Surgery*, 189 (1979): 683.

12. In a review of 35,381 cancer deaths in Cuyahoga County, Ohio, homes during the period 1957–1974, 65% of the people died in hospitals, 15% in nursing homes, and 20% at home. Arthur Flynn, "Where Do Cancer Patients Die?" *Journal of Community Health*, 5 (Winter 1979): 126. See also John M. Hinton, "Comparison of Places and Policies for Terminal Care," *Lancet*, 1 (1979): 29; Roger Pritchard, "Dying: Some Issues and Problems," *Annals of the New York Academy of Sciences, 164* (1969): 707.

13. Thomas, p. 2.

14. Raymond S. Duff and August B. Hollingshead, *Sickness and Society* (New York: Harper & Row, 1968), p. 307.

15. Anne R. Somers, "Long-Term Care for the Elderly and Disabled," *New England Journal of Medicine, 207* (1982): 221 (quoting Dorothy P. Rice of the National Center for Health Statistics).

16. Strauss and Glaser have developed a theory involving each patient's "dying trajectory" to describe this process. Barney G. Glaser and Anselm L. Strauss, *Time for Dying* (Hawthorne, NY: Aldine, 1968). "It plunges straight down, it moves slowly but steadily downward; it vacillates slowly, moving slightly up and down before diving downward radically; it moves slowly down at first, then hits a long plateau, then plunges abruptly to death." Anselm L. Strauss and Barney G. Glaser, "Patterns of Dying," in Brim, pp. 129, 131.

17. Peter G. Wilson, "Anxiety and Depression in Elderly and Dying Patients," in Marcus Reidenberg (Ed.), *Clinical Pharmacology of Symptom Control; The Medical Clinics of North America*, 66 (Sept. 1982): 1011. See generally, Patrick B. Friel, "Death and Dying," *Annals of Internal Medicine*, 97 (1982): 767.

18. Eric J. Cassell, "The Nature of Suffering and the Goals of Medicine," *New England Journal of Medicine*, 306 (1982): 639; Laurence B. McCullough, "Pain, Suffering and Life Extending Technologies," in Robert M. Veatch (Ed.), *Life Span* (New York: Harper & Row, 1979), p. 118.

19. Some of the techniques to control pain and other symptoms are given in Appendix B, pp. 275–297. St. Christopher's Hospice reports complete control of pain in more than 99% of its dying patients. Cicely M. Saunders, "Current Views on Pain Relief and Terminal Care," in Martin A. Swerdlow (Ed.), *The Therapy of Pain* (Philadelphia: J.B. Lippincott, 1981), p. 215.

Just as people have different understandings of death, so do they view pain differently.

According to Christian teaching, however, suffering, especially during the last moments of life, has a special place in God's saving plan; it is in fact a sharing in Christ's Pas-

sion and a union with the redeeming sacrifice which he offered in obedience to the Father's will. Therefore one must not be surprised if some Christians prefer to moderate their use of painkillers, in order to accept voluntarily at least a part of their suffering and thus associate themselves in a conscious way with the suffering of Christ crucified. Sacred Congregation for the Doctrine of Faith, *Declaration on Euthanasia* (Vatican City, 1980), p. 8.

20. Gerald Klerman has termed this hesitance on the part of physicians, "pharmacological Calvinism." Gerald L. Klerman, "Psychotropic Drugs as Therapeutic Agents," *Hastings Center Studies*, 2 (Jan. 1974): 91–92.

21. Marcia Angell, "The Quality of Mercy" (Editorial), *New England Journal of Medicine, 306* (1982): 98; Richard M. Marks and Edward J. Sachar, "Undertreatment of Medical Inpatients with Narcotic Analgesics," *Annals of Internal Medicine, 78* (1973): 173; Jane Porter and Hershel Jick, "Addiction Rate in Patients Treated with Narcotics," *New England Journal of Medicine, 302* (1980): 123.

22. Robert G. Twycross, "Relief of Pain," in Cicely M. Saunders (Ed.), *The Management of Terminal Disease* (London: Edward Arnold, 1978), p. 65.

23. Ned H. Cassem and Rege S. Steward, "Management and Care of the Dying Patient," *International Journal of Psychiatry in Medicine, 6* (1975): 293, 299; A.G.O. Crowther, "Management of Other Common Symptoms in the Terminally Ill," in Eric Wilkes (Ed.), *The Dying Patient* (Ridgewood, NJ: George A. Bogden & Son, 1982), p. 209; Mary J. Baines, "Control of Other Symptoms," in Saunders, p. 99.

24. Michele Vovelle, "Rediscovery of Death Since 1960," *Annals of the American Academy of Political & Social Science, 447* (1980): 89.

25. Elisabeth Kübler-Ross, *On Death and Dying* (New York: Macmillan, 1969).

26. Michael A. Simpson, "Therapeutic Uses of Truth," in Wilkes, pp. 255, 258; Ned H. Cassem, "The Dying Patient," in Thomas P. Hackett and Ned H. Cassem (Eds.), *Massachusetts General Hospital Handbook of General Hospital Psychiatry* (St. Louis: C.V. Mosby, 1978), p. 300.

27. Edwin S. Shneidman, "Death Work and Stages of Dying," in Edwin S. Shneidman (Ed.), *Death: Current Perspectives* (Palo Alto: Mayfield, 1976), p. 446.

28. See, e.g., C. M. Farquhar, "Attitudes and Beliefs Concerning Life and Death of Elderly Persons," *New Zealand Medical Journal, 92* (1980): 107; David L. Jackson and Stuart Youngner, "Patient Autonomy and 'Death with Dignity,'" *New England Journal of Medicine, 301* (1979): 404; L. Witzel, "Behavior of the Dying Patient," *British Medical Journal, 2* (1975): 81.

29. Immanuel Jakobovits, *Jewish Medical Ethics* (New York: Bloch, 1959), p. 46.

30. John Spiegel, "Cultural Variations in Attitudes Toward Death and Disease," in George H. Grosser et al. (Eds.),

The Threat of Impending Disaster (Cambridge, MA: M.I.T. Press, 1964), p. 297.

31. Simone de Beauvoir, *A Very Easy Death* (New York: G.P. Putnam's Sons, 1966), reprinted in Shneidman, pp. 523, 526.

32. Christopher Fry, *The Dark Is Light Enough* (London: Oxford University Press, 1954), p. 89.

33. Joseph Margolis, "Death," in *Negativities: The Limits of Life* (Columbus, OH: Charles E. Merrill, 1975), reprinted in Tom L. Beauchamp and Seymour Perlin (Eds.), *Ethical Issues in Death and Dying* (Englewood Cliffs, NJ: Prentice-Hall, 1978), pp. 357, 363.

34. Plato, "Phaedo," in Irwin Edman (Ed.), *The Works of Plato* (New York: Modern Library, 1928), p. 141.

35. "An appropriate death, in brief, is a death that someone might choose for himself—had he a choice." Avery D. Weisman, "Appropriate and Appropriated Death," in *On Dying and Denying: A Psychiatric Study of Terminality* (New York: Behavioral Publications, 1972), p. 41; Lauren E. Trombley, "A Psychiatrist's Response to a Life-Threatening Illness," in Shneidman, p. 506; H. Tristram Engelhardt, Jr., "Tractatus Artis Bene Moriendi Vivendique: Choosing Styles of Dying and Living," in Virginia Abernathy (Ed.), *Frontiers in Medical Ethics* (Cambridge, MA: Ballinger, 1980), p. 9.

36. Seneca, "Suicide," in *The Stoic Philosophy of Seneca*, Moses Hadas (Trans.) (New York: W.W. Norton, 1958), p. 506.

37. When 205 physicians in one study were presented with a hypothetical case, the range of assessments was striking, with those who favored and those against aggressive treatment offering the same reasons but projecting very different views of the patient's future. Robert A. Pearlman, Thomas S. Inui, and William Carter, "Variability in Physician Bioethical Decisionmaking: A Case Study of Euthanasia," *Annals of Internal Medicine, 97* (1982): 420.

38. See, e.g., Charles L. Bosk, *Forgive and Remember: Managing Medical Failure* (Chicago: University of Chicago Press, 1979).

39. See, e.g., Stephen L. Kuepper, *The Euthanasia Movement: A Brief History of the Organized Euthanasia Movement in the United States* (1979) (unpublished manuscript on file with the Society for the Right to Die, New York); Ivan Illich, "The Political Use of a Natural Death," *Hastings Center Studies, 2* (Jan. 1974): 3; Marya Mannes, *Last Rights: A Plea for the Good Death* (New York: William Morrow, 1974); Patrick Francis Sheehy, *On Dying With Dignity* (New York: Pinnacle Books, 1981). But see Jackson and Youngner.

40. See pp. 46–51 infra.

41. Robert M. Veatch, *Death, Dying and the Biological Revolution* (New Haven, CT: Yale University Press, 1976), pp. 277–305; Paul Ramsey, "The Indignity of Death with Dignity," *Hastings Center Report, 2* (May 1974): 47. See also Appendix B, pp. 275–297.

42. See, e.g., Daniel Callahan, "Natural Death and Public Policy," and James Childress, "Further Reflections on Natural Death and Public Policy," in Robert M. Veatch (Ed.), *Life Span: Values and Life-Extending Technologies* (San Francisco: Harper & Row, 1979), pp. 162, 176.

43. Natural Death Acts have usually tried to define a class of patients who have "incurable injury, diseases, or illness . . . where the application of life-sustaining procedures would serve only to prolong the dying process." Medical Treatment Decision Act, reprinted in Appendix D, pp. 313–317. The 1982 amendments to the Medicare program provide much more substantial reimbursement for "palliation and management" of "terminally ill" patients (defined as those for whom death is expected within six months) than for treatment of disease for these patients or for any treatment of other patients. §122, Part II, Tax Equity and Fiscal Responsibility Act, Pub. L. No. 97-248 (1982). These points are discussed more fully in Chapters Three and Four infra. See also Paul Ramsey, *The Patient as Person* (New Haven, CT: Yale University Press, 1970), p. 113.

44. "Physicians' predictions of prognosis were relatively inaccurate, with actual survival plus or minus one month coinciding with that predicted in only 16% of patients. Except in patients who were very ill and had short prognosis of three to four months, survival was consistently underestimated." Linda J. Aiken and Martita M. Marx, "Hospices: Perspectives on the Public Policy Debate," *American Psychologist, 37* (1982): 1271, 1275 (reporting data from J.W. Yates, F.P. McKegney, and L.E. Kun, "A Comparative Study of Home Nursing Care of Patients with Advanced Cancer," *Proceedings of the Third National Conference on Human Values of Cancer* (New York: American Cancer Society, 1982).

The subjective nature of prognosis affects the types of treatment that are encouraged, which in turn affects patients' outcome. In one study, physicians who preferred to intubate and artificially ventilate a patient with severe chronic lung disease projected that the patient would survive about 15 months; other physicians who decided against artificial ventilation when presented with the same case predicted that, even with artificial life support, the patient had only 6 months to live. Pearlman, Inui, and Carter. See also J. Englebert Dunphy, "Annual Discourse—On Caring for the Patient with Cancer," *New England Journal of Medicine, 295* (1976): 313, 314; Mark Siegler, "Pascal's Wager and the Hanging of Crepe," *New England Journal of Medicine, 293* (1975): 853; Arno G. Motulsky, "Biased Ascertainment and the Natural History of Disease," *New England Journal of Medicine, 298* (1978): 1196.

45. E. Mansell Pattison, "The Will to Live and the Expectation of Death," in E. Mansell Pattison, ed., *The Experience of Dying* (Englewood Cliffs, NJ: Prentice-Hall, 1977), p. 61.

46. President's Commission for the Study of Ethical Problems in Medicine and Biomedical and Behavioral Research, *Making Health Care Decisions* (Washington, DC: U.S. Government Printing Office, 1982).

47. President's Commission for the Study of Ethical Problems in Medicine and Biomedical and Behavioral Research, *Securing Access to Health Care* (Washington, DC: U.S. Government Printing Office, 1983).

Review Exercises

1. What is the difference between "whole brain death" and "persistent vegetative state"?

2. If a person has whole brain death, what kind of euthanasia is possible? Explain.

3. What is the difference between active and passive euthanasia?

4. Where do advance directives such as living wills and durable powers of attorney fit into the distinction between voluntary and nonvoluntary euthanasia?

5. What is the difference between ordinary and extraordinary measures of life support? If some measure of life support were rather common and inexpensive, would this necessarily make it an ordinary means of life support? Explain.

6. Label the following as examples of voluntary or nonvoluntary *and* active or passive euthanasia; if passive, are the measures described more likely to be considered ordinary or extraordinary measures of life support?

   a. A person who is dying asks to be given a fatal drug dose to bring about his death.

   b. A dying patient asks that no more chemotherapy be administered because it is doing nothing but prolonging her death, which is inevitable in a short time anyway.

   c. Parents of a newborn whose condition involves moderate retardation refuse permission for a simple surgery that would repair a physical anomaly inconsistent with continued life, and they let the infant die.

   d. A husband gives his wife a lethal overdose of her pain medicine because he does not want to see her suffer anymore.

   e. Doctors decide not to try to start artificial feeding mechanisms for their patient because they believe that it will be futile—that is, ineffective given the condition of their patient.

7. List the consequentialist concerns that could be given in arguing about whether or not the actions proposed in three of the scenarios in question 6 are justified.

8. Give some nonconsequentialist concerns that could be given in arguing about these same three scenarios.

Discussion Cases

1. *Respirator Removal.* Jim was an active person. He was a lawyer by profession. When he was forty-four years old, a routine physical revealed that he had a tumor on his right lung. After surgery to remove that lung he returned to a normal life. However, four years later a cancerous tumor was found in his other lung. He knew he had only months to live. Then came the last hospitalization. He was on a respirator. It was extremely uncomfortable for him, and he was frustrated by not being able to talk because of the tubes. After some thought he decided that he did not want to live out his last few weeks like this and asked to have the respirator removed. Because he was no longer able to breathe on his own, he knew this meant he would die shortly after it was removed.

Did Jim or the doctors who removed the respirator and then watched as Jim died as a result do anything wrong? Why or why not? Would there be any difference between this case and that of a person in a coma or persistent vegetative state whose wishes we do not know? Would it matter whether we considered the respirator ordinary or extraordinary means of life support? Which would it be in this case?

2. *Pill Overdose.* Mary Jones had a severe case of cerebral palsy. She now had spent twenty-eight years of life trying to cope with the varying dis-

abilities it caused. She could get around some-what in her motorized wheelchair. An aide fed her and took care of her small apartment. She had gone to junior college and earned a degree in sociology. She also had a mechanism whereby she could type on a computer. However, she had lately become weary with life. She saw no im-provement ahead and wanted to die. She had been receiving pain pills from her doctor. Now she asked for several weeks' worth of prescrip-tions so that she would not have to return for more so often. Her doctor suspected that she might be suicidal.

Should Mary Jones's doctor continue giving her the pills? Why or why not? Would she be as-sisting in Mary's suicide if she did? Does Mary Jones have a right to end her life if she chooses? Why or why not? Should her physician actually be able to administer some death-causing drug and not just provide the pills? Why or why not?

3. *Baby John Doe.* Sarah and Mike's baby boy was born with a defect called *spina bifida.* It con-sisted of an opening in the spine, and in his case was of the more severe kind in which the spinal cord also protruded through the hole. The open-ing was moderately high in the spine, and thus they were told that his neurological control be-low that level would be affected. He would have no bowel and bladder control and would not be able to walk unassisted. The cerebral spinal fluid had already started to back up into the cavity sur-rounding his brain, and his head was swelling. Doctors advised that they could have a shunt put in place to drain this fluid from the brain and prevent pressure on the brain. They could also have the spinal opening repaired. If they did not do so, however, the baby would probably die from the infection that would develop. Sarah and Mike are afraid of raising such a child and think that it also would not have a very easy life. In a few cases, however, children with this anomaly who do not have the surgery do not die, and then they are worse off than if the operation were done.

What should Sarah and Mike do? Why?

Selected Bibliography

Baird, Robert, and Stuart E. Rosenbaum (Eds.). *Euthana-sia: The Moral Issues.* Buffalo, NY: Prometheus, 1989.

Battin, M. Pabst. *Ethical Issues in Suicide.* Englewood Cliffs, NJ: Prentice-Hall, 1982.

————. *The Least Worst Death.* New York: Oxford Univer-sity Press, 1994.

Beauchamp, Tom L., and Robert M. Veatch. *Ethical Issues in Death and Dying.* Upper Saddle River, NJ: Prentice-Hall, 1996.

Beauchamp, Tom L. *Intending Death: The Ethics of As-sisted Suicide and Euthanasia.* Upper Saddle River, NJ: Prentice-Hall, 1996.

Behnke, John A., and Sissela Bok. *The Dilemmas of Eutha-nasia.* New York: Doubleday, Anchor, 1975.

Downing, A. B. (Ed.). *Euthanasia and the Right to Death: The Case for Voluntary Euthanasia.* New York: Humani-ties Press, 1969.

Grisez, Germain, and Joseph M. Boyle, Jr. *Life and Death with Liberty and Justice: A Contribution to the Euthana-sia Debate.* Notre Dame, IN: University of Notre Dame Press, 1979.

Keown, John (Ed.). *Euthanasia Examined: Ethical, Clini-cal and Legal Perspectives.* New York: Cambridge Uni-versity Press, 1996.

Kohl, Marvin (Ed.). *Beneficent Euthanasia.* Buffalo, NY: Prometheus, 1975.

Ladd, John. *Ethical Issues Relating to Life and Death.* New York: Oxford University Press, 1979.

Lynn, Joanne (Ed.). *By No Extraordinary Means: The Choice to Forgo Life-Sustaining Food and Water.* Bloom-ington: Indiana University Press, 1986.

Maguire, Daniel C. *Death by Choice.* New York: Dou-bleday, 1974.

Morgan, Robert, and Derrick Morgan (Eds.). *Death Rites: Law and Ethics at the End of Life.* New York: Routledge, 1994.

President's Commission for the Study of Ethical Prob-lems in Medicine and Biomedical and Behavioral Re-search. *Deciding to Forgo Life-Sustaining Treatment.* New York: Concern for Dying, 1983.

Russell, O. Ruth. *Freedom to Die: Moral and Legal Aspects of Euthanasia.* New York: Human Sciences Press, 1975.

Steinbock, Bonnie (Ed.). *Killing and Letting Die.* Engle-wood Cliffs, NJ: Prentice-Hall, 1980.

Walton, Douglas N. *On Defining Death: An Analytic Study of the Concept of Death in Philosophy and Medical Ethics.* Montreal: McGill-Queen, 1979.

Weir, Robert F. *Selective Non-treatment of Handicapped Newborns: Moral Dilemmas in Neonatal Medicine.* New York: Oxford University Press, 1984.

❧ *9* ❧

Abortion

Imagine the following scene. The setting is a women's medical clinic that performs abortions. Outside are demonstrators carrying placards. Some are shouting, "This is not a political or economic issue. This is a dead baby!"[1] Others echo, "Killing is wrong." One demonstrator explains, "We're volunteer sidewalk counselors to protect the unborn." Several women enter the clinic while trying to ignore the protesters. One young woman is accompanied by a young man. They, too, rush past the demonstrators, refusing the pamphlets they offer. "We want to give women like this one alternatives," the demonstrators explain. "They are naive. They do not know what they are doing. Many later regret their decisions to end the life of their unborn child." The young woman is upset. She acknowledges that her decision was difficult and that she nevertheless thought it was for the best. She is angry that others who do not know her or her situation are making her choice even more difficult. The demonstrators assume that she and other women are not capable of making decent moral decisions for themselves. Those who support women's right to choose abortion are also angry at those who harass the people entering such clinics and who threaten the doctors who perform abortions. Fewer young physicians, they point out, are now performing abortions even though it is a legal procedure. In March 1993 a doctor who performed abortions

was shot and killed by an antiabortion protester. Some in the prolife movement, however, disagree with the tactics of the more militant antiabortion groups. They believe that these tactics and the murder of the doctor hurt their cause. They preach nonviolence and urge respect for all persons, including the unborn.[2]

We continue to see such scenes broadcast on the evening news and described in the newspapers. Why? Abortion is an issue about which people have extremely strong opinions. Expressions of their opinions are often highly emotionally charged. Among the probable reasons why abortion is such a volatile issue is that it is a matter of life and death and involves beliefs about the very meaning of life itself. It is also a gender issue and touches our beliefs about the most intimate and powerful aspects of our lives as women and men and as mothers and fathers. Sometimes people's views are based on religious beliefs, but this is not always or necessarily the case. To complicate matters further, people do not always notice that there is a difference between asking about the morality of abortion and asking what the law ought or ought not to be in its regard. In addition, the language that is used in the debate over abortion often influences the debate. What is meant by "prolife"? Do not both those who oppose and those who condone abortion act in support of life? What is meant by "prochoice"? The position supporting a woman's right to choose abortion seems rightly labeled "prochoice." The phrases "proabortion" and "antichoice" have significantly different overtones than the phrases generally used. This shows how important is the language in which an ethical debate is couched. In this chapter we try to avoid labels and analyze the issues and arguments in such a way as to help us focus more clearly on the alternatives and the reasons supporting them.

What we say about the morality of abortion will depend on several issues. Some are strictly ethical matters and involve basic ethical perspectives, such as the nature and basis of moral rights. Others are factual matters, such as what happens at different stages of fetal development and what the likely consequences of certain actions are given particular social conditions. Others still are conceptual matters, such as the meaning of abortion or a person or a human being. We begin our analysis with certain factual matters concerning stages of fetal development and methods of abortion.

Stages of Fetal Development

When considering stages of fetal development, the label given to the developing fetus at particular stages is not likely to be relevant to any ethical argument because these are just names given for purposes of identification and communication. The newly fertilized egg is called a *zygote,* which simply means "joining together." When the ball of cells reaches the uterus some seven to ten days after fertilization, it is called a *blastocyst,* because a *blastula* is a fluid-filled cavity surrounded by a single layer of cells. From the second to eighth week of gestation it is called an *embryo,* as is any animal at this early stage of primitive tissue and organ development. From then on until birth it is called a *fetus,* which means "young unborn." We will simplify things and use the term *fetus* throughout development, but use of this term does not imply anything about its value or status. We can single out the following stages of fetal development (times are approximate).

- Day 1: Fertilization—Ovum (23 chromosomes) is penetrated by sperm (23 chromosomes); one cell is formed containing 46 chromosomes.

- Days 2–3: Passage through the fallopian tube; increasing cell division

- Days 7–10: Reaches uterus; a "ball of cells"

- Week 2: Embedding in uterine wall

- Weeks 2–8: Beginning and continuing development of organ systems (brain and spinal cord, heart and digestive tube) and structural features (for example, arm and leg buds)

- Weeks 6–8: Brain waves detectable; fetus about 1 inch long

- Weeks 12–16: "Quickening" (pregnant woman can feel movements); fetus about 5½ inches long

- Weeks 20–28: "Viability"—Fetus is able to exist apart from the mother, depending on size (2+ pounds) and lung development.

- Week 40: Birth

All changes during fetal development occur gradually. Even conception takes time as the sperm penetrates the egg and they come to form one cell. Any of these stages may or may not be morally relevant as we shall consider shortly.

Methods of Abortion

From early times people have known various methods of abortion. The Hippocratic Oath of the fourth century B.C. mentions it. When we speak of abortion, we mean induced abortion. This is to be distinguished from spontaneous abortion or what we generally call "miscarriage." Among the present-day methods of inducing abortion are the following.

- **Morning after pill:** Prevents blastocyst from embedding in uterine wall (the intrauterine device or IUD and some contraceptive pills operate in a similar way, causing the fertilized egg to be expelled by making the uterine wall inhospitable for implantation).

- **RU486 (mifepristone):** Drug developed in France, induces uterine contractions and the expelling of the embryo. Must be used within seven weeks of a missed menstrual period.[3]

- **Uterine or vacuum aspiration:** Dilation of cervix (opening of the uterus), and suction tube removal of uterine contents.

- **Dilation and curettage:** Dilation of cervix; uterus scraped with a spoon-shaped curette. This method is similar to the vacuum method except that it is performed somewhat later and requires that the fetus be dismembered and then removed.

- **Saline solution:** Replacing amniotic fluid with a solution of salt and water, which causes miscarriage.

- **Prostaglandin drugs:** Induces early labor.

- **Hysterotomy:** Similar to a cesarean section, used for later abortions; uncommon.

In 1992 approximately 1.5 million abortions were performed in the United States, 25.9 for every 1,000 women and 1 abortion for every 379 live births. (This compares to approximately 1 million in 1974.) Approximately 800,000 took place at less than 8 weeks gestation, another 580,000 from 9 to 12 weeks. Some 11 percent were for fetuses at 13 weeks or more of gestation.[4] One percent of the abortions in 1991 were for females under 15 years of age, 20 percent for ages 15 to 19, 34 percent for ages 20 to 24, 22 percent for ages 25 to 29, and 23 percent for those over 30. Seventeen percent were married and 83 percent were unmarried. Sixty-three percent of the women were white, and 37 percent were black or members of other racial groups.[5]

Abortion and the Law

Much of the contemporary debate about abortion centers on whether the law ought to permit abortion and, if so, what if any legal regulations ought to be placed on it. The relationship between morality and the law is often ignored in these debates. Sometimes it is assumed that if abortion is immoral, it ought to be illegal for that reason, or if it is morally permissible, it therefore ought to be legally permissible. As noted in the introduction to the chapter on euthanasia, this equivalence between morality and the law is questionable. We can think of actions that are possibly immoral, but which we would not want to be legally prohibited. For example, I may waste my talents but would not want the law to force me to develop and use them. However, many of our laws, such as civil rights laws, are grounded in moral reasons. What one believes the law should and should not do is bound up with an entire philosophy of law. Because this is an ethics text, we will not be able to explore this here. (Some treatment of this issue can be found in the following chapter's discussion of the legal regulation of pornography.) What we can do is note and be aware of the recent legislation regarding abortion. We can also note, as we summarize here, that many of the reasons given for these laws involve appeals to rights and other moral values.

Abortion has not always been condemned, even by churches now opposed to it.[6] Nor has it always been illegal, even in the United States. In fact, according to U.S. Supreme Court Justice Blackmun, writing in 1973, "At the time of the adoption of our Constitution, and throughout the major portion of the 19th century, abortion was viewed with less disfavor than under most American statutes currently in effect."[7] In the first half of the twentieth century most states passed laws regulating abortion or making it illegal, except in certain cases such as a pregnancy resulting from rape or incest or when the life or health of the pregnant woman was threatened. However, women continued to have abortions illegally and under dangerous conditions. In the early 1970s, a pregnant woman from Texas, given the fictitious name of Jane Roe, appealed the denial of a legal abortion. This case finally made its way to the U.S. Supreme Court, which ruled on it in 1973, and the decision has come to be called *Roe v. Wade*. In this decision, the Court stated that no state may prohibit abortion before the time of fetal viability. It stated that there was a fundamental "right to privacy" grounded in the Constitution, chiefly in the liberty and due process clauses of the Fourteenth Amendment. Privacy here does not refer to matters that must be kept secret or to what goes on in one's own home, but to a basic liberty, an ability or power to make decisions for oneself about what is one's own.[8] However, the Court noted that the state did have some interest in protecting what it called the "potential life" of the fetus as well as an interest in maternal health. (Note that the phrase "potential life" is not especially illuminating, because most people do not deny that the fetus is actually alive.) In the case of maternal health, this interest becomes "compelling" from the end of the first trimester (or third month) of pregnancy on, and in the case of the fetus's "potential life," from the time of viability on. The right to privacy was said not to be absolute but limited when these compelling state or social interests were at stake. The decision divided pregnancy into three trimesters and ruled that

1. from the end of the first trimester on, states could make laws to ensure the medical safety of the abortion procedures;
2. before the time of viability, about the end of the second trimester (the sixth month), the abortion decision should be left up to the pregnant woman and her doctor; and
3. from the time of viability on, states could prohibit abortion except in those cases in which the continued pregnancy would endanger the life or health of the pregnant woman.[9]

Since the 1973 Roe v. Wade decision, several other abortion-related decisions have been handed down by the U.S. Supreme Court. These have restricted Medicaid funding to cases in which the woman's life was at risk or the pregnancy was the result of rape or incest (1980, Harris v. McRae), or they have put other restrictions on the timing of an abortion and on its procedure. In Akron v. Center for Reproductive Health (1983), a state law that required a twenty-four-hour waiting period and notification of risks was held to be constitutional; and in Webster v. Reproductive Health Services (1989), a ban on the use of public facilities and employees for performing abortion and a test to determine fetal viability were also found to be constitutional. However, in the 1992 opinion concerning a Pennsylvania case, Planned Parenthood v. Casey, the Court again found some state restrictions to be permissible, but it also affirmed the basic decision in Roe v. Wade (see the end-of-chapter reading from Planned Parenthood). Noting that there had been no significant factual or legal changes or developments since the 1973 case, and that it was important that the Court not change significant opinions on which people had come to depend, the decision supported the legal right to privacy and abortion. It commented on the relation of abortion to the situation of equal opportunity for women. It also reiterated the state's interest in protecting life and argued that states could make regulations for such things as waiting periods designed to support this interest. However, it argued that these restrictions should not place an undue burden on women in the exercise of their constitutional right to privacy.

Although these Supreme Court decisions have not been unanimous, they seem to be attempts to balance concerns for the various moral values involved in abortion. In doing so, however, these decisions have made neither side in the abortion debate particularly happy. On the one hand, they stressed the values of privacy, liberty, and equal opportunity, and on the other hand, they concluded that some recognition ought to be given to the origins of human life. Because these are moral values reflected in the law, some of the issues regarding the morality of abortion will be relevant to what we think the law should or should not do here. In what follows, however, we will concentrate strictly on the question of the morality of abortion.[10]

Abortion: The Moral Question

Although the position that abortion ought to be a private matter and not a matter of law is debatable, it is much more difficult to make an argument that abortion is not a moral matter. After all, abortion involves issues of rights, happiness, and well-being, as well as the value of human life. If these things are morally relevant, then abortion is a moral matter. This is not to say that it is good or bad, simply morally important.

Rather than outlining so-called conservative, liberal, and moderate views on abortion, let us approach the issue somewhat differently. Then we can take a new look at it and not get caught up in labels. Suppose we consider two types of arguments both for and against abortion: arguments for which the moral status of the fetus is irrelevant and arguments for which it is relevant. We may suppose that all arguments regarding abortion hinge on this issue, but this is not the case. "Moral status of the fetus" is meant to cover questions about whether the fetus is a human being or whether it is a person, and whether the fetus has any value or any rights, including a right to life. We look first at arguments that do not concern themselves with the fetus's moral status.

Arguments That Do Not Depend on the Fetal-Personhood Issue

First, we will consider arguments for which the moral status of the fetus is irrelevant. These arguments are based on utilitarian reasoning and issues of persons' rights.

Utilitarian Reasoning

Many arguments that focus on something other than the moral status of the fetus are consequentialist in nature and broadly utilitarian. Arguments for abortion often cite the bad consequences that may result from a continued pregnancy—for example, loss of job or other opportunities for the pregnant woman, the suffering of the future child, the burden of caring for the child under particular circumstances, and so on. Some arguments against abortion also cite the loss of happiness and the future contributions of the being that is aborted.

According to act utilitarian reasoning, each case or action stands on its own, so to speak. Its own consequences determine whether it is good or bad, better or worse than other alternatives. Act utilitarians believe that the persons making the abortion decision must consider the likely consequences of the alternative actions—in other words, having or not having an abortion (as well as such considerations as where and when). Among the kinds of consequences to consider are health risks and benefits, positive or negative mental or psychological consequences, and financial and social aspects of the alternative choices. For example, a pregnant woman should consider questions such as these: What would be the effect on her of having the child versus ending the pregnancy? What are the consequences to any others affected? Would the child, if born, be likely to have a happy or unhappy life, and how would one determine this? How would an abortion or the child's birth affect her family, other children, the father, the grandparents, and so on?

Notice that the issue of whether the fetus (in the sense we are using it here) is a person or whether it is a human being is not among the things to consider when arguing from this type of consequentialist perspective. Abortion at a later stage of pregnancy might have different effects on people than at an earlier stage, and it might also have different effects on the fetus in terms of whether it might experience pain. It is the effects on the mother, child, and others that matter in utilitarian thinking, not the moral status of the fetus (what kind of value it has) or its ontological status (what kind of being we say it is) at that stage of development.[11] Also notice that on utilitarian or consequentialist grounds abortion sometimes would be permissible (the morally right thing to do) and sometimes not: It would depend on the consequences of the various sorts noted earlier. Moral judgments about abortion will be better or worse, according to this view, depending on the adequacy of the prediction of consequences.

Critics of utilitarian reasoning generally object to its seeming disregard of rights. They may point out that if we do not take the right to life seriously, then utilitarian reasoning may condone the taking of any life if the overall consequences of doing so are good! Thus, the critics might argue that the moral status of the fetus, such as whether it is the kind of being that has a right to life, is quite relevant to moral decisions about abortion. They would also have to address the matter of the rights of the pregnant woman (or others) and the problem of conflicts of rights.

Some Rights Arguments

Other arguments regarding abortion *do* consider the rights of persons but still maintain that the moral status of the fetus is irrelevant. It is irrelevant in the sense that it is not crucial for decisions about the morality of abortion, whether or not we think of the fetus as a person with full moral rights. The article on abortion by Judith Jarvis Thomson at the end of the chapter presents such an argument. She does assume for the purpose of argument that the fetus is a person from early on in pregnancy. But her conclusion is that abortion is still justified, even if the fetus is a person with a right to life (and she assumes it is also permissible if the fetus is not a person).[12] This is why the argument does not turn on what we say about the moral status of the fetus.

The question she poses is whether the pregnant woman has an obligation to sustain the life of the fetus through providing it with the means of life. To have us think about this, she asks us to consider an imaginary scenario. Suppose, she says, you wake up one morning and find yourself attached through various medical tubings to a famous violinist. You find out that during the night you have been kidnapped and hooked up to this violinist. The violinist has severe kidney problems, and the only way that his life can be saved is through being hooked up to another person so that the other person's kidneys will do the job of purifying his blood for some period of time until his own kidneys have recovered. The question Thomson poses is this: Would you be morally permitted or justified in "unplugging" the violinist, even though to do so would result in his death? Thomson argues that you would be

justified, in particular, because you had not consented to save the violinist. The point of this example applies most obviously to cases of rape. However, Thomson means it to apply more widely, and she uses other analogies to help make her point. One would only have a responsibility to save the violinist (or nurture the fetus) if one had agreed to do so. The consent that Thomson has in mind is a deliberate and planned choice. She argues that although it would be generous of you to save the life of the violinist (or the fetus), you are not obligated to do so. Her point is that no one has a right to use your body, even to save his own life, unless you give him that right. Such views are consistent with a position that stresses that women are persons and have a right to bodily integrity as do other persons, and that as persons they ought not to be used against their will for whatever purposes by others, even noble purposes such as the nurturing of children. Critics of this argument point out that it may apply at most to cases of rape, for in some other cases one might be said to implicitly consent to a pregnancy if one did what one knew might result in it. One response to this is that we do not always consider a person to have consented to chance consequences of their actions.

The persons' rights and utilitarian arguments are examples of arguments about abortion that do not depend on what we say about the moral status of the fetus, but other arguments hold this issue to be crucial. Some arguments for the moral permissibility of abortion as well as some against it rely in crucial ways on what is said about the fetus. We next consider some of these arguments.

Arguments That Depend on the Fetal-Personhood Issue

Not all arguments depend on what we say about the fetus as we have seen, but some abortion arguments turn on what is said about the moral status of the fetus. They ask such questions as: Is it a human being? A person? Alive? Let us for the moment focus not on these terms and what they might mean, but on the more general issue; that is, on the question of what kind of value or moral status the developing fetus has. Does it have a different status in various stages of development? If so, when does the status change, and why? (Further issues would include how to weigh its value or rights in comparison to other values or the rights of others.) I suggest that we examine a first approach and call it "Method I" and distinguish it from a broader approach that I will call "Method II." Briefly put, Method I focuses on the characteristics of the fetus and asks when it has what should be considered so significant that it is a person or has a new moral status from that point on. Method II asks a more general question. It asks us to think about what kind of beings of any sort, human or nonhuman, have some special moral status and possibly also rights such as a right to life. In this way it is also related to issues of animal rights (see Chapter 15).

Method I

In using this method we focus on fetal development and ask three things about possibly significant stages: (1) *What* is present? (2) *When* is this present (at what stage)? and (3) *Why* is this significant—in other words, why does this give this being special moral status? By "special moral status" we might mean various things. Among the most important would be whether the status were such that the fetus would be thought to have something like a right to life. If this were the case, then abortion would become morally problematic.[13]

Suppose we try Method I on various stages in fetal development and see what the arguments would look like. In each case let us consider the arguments for the position and then some criticisms of these arguments.

Conception or Fertilization   Fertilization, or when sperm penetrate the ovum, is the time at which many opponents of abortion say that the fetus has full moral status. The reason usually given is that this is when the fetus has the full genetic makeup from the combining of sperm and egg. In times past, people held that the egg provided the entire substance and the sperm only gave it a charge or impetus to grow, or that the sperm was "the little man" and only needed a place to grow and obtain nourishment, which the egg provided! We now know about the contribution of both sperm and ovum to the zygote. The argument for taking this stage as the morally significant one supposes an ontological argument something like this:[14] If we say that the resulting being that is born is a human being or person, and if there is no significant change in its development from its initial form, then it is the same kind of being all the way through the development period. Otherwise, we would be implying that different beings are succeeding one another during this process.

Critics of this position may point out that although fetal development is continuous, the bare genetic basis present at conception is not enough to constitute its being a person at that point. There is no structure or differentiation at this point, nothing that resembles a person in this initial form. There is not even an individual there. Consider, for example, what happens in the case of identical twinning. Before implantation, identical twins are formed by the splitting of cells in the early embryo. Each resulting twin has the same genetic makeup. Now, what are we to think of the original embryo? Suppose conception is the time when we are supposed to have an individual being. We will call him John. The twins that develop and later are born are Jim and Joe. What happened to John, if there was a John? Jim and Joe are two new individuals, genetically alike as twins, but also two different people. Is there a little of John in each of them? Or does the fact that there are two individuals after twinning mean that there was not any individual there before that time, that John never existed? Those who support conception as the crucial time at which we have a being with full moral status and rights must explain how there can be an individual at conception, at least in the case of twinning.

Detectable Brain Waves Another possibility for when a fetus might attain new moral status is that point at which brain waves begin to be detectable. The idea is reasonable given that the human brain is the locus of consciousness, language, and communication, and it is what makes us crucially different from other animals. Moreover, we now use the *cessation* of brain function as the determinant of death. Why should we not use the *beginning* of brain function as the beginning of an individual's life? We can detect brain activity between the sixth and eighth week of fetal development, which makes that point the significant time for this view.

Critics of this argument point out that brain activity develops gradually and no one time during its development can be singled out as unique. However, this may be only a practical problem. We might be satisfied with an approximation rather than a determinate time. Other questions about the type of brain function might also be raised. At six to eight weeks the brain is quite simple; only much later do those parts develop that are the basis of conscious function. At earlier stages the brain is arguably not that different from other animal brains in structure or function.

Quickening Usually, the pregnant woman can feel the fetus kick or move in approximately the fourth month of fetal development. This is what is meant by *quickening*. In former times, people may have thought there was no fetal movement before this time, and this would then be a more persuasive reason to consider this stage as crucial. Still, we could think of the movement present at this time as self-initiated movement because it now stems from a new level of brain development. This would make a better reason for considering this the beginning of the being's new life, for it would now be moving about on its own.

Critics will raise the same issue for this point as for brain development, namely, that there is no dramatic break in development of the ability of the fetus to move. Moreover, they might also point out that other animals and even plants move on their own, and this does not give them special moral status or a right to life. Furthermore, those who argue for animal rights usually do so because of their sentience, their ability to feel pleasure and pain, and not their ability to move.

Viability Viability is about the fifth month in fetal development, at which time the fetus is capable of existing apart from the pregnant woman or mother. All its organs and organ systems are sufficiently developed so that the fetus can function on its own. The last system to be functionally complete is the respiratory system. During previous stages of fetal development the fetus "breathes" amniotic fluid. One key element in lung development that enables the fetal lungs to breathe air is the secretion by the lungs of an agent called *surfactant*. In lay terms, the presence of this agent makes the lung tissue more elastic so that the lungs can expand, making inhalation and exhalation possible. Without a functioning respiratory system the fetus is not yet viable.

Why is the stage of viability singled out as the stage at which the fetus may take on a new moral status? Some answer that it is the capacity for *independent* existence that is the basis for the new status. However, if delivered at this time and left on its own, no infant would be able to survive. Perhaps the notion of *separate* existence is what is intended. The idea would be that the fetus is more clearly distinct from the mother before birth at this point. Or perhaps the notion of *completeness* is what is intended. Although the fetus is not fully formed at viability because much development takes place after birth, the argument might be that the viable fetus is sufficiently complete, enabling us to think of it as a new being.

Critics of viability can point again to the gradual nature of development and the seeming arbitrariness of picking out one stage of completeness as crucially different from the others. They also can point out that the viable fetus would still be dependent on others even if it were delivered at the point of viability. In addition, they can question the whole notion of making moral status a function of independence. We are all dependent on one another, and those who are more independent—just because of viability—have no greater value than those who are more dependent. Even someone dependent on machines is not for this reason less human, they might argue. Furthermore, the viable unborn fetus is still, in fact, dependent on the mother and does not have an existence separate from her. Birth, on these terms, would be a better time to pick than viability, they might argue, if it is separateness and independence that is crucial.

Each point in fetal development may provide a reasonable basis for concluding something about the moral status of the fetus. However, as is clear, none are problem-free. In any case, the whole idea of grounding moral status and rights on possessing certain characteristics may also be called into question. Let us consider this matter more broadly and look at another method, Method II, for thinking about the basis for moral status or worth.

Method II

If what we say about the fetus is crucial to a position about the morality of abortion, we may do well to compare what we say here to what we say about beings other than human fetuses. Why, for example, do we believe that people generally have rights? Are we significantly different from other animals such that we have unique moral status, simply because we are *human beings?* Or is the crucial determinant of special moral status or worth the ability to reason or think or imagine or dream? If so, then if there are other intelligent beings in the universe, would they have the same moral status as we do, even if they were not members of our species? Or suppose further that we consider cases in which human beings do not have the capacity for thought and reasoning and communication. Think, for example, of a newborn with anencephaly. This is a condition in which the newborn has no developed upper brain and thus will never be conscious or able to think. In fact, such an infant does not usually

live for long. But it is a human being biologically and not a member of some other species. Or take the case at the other end of life in which a person is in a permanent vegetative state. There is no doubt that the person is still human in the biological sense, but does this person lack human rights because he or she lacks some mental qualities that are the basis for rights? Finally, perhaps it is not actual ability to think or communicate but the potential for the development of these characteristics that grounds special moral worth and rights. A normal fetus would have this potentiality whereas a two-year-old dog would not. Of course, this depends on the level or type of thinking that is seen to be crucial, because dogs do have some type of mental capacity and some ability to communicate.

Taking each suggestion and giving it a name, we might have something like the following positions.[15] Each gives an answer to the question, What kind of beings have special moral status, which may include something like a right to life?[16]

Being Human According to one point of view, it is being a human being that counts—being a member of the human species. Now, using this criterion, we can note that human fetuses are members of the human species and conclude that they have equal moral status with all other human beings. The argument for this position might include something about the moral advance we make when we recognize that all humans have equal moral worth. This has not always been the case, such as when children or women were considered more as property than as human beings with equal and full moral status as humans. Nevertheless, questions can be raised about why only members of the human species are included here. If some other species of being were sufficiently like us in the relevant respects, then should they not be considered to have the same worth as members of our species? In considering this possibility, we may be better able to decide whether it is membership in a species or something else that grounds moral worth.

Being Like Human Beings Suppose that moral status (or personhood) depends on being a member of any species whose members have certain significant characteristics like human beings. But what characteristics are significant enough to ground high moral value and status, including rights? For example, consider the abilities to communicate, reason, and plan. Depending on how high a level of communicating, reasoning, and planning is required, perhaps other animals would qualify for the high moral status envisioned. Some chimpanzees and gorillas, for instance, can learn to communicate through sign language, according to some scientists. If there are beings elsewhere in the universe who are members of a different species but who can communicate, reason, and plan, then according to this criterion they too would have the same moral worth as humans. If a lower level of ability were used, then members of other animal species would also qualify.

These first two criteria are alike in that it is membership in a species that is the determinant of one's moral status. If any humans have this status, then they all do. If chimpanzees have this status, or Martians, then all members of their species also have this status. It does not matter what the individual member of the species is like or what individual capacities she or he possesses. On the other hand, perhaps it is not of what species you are a member but what individual characteristics you have that forms the basis of the special moral status with which we are concerned here. If this were the case, then there would be at least three other possible positions about the basis of moral status. These are as follows.

Potentiality Potentiality literally means "power." According to this criterion, all beings that have the power to develop certain key characteristics have full moral worth. Thus, if a particular fetus had the potential for developing the requisite mental capacities, this fetus would have full moral status. However, any fetus or other human being that does not have this potential (anencephalic infants or those in a permanent vegetative state, for example) does not have this status.

Yet how important is potential—and what, in fact, is it? Suppose that one had the potential for becoming a famous star or holding political office. Would one then have the same respect and rights due the actual star, say, or the legislator? Consider a fictitious story.[17] Suppose that we have a kitten that if left alone will grow into a mature cat. We also have a serum that if injected into the kitten will make it grow into a human being. After the injection, first the fur changes, then the tail goes, and so forth. Now if we ask whether the kitten had the potential to be a human being before the injection, we probably would say no, or that it had potential in only a very weak sense. But what would we say about the potential of the kitten to be a human being after it was injected? Only then, critics of the potentiality criterion might argue, would the potential for being a human being or person be relevant to treating the injected kitten differently than an ordinary kitten. In any case, the notion of potentiality may be morally significant, but supporters of this view must be able to address the issues raised by these criticisms.

Actuality At the other end of the spectrum is the view according to which potential for developing certain characteristics counts for nothing (or at least does not give one the kind of moral status about which we are concerned). Only the actual possession of the requisite characteristics is sufficient for full moral status. Again, it makes a significant difference to one's position here whether the characteristics are high level or low level. For example, if a rather high level of reasoning is required before an individual has the requisite moral status, then newborns probably would not be included, as well as many others.[18] Although the fetus, newborn infant, and extremely young child are human beings biologically, they are not yet persons or beings with the requisite moral status. They are not yet members of the moral community. There may be good reasons to treat them well and with respect, but it is not because they are persons with rights.

Evolving Value Finally, let us consider a position that is intermediate between the last two positions. The idea involved in it is that potential does count but not as much as actual possession of the significant characteristics. Furthermore, as the potential is gradually developed the moral status of the being also grows. This position could also be described in terms of competing interests and claims. The stronger the claim, the more it should prevail. If this is my book, then I have a stronger claim over it than you who would like to have the book.

In applying this criterion to fetal development, the conclusion would be that the early-term fetus has less moral value or moral status than the late-term fetus. Less of a claim or interest on the part of others is needed to override its claim to consideration. Moderately serious interests of the pregnant woman or of society could override the interests or claims of the early-term fetus, but it would take more serious interests to override the late-term fetus's claims. In the end, according to this view, when potentiality is sufficiently actualized, the fetus or infant has as much right as any other person. Although some people may view the evolving value position as a reasonable moral one, it would be more difficult to use it in a legal context in which claims and interests would need to be publicly weighed and compared.

We might note a view held by some feminists, a variant on this position. Most feminists support a woman's legal right to abortion, but they are not all happy with the rationale for it provided in *Roe v. Wade*.[19] For example, some worry that the "right to privacy" could be interpreted in ways detrimental to women. If this right is taken to imply that everything done in the privacy of one's home is out of the law's reach, then this would include some abuse of women and children.[20] Some feminists also have misgivings about the implications of some abortion supporters' views concerning the moral status of the fetus. Like the last of the five positions in

Method II, they argue that the fetus is surely human. It is both part and not part of the pregnant woman, but a separate being. Abortion is morally problematic, in some of these views, because the loss of an early form of human life is in fact loss of part of the mother's own life. However, this is not to imply that these views grant the fetus full moral status and rights. These critics do not necessarily conclude that abortion is morally impermissible.

These positions, as well as those summarized in Method I, are positions that focus on what to say about the status of the fetus. If the fetus does not have the requisite moral status, then abortion is probably morally permissible. If it does have that status, then abortion is morally problematic. If the fetus is said to have a somewhat in-between status, then the conclusion about abortion would be mixed. Again, these are positions that put the whole weight of the moral judgment about abortion on what status the fetus does or does not have. As the utilitarian and persons' rights arguments exemplified, there are other considerations about what counts in thinking about the morality of abortion. Finally, remember that unless you believe that everything that is immoral ought to be illegal, then even if abortion were in some case thought to be immoral, one would need to give further reasons about the purpose of law in order to conclude that it also ought to be illegal. So also if you believe that the only reason why something ought to be illegal is if it is immoral, then if abortion is morally permissible you should conclude that it ought to be legally permissible. From this point of view, there would be no other relevant legal considerations. Both views are problematic.

In the readings included in this chapter, Judith Jarvis Thomson provides several analogies to help us think about the morality of abortion, and Sidney Callahan raises questions about abortion from a prolife feminist perspective. The third reading is taken from a 1992 Supreme Court decision that affirmed the basic elements of *Roe v. Wade,* but added some new points.

Notes

1. From "Image" magazine, *San Francisco Examiner,* Oct. 25, 1992, 24.
2. Based on a report in the *New York Times,* March 7, 1993, B3, and March 11, 1993, A1.
3. The drug has been used by 200,000 European women and is recommended by the U.S. Food and Drug Administration as safe and effective. The FDA also noted that safe does not mean risk-free. The procedure occurs in two stages. Patients first take 600 milligrams of mifepristone, and then return two days later for 200 micrograms of misoprostol, which triggers contractions in 95 percent of the cases. In the other 5 percent, a surgical abortion would be recommended. See *New York Times* (July 20, 1996), p. A1, A11.
4. Statistical Abstracts of the United States, 1995. U.S. Department of Commerce, Bureau of the Census. U.S. Government Printing Office, p. 84. Tables 111, 112. The table for number of abortions includes the 1992 statistic, while the statistic of weeks of gestation was estimated from the table's most recent data which was for 1991.
5. Ibid.
6. In fact, it has also not always been condemned or treated as equivalent to the killing of a human being by one of its strongest opponents, the Catholic Church. Following the teachings of Thomas Aquinas, it held until perhaps the fifteenth to sixteenth centuries that the fetus was not human until some time after conception when the matter was suitable for the reception of a human soul. See John Noonan, *The Morality of Abortion* (Cambridge, MA: Harvard University Press, 1970), 18ff.
7. Justice Harry A. Blackmun, majority opinion in *Roe v. Wade,* United States Supreme Court. 410 U.S. 113 (1973).
8. See comments about this interpretation in Ronald Dworkin, "Feminists and Abortion," *New York Review of Books,* vol. XL, no. 11 (June 10, 1993): 27–29.
9. Blackmun, *Roe v. Wade.*
10. Further thoughts on the relation between morality and the law can be found in Chapter 10 and in the discussion of pornography.
11. Recall that rule utilitarian reasoning about abortion would be somewhat different. A rule utilitarian must consider which practice regarding abortion would be best. Whatever she judged to be the best practice, she should follow. She should mentally survey various possible practices or rules. Would the rule "No one should have an abortion" be likely to maximize happiness? Would the rule "No one should have an abortion unless the pregnancy threatens the mother's health or well-being" have better consequences overall? What about a rule that says "Persons who are in situations *x, y,* or *z* should have abortions"? How would too easy access to abortion affect our regard for the very young? How would the practice of abortion when the fetus has certain abnormalities affect our treatment of the physically or mentally disabled in general? How would a restrictive abortion policy affect women's ability to participate as equal human beings, enjoying jobs and other opportunities? Whichever practice or rule is likely to have the better net results (more good consequences and fewer bad ones) is the best practice.
12. Judith Jarvis Thomson, "A Defense of Abortion," *Philosophy and Public Affairs,* vol. 1, no. 1 (Fall 1971): 47–66.
13. Note that if the fetus had no right to life, then this would not automatically make abortion problem-free. See the comments in the last paragraph under "Method II."
14. An ontological argument is one having to do with the nature and identity of beings; *ontos* means "being."
15. This is based on notes of mine whose source I am unable to credit; regretfully, it was not retained!
16. Compare this discussion with similar discussions in Chapter 15 on animal rights and the environment. In particular, note the possible distinction between having moral value and having rights.
17. This is taken from Michael Tooley's article, "Abortion and Infanticide," *Philosophy and Public Affairs,* vol. 2, no. 1 (1972): 37–65.
18. This is the position of Mary Ann Warren, in "On the Moral and Legal Status of Abortion," *The Monist,* vol. 57, no. 1 (Jan. 1973): 43–61.
19. See the summary of these views in Dworkin, "Feminists and Abortion."
20. Note that this was not the interpretation of the "right to privacy" given earlier in this chapter. As based in the liberty clause of the Fourteenth Amendment, it was noted that it was a liberty right, the right or power to make one's own decisions about personal matters.

A Defense of Abortion

Judith Jarvis Thomson

Study Questions

1. What starting point for consideration of abortion does Thomson accept? Why?

2. Describe the violinist example. What argument could be made for keeping the violinist "plugged in"?

3. What is the so-called extreme position? How does it distinguish between directly killing and letting die?

4. How could the violinist case be a case of self-defense? How is abortion to save the mother's life similar to or different from this case?

5. What is the example of the child growing in the house supposed to show?

6. What is the example of Henry Fonda's cool hand supposed to show? The box of chocolates?

7. How does the people seeds example bring out the issue of consent or voluntariness?

8. What problems regarding the meaning of a right does Thomson's argument raise?

9. What is the point of the Good Samaritan example?

10. What, finally, is Thomson arguing for, and what is she not claiming?

M ost opposition to abortion relies on the premise that the fetus is a human being, a person, from the moment of conception. The premise is argued for, but, as I think, not well. Take, for example, the most common argument. We are asked to notice that the development of a human being from conception through birth into childhood is continuous; then it is said that to draw a line, to choose a point in this development and say "before this point the thing is not a person, after this point it is a person" is to make an arbitrary choice, a choice for which in the nature

From *Philosophy & Public Affairs*, vol. 1, no. 1 (Fall 1971): 47–66. © 1971 by Princeton University Press. Reprinted by permission of Princeton University Press.

of things no good reason can be given. It is concluded that the fetus is, or anyway that we had better say it is, a person from the moment of conception. But this conclusion does not follow. Similar things might be said about the development of an acorn into an oak tree, and it does not follow that acorns are oak trees, or that we had better say they are. Arguments of this form are sometimes called "slippery slope arguments"—the phrase is perhaps self-explanatory—and it is dismaying that opponents of abortion rely on them so heavily and uncritically.

I am inclined to agree, however, that the prospects for "drawing a line" in the development of the fetus look dim. I am inclined to think also that we shall probably have to agree that the fetus has already become a human person well before birth. Indeed, it comes as a surprise when one first learns how early in its life it begins to acquire human characteristics. By the tenth week, for example, it already has a face, arms and legs, fingers and toes; it has internal organs, and brain activity is detectable.[1] On the other hand, I think that the premise is false, that the fetus is not a person from the moment of conception. A newly fertilized ovum, a newly implanted clump of cells, is no more a person than an acorn is an oak tree. But I shall not discuss any of this. For it seems to me to be of great interest to ask what happens if, for the sake of argument, we allow the premise. How, precisely, are we supposed to get from there to the conclusion that abortion is morally impermissible? Opponents of abortion commonly spend most of their time establishing that the fetus is a person, and hardly any time explaining the step from there to the impermissibility of abortion. Perhaps they think the step too simple and obvious to require much comment. Or perhaps instead they are simply being economical in argument. Many of those who defend abortion rely on the premise that the fetus is not a person, but only a bit of tissue that will become a person at birth; and why pay out more arguments than you have to? Whatever the explanation, I suggest that the step they take is neither easy nor obvious, that it calls for closer examination than it is commonly given, and that when we do give it this closer examination we shall feel inclined to reject it.

I propose, then, that we grant that the fetus is a person from the moment of conception. How does the argument go from here? Something like this, I take it. Every person has a right to life. So the fetus has a right to life. No doubt the mother has a right to decide what shall happen in and to her body; everyone would grant that. But surely a person's right to life is stronger and more stringent than the mother's right to decide what happens in and to her body, and so outweighs it. So the fetus may not be killed; an abortion may not be performed.

It sounds plausible. But now let me ask you to imagine this. You wake up in the morning and find yourself back to back in bed with an unconscious violinist. A famous unconscious violinist. He has been found to have a fatal kidney ailment, and the Society of Music Lovers has canvassed all the available medical records and found that you alone have the right blood type to help. They have therefore kidnapped you, and last night the violinist's circulatory system was plugged into yours, so that your kidneys can be used to extract poisons from his blood as well as your own. The director of the hospital now tells you, "Look, we're sorry the Society of Music Lovers did this to you—we would never have permitted it if we had known. But still, they did it, and the violinist now is plugged into you. To unplug you would be to kill him. But never mind, it's only for nine months. By then he will have recovered from his ailment, and can safely be unplugged from you." Is it morally incumbent on you to accede to this situation? No doubt it would be very nice of you if you did, a great kindness. But do you have to accede to it? What if it were not nine months, but nine years? Or longer still? What if the director of the hospital says, "Tough luck, I agree, but you've now got to stay in bed, with the violinist plugged into you, for the rest of your life. Because remember this. All persons have a right to life, and violinists are persons. Granted you have a right to decide what happens in and to your body, but a person's right to life outweighs your right to decide what happens in and to your body. So you cannot ever be unplugged from him." I imagine you would regard this as outrageous, which suggests that something really is wrong with that plausible-sounding argument I mentioned a moment ago.

In this case, of course, you were kidnapped; you didn't volunteer for the operation that plugged the violinist into your kidneys. Can those who oppose abortion on the ground I mentioned make an exception for a pregnancy due to rape? Certainly. They can say that persons have a right to life only if they didn't come into existence because of rape; or they can say that all persons have a right to life, but that some have less of a right to life than others, in particular, that those who came into existence because of rape have less. But these statements have a rather unpleasant sound. Surely the question of whether you have a right to life at all, or how much of it you have, shouldn't turn on the question of whether or not you are the product of a rape. And in fact the people who oppose abortion on the ground I mentioned do not make this distinction, and hence do not make an exception in the case of rape.

Nor do they make an exception for a case in which the mother has to spend the nine months of her pregnancy in bed. They would agree that would be a great pity, and hard on the mother; but all the same, all persons have a right to life, the fetus is a person, and so on. I suspect, in fact, that they would not make an exception for a case in which, miraculously enough, the pregnancy went on for nine years, or even the rest of the mother's life.

Some won't even make an exception for a case in which continuation of the pregnancy is likely to shorten the mother's life; they regard abortion as impermissible even to save the mother's life. Such cases are nowadays very rare, and many opponents of abortion do not accept this extreme view. All the same, it is a good place to begin: A number of points of interest come out in respect to it.

1. Let us call the view that abortion is impermissible even to save the mother's life "the extreme view." I want to suggest first that it does not issue from the argument I mentioned earlier without the addition of some fairly powerful premises. Suppose a woman has become pregnant, and now learns that she has a cardiac condition such that she will die if she carries the baby to term. What may be done for her? The fetus, being a person, has a right to life, but as the mother is a person too, so has she a right to life. Presumably they have an equal right to life. How is it supposed to come out that an abortion may not be performed? If mother and child have an equal right to life, shouldn't we perhaps flip a coin? Or should we add to the mother's right to life her right to decide what happens in and to her body, which everybody seems to be ready to grant—the

sum of her rights now outweighing the fetus' right to life?

The most familiar argument here is the following. We are told that performing the abortion would be directly killing[2] the child, whereas doing nothing would not be killing the mother, but only letting her die. Moreover, in killing the child, one would be killing an innocent person, for the child has committed no crime, and is not aiming at his mother's death. And then there are a variety of ways in which this might be continued. (1) But as directly killing an innocent person is always and absolutely impermissible, an abortion may not be performed. Or, (2) as directly killing an innocent person is murder, and murder is always and absolutely impermissible, an abortion may not be performed.[3] Or, (3) as one's duty to refrain from directly killing an innocent person is more stringent than one's duty to keep a person from dying, an abortion may not be performed. Or, (4) if one's only options are directly killing an innocent person or letting a person die, one must prefer letting the person die, and thus an abortion may not be performed.[4]

Some people seem to have thought that these are not further premises which must be added if the conclusion is to be reached, but that they follow from the very fact that an innocent person has a right to life.[5] But this seems to me to be a mistake, and perhaps the simplest way to show this is to bring out that while we must certainly grant that innocent persons have a right to life, the theses in (1) through (4) are all false. Take (2), for example. If directly killing an innocent person is murder, and thus is impermissible, then the mother's directly killing the innocent person inside her is murder, and thus is impermissible. But it cannot seriously be thought to be murder if the mother performs an abortion on herself to save her life. It cannot seriously be said that she must refrain, that she must sit passively by and wait for her death. Let us look again at the case of you and the violinist. There you are, in bed with the violinist, and the director of the hospital says to you, "It's all most distressing, and I deeply sympathize, but you see this is putting an additional strain on your kidneys, and you'll be dead within the month. But you have to stay where you are all the same. Because unplugging you would be directly killing an innocent violinist, and that's murder, and that's impermissible." If anything in the world is true, it is that you do not commit murder, you do not do what is impermissible, if you reach around to your back and unplug yourself from that violinist to save your life.

The main focus of attention in writings on abortion has been on what a third party may or may not do in answer to a request from a woman for an abortion. This is in a way understandable. Things being as they are, there isn't much a woman can safely do to abort herself. So the question asked is what a third party may do, and what the mother may do, if it is mentioned at all, is deduced, almost as an afterthought, from what it is concluded that third parties may do. But it seems to me that to treat the matter in this way is to refuse to grant to the mother that very status of person which is so firmly insisted on for the fetus. For we cannot simply read off what a person may do from what a third party may do. Suppose you find yourself trapped in a tiny house with a growing child. I mean a very tiny house, and a rapidly growing child—you are already up against the wall of the house and in a few minutes you'll be crushed to death. The child on the other hand won't be crushed to death; if nothing is done to stop him from growing he'll be hurt, but in the end he'll simply burst open the house and walk out a free man. Now I could well understand it if a bystander were to say, "There's nothing we can do for you. We cannot choose between your life and his, we cannot be the ones to decide who is to live, we cannot intervene." But it cannot be concluded that you too can do nothing, that you cannot attack it to save your life. However innocent the child may be, you do not have to wait passively while it crushes you to death. Perhaps a pregnant woman is vaguely felt to have the status of house, to which we don't allow the right of self-defense. But if the woman houses the child, it should be remembered that she is a person who houses it.

I should perhaps stop to say explicitly that I am not claiming that people have a right to do anything whatever to save their lives. I think, rather, that there are drastic limits to the right of self-defense. If someone threatens you with death unless you torture someone else to death, I think you have not the right, even to save your life, to do so. But the case under consideration here is very different. In our case there are only two people involved, one whose life is threatened, and one who threatens it. Both are innocent: The one who is threatened is not threatened because of any fault, the one who threatens does not threaten because of any fault. For this reason we may feel that we bystanders cannot intervene. But the person threatened can.

In sum, a woman surely can defend her life against the threat to it posed by the unborn child, even if doing so involves its death. And this shows not merely that the theses in (1) through (4) are false; it shows also that the extreme view of abortion is false, and so we need not canvass any other possible ways of arriving at it from the argument I mentioned at the outset.

2. The extreme view could of course be weakened to say that while abortion is permissible to save the mother's life, it may not be performed by a third party, but only by the mother herself. But this cannot be right either. For what we have to keep in mind is that the mother and the unborn child are not like two tenants in a small house which has, by an unfortunate mistake, been rented to both: The mother owns the house. The fact that she does adds to the offensiveness of deducing that the mother can do nothing from the supposition that third parties can do nothing. But it does more than this: It casts a bright light on the supposition that third parties can do nothing. Certainly it lets us see that a third party who says "I cannot choose between you" is fooling himself if he thinks this is impartiality. If Jones has found and fastened on a certain coat, which he needs to keep him from freezing, but which Smith also needs to keep him from freezing, then it is not impartiality that says "I cannot choose between you" when Smith owns the coat. Women have said again and again "This body is my body!" and they have reason to feel angry, reason to feel that it has been like shouting into the wind. Smith, after all, is hardly likely to bless us if we say to him, "Of course it's your coat, anybody would grant that it is. But no one may choose between you and Jones who is to have it."

We should really ask what it is that says "no one may choose" in the face of the fact that the body that houses the child is the mother's body. It may be simply a failure to appreciate this fact. But it may be something more interesting, namely the sense that one has a right to refuse to lay hands on people, even where it would be just and fair to do so, even where justice seems to require that somebody do so. Thus justice might call for somebody to get Smith's coat back from Jones, and yet you have a right to refuse to be the one to lay hands on Jones, a right to refuse to do physical violence to him. This, I think, must be granted. But then what should be said is not "no one may choose,"

but only "I cannot choose," and indeed not even this, but "I will not act," leaving it open that somebody else can or should, and in particular that anyone in a position of authority, with the job of securing people's rights, both can and should. So this is no difficulty. I have not been arguing that any given third party must accede to the mother's request that he perform an abortion to save her life, but only that he may.

I suppose that in some views of human life the mother's body is only on loan to her, the loan not being one which gives her any prior claim to it. One who held this view might well think it impartiality to say "I cannot choose." But I shall simply ignore this possibility. My own view is that if a human being has any just, prior claim to anything at all, he has a just, prior claim to his own body. And perhaps this needn't be argued for here anyway, since, as I mentioned, the arguments against abortion we are looking at do grant that the woman has a right to decide what happens in and to her body.

But although they do grant it, I have tried to show that they do not take seriously what is done in granting it. I suggest the same thing will reappear even more clearly when we turn away from cases in which the mother's life is at stake, and attend, as I propose we now do, to the vastly more common cases in which a woman wants an abortion for some less weighty reason than preserving her own life.

3. Where the mother's life is not at stake, the argument I mentioned at the outset seems to have a much stronger pull. "Everyone has a right to life, so the unborn person has a right to life." And isn't the child's right to life weightier than anything other than the mother's own right to life, which she might put forward as ground for an abortion?

This argument treats the right to life as if it were unproblematic. It is not, and this seems to me to be precisely the source of the mistake.

For we should now, at long last, ask what it comes to, to have a right to life. In some views having a right to life includes having a right to be given at least the bare minimum one needs for continued life. But suppose that what in fact is the bare minimum a man needs for continued life is something he has no right at all to be given? If I am sick unto death, and the only thing that will save my life is the touch of Henry Fonda's cool hand on my fevered brow, then all the same, I have no right to be given the touch of Henry Fonda's cool hand on my fevered brow. It would be frightfully nice of him to fly in from the West Coast to provide it. It would be less nice, though no doubt well meant, if my friends flew out to the West Coast and carried Henry Fonda back with them. But I have no right at all against anybody that he should do this for me. Or again, to return to the story I told earlier, the fact that for continued life that violinist needs the continued use of your kidneys does not establish that he has a right to be given the continued use of your kidneys. He certainly has no right against you that you should give him continued use of your kidneys. For nobody has any right to use your kidneys unless you give him such a right; and nobody has the right against you that you shall give him this right—if you do allow him to go on using your kidneys, this is a kindness on your part, and not something he can claim from you as his due. Nor has he any right against anybody else that they should give him continued use of your kidneys. Certainly he had no right against the Society of Music Lovers that they should plug him into you in the first place. And if you now start to unplug yourself, having learned that you will otherwise have to spend nine years in bed with him, there is nobody in the world who must try to prevent you, in order to see to it that he is given something he has a right to be given.

Some people are rather stricter about the right to life. In their view, it does not include the right to be given anything, but amounts to, and only to, the right not to be killed by anybody. But here a related difficulty arises. If everybody is to refrain from killing that violinist, then everybody must refrain from doing a great many different sorts of things. Everybody must refrain from slitting his throat, everybody must refrain from shooting him—and everybody must refrain from unplugging you from him. But does he have a right against everybody that they shall refrain from unplugging you from him? To refrain from doing this is to allow him to continue to use your kidneys. It could be argued that he has a right against us that we should allow him to continue to use your kidneys. That is, while he had no right against us that we should give him the use of your kidneys, it might be argued that he anyway has a right against us that we shall not now intervene and deprive him of the use of your kidneys. I shall come back to third-party interventions later. But certainly the violinist has no right against you that you shall allow him to continue to use your kidneys. As I said, if you do allow him to use them, it is a kindness on your part, and not something you owe him.

The difficulty I point to here is not peculiar to the right of life. It reappears in connection with all the other natural rights; and it is something which an adequate account of rights must deal with. For present purposes it is enough just to draw attention to it. But I would stress that I am not arguing that people do not have a right to life—quite to the contrary, it seems to me that the primary control we must place on the acceptability of an account of rights is that it should turn out in that account to be a truth that all persons have a right to life. I am arguing only that having a right to life does not guarantee having either a right to be given the use of or a right to be allowed continued use of another person's body—even if one needs it for life itself. So the right to life will not serve the opponents of abortion in the very simple and clear way in which they seem to have thought it would.

4. There is another way to bring out the difficulty. In the most ordinary sort of case, to deprive someone of what he has a right to is to treat him unjustly. Suppose a boy and his small brother are jointly given a box of chocolates for Christmas. If the older boy takes the box and refuses to give his brother any of the chocolates, he is unjust to him, for the brother has been given a right to half of them. But suppose that, having learned that otherwise it means nine years in bed with that violinist, you unplug yourself from him. You surely are not being unjust to him, for you gave him no right to use your kidneys, and no one else can have given him any such right. But we have to notice that in unplugging yourself, you are killing him; and violinists, like everybody else, have a right to life, and thus in the view we were considering just now, the right not to be killed. So here you do what he supposedly has a right you shall not do, but you do not act unjustly to him in doing it.

The emendation which may be made at this point is this: The right to life consists not in the right not to be killed, but rather in the right not to be killed unjustly. This runs a risk of circularity, but never mind: It would enable us to square the fact that the violinist has a right to life with the fact that you do not act unjustly toward him in unplugging yourself, thereby killing him. For if you do not kill him unjustly, you do not violate his right to life, and so it is no wonder you do him no injustice.

But if this emendation is accepted, the gap in the argument against abortion stares us plainly in the face: It is by no means enough to show that the fetus is a person, and to remind us that all persons have a right to life—we need to be shown also that killing the fetus violates its right to life, i.e., that abortion is unjust killing. And is it?

I suppose we may take it as a datum that in the case of pregnancy due to rape the mother has not given the unborn person a right to the use of her body for food and shelter. Indeed, in what pregnancy should it be supposed that the mother has given the unborn person such a right? It is not as if there were unborn persons drifting about the world, to whom a woman who wants a child says "I invite you in."

But it might be argued that there are other ways one can have acquired a right to the use of another person's body than by having been invited to use it by that person. Suppose a woman voluntarily indulges in intercourse, knowing of the chance it will issue in pregnancy, and then she does become pregnant; is she not in part responsible for the presence, in fact the very existence, of the unborn person inside? No doubt she did not invite it in. But doesn't her partial responsibility for its being there itself give it a right to the use of her body?[6] If so, then her aborting it would be more like the boy's taking away the chocolates, and less like your unplugging yourself from the violinist—doing so would be depriving it of what it does have a right to, and thus would be doing it an injustice.

And then, too, it might be asked whether or not she can kill it even to save her own life: If she voluntarily called it into existence, how can she now kill it, even in self-defense?

The first thing to be said about this is that it is something new. Opponents of abortion have been so concerned to make out the independence of the fetus, in order to establish that it has a right to life, just as its mother does, that they have tended to overlook the possible support they might gain from making out that the fetus is dependent on the mother, in order to establish that she has a special kind of responsibility for it, a responsibility that gives it rights against her which are not possessed by any independent person—such as an ailing violinist who is a stranger to her.

On the other hand, this argument would give the unborn person a right to its mother's body only if her pregnancy resulted from a voluntary act, undertaken in full knowledge of the chance a pregnancy might result from it. It would leave out entirely the unborn person whose existence is due to rape. Pending the availability of some further argument, then, we would be left with the conclusion that unborn persons whose existence is due to rape have no right to the use of their mothers' bodies, and thus that aborting them is not depriving them of anything they have a right to and hence is not unjust killing.

And we should also notice that it is not at all plain that this argument really does go even as far as it purports to. For there are cases and cases, and the details make a difference. If the room is stuffy, and I therefore open a window to air it, and a burglar climbs in, it would be absurd to say, "Ah, now he can stay, she's given him a right to the use of her house—for she is partially responsible for his presence there, having voluntarily done what enabled him to get in, in full knowledge that there are such things as burglars, and that burglars burgle." It would be still more absurd to say this if I had had bars installed outside my windows, precisely to prevent burglars from getting in, and a burglar got in only because of a defect in the bars. It remains equally absurd if we imagine it is not a burglar who climbs in, but an innocent person who blunders or falls in. Again, suppose it were like this: Peopleseeds drift about in the air like pollen, and if you open your windows, one may drift in and take root in your carpets or upholstery. You don't want children, so you fix up your windows with fine mesh screens, the very best you can buy. As can happen, however, and on very, very rare occasions does happen, one of the screens is defective; and a seed drifts in and takes root. Does the personplant who now develops have a right to the use of your house? Surely not—despite the fact that you voluntarily opened your windows, you knowingly kept carpets and upholstered furniture, and you knew that screens were sometimes defective. Someone may argue that you are responsible for its rooting, that it does have a right to your house, because after all you could have lived out your life with bare floors and furniture, or with sealed windows and doors. But this won't do—for by the same token anyone can avoid a pregnancy due to rape by having a hysterectomy, or anyway by never leaving home without a (reliable!) army.

It seems to me that the argument we are looking at can establish at most that there are some cases in which the unborn person has a right to the use of its mother's body, and therefore some cases in which abortion is unjust killing. There is room for much discussion and argument as to precisely which, if any. But I think we should sidestep this issue and leave it open, for at any rate the argument certainly does not establish that all abortion is unjust killing.

5. There is room for yet another argument here, however. We surely must grant that there may be cases in which it would be morally indecent to detach a person from your body at the cost of his life. Suppose you learn that what the violinist needs is not nine years of your life, but only one hour: All you need do to save his life is spend one hour in that bed with him. Suppose also that letting him use your kidneys for that one hour would not affect your health in the slightest. Admittedly you were kidnapped. Admittedly you did not give anyone permission to plug him into you. Nevertheless it seems to me plain you ought to allow him to use your kidneys for that hour—it would be indecent to refuse.

Again, suppose pregnancy lasted only an hour, and constituted no threat to life or death [sic]. And suppose that a woman becomes pregnant as a result of rape. Admittedly she did not voluntarily do anything to bring about the existence of a child. Admittedly she did nothing at all which would give the unborn person a right to the use of her body. All the same it might well be said, as in the newly emended violinist story, that she ought to allow it to remain for that hour—that it would be indecent in her to refuse.

Now some people are inclined to use the term "right" in such a way that it follows from the fact that you ought to allow a person to use your body for the hour he needs, that he has a right to use your body for the hour he needs, even though he has not been given that right by any person or act. They may say that it follows also that if you refuse, you act unjustly toward him. This use of the term is perhaps so common that it cannot be called wrong; nevertheless it seems to me to be an unfortunate loosening of what we would do better to keep a tight rein on. Suppose that box of chocolates I mentioned earlier had not been given to both boys jointly, but was given only to the older boy. There he sits, stolidly eating his way through the box, his small brother watching enviously. Here we are likely to say "You ought not to be so mean. You ought to give your brother some of those chocolates." My own view is that it just does not follow from the truth of this that the brother has any right to any of the chocolates. If the boy refuses to give his brother any, he is greedy, stingy, callous—but not unjust. I suppose that the people I have in mind will say it does follow that the brother has a right to some of the chocolates, and thus that the boy does act unjustly if he refuses to give his brother any. But the effect of saying this is to obscure what we

should keep distinct, namely the difference between the boy's refusal in this case and the boy's refusal in the earlier case, in which the box was given to both boys jointly, and in which the small brother thus had what was from any point of view clear title to half.

A further objection to so using the term "right" that from the fact that A ought to do a thing for B, it follows that B has a right against A that A do it for him, is that it is going to make the question of whether or not a man has a right to a thing turn on how easy it is to provide him with it; and this seems not merely unfortunate, but morally unacceptable. Take the case of Henry Fonda again. I said earlier that I had no right to the touch of his cool hand on my fevered brow, even though I needed it to save my life. I said it would be frightfully nice of him to fly in from the West Coast to provide me with it, but that I had no right against him that he should do so. But suppose he isn't on the West Coast. Suppose he has only to walk across the room, place a hand briefly on my brow—and lo, my life is saved. Then surely he ought to do it, it would be indecent to refuse. Is it to be said, "Ah, well, it follows that in this case she has a right to the touch of his hand on her brow, and so it would be an injustice to him to refuse"? So that I have a right to it when it is easy for him to provide it, though no right when it's hard? It's rather a shocking idea that anyone's rights should fade away and disappear as it gets harder and harder to accord them to him.

So my own view is that even though you ought to let the violinist use your kidneys for the one hour he needs, we should not conclude that he has a right to do so—we should say that if you refuse, you are, like the boy who owns all the chocolates and will give none away, self-centered and callous, indecent in fact, but not unjust. And similarly, that even supposing a case in which a woman pregnant due to rape ought to allow the unborn person to use her body for the hour he needs, we should not conclude that he has a right to do so; we should conclude that she is self-centered, callous, indecent, but not unjust, if she refuses. The complaints are no less grave; they are just different. However, there is no need to insist on this point. If anyone does wish to deduce "he has a right" from "you ought," then all the same he must surely grant that there are cases in which it is not morally required of you that you allow that violinist to use your kidneys, and in which he does not have a right to use them, and in which you do not do him an injustice if you refuse. And so also for mother and unborn child. Except in such cases as the unborn person has a right to demand it—and we were leaving open the possibility that there may be such cases—nobody is morally required to make large sacrifices, of health, of all other interests and concerns, of all other duties and commitments, for nine years, or even for nine months, in order to keep another person alive.

6. We have in fact to distinguish between the two kinds of Samaritan: the Good Samaritan and what we might call the Minimally Decent Samaritan. The story of the Good Samaritan, you will remember, goes like this:

> A certain man went down from Jerusalem to Jericho, and fell among thieves, which stripped him of his raiment, and wounded him, and departed, leaving him half dead.
>
> And by chance there came down a certain priest that way; and when he saw him, he passed by on the other side.
>
> And likewise a Levite, when he was at the place, came and looked on him, and passed by on the other side.
>
> But a certain Samaritan, as he journeyed, came where he was; and when he saw him he had compassion on him.
>
> And went to him, and bound up his wounds, pouring in oil and wine, and set him on his own beast, and brought him to an inn, and took care of him.
>
> And on the morrow, when he departed, he took out two pence, and gave them to the host, and said unto him, "Take care of him; and whatsoever thou spendest more, when I come again, I will repay thee."

(Luke 10:30–35)

The Good Samaritan went out of his way, at some cost to himself, to help one in need of it. We are not told what the options were, that is, whether or not the priest and the Levite could have helped by doing less than the Good Samaritan did, but assuming they could have, then the fact they did nothing at all shows they were not even Minimally Decent Samaritans, not because they were not Samaritans, but because they were not even minimally decent.

These things are a matter of degree, of course, but there is a difference, and it comes out perhaps most clearly in the story of Kitty Genovese, who, as you will remember, was murdered while thirty-eight people watched or listened, and did nothing at all to help her. A Good Samaritan would have

rushed out to give direct assistance against the murderer. Or perhaps we had better allow that it would have been a Splendid Samaritan who did this, on the ground that it would have involved a risk of death for himself. But the thirty-eight not only did not do this, they did not even trouble to pick up a phone to call the police. Minimally Decent Samaritanism would call for doing at least that, and their not having done it was monstrous.

After telling the story of the Good Samaritan, Jesus said, "Go, and do thou likewise." Perhaps he meant that we are morally required to act as the Good Samaritan did. Perhaps he was urging people to do more than is morally required of them. At all events it seems plain that it was not morally required of any of the thirty-eight that he rush out to give direct assistance at the risk of his own life, and that it is not morally required of anyone that he give long stretches of his life—nine years or nine months—to sustaining the life of a person who has no special right (we were leaving open the possibility of this) to demand it.

Indeed, with one rather striking class of exceptions, no one in any country in the world is legally required to do anywhere near as much as this for anyone else. The class of exceptions is obvious. My main concern here is not the state of the law in respect to abortion, but it is worth drawing attention to the fact that in no state in this country is any man compelled by law to be even a Minimally Decent Samaritan to any person; there is no law under which charges could be brought against the thirty-eight who stood by while Kitty Genovese died. By contrast, in most states in this country women are compelled by law to be not merely Minimally Decent Samaritans, but Good Samaritans to unborn persons inside them. This doesn't by itself settle anything one way or the other, because it may well be argued that there should be laws in this country—as there are in many European countries—compelling at least Minimally Decent Samaritanism.[7] But it does show that there is a gross injustice in the existing state of the law. And it shows also that the groups currently working against liberalization of abortion laws, in fact working toward having it declared unconstitutional for a state to permit abortion, had better start working for the adoption of Good Samaritan laws generally, or earn the charge that they are acting in bad faith.

I should think, myself, that Minimally Decent Samaritan laws would be one thing, Good Samaritan laws quite another, and in fact highly improper. But we are not here concerned with the law. What we should ask is not whether anybody should be compelled by law to be a Good Samaritan, but whether we must accede to a situation in which somebody is being compelled—by nature, perhaps—to be a Good Samaritan. We have, in other words, to look now at third-party interventions. I have been arguing that no person is morally required to make large sacrifices to sustain the life of another who has no right to demand them, and this even where the sacrifices do not include life itself; we are not morally required to be Good Samaritans or anyway Very Good Samaritans to one another. But what if a man cannot extricate himself from such a situation? What if he appeals to us to extricate him? It seems to me plain that there are cases in which we can, cases in which a Good Samaritan would extricate him. There you are, you were kidnapped, and nine years in bed with that violinist lie ahead of you. You have your own life to lead. You are sorry, but you simply cannot see giving up so much of your life to the sustaining of his. You cannot extricate yourself, and ask us to do so. I should have thought that—in light of his having no right to the use of your body—it was obvious that we do not have to accede to your being forced to give up so much. We can do what you ask. There is no injustice to the violinist in our doing so.

7. Following the lead of the opponents of abortion, I have throughout been speaking of the fetus merely as a person, and what I have been asking is whether or not the argument we began with, which proceeds only from the fetus' being a person, really does establish its conclusion. I have argued that it does not.

But of course there are arguments and arguments, and it may be said that I have simply fastened on the wrong one. It may be said that what is important is not merely the fact that the fetus is a person, but that it is a person for whom the woman has a special kind of responsibility issuing from the fact that she is its mother. And it might be argued that all my analogies are therefore irrelevant—for you do not have that special kind of responsibility for that violinist, Henry Fonda does not have that special kind of responsibility for me. And our attention might be drawn to the fact that men and women both are compelled by law to provide support for their children.

I have in effect dealt (briefly) with this argument in section 4 above; but a (still briefer) recapitulation now may be in order. Surely we do not have any such "special responsibility" for a person unless we have

assumed it, explicitly or implicitly. If a set of parents do not try to prevent pregnancy, do not obtain an abortion, but rather take it home with them, then they have assumed responsibility for it, they have given it rights, and they cannot now withdraw support from it at the cost of its life because they now find it difficult to go on providing for it. But if they have taken all reasonable precautions against having a child, they do not simply by virtue of their biological relationship to the child who comes into existence have a special responsibility for it. They may wish to assume responsibility for it, or they may not wish to. And I am suggesting that if assuming responsibility for it would require large sacrifices, then they may refuse. A Good Samaritan would not refuse—or anyway, a Splendid Samaritan, if the sacrifices that had to be made were enormous. But then so would a Good Samaritan assume responsibility for that violinist; so would Henry Fonda, if he is a Good Samaritan, fly in from the West Coast and assume responsibility for me.

8. My argument will be found unsatisfactory on two counts by many of those who want to regard abortion as morally permissible. First, while I do argue that abortion is not impermissible, I do not argue that it is always permissible. There may well be cases in which carrying the child to term required only Minimally Decent Samaritanism of the mother, and this is a standard we must not fall below. I am inclined to think it a merit of my account precisely that it does not give a general yes or a general no. It allows for and supports our sense that, for example, a sick and desperately frightened fourteen-year-old schoolgirl, pregnant due to rape, may of course choose abortion, and that any law which rules this out is an insane law. And it also allows for and supports our sense that in other cases resort to abortion is even positively indecent. It would be indecent in the woman to request an abortion, and indecent in a doctor to perform it, if she is in her seventh month, and wants the abortion just to avoid the nuisance of postponing a trip abroad. The very fact that the arguments I have been drawing attention to treat all cases of abortion, or even all cases of abortion in which the mother's life is not at stake, as morally on a par ought to have made them suspect at the outset.

Secondly, while I am arguing for the permissibility of abortion in some cases, I am not arguing for the right to secure the death of the unborn child. It is easy to confuse these two things in that up to a certain point in the life of the fetus it is not able to survive outside the mother's body; hence removing it from her body guarantees its death. But they are importantly different. I have argued that you are not morally required to spend nine months in bed, sustaining the life of that violinist; but to say this is by no means to say that if, when you unplug yourself, there is a miracle and he survives, you then have a right to turn around and slit his throat. You may detach yourself even if this costs him his life; you have no right to be guaranteed his death, by some other means, if unplugging yourself does not kill him. There are some people who will feel dissatisfied by this feature of my argument. A woman may be utterly devastated by the thought of a child, a bit of herself, put out for adoption and never seen or heard of again. She may therefore want not merely that the child be detached from her, but more, that it die. Some opponents of abortion are inclined to regard this as beneath contempt—thereby showing insensitivity to what is surely a powerful source of despair. All the same, I agree that the desire for the child's death is not one which anybody may gratify, should it turn out to be possible to detach the child alive.

At this place, however, it should be remembered that we have only been pretending throughout that the fetus is a human being from the moment of conception. A very early abortion is surely not the killing of a person, and so is not dealt with by anything I have said here.

Notes

1. Daniel Callahan, *Abortion: Law, Choice and Morality* (New York, 1970), p. 373. This book gives a fascinating survey of the available information on abortion. The Jewish tradition in David M. Feldman, *Birth Control in Jewish Law* (New York, 1963), part 5; the Catholic tradition in John T. Noonan, Jr., "An Almost Absolute Value in History," in *The Morality of Abortion,* ed. John T. Noonan, Jr. (Cambridge, Mass., 1970).

2. The term "direct" in the arguments I refer to is a technical one. Roughly, what is meant by "direct kill-

ing" is either killing as an end in itself, or killing as a means to some end, for example, the end of saving someone else's life. See note 5 on this page, for an example of its use.

3. Cf. *Encyclical Letter of Pope Pius XI on Christian Marriage,* St. Paul Editions (Boston, n.d.), p. 32: "However much we may pity the mother whose health and even life is gravely imperiled in the performance of the duty allotted to her by nature, nevertheless what could ever be a sufficient reason for excusing in any way the direct murder of the innocent? This is precisely what we are dealing with here." Noonan (*The Morality of Abortion,* p. 43) reads this as follows: "What cause can ever avail to excuse in any way the direct killing of the innocent? For it is a question of that."

4. The thesis in (4) is in an interesting way weaker than those in (1), (2), and (3): They rule out abortion even in cases in which both mother and child will die if the abortion is not performed. By contrast, one who held the view expressed in (4) could consistently say that one needn't prefer letting two persons die to killing one.

5. Cf. the following passage from Pius XII, *Address to the Italian Catholic Society of Midwives:* "The baby in the maternal breast has the right to life immediately from God.—Hence there is no man, no human authority, no science, no medical, eugenic, social, economic or moral 'indication' which can establish or grant a valid juridical ground for a direct deliberate disposition of an innocent human life, that is a disposition which looks to its destruction either as an end or as a means to another end perhaps in itself not illicit.—The baby, still not born, is a man in the same degree and for the same reason as the mother" (quoted in Noonan, *The Morality of Abortion,* p. 45).

6. The need for a discussion of this argument was brought home to me by members of the Society of Ethical and Legal Philosophy, to whom this paper was originally presented.

7. For a discussion of the difficulties involved, and a survey of the European experience with such laws, see *The Good Samaritan and the Law,* ed. James M. Ratcliffe (New York, 1966).

Abortion and the Sexual Agenda: A Case for Prolife Feminism

Sidney Callahan

Study Questions

1. What is the primary general contention of prochoice feminists that Callahan wants to contest?

2. Explain what Callahan believes is involved in the contention that the right to choose abortion follows from a woman's right to control her own body.

3. How does Callahan respond to this view? Why does she believe that the analogies of organ transplants and parasites do not fit the case of pregnancy? How does she believe that justice requires concern for the fetus?

4. Summarize the prochoice view that free access to abortion is necessary for a woman to exercise autonomy.

5. How does Callahan respond to this view? In addition to individual agency and decisive action what else should the moral life involve?

6. What is meant by the contention that the value of fetal life is a conferred or constructed value?

7. How does Callahan respond to this contention? What does she think is the basis for human rights?

8. Explain the ways in which access to abortion is believed by some to be necessary for women to psychological well-being and full and equal membership in society.

9. Does Callahan agree with this goal of equality? Why does she not agree with the means?

T he abortion debate continues. In the latest and perhaps most crucial development, prolife feminists are contesting prochoice feminist claims that

Sidney Callahan, "Abortion and the Sexual Agenda: A Case for Prolife Feminism," *Commonweal*, vol. 113 (April 15, 1986), pp. 232–238. Reprinted with permission. © 1986 Commonweal Foundation.

abortion rights are prerequisites for women's full development and social equality. The outcome of this debate may be decisive for the culture as a whole. Prolife feminists, like myself, argue on good feminist principles that women can never achieve the fulfillment of feminist goals in a society permissive toward abortion.

These new arguments over abortion take place within liberal political circles. This round of intense intra-feminist conflict has spiraled beyond earlier right-versus-left abortion debates, which focused on "tragic choices," medical judgments, and legal compromises. Feminist theorists of the prochoice position now put forth the demand for unrestricted abortion rights as a *moral imperative* and insist upon women's right to complete reproductive freedom. They morally justify the present situation and current abortion practices. Thus it is all the more important that prolife feminists articulate their different feminist perspective.

These opposing arguments can best be seen when presented in turn. Perhaps the most highly developed feminist arguments for the morality and legality of abortion can be found in Beverly Wildung Harrison's *Our Right to Choose* (Beacon Press, 1983) and Rosalind Pollack Petchesky's *Abortion and Woman's Choice* (Longman, 1984). Obviously it is difficult to do justice to these complex arguments, which draw on diverse strands of philosophy and social theory and are often interwoven in prochoice feminists' own version of a "seamless garment." Yet the fundamental feminist case for the morality of abortion, encompassing the views of Harrison and Petchesky, can be analyzed in terms of four central moral claims: (1) the moral right to control one's own body; (2) the moral necessity of autonomy and choice in personal responsibility; (3) the moral claim for the contingent value of fetal life; (4) the moral right of women to true social equality.

1. The moral right to control one's own body. Prochoice feminism argues that a woman choosing an abortion is exercising a basic right of bodily integrity granted in our common law tradition. If she does not choose to be physically involved in the demands of a pregnancy and birth, she should not be compelled to be so against her will. Just because it is *her* body which is involved, a woman should have the right to terminate any pregnancy, which at this point in medical history is tantamount to terminating fetal life. No one can be forced to donate an organ or submit to other invasive physical procedures for however good a cause. Thus no woman should be subjected to "compulsory pregnancy." And it should be noted that in pregnancy much more than a passive biological process is at stake.

From one perspective, the fetus is, as Petchesky says, a "biological parasite" taking resources from the woman's body. During pregnancy, a woman's whole life and energies will be actively involved in the nine-month process. Gestation and childbirth involve physical and psychological risks. After childbirth a woman will either be a mother who must undertake a twenty-year responsibility for child rearing, or face giving up her child for adoption or institutionalization. Since hers is the body, hers the risk, hers the burden, it is only just that she alone should be free to decide on pregnancy or abortion.

The moral claim to abortion, according to the prochoice feminists, is especially valid in an individualistic society in which women cannot count on medical care or social support in pregnancy, childbirth, or child rearing. A moral abortion decision is never made in a social vacuum, but in the real life society which exists here and now.

2. The moral necessity of autonomy and choice in personal responsibility. Beyond the claim for individual *bodily* integrity, the prochoice feminists claim that to be a full adult *morally*, a woman must be able to make responsible life commitments. To plan, choose, and exercise personal responsibility, one must have control of reproduction. A woman must be able to make yes-or-no decisions about a specific pregnancy, according to her present situation, resources, prior commitments, and life plan. Only with such reproductive freedom can a woman have the moral autonomy necessary to make mature commitments, in the area of family, work, or education.

Contraception provides a measure of personal control, but contraceptive failure or other chance events can too easily result in involuntary pregnancy. Only free access to abortion can provide the necessary

guarantee. The chance biological process of an involuntary pregnancy should not be allowed to override all the other personal commitments and responsibilities a woman has: to others, to family, to work, to education, to her future development, health, or well-being. Without reproductive freedom, women's personal moral agency and human consciousness are subjected to biology and chance.

3. The moral claim for the contingent value of fetal life. Prochoice feminist exponents like Harrison and Petchesky claim that the value of fetal life is contingent upon the woman's free consent and subjective acceptance. The fetus must be invested with maternal valuing in order to become human. This process of "humanization" through personal consciousness and "sociality" can only be bestowed by the woman in whose body and psychosocial system a new life must mature. The meaning and value of fetal life are constructed by the woman; without this personal conferral there only exists a biological, physiological process. Thus fetal interests or fetal rights can never outweigh the woman's prior interest and rights. If a woman does not consent to invest her pregnancy with meaning or value, then the merely biological process can be freely terminated. Prior to her own free choice and conscious investment, a woman cannot be described as a "mother" nor can a "child" be said to exist.

Moreover, in cases of voluntary pregnancy, a woman can withdraw consent if fetal genetic defects or some other problem emerges at any time before birth. Late abortion should thus be granted without legal restrictions. Even the minimal qualifications and limitations on women embedded in *Roe v. Wade* are unacceptable—repressive remnants of patriarchal unwillingness to give power to women.

4. The moral right of women to full social equality. Women have a moral right to full social equality. They should not be restricted or subordinated because of their sex. But this morally required equality cannot be realized without abortion's certain control of reproduction. Female social equality depends upon being able to compete and participate as freely as males can in the structures of educational and economic life. If a woman cannot control when and how she will be pregnant or rear children, she is at a distinct disadvantage, especially in our male-dominated world.

Psychological equality and well-being is also at stake. Women must enjoy the basic right of a person to the free exercise of heterosexual intercourse and full sexual expression, separated from procreation. No less than males, women should be able to be sexually active without the constantly inhibiting fear of pregnancy. Abortion is necessary for women's sexual fulfillment and the growth of uninhibited feminine self-confidence and ownership of their sexual powers.

But true sexual and reproductive freedom means freedom to procreate as well as to inhibit fertility. Prochoice feminists are also worried that women's freedom to reproduce will be curtailed through the abuse of sterilization and needless hysterectomies. Besides the punitive tendencies of a male-dominated health-care system, especially in response to repeated abortions or welfare pregnancies, there are other economic and social pressures inhibiting reproduction. Genuine reproductive freedom implies that day care, medical care, and financial support would be provided mothers, while fathers would take their full share in the burdens and delights of raising children.

Many prochoice feminists identify feminist ideals with communitarian, ecologically sensitive approaches to reshaping society. Following theorists like Sara Ruddick and Carol Gilligan, they link abortion rights with the growth of "maternal thinking" in our heretofore patriarchal society. Maternal thinking is loosely defined as a responsible commitment to the loving nature of specific human beings as they actually exist in socially embedded interpersonal contexts. It is a moral perspective very different from the abstract, competitive, isolated, and principled rigidity so characteristic of patriarchy.

How does a prolife feminist respond to these arguments? Prolife feminists grant the good intentions of their prochoice counterparts but protest that the prochoice position is flawed, morally inadequate, and inconsistent with feminism's basic demands for justice. Prolife feminists champion a more encompassing moral ideal. They recognize the claims of fetal life and offer a different perspective on what is good for women. The feminist vision is expanded and refocused.

1. From the moral right to control one's own body to a more inclusive ideal of justice. The moral right to control one's own body does apply to cases of organ transplants, mastectomies, contraception, and sterilization; but it is not a conceptualization adequate for abortion. The abortion dilemma is caused by the fact that 266 days following a conception in one body, another body will emerge. One's own body no longer exists as a single unit but is engendering another

organism's life. This dynamic passage from conception to birth is genetically ordered and universally found in the human species. Pregnancy is not like the growth of cancer or infestation by a biological parasite; it is the way every human being enters the world. Strained philosophical analogies fail to apply: having a baby is not like rescuing a drowning person, being hooked up to a famous violinist's artificial life-support system, donating organs for transplant—or anything else.

As embryology and fetology advance, it becomes clear that human development is a continuum. Just as astronomers are studying the first three minutes in the genesis of the universe, so the first moments, days, and weeks at the beginning of human life are the subject of increasing scientific attention. While neonatology pushes the definition of viability ever earlier, ultrasound and fetology expand the concept of the patient *in utero*. Within such a continuous growth process, it is hard to defend logically any demarcation point after conception as the point at which an immature form of human life is so different from the day before or the day after, that it can be morally or legally discounted as a nonperson. Even the moment of birth can hardly differentiate a nine-month fetus from a newborn. It is not surprising that those who countenance late abortions are logically led to endorse selective infanticide.

The same legal tradition which in our society guarantees the right to control one's own body firmly recognizes the wrongfulness of harming other bodies, however immature, dependent, different looking, or powerless. The handicapped, the retarded, and newborns are legally protected from deliberate harm. Prolife feminists reject the suppositions that would except the unborn from this protection.

After all, debates similar to those about the fetus were once conducted about feminine personhood. Just as women, or blacks, were considered too different, too underdeveloped, too "biological," to have souls or to possess legal rights, so the fetus is now seen as "merely" biological life, subsidiary to a person. A woman was once viewed as incorporated into the "one flesh" of her husband's person; she too was a form of bodily property. In all patriarchal unjust systems, lesser orders of human life are granted rights only when wanted, chosen, or invested with value by the powerful.

Fortunately, in the course of civilization there has been a gradual realization that justice demands the powerless and dependent be protected against the uses of power wielded unilaterally. No human can be treated as a means to an end without consent. The fetus is an immature, dependent form of human life which only needs time and protection to develop. Surely, immaturity and dependence are not crimes.

In an effort to think about the essential requirements of a just society, philosophers like John Rawls recommend imagining yourself in an "original position," in which your position in the society to be created is hidden by a "veil of ignorance." You will have to weigh the possibility that any inequalities inherent in that society's practices may rebound upon you in the worst, as well as in the best, conceivable way. This thought experiment helps ensure justice for all.

Beverly Harrison argues that in such an envisioning of society everyone would institute abortion rights in order to guarantee that if one turned out to be a woman one would have reproductive freedom. But surely in the original position and behind the "veil of ignorance," you would have to contemplate the possibility of being the particular fetus to be aborted. Since everyone has passed through the fetal stage of development, it is false to refuse to imagine oneself in this state when thinking about a potential world in which justice would govern. Would it be just that an embryonic life—in half the cases, of course, a female life—be sacrificed to the right of a woman's control over her own body? A woman may be pregnant without consent and experience a great many penalties, but a fetus killed without consent pays the ultimate penalty.

It does not matter . . . whether the fetus being killed is fully conscious or feels pain. We do not sanction killing the innocent if it can be done painlessly or without the victim's awareness. Consciousness becomes important to the abortion debate because it is used as a criterion for the "personhood" so often seen as the prerequisite for legal protection. Yet certain philosophers set the standard of personhood so high that half the human race could not meet the criteria during most of their waking hours (let alone their sleeping ones). Sentience, self-consciousness, rational decision-making, social participation? Surely no infant, or child under two, could qualify. Either our idea of person must be expanded or another criterion, such as human life itself, be employed to protect the weak in a just society. Prolife feminists who defend the fetus emphatically identify with an immature state of growth passed through by themselves, their children, and everyone now alive.

It also seems a travesty of just procedures that a pregnant woman now, in effect, acts as sole judge of her own case, under the most stressful conditions. Yes, one can acknowledge that the pregnant woman will be subject to the potential burdens arising from a pregnancy, but it has never been thought right to have an interested party, especially the more powerful party, decide his or her own case when there may be a conflict of interest. If one considers the matter as a case of a powerful versus a powerless, silenced claimant, the prochoice feminist argument can rightly be inverted: since hers is the body, hers the risk, and hers the greater burden, then how in fairness can a woman be the sole judge of the fetal right to life?

Human ambivalence, a bias toward self-interest, and emotional stress have always been recognized as endangering judgment. Freud declared that love and hate are so entwined that if instant thought could kill, we would all be dead in the bosom of our families. In the case of a woman's involuntary pregnancy, a complex, long-term solution requiring effort and energy has to compete with the immediate solution offered by a morning's visit to an abortion clinic. On the simple, perceptual plane, with imagination and thinking curtailed, the speed, ease, and privacy of abortion, combined with the small size of the embryo, tend to make early abortions seem less morally serious—even though speed, size, technical ease, and the private nature of an act have no moral standing.

As the most recent immigrants from nonpersonhood, feminists have traditionally fought for justice for themselves and the world. Women rally to feminism as a new and better way to live. Rejecting male aggression and destruction, feminists seek alternative, peaceful, ecologically sensitive means to resolve conflicts while respecting human potentiality. It is a chilling inconsistency to see prochoice feminists demanding continued access to assembly-line, technological methods of fetal killing—the vacuum aspirator, prostaglandins, and dilation and evacuation. It is betrayal of feminism, which has built the struggle for justice on the bedrock of women's empathy. After all, "maternal thinking" receives its name from a mother's unconditional acceptance and nurture of dependent, immature life. It is difficult to develop concern for women, children, the poor and the dispossessed—and to care about peace—and at the same time ignore fetal life.

2. From the necessity of autonomy and choice in personal responsibility to an expanded sense of responsibility. A distorted idea of morality overemphasizes individual autonomy and active choice. Morality has often been viewed too exclusively as a matter of human agency and decisive action. In moral behavior persons must explicitly choose and aggressively exert their wills to intervene in the natural and social environments. The human will dominates the body, overcomes the given, breaks out of the material limits of nature. Thus if one does not choose to be pregnant or cannot rear a child, who must be given up for adoption, then better to abort the pregnancy. Willing, planning, choosing one's moral commitments through the contracting of one's individual resources becomes the premier model of moral responsibility.

But morality also consists of the good and worthy acceptance of the unexpected events that life presents. Responsiveness and response-ability to things unchosen are also instances of the highest human moral capacity. Morality is not confined to contracted agreements of isolated individuals. Yes, one is obligated by explicit contracts freely initiated, but human beings are also obligated by implicit compacts and involuntary relationships in which persons simply find themselves. To be embedded in a family, a neighborhood, a social system, brings moral obligations which were never entered into with informed consent.

Parent-child relationships are one instance of implicit moral obligations arising by virtue of our being part of the interdependent human community. A woman, involuntarily pregnant, has a moral obligation to the now-existing dependent fetus whether she explicitly consented to its existence or not. No prolife feminist would dispute the forceful observations of prochoice feminists about the extreme difficulties that bearing an unwanted child in our society can entail. But the stronger force of the fetal claim presses a woman to accept these burdens; the fetus possesses rights arising from its extreme need and the interdependency and unity of humankind. The woman's moral obligation arises both from her status as a human being embedded in the interdependent human community and her unique lifegiving female reproductive power. To follow the prochoice feminist ideology of insistent individualistic autonomy and control is to betray a fundamental basis of the moral life.

3. From the moral claim of the contingent value of fetal life to the moral claim for the intrinsic value of human life. The feminist prochoice position which claims that the value of the fetus is contingent upon the pregnant woman's bestowal—or willed, conscious "construction"—of humanhood is seriously flawed. The inadequacies of this position flow from the erroneous premises (1) that human value and rights can be granted by individual will; (2) that the individual woman's consciousness can exist and operate in an *a priori* isolated fashion; and (3) that "mere" biological, genetic human life has little meaning. Prolife feminism takes a very different stance toward life and nature.

Human life from the beginning to the end of development *has* intrinsic value, which does not depend on meeting the selective criteria or tests set up by powerful others. A fundamental humanist assumption is at stake here. Either we are going to value embodied human life and humanity as a good thing, or take some variant of the nihilist position that assumes human life is just one more random occurrence in the universe such that each instance of human life must explicitly be justified to prove itself worthy to continue. When faced with a new life, or an involuntary pregnancy, there is a world of difference in whether one first asks, "Why continue?" or "Why not?" Where is the burden of proof going to rest? The concept of "compulsory pregnancy" is as distorted as labeling life "compulsory aging."

In a sound moral tradition, human rights arise from human needs, and it is the very nature of a right, or valid claim upon another, that it cannot be denied, conditionally delayed, or rescinded by more powerful others at their behest. It seems fallacious to hold that in the case of the fetus it is the pregnant woman alone who gives or removes its right to life and human status solely through her subjective conscious investment or "humanization." Surely no pregnant woman (or any other individual member of the species) has created her own human nature by an individually willed act of consciousness, nor for that matter been able to guarantee her own human rights. An individual woman and the unique individual embryonic life within her can only exist because of their participation in the genetic inheritance of the human species as a whole. Biological life should never be discounted. Membership in the species, or collective human family, is the basis for human solidarity, equality, and natural human rights.

4. The moral right of women to full social equality from a prolife feminist perspective. Prolife feminists and prochoice feminists are totally agreed on the moral right of women to the full social equality so far denied them. The disagreement between them concerns the definition of the desired goal and the best means to get there. Permissive abortion laws do not bring women reproductive freedom, social equality, sexual fulfillment, or full personal development.

Pragmatic failures of a prochoice feminist position combined with a lack of moral vision are, in fact, causing disaffection among young women. Middle-aged prochoice feminists blamed the "big chill" on the general conservative backlash. But they should look rather to their own elitist acceptance of male models of sex and to the sad picture they present of women's lives. Pitting women against their own offspring is not only morally offensive, it is psychologically and politically destructive. Women will never climb to equality and social empowerment over mounds of dead fetuses, numbering now in the millions. As long as most women choose to bear children, they stand to gain from the same constellation of attitudes and institutions that will also protect the fetus in the woman's womb—and they stand to lose from the cultural assumptions that support permissive abortion. Despite temporary conflicts of interest, feminine and fetal liberation are ultimately one and the same cause.

Women's rights and liberation are pragmatically linked to fetal rights because to obtain true equality, women need (1) more social support and changes in the structure of society, and (2) increased self-confidence, self-expectations, and self-esteem. Society in general, and men in particular, have to provide women more support in rearing the next generation, or our devastating feminization of poverty will continue. But if a woman claims the right to decide by herself whether the fetus becomes a child or not, what does this do to paternal and communal responsibility? Why should men share responsibility for child support or child rearing if they cannot share in what is asserted to be the woman's sole decision? Furthermore, if explicit intentions and consciously accepted contracts are necessary for moral obligations, why should men be held responsible for what *they* do not voluntarily choose to happen? By prochoice reasoning, a man who does not want to have a child, or whose contraceptive fails, can be exempted from the responsibilities of fatherhood and child support. Traditionally, many men have been laggards in assuming parental responsibility and support for their children;

ironically, ready abortion, often advocated as a response to male dereliction, legitimizes male irresponsibility and paves the way for even more male detachment and lack of commitment.

For that matter, why should the state provide a system of day care or child support, or require workplaces to accommodate women's maternity and the needs of child rearing? Permissive abortion, granted in the name of women's privacy and reproductive freedom, ratifies the view that pregnancies and children are a woman's private individual responsibility. More and more frequently, we hear some version of this old rationalization: if she refuses to get rid of it, it's her problem. A child becomes a product of the individual woman's freely chosen investment, a form of private property resulting from her own cost-benefit calculation. The larger community is relieved of moral responsibility.

With legal abortion freely available, a clear cultural message is given: conception and pregnancy are no longer serious moral matters. With abortion as an acceptable alternative, contraception is not as responsibly used; women take risks, often at the urging of male sexual partners. Repeat abortions increase, with all their psychological and medical repercussions. With more abortion there is more abortion. Behavior shapes thought as well as the other way round. One tends to justify morally what one has done; what becomes commonplace and institutionalized seems harmless. Habituation is a powerful psychological force. Psychologically it is also true that whatever is avoided becomes more threatening; in phobias it is the retreat from anxiety-producing events which reinforces future avoidance. Women begin to see themselves as too weak to cope with involuntary pregnancies. Finally, through the potency of social pressure and the force of inertia, it becomes more and more difficult, in fact almost unthinkable, *not* to use abortion to solve problem pregnancies. Abortion becomes no longer a choice but a "necessity." . . .

New feminist efforts to rethink the meaning of sexuality, femininity, and reproduction are all the more vital as new techniques for artificial reproduction, surrogate motherhood, and the like present a whole new set of dilemmas. In the long run, the very long run, the abortion debate may be merely the opening round in a series of far-reaching struggles over the role of human sexuality and the ethics of reproduction. Significant changes in the culture, both positive and negative in outcome, may begin as local storms of controversy. We may be at one of those vaguely realized thresholds when we had best come to full attention. What kind of people are we going to be? Prolife feminists pursue a vision for their sisters, daughters, and granddaughters. Will their great-granddaughters be grateful?

Planned Parenthood v. Casey

From the Decision by Justices O'Connor, Kennedy, and Souter

Study Questions

1. What provisions of the Pennsylvania case were at issue in this U.S. Supreme Court case?

2. What is the basic conclusion of the majority opinion in *Planned Parenthood v. Casey*? What three aspects of *Roe v. Wade* did it affirm?

3. How did the justices compare the case of abortion to that of flag burning?

4. What do they believe is at the heart of the liberty protected by the Fourteenth Amendment to the Constitution?

5. What consequences to others are also at issue in an abortion decision, according to the justices?

6. What kinds of considerations should the court consider in deciding whether or not to overrule former decisions? Do the justices believe that such reasons apply in the case of *Roe*?

7. Do the justices believe that modern medical advances make some of *Roe's* elements obsolete?

8. Are political considerations sufficient for decisions in such cases? What else is needed for acceptance of court decisions?

9. In addition to protecting a woman's liberty, how may the state show respect and concern for the life of the unborn, according to this opinion?

10. What five elements are included in the summary of this decision?

Liberty finds no refuge in a jurisprudence of doubt. Yet 19 years after our holding that the Constitu-

tion protects a woman's right to terminate her pregnancy in its early stages, Roe v. Wade, 410 U.S. 113 (1973), that definition of liberty is still questioned. Joining the respondents as amicus curiae, the United States, as it has done in five other cases in the last decade, again asks us to overrule Roe.

At issue in these cases are five provisions of the Pennsylvania Abortion Control Act of 1982 as amended in 1988 and 1989. The Act requires that a woman seeking an abortion give her informed consent prior to the abortion procedure, and specifies that she be provided with certain information at least 24 hours before the abortion is performed. For a minor to obtain an abortion, the Act requires the informed consent of one of her parents, but provides for a judicial bypass option if the minor does not wish to or cannot obtain a parent's consent. Another provision of the Act requires that, unless certain exceptions apply, a married woman seeking an abortion must sign a statement indicating that she has notified her husband of her intended abortion. The Act exempts compliance with these three requirements in the event of a "medical emergency," which is defined in Sections 3203 of the Act. In addition to the above provisions regulating the performance of abortions, the Act imposes certain reporting requirements on facilities that provide abortion services. . . . State and Federal courts as well as legislatures throughout the union must have guidance as they seek to address this subject in conformance with the Constitution. Given these premises, we find it imperative to review once more the principles that define the rights of the woman and the legitimate authority of the state respecting the termination of pregnancies by abortion procedures.

After considering the fundamental constitutional questions resolved by Roe, principles of institutional integrity, and the rule of stare decisis, we are led to

Planned Parenthood v. Casey, U.S. Supreme Court Decision (Pennsylvania Case). 112 S. Ct., 2791, 1992.

conclude this: the essential holding of Roe v. Wade should be retained and once again reaffirmed.

It must be stated at the outset and with clarity that Roe's essential holding, the holding we reaffirm, has three parts. First is a recognition of the right of the woman to choose to have an abortion before viability and to obtain it without undue interference from the State. Before viability, the state's interests are not strong enough to support a prohibition of abortion or the imposition of a substantial obstacle to the woman's effective right to elect the procedure. Second is a confirmation of the state's power to restrict abortions after fetal viability if the law contains exceptions for pregnancies which endanger a woman's life or health. And third is the principle that the state has legitimate interests from the outset of the pregnancy in protecting the health of the woman and the life of the fetus that may become a child. These principles do not contradict one another; and we adhere to each. . . .

Men and women of good conscience can disagree, and we suppose some always shall disagree, about the profound moral and spiritual implications of terminating a pregnancy, even in its earliest stage. Some of us as individuals find abortion offensive to our most basic principles of morality, but that cannot control our decision. Our obligation is to define the liberty of all, not to mandate our own moral code. The underlying constitutional issue is whether the state can resolve these philosophic questions in such a definitive way that a woman lacks all choice in the matter, except perhaps in those rare circumstances in which the pregnancy is itself a danger to her own life or health, or is the result of rape or incest.

It is conventional constitutional doctrine that where reasonable people disagree the Government can adopt one position or the other. That theorem, however, assumes a state of affairs in which the choice does not intrude upon a protected liberty. Thus, while some people might disagree about whether or not the flag should be saluted, or disagree about the proposition that it may not be defiled, we have ruled that a state may not compel or enforce one view or the other.

Our cases recognize "the right of the individual, married or single, to be free from unwarranted governmental intrusion into matters so fundamentally affecting a person as the decision whether to bear or beget a child." Eisenstadt v. Baird. Our precedents "have respected the private realm of family life which the state cannot enter." Prince v. Massachusetts. These matters, involving the most intimate and personal choices a person may make in a lifetime, choices central to personal dignity and autonomy, are central to the liberty protected by the Fourteenth Amendment. At the heart of liberty is the right to define one's own concept of existence, of meaning, of the universe, and of the mystery of human life. Beliefs about these matters could not define the attributes of personhood were they formed under compulsion of the State.

These considerations begin our analysis of the woman's interest in terminating her pregnancy but cannot end it, for this reason: though the abortion decision may originate within the zone of conscience and belief, it is more than a philosophic exercise. Abortion is a unique act. It is an act fraught with consequences for others: for the woman who must live with the implications of her decision; for the persons who perform and assist in the procedure; for the spouse, family, and society which must confront the knowledge that these procedures exist, procedures some deem nothing short of an act of violence against innocent human life; and, depending on one's beliefs, for the life or potential life that is aborted. Though abortion is conduct, it does not follow that the State is entitled to proscribe it in all instances. That is because the liberty of the woman is at stake in a sense unique to the human condition and so unique to the law. The mother who carries a child to full term is subject to anxieties, to physical constraints, to pain that only she must bear. . . .

When this Court reexamines a prior holding, its judgment is customarily informed by a series of prudential and pragmatic considerations designed to test the consistency of overruling a prior decision with the ideal of the rule of law, and to gauge the respective costs of reaffirming and overruling a prior case. Thus, for example, we may ask whether the rule has proved to be intolerable simply in defying practical workability, whether the rule is subject to a kind of reliance that would lend a special hardship to the consequences of overruling and add inequity to the cost of repudiation, whether related principles of law have so far developed as to have left the old rule no more than a remnant of abandoned doctrine, or whether facts have so changed or come to be seen so differently, as to have robbed the old rule of significant application or justification.

So in this case we may inquire whether Roe's central rule has been found unworkable; whether the rule's limitation on a state power could be removed without serious inequity to those who have relied upon it or significant damage to the stability of the society governed by the rule in question; whether the law's growth in the intervening years has left Roe's central rule a doctrinal anachronism discounted by society; and whether Roe's premises of fact have so far changed in the ensuing two decades as to render its central holding somehow irrelevant or unjustifiable in dealing with the issue it addressed.

Although Roe has engendered opposition, it has in no sense proven "unworkable," representing as it does a simple limitation beyond which a state law is unenforceable. . . .

But to do this would be simply to refuse to face the fact that for two decades of economic and social developments, people have organized intimate relationships and made choices that define their views of themselves and their places in society, in reliance on the availability of abortion in the event that contraception should fail. The ability of women to participate equally in the economic and social life of the nation has been facilitated by their ability to control their reproductive lives. The Constitution serves human values, and while the effect of reliance on Roe cannot be exactly measured, neither can the certain cost of overruling Roe for people who have ordered their thinking and living around that case.

No evolution of legal principle has left Roe's doctrinal footings weaker than they were in 1973. No development of constitutional law since the case was decided has implicitly or explicitly left Roe behind as a mere survivor of obsolete constitutional thinking.

It will be recognized, of course, that Roe stands at an intersection of two lines of decisions, but in whichever doctrinal category one reads the case, the result for present purposes will be the same. The Roe Court itself placed its holding in the succession of cases most prominently exemplified by Griswold v. Connecticut. When it is so seen, Roe is clearly in no jeopardy, since subsequent constitutional developments have neither disturbed, nor do they threaten to diminish, the scope of recognized protection accorded to the liberty relating to intimate relationships, the family, and decisions about whether or not to beget or bear a child.

Roe, however, may be seen not only as an exemplar of Griswold liberty but as a rule (whether or not mistaken) of personal autonomy and bodily integrity, with doctrinal affinity to cases recognizing limits on governmental power to mandate medical treatment

or to bar its rejection. If so, our cases since Roe accord with Roe's view that a State's interest in the protection of life falls short of justifying any plenary override of individual liberty claims. . . .

We have seen how time has overtaken some of Roe's factual assumptions: advances in maternal health care allow for abortions safe to the mother later in pregnancy than was true in 1973, and advances in neonatal care have advanced viability to a point somewhat earlier. But these facts go only to the scheme of time limits on the realization of competing interests, and the divergences from the factual premises of 1973 have no bearing on the validity of Roe's central holding, that viability marks the earliest point at which the state's interest in fetal life is constitutionally adequate to justify a legislative ban on nontherapeutic abortions.

The soundness or unsoundness of that constitutional judgment in no sense turns on whether viability occurs at approximately 28 weeks, as was usual at the time of Roe, at 23 to 24 weeks, as it sometimes does today, or at some moment even slightly earlier in pregnancy, as it may if fetal respiratory capacity can somehow be enhanced in the future. Whenever it may occur, the attainment of viability may continue to serve as the critical fact, just as it has done since Roe was decided; which is to say that no change in Roe's factual underpinning has left its central holding obsolete, and none supports an argument for overruling it.

The sum of the precedential inquiry to this point shows Roe's underpinning unweakened in any way affecting its central holding. While it has engendered disapproval, it has not been unworkable. An entire generation has come of age free to assume Roe's concept of liberty in defining the capacity of women to act in society, and to make reproductive decisions; no erosion of principle going to liberty or personal autonomy has left Roe's central holding a doctrinal remnant; Roe portends no developments at odds with other precedent for the analysis of personal liberty; and no changes of fact have rendered viability more or less appropriate at the point at which the balance of interests tips. Within the bounds of normal stare decisis analysis, then, and subject to the considerations on which it customarily turns, the stronger argument is for affirming Roe's central holding, with whatever degree of personal reluctance any of us may have, not for overruling it. . . .

Our analysis would not be complete, however, without explaining why overruling Roe's central holding would not only reach an unjustifiable result under principles of *stare decisis*, but would seriously weaken the Court's capacity to exercise the judicial power and to function as the Supreme Court of a nation dedicated to the rule of law. To understand why this would be so it is necessary to understand the source of this Court's authority, the conditions necessary for its preservation, and its relationship to the country's understanding of itself as a constitutional Republic.

The root of American Governmental power is revealed most clearly in the instance of the power conferred by the Constitution upon the Judiciary of the United States and specifically upon this Court. As Americans of each succeeding generation are rightly told, the Court cannot buy support for its decisions by spending money and, except to a minor degree, it cannot independently coerce obedience to its decrees. The Court's power lies, rather, in its legitimacy, a product of substance and perception that shows itself in the people's acceptance of the Judiciary as fit to determine what the Nation's law means and to declare what it demands.

The underlying substance of this legitimacy is of course the warrant for the Court's decisions in the Constitution and the lesser sources of legal principle on which the Court draws. That substance is expressed in the Court's opinions, and our contemporary understanding is such that a decision without principled justification would be no judicial act at all. But even when justification is furnished by apposite legal principle, something more is required. Because not every conscientious claim of principled justification will be accepted as such, the justification claimed must be beyond dispute.

The Court must take care to speak and act in ways that allow people to accept its decisions on the terms the Court claims for them, as grounded truly in principle, not as compromises with social and political pressures having, as such, no bearing on the principled choices that the Court is obliged to make. Thus, the Court's legitimacy depends on making legally principled decisions under circumstances in which their principled character is sufficiently plausible to be accepted by the Nation.

The need for principled action to be perceived as such is implicated to some degree whenever this, or any other appellate court, overrules a prior case. This is not to say, of course, that this Court cannot give a perfectly satisfactory explanation in most cases. People understand that some of the Constitution's language is hard to fathom and that the Court's Justices are sometimes able to perceive significant facts or to understand principles of law that eluded their predecessors and that justify departures from existing decisions. However upsetting it may be to those most directly affected when one judicially derived rule replaces another, the country can accept some correction of error without necessarily questioning the legitimacy of the Court.

In two circumstances, however, the Court would almost certainly fail to receive the benefit of the doubt in overruling prior cases. There is, first, a point beyond which frequent overruling would overtax the country's belief in the Court's good faith. Despite the variety of reasons that may inform and justify a decision to overrule, we cannot forget that such a decision is usually perceived (and perceived correctly) as, at the least, a statement that a prior decision was wrong. There is a limit to the amount of error that can plausibly be imputed to prior courts. If that limit should be exceeded, disturbance of prior rulings would be taken as evidence that justifiable reexamination of principle had given way to drives for particular results in the short term. The legitimacy of the Court would fade with the frequency of its vacillation.

That first circumstance can be described as hypothetical; the second is to the point here and now. Where, in the performance of its judicial duties, the Court decides a case in such a way as to resolve the sort of intensely divisive controversy reflected in Roe and those rare, comparable cases, its decision has a dimension that the resolution of the normal case does not carry. It is the dimension present whenever the Court's interpretation of the Constitution calls the contending sides of a national controversy to end their national division by accepting a common mandate rooted in the Constitution.

The Court is not asked to do this very often, having thus addressed the nation only twice in our lifetime, in the decisions of Brown and Roe. But when the Court does act in this way, its decision requires an equally rare precedential force to counter the inevitable efforts to overturn it and to thwart its implementation. Some of those efforts may be mere unprincipled emotional reactions; others may proceed from principles worthy of profound respect.

But whatever the premises of opposition may be, only the most convincing justification under accepted standards of precedent could suffice to demonstrate that a later decision overruling the first was anything but a surrender to political pressure, and an unjustified repudiation of the principle on which the Court staked its authority in the first instance. So to overrule under fire in the absence of the most compelling reason to reexamine a watershed decision would subvert the Court's legitimacy beyond any serious questions. . . .

The Court's duty in the present case is clear. In 1973, it confronted the already divisive issue of governmental power to limit personal choice to undergo abortion, for which it provided a new resolution based on the due process guaranteed by the Fourteenth Amendment. Whether or not a new social consensus is developing on that issue, its divisiveness is no less today than in 1973 and pressure to overrule the decision, like pressure to retain it, has grown only more intense. A decision to overrule Roe's essential holding under the existing circumstances would address error, if error there was, at the cost of both profound and unnecessary damage to the Court's legitimacy, and to the Nation's commitment to the rule of law. It is therefore imperative to adhere to the essence of Roe's original decision, and we do so today.

From what we have said so far it follows that it is a constitutional liberty of the woman to have some freedom to terminate her pregnancy. We conclude that the basic decision in Roe was based on a constitutional analysis which we cannot now repudiate. The woman's liberty is not so unlimited, however, that from the outset the State cannot show its concern for the life of the unborn, and at a later point in fetal development the state's interest in life has sufficient force so that the right of the woman to terminate the pregnancy can be restricted. . . .

Yet it must be remembered that Roe v. Wade speaks with clarity in establishing not only the woman's liberty but also the state's "important and legitimate interest in potential life." That portion of the decision in Roe has been given too little acknowledgement and implementation by the Court in its subsequent cases.

Those cases decided that any regulation touching upon the abortion decision must survive strict scrutiny, to be sustained only if drawn in narrow terms to further a compelling state interest. Not all of the cases decided under that formulation can be reconciled with the holding in Roe itself that the state has legitimate interests in the health of the woman and in protecting the potential life within her.

In resolving this tension, we choose to rely upon Roe, as against the later cases. . . .

Some guiding principles should emerge. What is at stake is the woman's right to make the ultimate decision, not a right to be insulated from all others in doing so.

Regulations which do no more than create a structural mechanism by which the state, or the parent or guardian of a minor, may express profound respect for the life of the unborn are permitted, if they are not a substantial obstacle to the woman's exercise of the right to choose. Unless it has that effect on her right of choice, a state measure designed to persuade her to choose childbirth over abortion will be upheld if reasonably related to that goal.

Regulations designed to foster the health of a woman seeking an abortion are valid if they do not constitute an undue burden. That is to be expected in the application of any legal standard which must accommodate life's complexity. We do not expect it to be otherwise with respect to the undue burden standard. We give this summary:

(a) To protect the central right recognized by Roe v. Wave while at the same time accommodating the state's profound interest in potential life, we will employ the undue burden analysis as explained in this opinion. An undue burden exists, and therefore a provision of law is invalid, if its purpose or effect is to place a substantial obstacle in the path of a woman seeking an abortion before the fetus attains viability.

(b) We reject the rigid trimester framework of Roe v. Wade. To promote the state's profound interest in potential life, throughout pregnancy the state may take measures to ensure that the woman's choice is informed, and measures designed to advance this interest will not be invalidated as long as their purpose is to persuade the woman to choose childbirth over abortion. These measures must not be an undue burden on the right.

(c) As with any medical procedure, the state may enact regulations to further the health or safety of a woman seeking an abortion. Unnecessary health regulations that have the purpose or effect of presenting a substantial obstacle to a woman seeking an abortion impose an undue burden on the right.

(d) Our adoption of the undue burden analysis does not disturb the central holding of Roe v. Wade, and we reaffirm that holding. Regardless of whether exceptions are made for particular circumstances, a State may not prohibit any woman from making the ultimate decision to terminate her pregnancy before viability.

(e) We also reaffirm Roe's holding that "subsequent to viability, the State in promoting its interest in the potentiality of human life may, if it chooses, regulate, and even proscribe, abortion except where it is necessary, in appropriate medical judgment, for the preservation of the life or health of the mother." Roe v. Wade, 410 U.S., at 164–165.

Review Exercises

1. Outline the stages of fetal development.
2. Explain the conclusions of *Roe v. Wade* and *Planned Parenthood v. Casey.*
3. Give a utilitarian argument for abortion. Give one against abortion. Are these act or rule utilitarian arguments? Explain.
4. Describe how Thomson uses the violinist analogy to make an argument regarding the moral permissibility of abortion.
5. Use Method I to make one argument for abortion and one against.
6. Which of the following positions under Method II does each statement exemplify:
   a. Because this fetus has all the potential to develop the abilities of a person, it has all the rights of a person.
   b. Only when a being can think and communicate does it have full moral status. Because a fetus does not have these abilities, it has neither moral rights nor claims.
   c. If it is a human being, then it has full moral status and rights.
   d. Ability to feel pain gives a being full moral status. The fetus has this about the fifth or sixth month, so abortion is not morally justifiable beyond that stage.
   e. Early-term fetuses do not have as much moral significance as later-term fetuses because their potential is not as much developed as later.

Discussion Cases

1. *Abortion for Sex Selection.* It is now possible to determine the sex of one's child before birth. In the waiting room of a local women's clinic June has struck up a conversation with another woman, Ann. She finds out that each is there for an amniocentesis to determine the sex of her fetus. June reveals that she wants to know what sex it is because her husband and his family really want a boy. Because they plan to have only one child, they plan to end this pregnancy if it is a girl and try again. Ann tells her that her reason is different. She is a genetic carrier of a particular kind of muscular dystrophy. Duchene's muscular dystrophy is a sex-linked disease inherited through the mother with a 50 percent chance of each male child having the disease. Only males get the disease. The disease causes muscle weakness and often some mental retardation. It causes death through respiratory failure, usually in early adulthood. She does not want to risk having such a child, and this abnormality cannot yet be determined through prenatal testing. Thus, if the prenatal diagnosis reveals that her fetus is male, she plans to end this pregnancy.

What do you think of the use of prenatal diagnosis and abortion for purposes of sex selection in these or other cases? In India, ultrasound is commonly used for sex selection. Most abortions are of female fetuses. In fact, women are sometimes killed for not producing male children. What do you say about prenatal diagnosis in these circumstances?*

2. *Father's Consent to Abortion.* Jim and Sue had been planning to have a child for two years. Finally she had become pregnant. However, their marriage had been a rough one, and by the time she was in her third month of pregnancy they had decided to end their marriage and get a divorce. At that point they were both ambivalent about the pregnancy. They had both wanted the child. However, now things were different. Sue finally decided that she did not want to raise a

---

*I wish to thank a reviewer, Susan Armstrong of Humboldt State University, for this example. She notes that the killing of women in India for not producing male offspring is called "dowry death, and it has produced a missing two million Indian women."

child alone and did not want to raise Jim's child. She wanted to get on with her life. However, Jim had long wanted a child, and he realized that the developing fetus was partly his own because he had provided half the genetic basis for it. He did not want Sue to end the pregnancy. He wanted to keep and raise the child. The case was currently being heard by the court.

Although the primary decision is a legal one, do you think that Jim had any moral rights in this case or should the decision be strictly Sue's? Why or why not?

3. *Parental Consent to Abortion.* Judy is a high school sophomore and fifteen years old. She recently had become sexually active with her boyfriend. She does not want to tell him that she is now pregnant, and she does not feel that she can talk to her parents. They have been quite strict with her and would condemn her recent behavior. They also oppose abortion. Judy would like simply to end this pregnancy and start over with her life. However, in her state minors must get parental consent for an abortion. One reason is that this is a medical procedure and parents must consent for other medical procedures for their children.

What should Judy do? Do you agree that states should require parental consent for abortion for their minor children? Why or why not?

4. *Abortion and Economic Concerns.* Juanita works extremely hard. She is a domestic worker and cleans the homes of wealthy folks outside of the city. Her husband lost his job several months ago and has been unable to find work. Because of her low income, she is barely able to care for her three children. Recently she found out that she is pregnant with a fourth child. It is not that she did not try to prevent the pregnancy, but she was not able to say no to her husband. She does not tell him about the pregnancy because she thinks he would want her to have the baby. She feels that having an abortion is the only responsible thing to do.

How would you rate this reason among the others that people have for wanting an abortion? Should she tell her husband?

Selected Bibliography

Baird, Robert, and Stuart E. Rosenbaum (Eds.). *The Ethics of Abortion.* Buffalo, NY: Prometheus, 1989.

Brody, Baruch. *Abortion and the Sanctity of Life.* Cambridge, MA: MIT Press, 1975.

Callahan, Daniel. *Abortion: Law, Choice, and Morality.* New York: Macmillan, 1970.

Cohen, Marshall, Thomas Nagel, and Thomas Scanlon (Eds.). *The Rights and Wrongs of Abortion.* Princeton, NJ: Princeton University Press, 1974.

Colker, Ruth. *Abortion and Dialogue: Pro-Choice, Pro-Life, and American Law.* Bloomington: Indiana University Press, 1992.

Feinberg, Joel (Ed.). *The Problem of Abortion,* 2nd ed. Belmont, CA: Wadsworth, 1984.

Finnis, John, Judith Thomson, Michael Tooley, and Roger Wertheimer. *The Rights and Wrongs of Abortion.* Princeton, NJ: Princeton University Press, 1974.

Garfield, Jay L., and Patricia Hennessy. *Abortion: Moral and Legal Perspectives.* Amherst: University of Massachusetts Press, 1985.

Graber, Mark A. *Rethinking Abortion: Equal Choice, the Constitution, and Reproductive Politics.* Princeton, NJ: Princeton University Press, 1996.

Kamm, F. M. *Creation and Abortion: A Study in Moral and Legal Philosophy.* New York: Oxford University Press, 1992.

Luker, Kristin. *Abortion and the Politics of Motherhood.* Berkeley: University of California Press, 1984.

Nicholson, Susan. *Abortion and the Roman Catholic Church.* Knoxville, TN: Religious Ethics, 1978.

Noonan, John T., Jr. (Ed.). *The Morality of Abortion: Legal and Historical Perspectives.* Cambridge, MA: Harvard University Press, 1970.

Overall, Christine. *Ethics and Human Reproduction: A Feminist Analysis.* Boston: Allen & Unwin, 1988.

Perkins, Robert (Ed.). *Abortion: Pro and Con.* Cambridge, MA: Schenkman, 1974.

Podell, Janet (Ed.) *Abortion.* New York: H. W. Wilson, 1990.

Steinbock, Bonnie. *Life Before Birth: The Moral and Legal Status of Embryos and Fetuses.* New York: Oxford University Press, 1992.

Summer, L. W. *Abortion and Moral Theory.* Princeton, NJ: Princeton University Press, 1981.

Tietze, Christopher. *Induced Abortion: A World Review.* New York: Population Council, 1981.

Tooley, Michael. *Abortion and Infanticide.* New York: Oxford University Press, 1983.

❧ *10* ❧

Sexual Morality and Pornography

According to a recent study, three fourths of today's teenagers have had sexual relations by the time they are twenty years old.[1] Thirty-three percent of the boys surveyed and 27 percent of the girls had sex by the time they were fifteen. Furthermore, 15 percent of the teens had been sexual with five or more partners. The same study found that one-fourth of sexually active teens contract venereal disease every year, and that "about 20 [percent] of all AIDS patients are under 30," many of them having contracted the virus in their teens.[2] Many factors may contribute to the earlier and more widespread sexual activity of young people. Among the reasons cited are the lowered age of sexual maturity due to health and nutritional improvements over the last several decades, teenagers' increased freedom, and the sexual explicitness in today's TV, movies, and music.

On the one hand, many people are concerned about these trends in sexual activity, as well as by the trends in sexual explicitness. Moreover, sex is used to sell everything from blue jeans to perfume. Pornography is no longer found only in the back of the store or out-of-the-way places; it can now even be beamed into home televisions over telephone lines. Some believe that these trends are related to social problems, such as the fact that four out of seven marriages end in divorce. Some wonder if these trends are part

of an overall movement that denigrates human sexuality.

On the other hand, others argue that the kind of sexual freedom that we have today is preferable to the restrictive rules and negative views of sex of times past. Still, women are generally held to a different sexual standard than men, and what counts as acceptable for men may count as promiscuity for women. Perhaps too much is made of sex and sexual morality, as though it were the only moral issue. When we hear expressions such as "Doesn't he have any morals?" or "She has loose morals," the speakers most probably are referring to the person's sexual morals. But many other moral issues are arguably more important than sexual behavior.

Some of you might even be inclined to say that one's sexual behavior is not a moral matter at all. Is it not a private matter and too personal and individual to be a moral matter? To hold that it is not a moral matter, however, would seem to imply that our sexual lives are morally insignificant. Or it might imply that something has to be public or universal in order to have moral significance. However, I do not think that we would want to hold that personal matters cannot be moral matters. Furthermore, consider that sexual behavior lends itself to valuable experiences—those of personal relations, pleasure, fruitfulness and descendants, and self-esteem and enhancement. It also involves unusual opportunities for cruelty, deceit, unfairness, and selfishness. Because these are moral matters, sexual behavior must itself have moral significance.

Recent legal issues concerning gay rights have also highlighted issues related to sexual morality. In May 1996, the U.S. Supreme Court struck down a Colorado law that banned legal protection for homosexuals.[3] Supporters of the ban argued that the people of Colorado had a right to do what they could to preserve what they saw as traditional moral values. Those who sought to overturn the ban saw it as a matter of protection from discrimination and equal rights for all. The issue of legal recognition of same-sex marriage has also been the subject recently of heated debate, as has been the question of whether schools ought to give financial support to gay and lesbian clubs as they do other school organizations. Although these cases raise issues concerning the relation of law and morality (to be discussed later in this chapter), they also point to the divergence of views in society concerning whether certain kinds of sexual relations are morally approvable. In addition, they point out how difficult it is to keep personal moral matters separate from public social issues. It is primarily the issue of sexual morality that we address in this chapter. Issues related to discrimination and equality are treated in Chapter 11.

Conceptual Problems: What Is and Is Not Sexual

To discuss sexual morality, we might benefit from preliminary thinking about the subject of our discussion. Just what are we talking about when we speak of sexual pleasure, sexual desire, or sexual activity? Consider the meaning of the qualifier *sexual*. Suppose we said that behavior is sexual when it involves "pleasurable bodily contact with another." Will this do? This definition is quite broad. It includes passionate caresses and kisses as well as sexual intercourse. But it would not include activity that does not involve another individual, such as masturbation or looking at sexually stimulating pictures. It would also not include erotic dancing or erotic communications at a distance, because these activities do not involve physical contact with another. So the definition seems to be too narrow.

However, this definition is also too broad. It covers too much. Not all kisses or caresses are sexual, even though they are physical and can be pleasurable. And the contact sport of football is supposedly pleasurable for those who play it, but presumably not sexually pleasurable. It seems reasonable to think of sexual pleasure as pleasure that involves our so-called erogenous zones—those areas of the body that are sexually sensitive. Thus, only after a certain stage of biological development do we become capable of sexual passions or feelings. Could we then say that sexuality is necessarily bodily in nature? To answer this question, try the following thought experiment. Suppose we did not have bodies—in other words, suppose we were ghosts or spirits of some sort. Would we then be sexual beings? Could we experience sexual desire, for example? If we did, it would surely be different from that which we now experience. Moreover, it is not just that our own bodily existence seems required for us to experience sexual desire, but sexual desire for another would seem most properly to be for the embodied other. It cannot be simply the body of another that is desirable, or dead bodies generally would be sexually stimulating. It is an *embodied person* who is the normal object of sexual desire. This is not to say that bodily touching is necessary, as is clear from the fact that dancing can be sexy and phone conversations can be heated. Finally, if the body is so important for sexuality, we can also wonder whether there are any significant differences between male and female sexuality in addition to, and based on, genital and reproductive differences.

Let us also note one more conceptual puzzle. Many people refer to sexual intercourse as "making love." Some people argue that sexual intercourse should be accompanied by or be an expression of love, while others do not believe that this is necessary. Probably we would do best to consult the poets about the meaning of love. Briefly consider what you would regard as the difference between being in love (or falling in love) and loving someone. To "be in love" seems to suggest passivity. Similarly, to "fall in love" seems to be something that happens to a person. Supposedly one has little control over one's feelings and even some thoughts in such a state. One cannot get the other person out of one's mind. One is, so to speak, "head over heels in love" or "madly in love"; one has "fallen passionately in love." Yet comparing these notions to those of loving someone we may get a different result. To love someone is to be actively directed to that person's good. We want the best for him or her. In his essay on friendship in *Nicomachean Ethics*, Aristotle wrote that true friendship is different from that which is based on the usefulness of the friend or the pleasure one obtains from being with the friend. The true friend cares about his friend for the friend's own sake. According to Aristotle, "Those who wish well to their friends for their sake are most truly friends."[4] This kind of friendship is less common, he believed, though more lasting. For Aristotle and the Greeks of his time, true friendship was more or less reserved for men. One contribution an ethics of care makes to this discussion is just the importance of friendship that is available to all. Moreover, we need not be in love with someone to love them. We can love our friends, or parents, or children, and yet we are not in love with them. When considering what sex has to do with love, we would do well to consider the kind of love that is intended. It would also be well to ponder the possible link between a sexual relation and friendship.

Relevant Factual Matters

In addition to conceptual clarification, certain factual matters may also be relevant to what we say about matters of sexual morality. For example, would it not be morally significant to know the effects of celibacy or of restraining sexual urges? It is well known that Freud thought that if we repressed our sexual desires we would

either become neurotic or artists! Art, he argues, provides an emotional expressive outlet for repressed sexual feelings. Freudian theory about both sexual repression and the basis of art still has supporters—Camille Paglia, for example.[5] It also has not gone unchallenged. Knowing what the likely effects would be, both psychologically and physically, of sexual promiscuity might also be useful for thinking about sexual morality. Does separating sex and bodily pleasure from other aspects of oneself have any effect on a person's ability to have a more holistic and more fulfilling sexual experience? Furthermore, factual matters such as the likelihood of contracting a disease like AIDS would be important for what we say about the moral character of some sexual encounter. Our conclusions about many factual or empirical matters would seem to influence greatly what we say about sexual morality—that is, if the morality of sex, just like the morality of other human activities, is at least sometimes determined by the benefits and harms that result from it.

However, factual matters may be relevant only if we are judging the morality of actions on the basis of their consequences. If instead we adopt a nonconsequentialist moral theory such as Kant's, then our concerns will not be about the consequences of sexual behavior but about whether we are enhancing or using persons, for example, or being fair or unfair. If we adopt a natural law position, our concerns will again be significantly different, or at least based on different reasons. We will want to know whether certain sexual behavior fits or is befitting human nature.

In fact, the moral theory that we hold will even determine how we pose the moral question about sex. For example, if we are guided by a consequentialist moral theory such as utilitarianism, we will be likely to pose the moral question in terms of good or bad, better or worse sexual behavior. If we are governed by Kantian principles, then our questions will more likely be in terms of right or wrong, justifiable or unjustifiable sexual behavior. And if we judge from a natural law basis, we will want to know whether a particular sexual behavior is natural or unnatural, proper or improper, or even perverted. Let us consider each of these three ways of posing moral questions about sexual matters, and see some of the probable considerations appropriate to each type of reasoning.

Consequentialist or Utilitarian Considerations

If we were to take a consequentialist point of view—say that of an act utilitarian—we would judge our actions or make our decisions about how to behave sexually one at a time. In each case we would consider our alternatives and their likely consequences for all who would be affected by them. In each case we would consider who would benefit or suffer as well as the type of benefit or suffering. In sexual relations, we would probably want to consider physical, psychological, and social consequences. Considerations such as these are necessary for arguments that are consequentialist in nature. According to this perspective, the sexual practice or relation that has better consequences than other possibilities is the preferred one. Any practice in which the bad consequences outweigh the good consequences would be morally problematic.

Among the negative consequences to be avoided are physical harms, including sexually transmitted diseases such as syphilis, gonorrhea, and HIV. Psychic sufferings are no less real. There is the embarrassment caused by an unwanted sexual advance and the trauma of forced sex. Also to be considered are possible feelings of disappointment and foolishness for having false expectations or at being deceived or used. Pregnancy, though regarded in certain circumstances as a good or benefit, in other circumstances may be unwanted and can involve significant suffering. Some people might include as a negative consequence the effects on the family of certain sexual practices. In consequentialist reasoning, all the consequences count, and short-term benefit or pleasure may be outweighed by long-term suffering or pain. However, the pain caused to one per-son can also be outweighed by the pleasure given to another or others (the greater amount of pleasure by the rapist or rapists might outweigh the pain of the victim), and this is a major problem for this type of moral theory.

Many positive consequences or benefits also may come from sexual relations or activity. First of all, there is sexual pleasure itself. Furthermore, we may benefit both physically and psychologically from having this outlet for sexual urges and desires. It is relaxing. It enables us to appreciate other sensual things, and to be more passionate and perhaps even more compassionate. It may enhance our perceptions of the world. Colors can be brighter and individual differences more noticeable. For many people intimate sexual relations supposedly improve personal relations by breaking down barriers. However, one would think that this is likely to be so only where a good relationship already exists between the involved persons.

What about sex in the context of marriage and children? What about homosexual sexual relations? From a consequentialist point of view, there is nothing in the nature of sex itself that requires that it be heterosexual or occur only between married individuals or for reproductive purposes. In some cases, where the consequences would be better, sex should be reserved for a married relation. It would depend on the individual person. If particular individuals find sex fulfilling only in the context of a long-term or married relationship and where it is part of a desire to have children together, then this is what would be best for them. But this is not always the case, for people vary in how they are affected by different experiences. The social context and rules of a society may well make a difference. This may be especially true for homosexuality. Social acceptability or stigma will make a difference in whether people can be happy doing what they do. But it is happiness or pleasure and unhappiness or displeasure alone, from a classical consequentialist point of view, that determines the morality. In homosexual as well as in heterosexual relations, questions about whether monogamy is the best practice will be raised. Gay men and lesbian women, for example, have been known to disagree on this issue. So also when they have disagreed on whether disclosure of one's sexual orientation is a good thing, the debate has often turned on a disagreement about the likely consequences of doing so. Furthermore, because children are people too, the effects on them that might be produced by sexual activity must also play a role in consequentialist considerations. The availability of contraception now makes it easier to control these consequences, so offspring resulting from sexual relations are presumably (but not necessarily) more likely to be wanted and well cared for. Abortion and its consequences may also play a role in determining whether a particular sexual relation is good from this perspective.

Finally, consequentialist thinking has room for judging not only what is good and bad, or better and worse, but also what is worst and best. This perspective is entirely open to talk about better and worse sex or the best and worst. On utilitarian grounds the most pleasurable and most productive of overall happiness is the best. If one cannot have the ideal best, however, one should choose the best that is available, provided that this choice does not negatively affect one's ability to have the best. It is consistent with a consequentialist perspective to judge sexual behavior not in terms of what we must avoid to do right but in terms of what we should hope and aim for as the best. Nevertheless, in classical utilitarianism, the ideal is always to be thought of in terms of happiness or pleasure.

Nonconsequentialist or Kantian Considerations

Nonconsequentialist moral theories, such as that of Kant, would direct us to judge sexual actions as well as other actions in a way quite different from consequentialist theories. Although the golden rule is not strictly the same thing as the categorical imperative, there are similarities

between these two moral principles. According to both, as a person in sexual relation I should only do what would seem acceptable no matter whose shoes I were in or from whose perspective I judged. In the case of a couple, each person should consider what the sexual relation would look like from the other's point of view, and each should only proceed if a contemplated action or relation is also acceptable from that other viewpoint.

This looks like a position regarding sexual relations according to which anything is permissible sexually as long as it is agreed to by the participants. On some versions of Kantianism this would probably be so. The primary concern would then be whether the agreement was real. For example, we would want to know whether the participants were fully informed and aware of what was involved. Lying would certainly be morally objectionable. So also would other forms of deceit and refusal to inform. Not telling someone that one was married or that one had a communicable disease could also be forms of objectionable deceit, in particular when this information, if known, would make a difference to the other person's willingness to participate.

In addition, the relation would have to be freely entered into. Any form of coercion would be morally objectionable on Kantian grounds. What counts as coercion, just as what counts as deceit, is not always easy to say, both in general and in any concrete case. Certainly, physically forcing a person to engage in sexual intercourse against his or her will is coercion. We call it rape. However, some forms of "persuasion" may also be coercive. Threats to do what is harmful are coercive. For example, threatening to demote an employee or not promote him if he does not engage in a sexual relation, when he deserves the promotion and does not deserve the demotion, can be coercive. But more subtle forms of coercion also exist, including implied threats to withhold one's affection from the other or to break off a relationship. Perhaps even some offers or bribes are coercive, especially when what is promised is not only desirable but also something one does not have and cannot get along without. "I know that you are starving, and I will feed you if you have sex with me," is surely coercive.

Naturalness Considerations

Naturalistic moral theories hold that morality is grounded in human nature. That is good which furthers human nature or is fitting for it, and that is bad or morally objectionable which frustrates or violates or is inconsistent with human nature. How would such a theory be used to make moral judgments about sexual behavior? Obviously, the key is the description of human nature. In Chapter 6 on natural law theory we examined the Aristotelian and Thomistic versions and looked briefly at naturalness moralities more broadly.

In any use of human nature as a basis for determining what is good, a key issue will be describing human nature. To see how crucial this is, suppose that we examine a version of natural law theory that stresses the biological aspects of human nature. How would this require us to think about sexual morality? It would probably require us to note that an essential aspect of human nature is the orientation of the genital and reproductive system toward reproducing young. The very nature of heterosexual sexual intercourse (unless changed by accident or human intervention by sterilization or contraception) is to release male sperm into a female vagina and uterus. The sperm naturally tend to seek and penetrate an egg, fertilizing it and forming with the egg the beginning of a fetus, which develops naturally into a young member of the species. On this version of natural law theory, that which interferes with or seeks deliberately to frustrate this natural purpose of sexual intercourse as oriented toward reproduction is morally objectionable. Thus, contraception, masturbation, and homosexual sexual relations would be contrary to nature. Further arguments would be needed to show that sexual relations should take place only in marriage. These arguments would possibly have to do with the relation of sex and commitment, with the biological relation of the child to the parents, and with the necessary or best setting for the raising of children.

We could also envision other natural law–like arguments about sexual morality that are based on somewhat different notions of human nature. For example, we could argue that the natural purpose of sexual relations is pleasure, because nature has so constructed the nerve components of the genital system. Furthermore, the intimacy and naturally uniting aspect of sexual intercourse may provide a basis for arguing that this is its natural tendency—to unite people, to express their unity, or to bring them closer together.

As mentioned earlier, one of the most common arguments against homosexual sex is that it is unnatural, that it goes against nature. According to traditional natural law theory, although we differ individually in many ways, people share a common human nature. I may have individual inclinations, or things may be natural to me that are not natural to you, simply because of our differing talents, psychic traits, and other unique characteristics. Natural law theory tells us that certain things are right or wrong not because they further or frustrate our individual inclinations, but because they promote or work against our species' inclinations and aspects of our common human nature. When appealing to a traditional type of natural law theory to make judgments about homosexual behavior, we need to determine whether this is consistent with common human nature, not individual natures. The argument that gay men or lesbian women find relating sexually to members of their own sex "natural" to them as individuals, may or may not work as part of a natural law argument supporting that behavior. However, if one had a broader view of sexuality in its passionate, emotional, and social aspects, one could make a reasonable natural law argument that these are also aspects of a common human sexuality that is manifested in several ways, including homosexual sex. Historically, natural law arguments have not gone this way. But this is not to say that such an argument could not be reasonably put forth.

To believe that there is such a thing as sexual behavior that is consistent with human nature—or natural—also implies that there can be sexual behavior that is inconsistent with human nature or unnatural. Sometimes the term *perverted* has been used synonymously with unnatural. Thus, in the context of a discussion or analysis of natural law views about sexual morality we can also consider the question of whether there is such a thing as sexual perversion. This is not to say that notions of sexual perversion are limited to natural law theory, however. Perversion literally means turned against or away from something, usually away from some norm. Perverted sexual behavior would then be sexual behavior that departs from some norm for such behavior. "That's not normal," we say. By *norm* here we mean not just the usual type of behavior, for this depends on what in fact people do. Rather, by *norm* or *normal* we mean what coincides with a moral standard. If most human beings in a particular famine-ridden society died before the age of thirty-five, we could still say that this was abnormal because it was not the norm for human survival in most other societies.[6]

To consider whether there is a natural type of sexual behavior or desire, we might compare it with another appetite, namely, the appetite of hunger, whose natural object we might say is food. If a person were to eat pictures of food instead of food, this would generally be considered abnormal. Would we also say that a person who was satisfied with pictures of a sexually attractive person and used them as a substitute for a real person was in some sense abnormal or acting abnormally? This depends on whether there is such a thing as a normal sex drive and what its natural object would be. People have used the notion of normal sex drive and desire to say that things such as shoe fetishism (being sexually turned on by shoes) and desire for sex with animals or dead bodies are abnormal. One suggestion is that sexual desire in its normal form is for another individual and not just for the other but for the other's mutual and embodied response. In his essay, "Sexual Perversion," Thomas Nagel argues that there is such a thing as perverted sexual desire, and this is determined by comparison with a paradigm case or the norm for sexual desire. The norm is desire for the reciprocal embodied desire of another person.[7]

These notions of perverted versus normal sexual desire and behavior are notions that can belong in some loose way to a tradition that considers human nature as a moral norm. Like the utilitarian and Kantian moral traditions, natural law theory has its own way of judging sexual as well as other behavior. These three ways of judging sexual behavior are not necessarily incompatible with one another, however. We might find that some forms of sexual behavior are not only ill-fit for human nature, but also involve using another as a thing rather than treating her or him as a person, and additionally have bad consequences. Or we may find that what is most fitting for human nature is also what has the best consequences and treats persons with the respect due them. The more difficult cases will be those in which no harm comes to persons from a sexual relation, but they have nevertheless been used, or cases in which knowing consent is present but it is for activities that seem ill-fit for human nature or do not promise happiness, pleasure, or other benefits.

Pornography

It may seem problematic to include a discussion of pornography within a chapter on sexual morality. However, because pornography is usually defined in terms of sexual explicitness, including a discussion of it here is not unreasonable. Moreover, certain issues arise in both discussions—for example, issues of rape and coercion. Some pornography that is simply sexually explicit and erotic could be judged morally on the same grounds as other sexual behavior. However, pornography has become an especially problematic moral issue because it has often been viewed as more than a harmless erotic opportunity. Sometimes its suspect morality is the issue. Other times its supposed harmlessness is the issue. In addition to questions about the morality of pornography, we raise questions that we do not raise about sexual morality in general. That is, we also ask whether the law should regulate pornography in any way, and why or why not. For example, should the state or society restrict the use, sale, and making of pornography in general or certain types of pornography? Because it is the latter question that may be the more prominent, we focus on it here.

Before we start on this brief discussion of pornography and the law, we might usefully examine some problems we have in defining the subject matter. The term itself comes from the Greek roots *porno,* "prostitute," and *graphy,* "to write." This may be a strange association. However, some have pointed out that in much pornography women are treated as sexual servants or servicers in ways similar to the function of prostitutes. Pornography can be of many kinds, including writings, pictures or photographs, three-dimensional art forms, vocalizations (songs, phone conversations), live-person presentations, and even computerized games.

But what is pornography and what is not? Is it all in the mind of the perceiver, as one person's pornography is another person's art? In fact, legal definitions of pornography have usually tried to distinguish pornography from art. Suppose that we define pornography as "sexually explicit material that has as its primary purpose the stimulation of sexual excitement or interest." Compare this definition with one that says that pornography is "verbal or pictorial explicit representations of sexual behavior that . . . have as a distinguishing characteristic the degrading and demeaning portrayal of the role and status of the human female . . . as a mere sexual object to be exploited and manipulated sexually."[8] The first definition is morally neutral. It does not by definition imply that pornography is good or bad. It could be called a *descriptive* definition. It is also quite broad and would include both violent and nonviolent pornography. The second definition is not morally neutral, and it applies only to some types of such material. In the second, the question of the moral value of this pornography

is no longer totally open. Definitions of this type are *normative* or *value-laden* definitions. Still another definition is the legal one. This defines pornography as "obscenity." As such, it defines a type of pornography that is morally suspect and legally not protected as is other free speech. In fact, this term is used instead of pornography in the legal definition modeled after a 1954 version of the American Law Institute. In 1973, the U.S. Supreme Court in *Miller* v. *California* included this definition and defined obscenity as depictions or works that were "patently offensive" to local "community standards," that appeal to "prurient interests," and that taken as a whole lack "serious literary, artistic, political or scientific value."[9] This latter aspect of it is known as the LAPS test. In any case, whether we define pornography as degrading and immoral or in a more morally neutral way, the question of whether there should be laws regulating pornography is still open.

Liberty-Limiting Principles

To decide whether the law should regulate pornography, we need to have some idea about what sort of things we think the law should and should not regulate, and why. This is to raise, if only briefly, some issues in the philosophy of law or jurisprudence.[10] Let us rephrase the question somewhat before proceeding. We will assume a basic principle of liberty: that people ought to be able to do what they choose unless there is some reason to restrict their behavior by force of law. In other words, we are not asking whether the behavior is morally praiseworthy, but whether people should be free to act or should be prevented by law from doing so, whatever the moral character of the act.[11]

To think about this question in general and in relation to the issue of pornography, consider some possible options or positions. These can be called "liberty-limiting principles" because they are principles or norms for determining when the law may rightly restrict our liberty, and why.[12] One might support one or more than one of these principles.

The Harm Principle

According to the *harm principle,* the law may rightly restrict a person from doing what he wants in order to prevent him from harming others. According to J. S. Mill, this is the only reason that we may legitimately restrict people's behavior by legal force. According to Mill,

> the sole end for which mankind are warranted, individually or collectively, in interfering with the liberty of action of any of their number, is self-protection. That the only purpose for which power can be rightfully exercised over any member of a civilized community, against his will, is to prevent harm to others. His own good, either physical or moral, is not a sufficient warrant. He cannot rightfully be compelled to do or forbear because it will be better for him to do so, because it will make him happier, because, in the opinions of others, to do so would be wise, or even right. These are good reasons for remonstrating with him, or reasoning with him, or persuading him, or entreating him, but not for compelling him, or visiting him with any evil in case he do otherwise. To justify that, the conduct from which it is desired to deter him, must be calculated to produce evil to some one else. The only part of the conduct of any one, for which he is amenable to society, is that which concerns others. In the part which merely concerns himself, his independence is, of right, absolute. Over himself, over his own body and mind, the individual is sovereign.[13]

Essential to the nature as well as the application of this principle is the notion of harm. The paradigm notion of harm is physical harm. To cut off someone's arm or leg or damage her body in such a way that she dies is clearly to harm her. However, unless one views human beings as only physical beings, we must accept that we can be harmed in other ways as well, some of which clearly also have physical repercussions and some not obviously so. Thus, to threaten someone or otherwise harass them so that they seriously fear for their lives is to harm them psychologically. Damage also can be done to persons' reputations and livelihoods. People can be

harmed in subtle ways by the creation of a certain climate or ambience, a notion that is used in legal definitions of sexual harassment in the workplace. Moreover, some harms are more serious than others. Causing another to have a temporary rash is not as serious as causing her to have a life-threatening disease.

In applying this principle, we would have to decide when a harm is serious enough that the society ought to prevent individuals by force of law from causing that type of harm to others.[14] Moreover, the law would need to determine, among other things, what counts as causing a harm, how proximate the cause is, and who can be said to play a role in causing the harm. In addition, the harm principle may be formulated in such a way that liberty is thought to be so important that only strict proof of harm to others would be sufficient to justify restricting people from doing what they choose to do.

How would this liberty-limiting principle be applied in the case of pornography? One application would be to determine whether making, performing, viewing, or reading pornographic materials would lead people to harm others. For example, we would need to know whether viewing violent pornographic films leads people to engage in sexually violent acts. Obviously, violent pornography is sexually stimulating to some people. But does it take the place of real violence, or does it lead to it? There are anecdotal reports and some studies that suggest pornography leads to specific acts. In one study women reported that they were asked or forced by their mates to imitate sex acts that were depicted in pornography. One researcher who interviewed 114 convicted rapists "concluded that the scenes depicted in violent porn are repeated in rapists' accounts of their crimes." This included one who told his female victim, "You love being beaten. . . . You know you love it, tell me you love it. . . . I seen it all in the movies."[15] If this were true of the effects of certain violent types of pornography, then according to the harm principle there could be grounds for prohibiting it.

One critical issue here is the type and degree of "proof" required. For example, it has been reported that "young men shown sexually violent films and then asked to judge a simulated rape trial are less likely to vote for conviction than those who haven't seen the films." And "surveys of male college students who briefly watch porn report that thirty percent of the women they know would enjoy aggressively forced sex."[16] Does this prove that such pornography has an effect on people's attitudes about what is acceptable, or does it also show that this will lead people to act in certain harmful ways? If convicted rapists have had significantly more contact with pornographic materials than nonrapists, would this be sufficient to show that the pornography caused or was a contributing factor to the rapes? There could be an association between the two without one being the cause of the other. In logic you can learn about a fallacy labeled *post hoc, ergo propter hoc.* Roughly translated it means "after something, therefore because of something." This is regarded as a fallacy; just because one thing follows another (or is associated with it) does not mean that it was caused by it. For instance, Tuesday follows Monday but is not caused by it. But it also doesn't mean that there is no causal connection between frequently associated events. Even if there were a correlation between violent pornography and sexual violence, the cause might be some other thing that led to both the desire for violent pornography and the committing of sexual violence. On the other hand, if the other thing is the cause and the violence the symptom, it is not necessarily the case that we would attack the cause and not the symptom. Moreover, sexual violence is not the only possible harm that pornography can do. This is further discussed in the section on feminist views of pornography.

Finally, a society must provide a way of balancing interests or settling conflicts between people. Thus, in applying the harm principle we ought to consider whether in restricting a behavior to protect the interests of some we are negatively affecting the interests of others. It then would require us to compare the value of the interests and the cost of restrictions. Some people argue that in trying to define and restrict pornography the society risks impinging on valued free speech rights. For example, retired U.S. Supreme Court Justice Brennan has argued that it is in principle impossible to define pornography in such a way that it does not include legitimate free speech. In restricting pornography, he argued, we will also restrict free speech.[17] (On this issue see a different opinion in the reading from Catharine MacKinnon.) Yet we do restrict speech in many cases, including speech inciting to riot, and defamatory and fraudulent speech. We may also need to determine the value of free speech. Is it the expression itself, or is it for the sake of other goods such as knowledge or political power? The idea would be that allowing free speech enhances our ability to improve understanding by sharing opinions and ensures more democratic political participation. If these are the purposes of free speech, then if some sexual expression does not serve but hinders these purposes, then according to the harm principle there could be grounds for prohibiting it.

The Social Harm Principle

A second version of the harm principle, called the *social harm principle,* is sometimes confused with or not distinguished from the harm principle itself. The idea involved in this second liberty-limiting principle is that the law may prevent people from doing what they wish or choose when their action causes harm to society itself. For example, if a society is a theocracy, anything that will seriously erode the rule by religious leaders is a threat to that kind of society. If a society is a democracy, anything that seriously erodes public participation in political decision making is a threat to that society. The powerful role of lobbyists and money in the political process can be challenged in this regard. If a society is a free-market society, anything that seriously erodes market competition is a threat to it. Antitrust laws might be seen as an example of application of the social harm principle. (However, they might also be grounded in the harm principle.) In any society anything that seriously threatens its ability to defend itself would also threaten the continued existence of that society.

One need not believe that the social structure is a good one to use this principle. In fact, in some cases we could argue that the society in its present form should not endure, and threats to its continuation in that form are justified. Nevertheless, it is useful to distinguish the social harm principle from the harm principle, which tells us what the law may prevent us from doing to individuals, even many individuals. Thus, emitting harmful pollution from my factory may be regulated by society under the harm principle, for in regulating or preventing this pollution the factory owner is prevented from harming individuals, though not necessarily the society itself.

How would this principle apply to the issue of the legal regulation of pornography? According to some, pornography can be seen as a threat to society. One argument states that certain types of pornography weaken the ties of love and sex and thus also the family structure. If strong families are essential to a society, then pornography could be regulated for the good of the society itself.[18] But is this connection empirically substantiated? And are "strong families" of a particular sort essential to society? We would need to answer these questions to justify restricting pornography on the basis of this principle. If the society is essentially an egalitarian one, then one might argue that some types of pornography threaten its continued existence because pornography enforces views of women as subservient. Furthermore, as with all liberty-limiting principles, one would need to decide first whether the principle is valid for restricting people's liberty. Only if one believes that the principle is valid, would one go on to ask if a behavior is such a threat to an essential aspect of society that it can be rightly restricted by law. This would be true for the case of pornography as well as other acts and practices.

The Offense Principle

The *offense principle* holds that society may restrict people's choice to do what they want in order to prevent them from offending others. This principle may be considered to be a separate principle or a version of the harm principle. Here the harm is presumably a psychic one. According to those who support this principle, just as with the harm principle, only sufficiently offensive harms would be restricted. For example, we might consider that a public square display of nude corpses is sufficiently offensive to restrict this behavior. Not only the seriousness of the offense would have to be determined, but also how widely offensive it was. Anything that we do might offend someone. What is needed is some degree of universality for the offense to be restricted. Moreover, some people have argued that if this principle were to be used it would also have to involve another element—avoidability; that is, only those actions that would be unavoidable by people who would be offended by them could be restricted. Those that people could easily avoid would not be.

How would this principle be applied to pornography? First, instead of labeling certain explicit sexual material as pornographic, the term often used is *obscenity*. Obscenity has been as difficult to define as pornography. Among the phrases defining it, as noted earlier, is "patently offensive."[19] The question we then ask is whether pornography may be legally restricted on the grounds that it is offensive to some or to most people. We might want to consider whether it is offensive to a major part of a population or to some local community. Thus, also offensiveness, or serious offense, to women or to a specific racial group might be a sufficient basis for restriction. This relies on the criterion of universality.

As to the other criterion, avoidability, if live sex shows and materials were limited to a particular section of a city, for example, then the offense principle could not be used to justify banning them because this section could be avoided by people who would be offended. However, if there were displays in the public square or supermarket that people could not avoid, and should not have to avoid, then the offensive displays might be rightly restricted on this principle. However, as with the other principles, there remains the first and most basic question about whether the principle is a good one or not. Ought people to be restricted in doing what offends others in certain ways? If you answer, "No," then you need not go on to consider the details mentioned here. However, if you believe offenses to others are serious enough to warrant social restriction, then we would probably need to determine some limits in the application of this principle.

Legal Paternalism

According to the principle of *legal paternalism,* people's liberty may also be restricted to prevent them from doing harmful things to themselves. Granted that the kind and degree of harm would again have to be specified, the key element in this principle is its application to the individual. For instance, should the law be able to tell me that I must wear a car seatbelt when driving or a helmet when riding a motorcycle? There may be nonpaternalistic reasons behind some of the existing legislation in this area. If you are injured in an accident, it not only harms you, but also possibly others, for they may have to pay for your medical care. There may also be paternalistic reasons for such restraints. "We want to prevent you from harming yourself," say proponents of this type of law.

Just how or whether this principle might justify restriction on pornography is a tough question. The argument would have to be something like the following. Pornography is not good for you, and thus we can restrict your access to it. Whether pornography harms its users, and what kind of harm it might do, are matters open to question and argument. If people are forced into participation in pornographic activities and this participation is harmful to them, then the harm principle would come into play and be used to prevent those who would forcefully harm others.

Note that all of these principles are directed to adult behavior and restrictions on it. There are obviously further reasons to restrict the behavior of children, including restrictions on their freedom for their own good. The more problematic case is that of restricting the behavior of adults—behavior that is either harmless or not likely to harm anyone but themselves. To determine whether the principle of legal paternalism is a good principle, one would need to determine the role society ought to play in relation to individual citizens. Does or should society function as a kind of father (or mother) and look out to see that its "children" are not making foolish or unduly risky choices? Even if this principle were not accepted as valid, there would still be reasons for social intervention to inform people about the results of their choices. Thus, laws requiring truth in labeling and advertising would still be fitting, for they would be covered by the harm principle. This would restrict advertisers and sellers from harming users and buyers.

Legal Moralism

The final liberty-limiting principle is *legal moralism.* The idea is that the law may rightly act to prevent people from doing what is immoral just because it is immoral. It is easy to confuse this principle with the harm principle. We can agree that harming others may be immoral. But we need not focus on the immorality of harming them in order to say that the law can restrict this behavior because it falls under the harm principle. Thus, legal moralism usually applies to supposedly harmless immoralities or to so-called victimless crimes.

The principle of legal moralism involves a quite different notion of the purpose of law. It may view the state as a moral being in itself or as having a moral purpose. Puritans, for example, came to this country with one overriding purpose: to establish a new society that would be a moral example for all other nations to follow. Since the time of the Puritans, however, the relation between morality or religion and the state has been weakened in the United States. Laws promoting the separation of church and state exemplify this trend. Nevertheless, many elements of the original idea are present in our society, from the "In God We Trust" phrase on our money to the prayers beginning or ending various public services.

The application of this principle to the issue of pornography is basically as follows. If certain sorts of pornography are thought to be morally degrading or show an improper regard for sex, then on these grounds alone pornography can be restricted by law. Just whose view of what is morally right and wrong ought to be used will be a problem for the application of this principle. Those who support the principle will also want to consider the seriousness of the wrong, so as not to make all wrong actions subject to legal sanction. But, as in the case of the other principles, the first question to ask is whether the principle itself is valid. We would ask whether the immoral character of an action would be a good reason to restrict it by law and by the force of legal punishment.

Although this treatment of the liberty-limiting principles has taken place in the context of a discussion of pornography, the principles obviously apply more widely. Whether there should be legal restrictions on drug use, regulations for tobacco smoking, or laws regarding euthanasia and abortion are only a few of the matters that may depend on what we say about the relation of law and morality. You could now return to the chapters on euthanasia and abortion and ask about the particular liberty-limiting principles that might apply. Although thinking about the relation of the law and morality in terms of these principles is not the only way to pursue the issue, it is one approach that can help clarify our thinking.

Feminism and Pornography

In the last several years, many feminists have spoken out and written against pornography. Some feminists argue that certain forms of pornography, those that are simply erotica, are not objectionable. However, much of contemporary pornography, feminists believe, is much more problematic. They believe that pornography involving women often includes a degrading portrayal of women as subordinate and as wanting to be raped, bound, and bruised.[20] Music videos and album covers and lyrics provide examples of this today. It is not just the portrayal of degrading or abusive sex that feminists find objectionable, but that the portrayal is set in a context in which the harmful results of degrading women are not also shown. What they also find objectionable are portrayals with "implicit, if not explicit, approval and recommendation of sexual behavior that is immoral, i.e. that physically or psychologically violates the personhood of one of the participants."[21] A few incidents of this might be ignored, but if this type of pornographic material is widespread and mass produced, feminists argue, it can create a climate of support for attitudes that harm women. These attitudes can prevent women from occupying positions of equality and may also contribute to the lack of adequate social response to the abuse of women.

According to Andrea Dworkin, "Pornography creates attitudes that keep women second class citizens. . . . Porn teaches men that what they see reflects our natural attitudes."[22] She and lawyer Catharine MacKinnon have attempted to use civil rights and antidiscrimination laws to promote local ordinances restricting pornography. They view pornography as violating women's civil rights, including their right to be treated as equal citizens. That is because they believe that pornography by its very nature "eroticizes hierarchy. . . . It makes dominance and submission into sex." (See the reading from Catharine MacKinnon included in this chapter.) In some cases, laws have been enacted but later challenged in court and overturned as violations of free speech. If such restrictions involve a conflict of interests, then we would need to know which interests take precedence. For example, is the harm to women so serious that some restriction of free speech is justifiable? The answer to this question will at least partly depend on what we say about the purpose and value of free speech. Is self-expression a good in itself, or is the freedom to speak out a good because it promotes the free exchange of ideas or political freedoms? If it is the latter, then it will be more difficult to believe that pornography ought to come under legal protection as free speech. Rather, it would be judged in terms of the ends it promotes. If these ends include the undermining of the equality and dignity of women, then it would be even more difficult to make a case for its protection. However, as others have noted, the connection between pornography of various sorts and harms of these sorts is a difficult one to make. That is another reason why this issue will continue to be a matter of debate among people who care about these important values.

In this chapter's readings, Roger Scruton writes of the natural characteristics of sexual desire, Richard Mohr gives various responses to criticisms of the view that homosexuality is morally objectionable, and Catharine MacKinnon presents feminist criticisms of pornography.

Notes

1. From a telephone poll of 500 American teenagers taken for *Time*/CNN on April 13–14 by Yankelovich Partners Inc.; reported in *Time* (May 24, 1993), 60ff.

2. Ibid., 61.

3. *San Francisco Chronicle* (May 21, 1996), pp. A1, A13.

4. Aristotle, *Nicomachean Ethics*, Book VIII, Chap. 4.

5. Camille Paglia, *Sex, Art, and American Culture* (New York: Vintage Books, 1992).

6. There are obvious problems here with determining the norm because longevity is a function of nutrition and exercise as well as genetics. So also we might be inclined to consider norms for sexual behavior as partly a function of the setting or cultural conditions.

7. Thomas Nagel, "Sexual Perversion," *The Journal of Philosophy*, 66 (1969): 5–17.

8. From the Commission on Obscenity and Pornography, quoted in Helen Longino, "Pornography, Op-pression, and Freedom: A Closer Look," in *Take Back the Night: Women on Pornography* (New York: William Morrow, 1980).

9. U.S. Supreme Court. 413 U.S. 15, 24. This was based on the 1954 Model Penal Code of the American Law Institute.

10. Recall that we had raised similar questions about the distinction between moral questions about euthanasia or abortion and questions about what the law should or should not do, and we suggested strongly that these are two different types of question and need two different types of reasoning.

11. Note that this is not the only way to pose the question about the relation of law and morality. We might, for example, also want to know the more general purpose of a nation-state. Is it, for example, simply to keep order and prevent people from impinging on others' rights, or does it have a more positive purpose such as to "promote the general welfare"? We discuss this issue further in Chapter 13, "Economic Justice."

12. The names and ordering of these principles in writings on the subject vary. However, this is generally the type of division that is discussed. See, for example, Joel Feinberg, *Social Philosophy* (Englewood Cliffs, NJ: Prentice-Hall, 1973), 28–45.

13. John Stuart Mill, *On Liberty* (London, 1859).

14. The prevention can be through physical detention or through threat of punishment for nonconformity with the law. The issue of deterrent threats will be considered in the following chapter on legal punishment and the death penalty.

15. Study by Diana Scully, reported in *Newsweek* (March 18, 1985), 65.

16. Ibid., 62, studies by Edward Donnerstein.

17. See, for example, the minority opinion of Justice William Brennan in *Paris Adult Theatre I* v. *Slaton*, U.S. Supreme Court. 413 U.S. 49 (1973).

18. From the majority opinion in *Paris Adult Theatre I* v. *Slaton*.

19. *Roth* v. *United States* (1954) and *Miller* v. *California* (1973).

20. This is not to ignore pornography that involves homosexuals or children. There are obvious objections to using children.

21. Longino, "Pornography," op. cit.

22. *Newsweek* (March 18, 1985), 60.

Sexual Desire

Roger Scruton

Study Questions

1. Describe some of the views of sexual desire and erotic love found in modern philosophers as presented by Scruton.

2. According to Scruton, can animals experience sexual arousal? Explain.

3. How does Scruton describe the difference between sexual arousal in a stranger and someone who is known?

4. What does Scruton give as a crucial feature of "interpersonal intentionality"?

5. Is human embodiment a necessary feature of persons, according to Scruton? Explain.

6. How does Scruton use a comparison with carrots to explain an important aspect of sexual desire?

7. How does Scruton describe the "sexual" aspect of sexual desire?

8. According to Scruton, what is the relation between sexual desire and sexual arousal?

9. According to Scruton, why is orgasm not the aim of sexual desire?

10. What is the role of intimacy and love in the project of sexual desire, according to Scruton?

11. How does Scruton describe the phenomena of "falling in love"?

12. What does Scruton mean in asserting there is a biological basis to our sexual conduct?

In choosing to discuss sexual arousal, which is neither the origin nor the aim of sexual desire, I have entered the subject *in mediis rebus*. My intention has been to describe the most distinctive sexual phenomenon, and the one which most readily seems to lend itself to the theory that desire is a "biological"

Abridged with the permission of The Free Press, a division of Simon & Schuster, from *Sexual Desire: A Moral Philosophy of the Erotic* by Roger Scruton. © 1986 by Roger Scruton.

fact, rooted in the life which we share with animals. I have argued that sexual arousal is in fact an interpersonal response, founded in an epistemic intentionality. Hence only people can experience arousal, and only people—or imaginary people—can be the object of arousal. This does not mean that we should dismiss out of hand the similarities between the sexual behaviour of animals and that of human beings. Like animals we feel sexual urges; like animals we reproduce sexually; like animals we feel a need to unite through our sexual organs, and like animals we experience a compelling physical pleasure when we do so. But almost all comparisons besides those are apt to prove misleading. Animals are never sexually aroused; they do not feel sexual desire, nor do they have sexual fulfilment. Almost all that matters in sexual experience lies outside their capacities, not because they reach for it and fail to obtain it, but because they cannot reach for it.

It may seem odd to say that an animal can feel sexual urges, yet not be sexually aroused. But this is largely because we read into the mental states of animals those complex social dispositions which generate our actions. We see the aggressiveness of the bull as a kind of irascibility, even though it is evident that anger—the disposition to exact a penalty for injustice—is an emotion no bull can feel. For no bull possesses the fundamental concept (that of justice) upon which anger is founded. Anger can be felt only by persons, towards other persons, or towards things held to account as persons are. In like manner we may see the randiness of a dog as a kind of lust, or the mating ritual of a bird as a kind of courtship, even though there is no possibility of attributing to such creatures the mental equipment that would justify so dense a description of their behaviour. To those philosophers—like Mary Midgley[1]—who repeat that we must look at the similarities, I answer that we must look at the differences. And the place where these differences are most telling is in the sphere of personal, and interpersonal, existence, into which the lower animals cannot intrude. Even the description of the herding animals as "social," in so far as it implies a certain conception of "self" and "other" through which relations are mediated, is a false designation of their behaviour. That the organisation of the clan of gorillas *looks* social is obvious; but where are the laws and institutions, where the adjudications, where the disposition of rights, privileges and duties, which make up the social consciousness of man? Without rationality such things can never come into being, and while an ape may seem to possess them, he is in reality merely aping them. And likewise, all those attitudes which involve a "feeding back" into the individual experience of the social activity which creates our sense of self lie beyond the gorilla's competence—sexual desire included. . . .

The First-Person Perspective and Arousal

In sexual arousal the other appears to me, not merely as something affected by me, but as a perspective upon me. I am something *for* him, and he for me, and this thought is part of the foundation of what I feel. But we must distinguish two cases. It might be that some part of me, some quality of me, or some aspect of me, figures in his perspective. Or it might be that I appear to him. My hand, my arm, even my entire body, might appear to him either visibly or tactually, and yet I not appear to him, because he has not attached this appearance to a particular person—to a particular subject like himself. Suppose that you awake beside a strange body. You feel it, see its shape, hear its breathing, but for a long time it is no particular person for you, not even the person whose body it is. It may begin to exhibit those physical changes that signify arousal; and at the same time you may not know who is being aroused—you do not attribute this arousal to any particular person. And when you see this body as a particular person (you may even remember which person), there is a sudden and overwhelming change of aspect. Only then does this arousal come to have meaning *for* you, for only then does it become possible to respond to it as to another person. You are now seeing the body's condition as expressive of a particular perspective, and you might seek to be an object within that perspective, and the recipient of gestures that are expressive of another "I."

Embodiment

It seems . . . that certain involuntary changes in another's body are important elements in the generation and directing of desire. I have been describing a crucial feature of interpersonal intentionality: the

disposition to find the marks of another's perspective displayed on the surface of his body. A phenomenologist might refer to this as the thought of the "incarnation" (Sartre) or "embodiment" of the other; a Hegelian might describe it as the perception of the "body as spirit"—the body transparent, so to speak, to mental interpretation. Such descriptions add no genuine *theory* to what I have indicated. Indeed, . . . there can be no theory of such data which does not run the risk of abolishing them—the risk of replacing the concepts through which we experience the world with the more robust ideas that will explain them. The difficulty that now confronts us is that of "staying on the surface," so to speak: of giving a description of sexual desire that is sufficiently shallow to capture *what is wanted* by the subject. In order to achieve this result it will be necessary to refrain from theory (from any attempt to give the causality of what is described) for as long as possible. . . . I shall address myself to certain questions which might already have occurred to the reader, in order to show the errors that enter this subject, when scientific method is invoked prematurely.

Human embodiment is not a necessary feature of persons—for there are persons without human bodies and without corporeal identity of any kind, such as trading companies identifiable only by their books. (Ironically, these incorporeal persons are called "corporations" in law.) However, if there are to be persons at all, it is necessary that there should be embodied persons. For how can we identify the agency and responsibility that attach to companies if we cannot identify the physical actions of the embodied persons who represent them? Moreover, embodiment is an essential property of whatever possesses it—a property that a person could not cease to have without also ceasing to be. Indeed, it is arguable that, from the material (scientific) point of view, a person is *identical* with his body.[2] All those features of him which constitute his personal existence—action, thought, speech and response—are redescribed by the scientist as states, movements and changes in the body and brain. Any tolerable metaphysic of the human person must take seriously the suggestion that, by all our normal standards of identity, the "substance" from which human thought and action emanate and to which they ought to be ascribed is the human body. From the point of view of *material* understanding—the understanding of the objective structure and causality of events—self and body are one and the same.

From the point of view of intentional understanding, however, this identity seems to elude our grasp. I constantly identify myself without reference to my body, and in ways which seem to exclude the body. Moreover, I constantly react to you as though you were not identical with your body, but in some sense operating *through* your body, which is an *instrument* of your suffering and will. There arises, in our mutual transactions, the inescapable impression that each of us has a centre of existence which is not his body but his self. At the same time you are knowable to me only *through* your body and its effects, and when I attend to you, I attend directly and unhesitatingly to *it*.

In consequence, our experience of embodiment is incipiently dualistic. In a valuable study, Helmuth Plessner argues that I stand to my body in a relation that is at once instrumental and constitutive: I *have* my body, but I also *am* my body.[3] As a result I live in a state of tension with regard to my physical existence, while being at the same time wholly and completely bound to it.

Individualising Thought

Embodiment is a concept of intentional understanding; it expresses a feature of the human world that we instantly recognise and respond to, and all our references to one another are also, directly or obliquely, references to embodiment. It is doubtful, however, that any equivalent idea could feature in the *material* understanding of our condition. A science of man would refer to the human body as a particular biological organism. And often we need to see our bodies in that way—when injured, say, when speculating about exercise and diet, or as part of our contemplation of death. But, in doing so, we become estranged from our flesh, which ceases to appear to us as saturated with a first-person perspective. There is a tension between the scientific understanding of the human body and the intentional understanding of embodiment, which endorses the immediate tension contained within the experience of embodiment itself. We are "at home" in our bodies, we feel, but only because we have the lingering suspicion that we might have been elsewhere.

The idea of embodiment helps us to understand why involuntary transformations—"expressions"—have so important a function in mediating our interpersonal attitudes. In smiling, blushing, laughing and crying, it is precisely my loss of control over my body,

and its gain of control over me, that create the immediate experience of an incarnate person. The body ceases, at these moments, to be an *instrument,* and reasserts its natural rights as a person. In such expressions the face does not function merely as a bodily part, but as the whole person: the self is spread across its surface, and there "made flesh.". . .

The individualising intentionality of desire might not surprise us. For sexual desire is as much an interpersonal response as sexual arousal, and it is part of our perception of another as a person that we do not, as it were, see him merely as an instance of his kind, replaceable by whatever substitute. In all our dealings with people, the attitude of "respect for persons"—the injunction, in Kant's terms, to treat others as ends in themselves, and never as means only—leads us to attribute an irreplaceable value to those with whom we are brought into relation. An obvious contrast might be drawn here between sexual desire and the appetite for food.[4] My appetite for a dish of carrots is stilled by the possession of *any* (suitably arranged) dish of carrots. Someone who protests "No, I want Elspeth (name of a particular dish of carrots)," protests too much, and incoherently.

However, an important objection here occurs. As Bishop Butler argued in his attack upon hedonism,[5] what I want, while it is before me is *this* dish of carrots. I might indeed accept a substitute—but then I do so by coming to *want* the substitute. So why is this case any different from that of sexual desire? Is it not merely a convention that leads us to say that, when I transfer my appetite from this dish of carrots to that, there is only *one* appetite, with two successive objects, while, when I transfer my attentions from Elizabeth to Jane, there are two desires, differentiated precisely by their successive objects? In either case, surely, I could say both that there is one desire, and that there are two—everything will depend upon the purpose of my counting.

The response to that objection is long and complex. . . . But two things must be said at once, in order to dispel its immediate force. First, sexual desire is unlike my appetite for these carrots, in being *founded upon* an individuating thought. It is part of the very directedness of desire that a *particular* person is conceived as its object. Thus there arises the possibility—already discussed in relation to arousal—of mistakes of identity. Jacob's desire for Rachel seemed to be satisfied by his night with Leah, only to the extent that, and for as long as, Jacob imagined it was Rachel with whom he was lying. Likewise, I might reasonably apologise to my paramour's twin for mistaking her for her sister, not merely in the act of caressing her, but also in the impulse of desiring her. For in a crucial sense I did not desire *her*, but the other whom she resembles. The desire for a dish of carrots is not similarly dependent upon an individuating thought, and does not therefore give rise to errors of identity. To eat the wrong dish of carrots may be a social howler, but it is not a mistaken expression of desire—I really did desire the dish of carrots that I consumed. Of course I can make other mistakes in my appetites: I may discover that these are not carrots, say, or that they are carrots of a particularly nasty kind. But, in the relevant sense, these are not mistakes of *identity*.

. . . the human being is the *normal* object of desire. The object of desire must have, not just human flesh, but also the first-person perspective which serves to individualise him in his own eyes and in the eyes of his pursuer. To put it another way: unlike hunger, sexual desire is interested in the *embodiment* of the other, and not in his body. The interpersonal intentionality lies therefore in desire itself, and is not imposed by the accidental privations of our existence.

The First-Person Perspective in Desire

We may now put together our two major observations: first, that desire is directed towards the embodiment of the other, in the special sense of this term that I have tried to define. Secondly, that it has an inherently individualising intentionality. Both point in the same direction: both invite us to see the other's perspective as a fundamental part of the object of desire. For it is the perspective of the other that is made real to us in his embodiment, and which provides our most immediate image of his irreplaceable individuality. How things seem to him—we are apt to feel—they can only seem to *him*. For only *his* perspective expresses the self which he is.

Let us return to the discussion of the intentionality of desire. What is wanted by the person who desires another? I have already remarked on the difficulty in stating the aim of desire in propositional form. Although desire involves a strong sense of longing for another, there is no easy way of separating the longing from the individual person who is desired—no easy way of describing, in abstract terms, just what the other is supposed to do in order to satisfy me.

The Course of Desire

At the same time desire has a recognisable sexual focus—a focus on the sexual nature, and sexual parts, of another person. Although the other is treated as a person in the act of love, he is desired *as* a man, or *as* a woman. This is as true of homosexual as of heterosexual feeling, and is an ineliminable part of the excitement and drama of the sexual act. This act of union, I recognise, might have occurred with another of the same sex, and I approach the other partly as a representative of his sex.

This does not mean that I necessarily have a very clear conception of sex as a biological category. I may be unaware of the role of sex in reproduction, or of any other scientific fact about it. I may even be unaware that there are two sexes. Suppose that Jane has been brought up on an island inhabited only by women. It is still the case that, when she looks upon Miriam with the eyes of desire, she sees Miriam as one member of a kind. Miriam begins to be liked for her bodily parts—her eyes, her mouth, her way of moving or standing. These are "species-laden" characteristics, and bear the imprint of a biological kind, even though Jane's interest in them is an interest in the individual Miriam, and even though Jane may lack the concept either of species or of sexuality. When desire begins to focus, it is upon such things: it singles them out, and separates them from the thought that any other person's eyes, mouth or posture could have served just as well. In the very first movement of desire there is therefore a kind of paradox: the body of the other is interesting because it is one instance of a bodily kind; but the very interest which focuses upon it insists that it is no such thing, that it is unique, irreplaceable, the one and only object of this present emotion. This is yet another aspect of the tension that is present in our intentional understanding of embodiment.

Sexual interest in another has a natural tendency to gravitate, in the "course of desire," to his distinctively sexual parts: those parts which have a special role in the transmission of sexual pleasure. We must distinguish two ways in which this gravitation of interest may occur: the way of curious pleasure, as I shall call it, and the way of desire. Sexual curiosity is wholly unlike most normal curiosity. If I am curious as to the anatomy of the garfish, say, my curiosity may be satisfied by an experiment in dissection or by reading a textbook—by anything, in short, that conveys the requisite information. The information that satisfies my curiosity here also brings it to an end. Sexual curiosity, by contrast, renews itself endlessly; for the object of curiosity is not the bodily region as such, but the region "as inhabited by a pleased consciousness," and the pleasure is a dynamic thing, which has a constantly shifting significance in the experience of the person who feels it. Curiosity is in part directed towards his feeling, and therefore moves always onwards as his feeling evolves. . . .

The Aim of Desire

We are now in a position to describe the initial aim, and to indicate some of the further, longer-term projects which that aim implies. In true sexual desire, the aim is "union with the other," where "the other" denotes a particular person, with a particular perspective upon my actions. The reciprocity which is involved in this aim is achieved in the state of mutual arousal, and the interpersonal character of arousal determines the nature of the "union" that is sought. To put the matter shortly: the initial aim of desire is physical contact with the other, of the kind which is the object and the cause of arousal. No such quest for arousal enters into normal friendship or into the tender affection towards a child, even when these are focused on the embodiment of the object. Arousal is, therefore, the most important differential of desire.

In the light of our previous study of embodiment and the individualising intentionality of desire, we can see that the aim of desire, so described, must involve the other *essentially*. He cannot lend himself to my sexual purpose, without my purposes being focussed on him, as the particular person he is. It is he who is embodied in the creature whom I caress, and it is his perspective that is caught up in the compromising drama of arousal.

That is not to forbid the possibility of a sexuality that flits from object to object with orgiastic relish for novelty—the *Aphrodite pandemos* of unfettered lust. It is simply to point out, what is evidently true, that the "novelty" that is sought is not that of "new sensations," "new positions," "new contortions" or whatever—but that of *new people*. In other words, what is sought is a renewal of the *aim* of desire, with another person. And to renew the aim of desire is to begin again, with a new desire. Just how far this can be accomplished is another matter. Whatever the peculiarities of orgiastic desire, it is no exception to the rule that the other person enters essentially into the aim of desire.

Likewise with randiness, the state of the sailor who storms ashore, with the one thought "woman" in his body. His condition might be described as desire for a woman, but for no particular woman. Such a description, however, seriously misrepresents the transition that occurs when the woman is found and he is set on the path of satisfaction. For now he has found the woman whom he wants, whom he seeks to arouse and upon whom his thoughts and energies are focused. It would be better to say that, until that moment, he desired *no* woman. His condition was one of desiring to desire. And such was his need that he took an early opportunity to gratify his longing: to exchange the desire to desire for desire. It is an important feature of sexual desire that it should arise in this way from a generalised impulse. Nevertheless, desire is as distinct from the impulse that compels it as is anger from the excess of adrenalin. One should think of "sexual hunger" as one thinks of the hunger for conversation, not as an appetite, but as a predisposition towards an individualising response.

The aim of sexual desire does not stop short at "union." There is the further and developing project of sexual pleasure. Now arousal can be achieved without sexual pleasure, although pleasure requires arousal, both in the subject and in the object. Sexual pleasure is directed towards the arousal of the other, and a pleasure that does not require the other to be aroused—as when a man performs the sexual act on the body of a frigid witness—is perverted. The extreme case of such pleasure is that of the necrophiliac, and a man who is indifferent to his partner's pleasure is, in a sense, a disguised necrophiliac: if his excitement is in fact enhanced by the other's frigidity, it is because he can enjoy her only under the aspect of death. In his sexual behaviour, he in a sense wishes her dead.

Sexual pleasure carries the subject further along the path of arousal. It involves him still more deeply with the object of his delight, reinforcing his need for the other's response and for the other's increasing self-identification with the sexual act.

To see the orgasm as the aim of desire is as misguided as to see the exultation experienced by a player upon scoring a goal as the aim of football, rather than as a pleasurable offshoot of an aim fulfilled. But there is more to orgasm-worship than that: it is not *merely* the result of a false assimilation of desire to appetite. Spiritually speaking, it is also the sign of a peculiar and prevalent superstition: the belief that for every human activity there must be some single and evident experience which constitutes its success and which can be obtained not by virtue but by skill (to use an Aristotelian dichotomy). In other words, it results from the idea that sexual gratification is available to everyone, whatever his moral character, and can be achieved by technique. The roots of this superstition need not concern us—although Tocqueville's analysis of American democracy suggests that they may not be hard to trace.[6] But its consequences are of some importance. In order to be construed as matters of technique, human purposes must be sufficiently specific, and sufficiently circumscribed, to be the subject-matter of advice, in which end and means can be properly separated. The other person, on this view, cannot be described as the end of desire: he therefore figures as the means, as a substitute for whatever sophisticated appliance (*machine désirante*) might fulfil his functions better than himself. Such is the price of the ethos of "available success"—the ethos that sees every human project in terms of an equally distributed achievement.

The orgasm could not be the aim of sexual desire, even if it is sometimes the aim of what I have called "curious pleasure." The other person is not the means to satisfy desire, but part of the end of desire. Suppose a man were to masturbate, entertaining a stream of disjointed fantasies, occasionally wandering to the thought of his tax bill, his child's future and the scandalous behaviour of his neighbour's cat. The process might lead to orgasm and presumably has orgasm as its aim; but it is not an expression of desire. Imagine now the same man performing the same movements, but with his eyes fixed on the woman who undresses in the neighbouring window. Now there is a fantasy object of desire. What would enable us to say that the man really desires the woman? The very least is that he should seek to gain her interest and complicity in his act, or that he should entertain fantasies of her participation. He wants not just to do this thing, but to involve her in it. Of course, nobody with any sense could imagine that he could achieve his purpose in *this* way; his motive is likely to be not desire but curious pleasure, and the woman herself enters as a mere instrument in the fantasy which helps him to achieve his aim. Indeed, it is a feature of all such immodest, self-regarding sexual conduct that it tends to regard the other, not as the object, but as the instrument, of sexual release, so that the other cannot be the object of desire. Being treated in this way the other feels outraged and degraded, and under most systems of criminal law indecent exposure is treated as a serious personal assault.

There are two further stages on the way of desire that we must mention: the project of intimacy, and the fulfilment of desire in erotic love. Intimacy is the point to which the unveiling gestures of love-making are directed, and it is a project that is disclosed already in the first glances of desire. The glance which sets lovers apart from the crowd speaks in an undertone of things which are outside the sphere of others' knowledge. The project of intimacy arises automatically, although not inevitably, from the bond of desire. It is the point to which desire naturally leads, by its own devices. Generalised lust can be sustained only by complex strategies of replacement, such as those of the orgy, which prevent the passage from pleasure to intimacy—which prevent the carnal "knowledge" of the other. But it is a natural continuation of sexual pleasure to pursue such knowledge—to aim one's words, caresses and glances, as it were, into the heart of the other, and to know him from the inside, as a creature who is part of oneself.

Just as sexual pleasure tends to intimacy, so does intimacy tend to love—to a sense of commitment founded in the mutuality of desire. For the person who is compromised by his desire for another has acquired a crucial vulnerability: the vulnerability of one who has been overcome in his body by the embodied presence of another. This vulnerability is finally assuaged only in love (as Gilda, in *Rigoletto*, assuages her brief moment of arousal in the arms of the Duke of Mantua by sacrificing her life for him). It is through studying erotic love, therefore, that we shall be able to characterise in full the intentionality of desire.

Falling in Love

To understand "falling in love" one must see that its intentionality is a special case of the intentionality of desire. The person in love sees his beloved's personality in all his acts and gestures, and is, as we might express it, spellbound by them. The person who *falls* in love makes the reverse assimilation: he sees gestures and features which awaken his desire, and, in order that desire should justify the effort to which it at once commits him, he imagines a personality to fit what he sees. This is the "idealisation" of the object of desire. Thereafter all is discovery and deception, or, if his imagination triumphs, confirmation of the initial wish. Initially there is no distinction between love and "infatuation": the difference is revealed when the lover is submitted to a "trial"—and that is why true love requires a period of courtship. . . . The person who falls in love wants the smile, the words, the acts of the other to be "for him," in the sense of being done always in some measure for his sake. He feels, on perceiving the other, a premonition of "home": of that which is "mine by right." Garibaldi describes his first meeting with Anita thus:

> We remained silent and ecstatic, looking at each other, like two persons who do not see each other for the first time, and who seek in each other's features something which activates a memory.
> At last I saluted her, and said: "You must be mine." I spoke little Portuguese, and uttered the bold words in Italian. Nevertheless, I was magnetic in my insolence. I had made a knot that death alone could untie.[7]

Garibaldi's egoism in that passage is integral to this kind of love. He who falls in love wants an elaborate recognition of himself. He needs the other's personality to live up to his requirements—requirements that he himself barely understands, except through the intimation contained in the face at which he stares. The subject "falls in love" when he desires, and recognises in desire the possibility of love. He anticipates then the final consolation that will justify his trouble, and imagines the personality who will provide it. Love, here, is really an inspired guess: and it awaits what Stendhal called the moment of "crystallisation."[8]

There is a primitive experience upon which the lover frequently draws when entering this "magic" realm. He remembers some human creature who once tended him, whose hands and features were marked for him with the imprint of safety, intimacy and home. Thus many a face in later life appears already to prefigure some future intimacy, and we see in it, perhaps rightly, perhaps wrongly, not merely the presence of a certain perspective, but also the trajectory of our days within its view. This experience combines with sexual desire to overcome the natural obstacles to passion—the embarrassment and distrust which accompany the thought of so intimate a union. It releases us for union, and for the consolations which our covert memory has already prompted us to seek. Hence the "irresistible" nature of falling in love, which, by presenting us with the sense of something

totally new and totally overwhelming, merely sets us upon a trodden path, down which we run with old and indelible expectations. . . .

Sex and Gender

Men reproduce sexually, and, biologically speaking, reproduction is the function of the sexual act. That platitude has enormous consequences for our subject and two will be of particular concern to us. First, it is sometimes argued that the reproductive function of the sexual act is part of its nature *as an act*.[9] Hence sexual performance severed from its reproductive consequences—as in homosexual or contracepted intercourse—is a different act, intentionally and perhaps also morally, from the sexual act allied to its biological function. According to that view, reproduction is not only a biological but also a spiritual feature of the sexual act.

. . . [I] consider another, related thought, suggested by the biological destiny of human desire. It is evident that there are things which are not persons, with neither self-knowledge nor responsibility, which also reproduce sexually, and which are therefore compelled by whatever urge induces them to engage in the act of copulation, and rewarded by whatever pleasure accompanies its performance. We must surely be subject to the same urges, and the same pleasures, as govern the reproductive activities of other sexual beings. Why is that not the basic fact of sexual experience? There may indeed by interpersonal attitudes of the kind that I have described— attitudes of love and desire, attached by whatever cultural process to the basic urge to copulate. Nevertheless it is the urge which is fundamental, and which reveals the truth of our condition. . . .

The objection raises in its widest form the general subject of the relation between our erotic lives as persons and our sexual lives as animals. It therefore bears once again on the vexed question of embodiment: the question, how can one and the same thing be both a person and an animal?

[I] argue that there is indeed a biological basis to our sexual conduct; but I . . . reject the implication that it provides the core of sexual experience. The best way to understand the position for which I shall argue is in terms of an analogy. A tree grows in the soil, from which it takes its nourishment, and without which it would be nothing. And it would be almost nothing *to us* if it did not also spread itself in foliage, flower and fruit. In a similar way, human sexuality grows from the soil of the reproductive urge, from which it takes its life, and without which it would be nothing. Furthermore, it would be nothing *for us,* if it did not flourish in personal form, clothing itself in the flower and foliage of desire. When we understand each other as sexual beings, we see, not the soil which lies hidden beneath the leaves, but the leaves themselves, in which the matter of animality is intelligible, only because it has acquired a personal form. Animal and person are, in the end, inextricable, and just as the fact of sexual existence crucially qualifies our understanding of each other as persons, so does our personal existence make it impossible to understand sexuality in "purely animal" terms.

Notes

1. Mary Midgley, *Beast and Man* (London, 1979).
2. This thesis, a subtle variant of which was given by Aristotle in one of his greatest passages (*De Anima,* 403 a–b), has been defended in a variety of ways by recent philosophers. See especially Bernard Williams, "Are Persons Bodies?" in *Problems of the Self* (Cambridge, 1973).
3. Helmuth Plessner, *Lachen and Weinen,* 3rd ed. (Bern, 1961), James Spencer Churchill and Marjorie Grene (Trans.), *Laughing and Crying: A Study of the Limits of Human Behaviour* (Evanston, 1970).
4. My argument here parallels Nagel's ("Sexual Perversion," at pp. 42–43).
5. Bishop Butler, *Sermons* (London, 1726), sermon 1, "On the Social Nature of Man."
6. Alexis de Tocqueville, *De la democratie en Amerique* (Paris, 1835).
7. G. Garibaldi, *Memorie autobiografiche,* 7th ed. (Florence, 1888), p. 56.
8. Stendhal, *De l'amour* (Paris, 1891).
9. See G.E.M. Anscombe, "Contraception and Chastity," in *The Human World,* vol. II (1972).

Prejudice and Homosexuality

Richard D. Mohr

Study Questions

1. What kinds of discrimination do many gays and lesbians face?

2. Distinguish descriptive from normative or prescriptive morality. Which does Mohr believe we need to determine how gays ought to be treated?

3. How does Mohr evaluate certain religious opposition to homosexuality?

4. According to Mohr, is the claim that homosexuality is wrong because it is unnatural always a rationally based evaluation? Explain.

5. Does he believe that equating "unnatural" with "artificial" or "man-made" provides an adequate basis for condemning homosexuality? Explain.

6. What does he say of the argument that the "proper function" of sex is to produce children?

7. How does Mohr respond to the assertion that being homosexual is a matter of choice?

8. How does Mohr respond to the prediction that society would be harmed if it accepted homosexuality? How does he believe it might be benefited by such acceptance?

Who are gays anyway? A 1993 *New York Times–CBS* poll found that only one-fifth of Americans suppose that they have a friend or family member who is gay or lesbian. This finding is extraordinary given the number of practicing homosexuals in America. In 1948, Alfred Kinsey published a study of the sex lives of 12,000 white males. Its method was so rigorous that it set the standard for subsequent

From Richard D. Mohr, *The Little Book of Gay Rights* (Boston: Beacon Press, 1994). Revised version of previously published *Gay Basics.* Reprinted with permission of the author and Beacon Press.

statistical research across the social sciences, but its results shocked the nation: thirty-seven percent of the men had at least one homosexual experience to orgasm in their adult lives; an additional thirteen percent had homosexual fantasies to orgasm; four percent were exclusively homosexual in their practices; another five percent had virtually no heterosexual experience; and nearly one fifth had at least as many homosexual as heterosexual experiences. Kinsey's 1953 study of the sex lives of 8000 women found the occurrence of homosexual behavior at about half the rates for men. . . .

Gays are . . . subject to widespread discrimination in employment. Governments are leading offenders here. They do a lot of discriminating themselves, require that others do it, and set precedents favoring discrimination in the private sector. Lesbians and gay men are barred from serving in the armed forces. The federal government has also denied gays employment in the CIA, FBI, National Security Agency, and the state department. The government refuses to give security clearances to gays and so forces the country's considerable private sector military and aerospace contractors to fire employees known to be gay and to avoid hiring those perceived to be gay. State and local governments regularly fire gay teachers, policemen, firemen, social workers, and anyone who has contact with the public. Further, state licensing laws (though frequently honored only in the breech) officially bar gays from a vast array of occupations and professions—everything from doctors, lawyers, accountants, and nurses to hairdressers, morticians, even used car dealers.

Gays are subject to discrimination in a wide variety of other ways, including private-sector employment, public accommodations, housing, insurance of all types, custody, adoption, and zoning regulations that bar "singles" or "nonrelated" couples from living together. A 1988 study by the Congressional Office of Technology Assessment found that a third of America's insurance companies openly admit that they discriminate against lesbians and gay men. In nearly half the states, same-sex sexual behavior is illegal, so that the central role of sex to meaningful life is officially denied to lesbians and gay men.

Illegality, discrimination and the absorption by gays of society's hatred of them all interact to impede and, for some, block altogether the ability of gay men and lesbians to create and maintain significant personal relations with loved ones. Every facet of life is affected by discrimination. Only the most compelling reasons could justify it.

Many people think society's treatment of gays is justified because they think gays are extremely immoral. To evaluate this claim, different senses of "moral" must be distinguished. Some times by "morality" is meant the values generally held by members of a society—its mores, norms, and customs. On this understanding, gays certainly are not moral: lots of people hate them, and social customs are designed to register widespread disapproval of gays. The problem here is that this sense of morality is merely a descriptive one. On this understanding, every society has a morality—even Nazi society, which had racism and mob rule as central features of its "morality" understood in this sense. What is needed in order to use the notion of morality to praise or condemn behavior is a sense of morality that is prescriptive or normative.

As the Nazi example makes clear, that a belief or claim is descriptively moral does not entail that it is normatively moral. A lot of people in a society saying something is good, even over aeons, does not make it so. The rejection of the long history of socially approved and state-enforced slavery is another good example of this principle at work. Slavery would be wrong even if nearly everyone liked it. So consistency and fairness require that one abandon the belief that gays are immoral simply because most people dislike or disapprove of gays.

Furthermore, recent historical and anthropological research has shown that opinion about gays has been by no means universally negative. It has varied widely even within the larger part of the Christian era and even within the Church itself. There are even societies—current ones—where homosexual behavior is not only tolerated but is a universal compulsory part of male social maturation. Within the last thirty years, American society has undergone a grand turnabout from deeply ingrained, near total condemnation to near total acceptance on two emotionally charged "moral" or "family" issues—contraception and divorce. Society holds its current descriptive morality of gays not because it has to, but because it chooses to.

If popular opinion and custom are not enough to ground moral condemnation of homosexuality, perhaps religion can. Such arguments usually proceed along two lines. One claims that the condemnation is a direct revelation of God, usually through the Bible. The other claims to be able to detect condemnation in God's plan as manifested in nature; homosexuality (it is claimed) is "contrary to nature."

One of the more remarkable discoveries of recent gay research is that the Bible may not be as univocal in its condemnation of homosexuality as many have believed. Christ never mentions homosexuality. Recent interpreters of the Old Testament have pointed out that the story of Lot at Sodom is probably intended to condemn inhospitality rather than homosexuality.

Further, some of the Old Testament condemnations of homosexuality seem simply to be ways of tarring those of the Israelites' opponents who happen to accept homosexual practices when the Israelites themselves did not. If so, the condemnation is merely a quirk of history and rhetoric rather than a moral precept.

What does seem clear is that those who regularly cite the Bible to condemn an activity like homosexuality do so by reading it selectively. Do ministers who cite what they take to be condemnations of homosexuality in Leviticus maintain in their lives all the hygienic and dietary laws of Leviticus? If they cite the story of Lot at Sodom to condemn homosexuality, do they also cite the story of Lot in the Cave to praise incestuous rape? It seems then not that the Bible is being used to ground condemnations of homosexuality as much as society's dislike of homosexuality is being used to interpret the Bible.

Even if a consistent portrait of condemnation could be gleaned from the Bible, what social significance should it be given? One of the guiding principles of society, enshrined in the Constitution as a check against the government, is that decisions affecting social policy are not made on religious grounds. The Religious Right has been successful in stymieing sodomy-law reform, in defunding gay safe-sex literature and gay art, and in blocking the introduction of gay materials into school curriculums. If the real ground of the alleged immorality invoked by governments to discriminate against gays is religious (as it seems to be in these cases), then one of the major commitments of our nation is violated. Religious belief is a fine guide around which a person might organize his own life, but an awful instrument around which to organize someone else's life.

People also try to justify society's treatment of gays by saying they are unnatural. Though the accusation of unnaturalness looks whimsical, when applied to homosexuality, it is usually delivered with venom of forethought. It carries a high emotional charge, usually expressing disgust and evincing queasiness. Probably it is nothing but an emotional charge. For people get equally disgusted and queasy at all sorts of things that are perfectly natural, yet that could hardly be fit subjects for moral condemnation. Two typical examples in current American culture are some people's responses to mothers' suckling in public and to women who do not shave body hair. Similarly people fling the term "unnatural" against gays in the same breath and with the same force as when they call gays "sick" and "gross." When people have strong emotional reactions, as they do in these cases, without being able to give good reasons for them, they are thought of not as operating morally, but as being obsessed and manic. So the feelings of disgust that some people have toward gays will hardly ground a charge of immorality.

When "nature" is taken in technical rather than ordinary usages, it also cannot ground a charge of homosexual immorality. When unnatural means "by artifice" or "made by humans," it can be pointed out that virtually everything that is good about life is unnatural in this sense. The chief feature that distinguishes people from other animals is people's very ability to make over the world to meet their needs and desires. Indeed people's well-being depends upon these departures from nature. On this understanding of human nature and the natural, homosexuality is perfectly unobjectionable; it is simply a means by which some people adapt nature to fulfill their desires and needs.

Another technical sense of natural is that something is natural and so, good, if it fulfills some function in nature. On this view, homosexuality is unnatural because it violates the function of genitals, which is to produce babies. One problem with this view is that lots of bodily parts have lots of functions and just because some one activity can be fulfilled by only one organ (say, the mouth for eating), this activity does not condemn other functions of the organ to immorality (say, the mouth for talking, licking stamps, blowing bubbles, or having sex). So the possible use of the genitals to produce children does not, without more, condemn the use of the genitals for other purposes, say, achieving ecstasy and intimacy.

The functional view of nature will only provide a morally condemnatory sense to the unnatural if a thing which might have many uses has but one proper function to the exclusion of other possible functions.

But whether this is so cannot be established simply by looking at the thing. For what is seen is all its possible functions. The notion of function seemed like it might ground moral authority, but instead it turns out that moral authority is needed to define proper function.

Some people try to fill in this moral authority by appeal to the "design" or "order" of an organ, saying, for instance, that the genitals are designed for the purpose of procreation. But these people cheat intellectually if they do not make explicit who the designer and orderer is. If the "who" is God, we are back to square one—holding others accountable to one's own religious beliefs.

Further, ordinary moral attitudes about childbearing will not provide the needed supplement which would produce a positive obligation to use the genitals for procreation. Though there are local exceptions, society's general attitude toward a childless couple is that of pity not censure—even if the couple could have children. The pity may be an unsympathetic one, that is, not registering a course one would choose for oneself, but this does not make it a course one would require of others. The couple who discovers they cannot have children are viewed not as having thereby had a debt canceled, but rather as having to forgo some of the richness of life, just as a quadriplegic is viewed not as absolved from some moral obligation to hop, skip, and jump, but as missing some of the richness of life. Consistency requires then that, at most, gays who do not or cannot have children are to be pitied rather than condemned. What is immoral is the willful preventing of people from achieving the richness of life. Immorality in this regard lies with those social customs, regulations, and statutes that prevent lesbians and gay men from establishing blood or adoptive families, not with gays themselves.

Many gays would like to raise or foster children—perhaps those alarming number of gay kids who have been beaten up and thrown out of their "families" for being gay. And indeed many lesbian and gay male couples are now raising robust, happy families where children are the blessings of adoption, artificial insemination, or surrogacy. The country is experiencing something approaching a gay and lesbian babyboom.

Sometimes people attempt to establish authority for a moral obligation to use bodily parts in a certain fashion simply by claiming that moral laws are natural laws and vice versa. On this account, inanimate objects and plants are good in that they follow natural laws by necessity, animals follow them by instinct, and persons follow them by a rational will. People are special in that they must first discover the laws that govern them. Now, even if one believes the view—dubious in the post-Newtonian, post-Darwinian world—that natural laws in the usual sense ($e = mc^2$, for instance) have some moral content, it is not at all clear how one is to discover the laws in nature that apply to people.

On the one hand, if one looks to people themselves for a model—and looks hard enough—one finds amazing variety, including homosexual relations as a social ideal (as in upper-class fifth-century Athens) and even as socially mandatory (as in some Melanesian initiation rites today). When one looks to people, one is simply unable to strip away the layers of social custom, history, and taboo in order to see what's really there to any degree more specific than that people are the creatures that make over their world and are capable of abstract thought. That this is so should raise doubts that neutral principles are to be found in human nature that will condemn homosexuality.

On the other hand, if one looks to nature apart from people for models, the possibilities are staggering. There are fish that change sex over their lifetimes: should we "follow nature" and be operative transsexuals? Orangutans, genetically our next of kin, live completely solitary lives without social organization of any kind among adults: ought we to "follow nature" and be hermits? There are many species where only two members per generation reproduce: shall we be bees? The search in nature for people's purpose far from finding sure models for action is likely to leave one morally rudderless.

But (it might also be asked) aren't gays willfully the way they are? It is generally conceded that if sexual orientation is something over which an individual—for whatever reason—has virtually no control, then discrimination against gays is presumptively wrong, as it is against racial and ethnic classes.

Attempts to answer the question whether or not sexual orientation is something that is reasonably thought to be within one's own control usually appeal simply to various claims of the biological or "mental" sciences. But the ensuing debate over genes, hormones, hypothalamuses, twins, early childhood development, and the like is as unnecessary as it is currently inconclusive. All that is needed to answer the question is to look at the actual experience of lesbians and gay men in current society and it becomes fairly clear that sexual orientation is not likely a matter of choice.

On the one hand, the "choice" of the gender of a sexual partner does not seem to express a trivial desire which might as easily be fulfilled by a simple substitution of the desired object. Picking the gender of a sex partner is decidedly dissimilar, that is, to such activities as picking a flavor of ice cream. If an ice cream parlor is out of one's flavor, one simply picks another. And if people were persecuted, threatened with jail terms, shattered careers, loss of family and housing and the like for eating, say, rocky road ice cream, no one would ever eat it. Everyone would pick another easily available flavor. That gay people abide in being gay even in the face of persecution suggests that being gay is not a matter of easy choice.

On the other hand, even if establishing a sexual orientation is not like making a relatively trivial choice, perhaps it is relevantly like making the central and serious life-choices by which individuals try to establish themselves as being of some type or having some occupation. Again, if one examines gay experience, this seems not to be the general case. For one virtually never sees anyone setting out to become a homosexual, in the way one does see people setting out to become doctors, lawyers, and bricklayers. One does not find gays-to-be picking some end—"At some point in the future, I want to become a homosexual"—and then set about planning and acquiring the ways and means to that end, in the way one does see people deciding that they want to become lawyers, and then sees them plan what courses to take and what sort of temperaments, habits, and skills to develop in order to become lawyers. Typically gays-to-be simply find themselves having homosexual encounters and yet, at least initially, resisting quite strongly the identification of being homosexual. Such a person even very likely resists having such encounters, but ends up having them anyway. Only with time, luck, and great personal effort, but sometimes never, does the person gradually come to accept her or his orientation, to view it as a given material condition of life, coming as materials do with certain capacities and limitations. The person begins to act in accordance with his or her orientation and its capacities, seeing its actualization as a requisite for an integrated personality and as a central component of personal well-being. As a result, the experience of coming out to oneself has for gays the basic structure of a discovery, not the structure of a choice. And far from signaling immorality, coming out to others affords one of the few remaining opportunities in ever more bureaucratic, technological, and socialistic societies to manifest courage.

How would society at large be changed if gays were socially accepted? Suggestions to change social policy with regard to gays are invariably met with claims that to do so would invite the destruction of civilization itself: after all isn't that what did Rome in? Actually, Rome's decay paralleled not the flourishing of homosexuality but its repression under the later Christianized emperors. Predictions of American civilization's imminent demise have been as premature as they have been frequent. Civilization has shown itself to be rather resilient here, in large part because of the country's traditional commitments to respect for privacy, to individual liberties, and especially to people minding their own business. These all give society an open texture and the flexibility to try out things to see what works. And because of this, one now need not speculate about what changes reforms in gay social policy might bring to society at large. For many reforms have already been tried.

Half the states have decriminalized lesbian and gay male sex acts. Can you guess which of the following states still have sodomy laws: Wisconsin, Minnesota; New Mexico, Arizona; Vermont, New Hampshire; Nebraska, Kansas. One from each pair does and one does not have sodomy laws. And yet one would be hard pressed to point out any substantial social differences between the members of each pair. (If you're interested: it is the second of each pair with them.) Empirical studies have shown that there is no increase in other crimes in states that have decriminalized.

Neither has the passage of legislation barring discrimination against gays ushered in the end of civilization. Nearly a hundred counties and municipalities, including some of the country's largest cities (like Chicago and New York City) have passed such statutes, as have eight states: Wisconsin, Connecticut, Massachusetts, Hawaii, New Jersey, Vermont, California, and Minnesota. Again, no more brimstone has fallen in these places than elsewhere. Staunchly antigay cities, like Miami and Houston, have not been spared the AIDS crisis.

Berkeley, California, followed by a couple dozen other cities including New York, has even passed "domestic partner" legislation giving gay couples at least some of the same rights to city benefits as are held by heterosexually married couples, and yet Berkeley has not become more weird than it already was. A number of major universities (like Stanford and the University of Chicago) and respected corporations (like Levi Strauss and Company, the Montefiore Medical Center of New York, and Apple Computer, Inc.) are also following Berkeley's lead.

Seemingly hysterical predictions that the American family would collapse if such reforms would pass proved false, just as the same dire predictions that the availability of divorce would lessen the ideal and desirability of marriage proved unfounded. Indeed if current discrimination, which drives gays into hiding and into anonymous relations, ended, far from seeing gays destroying American families, one would see gays forming them.

Virtually all gays express a desire to have a permanent lover. But currently society and its discriminatory impulse make gay coupling very difficult. It is difficult for people to live together as couples without having their sexual orientation perceived in the public realm and so becoming targets for discrimination. Life in hiding is a pressure-cooker existence not easily shared with another. Members of nongay couples are here asked to imagine what it would take to erase every trace of their own sexual orientation for even just one week.

Even against oppressive odds, gays have shown an amazing tendency to nest. And those gay couples who have survived the odds show that the structure of more usual couplings is not a matter of destiny, but of personal responsibility. The so-called basic unit of society turns out not to be a unique immutable atom, but can adopt different parts, be adapted to different needs, and even be improved. Gays might even have a thing or two to teach others about divisions of labor, the relation of sensuality and intimacy, and the stages of development in such relations.

If discrimination ceased, gay men and lesbians would enter the mainstream of the human community openly and with self-respect. The energies that the typical gay person wastes in the anxiety of leading a day-to-day existence of systematic disguise would be released for use in personal flourishing. From this release would be generated the many spin-off benefits that accrue to a society when its individual members thrive.

Society would be richer for acknowledging another aspect of human diversity. Families with gay members would develop relations based on truth and trust rather than lies and fear. And the heterosexual majority would be better off for knowing that they are no longer trampling their gay friends and neighbors.

Finally and perhaps paradoxically, in extending to gays the rights and benefits it has reserved for its dominant culture, America would confirm its deeply held vision of itself as a morally progressing nation, a nation itself advancing and serving as a beacon for others—especially with regard to human rights. The words with which our national pledge ends—"with liberty and justice for all"—are not a description of the present, but a call for the future. America is a nation given to a prophetic political rhetoric which acknowledges that morality is not arbitrary and that justice is not merely the expression of the current collective will. It is this vision that led the black civil rights movement to its successes. Those senators and representatives who opposed that movement and its centerpiece, the 1964 Civil Rights Act, on obscurantist grounds, but who lived long enough and were noble enough came in time to express their heartfelt regret and shame at what they had done. It is to be hoped and someday to be expected that those who now grasp at anything to oppose the extension of that which is best about America to gays will one day feel the same.

Pornography, Civil Rights, and Speech

Catharine MacKinnon

Study Questions

1. What does MacKinnon believe to be the necessary content of pornography?

2. In addition, what does pornography do, according to MacKinnon?

3. What role does she believe pornography plays in gender inequality? In the construction of male and female sexuality?

4. What is meant by a "sex object"?

5. Why does she believe that many people are not able to see pornography as harmful?

6. What problems does MacKinnon believe feminists have with the 1973 legal definition of obscenity?

7. Why does she believe certain sexual depictions in serious art can still be harmful to women?

8. How does she distinguish obscenity from pornography in terms of its harm to women?

9. What, then, is her definition of pornography? How is this distinguished from erotica?

10. What kind of law does she believe pornography should fall under? Would this violate First Amendment free speech rights?

The content of pornography is one thing. There, women substantively desire dispossession and cruelty. We desperately want to be bound, battered, tortured, humiliated, and killed. Or, to be fair to the soft core, merely taken and used. This is erotic to the male point of view. Subjection itself, with self-determination ecstatically relinquished, is the content of women's sexual desire and desirability. Women are there to be violated and possessed, men to violate and possess us, either on screen or by camera or pen on behalf of the consumer. On a simple descriptive level,

the inequality of hierarchy, of which gender is the primary one, seems necessary for sexual arousal to work. Other added inequalities identify various pornographic genres or subthemes, although they are always added through gender: age, disability, homosexuality, animals, objects, race (including anti-Semitism), and so on. Gender is never irrelevant.

What pornography does goes beyond its content: it eroticizes hierarchy, it sexualizes inequality. It makes dominance and submission into sex. Inequality is its central dynamic; the illusion of freedom coming together with the reality of force is central to its working. Perhaps because this is a bourgeois culture, the victims must look free, appear to be freely acting. Choice is how she got there. Willing is what she is when she is being equal. It seems equally important that then and there she actually be forced and that forcing be communicated on some level, even if only through still photos of her in postures of receptivity and access, available for penetration. Pornography in this view is a form of forced sex, a practice of sexual politics, an institution of gender inequality.

From this perspective, pornography is neither harmless fantasy nor a corrupt and confused misrepresentation of an otherwise natural and healthy sexual situation. It institutionalizes the sexuality of male supremacy, fusing the erotization of dominance and submission with the social construction of male and female. To the extent that gender is sexual, pornography is part of constituting the meaning of that sexuality. Men treat women as who they see women as being. Pornography constructs who that is. Men's power over women means that the way men see women defines who women can be. Pornography is that way. Pornography is not imagery in some relation to a reality elsewhere constructed. It is not a distortion, reflection, projection, expression, fantasy, representation, or symbol either. It is a sexual reality.

In Andrea Dworkin's definitive work, *Pornography: Men Possessing Women*,[1] sexuality itself is a social construct gendered to the ground. Male dominance here is not an artificial overlay upon an underlying inalterable substratum of uncorrupted essential sexual being. Dworkin presents a sexual theory of gender inequality of which pornography is a constitutive practice. The way pornography produces its meaning constructs and defines men and women as such. Gender has no basis in anything other than the social reality its hegemony constructs. Gender is what gender means. The process that gives sexuality its male supremacist meaning is the same process through which gender inequality becomes socially real.

In this approach, the experience of the (overwhelmingly) male audiences who consume pornography is therefore not fantasy or simulation or catharsis but sexual reality, the level of reality on which sex itself largely operates. Understanding this dimension of the problem does not require noticing that pornography models are real women to whom, in most cases, something real is being done; nor does it even require inquiring into the systematic infliction of pornography and its sexuality upon women, although it helps. What matters is the way in which the pornography itself provides what those who consume it want. Pornography participates in its audience's eroticism through creating an accessible sexual object, the possession and consumption of which is male sexuality, as socially constructed; to be consumed and possessed as which, is female sexuality, as socially constructed; pornography is a process that constructs it that way.

The object world is constructed according to how it looks with respect to its possible uses. Pornography defines women by how we look according to how we can be sexually used. Pornography codes how to look at women, so you know what you can do with one when you see one. Gender is an assignment made visually, both originally and in everyday life. A sex object is defined on the basis of its looks, in terms of its usability for sexual pleasure, such that both the looking—the quality of the gaze, including its point of view—and the definition according to use become eroticized as part of the sex itself. This is what the feminist concept "sex object" means. In this sense, sex in life is no less mediated than it is in art. Men have sex with their image of a woman. It is not that life and art imitate each other; in this sexuality, they *are* each other.

To give a set of rough epistemological translations, to defend pornography as consistent with the equality of the sexes is to defend the subordination of women to men as sexual equality. What in the pornographic

view is love and romance looks a great deal like hatred and torture to the feminist. Pleasure and eroticism become violation. Desire appears as lust for dominance and submission. The vulnerability of women's projected sexual availability, that acting we are allowed (that is, asking to be acted upon), is victimization. Play conforms to scripted roles. Fantasy expresses ideology, is not exempt from it. Admiration of natural physical beauty becomes objectification. Harmlessness becomes harm. Pornography is a harm of male supremacy made difficult to see because of its pervasiveness, potency, and, principally, because of its success in making the world a pornographic place. Specifically, its harm cannot be discerned, and will not be addressed, if viewed and approached neutrally, because it *is* so much of "what is." In other words, to the extent pornography succeeds in constructing social reality, it becomes invisible as harm. If we live in a world that pornography creates through the power of men in a male-dominated situation, the issue is not what the harm of pornography is, but how that harm is to become visible. . . .

Obscenity law provides a very different analysis and conception of the problem of pornography.[2] In 1973 the legal definition of obscenity became that which the average person, applying contemporary community standards, would find that, taken as a whole, appeals to the prurient interest; that which depicts or describes in a patently offensive way—you feel like you're a cop reading someone's *Miranda* rights—sexual conduct specifically defined by the applicable state law; and that which, taken as a whole, lacks serious literary, artistic, political, or scientific value.[3] Feminism doubts whether the average person gender-neutral exists; has more questions about the content and process of defining what community standards are than it does about deviations from them; wonders why prurience counts but powerlessness does not and why sensibilities are better protected from offense than women are from exploitation; defines sexuality, and thus its violation and expropriation, more broadly than does state law; and questions why a body of law that has not in practice been able to tell rape from intercourse should, without further guidance, be entrusted with telling pornography from anything less. Taking the work "as a whole" ignores that which the victims of pornography have long known: legitimate settings diminish the perception of injury done to those whose trivialization and objectification they contextualize. Besides, and this is a heavy one, if a woman is subjected, why should it matter that the work has other value? Maybe what redeems the work's value is what enhances its injury to women, not to mention that existing standards of literature, art, science, and politics, examined in a feminist light, are remarkably consonant with pornography's mode, meaning, and message. And finally—first and foremost, actually—although the subject of these materials is overwhelmingly women, their contents almost entirely made up of women's bodies, our invisibility has been such, our equation as a sex *with* sex has been such, that the law of obscenity has never even considered pornography a women's issue.

Obscenity, in this light, is a moral idea, an idea about judgments of good and bad. Pornography, by contrast, is a political practice, a practice of power and powerlessness. Obscenity is ideational and abstract; pornography is concrete and substantive. The two concepts represent two entirely different things. Nudity, excess of candor, arousal or excitement, prurient appeal, illegality of the acts depicted, and unnaturalness or perversion are all qualities that bother obscenity law when sex is depicted or portrayed. Sex forced on real women so that it can be sold at a profit and forced on other real women; women's bodies trussed and maimed and raped and made into things to be hurt and obtained and accessed, and this presented as the nature of women in a way that is acted on and acted out, over and over; the coercion that is visible and the coercion that has become invisible—this and more bothers feminists about pornography. Obscenity as such probably does little harm.[4] Pornography is integral to attitudes and behavior of violence and discrimination that define the treatment and status of half the population. . . .

At the request of the city of Minneapolis, Andrea Dworkin and I conceived and designed a local human rights ordinance in accordance with our approach to the pornography issue. We define pornography as a practice of sex discrimination, a violation of women's civil rights, the opposite of sexual equality. Its point is to hold those who profit from and benefit from that injury accountable to those who are injured. It means that women's injury—our damage, our pain, our enforced inferiority—should outweigh their pleasure and their profits, or sex equality is meaningless.

We define pornography as the graphic sexually explicit subordination of women through pictures or words that also includes women dehumanized as

sexual objects, things, or commodities; enjoying pain or humiliation or rape; being tied up, cut up, mutilated, bruised, or physically hurt; in postures of sexual submission or servility or display; reduced to body parts, penetrated by objects or animals, or presented in scenarios of degradation, injury, torture; shown as filthy or inferior; bleeding, bruised, or hurt in a context that makes these conditions sexual.[5] Erotica, defined by distinction as not this, might be sexually explicit materials premised on equality.[6] We also provide that the use of men, children, or transsexuals in the place of women is pornography.[7] The definition is substantive in that it is sex-specific, but it covers everyone in a sex-specific way, so is gender neutral in overall design.

There is a buried issue within sex discrimination law about what sex, meaning gender, is. If sex is a *difference,* social or biological, one looks to see if a challenged practice occurs along the same lines; if it does, or if it is done to both sexes, the practice is not discrimination, not inequality. If, by contrast, sex has been a matter of *dominance,* the issue is not the gender difference but the difference gender makes. In this more substantive, less abstract approach, the concern with inequality is whether a practice *subordinates* on the basis of sex. The first approach implies that marginal correction is needed; the second requires social change. Equality, in the first view, centers on abstract symmetry between equivalent categories; the asymmetry that occurs when categories are not equivalent is not inequality, it is treating unlikes differently. In the second approach, inequality centers on the substantive, cumulative disadvantagement of social hierarchy. Equality for the first is nondifferentiation; for the second, nonsubordination.[8] Although it is consonant with both approaches, our antipornography statute emerges largely from an analysis of the problem under the second approach.

To define pornography as a practice of sex discrimination combines a mode of portrayal that has a legal history—the sexually explicit—with an active term that is central to the inequality of the sexes—subordination. Among other things, subordination means to be in a position of inferiority or loss of power, or to be demeaned or denigrated.[9] To be someone's subordinate is the opposite of being their equal. The definition does not include all sexually explicit depictions *of* the subordination of women. That is not what it says. It says, this which *does* that: the sexually explicit that subordinates women. To these active terms to capture what the pornography *does,* the definition adds a list of what it must also contain. This list, from our analysis, is an exhaustive description of what must be in the pornography for it to do what it does behaviorally. Each item in the definition is supported by experimental, testimonial, social, and clinical evidence. We made a legislative choice to be exhaustive and specific and concrete rather than conceptual and general, to minimize problems of chilling effect, making it hard to guess wrong, thus making self-censorship less likely, but encouraging (to use a phrase from discrimination law) voluntary compliance, knowing that if something turns up that is not on the list, the law will not be expansively interpreted.

The list in the definition, by itself, would be a content regulation.[10] But together with the first part, the definition is not simply a content regulation. It is a medium-message combination that resembles many other such exceptions to First Amendment guarantees.[11]

To focus what our law is, I will say what it is not. It is not a prior restraint. It does not go to possession. It does not turn on offensiveness. It is not a ban, unless relief for a proven injury is a "ban" on doing that injury again. Its principal enforcement mechanism is the civil rights commission, although it contains an option for direct access to court as well as de novo judicial review of administrative determinations, to ensure that no case will escape full judicial scrutiny and full due process. I will also not discuss various threshold issues, such as the sources of municipal authority, preemption, or abstention, or even issues of overbreadth or vagueness, nor will I defend the ordinance from views that never have been law, such as First Amendment absolutism. I will discuss the merits: how pornography by this definition is a harm, specifically how it is a harm of gender inequality, and how that harm outweighs any social interest in its protection by recognized First Amendment standards.[12]

This law aspires to guarantee women's rights consistent with the First Amendment by making visible a conflict of rights between the equality guaranteed to all women and what, in some legal sense, is now the freedom of the pornographers to make and sell, and their consumers to have access to, the materials this ordinance defines. Judicial resolution of this conflict, if the judges do for women what they have done for others, is likely to entail a balancing of the rights of women arguing that our lives and opportunities, including our freedom of speech and action, are constrained by—and in many cases flatly precluded by, in, and through—pornography, against those who argue that the pornography is harmless, or harmful only in part but not in the whole of the definition; or that it is more important to preserve the pornography than it is to prevent or remedy whatever harm it does.

In predicting how a court would balance these interests, it is important to understand that this ordinance cannot now be said to be either conclusively legal or illegal under existing law or precedent,[13] although I think the weight of authority is on our side. This ordinance enunciates a new form of the previously recognized governmental interest in sex equality. Many laws make sex equality a governmental interest.[14] Our law is designed to further the equality of the sexes, to help make sex equality real. Pornography is a practice of discrimination on the basis of sex, on one level because of its role in creating and maintaining sex as a basis for discrimination. It harms many women one at a time and helps keep all women in an inferior status by defining our subordination as our sexuality and equating that with our gender. It is also sex discrimination because its victims, including men, are selected for victimization on the basis of their gender. But for their sex, they would not be so treated.[15]

Notes*

1. Andrea Dworkin, *Pornography: Men Possessing Women* (1981).

2. For a fuller development of this critique, see "Not a Moral Issue" (Chapter 13 in original source).

3. *Miller v. California,* 413 U.S. 15, 24 (1973).

4. See the *Report of the Presidential Commission on Obscenity and Pornography* (1970).

5. For the specific statutory language, see "Not a Moral Issue," note 1.

6. See, e.g., Gloria Steinem, "Erotica v. Pornography," in *Outrageous Acts and Everyday Rebellions* 219 (1983).

7. See Indianapolis Ordinance, "Not a Moral Issue," note 1.

8. See Catharine A. MacKinnon, *Sexual Harassment of Working Women* 101–141 (1979).

---

*Some notes have been deleted and the remaining ones renumbered.—ED.

9. For a lucid discussion of subordination, see Andrea Dworkin, "Against the Male Flood: Censorship, Pornography, and Equality," 8 *Harvard Women's Law Journal* 1 (1985).

10. If this part stood alone, it would, along with its support, among other things, have to be equally imposed—an interesting requirement for an equality law, but arguably met by this one. See *Carey v. Brown,* 447 U.S. 455 (1980); *Police Department of Chicago v. Mosley,* 408 U.S. 92 (1972); Kenneth Karst, "Equality as a Central Principle in the First Amendment," 43 *University of Chicago Law Review* 20 (1975).

11. See *KPNX Broadcasting Co. v. Arizona Superior Court,* 459 U.S. 1302 (1982) (Rehnquist as Circuit Justice denied application to stay Arizona judge's order that those involved with heavily covered criminal trial avoid direct contact with press; mere potential confusion from unrestrained contact with press is held to justify order); *New York v. Ferber,* 458 U.S. 747 (1982) (child pornography, defined as promoting sexual performance by a child, can be criminally banned as a form of child abuse); *F.C.C. v. Pacific Found.,* 438 U.S. 726 (1978) ("indecent" but not obscene radio broadcasts may be regulated by F.C.C. through licensing); *Young v. American Mini Theatres, Inc.,* 427 U.S. 50 (1976) (exhibition of sexually explicit "adult movies" may be restricted through zoning ordinances); *Gertz v. Robert Welch, Inc.,* 418 U.S. 323, 347 (1974) (state statute may allow private persons to recover for libel without proving actual malice so long as liability is not found without fault); *Pittsburgh Press Co. v. Human Relations Comm'n,* 413 U.S. 376 (1973) (sex-designated help-wanted columns conceived as commercial speech may be prohibited under local sex discrimination ordinance); *Miller v. California,* 413 U.S. 15, 18 (1973) (obscenity unprotected by First Amendment in case in which it was "thrust by aggressive sales action upon unwilling [viewers]. . . ."); *Red Lion Broadcasting Co. v. F.C.C.,* 395 U.S. 367, 387 (1969) (F.C.C. may require broadcasters to allow reply time to vindicate speech interests of the public: "The right of free speech of a broadcaster, the user of a sound truck, or any other individual does not embrace a right to snuff out the free speech of others."); *Ginzburg v. United States,* 383 U.S. 463, 470 (1966) (upholding conviction for mailing obscene material on "pandering" theory: "[T]he purveyor's sole emphasis [is] on the sexually provocative aspects of his publications."); *Roth v. United States,* 354 U.S. 476, 487 (1957) (federal obscenity statute is found valid; obscene defined as "material which deals with sex in a manner appealing to prurient interest"); *Beauharnais v. Illinois,* 343 U.S. 250 (1952) (upholding group libel statute); *Chaplinsky v. New Hampshire,* 315 U.S. 568 (1942) (a state statute outlawing "fighting words" likely to cause a breach of peace is not unconstitutional under the First Amendment); *Near v. Minnesota,* 283 U.S. 697 (1931) (Minnesota statute permitting prior restraint of publishers who regularly engage in publication of defamatory material is held unconstitutional; press freedom outweighs prior restraints in all but exceptional cases, such as national security or obscenity); for one such exceptional case, see *United States v. Progressive, Inc.,* 486 F. Supp. 5 (W.D. Wis. 1979) (prior restraint is allowed against publication of information on how to make a hydrogen bomb, partially under "troop movements" exception); *Schenck v. United States,* 249 U.S. 47, 52 (1919) ("clear and present dangers" excepted from the First Amendment: "The most stringent protection of free speech would not protect a man in falsely shouting fire in a theatre and causing a panic.")

12. See *Young v. American Mini Theatres, Inc.,* 427 U.S. 50 (1976); *Pittsburgh Press Co. v. Human Relations Comm'n,* 413 U.S. 376 (1973); *Konigsberg v. State Bar of California,* 366 U.S. 36, 49–51 (1961).

13. After the delivery of [. . . this] Lecture, an Indiana federal court declared the ordinance unconstitutional in a facial challenge brought by the "Media Coalition," an association of publishers and distributors. The ordinance is repeatedly misquoted, and the misquotations are underscored to illustrate its legal errors. Arguments not made in support of the law are invented and attributed to the city and found legally inadequate. Evidence of harm before the legislature is given no weight at all, while purportedly being undisturbed, as an absolutist approach is implicitly adopted, unlike any existing Supreme Court precedent. To the extent that existing law, such as obscenity law, overlaps with the ordinance, even it would be invalidated under this ruling. And clear law on sex equality is flatly misstated. The opinion permits a ludicrous suit by mostly legitimate trade publishers, parties whose interests are at most tenuously and remotely implicated under the ordinance, to test a law that directly and importantly would affect others, such as pornographers and their victims. The decision also seems far more permissive toward racism than would be allowed in a concrete case even under existing law, and displays blame-the-victim misogyny: "Adult women generally have the capacity to protect themselves from participating in and being personally victimized by pornography . . ." *American Booksellers v. Hudnut,* 598 F. Supp. 1316, 1334 (S.D. Ind. 1984). For subsequent developments, see "The Sexual Politics of the First Amendment."

14. See e.g., Title IX of the Educ. Amends. of 1972, 20 U.S.C. §§1681–1686 (1972); Equal Pay Act, 29 U.S.C. §§206(d) (1963); Title VII of the Civil Rights Act of 1964, 42 U.S.C. §§2000e to 2000e17 (1976). Many states have equal rights amendments to their constitutions, see Barbara Brown and Ann Freedman, "Equal

Rights Amendment: Growing Impact on the States," 1 *Women's Rights Law Reporter* 1.63, 1.63–1.64 (1974); many states and cities, including Minneapolis and Indianapolis, prohibit discrimination on the basis of sex. See also *Roberts* v. *United States Jaycees*, 468 U.S. 609 (1984) (recently recognizing that sex equality is a compelling state interest); *Frontiero* v. *Richardson*, 411 U.S. 677 (1973); *Reed* v. *Reed*, 404 U.S. 71 (1971); U.S. Const. amend. XIV.

15. See *City of Los Angeles* v. *Manhart*, 435 U.S. 702, 711 (1978) (city water department's pension plan was found discriminatory in its "treatment of a person in a manner which but for that person's sex would be different"). See also *Orr* v. *Orr*, 440 U.S. 268 (1979); *Barnes* v. *Costle*, 561 F.2d 983 (D.C. Cir. 1977).

Review Exercises

1. Distinguish "conceptual" and "factual" matters regarding sexual morality. What is the difference between them?

2. What are some factual matters that would be relevant for consequentialist arguments regarding sexual behavior?

3. According to a Kantian type of morality, we ought to treat persons as persons. Deceit and coercion violate this requirement. On this view, what kinds of things regarding sexual morality would be morally objectionable?

4. How would a natural law theory be used to judge sexual behavior? Explain.

5. What is meant by the term *perversion*? How would this notion be used to determine whether there was or was not something called "sexual perversion"?

6. Distinguish normative and descriptive definitions of pornography.

7. Label each of the statements below regarding the legal regulation of pornography as examples of one of the types of "liberty-limiting principles."

   a. It is important to any society that its citizens be self-disciplined. One area of self-discipline is sexual behavior. Thus a society in its own interest may make legal regulations regarding sexual matters, including pornography.

   b. Only if pornography can be proven to lead people to commit sexual assaults on others can it rightly be restricted by law.

   c. Pornography manifests sexual immaturity, and a society should not encourage such immaturity in its members and thus may limit pornography.

   d. Pornography depicts improper and degrading sex acts and thus should be legally banned.

   e. Just as we prevent people from walking nude in public places because it upsets people, so pornography should not be allowed in public places.

8. To which types of pornography do feminists object and why?

Discussion Cases

1. *Date Rape?* The students at a local university had heard much about date rape, what it was, what could lead to it, and that it was morally wrong and legally a crime. However, they were not always so clear about what counted as true consent to a sexual relation or experience. John insisted that unless the other person clearly said "no," then consent should be implied. Amy said it was not so easy as that. Sometimes the issue comes up too quickly for a person to realize what is happening. The person has voluntarily gone along up to a certain point and may even be ambiguous about proceeding further. Bill insisted that he would want a clear expression of a positive desire to go on for him to consider there to be a real consent. He also said that guys could also be ambiguous and in some cases not actually want to get involved sexually and be talked into it against their will by their partner.

What do you think is required for true consent to a sexual involvement?

2. *Pornographic Lyrics.* One of the latest hot hits on the ABC label has been said by certain women's groups to be pornographic. It uses explicit sexual language. It uses crude language to describe women's genitalia. It also suggests that

it is all right to sexually abuse women and that they like to be treated this way. The women's groups want the album banned as pornography that harms women. The music company is protesting that this is a free country and that this is simply free speech. You might not like it and it may be tasteless, they argue, but consumers who find it so do not have to buy it.

Do you agree with the record company or the women's groups? Why?

Selected Bibliography

Assiter, Alison. *Pornography, Feminism and Individualism.* Cambridge, MA: Unwin Hyman, 1990.

Atkinson, Ronald. *Sexual Morality.* New York: Harcourt Brace & World, 1965.

Baker, Robert, and Frederick Elliston (Eds.). *Philosophy and Sex.* Buffalo, NY: Prometheus Books, 1984.

Batchelor, Edward (Ed.). *Homosexuality and Ethics.* New York: Pilgrim Press, 1980.

Berger, Fred R. *Freedom of Expression.* Belmont, CA: Wadsworth, 1980.

Bertocci, Peter A. *Sex, Love, and the Person.* New York: Sheed & Ward, 1967.

Burstyn, Varda (Ed.). *Women Against Censorship.* Vancouver, BC: Douglas & McIntyre, 1985.

Copp, David, and Susan Wendell. *Pornography and Censorship.* Buffalo, NY: Prometheus, 1983.

Devlin, Patrick. *The Enforcement of Morals.* New York: Oxford University Press, 1965.

Dworkin, Ronald M. (Ed.) *The Philosophy of Law.* New York: Oxford University Press, 1977.

Feinberg, Joel. *Offense to Others.* New York: Oxford University Press, 1985.

Holbrook, David (Ed.). *The Case Against Pornography.* New York: Library Press, 1973.

Hunter, J. F.M. *Thinking about Sex and Love.* Toronto: Macmillan, 1980.

Kosnik, Anthony, et al. *Human Sexuality: New Directions in American Catholic Thought.* New York: Paulist Press, 1977.

Lederer, Laura (Ed.). *Take Back the Night: Women on Pornography.* New York: Morrow, 1980.

Leiser, Burton. *Liberty, Justice and Morals,* 2nd ed. New York: Macmillan, 1979.

MacKinnon, Catharine. *Feminism Unmodified.* Cambridge, MA: Harvard University Press, 1987.

Nagel, Thomas. "Sexual Perversion," in *The Journal of Philosophy,* vol. 66 (1969).

Paglia, Camille. *Sex, Art, and American Culture.* New York: Vintage, 1992.

Soble, Alan (Ed.). *The Philosophy of Sex.* Totowa, NJ: Littlefield, Adams, 1980.

Stewart, Robert (Ed.). *Philosophical Perspectives on Sex and Love.* New York: Oxford University Press, 1995.

Taylor, Richard. *Having Love Affairs.* Buffalo, NY: Prometheus, 1982.

Tong, Rosemarie. *Women, Sex, and the Law.* Totowa, NJ: Rowman & Allanheld, 1984.

U.S. Department of Justice. *Attorney General's Commission on Pornography.* Final Report, July 1986.

Vanoy, Russell. *Sex Without Love.* Buffalo, NY: Prometheus, 1980.

Whiteley, C. H., and W. N. Whiteley. *Sex and Morals.* New York: Basic Books, 1967.

❧ 11 ❧

Equality and Discrimination

Not long ago a couple dozen secret service agents were in Annapolis, Maryland, to prepare for the visit of the president. They stopped at a local fast food restaurant for breakfast. They sat at three tables, and all ordered at the same time. Those agents sitting at two of the tables were served shortly. Those at the third table waited. The others were served seconds. Those at the third table waited. They also reminded the server that they had not yet been served. They did so again. After fifty-five minutes, they were still not served and all had to leave. Those at the third table were all African Americans. All but one of the agents at the other two tables were white. This event took place not in 1860 or 1900 or 1960 but in 1993![1]

Although we have not completely eliminated racism and sexism from our society, we like to think there is less of it today than thirty years ago. But how do we know? We read about insults like the one described here. We look at statistics of various sorts and examine our own experience. We look at our surroundings, our schools, our neighborhoods, our associations to see if there is more racial integration and more equality among women and men and people of color in positions and offices. And what do we find? We still hear comments such as the following: "You probably don't know the answer to that question, Mary, because it's a little techni-

cal." "We can't expect much from him because he is from that section of town." "She's a looker; let's hire her." "They're all lazy, or . . . ." "I'm just reporting to you what I heard, that all the women there are . . . ." Are these harmless comments, unintentionally racist or sexist remarks, or examples of prevalent and harmful attitudes?[2]

In a study by CNN, fifty males and fifty females were sent to several reputable investment firms. Those in the thirty-to-forty-five age group, both males and females, each had $25,000 to invest, and those in the fifty and older age group had $50,000. The women were treated more courteously, and they were seen sooner than the men. However, they were also taken less seriously. For example, they were less often asked about their risk comfort level, a key to investment counseling.[3]

We then look at the statistics regarding gender equality, and what do they tell us? Although the data can be structured in such a way as to be deceptive, some numbers continue to be repeated and thus are generally reliable. For example, thirty years after the 1963 Equal Pay Act was enacted, the U.S. Bureau of the Census found that "the average woman earned only 53 cents for every dollar paid to a man."[4] The survey from which this figure was derived used the average salary for men and women working in twelve categories of employment, among them executive and administrative jobs, positions in sales and transportation, and service workers and laborers. Even when the mean or middle salary was used, women still earned 30 cents less on the dollar than men. "From 1985 to 1990, women's wages crept up one penny a year, and in 1990 they slid two cents," *Working Woman* magazine reported.[5]

Although traditional men's jobs are now more open to women, many types of jobs still tend to be sex-segregated, with women's jobs generally paying less than men's. For example, most janitors are men and most household cleaners are women. Even in jobs such as sales and retail, women sell smaller things such as cosmetics, and men sell bigger things such as cars—and they make higher commissions. In 1994, U.S. women were only 8.3 percent of engineers and 24 percent of lawyers, while they were 93 percent of registered nurses and 74 percent of noncollege and university teachers.[6] The twelfth annual survey (for 1995) of executive compensation for northern California's 52 largest companies, reported that 84 of the executives received $1 million or more. Every one of the 84 executives pictured in the news report was a white male.[7] "Despite large structural changes in the economy and major anti-discrimination legislation, the economic well-being of women in comparison with that of men did not improve between 1959 and 1983."[8] More recently, however, women may be making some gains. In the first half of 1993 "women's hourly wages reached 78 percent of men's, a historic high," and between 1989 and 1993 women's median wages (after adjusting for inflation) grew 2 percent, while men's dropped 5 percent.[9] There are more women with children in the workforce than ever before. Approximately 75 percent of women whose youngest children are under eighteen work outside the home, and 55 percent of those with children under age three do so.[10] They continue to feel the pull of work and home more than men, and still are more responsible for the "second shift" work: housework. Other discussions of discrimination could focus on the increasing feminization of poverty (of single

mothers and divorcees) and the incidence of physical and sexual abuse of women.

Is the situation any different for race relations? Most whites, for example, believe that "racial prejudice is declining," but African Americans disagree. "They perceive much more lingering prejudice than whites do . . . [and] are more than twice as likely to attribute blacks' disadvantaged state to discrimination as to personal faults."[11] In 1993, 33.1 percent of blacks were below the poverty line compared to 12.2 percent of whites.[12] Both groups showed some gain in the 1995 statistics, with 29.3 percent of blacks below the poverty line. This is also an improvement over 1970, when 39 percent of blacks had incomes below the poverty line.[13] Just as with women, there is some good news in terms of the percentage of African Americans who hold managerial and professional jobs. Yet black unemployment is twice as high as white unemployment, and "white men were three to four times more likely than black men, and white women were about twice as likely as African American women, to attend college from 1955 to 1969."[14] Statistics for 1996 show that of the 33.5 million blacks in the United States (compared to 30.3 million in 1990), 73.8 percent of those 25 and older had completed high school (compared to 63.1 percent in 1990). In 1995, 86 percent of blacks aged 25 to 29 had graduated from high school, approximately the same percentage as young whites. Yet the "median income of black men working year-round, full time, was $25,350. In 1994, [it was] 72 percent of the figure for non-Hispanic white men." In that same year, black women earned 85 percent of non-Hispanic white women.[15] Other indicator areas such as residential integration or segregation and funding for schools confirm this pattern. After decades of attempting to make progress in the integration of schools, there is now more segregation than in 1970. "Nationally, fully a third of black public school students attend schools where the enrollment is 90 percent to 100 percent minority."[16] Detroit's public school system, for example, is now 94 percent minority students.

Similar patterns and problems exist for people of Hispanic origin. Census bureau findings for 1995 showed 30 percent of Hispanics below the poverty line, compared with 22 percent in 1970. Since 1990, their earnings fell by 5.1 percent.[17] According to the report "Educational Attainment in the United States: March 1995," Hispanic adults aged 25 to 29 lagged behind both blacks and whites. A "smaller percentage of Hispanics held high school diplomas in 1995 than held them in 1992, and the proportion of Hispanics who have completed four years of college has dropped by nearly 20 percent since 1988." This fact may not be a function only of a large influx of Hispanic immigrants during this period, for two thirds of all Hispanic students are native-born.[18]

Asian Americans face other problems of misunderstanding and prejudice even though their academic achievements have been phenomenal. Figures for median income for Asian Americans are often deceiving, especially when citing median family income, for there may be three to five household workers contributing to that income. The mentally and physically disabled today are more integrated into society than in decades past, but they continue to be judged more by their disabilities than their abilities. It has been reported that 85 percent of Americans surveyed "favor equal treatment in the workplace for homosexuals and heterosexuals." In 1996, 313 companies, 36 cities, 12 counties, and four states had extended health benefits to gay partners of their employees.[19] Although progress has been made in the area of discrimination, we need not look far to find examples of practices that should be changed. However, not everyone agrees on which practices these are and what changes should be made and why.

Civil Rights Laws: A Brief History

We would like to think that civil rights laws enacted throughout the history of the United States and other Western countries have lessened racial injustice and promoted equal treatment for all citizens. Consider the following highlights of U.S. civil rights–related legislation.

- 1868 The Fourteenth Amendment to the Constitution, the equal protection clause, declared that no state may "deny to any person within its jurisdiction the equal protection of the law." This followed the Thirteenth Amendment in 1865, which prohibited slavery.

- 1920 The Nineteenth Amendment to the Constitution gave women the right to vote. This followed efforts and demonstrations by the suffragettes and the enactment of state laws giving this right to women.

- 1954 The U.S. Supreme Court ruling *Brown* v. *Board of Education* overturned the "separate but equal" schooling decision of the Court's 1896 *Plessy* v. *Ferguson* ruling.

- 1959 Vice President Richard Nixon ordered preferential treatment for qualified blacks in jobs with government contractors. In an executive order in 1961, President John F. Kennedy called for affirmative action in government hiring, and in 1965 President Lyndon Johnson issued enforcement procedures such as goals and timetables for hiring women and underrepresented minorities.

- 1963 The Equal Pay Act required equal pay for substantially equal work by companies engaged in production for commerce.

- 1964 The Civil Rights Act, Title VII, prohibited discrimination in employment by private employers, employment agencies, and unions with fifteen or more employees. It prohibited the sex segregation of jobs, and it required that there be a Bona Fide Occupational Qualification (BFOQ) to allow preference of specific group members for jobs, as with jobs for wet nurses or clothing models.

- 1978 The U.S. Supreme Court ruling *Bakke* v. *U.C. Davis Medical School* forbid the use of racial quotas in school admissions but allowed some consideration of race in admissions decisions. Recently, this decision has been challenged by the 1995 decision *Adarand* v. *Pena.*

According to this 5–4 decision, racial classifications must come under "strict scrutiny" to be acceptable. University use of racial classifications in the interest of achieving a diverse student body, which was acceptable under *Bakke,* might not pass this stricter test. However, affirmative action as a means to remedy the lingering effects of past discrimination might pass. This was allowed in the 1979 Court decision *Weber* v. *Kaiser Aluminum,* which permitted a company to remedy its past discriminatory practices by using race as a criterion for admission to special training programs. These programs were aimed at ensuring that a percentage of black persons equal to that in the local labor force would be moved up to managerial positions in the company.

■ 1991 The Congressional Civil Rights Act required that businesses using employment practices that had a discriminatory impact (even if unintentional) must show that there is a business necessity for the practice, or else the business must reform its practices to eliminate this impact.[20] Quotas were forbidden except when required by court order for rectifying wrongful past or present discrimination. Sexual harassment was also noted as a form of discrimination. Although cases of sexual harassment began to appear in court in the late 1970s, the concept is still being defined by the courts. Two forms of this harassment are generally recognized: One promises employment rewards for sexual favors and the other creates a "hostile work environment."

These are just a few of the highlights of the last 150 years of civil rights laws as enacted by various government bodies and persons. They have played a major role in the way we carry on our social and economic life together. Other laws and court decisions relating to housing, lending, and busing of school students could also be cited. Laws have been designed to prevent discrimination on the basis of not only race and sex, but also religion, age, disability, and sexual orientation.[21] Many of these laws rely on and are based on legal precedent. But they also are grounded in moral notions such as equality and justice and fairness. In this chapter we will examine some of the moral notions and arguments that play a role in discussions about what a just society should be like.

Racism and Sexism

Some time ago I came across an article entitled, "What's Wrong with Racism?" It is an intriguing title. To answer the question, we ought first to ask, What is racism? Race is a somewhat arbitrary classification by which we group people according to selected sets of characteristics and geographical origins. Although in times past people were divided into three races, more recently nine geographically based races have been recognized.[22] However, some people hold that "the biological category of race is virtually meaningless." This is because "the human species shares a common gene pool, and while there is obvious phenotypic variation, it cannot be classified into distinct racial types—there is more variation within currently labeled racial groups than between groups."[23] Nevertheless, classifying people on the basis of certain phenotypic variation or race is not in itself racism. First of all, racism involves making race a significant factor about the person, more important, say, than height or strength. Race becomes a key identifying factor. It sets people of one race apart from people of other races, making us think of "us and them" on the basis of this classification.

Still, this is not a sufficiently distinguishing characteristic of racism. Racism also involves the denigration of people of a certain race, simply because they are members of that race. It involves believing that all persons of that race are inferior to persons of other races in some way. Does this necessarily make racism wrong? In the abstract, it would seem that believing that someone is shorter than another or less strong is not necessarily objectionable, especially if the belief is true.

However, what we presume makes racism wrong is that it involves making false judgments about people. It also involves value judgments about their worth as persons. A similar definition could be given of sexism, namely, having false beliefs about people or devaluing them because of their sex. It also involves power and oppression, for those groups that are devalued by racism are also likely to be treated accordingly.

Furthermore, racism and sexism are not the same as prejudice. Prejudice is making judgments or forming beliefs before knowing the truth about something or someone. These prejudgments might accidentally be correct beliefs. However, the negative connotation of the term *prejudice* indicates that these beliefs or judgments are formed without adequate information and are also mistaken. Moreover, prejudice in this context may also be a matter of judging an individual on the basis of judgments about the characteristics of a group to which he or she belongs. They are supposedly false generalizations. Thus, if I think that all people of a certain race or sex like to drink warm beer because I have seen some of that group do so, I am making a false generalization, one without adequate basis in the facts. Racism or sexism, while different from prejudice, may follow from prejudiced beliefs.

Knowing what racism is, we can then answer the question, What is wrong with racism? We believe racism, like sexism, is wrong because it is unjust or unfair. It is also wrong because it is harmful to people. The racist or sexist treats people of a particular race or sex differently and less well simply because of their race or sex.

Yet we have not gotten to the root of what is wrong with racism or sexism. Suppose that our views about members of a group are not based on prejudice but on an objective factual assessment about the group. For example, if men differ from women in significant ways—and surely they do—then is this not a sufficient reason to treat them differently? There is a moral principle that can be used to help us think about this issue. It is called the *principle of equality*. The general idea embodied in this principle is that we should treat equals equally and we may treat unequals unequally. In analyzing this principle we will be able to clarify what is meant by discrimination, and whether or why it is morally objectionable. We will also be able to consider what is meant by affirmative action or reverse discrimination, and analyze the arguments for and against it.

The Principle of Equality

The principle of equality can be formulated in various ways. Consider the following formulation:

It is unjust to treat people differently in ways that deny to some of them significant social benefits unless we can show that there is a difference between them that is relevant to the differential treatment.

To understand the meaning of this principle, we will focus on the emphasized parts of it.

Justice

First we notice that the principle is a principle of justice. It tells us that certain actions or practices that treat people unequally are unjust, and others presumably are just. To understand this principle fully, we would need to explore further the concept of justice. Here we do so only briefly. (Further treatment of the nature of justice occurs in Chapter 12.) Consider, for instance, our symbols of justice. Outside the Supreme Court in Washington, D.C., is a statue of a woman. She is blindfolded and holds a scale in one hand. The idea of the blindfold is that justice is blind—in other words, it is not biased. It does not favor one person over another on the basis of irrelevant characteristics. The same laws are supposed to apply to all equally. The scale indicates that justice may involve not equality but proportionality. It requires that treatment of persons be according to what is due them on some grounds. Therefore, it requires that there be valid reasons for differential treatment.

Social Benefits and Harms

We are not required to justify treating people differently from others in every case. For example, I may give personal favors to my friends or family and not to others without having to give a reason. However, sometimes social policy effectively treats people differently in ways that penalize or harm some and benefit others. This harm can be obvious or it can be subtle. In addition, there is a difference between primary racism or sexism and secondary racism or sexism.[24] In primary racism or sexism, people are singled out and directly penalized simply because they are a member of a particular race or sex, as when they are denied school admissions or promotions just because of this characteristic. In secondary racism or sexism, criteria for benefit or harm are used that do not directly apply to members of particular groups, but only indirectly affect them. Thus, the policy "last hired, first fired" is likely to have such an effect. Such policies may be allowed in the workplace or other social settings, policies that may seem harmless but actually have a harmful effect on certain groups. What we now label "sexual harassment" is an example of harmful discriminatory practices. This aspect of the principle of equality, then, directs us to consider the ways in which social benefits and penalties or harms sometimes occur for reasons that are not justified.

Proof

The principle states that we must show, or prove, that certain differences exist that justify treating people differently in socially significant ways. The principle can be stronger or weaker, depending on the kind of proof of differences required by it. It is not acceptable to treat people on the basis of differences that we only think or suspect exist. Scientific studies of sex differences, for example, must be provided to show that certain sex differences actually exist.

Real Differences

The principle of equality requires that we show or prove that actual differences exist between the people that we would treat differently. Many sex differences are obvious and others that are not obvious have been confirmed by empirical studies, such as differences in metabolism rate, strength

and size, hearing acuity, shoulder structure, and disease susceptibility. However, it is unlikely that these differences would be relevant for any differential social treatment. Those that would be relevant are differences such as type of intellectual ability, aggressiveness, or nurturing capacity.

We might look to scientific studies of sex differences to help us determine whether any such possibly relevant sex differences exist. Women have been found to do better on tests that measure verbal speed and men to do better on being able to imagine what an object would look like if it were rotated. It has recently been discovered that men and women use different parts of their brains to do the same tasks. For example, to recognize whether nonsense words rhyme, men used a tiny area in the front left side of the brain, while women used a comparable section of the right side.[25] Whether this difference has a wider significance for different types of intelligence is a matter of some debate. So also are the studies of aggressiveness. Testosterone has been shown to increase size and strength, but whether it also makes males more aggressive than females is disputed. This is not only because of the difficulties we have in tracing physical causation, but also because of our uncertainty about just what we mean by aggressiveness.

However, most studies that examine supposed male and female differences also look at males and females after they have been socialized. Thus, it is not surprising that they find the differences that they do. Suppose that a study found that little girls play with dolls and make block enclosures while little boys prefer trucks and use the blocks to build imaginary adventure settings. Would this necessarily mean there is some innate difference that is the cause of this? If there were such differences and if they were innate, this may be relevant to how we would structure education and some aspects of society. We might prefer women for the job of nurse or early child care provider, for example. We might provide women but not men with paid child care leave.[26]

However, if we cannot prove that these or any such characteristics are by nature rather than by nurture, then we are left with the following type of problem. Suppose that for many years we have thought that females had lesser mathematical abilities than males. Thus, in our educational practices we would not expect females to have these abilities, and teachers would tend to treat their male and female mathematics students differently. For instance, in a 1987 study, female students in the fourth through seventh grades who ranked high in mathematics were found to be "less likely to be assigned to high-ability groups by their teachers than were males with comparable scores."[27] Suppose that at a later point we tested people on mathematical ability and found a difference between the male and female scores. Would that mean we could justly prefer one group over the other for positions and jobs that required this skill? It would seem that if we wanted the jobs done well, we should do this. But suppose also that these jobs were the highest-paying and had the greatest esteem and power connected with them. Socialization has contributed to people's being more or less well qualified for valued positions like these in society. We should consider whether our social institutions perpetuate socially induced disadvantages. Using the principle of equality, we could rightly criticize such a system of reward for socially developed skills as unfair because first it causes certain traits in people, and then it penalizes them for having those traits!

Relevant Differences

The principle of equality requires more than showing that there are differences between people that are real and not just socially learned differences before we are justified in treating them differently. It also requires that the differences must be relevant. This is the idea embodied in the BFOQ of the 1964 Civil Rights Act mentioned earlier. For example, if it could be shown that women were by nature better at bricklaying than men, then this would be a "real" difference between them. Although we might then be justified in preferring women for the job of brick-

layer, we would not be justified in using this difference to prefer women for the job of airline pilot. On the other hand, if men and women think differently and if certain jobs require these particular thinking skills, then according to the principle of equality we may well prefer those with these skills for the jobs.

The relevance of a talent or characteristic or skill to a job is not an easy matter to determine. For example, is upper body strength an essential skill for the job of firefighter or police officer? Try debating this one with a friend. In answering this question, it would be useful to determine what kinds of things firefighters usually have to do, what their equipment is like, and so forth. Similarly, with the job of police officer we might ask how much physical strength is required and how important are other physical or psychological skills or traits. And is being an African American or Asian or female an essential qualification for a position as university teacher of courses in black studies or Asian or women's studies? It may not be an essential qualification, but some people argue that this does help qualify a person because she or he is more likely to understand the issues and problems with which the course deals. Nevertheless, this view has not gone unchallenged.

In addition to determining what characteristics or skills are relevant to a particular position, we must be able to assess adequately whether particular persons possess these characteristics or skills. Designing tests to assess this presents a difficulty. Prejudice may play a role in such assessments. For instance, how do we know whether someone works well with people or has sufficient knowledge of the issues that ought to be treated in a women's studies course? This raises another issue. Should or must we always test or judge people as individuals, or is it ever permissible to judge an individual as a member of a particular group? The principle of equality seems better designed for evaluating differential group treatment than differential treatment of individuals. This is just one issue that can be raised to challenge the principle of equality.

Challenges to the Principle

The first problem this principle faces stems from the fact that those group differences that are both real and relevant to some differential treatment are often, if not always, *average* differences. In other words, a characteristic may be typical of a group of people, but it may not belong to every member of the group. Consider height. Men are typically taller than women. Nevertheless, some women are taller than some men. Even if women were typically more nurturing than men, it would still be likely or at least possible that some men would be more nurturing than some women. Thus, it would seem that we ought to consider what characteristics an individual has rather than what is typical of the group to which he or she belongs. This would only seem to be fair or just. What, then, of the principle of equality as an adequate or usable principle of justice? It would seem to require us to do unfair things—specifically, to treat people as members of a group rather than as individuals.

Are we ever justified in treating someone differently because of her membership in a group and because of that group's typical characteristics—even if that person does not possess those characteristics? We do this in some cases, and presumably think that it is not unjust. Consider our treatment of people as members of an age group, say, for purposes of driving or voting. We have rules that require that a person must be at least fifteen years old to obtain a driver's permit or license. But is it not true that some individuals who are fourteen would be better drivers than some individuals who are eighteen? Yet we judge them on the basis of a group characteristic rather than their individual abilities. Similarly, in the United States we require that persons be eighteen years of age before they can vote. However, some persons who are less than eighteen would be more intelligent voters than some over eighteen. Is it not unjust to treat persons differently simply because of their age group rather than on the basis of their own individual characteristics and abilities?

Consider possibilities for determining when treating people as members of a group is unfair or wrong and when it is justified. Take our two examples. If an individual is well qualified to drive, but not yet fifteen or sixteen, then she has only to wait one year. This causes no great harm to her. Nor is any judgment made about her natural abilities. Even those fifteen and older have to take a test on which they are judged as individuals and not just as members of a group. Furthermore, suppose that we tried to judge people as individuals for the purposes of voting. We would need to develop a test of "intelligent voting ability." Can you imagine what political and social dynamite this testing would be? The cost to our democracy of instituting such a policy would be too great, while the cost to the individual to be judged as a member of an age group and wait a couple years to vote is minimal. Thus, this practice does not seem unduly unfair.

However, if real and relevant sex differences existed, and if we treated all members of one sex alike on the basis of some characteristic typical of their group rather than on the basis of their characteristics as individuals, this would involve both significant costs and significant unfairness. It would be of great social cost to society not to consider applicants or candidates because of their sex; these individuals might otherwise make great contributions to society. In addition, those who are denied consideration could rightly complain that it was unfair to deny them a chance at a position for which they qualified, something that would also affect them their whole lives. Thus, we could argue that the ideal of the principle of equality is generally valid, but that it would need to be supplemented by considerations concerning when it would be permissible to judge a person as a member of a group.

The second challenge to the principle of equality, or to its application, can be found in the debates over *preferential treatment* programs. Could not those people who support these programs claim that past discrimination was, in fact, a relevant difference between groups of people and that we would thus be justified in treating people differently on this basis? Preferential treatments would be designed to benefit those who are members of groups that have been discriminated against in the past. We will look shortly at the various forms of affirmative action and the arguments for and against them. It is useful here, however, to note the way in which the principle of equality might be used to justify some of these programs. The claim would be that being a member of a group was a sufficient reason to treat someone in a special way. Would we need to show that every member of that group was in some way harmed or affected by past discrimination? Some individual members of particular groups would not obviously have been harmed by past discrimination. However, we should also be aware of the subtle ways in which group or community membership affects a person and the subtle ways in which they might thus be harmed by it. On the other hand, the attempt to use the principle of equality to justify preferential treatment of members of certain groups would contradict the aspect of the principle of equality that requires that the differences justifying differential treatment were real—in other words, caused by nature rather than by nurture—as well as significant.

The third problem users of the principle of equality must address concerns the equality–inequality dilemma. We can exemplify this by using sex or gender differences, but it could also be applied to cultural differences. Women have sought equality with men in the workplace, education, and public life generally. At the same time, they remain the primary child care providers, placing them at an inevitable disadvantage in terms of advancement in professions and so forth. Some feminists have argued that the liberal notion of equality can be detrimental to women.[28] Rather than think of women as similar to men, or use only a formal notion of equality devoid of content, some feminists argue for a more concrete notion of a person.[29] Thus, differences between males and females in such areas as parental responsibilities would be relevant to the justness of requirements for professional advancement.

Issues of multiculturalism also could be raised here. (See the article by Lawrence Blum in this chapter.) Sometimes a person identifies him- or herself more by ethnic background than by race. "Whereas race is used for socially marking groups based on physical differences, ethnicity allows for a broader range of affiliation, based for example on shared language, shared place of origin, or shared religion."[30] We live in a complex society in which there are many forms of cultural expression and heritage. To what extent should this cultural heritage be acknowledged and encouraged? Problems arise, for example, in education and its content as in debates about how to present history to young children and what to include in literary canons. Obviously, this is an area that raises many issues for heated debate. However, keep in mind that there probably ought to be some balance between equal treatment under the law and basic civility toward all on the one hand, and acknowledging our differences and respecting the contributions that we all make because of the ways in which we differ on the other.

Affirmative Action and Preferential Treatment

As mentioned earlier in the summary of civil rights legislation, the use of the term *affirmative action* and the policy itself originated more than three decades ago. Disputes about the justification of these practices continue, however. The first thing to note about affirmative action is that it comes in many forms. The idea suggested by the term is that to remedy certain injustices we need to do more than follow the negative requirement "Don't discriminate" or "Stop discriminating." The basic argument given for doing something more is usually that the other way will not or has not worked. Psychological reasons may be cited, for example, that discrimination and prejudice are so ingrained in people that they cannot help discriminating and do not even recognize when they are being discriminatory or prejudiced. Social and political reasons can also be given, for example, that the discrimination is institutionalized. Many rules and practices have a built-in discriminatory impact, such as the discriminatory result of the seniority system. (See the selection from Robert Fullinwider included here.) The only way to change things, the argument goes, is to do something more positive.

But what are we to do? There are many possibilities. One is to make a greater positive effort to find qualified persons. Thus in hiring, a company might place ads in minority newspapers. In college admissions, counselors might be sent to schools with heavy student populations of underrepresented minority groups, or invite the students to campus, or give them special invitations to apply. Once the pool is enlarged, then all in the pool would be judged by the same criteria, and no special preferences would be given on the basis of race or sex.

Other versions of affirmative action involve what has come to be known as *preferences*. Preference or some special favoring or a plus factor could be given to minority group members or women who were equally well qualified with the other finalists to give them some edge. Preference may also be given for minority group members or women who were somewhat less well qualified than other applicants. In either case it is clear that determining equality of qualification is in itself a problem. One reason for this is that applicants for a position that has several qualifications are usually stronger on some qualifications and weaker on others. Another is the difficulty of deciding just what qualifications are necessary or important for some position. Although those people who support and oppose preferences seem to imply that it is an easy matter to determine this, it is not at all that simple.

Other forms of affirmative action also exist. For example, companies or institutions may establish goals and quotas to be achieved for increasing minority or female representation. *Goals* are usually thought of as ideals that we aim for but are not absolutely required to reach. Goals can be formulated in terms of percentages or numbers. As of now, for example, U.S. federal contractors and all institutions with fifty or more employees and who receive federal funds of $50,000 or more must adopt affirmative action

plans. These plans have sometimes involved setting goals for increasing the number of underrepresented minority members and women so that it might more closely reflect their percentage in the local labor pool. Companies might have specific recruiting plans for reaching their goals. These plans could, but would not necessarily, involve preferential treatments. *Quotas,* in contrast, are usually fixed percentages or numbers that a company intends to actually reach. Thus, a university or professional school might set aside a fixed number of slots for its incoming first-year class that would be for certain minority group members (note the Bakke and Weber cases mentioned earlier). The institution would fill these positions even if this meant admitting persons with lesser overall scores or points in the assessment system.

In summary, the following types of affirmative action can be specified:

1. Enlarging the pool of applicants, then hiring on the basis of competence.
2. Giving preferences among equally qualified applicants.
3. Giving preferences for less qualified applicants.
4. Setting goals or ideal numbers for which to aim; these need not involve preferences.
5. Setting quotas or fixed numbers to actually attain; these usually do involve preferences.

The next question, then, to ask ourselves is, Are these practices good or bad, justified or unjustified? All of them, or some of them, or none of them? In any discussion of affirmative action, it is important to specify what kind of practice one favors or opposes. Let us examine the arguments for and against the various types of affirmative action in terms of the reasons given to support them. These again can be easily divided into consequentialist and nonconsequentialist types of arguments.

Consequentialist Considerations

Arguments both for and against various affirmative action programs have relied on consequentialist considerations for their justification. These considerations are broadly utilitarian in nature. The question is whether such programs do more good than harm or more harm than good. Those people who argue in favor of these programs urge the following sorts of considerations: These programs benefit us all. We live in a multiracial society and benefit from mutual respect and harmony. We all bring diverse backgrounds to our employment and educational institutions, and we all benefit from the contributions of people who have a variety of diverse perspectives. Our law schools should have representation from all of the people who need adequate representation in society. We need to break the vicious circle of discrimination, disadvantage, and inequality. Past discrimination has put women and some minority group members at a continuing disadvantage. Unless something is done, they will never be able to compete on an equal basis or to have an equal chance or equal opportunity. Family plays a crucial role in what chances a child has.[31] To put it simply, low family income leads to poorer education for children, which leads to lower-paying jobs, which leads to low family income, and so on and so on. Affirmative action is one way to break the vicious circle of disadvantage. Children need role models to look up to. They need to know that certain types of achievement and participation are possible for them. Otherwise, they will not have hope and not work to be what they can become. Without affirmative action programs, supporters argue, things are not likely to change. Discrimination is so entrenched that drastic measures are needed to overcome it. The statistics show that while some progress has been made, a great gap continues in the major indicators of success between members of certain minority groups and women and others in the society. These are just some of the good results from affirmative action that its supporters might cite.

Those people who argue against affirmative action on consequentialist grounds believe that the programs do not work or do more harm than good. They cite statistics showing that these pro-grams have benefited middle-class African Americans, for example, but not the lower class. "The most disadvantaged black people are not in a position to benefit from preferential admission."[32] Unless affirmative action admissions programs are accompanied by other aid, both financial and tutorial, they are often useless or wasted. Some critics point out that lawsuits filed under the 1964 Civil Rights Act have done more than affirmative action to increase the percentage of blacks in various white collar positions.[33] There is also the likelihood of stigma attached to those who have been admitted or hired through affirmative action programs. This can be debilitating to those who are chosen on this basis. Black neoconservatives, for example, argue that quotas and racially weighted tests "have psychologically handicapped blacks by making them dependent on racial-preference programs rather than their own hard work."[34] Those who oppose affirmative action programs also cite the increased racial tension that they believe results from these programs: in effect, a white male backlash against women and members of minority groups.

The key to evaluating these consequentialist arguments both for and against affirmative action is in examining the validity of their assessments and predictions. What, in fact, have college admissions affirmative action programs achieved? Have they achieved little because they benefit those who least need it and might have succeeded without them, or have they actually brought more disadvantaged into the system and into better and higher-paying jobs, thus helping break the vicious circle? Have they increased racial harmony by increasing diversity in the workforce and in various communities, or have they only led to increasing racial tensions? These are difficult matters to assess. Here is another place where ethical judgments depend on empirical information drawn from the various sciences or other disciplines. The consequentialist argument for affirmative action programs will succeed if it can be shown that there is no better way to achieve the goods the programs are designed to achieve and that the good done by these affirmative action programs, or at least some of them, outweighs any harm they cause, including some racial tension and some misplaced awards. The consequentialist argument against affirmative action programs will succeed if it can be shown that there are better ways to achieve the same good ends, or that the harm that they create outweighs the good achieved by them.

Nonconsequentialist Considerations

However, not all arguments regarding affirmative action programs are based on appeals to consequences. Some arguments appeal to considerations of justice. For instance, some people argue for affirmative action programs on the grounds that they provide justice, a way of making compensation for past wrongs done to members of certain groups. People have been harmed and wronged by past discrimination, and we now need to make up for that by benefiting them, by giving them preferential treatment. However, it is difficult to know how preferential treatment can right a past wrong. We may think of it as undoing the past harm done. Then we find that it is often difficult to undo the harm. How does one really prevent or erase results such as the loss of self-esteem and confidence in the minority child who asks, "Mom, am I as good as the white kid?" or in the little girl who says, "I can't do that; I'm a girl."[35] This interpretation of making compensation then becomes a matter of producing good consequences or eliminating bad ones. It is a matter of trying to change the results of past wrongs. Thus, if making compensation is to be a nonconsequentialist reason, it must involve a different sense of righting a wrong, a sense of justice being done in itself whether or not it makes any difference in the outcome.

Some people also argue against affirmative action on grounds of its injustice. They appeal to the principle of equality, arguing that race and sex are irrelevant characteristics. Just as it was wrong in the past to use these characteristics to deny people equal chances, so it is also wrong in the present, even if it is used this time to give them preferences. Race and sex are not differences that should count in treating people differently to deny some benefits and to grant them to others. Preferences for some also mean denial to others. For this reason preferential treatment programs have sometimes been labeled *reverse discrimination*. Moreover, opponents of affirmative action criticize the use of compensatory justice arguments. In a valid use of the principles of compensatory justice, they might argue, those and only those wronged should be compensated, and those and only those responsible for the wrong should be made to pay. But some programs of affirmative action have actually compensated people regardless of whether they themselves have been harmed by past discriminatory practices. They have also required that some people pay who have not been responsible for the past discrimination. Those who lose out in affirmative action programs, they argue, may not have ever been guilty of discrimination or may not have wronged anyone.

The arguments for affirmative action based on considerations of justice will succeed only if those people who make them can also make a case for the justice of the programs, that they do in fact compensate those who have been wronged, even if they have been affected by discrimination in ways that are not immediately obvious, and it is not unjust if other people have to pay. Supporters may cite the fact that those who lose out are not badly harmed for they have other opportunities and are not demeaned by their loss. Though they have not intentionally wronged anyone, they have likely been the beneficiaries of past discrimination.

The arguments against affirmative action based on considerations of justice will succeed only if they can respond to these claims and make the principle of equality work for their case. They may cite the matter of consistency in applying the principle, for example. But if they rely primarily on the harms done by continuing to use race or sex as a characteristic that grounds differential treatment, they will be appealing to a consequentialist consideration and must be judged on that basis. To answer this question, the more basic issues of the moral status of considerations of justice would need to be addressed. Further treatment of justice in this text occur in Chapters 12 and 13.

In the readings included in this chapter, Lawrence Blum discusses the meaning and value of multiculturalism, and Lisa Newton and Robert Fullinwider disagree over whether affirmative action is a justifiable social practice.

Notes

1. Reported on the CBS "Evening News," May 24, 1993, and in the *New York Times,* May 25, 1993, A6.
2. These are examples of what Mary Rowe calls "micro-inequities, . . . tiny, damaging characteristics of an environment." "Barriers to Equality: The Power of Subtle Discrimination to Maintain Unequal Opportunity," in *Social Ethics,* 4th ed., Thomas Mappes and Jane Zembaty (Eds.) (New York: McGraw-Hill, 1992), 296–305.
3. Reported on CNN, May 24, 1993.
4. Reported in the *San Francisco Chronicle,* March 28, 1993, A1 and A6.
5. Ibid., A6.
6. *Statistical Abstracts of the United States, 1995.* U.S. Department of Commerce, Bureau of the Census. U.S. Government Printing Office, p. 411, table No. 649.
7. *San Francisco Chronicle* (June 24, 1996), pp. B1–B4. One woman was actually on the list but was not pictured.
8. Victor R. Fuchs, "Sex Differences in Economic Well-Being," *Science* 232 (April 25, 1986): 459. Contributing to this conclusion, Fuchs cites the increase in unmarried women who are dependent on their own income and caring for children. Their leisure and also access to goods declined.
9. From a study of wage trends by the Economic Policy Institute, Washington, D.C., as reported in the *San Francisco Chronicle,* Aug. 20, 1993, A4.
10. A recent analysis of the Bureau of Labor Statistics, reported in the *New York Times,* Sept. 2, 1992, A16.
11. Jennifer L. Hochschild, "Race, Class, Power, and Equal Opportunity," in *Equal Opportunity,* Norman E. Bowie (Ed.) (Boulder, CO: Westview, 1988), 76.
12. *Statistical Abstracts of the United States, 1995.* U.S. Department of Commerce, Bureau of the Census. U.S. Government Printing Office, p. 483, table No. 750. These figures were up for both groups since

1979. See discussion of the gap between rich and poor in Chapter 12.
13. *New York Times* (Sept. 17, 1996), p. A1. Bureau of the Census Report.
14. Hochschild, op. cit., pp. 78–79. See also *Statistics Record of Black America,* Carroll P. Horton and Jessie Carney (Eds.) (Detroit: Gale Research, 1990).
15. *New York Times* (June 11, 1996), p. A11.
16. James S. Kunen, "The End of Integration," *Time* (April 29, 1996), p. 39.
17. *New York Times* (Sept. 27, 1996), p. A11.
18. *New York Times* (Sept. 6, 1996), p. A8.
19. *New York Times* (Sept. 18, 1996).
20. This aspect of the bill confirmed the "disparate impact" notion of the 1971 U.S. Supreme Court ruling in *Griggs* v. *Duke Power Company,* which required companies to revise their business practices that perpetuated past discrimination. This was weakened by the Court's 1989 ruling in *Wards Cove Packing Co.* v. *Antonio,* which among other things put the burden of proof on the employee to show that the company did not have a good reason for some discriminatory business practice.
21. We could also cite legislation aimed against discrimination on the basis of age and the disabled: for example, the Age Discrimination Act (1967) and the Americans with Disabilities Act (1991).
22. These are African (Negroid), American Indian, Asian, Australian, European (Caucasoid or Caucasian), Indian, Melanesian, Micronesian, and Polynesian. *The World Book Encyclopedia* 16 (Chicago: World Book, 1981), 52–53.
23. Alaka Wali, "Multiculturalism: An Anthropological Perspective," *Report from the Institute for Philosophy and Public Policy,* vol. 12, no. 1 (Spring/Summer 1992), p. 7.
24. See Mary Ann Warren, "Secondary Sexism and Quota Hiring," *Philosophy and Public Affairs,* vol. 6, no. 3 (Spring 1977): 240–261.
25. Gina Kolata, "Men and Women Use Brain Differently, Study Discovers," *New York Times* (Feb. 16, 1995), p. A8.
26. It is interesting in this regard that the 1993 federal Family Leave Bill allows both men and women to take unpaid leave to take care of a sick child or other close relative without losing their jobs or their medical insurance.
27. M. T. Hallinan and A. B. Sorensen, *Sociological Education,* vol. 60, note 63 (1987), as reported in *Science* 237 (July 24, 1987): 350.
28. *New York Times* (February 16, 1995), pp. A1, 8.
29. Iris Marion Young, "Polity and Group Difference: A Critique of the Ideal of Universal Citizenship," in

Feminism and Political Theory, Sunstein Cass (Ed.) (Chicago: University of Chicago Press, 1990). Cited in an unpublished manuscript by Jennifer MacKinnon, "Rights and Responsibilities: A Reevaluation of Parental Leave and Child Care in the United States," Spring 1993.

30. Alaka Wali, "Multiculturalism," op. cit., p. 7.

31. See James Fishkin, *Justice, Equal Opportunity and the Family* (New Haven, CT: Yale University Press, 1983), for documentation and analysis.

32. Stephen Carter, *Reflections of an Affirmative Action Baby* (New York: Basic Books, 1991).

33. Professor Jonathan Leonard, cited in the *San Francisco Examiner,* Sept. 29, 1991.

34. *Time* (May 27, 1991): 23.

35. A parent's report.

Philosophy and the Values of a Multicultural Community

Lawrence A. Blum

Study Questions

1. In what two ways does Blum believe philosophy can contribute to the debate over cultural diversity in education?

2. What three distinct values does Blum believe are desirable in a multiracial, multicultural campus?

3. What does the author mean by "racism"? According to this definition, why are affirmative action programs, minority exclusiveness, and stereotyping not necessarily racist, according to Blum?

4. Are all forms of racism as he defines it equally wrong, according to Blum? Explain.

5. How does multiculturalism go beyond cultural pluralism, as Blum understands these practices?

6. What are some other difficulties regarding the definition of multiculturalism that Blum briefly mentions?

7. What is the difference between the approach to study of different cultures of multiculturalism and antiracism, according to Blum?

8. How is each a partial perspective, and how do they complement each other? How also can they be mutually supportive, according to Blum?

9. What more does a sense of genuine community involve, according to Blum?

10. Why does Blum believe that neither antiracism nor multiculturalism guarantees a sense of community and may, in fact, be divisive?

Many philosophers are wary about recent calls for greater cultural diversity in university curricula, especially demands that non-Western traditions and modes of thought be given significant recognition. Philosophy departments are often among the last to institute such changes and to join interdisciplinary efforts at implementing this diversity. But I will argue that attention to multiculturalism should be seen as a boon to philosophy.

Philosophy can come into the educational debate over cultural diversity in two places. One concerns philosophy as a specific intellectual discipline among others, and the way diversity is to be explained, justified, and incorporated within its courses. The other is philosophy as contributing to the overall

Lawrence A. Blum, "Philosophy and the Values of a Multicultural Community," *Teaching Philosophy, 14,* no. 2 (June 1991), pp. 127–134. Reprinted by permission of Philosophy Documentation Center, Bowling Green State University.

exploration of the issues of multiculturalism as they apply not only to course content but to the classroom and the university as multiracial and multicultural communities of learning. Important as the first is, we should not confine ourselves to a narrow disciplinary focus but should see philosophy as having its role to play in creating what the recent Carnegie Foundation Report "Campus Life: In Search of Community" expressed as a community which is, among other things, just, caring, open, and civil.[1] Taking this role seriously can also show how philosophy can expand to include issues of race, culture, and ethnicity into many courses in ethics, social, and political philosophy, and perhaps other areas of philosophy as well. I would like to begin such an exploration of philosophy and multicultural community today.

I will discuss three distinct values desirable in a multiracial, multicultural campus. They are: (1) opposition to racism, (2) multiculturalism, (3) sense of community, connection, or common humanity. These values are seldom clearly distinguished, and are often entirely run together, defeating clear thought about the real goals and possibilities of multicultural communities.[2] Failure to make these distinctions blinds us both to possible tensions among these distinct values and to the raising of the question of how best to realize them all so as to minimize that tension.

1. Opposition to Racism

The notion of "racism" is highly charged emotionally, and the term is used in contemporary parlance in a number of ways. There has been a well-documented increase in what are unquestionably racist incidents on campus, but also frequent yet more controversial *charges* of racism for any number of remarks and behavior. I want to suggest that the core meaning of "racism" is connected with the *domination or victimization* of some groups by others, and with the notion of the subordinate groups as inferior or less worthy than the dominant group. I will call an act or reaction "racist" if it expresses a notion of a member of a different racial group as being inferior.[3]

On this view the following phenomena, often called "racist" by many students, are not (necessarily, or usually) racist: (1) Departure from pure meritocratic justice: Affirmative action programs which prefer a minority student with lower test scores to a Caucasian student with higher ones. (2) Minority exclusiveness: Black students sitting together in the college dining room, thereby making it uncomfort-

able for whites to join them. (3) Stereotyping: A white student's unthinkingly assuming that a Latino student is from a lower socio-economic background than his own.

None of these actions express beliefs of superiority toward other groups; this is why they should not (I suggest) be called "racist." This does not mean that these actions and policies cannot be criticized as violating some other moral value appropriate to multiracial communities, especially college communities. My point is precisely that there are several values relevant to a multiracial community—values which are distinct from one another.

While all racism is bad, on the definition of racism as dominance-attitude, not all manifestations of racism are *equally* bad. To oversimplify a complex issue here, racist attitudes which lend support to an existing structure of racism in which the possessor of the racist attitude is a member of a dominant group are worse than racist attitudes of a member of a subordinate group toward a member of a dominant group, for the latter do not support an existing structure of domination. For example, beliefs and doctrines of Caucasian inferiority to people of color are genuinely racist and worthy of condemnation. Yet these manifestations of racism toward whites are not *as* bad, dangerous, or condemnable as doctrines of white superiority to people of color (or attitudes expressing those doctrines), since the latter, and not the former, play a role in supporting actual structures of domination. The source of the value asymmetry here is that racism supporting existing subordination invokes and reinforces the social weight of this structure of dominance, bringing it down against its victim, and thus (other things being equal) more deeply shames and harms its victim than does subordinate-to-dominant racism, which does not carry that social and historical resonance. (The different force of the formally similar expressions "honkie" and "nigger" illustrates this point.)[4]

This asymmetry helps clarify the frequent mutual incomprehension between white and non-white students concerning racism. Many black students tend to think of racism solely as a phenomenon of whites against blacks or other non-whites. White students by contrast tend to equate—and condemn equally—all attitudes of racial insult, exclusion, or differentiation, by any racial group toward any other.

Aside from the point made earlier that some of what these white students call "racism" is not actually racism (according to my account), each group holds part of the truth. The non-white students see that the core and most socially dangerous phenomenon of racism is the actual, historical domination or victimization of one group by another, and attitudes of superiority (whether conscious or not) which directly support that domination. Many white students fail entirely to see this, not acknowledging—or not acknowledging the significance of—continuing subordinate status (in the United States) of people of color.

The white students, on the other hand, are correct to see clearly that *all* manifestations of racial contempt and superiority are worthy of condemnation, precisely because they are the *sorts* of attitudes which do underpin racial subordination. The non-white students' attitude has the effect of entirely letting non-whites off the hook for objectionable attitudes of superiority or contempt toward other groups.[5]

To state briefly what is involved in learning to oppose racism, and in embodying that value in an educational community: There is a philosophical component involved in understanding why racism is wrong, involving among other things learning how racism damages its victims; but learning the psychological, sociological, economic, and historical dynamics of racism and of resistance to it are essential as well. Public condemnation of racism on the campus is also essential.

2. Multiculturalism

Like "racism," this is a term of great currency and imprecise usage. I will use it to encompass the following two components: (a) understanding and valuing one's own cultural heritage, and (b) having respect for and interest in the cultural heritage of members of groups other than one's own. Note that condition (b) takes multiculturalism beyond what is often referred to as "cultural pluralism"—a situation in which different groups are each turned inward into their own group, valuing and learning about their own cultural heritage but being indifferent to that of others. While the idea of cultural pluralism perhaps contains the notion of tolerance for and recognition of the right of others to pursue their own cultural exploration and learning, "multiculturalism" as I am understanding it goes beyond this to encompass a positive interest in and respect for other cultures.

Often the initial association with "cultural diversity" or "multiculturalism"—for example when im-

plying a policy to diversify the curriculum—is as (1) giving non-Caucasian students an understanding of and validation of their own cultural heritages (and thereby also broadening the sense of inclusion in the university's intellectual enterprise), and (2) expanding Caucasian students' intellectual horizons and reducing their ethnocentrism. Yet these two albeit crucial goals do not comprise the whole of what I mean by "multiculturalism." For in addition, my definition implies that members of *every* group (whites and non-whites alike) be involved in overcoming their own ethnocentrism, one possible curricular implication being that every student ought to study, say, two cultures other than her own.

Bypassing for this short presentation further difficulties regarding the definition of multiculturalism (e.g., what constitutes a "culture," which cultures should count for curricular and noncurricular attention, how respect for different cultures is consistent with criticism of them), I want to focus on how what I have called *multiculturalism* is a distinct value from what I have called *opposition to racism*, yet how both are essential in a multiracial community. First, each involves looking at the same group through distinct lenses. From the viewpoint of anti-racism, groups are divided into dominant and subordinate. From an anti-racist perspective, to study for example Native Americans or African Americans involves looking at the way these groups have been oppressed, undermined, damaged, and the like by white America, at the beliefs and policies which have supported this mistreatment, and at the subordinate group's resistance to this subordination. It is to study subordinate groups primarily in their role as victims and resisters.

By contrast, to learn about cultural groups from a multicultural perspective involves studying the group's customs, rituals, language, systems of thought and religion, forms of cultural expression, accomplishments and contributions to the wider societies of which they are a part, and the like. The contrast resides not so much in distinct aspects of the groups in question focused on by the multicultural *versus* the anti-racist perspective; for subordinate groups' forms of cultural expressions are often so intimately bound up with their oppressed status and history that no simple delineation is possible. (Consider, for example, Afro-American music, Jewish humor.) The point is that both anti-racism and multiculturalism bring an analytical perspective on the study of cultural groups that the other lacks.

"Multiculturalism" is the preferred rubric of many educators.[6] But multiculturalism without anti-racism projects a world (or society) of cultural groups, each with its own way of life, forms of cultural expression, accomplishments and the like, all existing on something like an equal level. While this sense of equality—to teach and learn informed respect for every culture—may be appropriately (if only roughly) seen as an appropriate aspiration taken purely by itself, it obscures the fact that in our world and our society some of these cultures have been subordinated, undermined, and mistreated by other ones. It is as if one could just affirm that each group is equal, without taking into account the fact that in the world they are not treated as equal; it is this lack of equality that the anti-racist perspective keeps before us.

At the same time, the anti-racist perspective is also by itself incomplete. First, seeing a culture in terms of its victimization—or even its victimization and its resistance to that victimization—is an only partial perspective on that culture, omitting (or omitting important dimensions of) cultural expression and accomplishment. Second, the value perspective of anti-racism is itself only partial. To see that racism is wrong—and to firmly believe that it is wrong—is not the same as, and does not even require, actually having a positive appreciation for the culture of the subordinate group. In fact it is possible to be genuinely anti-racist while knowing little about the cultures of different groups that have been discriminated against. For example, many European, Christian, rescuers of Jews during the Nazi occupation expressed a fully anti-racist outlook in attempting their noble and dangerous rescue efforts; but few had genuine respect for Jews as a distinct cultural/religious group.[7]

While I have been arguing for the distinctness of anti-racism and multiculturalism as goals and values, they are also, or can be, mutually supportive. Learning to value a different culture can certainly help to bring home to a student the wrongness of that culture's mistreatment (even if the student were already in agreement on the abstract point that racism is wrong). It can awaken students for whom opposition to racism does not run very deep to the humanity of others—in its particular manifestation in the culture being studied. Both anti-racism and multiculturalism involve taking those outside one's own group seriously. Though they do so in different ways, both have the power to combat egoism and ethnocentrism.

3. Sense of Community, Connection, or Common Humanity

In addition to exemplifying the values of opposition to racism and multiculturalism, one also wants the college community to constitute and to foster a cross-racial sense of connection or community. At first glance, this might not seem a distinct value. For isn't opposition to racism grounded in a sense of common humanity? Isn't racism wrong because it violates that common humanity? And doesn't the mutual respect involved in multiculturalism also express a sense of community?

But a sense of (cross-racial) community is, I want to argue, a distinct value. For a genuinely anti-racist individual does not necessarily have a sense of connection to those of another race, even while she or he regards those others as equals. For this sense of community can be negated not only by regarding others as *inferior* but simply by experiencing them as "other," as apart from, distant from, oneself, as persons one does not feel comfortable with because they are not members of one's own group.

It seems clear that many college students do not feel a genuine or full sense of cross-racial community, even though these same students are not racist in the sense defined here; they do not regard the other groups as inferior. Yet to be a genuine *community,* and not just a collection of people seeing each other as equals, a learning community must embody more than anti-racism.

There are ways of teaching and learning about racism which may fail to create, or even to hinder, a cross-racial sense of community. These ways reinforce a "we/they" consciousness in both the white and the non-white students; for example, never mentioning whites who stood against racism but projecting simply a (not really incorrect, but only partial) image of racism as "white oppressing black." It is undoubtedly true that learning about racism and why it is wrong has the inherent potentiality to undermine or strain this sense of connection. And classes on this subject might find ways within the pedagogical structure of the class to meliorate that effect—for example by having cross-racial groups work on class projects. Ultimately, however, such classes are necessary to help reconstruct or create a sense of community at a more informed level. Without a firm anti-racist component, any sense of cross-racial community will fail to involve true equals.

A sense of (cross-racial) connection is distinct from multiculturalism as well, even though multiculturalism teaches respect for others. The more minimal condition of valuing one's own culture and tradition goes nowhere toward creating a sense of cross-racial community, and its inward-turning can serve to undermine that connection (though at the same time for some minority students this aspect of multiculturalism might be a necessary condition for their being able to experience a sense of connection with white students—from a base of cultural self-respect).

Even including the second condition of multiculturalism (respect for other cultures) does not guarantee a sense of community. For there are ways of presenting other cultures which can simultaneously promote a sense of respect yet of distance from members of that culture—for example placing too much emphasis on the self-enclosed, self-coherent, and differentness of each culture. Such a presentation would be *intellectually* deficient in not recognizing the multiplicity within each culture, its changes over time, its influences from other cultures, and (in most cases) values or elements it shares with other cultures. But my point here is that this intellectual error also has the unfortunate moral effect of helping to create or perpetuate among students a sense of distance between members of different cultures.

Recognizing these potentially divisive or distancing effects of both anti-racism and multiculturalism has been one source of opposition to both of them. "Why don't we just emphasize commonalities among our students, and reinforce them through a curriculum emphasizing a common Western and national tradition," say some (for example, occasionally in the "Point of View" column of the *Chronicle of Higher Education*). But ignoring both racism and genuinely culturally distinct sources of identity will not make these go away. Moreover, as I have tried to argue, both anti-racism and multiculturalism represent distinct and worthy goals, which an educational community must uphold and institutionalize. Any sense of community in the absence of a recognition of these values will in any case be a false and deceptive one.

What is necessary, I suggest, is to take seriously the three distinct goals, to recognize that it may not always be possible to realize all simultaneously, but to search for ways—in the curriculum, the classroom, and the organization of life on campus—to minimize the conflict among them, and to teach those values in ways that do mutually enhance one another to the greatest extent possible.

What I have presented here is a mere sketch of a nest of complex philosophical and value issues concerning multi-racial college classrooms and communities. Philosophy should not cede the discussion of these issues to social scientists, historians, and literature teachers, as we have tended to do. There is clarificatory and constructive work to be done here to which philosophy brings a necessary perspective. That work needs to be done in various courses in moral, social, and political philosophy, as well as in contributions to campus-wide debate.

Notes

1. Carnegie Foundation for the Advancement of Teaching, *Campus Life: In Search of Community* (1990).

2. For example, the excellent Carnegie study mentioned above takes up racial/cultural issues primarily in its "A Just Community" chapter, misleadingly implying a conceptual unity to the distinct issues of access and retention, ignorance of groups and traditions other than one's own, outright discrimination, and minority in-group exclusiveness.

3. To simplify, I will continue to use the language of "dominant/subordinate," though this bypasses not insignificant differences among the terms "subordination," "victimization," "exploitation," "oppression," being "dominated," being "discriminated against," being "mistreated," being an "object of injustice"—all of which terms are used in this context.

4. This too-brief account of moral asymmetries in manifestations of racism is spelled out in my (unpublished) talk in the "Ethics and Society" Lecture Series, Stanford University, April 1990.

5. Note that the forgoing analysis does not concern racism of one subordinate or vulnerable group toward another—e.g., Koreans toward blacks, or blacks toward Jews. This complex matter is discussed in the manuscript mentioned in the previous footnote.

6. Cf. the excellent article defending multicultural education, but in distinction from and even denial of the anti-racist perspective by Diane Ravitch, "Diversity and Democracy: Multicultural Education in America," *American Educator* (Spring 1990).

7. On this see the L. Blum "Altruism and the Moral Value of Rescue: Resisting Persecution, Racism, and Genocide," in L. Baron, L. Blum, D. Krebs, P. Oliner, S. Oliner and Z. Smolenska, *Embracing the Other: Philosophical, Psychological, and Historical Perspectives on Altruism* (New York: NYU Press, 1992).

Reverse Discrimination as Unjustified

Lisa Newton

Study Questions

1. How are justice, the rule of law, and citizenship related in the view of Aristotle?

2. What did this ideal of citizenship look like when it became a moral ideal, according to Newton?

3. How does Newton believe that preferential treatment undermines justice?

4. What practical problems does she envision with regard to favoring members of minority groups in order to make restitution to them for past discrimination?

5. What problems does she envision for determining when restitution is enough?

6. Does she believe that individuals or groups can be said to have rights that are not recognized by the law? How does this relate to the issue of restitution through preferential treatment?

I have heard it argued that "simple justice" requires that we favor women and blacks in employment and educational opportunities, since women and blacks were "unjustly" excluded from such opportunities for so many years in the not so distant past. It is a strange argument, an example of a possible implication of a true proposition advanced to dispute the proposition itself, like an octopus absentmindedly slicing off his head with a stray tentacle. A fatal confusion underlies this argument, a confusion fundamentally relevant to our understanding of the notion of the rule of law.

Two senses of justice and equality are involved in this confusion. The root notion of justice, progenitor of the other, is the one that Aristotle (*Nichomachean Ethics* 5.6; Politics 1.2; 3.1) assumes to be the foundation and proper virtue of the political association. It is the condition which free men establish among

themselves when they "share a common life in order that their association bring them self-sufficiency"—the regulation of their relationship by law, and the establishment, by law, of equality before the law. Rule of law is the name and pattern of this justice; its equality stands against the inequalities—of wealth, talents, etc.—otherwise obtaining among its participants, who by virtue of that equality are called "citizens." It is an achievement—complete, or, more frequently, partial—of certain people in certain concrete situations. It is fragile and easily disrupted by powerful individuals who discover that the blind equality of rule of law is inconvenient for their interests. Despite its obvious instability, Aristotle assumed that the establishment of justice in this sense, the creation of citizenship, was a permanent possibility for men and that the resultant association of citizens was the natural home of the species. At levels below the political association, this rule-governed equality is easily found; it is exemplified by any group of children agreeing together to play a game. At the level of the political association, the attainment of this justice is more difficult, simply because the stakes are so much higher for each participant. The equality of citizenship is not something that happens of its own accord, and without the expenditure of a fair amount of effort it will collapse into the rule of a powerful few over an apathetic many. But at least it has been achieved, at some times in some places; it is always worth trying to achieve, and eminently worth trying to maintain, wherever and to whatever degree it has been brought into being.

Aristotle's parochialism is notorious; he really did not imagine that persons other than Greeks could associate freely in justice, and the only form of association he had in mind was the Greek polis. With the decline of the polis and the shift in the center of political thought, his notion of justice underwent a sea change. To be exact, it ceased to represent a political type and became a moral ideal: the ideal of equality as we know it. This ideal demands that all men be included in citizenship—that one Law govern all equally, that all men regard all other men as fellow

From *Ethics*, vol. 83, no. 4 (July 1973): 308–312.
©1973 by The University of Chicago Press. Reprinted by permission.

citizens, with the same guarantees, rights, and protections. Briefly, it demands that the circle of citizenship achieved by any group be extended to include the entire human race. Properly understood, its effect on our association can be excellent: it congratulates us on our achievement of rule of law as a process of government but refuses to let us remain complacent until we have expanded the associations to include others within the ambit of the rules, as often and as far as possible. While one man is a slave, none of us may feel truly free. We are constantly prodded by this ideal to look for possible unjustifiable discrimination, for inequalities not absolutely required for the functioning of the society and advantageous to all. And after twenty centuries of pressure, not at all constant, from this idea, it might be said that some progress has been made. To take the cases in point for this problem, we are now prepared to assert, as Aristotle would never have been, the equality of sexes and of persons of different colors. The ambit of American citizenship, once restricted to white males of property, has been extended to include all adult free men, then all adult males including ex-slaves, then all women. The process of acquisition of full citizenship was for these groups a sporadic trail of half-measures, even now not complete; the steps on the road to full equality are marked by legislation and judicial decisions which are only recently concluded and still often not enforced. But the fact that we can now discuss the possibility of favoring such groups in hiring shows that over the area that concerns us, at least, full equality is presupposed as a basis for discussion. To that extent, they are full citizens, fully protected by the law of the land.

It is important for my argument that the moral ideal of equality be recognized as logically distinct from the condition (or virtue) of justice in the political sense. Justice in this sense exists among a citizenry, irrespective of the number of the populace included in that citizenry. Further, the moral ideal is parasitic upon the political virtue, for "equality" is unspecified—it means nothing until we are told in what respect that equality is to be realized. In a political context, "equality" is specified as "equal rights"—equal access to the public realm, public goods and offices, equal treatment under the law—in brief, the equality of citizenship. If citizenship is not a possibility, political equality is unintelligible. The ideal emerges as a generalization of the real condition and refers back to that condition for its content.

Now, if justice (Aristotle's justice in the political sense) is equal treatment under law for all citizens, what is injustice? Clearly, injustice is the violation of that equality, discriminating for or against a group of citizens, favoring them with special immunities and privileges or depriving them of those guaranteed to the others. When the southern employer refuses to hire blacks in white-collar jobs, when Wall Street will only hire women as secretaries with new titles, when Mississippi high schools routinely flunk all black boys above ninth grade, we have examples of injustice, and we work to restore the equality of the public realm by ensuring that equal opportunity will be provided in such cases in the future. But of course, when the employers and the schools favor women and blacks, the same injustice is done. Just as the previous discrimination did, this reverse discrimination violates the public equality which defines citizenship and destroys the rule of law for the areas in which these favors are granted. To the extent that we adopt a program of discrimination, reverse or otherwise, justice in the political sense is destroyed, and none of us, specifically affected or not, is a citizen, a bearer of rights—we are all petitioners for favors. And to the same extent, the ideal of equality is undermined, for it has content only where justice obtains, and by destroying justice we render the ideal meaningless. It is, then, an ironic paradox, if not a contradiction in terms, to assert that the ideal of equality justifies the violation of justice; it is as if one should argue, with William Buckley, that an ideal of humanity can justify the destruction of the human race.

Logically, the conclusion is simple enough: all discrimination is wrong prima facie because it violates justice, and that goes for reverse discrimination too. No violation of justice among the citizens may be justified (may overcome the prima facie objection) by appeal to the ideal of equality, for that ideal is logically dependent upon the notion of justice. Reverse discrimination, then, which attempts no other justification than an appeal to equality, is wrong. But let us try to make the conclusion more plausible by suggesting some of the implications of the suggested practice of reverse discrimination in employment and education. My argument will be that the problems raised there are insoluble, not only in practice but in principle.

We may argue, if we like, about what "discrimination" consists of. Do I discriminate against blacks if I admit none to my school when none of the black applicants are qualified by the tests I always give? How far must I go to root out cultural bias from my application forms and tests before I can say that I have not discriminated against those of different cultures? Can I assume that women are not strong enough to be roughnecks on my oil rigs, or must I test them individually? But this controversy, the most popular and well-argued aspect of the issue, is not as fatal as two others which cannot be avoided: if we are regarding the blacks as a "minority" victimized by discrimination, what is a "minority"? And for any group—blacks, women, whatever—that has been discriminated against, what amount of reverse discrimination wipes out the initial discrimination? Let us grant as true that women and blacks were discriminated against, even where laws forbade such discrimination, and grant for the sake of argument that a history of discrimination must be wiped out by reverse discrimination. What follows?

First, are there other groups which have been discriminated against? For they should have the same right of restitution. What about American Indians, Chicanos, Appalachian Mountain whites, Puerto Ricans, Jews, Cajuns, and Orientals? And if these are to be included, the principle according to which we specify a "minority" is simply the criterion of "ethnic (sub) group," and we're stuck with every hyphenated American in the lower-middle class clamoring for special privileges for his group—and with equal justification. For be it noted, when we run down the Harvard roster, we find not only a scarcity of blacks (in comparison with the proportion in the population) but an even more striking scarcity of those second-, third-, and fourth-generation ethnics who make up the loudest voice of Middle America. Shouldn't they demand their share? And eventually, the WASPs will have to form their own lobby, for they too are a minority. The point is simply this: there is no "majority" in America who will not mind giving up just a bit of their rights to make room for a favored minority. There are only other minorities, each of which is discriminated against by the favoring. The initial injustice is then repeated dozens of times, and if each minority is granted the same right of restitution as the others, an entire area of rule governance is dissolved into a pushing and shoving match between self-interested groups. Each works to catch the public eye and political popularity by whatever means of advertising and power politics lend themselves to the effort, to capitalize as much as possible on temporary popularity until the restless mob picks another group to feel sorry for. Hardly an edifying spectacle, and in the long run no one can benefit: the pie is no larger—it's just that instead of setting up and enforcing rules for getting a piece, we've turned the contest into a free-for-all, requiring much more effort for no larger a reward. It would be in the interests of all the participants to reestablish an objective rule to govern the process, carefully enforced and the same for all.

Second, supposing that we do manage to agree in general that women and blacks (and all the others) have some right of restitution, some right to a privileged place in the structure of opportunities for a while, how will we know when that while is up? How much privilege is enough? When will the guilt be gone, the price paid, the balance restored? What recompense is right for centuries of exclusion? What criterion tells us when we are done? Our experience with the Civil Rights movement shows us that agreement on these terms cannot be presupposed: a process that appears to some to be going at a mad gallop into a black takeover appears to the rest of us to be at a standstill. Should a practice of reverse discrimination be adopted, we may safely predict that just as some of us begin to see "a satisfactory start toward righting the balance," others of us will see that we "have already gone too far in the other direction" and will suggest that the discrimination ought to be reversed again. And such disagreement is inevitable, for the point is that we could not possibly have any criteria for evaluating the kind of recompense we have in mind. The context presumed by any discussion of restitution is the context of rule of law: law sets the rights of men and simultaneously sets the method for remedying the violation of those rights. You may exact suffering from others and/or damage payments for yourself if and only if the others have violated your rights; the suffering you have endured is not sufficient reason for them to suffer. And remedial rights exist only where there is law: primary human rights are useful guides to legislation but cannot stand as reasons for awarding remedies for injuries sustained. But then, the context presupposed by any discussion of restitution is the context of preexistent full citizenship. No remedial rights could exist for the excluded; neither in law nor in logic does there exist a right to sue for a standing to sue.

From these two considerations, then, the difficulties with reverse discrimination become evident. Restitution for a disadvantaged group whose rights under the law have been violated is possible by legal means, but restitution for a disadvantaged group whose grievance is that there was no law to protect them simply is not. First, outside of the area of justice defined by the law, no sense can be made of "the group's rights," for no law recognizes that group or the individuals in it, qua members, as bearers of rights (hence any group can constitute itself as a disadvantaged minority in some sense and demand similar restitution). Second, outside of the area of protection of law, no sense can be made of the violation of rights (hence the amount of the recompense cannot be decided by any objective criterion). For both reasons, the practice of reverse discrimination undermines the foundation of the very ideal in whose name it is advocated; it destroys justice, law, equality, and citizenship itself, and replaces them with power struggles and popularity contests.

Affirmative Action and Fairness

Robert K. Fullinwider

Study Questions

1. How did the issue of quotas arise in the case of Weber and Kaiser Aluminum and George Bush's veto of the 1990 Civil Rights Act?

2. How did William Bradford Reynolds describe the differences between equality of opportunity and equality of results?

3. According to Fullinwider, why did twenty years of federal judges' decisions support programs of affirmative action?

4. Why does he believe that good intentions not to discriminate are not enough to eliminate discrimination?

5. What did the *Griggs* v. *Duke Power Company* require of businesses?

6. How does the question about whether discrimination is "shallow" or "deep" or "transparent" or "opaque" play a role in Fullinwider's argument?

7. For what purpose does he use the analogy of the Land of the Giants?

From the *Report from the Institute for Philosophy and Public Policy*, vol. 11, no. 1 (Winter 1991): 10–13. © 1991 by the Institute for Philosophy and Public Policy. Reprinted with permission.

I begin by talking about four white men: David Duke, Brian Weber, William Bradford Reynolds, and George Bush.

. . . A former Klansman, a former leader of a white supremacist party, a purveyor of neo-Nazi literature, and now a representative in the state legislature, Duke took 40 percent of the vote in the 1990 senatorial primary in Louisiana—40 percent of the vote, 60 percent of the white vote. The main theme of his campaign: the injustice of affirmative action, the need for civil rights for whites. He tapped into something deep. He touched a nerve.

Brian Weber is also from Louisiana. In the 1970s he worked at a Kaiser Company chemical plant. That plant, like industry in general in the South, had a segregated work force. All of its black employees were relegated to a handful of unskilled jobs. There were none in the high-paying craft occupations. Moreover, given the company's rules and practices, little was likely to change. Kaiser hired craft workers by going outside the plant, using a regional labor market in which almost all workers trained in the crafts were white. The chemical workers' union and the company agreed to a plan to change things: the company would henceforth train its own craft workers instead of hiring from the outside, and it set up an on-the-job training program, admitting plant workers into the program from two lists—a white list and a black list. For every white worker admitted, one black worker would be admitted—until 30 percent of the craft workers at the plant were black. An explicit racial criterion. A quota.

In Brian Weber's eyes, this was unjustified reverse discrimination. He brought suit in federal court, and in 1979 the Supreme Court found in favor of the company.

There is a real irony in Weber's lawsuit. Weber himself was an unskilled worker at the plant. Had the company maintained its practice of going to outside markets for craft workers, Brian Weber would never have risen very far within the plant. The new program meant that he now had a chance to advance himself; he only had to wait his turn. No matter. The racial preferences in the program touched a nerve. They weren't tolerable. They had to go.

Nor, for George Bush, is the mere threat of preferences in favor of blacks or women acceptable. In October 1990 he vetoed the new Civil Rights Act, which would have clarified certain standards of proof in civil rights lawsuits. His objection was that these standards of proof made it hard for firms to defend themselves against charges of discrimination. Consequently, some firms might be tempted to avoid discrimination charges by using quotas—giving racial or gender preferences to make sure their work forces had the right racial or gender profile. This possibility was enough to cause the president to reject the bill.

Why Quotas Are Anathema

What is it, though, that makes a program like Kaiser's intolerable? What makes the mere risk of preferences unacceptable? Why is the Q-word anathema? That question brings me to the last man I'll talk about, William Bradford Reynolds. Reynolds headed the Office of Civil Rights in the Department of Justice during the Reagan Administration, and was that administration's leading spokesman on affirmative action and against quotas.

The debate about preferential treatment, he said, is between those (like himself) who believe in *equality of opportunity* and those who believe in *equality of results*. Those who *oppose* preferential treatment believe in individual rights and a colorblind, gender-blind society. Those who *support* quotas believe in group rights and dividing up social benefits by race and gender. That's the way Reynolds put it.

Putting the matter this way is politically effective for opponents of affirmative action. Individual rights,

equality of opportunity, success through effort and merit, reward because of what you do, not who you are—these values are as American as apple pie. Opposing preferential treatment isn't opposing racial and gender justice; it's just opposing an alien philosophy, an un-American ideology.

There may well be people who support preferential treatment because they believe in equality of results for its own sake, because they believe in group rights, or because they want a society shaped around color and gender. But the federal judges of this country are certainly not among those people, and it is federal courts who for twenty years have created or sustained the various parts of affirmative action, including the occasional use of quotas and preferences. Why have they done this? By their own account, to *prevent* discrimination and *secure* equality of opportunity.

Reynolds says that using racial and sexual preferences to end discrimination is nonsense; the way to end discrimination is not to discriminate in reverse but simply to *stop discriminating*. Exactly—if we can. If we can stop discriminating. That's the rub. And that's the problem courts ran into.

Can't We Just Stop Discriminating?

It takes more than good will and good intentions not to discriminate. It takes capability as well, and that may be hard to come by. To see what I'm talking about, let's look back at a company like Kaiser after the Civil Rights Act of 1964 outlawed discrimination in employment. The company may have employed no blacks at all. The sign in the window said: "No blacks apply." Now, how does the company comply with the law and stop discriminating? It takes the sign out of the window and says, "If blacks apply and meet all requirements, we will hire them." And suppose it is sincere. Is that enough?

Look at how other aspects of company policy may work. Suppose the company only advertises its jobs by word of mouth. It posts job openings on the bulletin board and lets the grapevine do the rest. Then few blacks will ever hear of openings since all the workers are white—a fact reflecting, of course, the company's past discrimination. A company policy not itself designed to keep blacks out nevertheless does exactly that. Or suppose that the company requires each applicant to provide a letter of recommendation from some current or former employee. All the current and former employees are white, so this policy, too, is going to exclude blacks. Taking the sign out of the window changes nothing at all.

This is what courts encountered when they began adjudicating civil rights cases in the 1960s. Because the system of discrimination has been so thorough and in place for so long, it was like the child's spinning top, which keeps on spinning even after you take your hand away. Ordinary business practices let a firm's prior discrimination keep reproducing itself—and that reproduction, whether intended or not, is *itself* discrimination. So concluded a unanimous Supreme Court in the landmark 1971 case *Griggs* v. *Duke Power Company*. In order to comply with the law, businesses must look at all parts of their operations—job classifications, work rules, seniority systems, physical organization, recruitment and retention policies, everything—and revise, where possible, those elements that reproduce past discrimination. That's the core idea of affirmative action, as it was born in the early 1970s from the experience of courts trying to assure nondiscrimination and equal opportunity, and as extended through federal rules to all recipients of government contracts and funds.

Make a plan (these rules say) that establishes a system for monitoring your workplace and operations; that changes procedures and operations where you see they may have discriminatory impact; and that predicts what your work force would look like were you successfully nondiscriminating, so you will have some measure of the success or failure of your efforts.

Those are the basic elements of affirmative action. They are surely reasonable. Even William Bradford Reynolds accepted most of this. Why is there ever a need for more? Why is there ever a need actually to impose racial or gender quotas? Or to risk their being adopted by firms?

Because sometimes it takes strong measures for us to see how to do what is needed to secure the reality of equal opportunity, not just its form. If we've built a whole world around discrimination, then many of the ways the world discriminates may not be visible to us even when we go looking. We may not be able to see all the ways our business practices exclude women and blacks from the workplace or detract from their performance there until the workplace is actually changed by having women and blacks in it. And one quick way of changing the composition of the workplace is through quotas.

Courts have sometimes—not often—resorted to quotas when they were convinced that an institution was simply not capable of identifying and changing all the features of its practices that discriminate. Often the quotas have been imposed on companies or municipal agencies whose own histories showed them completely unwilling to make anything but token changes. But sometimes they've been imposed where the sheer inertial weight of company culture and organization convinced the court that the company would never be able to find "qualified" minorities or women, no matter how hard it tried. The culture itself had to be changed by putting minorities and women in roles from which they had been excluded.

Here is where the real issue lies. It is about the nature and sweep of discrimination. Do we think discrimination is a relatively *shallow* or a very *deep* phenomenon? Do we think discrimination is *transparent* or *opaque*? The answer need not be a flat yes or no. Perhaps in some places discrimination is shallow, in some places deep; in some circumstances transparent, in others opaque. If discrimination is shallow and transparent, then modest affirmative action should be enough to cure it: we look for, find, and eliminate practices that are reproducing the effects of past discrimination. But if discrimination is deep and opaque, then we may not be able to find it even when we look, and more robust forms of affirmative action may be necessary. We may need rather sharp assistance to *see* the way our practices work to exclude and oppress. We may need to be shocked or shaken out of our old habits, to have our consciousness raised.

This, I think, is the heart of the controversy about affirmative action. The difference is not that some people want equal opportunity and some want equality of results, that some believe in individual rights and some believe in group entitlements. The difference is that some think discrimination is always transparent and shallow while others think it is—sometimes, at least, in some sectors or institutions—deep, enduring, and opaque.

The Land of the Giants

To drive home this point about the opacity of discrimination and how it can subvert good will and good intentions, I ask you to go through some thought experiments with me. Start with a simple fantasy. Imagine we were suddenly all transported to the land of the Giants. They would be puzzled and wonder what in the world to make of us; and in short order they would probably conclude that, though we were like them in many ways, still we were quite incapable, incompetent, *inferior* creatures—for although we have our charming side, we really can't manage to do well even the simplest tasks in Giant Land. We just don't measure up. Perhaps it's just our nature to be helpless, the Giants conclude. We must have been some unfortunate quirk in God's creation.

But we would know that the problem does not lie in us, it lies in the fact that everything in Giant Land is built to the scale of Giants. That world is built for Giants and of course we don't do well in that world—but give us back the world built for us and see what we can do! We can even outperform Giants!

What's my point? It's that the Giants see *their* world as *the* world. They just naturally measure us against it, so they see the problem to be in *us*.

This is just fantasy, you say, and besides, the Giants wouldn't have been so dense. If you think not, then turn to a second example—a real one.

Twenty-five years ago, we tended to think that people in wheelchairs couldn't do much. It was a shame they were in wheelchairs—it wasn't their fault—but it meant that they were incapable of doing what most of the rest of us did. They were very limited in their mobility, thus not qualified for most jobs. And so they were excluded. Left out. Omitted.

Why did we think that? Not because we disliked people in wheelchairs. It was because, when they had trouble performing operations we do easily, we naturally attributed the trouble to *them*—to *their* condition—because we just took the world as it was for granted. And how was that world? It was a world of *curbs*. Curbs everywhere.

Now, curbs are not supplied by nature. The world of curbs was made—made by and for us, the walking, running, jumping types. It took federal law that mandated tearing up the sidewalks at nearly every intersection in this country to jar us into realizing that many of the problems people in wheelchairs faced lay not in them but in the fact that *we* had *made* a world that excluded them, and then, like the Giants, had assumed *that* world was *the* world.

Unavoidable Unfairness

The world of Giants—the world of curbs—the world of whites and men: imagine, if you will, a world built over a long time by and for men, by and for whites. In that world there would be a thousand and one impediments to women and blacks working effectively and successfully. That world and its institutions would be suffused through and through with inhospitality to blacks and women—just as Giant Land was inhospitable to us little people, and Curb World was inhospitable to wheelchair people. Imagine that world—or do you have to imagine it? That's the world we still live in, isn't it?

Isn't it plausible that strong measures may be needed to change it? Are those strong measures, if they involve racial or gender preferences, unfair to white men? Of course they are. Well, doesn't that settle the matter? It would if we could always be fair without sometimes being unfair. Does that sound puzzling?

Think a moment. What are our options? Consider the civil rights bill George Bush vetoed. . . . If we set high burdens of proof on businesses, some of them may resort to quotas—and that's unfair discrimination. But if we don't set high standards, some businesses won't make the necessary effort to change practices that still hinder blacks and women—and *that's* unfair discrimination. Sometimes we may be faced only with the choice of risking unfairness in one direction or risking it in another. Sometimes we may have no choice except to impose one unfairness or allow another to persist. Then what do we do?

President Bush vetoed the civil rights bill because it created the risk of quotas. Does he believe, then, that vetoing it creates no risks that some blacks and women will continue to be discriminated against, or is the unspoken premise this: that the risk of victimization is tolerable if the victims are not white men?

Review Exercises

1. In the history of affirmative action and civil rights legislation:
   a. When were the terms *preferential treatment* and *affirmative action* first used?
   b. What is the difference between the Equal Pay Act and Title VII of the 1964 Civil Rights Act?
   c. Has the U.S. Supreme Court ever forbidden the use of racial quotas? Approved them?
2. What is meant by *racism*? *sexism*? Are there any other similar "ism"s?

3. Explain the five different elements of the principle of equality as it was given here.

4. What is the difference between individual, group, and average differences? How are these an issue in the application of the principle of equality?

5. What is "affirmative action," and why does it have this name? Give five different types of affirmative action. Which of them involve or may involve giving preferential treatment?

6. Summarize the consequentialist arguments for and against affirmative action.

7. Summarize the nonconsequentialist arguments for and against affirmative action.

Discussion Cases

1. *Preferences in Hiring.* XYZ University has an opening in its philosophy department. Currently the full-time faculty in this department is all male. The department has received 200 applications for this position. It has been advised by the dean that because the student body is half female, it should seek a woman to fill this position. The school is also under affirmative action guidelines because it receives federal funding for some of its programs. The faculty members have agreed to consider seriously the several applications from females that they have received. The qualifications for the position, the field of specialization, has been advertised. But there are several other ways in which the position is open. The list has been narrowed to ten top candidates. Two of these are women. All ten are well qualified in their own ways. The department is split on what to do. Some members believe that because all ten are well qualified, they should choose one of the two women. The other members believe that the most qualified of the final group do not include the two women.

What do you think they should do? Why?

2. *Campus Diversity.* During the last couple of decades, colleges and universities have tried to increase their numbers of minority students by various forms of affirmative action. At campus X this has led to no small amount of dissension. Some students complain that the policy of accepting students with lower SAT and other scores just because of their race or minority status is unfair. Others believe that the diversity that results from such policies is good for everyone because we should learn to live together and a university campus should be a place to do this. Still there is some question even among this group as to how well the integration is working. Furthermore, a different type of problem has recently surfaced. Because Asian Americans were represented in numbers greater than their percentage of the population, some universities were restricting the percentage they would accept even when their scores were higher than others they did accept.

Do you think that diversity ought to be a goal of campus admissions? Or do you believe that only academic qualifications ought to count? Why?

Selected Bibliography

Bell, Linda A., and David Blumenfeld (Eds.). *Overcoming Racism and Sexism.* Lanham, MD: Rowman & Littlefield, 1995.

Bergmann, Barbara R. *In Defense of Affirmative Action.* New York: Basic Books, 1995.

Bishop, Sharon, and Marjorie Weinzweig. *Philosophy and Women.* Belmont, CA: Wadsworth, 1979.

Bittker, Boris. *The Case for Black Reparations.* New York: Random House, 1973.

Blackstone, William, and Robert Heslep. *Social Justice and Preferential Treatment.* Athens: University of Georgia Press, 1977.

Bowie, Norman E. (Ed.). *Equal Opportunity.* Boulder, CO: Westview, 1988.

Bravo, Ellen, and Ellen Casedy. *The 9 to 5 Guide to Combating Sexual Harassment.* New York: Wiley, 1992.

Cohen, Marshall, Thomas Nagel, and Thomas Scanlon (Eds.). *Equality and Preferential Treatment.* Princeton, NJ: Princeton University Press, 1976.

DeCrow, Karen. *Sexist Justice*. New York: Vintage, 1975.

Faludi, Susan. *Backlash: The Undeclared War Against American Women*. New York: Crown, 1991.

Ferguson, Ann. *Sexual Democracy: Women, Oppression, and Revolution*. Boulder, CO: Westview, 1991.

Fishkin, James. *Justice, Equal Opportunity and the Family*. New Haven, CT: Yale University Press, 1983.

Francis, Leslie Pickering. *Sexual Harassment in Academe*. Lanham, MD: Rowman & Littlefield, 1996.

Friedman, Marilyn, and Jan Narveson. *Political Correctness: For and Against*. Lanham, MD: Rowman & Littlefield, 1994.

Frye, Marilyn. *The Politics of Reality*. New York: Crossing, 1983.

Fullinwider, Robert. *The Reverse Discrimination Controversy*. Totowa, NJ: Rowman & Littlefield, 1980.

Garry, Ann, and Marilyn Pearsall (Eds.). *Women, Knowledge, and Reality: Explorations in Feminist Philosophy*. Boston: Unwin Hyman, 1989.

Gilligan, Carol. *In a Different Voice*. Cambridge, MA: Harvard University Press, 1987.

Goldberg, Steven. *The Inevitability of Patriarchy*. New York: William Morrow, 1973.

Goldman, Alan. *Justice and Reverse Discrimination*. Princeton, NJ: Princeton University Press, 1979.

Gross, Barry R. (Ed.). *Reverse Discrimination*. Buffalo, NY: Prometheus, 1977.

Hooks, Bell. *Ain't I a Woman: Black Women and Feminism*. Boston: South End, 1981.

Jaggar, Alison. *Feminist Politics and Human Nature*. Sussex, NJ: Rowman & Littlefield, 1983.

Kittay, Eva, and Diana Meyers (Eds.). *Women and Moral Theory*. Sussex, NJ: Rowman & Littlefield, 1987.

Kymlicka, Will. *Multicultural Citizenship: A Liberal Theory of Minority Rights*. New York: Oxford University Press, 1995.

Maccoby, E., and C. Jacklin. *The Psychology of Sex Differences*. Palo Alto, CA: Stanford University Press, 1974.

MacKinnon, Catharine A. *Sexual Harassment of Working Women: A Case of Sex Discrimination*. New Haven, CT: Yale University Press, 1979.

Mill, John Stuart. *On the Subjection of Women*. New York: Frederick A. Stokes, 1911.

Murray, Charles. *Losing Ground*. New York: Basic Books, 1984.

Noddings, Nel. *Women and Evil*. Berkeley: University of California Press, 1989.

Rae, Douglas. *Equalities*. Cambridge, MA: Harvard University Press, 1981.

Rakowski, Eric. *Equal Justice*. New York: Oxford University Press, 1991.

Remick, H. *Comparable Worth and Wage Discrimination*. Philadelphia: Temple University Press, 1985.

Sowell, Thomas. *The Economics and Politics of Race: An International Perspective*. New York: William Morrow, 1983.

Sterba, James P. *Justice: Alternative Political Perspectives*, 2nd ed. Belmont, CA: Wadsworth, 1992.

Tong, Rosemarie. *Feminine and Feminist Ethics*. Belmont, CA: Wadsworth, 1993.

Veatch, Robert M. *The Foundations of Justice: Why the Retarded and the Rest of Us Have Claims to Equality*. New York: Oxford University Press, 1986.

Young, Iris Marion. *Justice and the Politics of Difference*. Princeton, NJ: Princeton University Press, 1990.

❧ *12* ❧

Economic Justice

Perhaps you have heard something like the following dialogue. It might be carried on between a student majoring in business (Betty Business Major) and another majoring in philosophy (Phil Philosophy Major).

Betty: I think that people have a right to make and keep as much money as they can as long as they do not infringe on others' rights. Thus, we should not be taxing the rich to give to the poor.

Phil: Is it fair that some people are born with a silver spoon in their mouth and others are not? The poor often have not had a chance to get ahead. Society owes them that much. They are persons just like everyone else.

Betty: But how could we guarantee that they will not waste what we give them? In any case, it is just not right to take the money of those who have worked hard for it and redistribute it. They deserve to keep it.

Phil: Why do they deserve to keep what they have earned? If they are in the position that they are in because of the good education and good example provided by their parents, how do they themselves deserve what they can get with that?

Betty: In any case, if we take what such people have earned, whether they deserve it or not, they will have no incentive to work. Profits are what make the economy of a nation grow.

Phil: And why is that so? Does this imply that the only reason people work is for their own self-interest? That sounds like good old capitalism to me, as your idol Adam Smith would have it. But is a capitalistic system a just economic system?

Betty: Justice does not seem to me to require that everyone have equal amounts of wealth. If justice is fairness, as some of your philosophers say, it is only fair and therefore just that people get out of the system what they put into it. And, besides, there are other values. We value freedom, too, don't we? People ought to be free to work and keep what they earn.

Phil: This sounds like where I came in. We are now back to square one!

The issues touched on in this conversation belong to a group of issues that fall under the topic of what has been called "economic justice." There are others as well. For example, do people have a right to a job and good wages? Is welfare aid to the poor a matter of charity or justice? Is an economic system that requires a pool of unemployed workers a just system? Is it fair to tax the rich more heavily than the middle class? Between 1969 and 1994 in the United States the gap between the incomes of the top earners and the working class and poor widened. According to the 1995 Bureau of the Census report, "A Brief Look at Postwar U.S. Income Inequality," during that twenty-five-year period, "the share of the nation's aggregate income that went to the top 20 percent of its households increased to 46.9 percent from 40.5 percent," and the share earned by the rest of the households either remained the same or decreased.[1] The gap between the rich and the poor is and has been widening for some time. In fact, throughout the history of this country, the richest sector of the population has owned a portion of wealth out of all proportion to its size. In mid-nineteenth-century New York, for example, the richest 4 percent owned 81 percent of all wealth, and in small East Coast towns and rural areas they owned 90 percent.[2] This difference was attributed to the rise of capitalism and the beginnings of industrialization. The more recent continuing gap is thought to result partly from the increase in high-skilled and computer-assisted technological jobs and the decline of low-skilled manufacturing jobs. Social welfare programs have helped to bridge the gap, but these are now under fire. Is there anything wrong with this kind of economic inequality, which is increasingly a factor throughout the industrialized world? This chapter will address some of the underlying ethical issues that play a role in answering such questions. It will focus on questions of economic justice within a nation, leaving the larger issues of international economic justice to the following chapter.

It is important to distinguish justice and certain other moral notions. For example, justice is not the same as charity. It is one thing to say that a community, like a family, out of concern for its poorer members will help them when they are in need. But is helping people in need ever a matter of justice? If we say that it is, we imply that it is not morally optional. We can think of *justice* here as the giving of what is rightly due, and *charity* as what is above and beyond the requirements of justice. Furthermore, justice is not the

only relevant moral issue in economic matters. Efficiency and liberty are also moral values that play a role in discussions on ethics and economics. When we say that a particular economic system is efficient, we generally mean that it produces a maximum amount of desired goods and services, or the most value for the least cost. Thus, some people say that a free-market economy is a good economic system because it is the most efficient system, the one best able to create wealth. But it is quite another question to ask whether such a system is also a just system. Nevertheless, efficiency is important, and so too is freedom or liberty. If we could have the most just and perhaps even the most efficient economic system in the world, would it be worth it if we were not also free to make our own decisions about many things, including how to earn a living and what to do with our money?

In this chapter we will be discussing what is generally termed *distributive justice*. Distributive justice has to do with how goods are allocated among persons, for example, who and how many people have what percentage of the goods or wealth in a society. Thus, suppose that in some society 5 percent of the people possessed 90 percent of the wealth, and the other 95 percent of the people possessed the other 10 percent of the wealth. Asking whether this arrangement would be just is raising a question of distributive justice. Now how would we go about answering this question? It does seem that this particular distribution of wealth is quite unbalanced. But must a distribution be equal for it to be just? To answer this question, we can examine two quite different ways of approaching distributive justice. One is what we can call a *process view*, and the other is an *end state view*.

Process or End State Distributive Justice

According to some philosophers, any economic distribution (or any system that allows a particular economic distribution) is just if the process by which it comes about is just. Some call this *procedural justice*. For example, if the wealthy 5 percent of the people got their 90 percent of the wealth fairly—they competed for jobs, they were honest, they did not take what was not theirs—then what they earned would be rightly theirs. In contrast, if the wealthy obtained their wealth through force or fraud, then their possession of such wealth would be unfair. But there would be nothing unfair or unjust about the uneven distribution in itself. (See the reading selection by Robert Nozick for an example of elements of this view.) We might suspect that because talent is more evenly distributed, there is something suspicious about this uneven distribution of wealth. We might suspect that coercion or unjust taking or unfair competition or dishonesty was involved. Now, some people are wealthy because of good luck and fortune, and others are not wealthy because of bad economic luck. However, on this view, those who keep money that through luck or good fortune falls to them from the sky, so to speak, are not being unjust in keeping it even when others are poor.

Others believe that the process by which people attain wealth is not the only consideration relevant to determining the justice of an economic distribution. They believe that we should also look at the way things turn out, the end state, or resulting distribution of wealth in a society, and ask about its fairness. Suppose that the lucky persons possessed the 95 percent of the wealth through inheritance, for example. Would it be fair for them to have so much wealth when others in the society were extremely poor? How would we judge whether such an arrangement was fair? We would look to see if there is some good reason why the wealthy are wealthy. Did they work hard for it? Did they make important social contributions? These might be nonarbitrary or good reasons for the wealthy to possess their wealth rightly or justly. However, if they are wealthy while others are poor because they, unlike the others, were born of a certain favored race or sex or eye color or height, then we might be inclined to say that their having more is not fair. What reasons, then, justify differences in wealth?

Several different views exist on this issue. Radical *egalitarians* deny that there is any good reason why some people should possess greater wealth than others. Their reasons for this view vary. They might stress that human beings are essentially alike as human and that this is more important than any differentiating factors about them, including their talents and what they do with them. They might use religious or semireligious reasons such as that the earth is given to all of us equally, and we all thus have an equal right to the goods derived from it. Even egalitarians, however, must decide what it is that they believe should be equal. Should there be equality of wealth and income or equality of satisfaction or welfare, for example? These are not the same. Some people have little wealth or income but nevertheless are quite satisfied, while others who have great wealth or income are quite dissatisfied. Some have champagne tastes, and others are satisfied with beer!

On the other hand, at least some basic differences between people should make a difference in what distribution of goods is thought to be just. For example, some people simply have different *needs* than others. People are not identical physically, and some of us need more food and different kinds of health care than others. Karl Marx's "To each according to his need" captures something of this variant of egalitarianism.[3] Nevertheless, why only this particular differentiating factor—need—should justify differences in wealth is puzzling. In fact, we generally would tend to pick out others as well, differences in merit, achievement, effort, or contribution.

Suppose, for example, that Jim uses his talent and education and produces a new electronic device that allows people to transfer their thoughts to a computer directly. This device would alleviate the need to type or write the thoughts—at least, initially. People would value this device, surely, and Jim would probably make a great deal of money from his invention. Would not Jim have a right to or *merit* this money? Would it not be fair that he had this money and others who did not come up with such a device had less? It would seem so. But let us think about why we might say so. Is it because Jim had an innate or *native talent* that others did not have? Then through no fault of their own, those without the talent would have less. Jim would have had nothing to do with his having been born with this talent and thus becoming wealthy.

Perhaps it is because Jim not only had the talent but also used it. He put a great deal of *effort* into it. He studied electronics and brain anatomy for many years, and spent years working on the invention itself in his garage. His own effort, time, and study were his own contribution. Would this be a good reason to say that he deserved the wealth that he earned from it? This might seem reasonable, if we did not also know that the particular education that he had and his motivation might have also been in some ways gifts of his circumstance and family upbringing. Furthermore, effort alone would not be a good reason for monetary reward, or else John, whom it took three weeks to make a pair of shoes, should be paid more than Jeff, who did them up in three hours. This would be similar to the student who asks for a higher grade because of all the effort and time he spent on study for the course, when in fact the result was more consistent with the lower grade.

Finally, perhaps Jim should have the rewards of his invention because of the nature of his *contribution,* because of the product he made and its value to people. Again, this seems at first reasonable, and yet there are also fairness problems here. Suppose that he had produced this invention before there were computers. The invention would be wonderful but not valued by people for they could not use it. Or suppose that others at the same time produced similar inventions. Then this happenstance would also lessen the value of the product and its monetary reward. He could rightly say that it was unfair that he did not reap a great reward from his invention just because he happened to be born at the wrong time or finished his invention a little late. This may be just bad luck. But is it also unfair? Furthermore, it is often difficult to know how to

value particular contributions to a jointly produced product or result. How do we measure and compare the value of the contributions of the person with the idea, the money, the risk takers, and so forth so as to know what portion of the profits are rightly due them? Marxists are well known for their claim that the people who own the factory or have put up the money for a venture profit from the workers' labor unfairly or out of proportion to their own contribution.

It may not be possible to give a nonproblematic basis for judging when an unequal distribution of wealth in a society is fair by appealing to considerations of merit, achievement, effort, or contribution. However, perhaps some combination of process and end state view and some combination of factors as grounds for distribution can be found. At least this discussion will provide a basis for critically evaluating simple solutions.

Equal Opportunity

Another viewpoint on economic justice does not fit easily under the category of process or end state views. In this view, the key to whether an unequal distribution of wealth in a society is just is whether people have a fair chance to attain those positions of greater income or wealth; that is, equality of wealth is not required, only equal opportunity to attain it. The notion of equal opportunity is symbolized by the Statue of Liberty in New York Harbor. It sits on Ellis Island, where historically new immigrants to America were processed. The idea symbolized was one of hope, namely, that in this country all people had a chance to make a good life for themselves provided that they worked hard. But just what is involved in the notion of equal opportunity, and is it a realizable goal or ideal?

Literally, it involves both opportunities and some sort of equality of chances to attain them. An opportunity is a chance to attain some benefit or goods. People have equal chances to attain these first of all when there are no barriers to prevent them from attaining the goods. Opportunities can still be said to be equal if barriers exist as long as they are equal. Clearly, if racism or prejudice prevents some people from having similar chances to attain valued goals or positions in a society, then there is not equal opportunity for those who are its victims. If women have twice the family responsibilities as men, will they have effective equal opportunity to compete professionally?

According to James Fishkin, if there is equal opportunity in my society, "I should not be able to enter a hospital ward of healthy newborn babies and, on the basis of class, race, sex, or other arbitrary native characteristics, predict the eventual positions in society of those children."[4] However, knowing what we do about families and education and real-life prospects of children, we know how difficult this ideal would be to realize. In reality, children do not start life with equal chances. Advantaged families give many educational, motivational, and experiential advantages to their children that children of disadvantaged families do not have, and this makes their opportunities effectively unequal. Schooling has a great impact on equal opportunity. However, funding per pupil on schooling in this country varies greatly according to locale. For example, "in Chicago the city average for 1988–89 was $5,265, while in surrounding suburbs the averages were often 50 percent more." In Camden, New Jersey, $3,538 was spent per pupil, while in West Orange and Princeton the levels were twice that.[5]

This version of equal opportunity is a starting-gate theory. It assumes that if people had equal starts, then they would have equal chances. Bernard Williams provides an example.[6] In an imaginary society he describes, a class of skillful warriors has for generations held all of the highest positions and passed them on to their offspring. At some point, the warriors decide to let all people compete for membership in their class. The children of the warrior class are much stronger and better nourished than other children who, not surprisingly, fail to gain entrance to the warrior class. Would these children have had effective equality of opportunity to gain entrance to the warrior class and its benefits? Even if the competition was formally fair, the outside chil-

dren were handicapped and had no real chance of winning. But how could initial starting points then be equalized? Perhaps by providing special aids or help to the other children to prepare them for the competition. Applying this example to our real-world situation would mean that society should give special aid to the children of disadvantaged families if it wants to ensure equal opportunity. According to James Fishkin, however, to do this effectively would require serious infringements on family autonomy. Is the goal of equal opportunity then unrealizable without threatening other values such as family autonomy? Even if the ideal of equal opportunity were unattainable, however, this would not imply that we should do nothing, or that we should not at least do what would make opportunity more equal.

Four Political and Economic Theories

One further way to approach the general topic of economic justice and to understand some of the values at issue in economic systems is to compare the theories that go by the labels of *libertarianism, capitalism, socialism,* and *modern liberalism.* These theories can be differentiated from one another not only by basic definitions but also by the different emphasis that they place on the values of liberty, efficiency, and justice. They also are differentiated by how they favor or disfavor process or end state views of distributive justice. These values and these views of distributive justice will become clearer if we examine these theories briefly.

Libertarianism

Libertarianism is a political theory about both the importance of liberty in human life, and the role of government. Although a political party goes under this name and draws on the theory of libertarianism, we will examine the theory itself. Libertarians believe that we are free when we are not constrained or restrained by other people. Sometimes this type of liberty is referred to as a basic right to noninterference. Thus, if you stand in the doorway and block my exit, you are violating my liberty to go where I wish. However, if I fall and break my leg and am unable to exit the door, my liberty rights are violated by no one. The doorway is open and unblocked, and I am free to go out. I cannot simply because of my injury.

According to libertarianism, government has but a minimal function, an administrative function. It should provide an orderly place where people can go about their business. It does have an obligation to ensure that people's liberty rights are not violated, that people do not block freeways (if not doorways), and so forth. However, it has no obligation to see that my broken leg is repaired so that I can walk where I please. In particular, it has no business taking money from you to pay for my leg repair or any other good that I might like to have or even need. This may be a matter of charity or something that charities should address, but it is not a matter of social justice or obligation.

Libertarians would more likely support a process view of distributive justice than an end state view. Any economic arrangement would be just so long as it resulted from a fair process of competition, and so long as people did not take what is not theirs or get their wealth by fraudulent or coercive means. Libertarians do not believe, however, that governments should be concerned with end state considerations. They should not try to even out any imbalance between rich and poor that might result from a fair process. They should not be involved in any redistribution of wealth. Libertarianism is a theory about the importance of liberty, of rights to noninterference by others, and of the proper role of government. Libertarians also have generally supported capitalist free-market economies, thus some brief comments about this type of economic system and the values that support it are appropriate here.

Capitalism

Capitalism is an economic system in which individuals or business corporations (not the government, or community, or state) own and control much or most of the country's capital. Capital is the wealth or raw materials, factories, and so forth that are used to produce more wealth. Capitalism is also usually associated with a free-enterprise system, an economic system that allows people freedom to set prices and determine production, and to make their own choices about how to earn and spend their incomes. Sometimes this is also referred to as a *market economy* in which people are motivated by profit and engage in competition, and in which value is a function of supply and demand.

Certain philosophical values and beliefs also undergird this system. Among these can be a libertarian philosophy that stresses the importance of liberty and limited government. Certain beliefs about the nature of human motivation also are implicit—for example, that people are motivated by self-interest. Some argue that capitalism and a free-market economy constitute the best economic system because it is the most efficient one, producing greater wealth for more people than any other system. People produce more and better, they say, when something is in it for them or their families, or when what they are working for is their own. Moreover, we will usually make only what people want, and we know what people want by what they are willing to buy. So people make their mousetraps and their mind-reading computers, and we reward them for giving us what we want by buying their products. Exemplifying this outlook is the view of economist Milton Friedman that the purpose of a business is to maximize profits, "to use its resources and engage in activities designed to increase its profits. . . ."[7] It is a further point, however, to assert that people have a right in justice to the fruits of their labors. Although libertarian and other supporters of capitalism will stress process views of justice, when end state criteria for distributive justice are given, it is most often *meritocratic criteria,* according to which people are judged to deserve what they merit or earn.

Socialism

Socialism is an economic system, political movement, and social theory. It holds that government should own and control most of a nation's resources. According to this theory, there should be public ownership of land, factories, and other means of production. Socialism criticizes capitalism because of its necessary unemployment and poverty, unpredictable business cycles, and inevitable conflicts between workers and owners of the means of production. Rather than allowing the few to profit often at the expense of the many, socialism holds that government should engage in planning and adjust production to the needs of all of the people. Justice is stressed over efficiency, but central planning is thought to contribute to efficiency as well as justice. Socialism generally is concerned with end state justice and is egalitarian in orientation, allowing only for obvious differences among people in terms of their different needs. It holds that it is not only external constraints that limit people's liberty. True liberty or freedom also requires freedom from other internal constraints. Among these are the lack of the satisfaction of basic needs, and poor education and health care. These needs must be addressed by government.

One key distinction between a libertarian and a socialist conception of justice is that the former recognizes only *negative rights* and the latter stresses *positive rights*.[8] Negative rights are rights not to be harmed in some way. Because libertarians take liberty as a primary value, they stress the negative right of people not to have their liberty restricted by others. These are rights of noninterference. In the economic area, they support economic liberties that create wealth, and they believe that people should be able to dispose of their wealth as they choose. For the libertarian, government's role is to protect negative rights, not positive rights. Contrary to this view, socialists believe that government should not only protect people's negative rights not to be interfered with but also attend to their positive rights to be given basic necessities. Consequently, a right to life must not only involve a right not to be killed but a right to what is necessary to live, namely, food, clothing, and shelter. Positive rights to be helped or benefited are sometimes called "wel-

fare rights." Those favoring such a concept of rights may ask what a right to life would amount to if one had not the means to live. Positive economic rights would be rights to basic economic subsistence. Those favoring positive rights would allow for a variety of ways to provide for this from outright grants to incentives of various sorts.

None of these three systems is problem-free. *Socialism,* at least in recent times, often has not lived up to the ideals of its supporters. Central planning systems have failed as society becomes more complex and participates in international economic systems. Socialist societies have tended in some cases to become authoritarian, for it is difficult to get voluntary consent to centrally decided plans for production and other policies. Basic necessities may be provided for all, but their quality has often turned out to be low. *Capitalism* and a free-market economy also are open to moral criticism. Many people, through no fault of their own, cannot or do not compete well and fall through the cracks. Unemployment is a natural part of the system, but it is also debilitating. Of what use is the liberty to vote or travel if one cannot take advantage of this freedom? Where is the concern for the basic equality of persons or the common good? *Libertarianism* has been criticized for failing to notice that society provides the means by which individuals do seek their own good—for example, by means of transportation and communication. It fails to notice that state action is needed to protect liberty rights and rights to security, property, and litigation. It must at least admit social welfare in terms of publicly funded compulsory primary education.[9] It also may be criticized for ignoring the impact of initial life circumstance on the equal chances of individuals to compete fairly for society's goods.

Let us consider whether a mixed form of political and economic system might be better. We shall call it "modern liberalism," even though the term *liberalism* has meant many things to many people. One reason for using this name is that it is the one given to the views of one philosopher who exemplifies it and whose philosophy we shall also treat here, namely, John Rawls.

Modern Liberalism

Modern liberalism follows in the footsteps of the classical liberalism of John Stuart Mill, John Locke, and Adam Smith with their stress on liberty rights. However, it also stresses the primacy of justice. Suppose we were to attempt to combine the positive elements of libertarianism, capitalism, and socialism. What would we pull from each? Liberty, or the ability to be free from unjust constraint by others, the primary value stressed by libertarianism, would be one value to preserve. However, we may want to support a fuller notion of liberty that also recognizes the power of internal constraints. We might want, too, to recognize both positive and negative rights and hold that government ought to play some role in supporting the former as well as the latter. Stress on this combination of elements characterizes modern liberalism.

In writing the American *Declaration of Independence,* Thomas Jefferson had prepared initial drafts. In one of these, when writing about the purpose of government and the inalienable rights to life, liberty, and happiness, he wrote, "in order to *secure these ends* governments are instituted among men." In the final draft the phrase is "in order to *secure these rights* governments are instituted among men."[10] In some ways these two versions of the purpose of government, according to Jefferson, parallel the two versions of determining when a distribution of wealth is just—the end state view and a stress on positive rights ("to secure these ends"), and the process view and a focus on negative rights of noninterference ("to secure these rights"). Whichever we believe to be more important will determine what view we have of the role of government in securing economic justice.

We would want our economic system to be efficient as well as just. Thus, our system would probably allow capitalist incentives and inequalities of wealth. However, if we value positive rights we would also be concerned about the least advantaged members of the society. Companies and corporations would be regarded as guests in society, because they benefit from the society as well as contribute to it. They could be thought to owe something in return to the community—as a matter of justice and not just as something in their own best interest. Would this describe the just society? What would you add or subtract?

John Rawls's Theory of Justice

Among the most discussed works on justice of the last two decades is John Rawls's 1971 book, *A Theory of Justice.*[11] In summarizing the basic ideas in this book, we can review elements of the theories discussed earlier.

According to Rawls, justice is fairness. It is also the *first virtue* of social institutions as truth is of scientific systems; that is, it is most important for scientific systems to be true or well supported. They may be elegant or interesting or in line with our other beliefs, but that is not the primary requirement for their acceptance. Something similar would be the case for social and economic institutions. We would want them to be efficient, but it would be even more important that they be just. But what is justice, and how do we know whether an economic system is just? Rawls sought to develop a set of principles or guidelines that we could apply to our institutions, enabling us to judge whether they are just or unjust. But how could we derive, or where could we find, valid principles of justice?

Rawls used an imaginary device called the "original position." He said that if we could imagine people in some initial fair situation and determine what they would accept as principles of justice, then these principles would be valid ones. In other words, we would first have our imaginary people so situated or described that they could choose fairly. We then would ask what they would be likely to accept. To make their choice situation fair, we would have to eliminate all bias from their choosing. Suppose that we were those people in the imaginary original position. If I knew that I was a college professor and was setting up principles to govern my society, then I would be likely to set them up so that college professors would do very well. If I knew that I had a particular talent for music or sports, for example, I might be likely to bias the principles in favor of people with these talents, and so on. To eliminate such bias, then, the people in the original position must not be able to know biasing things about themselves. They must not know their age, sex, race, talents, and so on. They must, as he says, choose from behind what he calls a "veil of ignorance."

If people could choose under such conditions, what principles of justice would they choose? We need not think of these people as selfless. They want what all people want of the basic goods of life. And as persons, their liberty is especially important to them. If they also chose rationally, rather than out of spite or envy, then what would they choose? Rawls believes that they would choose two principles; the first has to do with their political liberties, and the second concerns economic arrangements. Although he varies the wording of the principles, according to a more developed version they are as follows:

1. Each person is to have an equal right to the most extensive total system of equal basic liberties compatible with a similar system of liberty for all.
2. Social and economic inequalities are to be arranged so that they are
   a. to the greatest benefit of the least advantaged . . . , and
   b. attached to offices and positions open to all under conditions of fair equality of opportunity.[12]

Rawls believes that if people were considering an imaginary society in which to live and for which they were choosing principles of justice, and if they did not know who they would be in the society, they would require that there be *equality of liberties*; that is, they would not be willing to be the persons who had less freedom than others. They would want as much say about matters in their society that affect them as any others. This is because of the importance of liberty to all persons as persons. When it comes to wealth, however, Rawls believes that these people would accept *unequal wealth* provided certain conditions were met. They would be willing that some would be richer and some would not be so rich provided that the not so rich are better off than they otherwise would be if all had equal amounts of wealth.

You can test yourself to see if your choices coincide with Rawls's belief about people accepting unequal wealth. The table below shows the number of people at three different wealth levels (high, medium, and low) in three societies. If you had to choose, to which society would you want to belong?

If you chose society A, you are a risk taker. According to Rawls, you do not know what your chances are of being in any of the three positions in the society. You do not know whether your chances of being in the highest group are near zero or whether your chances of being in the lowest group are very good. Your best bet when you do not know what your chances are, and you do want the goods that these numbers represent, is to choose society B. In society B, no matter what position you are in you will do better than any position in society C. And because you do not know what your chances are of being in

Wealth Levels	Society A	Society B	Society C
High income	100,000	700	100
Medium income	700	400	100
Low income	50	200	100

the lowest group, even if you were in the lowest position in society B, you would be better off than in the lowest position in either group A or C. This is a "maximin" strategy: In choosing under uncertainty, you choose that option with the best worst or minimum position.

Now what is the relevance of this to his second principle of justice and his method of deriving it? It is this. When the people in the original position choose, they do not know who they are, and so they will not bias the outcome in their favor. They do not know in what position they will be in the society for which they are developing principles. Thus, they will look out for the bottom position in that society. They will think to themselves that if they were in that lowest position in their society, they would accept that some people are more wealthy than they, provided that they themselves were thereby also better off. Thus, the first part of the second principle of justice, which addresses the improvement of the least advantaged, is formulated as it is.

Another reason why Rawls believes there must be some special concern in justice to provide for the least advantaged is what he calls the "redress of nature." Nature, so to speak, is arbitrary in doling out initial starting points in life. Some people start off quite well and others are less fortunate. Justice opposes arbitrariness. If inequalities are to be just, then there must be some good reason for them. But there seemingly is no good reason that some are born wealthy and some poor. If some are born into unfortunate circumstances, it is through no fault of their own but merely because of the arbitrariness of the circumstances of their birth. Justice requires that something be done about this. Thus, again justice requires some special concern about the lot of the least advantaged, and this is part of the requirement for a just society that has inequality of wealth.

The second part of the second principle is an equal opportunity principle. For the institutions in a society that allow inequality of income and wealth to be just, that society must provide equal opportunity for those with the interest and

talent to attain the positions to which the greater wealth is attached. As noted in our earlier discussion about equal opportunity, there remain problems with the justness of reward on the basis of talent itself, if naturally endowed talent is arbitrary. However, to do otherwise and require equal opportunity for all no matter what their talents would violate the demands of efficiency and most probably would not be something that persons in the original position would accept.

In a more recent work, *Political Liberalism,* Rawls points out that his two principles of justice would not necessarily be those chosen by any persons whatsoever. They are rather the principles most likely to be accepted by people who are brought up in the traditions and institutions of a modern democratic society.[13] Modern democratic societies are pluralistic—that is, their people will have many different and irreconcilable sets of moral and religious beliefs. How, then, would they ever agree on substantive matters of justice? Consider what goes on during presidential elections in the United States. People have and manifest extremely strong and diverse political and moral beliefs, yet as members of a modern democratic society they will also share certain political values. One is that for a political system to be legitimate it must have rules that determine a system of fair cooperation for mutual advantage by members who are regarded as free and equal persons. This conception is modeled by the original position, which gives us the two principles of justice, the first specifying that people have equal political liberties and the second laying down conditions for unequal distribution of wealth, namely, principles of equal opportunity and the improvement of the least advantaged. A free-market system must be limited by the concerns of justice, which is the primary virtue of social institutions.[14]

This discussion will no doubt fail to provide easy answers for the questions regarding economic justice posed at the beginning of this chapter. However, answering questions such as these does depend on clarification of such matters as the meaning and basis of distributive justice and the relative values of efficiency, justice, and liberty. By summarizing some possibilities here, I hope to have provided you with a way to approach the more concrete matters of economic justice.

In the readings included in this chapter, the views of John Rawls as they appear in *A Theory of Justice* can be found. Susan Okin raises questions about whether theories of justice adequately take account of gender and the family. Robert Nozick discusses an entitlement theory of justice.

Notes

1. *New York Times* (August 20, 1996), p. A1. Also see Mickey Kaus, "For a New Equality," *The New Republic* (May 7, 1990), p. 19.
2. *New York Times* (December 19, 1995).
3. We associate the saying "From each according to his ability, to each according to his need" with Karl Marx. However, it originated with the "early French socialists of the Utopian school, and was officially adopted by German socialists in the Gotha Program of 1875." Nicholas Rescher, *Distributive Justice* (Indianapolis, IN: Bobbs-Merrill, 1966), 73–83.
4. James Fishkin, *Justice, Equal Opportunity, and the Family* (New Haven, CT: Yale University Press, 1983), 4.
5. Jonathan Kozol, *Savage Inequalities* (New York: Crown, 1991).
6. Bernard Williams, "The Idea of Equality," in *Philosophy, Politics and Society,* Second Series, Peter Laslett and W. G. Runciman (Eds.) (Oxford: Basil Blackwell, 1962), 110–131.
7. Milton Friedman, *Capitalism and Freedom* (Chicago: University of Chicago Press, 1982), 133.
8. This distinction has been stressed by Philippa Foot in her article, "Killing and Letting Die," in *Abortion: Moral and Legal Perspectives,* Jay Garfield (Ed.) (Amherst: University of Massachusetts Press, 1984), 178–185. This distinction is the subject of some debate among recent moral philosophers.
9. Stephen Holmes, "Welfare and the Liberal Conscience," *Report from the Institute for Philosophy and Public Policy,* vol. 15, no. 1 (Winter 1995), pp. 1–6.
10. Morton White, *The Philosophy of the American Revolution* (New York: Oxford University Press, 1978), 161.
11. John Rawls, *A Theory of Justice* (Cambridge, MA: Harvard University Press, 1971).
12. Ibid., 302.
13. John Rawls, *Political Liberalism* (New York: Columbia University Press, 1993). This work is a collection of some of Rawls's essays and lectures over the previous two decades, together with an overview introduction and several new essays.
14. Rawls, "The Primacy of the Right over the Good," in *Political Liberalism.*

Justice as Fairness

John Rawls

Study Questions

1. What does Rawls mean when he states that justice is the first virtue of social institutions?

2. How does Rawls describe the social contract idea that he intends to use to develop his theory of justice?

3. How does he describe what he calls "the original position" and the "veil of ignorance" from behind which people in the original position must choose?

4. How is the original position supposed to correspond to the notion of justice as fairness?

5. What are the people in the original position supposed to choose?

6. What has their choice from this situation to do with the voluntary cooperation of individuals in a society?

7. What two principles does Rawls believe the people in the original position would choose? Compare this first statement with the formulation later in this reading.

8. According to these principles, can the good of some or the majority justify the hardship of a minority?

9. What are some advantages of contract language for a theory of justice, according to Rawls?

10. What is Rawls's justification for the "veil of ignorance"?

11. What does Rawls mean when he states that our principles must be made to match our considered convictions about justice and vice versa, going back and forth between these two until we achieve a reflective equilibrium?

12. In his final formulation of the principles in this reading, what does Rawls mean by "equal liberties"? What does the second principle require? What are the primary goods to which it refers?

13. Do the principles allow that liberties be curtailed for the sake of economic gains?

14. How do the principles illustrate a tendency toward equality? Explain this in regard to the principle of "redress."

The Role of Justice

Justice is the first virtue of social institutions, as truth is of systems of thought. A theory however elegant and economical must be rejected or revised if it is untrue; likewise laws and institutions no matter how efficient and well-arranged must be reformed or abolished if they are unjust. Each person possesses an inviolability founded on justice that even the welfare of society as a whole cannot override. For this reason justice denies that the loss of freedom for some is made right by a greater good shared by others. It does not allow that the sacrifices imposed on a few are outweighed by the larger sum of advantages enjoyed by many. Therefore in a just society the liberties of equal citizenship are taken as settled; the rights secured by justice are not subject to political bargaining or to the calculus of social interests. The only thing that permits us to acquiesce in an erroneous theory is the lack of a better one; analogously, an injustice is

From John Rawls, *A Theory of Justice* (Cambridge, MA: Belknap Press of Harvard University Press), 3–4, 11–22, 60–65, 100–102. © 1971 by the President and Fellows of Harvard College. Reprinted by permission of the publishers.

tolerable only when it is necessary to avoid an even greater injustice. Being first virtues of human activities, truth and justice are uncompromising.

These propositions seem to express our intuitive conviction of the primacy of justice. No doubt they are expressed too strongly. In any event I wish to inquire whether these contentions or others similar to them are sound, and if so how they can be accounted for. To this end it is necessary to work out a theory of justice in the light of which these assertions can be interpreted and assessed. . . .

The Main Idea of the Theory of Justice

My aim is to present a conception of justice which generalizes and carries to a higher level of abstraction the familiar theory of the social contract as found, say, in Locke, Rousseau, and Kant.[1] In order to do this we are not to think of the original contract as one to enter a particular society or to set up a particular form of government. Rather, the guiding idea is that the principles of justice for the basic structure of society are the object of the original agreement. They are the principles that free and rational persons concerned to further their own interests would accept in an initial position of equality as defining the fundamental terms of their association. These principles are to regulate all further agreements; they specify the kinds of social cooperation that can be entered into and the forms of government that can be established. This way of regarding the principles of justice I shall call justice as fairness.

Thus we are to imagine that those who engage in social cooperation choose together, in one joint act, the principles which are to assign basic rights and duties and to determine the division of social benefits. Men are to decide in advance how they are to regulate their claims against one another and what is to be the foundation charter of their society. Just as each person must decide by rational reflection what constitutes his good, that is, the system of ends which it is rational for him to pursue, so a group of persons must decide once and for all what is to count among them as just and unjust. The choice which rational men would make in this hypothetical situation of equal liberty, assuming for the present that this choice problem has a solution, determines the principles of justice.

In justice as fairness the original position of equality corresponds to the state of nature in the traditional theory of the social contract. This original position is not, of course, thought of as an actual historical state of affairs, much less as a primitive condition of culture. It is understood as a purely hypothetical situation characterized so as to lead to a certain conception of justice.[2] Among the essential features of this situation is that no one knows his place in society, his class position or social status, nor does anyone know his fortune in the distribution of natural assets and abilities, his intelligence, strength, and the like. I shall even assume that the parties do not know their conceptions of the good or their special psychological propensities. The principles of justice are chosen behind a veil of ignorance. This ensures that no one is advantaged or disadvantaged in the choice of principles by the outcome of natural chance or the contingency of social circumstances. Since all are similarly situated and no one is able to design principles to favor his particular condition, the principles of justice are the result of a fair agreement or bargain. For given the circumstances of the original position, the symmetry of everyone's relations to each other, this initial situation is fair between individuals as moral persons, that is, as rational beings with their own ends and capable, I shall assume, of a sense of justice. The original position is, one might say, the appropriate initial status quo, and thus the fundamental agreements reached in it are fair. This explains the propriety of the name "justice as fairness": it conveys the idea that the principles of justice are agreed to in an initial situation that is fair. The name does not mean that the concepts of justice and fairness are the same, any more than the phrase "poetry as metaphor" means that the concepts of poetry and metaphor are the same.

Justice as fairness begins, as I have said, with one of the most general of all choices which persons might make together, namely, with the choice of the first principles of a conception of justice which is to regulate all subsequent criticism and reform of institutions. Then, having chosen a conception of justice, we can suppose that they are to choose a constitution and a legislature to enact laws, and so on, all in accordance with the principles of justice initially agreed upon. Our social situation is just if it is such that by this sequence of hypothetical agreements we would have contracted into the general system of rules which defines it. Moreover, assuming that the original position does determine a set of principles (that is, that a particular conception of justice would

be chosen), it will then be true that whenever social institutions satisfy these principles those engaged in them can say to one another that they are cooperating on terms to which they would agree if they were free and equal persons whose relations with respect to one another were fair. They could all view their arrangements as meeting the stipulations which they would acknowledge in an initial situation that embodies widely accepted and reasonable constraints on the choice of principles. The general recognition of this fact would provide the basis for a public acceptance of the corresponding principles of justice. No society can, of course, be a scheme of cooperation which men enter voluntarily in a literal sense; each person finds himself placed at birth in some particular position in some particular society, and the nature of this position materially affects his life prospects. Yet a society satisfying the principles of justice as fairness comes as close as a society can to being a voluntary scheme, for it meets the principles which free and equal persons would assent to under circumstances that are fair. In this sense its members are autonomous and the obligations they recognize self-imposed.

One feature of justice as fairness is to think of the parties in the initial situation as rational and mutually disinterested. This does not mean that the parties are egoists, that is, individuals with only certain kinds of interests, say in wealth, prestige, and domination. But they are conceived as not taking an interest in one another's interests. They are to presume that even their spiritual aims may be opposed, in the way that the aims of those of different religions may be opposed. Moreover, the concept of rationality must be interpreted as far as possible in the narrow sense, standard in economic theory, of taking the most effective means to given ends. I shall modify this concept to some extent, as explained later . . . , but one must try to avoid introducing into it any controversial ethical elements. The initial situation must be characterized by stipulations that are widely accepted.

In working out the conception of justice as fairness one main task clearly is to determine which principles of justice would be chosen in the original position. To do this we must describe this situation in some detail and formulate with care the problem of choice which it presents. These matters I shall take up in the immediately succeeding chapters. It may be observed, however, that once the principles of justice are thought of as arising from an original agreement in a situation of equality, it is an open question whether the principle of utility would be acknowledged. Offhand it hardly seems likely that persons who view themselves as equals, entitled to press their claims upon one another, would agree to a principle which may require lesser life prospects for some simply for the sake of a greater sum of advantages enjoyed by others. Since each desires to protect his interests, his capacity to advance his conception of the good, no one has a reason to acquiesce in an enduring loss for himself in order to bring about a greater net balance of satisfaction. In the absence of strong and lasting benevolent impulses, a rational man would not accept a basic structure merely because it maximized the algebraic sum of advantages irrespective of its permanent effects on his own basic rights and interests. Thus it seems that the principle of utility is incompatible with the conception of social cooperation among equals for mutual advantage. It appears to be inconsistent with the idea of reciprocity implicit in the notion of a well-ordered society. Or, at any rate, so I shall argue.

I shall maintain instead that the persons in the initial situation would choose two rather different principles: the first requires equality in the assignment of basic rights and duties, while the second holds that social and economic inequalities, for example inequalities of wealth and authority, are just only if they result in compensating benefits for everyone, and in particular for the least advantaged members of society. These principles rule out justifying institutions on the grounds that the hardships of some are offset by a greater good in the aggregate. It may be expedient but it is not just that some should have less in order that others may prosper. But there is no injustice in the greater benefits earned by a few provided that the situation of persons not so fortunate is thereby improved. The intuitive idea is that since everyone's well-being depends upon a scheme of cooperation without which no one could have a satisfactory life, the division of advantages should be such as to draw forth the willing cooperation of everyone taking part in it, including those less well situated. Yet this can be expected only if reasonable terms are proposed. The two principles mentioned seem to be a fair agreement on the basis of which those better endowed, or more fortunate in their social position, neither of which we can be said to deserve, could expect the willing cooperation of others when some workable scheme is a necessary condition of the welfare of all.[3] Once we decide to look for a conception of justice that nullifies the accidents of natural endowment and the contingencies of social circumstance as counters in the quest for political and economic advantage, we are led to these principles. They express the result of leaving aside those aspects of the social world that seem arbitrary from a moral point of view.

The problem of the choice of principles, however, is extremely difficult. I do not expect the answer I shall suggest to be convincing to everyone. It is, therefore, worth noting from the outset that justice as fairness, like other contract views, consists of two parts: (1) an interpretation of the initial situation and of the problem of choice posed there, and (2) a set of principles which, it is argued, would be agreed to. One may accept the first part of the theory (or some variant thereof), but not the other, and conversely. The concept of the initial contractual situation may seem reasonable although the particular principles proposed are rejected. To be sure, I want to maintain that the most appropriate conception of this situation does lead to principles of justice contrary to utilitarianism and perfectionism, and therefore that the contract doctrine provides an alternative to these views. Still, one may dispute this contention even though one grants that the contractarian method is a useful way of studying ethical theories and of setting forth their underlying assumptions.

Justice as fairness is an example of what I have called a contract theory. Now there may be an objection to the term "contract" and related expressions, but I think it will serve reasonably well. Many words have misleading connotations which at first are likely to confuse. The terms "utility" and "utilitarianism" are surely no exception. They too have unfortunate suggestions which hostile critics have been willing to exploit; yet they are clear enough for those prepared to study utilitarian doctrine. The same should be true of the term "contract" applied to moral theories. As I have mentioned, to understand it one has to keep in mind that it implies a certain level of abstraction. In particular, the content of the relevant agreement is not to enter a given society or to adopt a given form of government, but to accept certain moral principles. Moreover, the undertakings referred to are purely hypothetical: a contract view holds that certain principles would be accepted in a well-defined initial situation.

The merit of the contract terminology is that it conveys the idea that principles of justice may be conceived as principles that would be chosen by rational persons, and that in this way conceptions of justice may be explained and justified. The theory of justice is a part, perhaps the most significant part, of the theory of rational choice. Furthermore, principles of justice deal with conflicting claims upon the advantages won by social cooperation; they apply to the relations among several persons or groups. The word "contract" suggests this plurality as well as the condition that the appropriate division of advantages must be in accordance with principles acceptable to all parties. The condition of publicity for principles of justice is also connoted by the contract phraseology. Thus, if these principles are the outcome of an agreement, citizens have a knowledge of the principles that others follow. It is characteristic of contract theories to stress the public nature of political principles. Finally there is the long tradition of the contract doctrine. Expressing the tie with this line of thought helps to define ideas and accords with natural piety. There are then several advantages in the use of the term "contract." With due precautions taken, it should not be misleading.

A final remark. Justice as fairness is not a complete contract theory. For it is clear that the contractarian idea can be extended to the choice of more or less an entire ethical system, that is, to a system including principles for all the virtues and not only for justice. Now for the most part I shall consider only principles of justice and others closely related to them; I make no attempt to discuss the virtues in a systematic way. Obviously if justice as fairness succeeds reasonably well, a next step would be to study the more general view suggested by the name "rightness as fairness." But even this wider theory fails to embrace all moral relationships, since it would seem to include only our relations with other persons and to leave out of account how we are to conduct ourselves toward animals and the rest of nature. I do not contend that the contract notion offers a way to approach these questions which are certainly of the first importance; and I shall have to put them aside. We must recognize the limited scope of justice as fairness and of the general type of view that it exemplifies. How far its conclusions must be revised once these other matters are understood cannot be decided in advance.

The Original Position and Justification

I have said that the original position is the appropriate initial status quo which insures that the fundamental agreements reached in it are fair. This fact yields the name "justice as fairness." It is clear, then, that I want to say that one conception of justice is more reasonable than another, or justifiable with respect to it, if rational persons in the initial situation would choose its principles over those of the other for the role of justice. Conceptions of justice are to be ranked by their acceptability to persons so circumstanced. Understood in this way the question of justification is settled by working out a problem of deliberation: we have to ascertain which principles it would be rational to adopt given the contractual situation. This connects the theory of justice with the theory of rational choice.

If this view of the problem of justification is to succeed, we must, of course, describe in some detail the nature of this choice problem. A problem of rational decision has a definite answer only if we know the beliefs and interests of the parties, their relations with respect to one another, the alternatives between which they are to choose, the procedure whereby they make up their minds, and so on. As the circumstances are presented in different ways, correspondingly different principles are accepted. The concept of the original position, as I shall refer to it, is that of the most philosophically favored interpretation of this initial choice situation for the purposes of a theory of justice.

But how are we to decide what is the most favored interpretation? I assume, for one thing, that there is a broad measure of agreement that principles of justice should be chosen under certain conditions. To justify a particular description of the initial situation one shows that it incorporates these commonly shared presumptions. One argues from widely accepted but weak premises to more specific conclusions. Each of the presumptions should by itself be natural and plausible; some of them may seem innocuous or even trivial. The aim of the contract approach is to establish that taken together they impose significant bounds on acceptable principles of justice. The ideal outcome would be that these conditions determine a unique set of principles; but I shall be satisfied if they suffice to rank the main traditional conceptions of social justice.

One should not be misled, then, by the somewhat unusual conditions which characterize the original position. The idea here is simply to make vivid to ourselves the restrictions that it seems reasonable to impose on arguments for principles of justice, and therefore on these principles themselves. Thus it seems reasonable and generally acceptable that no one should be advantaged or disadvantaged by natural fortune or social circumstances in the choice of principles. It also seems widely agreed that it should be impossible to tailor principles to the circumstances of one's own case. We should insure further that particular inclinations and aspirations, and persons' conceptions of their good do not affect the principles adopted.

The aim is to rule out those principles that it would be rational to propose for acceptance, however little the chance of success, only if one knew certain things that are irrelevant from the standpoint of justice. For example, if a man knew that he was wealthy, he might find it rational to advance the principle that various taxes for welfare measures be counted unjust; if he knew that he was poor, he would most likely propose the contrary principle. To represent the desired restrictions one imagines a situation in which everyone is deprived of this sort of information. One excludes the knowledge of those contingencies which sets men at odds and allows them to be guided by their prejudices. In this manner the veil of ignorance is arrived at in a natural way. This concept should cause no difficulty if we keep in mind the constraints on arguments that it is meant to express. At any time we can enter the original position, so to speak, simply by following a certain procedure, namely, by arguing for principles of justice in accordance with these restrictions.

It seems reasonable to suppose that the parties in the original position are equal. That is, all have the same rights in the procedure for choosing principles; each can make proposals, submit reasons for their acceptance, and so on. Obviously the purpose of these conditions is to represent equality between human beings as moral persons, as creatures having a conception of their good and capable of a sense of justice. The basis of equality is taken to be similarity in these two respects. Systems of ends are not ranked in value; and each man is presumed to have the requisite ability to understand and to act upon whatever principles are adopted. Together with the veil of ignorance, these conditions define the principles of justice as those which rational persons concerned to advance their interests would consent to as equals when none are known to be advantaged or disadvantaged by social and natural contingencies.

There is, however, another side to justifying a particular description of the original position. This is to see if the principles which would be chosen match our considered convictions of justice or extend them in an acceptable way. We can note whether applying these principles would lead us to make the same judgments about the basic structure of society which we now make intuitively and in which we have the greatest confidence; or whether, in cases where our present judgments are in doubt and given with hesitation, these principles offer a resolution which we can affirm on reflection. There are questions which we feel sure must be answered in a certain way. For example, we are confident that religious intolerance and racial discrimination are unjust. We think that we have examined these things with care and have reached what we believe is an impartial judgment not likely to be distorted by an excessive attention to our own interests. These convictions are provisional fixed points which we presume any conception of justice must fit. But we have much less assurance as to what is the correct distribution of wealth and authority. Here we may be looking for a way to remove our doubts. We can check an interpretation of the initial situation, then, by the capacity of its principles to accommodate our firmest convictions and to provide guidance where guidance is needed.

In searching for the most favored description of this situation we work from both ends. We begin by describing it so that it represents generally shared and preferably weak conditions. We then see if these conditions are strong enough to yield a significant set of principles. If not, we look for further premises equally reasonable. But if so, and these principles match our considered convictions of justice, then so far well and good. But presumably there will be discrepancies. In this case we have a choice. We can either modify the account of the initial situation or we can revise our existing judgments, for even the judgments we take provisionally as fixed points are liable to revision. By going back and forth, sometimes altering the conditions of the contractual circumstances, at others withdrawing our judgments and conforming them to principle, I assume that eventually we shall find a description of the initial situation that both expresses reasonable conditions and yields principles which match our considered judgments duly pruned and adjusted. This state of affairs I refer to as reflective equilibrium.[4] It is an equilibrium because at last our principles and judgments coincide; and it is reflective since we know to what principles our judgments conform and the premises of their derivation. At the moment everything is in order. But this equilibrium is not necessarily stable. It is liable to be upset by further examination of the conditions which should be imposed on the contractual situation and by particular cases which may lead us to revise our judgments. Yet for the time being we have done what we can to render coherent and to justify our convictions of social justice. We have reached a conception of the original position.

I shall not, of course, actually work through this process. Still, we may think of the interpretation of the original position that I shall present as the result of such a hypothetical course of reflection. It represents the attempt to accommodate within one scheme both reasonable philosophical conditions on principles as well as our considered judgments of justice. In arriving at the favored interpretation of the initial situation there is no point at which an appeal is made to self-evidence in the traditional sense either of general conceptions or particular convictions. I do not claim for the principles of justice proposed that they are necessary truths or derivable from such truths. A conception of justice cannot be deduced from self-evident premises or conditions on principles; instead, its justification is a matter of the mutual support of many considerations, of everything fitting together into one coherent view.

A final comment. We shall want to say that certain principles of justice are justified because they would be agreed to in an initial situation of equality. I have emphasized that this original position is purely hypothetical. It is natural to ask why, if this agreement is never actually entered into, we should take any interest in these principles, moral or otherwise. The answer is that the conditions embodied in the description of the original position are ones that we do in fact accept. Or if we do not, then perhaps we can be persuaded to do so by philosophical reflection. Each aspect of the contractual situation can be given supporting grounds. Thus what we shall do is collect together into one conception a number of conditions on principles that we are ready upon due consideration to recognize as reasonable. These constraints express what we are prepared to regard as limits on fair terms of social cooperation. One way to look at the idea of the original position, therefore, is to see it as an expository device which sums up the meaning of these conditions and helps us to extract their consequences. On the other hand, this conception is also an intuitive notion that suggests its own elabo-

ration, so that led on by it we are drawn to define more clearly the standpoint from which we can best interpret moral relationships. We need a conception that enables us to envision our objective from afar: the intuitive notion of the original position is to do this for us. . . .[5]

Two Principles of Justice

I shall now state in a provisional form the two principles of justice that I believe would be chosen in the original position. In this section I wish to make only the most general comments, and therefore the first formulation of these principles is tentative. As we go on I shall run through several formulations and approximate step by step the final statement to be given much later. I believe that doing this allows the exposition to proceed in a natural way.

The first statement of the two principles reads as follows.

> First: each person is to have an equal right to the most extensive basic liberty compatible with a similar liberty for others.

> Second: social and economic inequalities are to be arranged so that they are both (a) reasonably expected to be to everyone's advantage, and (b) attached to positions and offices open to all. . . .

By way of general comment, these principles primarily apply, as I have said, to the basic structure of society. They are to govern the assignment of rights and duties and to regulate the distribution of social and economic advantages. As their formulation suggests, these principles presuppose that the social structure can be divided into two more or less distinct parts, the first principle applying to the one, the second to the other. They distinguish between those aspects of the social system that define and secure the equal liberties of citizenship and those that specify and establish social and economic inequalities. The basic liberties of citizens are, roughly speaking, political liberty (the right to vote and to be eligible for public office) together with freedom of speech and assembly; liberty of conscience and freedom of thought; freedom of the person along with the right to hold (personal) property; and freedom from arbitrary arrest and seizure as defined by the concept of the rule of law. These liberties are all required to be equal by the first principle, since citizens of a just society are to have the same basic rights.

The second principle applies, in the first approximation, to the distribution of income and wealth and to the design of organizations that make use of differences in authority and responsibility, or chains of command. While the distribution of wealth and income need not be equal, it must be to everyone's advantage, and at the same time, positions of authority and offices of command must be accessible to all. One applies the second principle by holding positions open, and then, subject to this constraint, arranges social and economic inequalities so that everyone benefits.

These principles are to be arranged in a serial order with the first principle prior to the second. This ordering means that a departure from the institutions of equal liberty required by the first principle cannot be justified by, or compensated for, by greater social and economic advantages. The distribution of wealth and income, and the hierarchies of authority, must be consistent with both the liberties of equal citizenship and equality of opportunity.

It is clear that these principles are rather specific in their content, and their acceptance rests on certain assumptions that I must eventually try to explain and justify. A theory of justice depends upon a theory of society in ways that will become evident as we proceed. For the present, it should be observed that the two principles (this holds for all formulations) are a special case of a more general conception of justice that can be expressed as follows.

> All social values—liberty and opportunity, income and wealth, and the bases of self-respect—are to be distributed equally unless an unequal distribution of any, or all, of these values is to everyone's advantage.

Injustice, then, is simply inequalities that are not to the benefit of all. Of course, this conception is extremely vague and requires interpretation.

As a first step, suppose that the basic structure of society distributes certain primary goods, that is, things that every rational man is presumed to want. These goods normally have a use whatever a person's rational plan of life. For simplicity, assume that the chief primary goods at the disposition of society are rights and liberties, powers and opportunities, income and wealth. . . . There the primary good of self-respect has a central place. These are the social primary goods. Other primary goods such as health and vigor, intelligence and imagination, are natural goods; although their possession is influenced by the basic structure, they are not so directly under its control. Imagine, then, a hypothetical initial arrangement in which all the social primary goods are equally distributed: everyone has similar rights and duties, and income and wealth are evenly shared. This state of affairs provides a benchmark for judging improvements. If certain inequalities of wealth and organizational powers would make everyone better off than in this hypothetical starting situation, then they accord with the general conception.

Now it is possible, at least theoretically, that by giving up some of their fundamental liberties men are sufficiently compensated by the resulting social and economic gains. The general conception of justice imposes no restrictions on what sort of inequalities are permissible; it only requires that everyone's position be improved. We need not suppose anything so drastic as consenting to a condition of slavery. Imagine instead that men forego certain political rights when the economic returns are significant and their capacity to influence the course of policy by the exercise of these rights would be marginal in any case. It is this kind of exchange which the two principles as stated rule out; being arranged in serial order they do not permit exchanges between basic liberties and economic and social gains. The serial ordering of principles expresses an underlying preference among primary social goods. When this preference is rational so likewise is the choice of these principles in this order.

In developing justice as fairness I shall, for the most part, leave aside the general conception of justice and examine instead the special case of the two principles in serial order. The advantage of this procedure is that from the first the matter of priorities is recognized and an effort made to find principles to deal with it. One is led to attend throughout to the conditions under which the acknowledgment of the absolute weight of liberty with respect to social and economic advantages, as defined by the lexical order of the two principles, would be reasonable. Offhand, this ranking appears extreme and too special a case to be of much interest; but there is more justification for it than would appear at first sight. Or at any rate, so I shall maintain. . . . Furthermore, the distinction between fundamental rights and liberties and economic and social benefits marks a difference among primary social goods that one should try to exploit. It suggests an important division in the social system. Of course, the distinctions drawn and the ordering proposed are bound to be at best only approximations. There are surely circumstances in which they fail. But it is essential to depict clearly the main lines of a reasonable conception of justice; and under many conditions anyway, the two principles in serial order may serve well enough. When necessary we can fall back on the more general conception.

The fact that the two principles apply to institutions has certain consequences. Several points illustrate this. First of all, the rights and liberties referred to by these principles are those which are defined by the public rules of the basic structure. Whether men are free is determined by the rights and duties established by the major institutions of society. Liberty is a certain pattern of social forms. The first principle simply requires that certain sorts of rules, those defining basic liberties, apply to everyone equally and that they allow the most extensive liberty compatible with a like liberty for all. The only reason for circumscribing the rights defining liberty and making men's freedom less extensive than it might otherwise be is that these equal rights as institutionally defined would interfere with one another.

Another thing to bear in mind is that when principles mention persons, or require that everyone gain from an inequality, the reference is to representative persons holding the various social positions, or offices, or whatever, established by the basic structure. Thus in applying the second principle I assume that it is possible to assign an expectation of well-being to representative individuals holding these positions. This expectation indicates their life prospects as viewed from their social station. In general, the expectations of representative persons depend upon the distribution of rights and duties throughout the basic structure. When this changes, expectations change. I assume, then, that expectations are connected: by raising the prospects of the representative man in one position we presumably increase or decrease the prospects of representative men in other positions. Since it applies to institutional forms, the second principle (or rather the first part of it) refers to the expectations of representative individuals. As I shall discuss below, neither principle applies to distributions of particular goods to particular individuals who may be identified by their proper names. The situation where someone is considering how to allocate certain commodities to needy persons who are known to him is not within the scope of the principles. They are meant to regulate basic institutional arrangements. We must not assume that there is much similarity from the standpoint of justice between an administrative allotment of goods to specific persons and the appropriate design of society. Our common sense intuitions for the former may be a poor guide to the latter.

Now the second principle insists that each person benefit from permissible inequalities in the basic structure. This means that it must be reasonable for each relevant representative man defined by this structure, when he views it as a going concern, to prefer his prospects with the inequality to his prospects without it. One is not allowed to justify differences in income or organizational powers on the ground that the disadvantages of those in one position are outweighed by the greater advantages of those in another. Much less can infringements of liberty be counterbalanced in this way. Applied to the basic structure, the principle of utility would have us maximize the sum of expectations of representative men (weighted by the number of persons they represent, on the classical view); and this would permit us to compensate for the losses of some by the gains of others. Instead, the two principles require that everyone benefit from economic and social inequalities. . . .

The Tendency to Equality

I wish to conclude this discussion of the two principles by explaining the sense in which they express an egalitarian conception of justice. Also I should like to forestall the objection to the principle of fair opportunity that it leads to a callous meritocratic society. In order to prepare the way for doing this, I note several aspects of the conception of justice that I have set out.

First we may observe that the difference principle gives some weight to the considerations singled out by the principle of redress. This is the principle that undeserved inequalities call for redress; and since inequalities of birth and natural endowment are undeserved, these inequalities are to be somehow compensated for.[6] Thus the principle holds that in order to treat all persons equally, to provide genuine equality of opportunity, society must give more attention to those with fewer native assets and to those born into the less favorable social positions. The idea is to redress the bias of contingencies in the direction of equality. In pursuit of this principle greater resources might be spent on the education of the less rather than the more intelligent, at least over a certain time of life, say the earlier years of school.

Now the principle of redress has not to my knowledge been proposed as the sole criterion of justice, as the single aim of the social order. It is plausible as most such principles are only as a prima facie principle, one that is to be weighed in the balance with others. For example, we are to weigh it against the principle to improve the average standard of life, or to advance the common good.[7] But whatever other principles we hold, the claims of redress are to be taken into account. It is thought to represent one of the elements in our conception of justice. Now the difference principle is not of course the principle of redress. It does not require society to try to even out handicaps as if all were expected to compete on a fair basis in the same race. But the difference principle would allocate resources in education, say, so as to improve the long-term expectation of the least favored. If this end is attained by giving more attention to the better endowed, it is permissible; otherwise not. And in making this decision, the value of education should not be assessed only in terms of economic efficiency and social welfare. Equally if not more important is the role of education in enabling a person to enjoy the culture of his society and to take part in its affairs, and in this way to provide for each individual a secure sense of his own worth.

Thus although the difference principle is not the same as that of redress, it does achieve some of the intent of the latter principle. It transforms the aims of the basic structure so that the total scheme of institutions no longer emphasizes social efficiency and technocratic values. We see then that the difference principle represents, in effect, an agreement to regard the distribution of natural talents as a common asset and to share in the benefits of this distribution whatever it turns out to be. Those who have been favored by nature, whoever they are, may gain from their good fortune only on terms that improve the situation of those who have lost out. The naturally advantaged are not to gain merely because they are more gifted, but only to cover the costs of training and education and for using their endowments in ways that help the less fortunate as well. No one deserves his greater natural capacity nor merits a more favorable starting place in society. But it does not follow that one should eliminate these distinctions. There is another way to deal with them. The basic structure can be arranged so that these contingencies work for the good of the least fortunate. Thus we are led to the difference principle if we wish to set up the social system so that no one gains or loses from his arbitrary place in the distribution of natural assets or his initial position in society without giving or receiving compensating advantages in return.

In view of these remarks we may reject the contention that the ordering of institutions is always defective because the distribution of natural talents and the contingencies of social circumstance are unjust, and this injustice must inevitably carry over to human arrangements. Occasionally this reflection is offered as an excuse for ignoring injustice, as if the refusal to acquiesce in injustice is on a par with being unable to accept death. The natural distribution is neither just nor unjust; nor is it unjust that men are born into society at some particular position. These are simply natural facts. What is just and unjust is the way that institutions deal with these facts. Aristocratic and caste societies are unjust because they make these contingencies the ascriptive basis for belonging to more or less enclosed and privileged social classes. The basic structure of these societies incorporates the arbitrariness found in nature. But there is no necessity for men to resign themselves to these contingencies. The social system is not an unchangeable order beyond human control but a pattern of human action. In justice as fairness men agree to share one another's fate. In designing institutions they undertake to avail themselves of the accidents of nature and social circumstance only when doing so is for the common benefit. The two principles are a fair way of meeting the arbitrariness of fortune; and while no doubt imperfect in other ways, the institutions which satisfy these principles are just.

Notes*

1. As the text suggests, I shall regard Locke's *Second Treatise of Government,* Rousseau's *The Social Contract,* and Kant's ethical works beginning with *The Foundations of the Metaphysics of Morals* as definitive of the contract tradition. For all of its greatness, Hobbes's *Leviathan* raises special problems. A general historical survey is provided by J. W. Gough, *The Social Contract,* 2nd ed. (Oxford, The Clarendon Press, 1957), and Otto Gierke, *Natural Law and the Theory of Society,* trans. with an introduction by Ernest Barker (Cambridge, The University Press, 1934). A presentation of the

---

*Some of the notes have been deleted and the remaining ones renumbered.—ED.

contract view as primarily an ethical theory is to be found in G. R. Grice, *The Grounds of Moral Judgment* (Cambridge, The University Press, 1967). See also §19, note 30.

2. Kant is clear that the original agreement is hypothetical. See *The Metaphysics of Morals,* pt. I (Rechtslehre), especially §§47, 52; and pt. II of the essay "Concerning the Common Saying: This May Be True in Theory but It Does Not Apply in Practice," in Kant's *Political Writings,* ed. Hans Reiss and trans. by H. B. Nisbet (Cambridge, The University Press, 1970), pp. 73–87. See Georges Vlachos, *La Pensée politique de Kant* (Paris, Presses Universitaires de France, 1962), pp. 326–335; and J. G. Murphy, *Kant: The Philosophy of Right* (London, Macmillan, 1970), pp. 109–112, 133–136, for a further discussion.

3. For the formulation of this intuitive idea I am indebted to Allan Gibbard.

4. The process of mutual adjustment of principles and considered judgments is not peculiar to moral philosophy. See Nelson Goodman, *Fact, Fiction, and Forecast* (Cambridge, Mass., Harvard University Press, 1955), pp. 65–68, for parallel remarks concerning the justification of the principles of deductive and inductive inference.

5. Henri Poincaré remarks: "Il nous faut une faculté qui nous fasse voir le but de loin, et, cette faculté, c'est l'intuition." *La Valeur de la science* (Paris, Flammarion, 1909), p. 27.

6. See Herbert Spiegelberg, "A Defense of Human Equality," *Philosophical Review,* vol. 53 (1944), pp. 101, 113–123; and D. D. Raphael, "Justice and Liberty," *Proceedings of the Aristotelian Society,* vol. 51 (1950–1951), pp. 187f.

7. See, for example, Spiegelberg, pp. 120f.

Justice and Gender

Susan Moller Okin

Study Questions

1. What does Okin mean when she speaks of the gendered structure of the family and marriage as major hindrances to justice for women? What are some of the examples of this she provides?

2. What does she mean by "construction of gender"?

3. Why is the neglect of the problem of justice and gender by contemporary political theorists puzzling to Okin?

4. What is the "separate spheres tradition" that she believes is wrongly continued by these theorists?

5. For what three reasons does she believe this state of affairs is unacceptable?

6. Why does Okin believe that feminists also should give attention to an ethics of rights and not simply an ethics of care?

7. What kinds of things does she believe are essential if we are to have real equality of opportunity? How does the situation of the family today create problems of equal opportunity for women?

8. How does Okin believe that the family teaches injustice to children? Has this been recognized by theorists of the past or present?

9. What is her assessment of Rawls's treatment of the family and justice?

10. Why is education for justice in the family important, according to Okin?

We as a society pride ourselves on our democratic values. We don't believe people should be constrained by innate differences from being able to achieve desired positions of influence or to improve their well-being; equality of opportunity is our professed aim. The Preamble to our Constitution stresses the importance of justice, as well as the general

From Susan Moller Okin, *Justice, Gender, and the Family* (New York: Basic Books, 1989), 3–9, 14–19, 21–22. ©1989 by Basic Books, Inc. Reprinted by permission of Basic Books, a division of HarperCollins Publishers, Inc.

welfare and the blessings of liberty. The Pledge of Allegiance asserts that our republic preserves "liberty and justice for all."

Yet substantial inequalities between the sexes still exist in our society. In economic terms, full-time working women (after some very recent improvement) earn on average 71 percent of the earnings of full-time working men. One-half of poor and three-fifths of chronically poor households with dependent children are maintained by a single female parent. The poverty rate for elderly women is nearly twice that for elderly men.[1] On the political front, two out of a hundred U.S. senators are women, one out of nine justices seems to be considered sufficient female representation on the Supreme Court, and the number of men chosen in each congressional election far exceeds the number of women elected in the entire history of the country. Underlying and intertwined with all these inequalities is the unequal distribution of the unpaid labor of the family.

An equal sharing between the sexes of family responsibilities, especially child care, is "the great revolution that has not happened."[2] Women, including mothers of young children, are, of course, working outside the household far more than their mothers did. And the small proportion of women who reach high-level positions in politics, business, and the professions command a vastly disproportionate amount of space in the media, compared with the millions of women who work at low-paying, dead-end jobs, the millions who do part-time work with its lack of benefits, and the millions of others who stay home performing for no pay what is frequently not even acknowledged as work. Certainly, the fact that women are doing more paid work does not imply that they are more equal. It is often said that we are living in a postfeminist era. This claim, due in part to the distorted emphasis on women who have "made it," is false, no matter which of its meanings is intended. It is certainly not true that feminism has been vanquished, and equally untrue that it is no longer needed because its aims have been fulfilled. Until there is justice within the family, women will not be able to gain equality in politics, at work, or in any other sphere.

. . . The typical current practices of family life, structured to a large extent by gender, are not just. Both the expectation and the experience of the division of labor by sex make women vulnerable.

. . . A cycle of power relations and decisions pervades both family and workplace, each reinforcing the inequalities between the sexes that already exist within the other. Not only women, but children of both sexes, too, are often made vulnerable by gender-structured marriage. One-quarter of children in the United States now live in families with only one parent—in almost 90 percent of cases, the mother. Contrary to common perceptions—in which the situation of never-married mothers looms largest—65 percent of single-parent families are a result of marital separation or divorce.[3] Recent research in a number of states has shown that, in the average case, the standard of living of divorced women and the children who live with them plummets after divorce, whereas the economic situation of divorced men tends to be better than when they were married.

A central source of injustice for women these days is that the law, most noticeably in the event of divorce, treats more or less as equals those whom custom, workplace discrimination, and the still conventional division of labor within the family have made very unequal. Central to this socially created inequality are two commonly made but inconsistent presumptions: that women are primarily responsible for the rearing of children; and that serious and committed members of the work force (regardless of class) do not have primary responsibility, or even shared responsibility, for the rearing of children. The old assumption of the workplace, still implicit, is that workers have wives at home. It is built not only into the structure and expectations of the workplace but into other crucial social institutions, such as schools, which make no attempt to take account, in their scheduled hours or vacations, of the fact that parents are likely to hold jobs.

Now, of course, many wage workers do not have wives at home. Often, they are wives and mothers, or single, separated, or divorced mothers of small children. But neither the family nor the workplace has taken much account of this fact. Employed wives still do by far the greatest proportion of unpaid family work, such as child care and housework. Women are far more likely to take time out of the workplace or to work part-time because of family responsibilities than are their husbands or male partners. And they are much more likely to move because of their husbands' employment needs or opportunities than their own. All these tendencies, which are due to a number of factors, including the sex segregation and discrimination of the workplace itself, tend to be cyclical in their effects: wives advance more slowly than their husbands at work and thus gain less seniority, and the discrepancy between their wages increases over time.

Then, because both the power structure of the family and what is regarded as consensual "rational" family decision making reflect the fact that the husband usually earns more, it will become even less likely as time goes on that the unpaid work of the family will be shared between the spouses. Thus the cycle of inequality is perpetuated. Often hidden from view within a marriage, it is in the increasingly likely event of marital breakdown that socially constructed inequality of married women is at its most visible.

This is what I mean when I say that gender-structured marriage *makes* women vulnerable. These are not matters of natural necessity, as some people would believe. Surely nothing in our natures dictates that men should not be equal participants in the rearing of their children. Nothing in the nature of work makes it impossible to adjust it to the fact that people are parents as well as workers. That these things have not happened is part of the historically, socially constructed differentiation between the sexes that feminists have come to call *gender*. We live in a society that has over the years regarded the innate characteristic of sex as one of the clearest legitimizers of different rights and restrictions, both formal and informal. While the legal sanctions that uphold male dominance have begun to be eroded in the past century, and more rapidly in the last twenty years, the heavy weight of tradition, combined with the effects of socialization, still works powerfully to reinforce sex roles that are commonly regarded as of unequal prestige and worth. The sexual division of labor has not only been a fundamental part of the marriage contract, but so deeply influences us in our formative years that feminists of both sexes who try to reject it can find themselves struggling against it with varying degrees of ambivalence. Based on this linchpin, "gender"—by which I mean the *deeply entrenched institutionalization of sexual difference*—still permeates our society.

The Construction of Gender

Due to feminism and feminist theory, gender is coming to be recognized as a social factor of major importance. Indeed, the new meaning of the word reflects the fact that so much of what has traditionally been thought of as a sexual difference is now considered by many to be largely socially produced.[4] Feminist scholars from many disciplines and with radically different points of view have contributed to the enterprise of making gender fully visible and compre-

hensible. At one end of the spectrum are those whose explanations of the subordination of women focus primarily on biological difference as causal in the construction of gender,[5] and at the other end are those who argue that biological difference may not even lie at the core of the social construction that is gender[6]; the views of the vast majority of feminists fall between these extremes. The rejection of biological determinism and the corresponding emphasis on gender as a social construction characterize most current feminist scholarship. Of particular relevance is work in psychology, where scholars have investigated the importance of female primary parenting in the formation of our gendered identities,[7] and in history and anthropology,[8] where emphasis has been placed on the historical and cultural variability of gender. Some feminists have been criticized for developing theories of gender that do not take sufficient account of differences *among* women, especially race, class, religion, and ethnicity.[9] While such critiques should always inform our research and improve our arguments, it would be a mistake to allow them to detract our attention from gender itself as a factor of significance. Many injustices are experienced by women *as women*, whatever the differences among them and whatever other injustices they also suffer from. The past and present gendered nature of the family, and the ideology that surrounds it, affects virtually all women, whether or not they live or ever lived in traditional families. Recognizing this is not to deny or de-emphasize the fact that gender may affect different subgroups of women to a different extent and in different ways.

The potential significance of feminist discoveries and conclusions about gender for issues of social justice cannot be overemphasized. They undermine centuries of argument that started with the notion that not only the distinct differentiation of women and men but the domination of women by men, being natural, was therefore inevitable and not even to be considered in discussions of justice. As I shall make clear in later chapters, despite the fact that such notions cannot stand up to rational scrutiny, they not only still survive but flourish in influential places.

During the same two decades in which feminists have been intensely thinking, researching, analyzing, disagreeing about, and rethinking the subject of gender, our political and legal institutions have been increasingly faced with issues concerning the injustices of gender and their effects. These issues are being decided within a fundamentally patriarchal system, founded in a tradition in which "individuals" were assumed to be male heads of households. Not surprisingly, the system has demonstrated a limited capacity for determining what is just, in many cases involving gender. Sex discrimination, sexual harassment, abortion, pregnancy in the workplace, parental leave, child care, and surrogate mothering have all become major and well-publicized issues of public policy, engaging both courts and legislatures. Issues of family justice, in particular—from child custody and terms of divorce to physical and sexual abuse of wives and children—have become increasingly visible and pressing, and are commanding increasing attention from the police and court systems. There is clearly a major "justice crisis" in contemporary society arising from issues of gender.

Theories of Justice and the Neglect of Gender

During these same two decades, there has been a great resurgence of theories of social justice. Political theory, which had been sparse for a period before the late 1960s except as an important branch of intellectual history, has become a flourishing field, with social justice as its central concern. Yet, remarkably, major contemporary theorists of justice have almost without exception ignored the situation I have just described. They have displayed little interest in or knowledge of the findings of feminism. They have largely bypassed the fact that the society to which their theories are supposed to pertain is heavily and deeply affected by gender, and faces difficult issues of justice stemming from its gendered past and present assumptions. Since theories of justice are centrally concerned with whether, how, and why persons should be treated differently from one another, this neglect seems inexplicable. These theories are *about* which initial or acquired characteristics or positions in society legitimize differential treatment of persons by social institutions, laws, and customs. They are *about* how and whether and to what extent beginnings should affect outcomes. The division of humanity into two sexes seems to provide an obvious subject for such inquiries. But, as we shall see, this does not strike most contemporary theorists of justice, and their theories suffer in both coherence and relevance because of it. This book is about this remarkable case of neglect. It is also an attempt to rectify it, to point the way toward a more fully hu-

manist theory of justice by confronting the question, "How just is gender?"

Why is it that when we turn to contemporary theories of justice, we do not find illuminating and positive contributions to this question? How can theories of justice that are ostensibly about people in general neglect women, gender, and all the inequalities between the sexes? One reason is that most theorists *assume*, though they do not discuss, the traditional, gender-structured family. Another is that they often employ gender-neutral language in a false, hollow way. . . .

The Hidden Gender-Structured Family

In the past, political theorists often used to distinguish clearly between "private" domestic life and the "public" life of politics and the marketplace, claiming explicitly that the two spheres operated in accordance with different principles. They separated out the family from what they deemed the subject matter of politics, and they made closely related, explicit claims about the nature of women and the appropriateness of excluding them from civil and political life. Men, the subjects of the theories, were able to make the transition back and forth from domestic to public life with ease, largely because of the functions performed by women in the family.[10] When we turn to contemporary theories of justice, superficial appearances can easily lead to the impression that they are inclusive of women. In fact, they continue the same "separate spheres" tradition, by ignoring the family, its division of labor, and the related economic dependency and restricted opportunities of most women. The judgment that the family is "nonpolitical" is implicit in the fact that it is simply not discussed in most works of political theory today. In one way or another, as will become clear in the chapters that follow, almost all current theorists continue to assume that the "individual" who is the basic subject of their theories is the male head of a fairly traditional household. Thus the application of principles of justice to relations between the sexes, or within the household, is frequently, though tacitly, ruled out from the start. In the most influential of all twentieth-century theories of justice, that of John Rawls, family life is not only assumed, but is assumed to be just—and yet the prevalent gendered division of labor within the family is neglected, along with the associated distribution of power, responsibility, and privilege. . . .[11]

Gender as an Issue of Justice

For three major reasons, this state of affairs is unacceptable. The first is the obvious point that women must be fully included in any satisfactory theory of justice. The second is that equality of opportunity, not only for women but for children of both sexes, is seriously undermined by the current gender injustices of our society. And the third reason is that, as has already been suggested, the family—currently the linchpin of the gender structure—must be just if we are to have a just society, since it is within the family that we first come to have that sense of ourselves and our relations with others that is at the root of moral development.

Counting Women In

When we turn to the great tradition of Western political thought with questions about the justice of the treatment of the sexes in mind, it is to little avail. Bold feminists like Mary Astell, Mary Wollstonecraft, William Thompson, Harriet Taylor, and George Bernard Shaw have occasionally challenged the tradition, often using its own premises and arguments to overturn its explicit or implicit justification of the inequality of women. But John Stuart Mill is a rare exception to the rule that those who hold central positions in the tradition almost never question the justice of the subordination of women.[12] This phenomenon is undoubtedly due in part to the fact that Aristotle, whose theory of justice has been so influential, relegated women to a sphere of "household justice"—populated by persons who are not fundamentally equal to the free men who participate in political justice, but inferiors whose natural function is to serve those who are more fully human. The liberal tradition, despite its supposed foundation of individual rights and human equality, is more Aristotelian in this respect than is generally acknowledged.[13] In one way or another, almost all liberal theorists have assumed that the "individual" who is the basic subject of the theories is the male head of a patriarchal household.[14] Thus they have not usually considered applying the principles of justice to women or to relations between the sexes.

When we turn to contemporary theories of justice, however, we expect to find more illuminating and positive contributions to the subject of gender and justice. As the omission of the family and the falseness of their gender-neutral language suggest, however, mainstream contemporary theories of justice do not address the subject any better than those of the past. Theories of justice that apply to only half of us simply won't do; the inclusiveness falsely implied by the current use of gender-neutral terms must become real. Theories of justice must apply to all of us, and to all of human life, instead of *assuming* silently that half of us take care of whole areas of life that are considered outside the scope of social justice. In a just society, the structure and practices of families must afford women the same opportunities as men to develop their capacities, to participate in political power, to influence social choices, and to be economically as well as physically secure.

Unfortunately, much feminist intellectual energy in the 1980s has gone into the claim that "justice" and "rights" are masculinist ways of thinking about morality that feminists should eschew or radically revise, advocating a morality of care.[15] The emphasis is misplaced, I think, for several reasons. First, what is by now a vast literature on the subject shows that the evidence for differences in women's and men's ways of thinking about moral issues is not (at least yet) very clear; neither is the evidence about the source of whatever differences there might be.[16] It may well turn out that any differences can be readily explained in terms of roles, including female primary parenting, that are socially determined and therefore alterable. There is certainly no evidence—nor could there be, in such a gender-structured society—for concluding that women are somehow naturally more inclined toward contextuality and away from universalism in their moral thinking, a false concept that unfortunately reinforces the old stereotypes that justify separate spheres. . . .

. . . I think the distinction between an ethic of justice and an ethic of care has been overdrawn. The best theorizing about justice, I argue, has integral to it the notions of care and empathy, of thinking of the interests and well-being of others who may be very different from ourselves. It is, therefore, misleading to draw a dichotomy as though they were two contrasting ethics. The best theorizing about justice is not some abstract "view from nowhere," but results from the carefully attentive consideration of *everyone's* point of view. This means, of course, that the best theorizing about justice is not good enough if it does not, or cannot readily be adapted to, include women and their points of view as fully as men and their points of view.

Gender and Equality of Opportunity

The family is a crucial determinant of our opportunities in life, of what we "become." It has frequently been acknowledged by those concerned with real equality of opportunity that the family presents a problem.[17] But though they have discerned a serious problem, these theorists have underestimated it because they have seen only half of it. They have seen that the disparity among families in terms of the physical and emotional environment, motivation, and material advantages they can give their children has a tremendous effect upon children's opportunities in life. We are not born as isolated, equal individuals in our society, but into family situations: some in the social middle, some poor and homeless, and some superaffluent; some to a single or soon-to-be-separated parent, some to parents whose marriage is fraught with conflict, some to parents who will stay together in love and happiness. Any claims that equal opportunity exists are therefore completely unfounded. Decades of neglect of the poor, especially of poor black and Hispanic households, accentuated by the policies of the Reagan years, have brought us farther from the principles of equal opportunity. To come close to them would require, for example, a high and uniform standard of public education and the provision of equal social services—including health care, employment training, job opportunities, drug rehabilitation, and decent housing—for all who need them. In addition to redistributive taxation, only massive reallocations of resources from the military to social services could make these things possible.

But even if all these disparities were somehow eliminated, we would still not attain equal opportunity for all. This is because what has not been recognized as an equal opportunity problem, except in feminist literature and circles, is the disparity *within* the family, the fact that its gender structure is itself a major obstacle to equality of opportunity. This is very important in itself, since one of the factors with most influence on our opportunities in life is the social significance attributed to our sex. The opportunities of girls and women are centrally affected by the structure and practices of family life, particularly by the fact that women are almost invariably primary parents. What nonfeminists who see in the family an obstacle to equal opportunity have *not* seen is that the extent to which a family is gender-structured can make the sex we belong to a relatively insignificant aspect of our identity and our life prospects or an all-pervading one. This is because so much of the social construction of gender takes place in the family, and particularly in the institution of female parenting.

Moreover, especially in recent years, with the increased rates of single motherhood, separation, and divorce, the inequalities between the sexes have *compounded* the first part of the problem. The disparity among families has grown largely because of the impoverishment of many women and children after separation or divorce. The division of labor in the typical family leaves most women far less capable than men of supporting themselves, and this disparity is accentuated by the fact that children of separated or divorced parents usually live with their mothers. The inadequacy—and frequent nonpayment—of child support has become recognized as a major social problem. Thus the inequalities of gender are now directly harming many children of both sexes as well as women themselves. Enhancing equal opportunity for women, important as it is in itself, is also a crucial way of improving the opportunities of many of the most disadvantaged children.

As there is a connection among the parts of this problem, so is there a connection among some of the solutions: much of what needs to be done to end the inequalities of gender, and to work in the direction of ending gender itself, will also help to equalize opportunity from one family to another. Subsidized, high-quality day care is obviously one such thing; another is the adaptation of the workplace to the needs of parents. . . .

The Family as a School of Justice

One of the things that theorists who have argued that families need not or cannot be just, or who have simply neglected them, have failed to explain is how, within a formative social environment that is *not* founded upon principles of justice, children can learn to develop that sense of justice they will require as citizens of a just society. Rather than being one among many co-equal institutions of a just society, a family is its essential foundation.

It may seem uncontroversial, even obvious, that families must be just because of the vast influence they have on the moral development of children. But this is clearly not the case. I shall argue that unless the first and most formative example of adult interaction usually experienced by children is one of justice and reciprocity, rather than one of domination and manipulation or of unequal altruism and one-sided self-sacrifice, and unless they themselves are treated with concern and respect, they are likely to be considerably hindered in becoming people who are guided by principles of justice. Moreover, I claim, the sharing of roles by men and women, rather than the division of roles between them, would have a further positive impact because the experience of *being* a physical and psychological nurturer—whether of a child or of another adult—would increase that capacity to identify with and fully comprehend the viewpoints of others that is important to a sense of justice. In a society that minimized gender this would be more likely to be the experience of all of us.

Almost every person in our society starts life in a family of some sort or other. Fewer of these families now fit the usual, though by no means universal, standard of previous generations, that is, wageworking father, homemaking mother, and children. More families these days are headed by a single parent; lesbian and gay parenting is no longer so rare; many children have two wageworking parents, and receive at least some of their early care outside the home. While its forms are varied, the family in which a child is raised, especially in the earliest years, is clearly a crucial place for early moral development and for the formation of our basic attitudes to others. It is, potentially, a place where we can *learn to be just*. It is especially important for the development of a sense of justice that grows from sharing the experiences of others and becoming aware of the points of view of others who are different in some respects from ourselves, but with whom we clearly have some interests in common.

The importance of the family for the moral development of individuals was far more often recognized by political theorists of the past than it is by those of the present. Hegel, Rousseau, Tocqueville, Mill, and Dewey are obvious examples that come to mind. Rousseau, for example, shocked by Plato's proposal to abolish the family, says that it is

> as though there were no need for a natural base on which to form conventional ties; as though the love of one's nearest were not the principle of the love one owes the state; as though it were not by means of the small fatherland which is the family that the heart attaches itself to the large one.[18]

Defenders of both autocratic and democratic regimes have recognized the political importance of different family forms for the formation of citizens. On the one hand, the nineteenth-century monarchist Louis de Bonald argued against the divorce reforms of the French Revolution, which he claimed had weakened the patriarchal family, on the grounds that "in order to keep the state out of the hands of the people, it is necessary to keep the family out of the hands of women and children."[19] Taking this same line of thought in the opposite direction, the U.S. Supreme Court decided in 1879 in *Reynolds* v. *Nebraska* that familial patriarchy fostered despotism and was therefore intolerable. Denying Mormon men the freedom to practice polygamy, the Court asserted that it was an offense "subversive of good order" that "leads to the patriarchal principle, . . .[and] when applied to large communities, fetters the people in stationary despotism, while that principle cannot long exist in connection with monogamy. . . .[20]

Most theorists of the past who stressed the importance of the family and its practices for the wider world of moral and political life by no means insisted on congruence between the structures or practices of the family and those of the outside world. Though concerned with moral development, they bifurcated public from private life to such an extent that they had no trouble reconciling inegalitarian, sometimes admittedly unjust, relations founded upon sentiment within the family with a more just, even egalitarian, social structure outside the family. Rousseau, Hegel, Tocqueville—all thought the family was centrally important for the development of morality in citizens, but all defended the hierarchy of the marital structure while spurning such a degree of hierarchy in institutions and practices outside the household. Preferring instead to rely on love, altruism, and generosity as the basis for family relations, none of these theorists argued for *just* family structures as necessary for socializing children into citizenship in a just society. . . .

Contemporary theorists of justice, with few exceptions, have paid little or no attention to the question of moral development—of how we are to *become* just. Most of them seem to think, to adapt slightly Hobbes's notable phrase, that just men spring like mushrooms from the earth.[21] Not surprisingly, then, it is far less often acknowledged in recent than in past theories that the family is important for moral development, and especially for instilling a sense of justice. As I have already noted, many theorists pay no attention at all to either the family or gender. In the rare case that the issue of justice within the family is given any sustained attention, the family is not viewed as a potential school of social justice.[22] In the rare case that a theorist pays any sustained attention to the development of a sense of justice or morality, little if any attention is likely to be paid to the family.[23] Even in the rare event that theorists pay considerable attention to the family *as* the first major locus of moral socialization, they do not refer to the fact that families are almost all still thoroughly gender-structured institutions.[24]

Among major contemporary theorists of justice, John Rawls alone treats the family seriously as the earliest school of moral development. He argues that a just, well-ordered society will be stable only if its members continue to develop a sense of justice. And he argues that families play a fundamental role in the stages by which this sense of justice is acquired. From the parents' love for their child, which comes to be reciprocated, comes the child's "sense of his own value and the desire to become the sort of person that they are."[25] The family, too, is the first of that series of "associations" in which we participate, from which we acquire the capacity, crucial for a sense of justice, to see things from the perspectives of others. . . . This capacity—the capacity for empathy—is essential for maintaining a sense of justice of the Rawlsian kind. For the perspective that is necessary for maintaining a sense of justice is not that of the egoistic or disembodied self, or of the dominant few who overdetermine "our" traditions or "shared understandings,". . . but rather the perspective of every person in the society for whom the principles of justice are being arrived at. . . . The problem with Rawls's rare and interesting discussion of moral development is that it rests on the unexplained *assumption* that family institutions are just. If gendered family institutions are *not* just, but are, rather, a relic of caste or feudal societies in which responsibilities, roles, and resources are distributed, not in accordance with the principles of justice he arrives at or with any other commonly respected values, but in accordance with innate differences that are imbued with enormous social significance, then Rawls's theory of moral development would seem to be built on uncertain ground. This problem is exacerbated by suggestions in some of Rawls's most recent work that families are "private institutions," to which it is not appropriate

to apply standards of justice. But if families are to help form just individuals and citizens, surely they must be *just families*.

In a just society, the structure and practices of families must give women the same opportunities as men to develop their capacities, to participate in political power and influence social choices, and to be economically secure. But in addition to this, families must be just because of the vast influence that they have on the moral development of children. The family is the primary institution of formative moral development. And the structure and practices of the family must parallel those of the larger society if the sense of justice is to be fostered and maintained. While many theorists of justice, both past and present, appear to have denied the importance of at least one of these factors, my own view is that both are absolutely crucial. A society that is committed to equal respect for all of its members, and to justice in social distributions of benefits and responsibilities, can neither neglect the family nor accept family structures and practices that violate these norms, as do current gender-based structures and practices. It is essential that children who are to develop into adults with a strong sense of justice and commitment to just institutions spend their earliest and most formative years in an environment in which they are loved and nurtured, *and* in which principles of justice are abided by and respected.

Notes*

1. U.S. Department of Labor, *Employment and Earnings: July 1987* (Washington, D.C.: Government Printing Office, 1987); Ruth Sidel, *Women and Children Last: The Plight of Poor Women in Affluent America* (New York: Viking, 1986), pp. xvi, 158. See also David T. Ellwood, *Poor Support: Poverty in the American Family* (New York: Basic Books, 1988), pp. 84–85, on the chronicity of poverty in single-parent households. . . .

2. Shirley Williams, in Williams and Elizabeth Holtzman, "Women in the Political World: Observations," *Daedalus* 116, no. 4 (Fall 1987): 30.

3. Twenty-three percent of single parents have never been married and 12 percent are widowed. (U.S. Bureau of the Census, Current Population Reports, *Household and Family Characteristics: March 1987* [Washington, D.C.: Government Printing Office, 1987], p. 79). In 1987, 6.8 percent of children under eighteen were

---

*Some notes have been deleted and the remaining ones renumbered.—ED.

living with a never-married parent. ("Study Shows Growing Gap Between Rich and Poor," *New York Times,* March 23, 1989, p. A24). The proportions for the total population are very different from those for black families, of whom in 1984 half of those with adult members under thirty-five years of age were maintained by single, female parents, three-quarters of whom were never married. Frank Levy, *Dollars and Dreams: The Changing American Income Distribution* (New York: Russell Sage, 1987), p.156.

4. As Joan Scott has pointed out, gender was until recently used only as a grammatical term. See "Gender: A Useful Category of Historical Analysis," in Joan Wallach Scott, *Gender and the Politics of History* (New York: Columbia University Press, 1988), p. 28, citing Fowler's *Dictionary of Modern English Usage.*

5. Among Anglo-American feminists see, for example, Mary Daly, *Gyn/Ecology: The Metaethics of Radical Feminism* (Boston: Beacon Press, 1978); Susan Griffin, *Woman and Nature: The Roaring Inside Her* (New York: Harper & Row, 1978). For a good, succinct discussion of radical feminist biological determinism, see Alison Jaggar, *Feminist Politics and Human Nature* (Totowa, NJ: Rowman & Allanheld, 1983).

6. See, for example, Sylvia Yanagisako and Jane Collier, "The Mode of Reproduction in Anthropology," in *Theoretical Perspectives on Sexual Difference,* Deborah Rhode (Ed.) (New Haven, CT: Yale University Press, 1990).

7. Nancy Chodorow, *The Reproduction of Mothering: Psychoanalysis and the Sociology of Gender* (Berkeley: University of California Press, 1978); Dorothy Dinnerstein, *The Mermaid and the Minotaur: Sexual Arrangements and Human Malaise* (New York: Harper & Row, 1976). . . .

8. Linda Nicholson, *Gender and History* (New York: Columbia University Press, 1986); Michelle Z. Rosaldo, "The Use and Abuse of Anthropology," *Signs* 5, no. 3 (1980); Joan Wallach Scott, *Gender and the Politics of History* (New York: Columbia University Press, 1986).

9. For such critiques, see Bell Hooks, *Ain't I a Woman: Black Women and Feminism* (Boston: South End Press, 1981), and *Feminist Theory: From Margin to Center* (Boston: South End Press, 1984); Elizabeth V. Spelman, *Inessential Woman: Problems of Exclusion in Feminist Thought* (Boston: Beacon Press, 1989).

10. There is now an abundant literature on the subject of women, their exclusion from nondomestic life, and the reasons given to justify it, in Western political theory. See, for example, Lorenne J. Clark and Lynda Lange (Eds.), *The Sexism of Social and Political Thought* (Toronto: University of Toronto Press, 1979); Jean Bethke Elshtain, *Public Man, Private Woman: Women in Social and Political Thought* (Princeton, NJ: Princeton University Press, 1981); Genevieve Lloyd, *The Man of Reason: "Male" and "Female" in Western Philosophy* (Minneapolis: University of Minnesota Press, 1984); Mary O'Brien, *The Politics of Reproduction* (London: Routledge & Kegan Paul, 1981); Susan Moller Okin, *Women in Western Political Thought* (Princeton, NJ: Princeton University Press, 1979); Carole Pateman, "Feminist Critiques of the Public/Private Dichotomy," in *Public and Private in Social Life,* S. Benn and G. Gaus (Eds.) (London: Croom Helm, 1983); Carole Pateman and Elizabeth Gross (Eds.), *Feminist Challenges: Social and Political Theory* (Boston: Northeastern University Press, 1987); Carole Pateman, *The Sexual Contract* (Stanford, CA: Stanford University Press, 1988); Carole Patemen and Mary L. Shanley (Eds.), *Feminist Critiques of Political Theory* (Oxford, UK: Polity Press, in press).

11. Bruce Ackerman, *Social Justice in the Liberal State* (New Haven, CT: Yale University Press, 1980); Ronald Dworkin, *Taking Rights Seriously* (Cambridge, MA: Harvard University Press, 1977); William Galston, *Justice and the Human Good* (Chicago: University of Chicago Press, 1980); Alasdair MacIntyre, *After Virtue* (Notre Dame, IN: University of Notre Dame Press, 1981), and *Whose Justice? Which Rationality?* (Notre Dame: University of Notre Dame Press, 1988); Robert Nozick, *Anarchy, State, and Utopia* (New York: Basic Books, 1974); Roberto Unger, *Knowledge and Politics* (New York: The Free Press, 1975), and *The Critical Legal Studies Movement* (Cambridge, MA: Harvard University Press, 1986).

12. I have analyzed some of the ways in which theorists in the tradition avoided considering the justice of gender in "Are Our Theories of Justice Gender-Neutral?" in *The Moral Foundations of Civil Rights,* Robert Fullinwider and Claudia Mills (Eds.) (Totowa, NJ: Rowman & Littlefield, 1986).

13. See Judith Hicks Stiehm, "The Unit of Political Analysis: Our Aristotelian Hangover," in *Discovering Reality: Feminist Perspectives on Epistemology, Metaphysics, Methodology, and Philosophy of Science,* Sandra Harding and Merrill B. Hintikka (Eds.) (Dordrecht, Holland: Reidel, 1983).

14. See Carole Pateman and Theresa Brennan, "'Mere Auxiliaries to the Commonwealth': Women and the Origins of Liberalism," *Political Studies* 27, no. 2 (June 1979); also Susan Moller Okin, "Women and the Making of the Sentimental Family," *Philosophy and Public Affairs* 11, no. 1 (Winter 1982). This issue is treated at much greater length in Pateman, *The Sexual Contract.*

15. This claim, originating in the moral development literature, has significantly influenced recent feminist moral and political theory. Two central books are Carol Gilligan, *In a Different Voice* (Cambridge, MA: Harvard

University Press, 1982); and Nel Noddings, *Caring: A Feminine Approach to Ethics and Moral Education* (Berkeley: University of California Press, 1984). For the influence of Gilligan's work on feminist theory, see, for example, Seyla Benhabib, "The Generalized and the Concrete Other: The Kohlberg-Gilligan Controversy and Feminist Theory," in *Feminism as Critique*, Benhabib and Drucilla Cornell (Eds.) (Minneapolis: University of Minnesota Press, 1987); Lawrence Blum, "Gilligan and Kohlberg: Implications for Moral Theory," *Ethics* 98, no. 3 (1988); and Eva Kittay and Diana Meyers (Eds.), *Women and Moral Theory* (Totowa, NJ: Rowman & Allenheld, 1986). For a valuable alternative approach to the issues, and an excellent selective list of references to what has now become a vast literature, see Owen Flanagan and Kathryn Jackson, "Justice, Care and Gender: The Kohlberg-Gilligan Debate Revisited," *Ethics* 97, no. 3 (1987).

16. See, for example, John M. Broughton, "Women's Rationality and Men's Virtues: A Critique of Gender Dualism in Gilligan's Theory of Moral Development," *Social Research* 50, no. 3 (1983). . . .

17. See esp. James Fishkin, *Justice, Equal Opportunity and the Family* (New Haven, CT: Yale University Press, 1983); Phillips, *Just Social Order*, esp. pp. 346–49; Rawls, *Theory*, pp. 74, 300–301, 511–12.

18. Jean-Jacques Rousseau, *Emile: or On Education*, trans. Allan Bloom (New York: Basic Books, 1979), p. 363.

19. Louis de Bonald, in *Archives Parlementaires*, 2e série (Paris, 1869) vol. 15, p. 612; cited and translated by Roderick Phillips, "Women and Family Breakdown in Eighteenth-Century France: Rouen 1780–1800," *Social History* 2 (1976): 217.

20. *Reynolds v. Nebraska*, 98 U.S. 145 (1879), 164, 166. "Gender Dualism in Gilligan's Theory of Moral Development," *Social Research* 50, no. 3 (1983); Owen Flanagan, *Varieties of Moral Personality: Ethics and Psychological Realism* (Cambridge, MA: Harvard University Press, forthcoming), ch. 8; Catherine G. Greeno and Eleanor E. Maccoby, "How Different Is the 'Different Voice'?" and Gilligan's reply, *Signs* 11, no. 2 (1986); Debra Nails, "Social-Scientific Sexism: Gilligan's Mismeasure of Man," *Social Research* 50, no. 3 (1983); Joan Tronto, "Women's Morality: Beyond Gender Difference to a Theory of Care," *Signs* 12, no. 4 (1987); Lawrence J. Walker, "Sex Differences in the Development of Moral Reasoning: A Critical Review," *Child Development* 55 (1984).

21. Hobbes writes of "men . . . as if but even now sprung out of the earth . . . like mushrooms." "Philosophical Rudiments Concerning Government and Society," in *The English Works of Thomas Hobbes*, Sir William Molesworth (Ed.) (London: John Bohn, 1966), vol. 2, p. 109.

22. For example, Walzer, *Spheres of Justice*; chap. 9, "Kinship and Love."

23. See Alan Gewirth, *Reason and Morality* (Chicago: University of Chicago Press, 1978). He discusses moral development from time to time, but places families within the broad category of "voluntary associations" and does not discuss gender roles within them.

24. This is the case with both Rawls's *A Theory of Justice* (Cambridge, MA: Harvard University Press, 1971), . . . , and Phillips's sociologically oriented *Toward a Just Social Order*, as discussed above.

25. Rawls, *Theory*, p. 465.

Distributive Justice

Robert Nozick

Study Questions

1. According to Nozick, why can the term *distributive justice* be misleading? What term does Nozick propose to use instead?

2. What does Nozick mean by the principle of justice in acquisition? In addition to the acquisition of holdings, how can one also transfer holdings?

3. According to Nozick, under what conditions would a person be justly entitled to something?

4. What are some impermissible methods of coming to possess or hold things?

5. According to Nozick, what questions does past injustice raise for present holders? How would the principle of rectification apply here?

6. What is the difference between Nozick's historical account of justice and a current time-slice view? Why does he believe the latter view does

not give the whole story about what is and is not just?

7. What does Nozick mean by a patterned principle of distribution? Give some examples. Are his own principles patterned? Explain.

8. According to Nozick, how does liberty upset patterns of distribution? How does the Wilt Chamberlain example demonstrate this? How does this fact thwart patterned principles?

9. For what reason does Nozick discuss families in this context?

10. What does Nozick think of taxation of earnings from labor and the use of this money to benefit the poor?

The term "distributive justice" is not a neutral one. Hearing the term "distribution," most people presume that some thing or mechanism uses some principle or criterion to give out a supply of things. Into this process of distributing shares some error may have crept. So it is an open question, at least, whether *redistribution* should take place; whether we should do again what has already been done once, though poorly. However, we are not in the position of children who have been given portions of pie by someone who now makes last minute adjustments to rectify careless cutting. There is no *central* distribution, no person or group entitled to control all the resources, jointly deciding how they are to be doled out. What each person gets, he gets from others who give to him in exchange for something, or as a gift. In a free society, diverse persons control different resources, and new holdings arise out of the voluntary exchanges and actions of persons. There is no more a distributing or distribution of shares than there is a distributing of mates in a society in which persons choose whom they shall marry. The total result is the product of many individual decisions which the different individuals involved are entitled to make. Some uses of the term "distribution," it is true, do not imply a previous distributing appropriately judged by some criterion (for example, "probability distribution"); nevertheless, despite the title of this chapter,

it would be best to use a terminology that clearly is neutral. We shall speak of people's holdings; a principle of justice in holdings describes (part of) what justice tells us (requires) about holdings. I shall state first what I take to be the correct view about justice in holdings, and then turn to the discussion of alternate views.[1]

Section 1 The Entitlement Theory

The subject of justice in holdings consists of three major topics. The first is the *original acquisition of holdings,* the appropriation of unheld things. This includes the issues of how unheld things may come to be held, the process, or processes, by which unheld things may come to be held, the things that may come to be held by these processes, the extent of what comes to be held by a particular process, and so on. We shall refer to the complicated truth about this topic, which we shall not formulate here, as the principle of justice in acquisition. The second topic concerns the *transfer of holdings* from one person to another. By what processes may a person transfer holdings to another? How may a person acquire a holding from another who holds it? Under this topic come general descriptions of voluntary exchange, and gift and (on the other hand) fraud, as well as reference to particular conventional details fixed upon in a given society. The complicated truth about this subject (with placeholders for conventional details) we shall call the principle of justice in transfer. (And we shall suppose it also includes principles governing how a person may divest himself of a holding, passing it into an unheld state.)

If the world were wholly just, the following inductive definition would exhaustively cover the subject of justice in holdings.

1. A person who acquires a holding in accordance with the principle of justice in acquisition is entitled to that holding.

2. A person who acquires a holding in accordance with the principle of justice in transfer, from someone else entitled to the holding, is entitled to the holding.

3. No one is entitled to a holding except by (repeated) applications of 1 and 2.

The complete principle of distributive justice would say simply that a distribution is just if everyone is entitled to the holdings they possess under the distribution.

A distribution is just if it arises from another just distribution by legitimate means. The legitimate means of moving from one distribution to another are specified by the principle of justice in transfer. The legitimate first "moves" are specified by the principle of justice in acquisition.[2] Whatever arises from a just situation by just steps is itself just. The means of change specified by the principle of justice in transfer preserve justice. As correct rules of inference are truth-preserving, and any conclusion deduced via repeated application of such rules from only true premises is itself true, so the means of transition from one situation to another specified by the principle of justice in transfer are justice-preserving, and any situation actually arising from repeated transitions in accordance with the principle from a just situation is itself just. The parallel between justice-preserving transformations and truth-preserving transformations illuminates where it fails as well as where it holds. That a conclusion could have been deduced by truth-preserving means from premises that are true suffices to show its truth. That from a just situation a situation *could* have arisen via justice-preserving means does *not* suffice to show its justice. The fact that a thief's victims voluntarily *could* have presented him with gifts does not entitle the thief to his ill-gotten gains. Justice in holdings is historical; it depends upon what actually has happened. We shall return to this point later.

Not all actual situations are generated in accordance with the two principles of justice in holdings: the principle of justice in acquisition and the principle of justice in transfer. Some people steal from others, or defraud them, or enslave them, seizing their product and preventing them from living as they choose, or forcibly exclude others from competing in exchanges. None of these are permissible modes of transition from one situation to another. And some persons acquire holdings by means not sanctioned by the principle of justice in acquisition. The existence of past injustice (previous violations of the first two principles of justice in holdings) raises the third major topic under justice in holdings: the rectification of injustice in holdings. If past injustice has shaped present holdings in various ways, some identifiable and some not, what now, if anything, ought to be done to rectify these injustices? What obligations do the performers of injustice have toward those whose position is worse than it would have been had the injustice not been done? Or, than it would have been had compensation been paid promptly? How, if at all, do things change if the beneficiaries and those made worse off are not the direct parties in the act of injustice, but, for example, their descendants? Is an injustice done to someone whose holding was itself based upon an unrectified injustice? How far back must one go in wiping clean the historical slate of injustices? What may victims of injustice permissibly do in order to rectify the injustices being done to them, including the many injustices done by persons acting through their government? I do not know of a thorough or theoretically sophisticated treatment of such issues.[3] Idealizing greatly, let us suppose theoretical investigation will produce a principle of rectification. This principle uses historical information about previous situations and injustices done in them (as defined by the first two principles of justice and rights against interference), and information about the actual course of events that flowed from these injustices, until the present, and it yields a description (or descriptions) of holdings in the society. The principle of rectification presumably will make use of its best estimate of subjunctive information about what would have occurred (or a probability distribution over what might have occurred, using the expected value) if the injustice had not taken place. If the actual description of holdings turns out not to be one of the descriptions yielded by the principle, then one of the descriptions yielded must be realized.[4]

The general outlines of the theory of justice in holdings are that the holdings of a person are just if he is entitled to them by the principles of justice in acquisition and transfer, or by the principle of rectification of injustice (as specified by the first two principles). If each person's holdings are just, then the total set (distribution) of holdings is just. To turn these general outlines into a specific theory we would have to specify the details of each of the three principles of justice in holdings: the principle of acquisition of holdings, the principle of transfer of holdings, and the principle of rectification of violations of the first two principles. I shall not attempt that task here.

Historical Principles and End-Result Principles

The general outlines of the entitlement theory illuminate the nature and defects of other conceptions of distributive justice. The entitlement theory of justice in distribution is *historical*; whether a distribution is just depends upon how it came about. In contrast, *current time-slice principles* of justice hold that the justice of a distribution is determined by how things are distributed (who has what) as judged by some *structural* principle(s) of just distribution. A utilitarian who judges between any two distributions by seeing which has the greater sum of utility and, if the sums tie, applies some fixed equality criterion to choose the more equal distribution, would hold a current time-slice principle of justice. As would someone who had a fixed schedule of trade-offs between the sum of happiness and equality. According to a current time-slice principle, all that needs to be looked at, in judging the justice of a distribution, is who ends up with what; in comparing any two distributions one need look only at the matrix presenting the distributions. No further information need be fed into a principle of justice. It is a consequence of such principles of justice that any two structurally identical distributions are equally just. (Two distributions are structurally identical if they present the same profile, but perhaps have different persons occupying the particular slots. My having ten and your having five, and my having five and your having ten are structurally identical distributions.) Welfare economics is the theory of current time-slice principles of justice. The subject is conceived as operating on matrices representing only current information about distribution. This, as well as some of the usual conditions (for example, the choice of distribution is invariant under relabeling of columns), guarantees that welfare economics will be a current time-slice theory, with all of its inadequacies.

Most persons do not accept current time-slice principles as constituting the whole story about distributive shares. They think it relevant in assessing the justice of a situation to consider not only the distribution it embodies, but also how that distribution came about. If some persons are in prison for murder or war crimes, we do not say that to assess the justice of the distribution in the society we must look only at what this person has, and that person has, and that person has, . . . at the current time. We think it relevant to ask whether someone did something so that he *deserved* to be punished, deserved to have a lower share. Most will agree to the relevance of further information with regard to punishments and penalties. Consider also desired things. One traditional socialist view is that workers are entitled to the product and full fruits of their labor; they have earned it; a distribution is unjust if it does not give the workers what they are entitled to. Such entitlements are based upon some past history. No socialist holding this view would find it comforting to be told that because the actual distribution A happens to coincide structurally with the one he desires D, A therefore is no less just than D; it differs only in that the "parasitic" owners of capital receive under A what the workers are entitled to under D, and the workers receive under A what the owners are entitled to under D, namely very little. This socialist rightly, in my view, holds onto the notions of earning, producing, entitlement, desert, and so forth, and he rejects current time-slice principles that look only to the structure of the resulting set of holdings. (The set of holdings resulting from what? Isn't it implausible that how holdings are produced and come to exist has no effect at all on who should hold what?) His mistake lies in his view of what entitlements arise out of what sorts of productive processes.

We construe the position we discuss too narrowly by speaking of *current* time-slice principles. Nothing is changed if structural principles operate upon a time sequence of current time-slice profiles and, for example, give someone more now to counterbalance the less he has had earlier. A utilitarian or an egalitarian or any mixture of the two over time will inherit the difficulties of his more myopic comrades. He is not helped by the fact that *some* of the information others consider relevant in assessing a distribution is reflected, unrecoverably, in past matrices. Henceforth, we shall refer to such unhistorical principles of distributive justice, including the current time-slice principles, as *end-result principles* or *end-state principles*.

In contrast to end-result principles of justice, *historical principles* of justice hold that past circumstances or actions of people can create differential entitlements or differential deserts to things. An injustice can be worked by moving from one distribution to another structurally identical one, for the second, in profile the same, may violate people's entitlements or deserts; it may not fit the actual history.

Patterning

The entitlement principles of justice in holdings that we have sketched are historical principles of justice. To better understand their precise character, we shall distinguish them from another subclass of the historical principles. Consider, as an example, the principle of distribution according to moral merit. This principle requires that total distributive shares vary directly with moral merit; no person should have a greater share than anyone whose moral merit is greater. (If moral merit could be not merely ordered but measured on an interval or ratio scale, stronger principles could be formulated.) Or consider the principle that results by substituting "usefulness to society" for "moral merit" in the previous principle. Or instead of "distribute according to moral merit," or "distribute according to usefulness to society," we might consider "distribute according to the weighted sum of moral merit, usefulness to society, and need," with the weights of the different dimensions equal. Let us call a principle of distribution *patterned* if it specifies that a distribution is to vary along with some natural dimension, weighted sum of natural dimensions, or lexicographic ordering of natural dimensions. And let us say a distribution is patterned if it accords with some patterned principle. (I speak of natural dimensions, admittedly without a general criterion for them, because for any set of holdings some artificial dimensions could be gimmicked up to vary along with the distribution of the set.) The principle of distribution in accordance with moral merit is a patterned historical principle, which specifies a patterned distribution. "Distribute according to I.Q." is a patterned principle that looks to information not contained in distributional matrices. It is not historical, however, in that it does not look to any past actions creating differential entitlements to evaluate a distribution; it requires only distributional matrices whose columns are labeled by I.Q. scores. The distribution in a society, however, may be composed of such simple patterned distributions, without itself being simply patterned. Different sectors may operate different patterns, or some combination of patterns may operate in different proportions across a society. A distribution composed in this manner, from a small number of patterned distributions, we also shall term "patterned." And we extend the use of "pattern" to include the overall designs put forth by combinations of end-state principles.

Almost every suggested principle of distributive justice is patterned: to each according to his moral merit, or needs, or marginal product, or how hard he tries, or the weighted sum of the foregoing, and so on. The principle of entitlement we have sketched is

not patterned.[5] There is no one natural dimension or weighted sum or combination of a small number of natural dimensions that yields the distributions generated in accordance with the principle of entitlement. The set of holdings that results when some persons receive their marginal products, others win at gambling, others receive a share of their mate's income, others receive gifts from foundations, others receive interest on loans, others receive gifts from admirers, others receive returns on investment, others make for themselves much of what they have, others find things, and so on, will not be patterned. Heavy strands of patterns will run through it; significant portions of the variance in holdings will be accounted for by pattern-variables. If most people most of the time choose to transfer some of their entitlements to others only in exchange for something from them, then a large part of what many people hold will vary with what they held that others wanted. More details are provided by the theory of marginal productivity. But gifts to relatives, charitable donations, bequests to children, and the like, are not best conceived, in the first instance, in this manner. Ignoring the strands of pattern, let us suppose for the moment that a distribution actually arrived at by the operation of the principle of entitlement is random with respect to any pattern. Though the resulting set of holdings will be unpatterned, it will not be incomprehensible, for it can be seen as arising from the operation of a small number of principles.

Now suppose that Wilt Chamberlain is greatly in demand by basketball teams, being a great gate attraction. (Also suppose contracts run only for a year, with players being free agents.) He signs the following sort of contract with a team: In each home game, twenty-five cents from the price of each ticket of admission goes to him. (We ignore the question of whether he is "gouging" the owners, letting them look out for themselves.) The season starts, and people cheerfully attend his team's games; they buy their tickets, each time dropping a separate twenty-five cents of their admission price into a special box with Chamberlain's name on it. They are excited about seeing him play; it is worth the total admission price to them. Let us suppose that in one season one million persons attend his home games, and Wilt Chamberlain winds up with $250,000, a much larger sum than the average income and larger even than anyone else has. Is he entitled to this income? Is this new distribution D_2, unjust? If so, why? There is *no* question about whether each of the people was entitled to the control over the resources they held in D_1; because that was the distribution (your favorite) that (for the purposes of argument) we assumed was acceptable. Each of these persons *chose* to give twenty-five cents of their money to Chamberlain. They could have spent it on going to the movies, or on candy bars, or on copies of *Dissent* magazine, or of *Monthly Review*. But they all, at least one million of them, converged on giving it to Wilt Chamberlain in exchange for watching him play basketball. If D_1 was a just distribution, and people voluntarily moved from it to D_2, transferring parts of their shares they were given under D_1 (what was it for if not to do something with?), isn't D_2 also just? If the people were entitled to dispose of the resources to which they were entitled (under D_1), didn't this include their being entitled to give it to, or exchange it with, Wilt Chamberlain? Can anyone else complain on grounds of justice? Each other person already has his legitimate share under D_1. Under D_1, there is nothing that anyone has that anyone else has a claim of justice against. After someone transfers something to Wilt Chamberlain, third parties *still* have their legitimate shares; *their* shares are not changed. By what process could such a transfer among two persons give rise to a legitimate claim of distributive justice on a portion of what was transferred, by a third party who had no claim of justice on any holding of the others *before* the transfer?[6] To cut off objections irrelevant here, we might imagine the exchanges occurring in a socialist society, after hours. After playing whatever basketball he does in his daily work, or doing whatever other daily work he does, Wilt Chamberlain decides to put in *overtime* to earn additional money. (First his work quota is set; he works time over that.) Or imagine it is a skilled juggler people like to see, who puts on shows after hours.

Why might someone work overtime in a society in which it is assumed their needs are satisfied? Perhaps because they care about things other than needs. I like to write in books that I read, and to have easy access to books for browsing at odd hours. It would be very pleasant and convenient to have the resources of Widener Library in my back yard. No society, I assume, will provide such resources close to each person who would like them as part of his regular allotment (under D_1). Thus, persons either must do without some extra things that they want, or be allowed to do something extra to get some of these

things. On what basis could the inequalities that would eventuate be forbidden? Notice also that small factories would spring up in a socialist society, unless forbidden. I melt down some of my personal possessions (under D_1) and build a machine out of the material. I offer you, and others, a philosophy lecture once a week in exchange for your cranking the handle on my machine, whose products I exchange for yet other things, and so on. (The raw materials used by the machine are given to me by others who possess them under D_1, in exchange for hearing lectures.) Each person might participate to gain things over and above their allotment under D_1. Some persons even might want to leave their job in socialist industry and work full time in this private sector. I shall say something more about these issues in the next chapter. Here I wish merely to note how private property even in means of production would occur in a socialist society that did not forbid people to use as they wished some of the resources they are given under the socialist distribution D_1.[7] The socialist society would have to forbid capitalist acts between consenting adults.

The general point illustrated by the Wilt Chamberlain example and the example of the entrepreneur in a socialist society is that no end-state principle or distributional patterned principle of justice can be continuously realized without continuous interference with people's lives. Any favored pattern would be transformed into one unfavored by the principle, by people choosing to act in various ways; for example, by people exchanging goods and services with other people, or giving things to other people, things the transferrers are entitled to under the favored distributional pattern. To maintain a pattern one must either continually interfere to stop people from transferring resources as they wish to, or continually (or periodically) interfere to take from some persons resources that others for some reason chose to transfer to them. (But if some time limit is to be set on how long people may keep resources others voluntarily transfer to them, why let them keep these resources for *any* period of time? Why not have immediate confiscation?) It might be objected that all persons voluntarily will choose to refrain from actions which would upset the pattern.

Redistribution and Property Rights

Apparently, patterned principles allow people to choose to expend upon themselves, but not upon others, those resources they are entitled to (or rather, receive) under some favored distributional pattern D_1. For if each of several persons chooses to expend some of his D_1 resources upon one other person, then that other person will receive more than his D_1 share, disturbing the favored distributional pattern. Maintaining a distributional pattern is individualism with a vengeance! Patterned distributional principles do not give people what entitlement principles do, only better distributed. For they do not give the right to choose what to do with what one has; they do not give the right to choose to pursue an end involving (intrinsically, or as a means) the enhancement of another's position. To such views, families are disturbing; for within a family occur transfers that upset the favored distributional pattern. Either families themselves become units to which distribution takes place, the column occupiers (on what rationale?), or loving behavior is forbidden. We should note in passing the ambivalent position of radicals toward the family. Its loving relationships are seen as a model to be emulated and extended across the whole society, at the same time that it is denounced as a suffocating institution to be broken and condemned as a focus of parochial concerns that interfere with achieving radical goals. Need we say that it is not appropriate to enforce across the wider society the relationships of love and care appropriate within a family, relationships which are voluntarily undertaken?[8] Incidentally, love is an interesting instance of another relationship that is historical, in that (like justice) it depends upon what actually occurred. An adult may come to love another because of the other's characteristics; but it is the other person, and not the characteristics, that is loved.[9] The love is not transferrable to some else with the same characteristics, even to one who "scores" higher for these characteristics. And the love endures through changes of the characteristics that gave rise to it. One loves the particular person one actually encountered. Why love is historical, attaching to persons in this way and not to characteristics, is an interesting and puzzling question.

Proponents of patterned principles of distributive justice focus upon criteria for determining who is to receive holdings; they consider the reasons for which someone should have something, and also the total picture of holdings. Whether or not it is better to give than to receive, proponents of patterned principles ignore giving altogether. In considering the distribu-

tion of goods, income, and so forth, their theories are theories of recipient justice; they completely ignore any right a person might have to give something to someone. Even in exchanges where each party is simultaneously giver and recipient, patterned principles of justice focus only upon the recipient role and its supposed rights. Thus discussions tend to focus on whether people (should) have a right to inherit, rather than on whether people (should) have a right to bequeath or on whether persons who have a right to hold also have a right to choose that others hold in their place. I lack a good explanation of why the usual theories of distributive justice are so recipient oriented; ignoring givers and transferrers and their rights is of a piece with ignoring producers and their entitlements. But why is it *all* ignored?

Patterned principles of distributive justice necessitate *re*distributive activities. The likelihood is small that any actual freely-arrived-at set of holdings fits a given pattern; and the likelihood is nil that it will continue to fit the pattern as people exchange and give. From the point of view of an entitlement theory, redistribution is a serious matter indeed, involving, as it does, the violation of people's rights. (An exception is those takings that fall under the principle of the rectification of injustices.) From other points of view, also, it is serious.

Taxation of earnings from labor is on a par with forced labor.[10] Some persons find this claim obviously true: taking the earnings of *n* hours labor is like taking *n* hours from the person; it is like forcing the person to work *n* hours for another's purpose. Others find the claim absurd. But even these, *if* they object to forced labor, would oppose forcing unemployed hippies to work for the benefit of the needy.[11] And they would also object to forcing each person to work five extra hours each week for the benefit of the needy. But a system that takes five hours' wages in taxes does not seem to them like one that forces someone to work five hours, since it offers the person forced a wider range of choice in activities than does taxation in kind with the particular labor specified. (But we can imagine a gradation of systems of forced labor, from one that specifies a particular activity, to one that gives a choice among two activities, to . . . ; and so on up.) Furthermore, people envisage a system with something like a proportional tax on everything above the amount necessary for basic needs. Some think this does not force someone to work extra hours, since there is no fixed number of extra hours he is forced to work, and since he can avoid the tax entirely by earning only enough to cover his basic needs. This is a very uncharacteristic view of forcing for those who *also* think people are forced to do something *whenever* the alternatives they face are considerably worse. However, *neither* view is correct. The fact that others intentionally intervene, in violation of a side constraint against aggression, to threaten force to limit the alternatives, in this case to paying taxes or (presumably the worse alternative) bare subsistence, makes the taxation system one of forced labor and distinguishes it from other cases of limited choices which are not forcings.[12]

Notes*

1. The reader who has looked ahead and seen that the second part of this chapter discusses Rawls' theory mistakenly may think that every remark or argument in the first part against alternative theories of justice is meant to apply to, or anticipate, a criticism of Rawls' theory. This is not so; there are other theories also worth criticizing.

2. Applications of the principle of justice in acquisition may also occur as part of the move from one distribution to another. You may find an unheld thing now and appropriate it. Acquisitions also are to be understood as included when, to simplify, I speak only of transitions by transfers.

3. See, however, the useful book by Boris Bittker, *The Case for Black Reparations* (New York: Random House, 1973).

4. If the principle of rectification of violations of the first two principles yields more than one description of holdings, then some choice must be made as to which of these is to be realized. Perhaps the sort of considerations about distributive justice and equality that I argue against play a legitimate role in *this* subsidiary choice. Similarly, there may be room for such considerations in deciding which otherwise arbitrary features a statute will embody, when such features are unavoidable because other considerations do not specify a precise line; yet a line must be drawn.

5. One might try to squeeze a patterned conception of distributive justice into the framework of the entitlement conception, by formulating a gimmicky obligatory "principle of transfer" that would lead to the pattern. For example, the principle that if one has more than the mean income one must transfer everything one holds above the mean to persons below the mean so as to bring them up to (but not over) the mean. We can formulate a criterion for a "principle of transfer"

to rule out such obligatory transfers, or we can say that no correct principle of transfer, no principle of transfer in a free society will be like this. The former is probably the better course, though the latter also is true.

Alternatively, one might think to make the entitlement conception instantiate a pattern, by using matrix entries that express the relative strength of a person's entitlements as measured by some real-valued function. But even if the limitation to natural dimensions failed to exclude this function, the resulting edifice would *not* capture our system of entitlements to *particular* things.

6. Might not a transfer have instrumental effects on a third party, changing his feasible options? (But what if the two parties to the transfer independently had used their holdings in this fashion?) I discuss this question below, but note here that this question concedes the point for distributions of ultimate intrinsic noninstrumental goods (pure utility experiences, so to speak) that are transferrable. It also might be objected that the transfer might make a third party more envious because it worsens his position relative to someone else. I find it incomprehensible how this can be thought to involve a claim of justice....

Here ... a theory which incorporates elements of pure procedural justice might find what I say acceptable, if kept in its proper place; that is, if background institutions exist to ensure the satisfaction of certain conditions on distributive shares. But if these institutions are not themselves the sum or invisible-hand result of people's voluntary (nonaggressive) actions, the constraints they impose require justification. At no point does our argument assume any background institutions more extensive than those of the minimal night-watchman state, a state limited to protecting persons against murder, assault, theft, fraud, and so forth.

7. See the selection from John Henry MacKay's novel, *The Anarchists,* reprinted in Leonard Krimmerman and Lewis Perry (Eds.), *Patterns of Anarchy* (New York: Doubleday Anchor Books, 1966), in which an individualist anarchist presses upon a communist anarchist the following question: "Would you, in the system of society which you call 'free Communism' prevent individuals from exchanging their labor among themselves by means of their own medium of exchange? And further: Would you prevent them from occupying land for the purpose of personal use?" The novel continues: "[the] question was not to be escaped. If he answered 'Yes!' he admitted that society had the right of control over the individual and threw overboard the autonomy of the individual which he had always zealously defended; if on the other hand, he answered 'No!' he admitted the right of private prop-

erty which he had just denied so emphatically . . . . Then he answered 'In Anarchy any number of men must have the right of forming a voluntary association, and so realizing their ideas in practice. Nor can I understand how any one could justly be driven from the land and house which he uses and occupies . . . every serious man must declare himself: for Socialism, and thereby for force and against liberty, or for Anarchism, and thereby for liberty and against force.'" In contrast, we find Noam Chomsky writing, "Any consistent anarchist must oppose private ownership of the means of production," "the consistent anarchist then . . . will be a socialist . . . of a particular sort." Introduction to Daniel Guerin, *Anarchism: From Theory to Practice* (New York: Monthly Review Press, 1970), pages xiii, xv.

8. One indication of the stringency of Rawls' difference principle, which we attend to in the second part of this chapter, is its inappropriateness as a governing principle even within a family of individuals who love one another. Should a family devote its resources to maximizing the position of its least well off and least talented child, holding back the other children or using resources for their education and development only if they will follow a policy through their lifetimes of maximizing the position of their least fortunate sibling? Surely not. How then can this even be considered as the appropriate policy for enforcement in the wider society? (I discuss below what I think would be Rawls' reply: that some principles apply at the macro level which do not apply to microsituations.)

9. See Gregory Vlastos, "The Individual as an Object of Love in Plato" in his *Platonic Studies* (Princeton, NJ: Princeton University Press, 1973), pp. 3–34.

10. I am unsure as to whether the arguments I present below show that such taxation merely *is* forced labor; so that "is on a par with" means "is one kind of." Or alternatively, whether the arguments emphasize the great similarities between such taxation and forced labor, to show it is plausible and illuminating to view such taxation in the light of forced labor. This latter approach would remind one of how John Wisdom conceives of the claims of metaphysicians.

11. Nothing hangs on the fact that here and elsewhere I speak loosely of *needs*, since I go on, each time, to reject the criterion of justice which includes it. If, however, something did depend upon the notion, one would want to examine it more carefully. For a skeptical view, see Kenneth Minogue, *The Liberal Mind* (New York: Random House, 1963), pp. 103–112.

12. Further details which this statement should include are contained in my essay "Coercion," in *Philosophy, Science, and Method*, S. Morgenbesser, P. Suppes, and M. White (Eds.) (New York: St. Martin, 1969).

Review Exercises

1. What is the difference between a process view of distributive justice and an end state view?

2. Discuss the meaning and problems associated with the use of the end state view criteria of merit, achievement, effort, and contribution.

3. What is the literal meaning of "equal opportunity"? What criterion does Fishkin use for judging whether it exists? What is Bernard Williams's "starting gate theory" of equal opportunity?

4. Explain the libertarian position on liberty and the role of government.

5. What are the basic differences between capitalism and socialism as social and economic theories?

6. What is Rawls's "original position," and what role does it play in his derivation of principles of justice?

7. What is Rawls's "maximin" principle, and how is it related to his second principle of justice?

Discussion Cases

1. *The Homeless.* Joe was laid off two years ago at the auto repair company where he had worked for fifteen years. For the first year he tried to get another job. He read the want ads and left his application at local employment agencies. After that he gave up. He had little savings and soon had no money for rent. He has been homeless now for about a year. He will not live in the shelters because they are crowded and noisy. As time goes by, he has less and less chance of getting back to where he was before. He drinks now when he can to forget the past and escape from the present. Others whom he meets on the streets are mentally retarded or psychologically disturbed. He realizes that the city does some things to try to help people like him. However, there is little money, and the numbers of homeless people seem to be growing.

Does society have any responsibility to do anything for people like Joe? Why or why not?

2. *Rights to Keep What One Earns.* Gene and his co-workers have been talking over lunch about how their taxes have continued to rise. Some complain that the harder they work, the less they are making. Others are upset because their taxes are going to pay for things that they do not believe the government should support by our tax dollars. For example, they believe that the government should not give money to support the arts. That should be a matter of charity. "Why should they support museums or the opera when they do not ever go to them?" they argue. They also complain that they work hard but that their income is being used to take care of others who could but do not work themselves.

Are they right? Why?

Selected Bibliography

Ackerman, Bruce A. *Social Justice in the Liberal State.* New Haven, CT: Yale University Press, 1980.

———. *The Future of Liberal Revolution.* New Haven, CT: Yale University Press, 1992.

Arthur, John, and William Shaw (Eds.). *Justice and Economic Distribution,* 2nd ed. Englewood Cliffs, NJ: Prentice-Hall, 1991.

Bowie, Norman (Ed.). *Equal Opportunity.* Boulder, CO: Westview, 1988.

Cauthen, Kenneth. *The Passion for Equality.* Totowa, NJ: Rowman & Littlefield, 1987.

Daniels, Norman. *Reading Rawls.* New York: Basic Books, 1976.

Ferguson, Ann. *Sexual Democracy: Women, Oppression, and Revolution.* Boulder, CO: Westview, 1991.

Fishkin, James S. *The Dialogue of Justice.* New Haven, CT: Yale University Press, 1992.

———. *Justice, Equal Opportunity, and the Family.* New Haven, CT: Yale University Press, 1983.

Frankel Paul, Ellen, et al. *Equal Opportunity.* London: Basil Blackwell, 1987.

Friedman, Milton. *Capitalism and Freedom.* Chicago: University of Chicago Press, 1962.

Gutman, Amy. *Liberal Equality.* Cambridge, UK: Cambridge University Press, 1980.

Harrington, Michael. *Socialism Past and Future.* New York: Arcade, 1989.

Haslett, David W. *Capitalism with Morality.* New York: Oxford University Press, 1994.

Held, Virginia (Ed.). *Property, Profits, and Economic Justice.* Belmont, CA: Wadsworth, 1980.

Jaggar, Alison. *Feminist Politics and Human Nature.* Totowa, NJ: Rowman & Littlefield, 1983.

Jencks, Christopher. *Inequality.* New York: Basic Books, 1972.

MacKinnon, Catharine. *Toward a Feminist Theory of the State.* Cambridge, MA: Harvard University Press, 1989.

Narveson, Jan. *The Libertarian Idea.* Philadelphia: Temple University Press, 1989.

Nielsen, Kai. *Equality and Liberty: A Defense of Radical Egalitarianism.* Totowa, NJ: Rowman & Littlefield, 1984.

Nozick, Robert. *Anarchy, State, and Utopia.* New York: Basic Books, 1974.

Okin, Susan Moller. *Gender and Justice.* New York: Basic Books, 1982.

Paul, Jeffrey, and Ellen Frankel Paul (Eds.). *Economic Rights.* New York: Cambridge University Press, 1993.

Rae, Douglas, et al. *Equalities.* Cambridge, MA: Harvard University Press, 1981.

Rakowski, Eric. *Equal Justice.* New York: Oxford University Press, 1991.

Regan, Tom (Ed.). *Just Business: New Introductory Essays in Business Ethics.* Philadelphia: Temple University Press, 1983.

Shue, Henry. *Basic Rights: Subsistence, Affluence, and U.S. Foreign Policy.* Princeton, NJ: Princeton University Press, 1980.

Sterba, James P. *How to Make People Just.* Lanham, MD: Rowman & Littlefield, 1988.

———. *How to Make People Just.* Totowa: Rowman & Littlefield, 1988.

———. *Justice: Alternative Political Perspectives,* 2nd ed. Belmont, CA: Wadsworth, 1992.

Veatch, Robert M. *The Foundations of Justice: Why the Retarded and the Rest of Us Have Claims to Equality.* New York: Oxford University Press, 1986.

Walzer, Michael. *The Spheres of Justice.* New York: Basic Books, 1983.

Young, Iris Marion. *Justice and the Politics of Difference.* Princeton, NJ: Princeton University Press, 1990.

❧ *13* ❧

Legal Punishment

In 1994 in the United States, 18,382 violent crimes were committed for every 100,000 inhabitants.[1] This was down 2.2 percent from 1990. Of all crimes reported, slightly more than half were for larceny and theft, 19.4 percent for burglary, 11 percent for motor vehicle theft, 8 percent for assault, 4.4 percent for robbery, 0.7 percent for forcible rape, and 0.2 percent for murder. Although the murder rate in recent years has gone down slightly, it is still twice what it was 30 years ago. Firearms were used in 7 of 10 murders in 1994, and 58 percent of these were handguns. Almost half of the women who are killed each year are killed by their current or former husbands or boyfriends. In contrast, only 6 percent of men killed are killed by wives or girlfriends.[2] In 1994, the arrests for violent crime in the United States among 14 to 17 year olds was up 46.3 percent over 1989, those 18 to 24 were up 12 percent, and those 25 years and older rose 12.6 percent. As of 1993, 35 percent of the people in U.S. prisons were functionally illiterate, and 61 percent were there because of narcotics offenses.[3] Some experts believe that by the year 2000 three-fourths of the people in U.S. prisons will be there for drug-related crimes.[4] There are many different assessments of the causes of crime and its increase or decrease. As we will see, these causes, as well as the overall statistics on crime rates and types,

may be relevant to the moral judgments that we make about legal punishment.

The United States has the highest rate of incarceration in the world; in 1991, 455 people were in prison for every 100,000 residents. This compares to an average rate in Europe of 35 to 120 per 100,000. Currently, the United States has more than 1 million persons in its various federal, state, and local jails and prisons. The cost annually to imprison these persons was recently about $16 billion.[5] The states with the highest numbers in prison in 1988 were California, New York, and Texas. Those with the highest rates of incarceration per population were Nevada, South Carolina, and Louisiana. The United States is now almost alone among Western countries in retaining the death penalty as a form of legal punishment. West Germany abolished the death penalty in the 1940s, Britain in the 1960s, and Canada in the 1970s. For people in these countries, the issue may be settled, but in the United States it continues to be a matter of heated debate. The difficulties are illustrated by the following case.

In April 21, 1992, the first person to be executed in California in twenty-five years was put to death in the gas chamber at San Quentin prison. No one had been executed in that state since 1968. In fact, in that year only one person had been executed in the entire United States, the number having gradually declined from a high of 199 persons executed in 1935. By 1968, a majority of people in the country opposed the death penalty. Not long after this, in 1972, the U.S. Supreme Court revoked the death penalty, ruling that it had become too "arbitrary and capricious" and thus violated the Constitution's ban on cruel and unusual punishment.[6] By 1976, however, the mood of the country had again begun to change. In that year the High Court reinstated the death penalty in *Gregg* v. *Georgia*, arguing that it did not violate the Eighth Amendment's ban on cruel and unusual punishment and thus could be constitutionally applied for convicted murderers. The reasons for this new change are uncertain. It is not clear that it was simply a concern about a rising crime rate. Support for the death penalty has continued, as evidenced by a 1991 poll that found 71 percent of the population in favor of it.[7] However, a 1986 poll also found that 74 percent of the respondents felt that the death penalty was too arbitrary, and 47 percent said that it was "racially and economically unfair."[8] On February 3, 1997, the American Bar Association, the largest and most influential organization of lawyers in the United States, voted for a moratorium on executions until greater fairness in the process could be assured, especially in the quality of representation that defendants receive.[9]

The person executed in 1992 in San Quentin was Robert Alton Harris. In 1979, Harris was tried and convicted for killing two San Diego teenagers. He and his brother were planning a robbery and needed a getaway car. They saw the two boys at a fast-food restaurant and forced them to drive to a deserted area. According to Harris's brother, Robert resisted the teens' pleas for mercy and shot them to death. Later he bragged and laughed about the killing and said that to finish things off he had eaten the boys' hamburgers. The killings were especially gratuitous and heartless. Harris seemed not to have any feeling for his victims. For proponents of the death penalty he was a justifiable subject for execution, an irreformably vicious murderer.

In fact, if a person's early childhood plays a role or has a strong causal effect on a person's later behavior, then Harris's actions were not surprising or unpredictable. His father was a drunk who often abused his mother and Robert's sisters.[10] In one rage, he had kicked the mother, causing Robert's premature birth. When Robert was two years old, his father slapped him across the dinner table, causing him to fall out of his high chair and have convulsions. He then proceeded to choke Robert, but the child survived. The family worked as migrant farm hands, sleeping in tents or in their car. When he was fourteen years old, Robert's mother put him out of the car and just drove away. He kicked around for years. In 1975 he killed a roommate of his older brother, for which he served two and one-half years for manslaughter. The killing of the two teenagers occurred just six months after he was paroled. After his conviction for the murder of the boys, Harris's case went through a typical appeals history in the California courts and the U.S. Supreme Court. The appeals process lasted thirteen years. By the time of his 1992 execution, he had survived four other execution dates. Opponents of the death penalty argued that Harris himself was also a victim and should not be held totally blameworthy or responsible for his crimes. Proponents of the death penalty, on the other hand, cite cases like that of Harris as an example of a system gone wrong. It is just this sort of case, they argue, that makes capital cases so expensive.

The cost for a sentence of life in prison is now estimated to be about $800,000 per person, but the cost of a death penalty case is between $2 and $5 million. In 1985, after several years of trying, the Kansas legislature passed a death penalty bill. However, when legislators figured out that it was likely to cost the state about $10 million in the first year and $50 million by 1990, they repealed it. Those who protested the death penalty argue that the long appeals process results from strong moral opposition to state-sanctioned killing. Indeed, moral sentiments on this issue are strong on both sides.

To know what to think about cases like this and the various crime statistics, we need to examine some of the reasons given for the practice of legal punishment itself. Only then can we also appreciate the nature and strength of the arguments for and against the death penalty.

The Nature of Legal Punishment

The most visible form of legal criminal punishment is imprisonment. However, we also punish with fines, forced work, and corporal punishment, including death. What we want to examine here is not any sort of punishment, only legal punishment. Eight-year-old Jimmy's parents can punish him with no TV for a week for a failing grade, and I can punish myself for a momentary caloric indulgence. Legal punishment is like parental and self-punishment in that it is designed to "hurt." If something is gladly accepted or enjoyed, then it is not really punishment.

However, legal punishment is distinct in several ways from other forms of punishment. Legal punishment must follow legal rules of some sort. It is authorized by a legal authority and follows a set of rules for who is punished, how, and how much. Lynching is not legal punishment. Furthermore, "Every dog gets his first bite," as the old saying goes. You must first commit the crime or be suspected of it. Whatever we say about the justification of detaining people before they commit (or we think they will commit) a crime, it is not punishment. Punishment of any sort presumes someone has done something to merit the penalty. In the case of legal punishment, it is a penalty for doing what the law forbids. Law, by its very nature, must have some sanction, some threat attached to breaking it, or else it loses its force. Without such force, it may be a request, but it is not law.

Thus, we can say that legal punishment is the state's infliction of harm or pain on those who break the law according to a set of legally established rules. But is such a practice justified? What gives a society the right to inflict the pain of punishment on any of its members? In asking this, we are asking a moral and not just a legal question. Is legal punishment of some sort morally justifiable? If so, why?

The Deterrence Argument

One answer to the question of whether legal punishment is morally justifiable is, "Yes, if (and only if) the punishment could be fashioned to prevent or deter crime." The general idea involved in this first rationale for legal punishment is related to both the *nature of law* and *its purpose*. For a law to be a law and not just a request, sanctions must be attached to it. It must have force behind it. Moreover, as we have seen from the discussion in Chapter 10, law has many possible purposes. One purpose is to prevent people from harming others. Our laws presumably are directed to achieving some good. Having penalties as sanctions attached to breaking these laws helps to ensure that the good intended by the laws will be achieved. Of course, not all laws are good laws. However, the idea is that we want not only to have good laws, but also to have them enforced in ways that make them effective.

Legal punishment, according to this reasoning, is for the purpose of *preventing* people from breaking the law, *deterring* them from doing so, or both. Broadly interpreted, the deterrence argument involves these two mechanisms. We can prevent crime by detaining would-be or actual criminals, that is, by simply holding them somewhere so that they cannot do social damage. We can also prevent crime by means such as increased street lighting, more police officers, and stricter handgun laws. We can deter crime by holding out a punishment as a threat, so as to persuade those who contemplate breaking the law not to do so. If a punishment works as a deterrent, it works in a particular way, through the would-be law breaker's thought and decision-making processes. One considers the possibility of being punished for doing some contemplated action and concludes that the gain achieved from the act is not worth the price to be paid, namely, the punishment. Then one acts accordingly.

Problematic Aspects

If deterrence works in this way, we can also notice that it is not likely to work in some cases. It is not likely to deter crimes of passion, in which people are overcome, if you will, by strong emotions. Not only are they not in the mood to calculate the risks versus the benefits, but also they are unlikely to stop themselves from continuing to act as they will. Punishment as a threat is also not likely to work in cases where people do calculate the risks and the benefits, and they think the benefits are greater than the risks. These would be cases in which the risks of being caught and punished are perceived as small and the reward or benefit is great. The benefit could be financial or the reward of group or gang respect. It might also be the reward of having done what one believed to be right, as in acts of civil disobedience, or in support of any cause whether actually good or bad. While punishment does not deter in some cases, in others presumably people will be motivated by the threat of punishment. A system of legal punishment will be worthwhile if it works for the greater majority, even if not for all, and if there are no bad consequences that outweigh the good ones.

The issue of cost and benefit also helps make another point about the deterrence rationale for legal punishment: Punishment, in this view, is *externally related* to law breaking. In other words, it is not essential. If something else works better than punishment, then that other means ought to be used either as a substitution for punishment or in addition to it. Some argue that punishment itself does not work. But punishment combined with rehabilitation, job training, or psychological counseling might be effective. However, if a punishment system is not working, then, in this view, it is not morally justifiable, for the whole idea is not to punish for punishment's sake but to achieve the goal of law enforcement. On utilitarian grounds, pain is never good in itself. Thus, if punishment involves suffering it must be justified. The suffering must be outweighed by the good to be achieved by it.

The deterrence argument has a more serious problem: Some people morally object to using this rationale as the sole grounds for legal punishment. For example, if the whole purpose is to enforce the law, and a particular form of punishment will actually work and work better than other measures to achieve the desired deterrent effect, then it would seem that we ought to use it. Suppose that a community has a particularly vexing problem with graffiti. To clean it up is costing the community scarce resources that could be better spent elsewhere. To get rid of the problem, suppose the community decides to institute a program whereby it would randomly pick up members of particular gangs believed to be responsible for the graffiti and punish these individuals with floggings in the public square. Or suppose that cutting off their hands would work better! We would surely have serious moral objections to this program. One objection would be that these particular individuals may not themselves have been responsible for the defacing. They were just picked at random because of suspicion. Another would be that the punishment seems all out of proportion to the offense. However, in itself (or in principle), on deterrence grounds there would be nothing essentially wrong with this program of law enforcement. It would not be necessary that the individual herself be guilty or that the punishment fit the crime. What would be crucial to determine is whether this punishment worked or worked better than alternative forms.

There is another version of the deterrence argument, and it has to do with how deterrence is supposed to work. According to this view, legal punishment is part of a system of social moral education. A society has a particular set of values. One way in which it can instill these values in its members from their youth is to establish punishments for those who undermine them. If private property is valued, society should punish those who damage or take others' property. These punishments would then become a deterrent in the sense that they had helped individuals internalize social values, giving them internal prohibitions against violating them. Key to evaluating this view is to determine whether punishment does work in this fashion. What does punishment teach the young and the rest of us? Does it help us internalize values, and does it motivate us? The way that the system is administered can also send a message, and in some cases it might be the wrong message. For example, if legal punishment is not applied fairly, then the lesson that some might learn may not be the one we would hope for.

The Retributivist Argument

The second primary rationale for legal punishment is retribution. On the retributivist view, legal punishment is justified as a means of making those responsible for a crime or harm pay for it. We can understand the idea embodied in this rationale in several ways. It is an argument that uses the concept of justice. Thus, a proponent might say that because someone caused a great deal of pain or harm to another, it is only just or fair that he suffer similarly or proportionately to the harm or pain he caused the other person. Or we might say that she deserves to suffer because she made her victim suffer. The punishment is only just or a fair recompense. In this view, punishment is *internally related* to the wrongful conduct. One cannot, as in the case of the deterrence argument, say that if something else works better than punishment, then that is what ought to be done. Here the punishing itself is essential for justice to be done.

Let us examine this reasoning a bit further. It is based on a somewhat abstract notion of justice. We punish to right a wrong or restore some original state. However, in many cases we cannot really undo the suffering of the victim by making the perpetrator suffer. One can pay back the money or return the property to its original state before it was damaged. But even in these cases there are other harms that cannot be undone, such as the victim's lost sense of privacy or security. Thus, the erasing, undoing, or righting of the wrong is of some other abstract or metaphysi-

cal type. It is difficult to explain, but supporters of this rationale for punishment believe that we do have some intuitive sense of what we mean when we say "justice was done."

According to the retributivist view, payment must be made in some way that is equivalent to the crime or harm done. Writers distinguish two senses of equivalency, an *egalitarian* and a *proportional* sense. With egalitarian equivalency, one is required to pay back something identical or almost identical to what was taken. If you make someone suffer two days, then you should suffer two days. However, it would also mean that if you caused someone's arm to be amputated, then your arm should also be cut off. Thus, this version is often given the label *lex talionis*. Translated literally, it means the "law of the talon," of the bird of prey's claw. We also call it the "law of the jungle" or taking "an eye for an eye."

Proportional equivalency holds that what is required in return is not something more or less identical to the harm done or pain caused, but something proportional. In this version, we can think of harms or wrongs as matters of degree, namely, of bad, worse, and worst. Punishments are also scaled from the minimal to the most severe. In this view, punishment must be proportional to the degree of the seriousness of the crime.

Obviously there are serious problems, both practical and moral, with the lex talionis version of the retributivist view. In some cases—for example, in the case of multiple murders—it is not possible to deliver something in like kind, for one cannot kill the murderer more than once. We would presumably also have some moral problems with torturing the torturer or raping the rapist. If one objects to this version of the retributivist view, then one would not necessarily have to object to the proportional version, however.

We should also notice that the retributivist justification of legal punishment does respond to two major problems that the deterrence argument has: that is, it is essential from this point of view that the payment or punishment be just. For it to be just, it must fit both the perpetrator and the crime. First, it must fit the perpetrator in the following ways. Only those responsible for a crime should be punished, and only to the degree that they are responsible. It would be important from this perspective that guilt be proved, and that we not single out likely suspects or representatives of a group so as to make an example of them or use them to intimidate the other group members as in our graffiti example. It would also be important that the punishment fit the person in terms of the degree of his responsibility. This requirement would address the concerns that we have about accomplices to a crime and also about the mental state of the criminal. Diminished mental capacity, mitigating circumstances, and duress, which lessen a person's responsibility, are significant elements of our criminal punishment system.

Second, it is essential in the retributive view that the punishment fit the crime. Defacing property is not a major wrong or harm and thus should not be punished with amputation of the perpetrator's hand, however well that might work to deter the graffiti artists. This view then requires that we do have a sense of what is more or less serious among crimes and also among punishments so that they can be well matched.

Problematic Aspects

Just as in the case of the deterrence argument, the retributivist argument regarding legal punishment has problematic aspects. We have already referred to one such problem—the fact that punishing the perpetrator does not concretely undo the wrong done to the victim. If there is undoing, it is only in some abstract or perhaps metaphysical sense. Those people who defend this argument would have to explain in what sense the balance is restored or the wrong righted by punishment. However, the retributivist would not have any problem with those who point out that a particular form of punishment does not work. According to a retributivist, this is not the primary reason to punish. Someone should be punished as a way of making satisfaction or restitution even if it does them or others no good.

A more common objection to the retributivist view is that it amounts to a condoning of revenge. To know whether this were true or not, we would have to clarify what we mean by revenge. Suppose we mean that particular people—say, a victim or her family—will get a sense of satisfaction in seeing the wrongdoer punished. But the retributivist view is arguably based on a different sense of justice. Only if it is might a reasonable argument for punishment on this basis be provided. However, some may question whether any type of justice exists that is not a matter of providing emotional satisfaction to victims or others enraged by a wrong done to them.

Finally, we can wonder whether the retributivist view provides a good basis for a system of legal punishment. Is the primary purpose of such a system to see that justice is done? Do we not have a system of legal punishment to ensure social order and safety? If so, it would seem that the deterrence argument is the best reason for having any system of legal punishment. One solution to this problem about which justification for legal punishment is the better one, is to use both.[11] In designing this system, we can retain consequentialist and thus deterrence and prevention reasons for having a legal punishment system, and consider first what works to deter and prevent crimes. However, we then can bring in our retributivist concerns to determine who is punished (only those guilty and to the extent that they are guilty) and how much (the punishment fitting the crime). In fashioning the punishment system, however, there may be times when we need to determine which rationale takes precedence. For example, in setting requirements for conviction of guilt, we may need to know how bad it is to punish an innocent person. We may decide to give precedence to the retributivist rationale and then make the requirements for conviction of guilt very strenuous, requiring unanimous jury verdicts and guilt beyond a reasonable doubt. In so doing, we also let some guilty people go free and thus run the risk of lessening the deterrent effect of the punishment system. Or we may decide to give precedence to the deterrence rationale. We thus may weaken the requirements for conviction so that we may catch and punish more guilty people. In doing so, however, we run the risk of also punishing more innocent persons.

Punishment and Responsibility

A key element of our legal punishment system and practice is the supposed tie between punishment and responsibility. Responsibility is essential for punishment from the retributivist point of view. The retributivist believes it is unjust to punish those who are not responsible for a crime. This can also be supported on deterrence grounds, for it probably would work better to punish only those who are responsible: Otherwise, who would have respect for or obey the law if we could be punished whether or not we obeyed it? Responsibility is essential from the retributivist point of view, but only possibly important from the deterrence point of view.

Thus, our legal punishment system contains defenses that are grounded in the requirement that a person be responsible to be punished. For example, the defense of duress can be viewed this way. If a person were forced to commit a crime, either physically forced or under threat to life, then we would probably say that that person was not responsible. The person may have committed the crime, but that is not enough. We do not have a system of strict liability in which the only issue is whether or not you actually did or caused something.

One of the most problematic defenses in our criminal justice system may well be the insanity defense. It involves a plea and a finding of "not guilty by reason of insanity." This defense has a long history going back at least into the nineteenth century in England with the *M'Naughton Rule* (1843). According to this rule, persons are not responsible for their actions if they did not know what they were doing or did not know that it was wrong. This is often referred to as the "right from wrong test." Since that time, other attempts have also been made to list the conditions under which persons should not be held re-

sponsible for their actions. One example is the "irresistible impulse test." The idea underlying this test for insanity is that sometimes persons are not able to control their conduct and thus act through no fault of their own. Of course, if a person does what he knows will put him in a condition in which he will not be able to control himself and then he unlawfully harms others, then he is held responsible. Thus, the person who drinks and then drives and harms another is held legally liable. However, the person who has some biochemical imbalance that prevents her from controlling her conduct would not be in the same position. In some cases, the insanity defense has been defined in medical terms when the behavior is said to be the result of mental disease. Thus, the *Durham Rule* defines insanity as the "product of mental disease or defect," some sort of abnormal mental condition that affects mental and emotional processes and impairs behavior controls. In our current criminal justice system, mental competence is one requirement for criminal liability. It is called the *mens rea,* or mental element.

Common criticisms of the insanity defense revolve around our ability to determine whether someone is mentally insane or incompetent. Can't someone feign this? How do psychiatrists or other experts really know whether a person knows what she is doing? However, if we could diagnose these conditions, a more basic question would still remain, namely, would the conditions diminish or take away responsibility? If so, then would punishment be appropriate? In the extreme case in which a person has a serious brain condition that prevented normal mental function, we assume that this would excuse him from full responsibility. He may, however, be dangerous, and this may be another reason to detain him.

Some people have criticized the entire notion of mental illness, especially as it is used in criminal proceedings. They are concerned about the results of a finding such as "not guilty by reason of insanity." For example, it may result in indeterminate sentences for minor crimes, because one must remain in custody in a criminal mental institution until sane. Others find the whole idea wrongheaded and dangerous. For example, Thomas Szasz believes that we have sometimes used this diagnosis of mental illness to categorize and stigmatize people who are simply different.[12] He finds this diagnosis to be often a dangerous form of social control.

Some of us also tend to look at some heinous crime and say that "no sane person could have done that!" Or we say that a certain crime was "sick." We use the horror of the crime, its serious wrongness, to conclude that the person committing it must be mentally diseased. One problem with this conclusion is that it implies that the person is not responsible. However, are we not then implying that no one who does evil things is responsible for what they do? If so, then perhaps they should not be punished. The connection between punishment and responsibility is not only central to our system of legal punishment, but also an important element of a morality of legal punishment. In fact, if all acts were determined, and no one of us was responsible for what we do (in the sense that we could have done otherwise), then it would seem that punishment as such (at least in the retributive sense of giving someone what was due them) would seem never to be appropriate.

The Death Penalty

We now return to a discussion of the death penalty. Throughout history people have been executed for various, and often political, reasons. The forms have also varied and have included death by guillotine, hanging, firing squad, electrocution, the gas chamber, and now lethal injection. Lethal injection was first permitted by the U.S. Supreme Court for an Oklahoma case in 1985, and it is now an option in 22 states.[13] As noted above, West Germany abolished the death penalty in the 1940s, Britain in the 1960s, and Canada in the 1970s; also as noted earlier, the U.S. High Court restored the death penalty in 1976. It has ruled that murder accomplices who showed "reckless indifference" for human life

could be subject to the death penalty. The Court also concluded that if the death penalty is carried out in racially discriminatory ways, this does not violate the Constitution![14] Still, 12 states have no death penalty, and another four have not yet imposed it. In 13 states, mostly in the South, more than 200 people were executed between 1977 and 1992 (more than 60 in Texas alone). In 1993, 2,713 persons were on death rows in the various states.[15] The same two arguments regarding legal punishment—deterrence and retribution—generally are used in arguments about the death penalty. We will return now to these rationales and see what considerations would be relevant to arguments for and against the death penalty.

On Deterrence Grounds

Is the death penalty a deterrent? Does it prevent people from committing certain capital crimes? Consider first the issue of prevention. One would think that at least there is certainty here. If you execute someone, that person will be prevented from committing any future crimes—murders, for example—because he will be dead. However, on a stricter interpretation of the term *prevent*, this may not necessarily be so.[16] Suppose that we meant by preventing X from doing Y, that we stop X from doing what she would have done, namely, Y. Next we ask whether by executing a convicted murderer we prevent that person from committing any further murders. The answer is, "Maybe." If that person would have committed another murder, then we do prevent him from doing so. If that person would not have committed another murder, then we would not have prevented him from doing so. In general, by executing all convicted murderers we would, strictly speaking, have prevented some of them (those who would have killed again) but not others (those who would not have killed again) from doing so. How many? It is difficult to tell. Those who support the death penalty will insist that it will have been worth it, no matter how small the number of murders being prevented, because the people executed are convicted murderers anyway. The last point must mean that their lives are not worth that much!

What about the deterrence argument for the death penalty? If having the death penalty deters would-be murderers from committing their crimes, then it will have been worth it, according to this rationale. Granted, it would not deter those who kill out of passion or those murders committed by risk takers, but it would deter others. This argument depends on showing that the death penalty is an effective deterrent. There are two kinds of resources to use to make this case. One is to appeal to our own intuitions about the value of our lives, that we would not do what would result in our own death. Threats of being executed would deter us, and thus we think they would also deter others. It is more likely, however, that reasons other than fear of the death penalty restrain most of us from killing others.

The other resource for making the case for the death penalty's deterrent effect is to use comparisons. For example, we could compare two jurisdictions, say, two states: One has the death penalty, and one does not. If we find that in the state with the death penalty there are fewer murders than in the state without the death penalty, can we assume that the death penalty has made the difference and is thus a deterrent? Not necessarily. Perhaps it was something else about the state with the death penalty that accounted for the lesser incidence of murder. For example, the lower homicide rate could be the result of good economic conditions or a culture that has strong families or religious institutions. Something similar could be true of the state with a higher incidence of homicide. The cause in this case could be factory closings or other poor economic conditions. So, also, if there were a change in one jurisdiction from no death penalty to death penalty (or the opposite), and the statistics regarding homicides also changed, then we might conclude that the causal factor was the change in the death penalty status. But again this is not necessarily so. For example, the murder rate in Canada actually declined after it abolished the

death penalty in 1976.[17] Other studies found no correlation between having or instituting or abolishing the death penalty and the rate of homicide.[18]

To make a good argument for the death penalty on deterrence grounds, a proponent would have to show that it works in this fashion. In addition, the proponent would have to show that the death penalty works better than life in prison without the possibility of parole. If we do not know for sure, we can ask what are our options. If we have the death penalty and it does not provide an effective deterrent, then we will have executed people for no good purpose. If we do not have the death penalty and it would have been an effective deterrent, then we risk the lives of innocent victims who otherwise would have been saved. Because this is the worse alternative, some argue, we ought to retain the death penalty.[19]

On Retributivist Grounds

As we have already noted, according to the retributivist argument for legal punishment, we ought to punish people in order to make them pay for the wrong or harm they have done. Those who argue for the death penalty on retributivist grounds must show that it is a fitting punishment and the only fitting punishment for certain crimes and criminals. This is not necessarily an argument based on revenge, that the punishment of the wrongdoer gives others satisfaction. It appeals rather to a sense of justice and an abstract righting of wrongs done. Again, there are two different versions of the retributive principle: egalitarian (or lex talionis) and proportional. The egalitarian version says that the punishment should equal the crime. An argument for the death penalty would attempt to show that the only fitting punishment for someone who takes a life is that her own life be taken in return. The value of a life is not equivalent to anything else, thus even life in prison is not sufficient payment for taking a life. On this view, however, it would seem that the only crime deserving of the death penalty would be murder. It is interesting to note that homicide is not the only crime for which we have assigned the death penalty. We have also done so for treason and rape. Currently, only some types of murder are thought by proponents of the death penalty to deserve this form of punishment. As noted in the earlier critique of the lex talionis view, strict equality of punishment would be not only impractical in some cases, but also morally problematic.

Perhaps a more acceptable argument could be made on grounds of proportionality. In this view, death is the only fitting punishment for certain crimes. Certain crimes are worse than all others, and these should receive the worst or most severe punishment. Surely, some say, death is a worse punishment than life in prison. However, some people argue that spending one's life in prison is worse. This form of the retributivist principle would not require that the worst crimes receive the worst possible punishment. It only requires that of the range of acceptable punishments, the worst crimes receive the top punishment on the list. Death by prolonged torture might be the worst punishment. But it is unlikely that we would put that at the top of our list. So, also, death could but need not be included on that list.

Using the retributivist rationale, one would need to determine the most serious crimes. Can these be specified and a good reason given as to why they are the worst crimes? Multiple murders would be worse than single ones, presumably. Murder with torture or of certain people might also be found to be among the worst crimes. What about treason? What about huge monetary swindles? What about violation of laws against weapons sales to certain foreign governments? We do rate degrees of murder. We distinguish murder in the first degree from murder in the second degree. The first is worse because the person not only deliberately intended to kill the victim, but also did it out of malice. These are distinguished from manslaughter, which is killing also, both its voluntary and involuntary forms. The idea supposedly is that the kind of personal and moral involvement makes a difference, such that the more planning and intention and deliberate-

ness, the more truly the person owned the act. In addition, the more malicious crime is thought to be worse. Critics of the death penalty sometimes argue that such rational distinctions are difficult if not impossible to make in practice. However, unless it is impossible in principle or by its very nature, supporters could continue to refine the current distinctions.

Other Concerns

Not all arguments for and against the death penalty come easily or neatly under the headings of deterrence or retributivist arguments. Some, for example, appeal to the uniqueness of the action by which society deliberately takes the life of a human being. People die all the time. But for some individuals or for the state's representatives to deliberately end the experience and thoughts and feelings of a living human being is the gravest of actions, they argue. As mentioned previously, most Western nations no longer have a death penalty. Some have given it up because they believe it to be uncivilized, brutalizing, degrading, barbarous, and dehumanizing. The one put to death, depending on the form of execution, gasps for air, strains, and shakes uncontrollably. The eyes bulge, the blood vessels expand, and sometimes more than one try is needed to complete the job. Death by lethal injection is arguably more humane. Yet it calls to mind the young person who was brought into the emergency room suffering from a gunshot wound and who was amazed at how much it hurt. On TV, she said, people get shot all the time and often just get up and go on. The person who is put to death by lethal injection would seem to be just going to sleep. That doesn't seem so bad!

Other opponents of the death penalty appeal to religious reasons, declaring the wrongness of "playing God." Only God can take a life, they argue. Another argument appeals to the inalienable right to life possessed by all human beings. Critics of this argument assert that those who deliberately kill other human beings forfeit their own right to life. Consider, further, whether a condemned prisoner should have the right to choose his own means of execution. Not long ago a convicted murderer in Oregon asked to be hanged![20] Do some forms of execution (guillotine, for example) violate the Eighth Amendment's ban on cruel and unusual punishment? Should executions become public or videotaped for purposes of information and instruction? When we ask questions such as these, our views on the death penalty and our reasons for supporting or opposing it will be put to the test, which is probably not a bad thing.

In the readings in this chapter, Hugo Bedau discusses general matters about the purposes of legal punishment. Ernest van den Haag, a supporter of the death penalty, attempts to answer many of the arguments of those who oppose it. Finally, Robert Johnson describes what happens in the process of carrying out executions today.

Notes

1. "Crime in the United States, 1994," U.S. Department of Justice, Federal Bureau of Investigation (Nov. 19, 1995), p. 9.
2. *Time* (Feb. 7, 1994); *New York Times* (March 31, 1997), A1.
3. "Crime in the United States, 1994," pp. 8, 17. *New York Times* (June 24, 1996), pp. A1, A7. *Time* (Feb. 7, 1994), pp. 56, 58.
4. HBO Special, May 25, 1993.
5. *San Francisco Examiner, Image* Magazine (Jan. 8, 1989): 19–23.
6. U.S. Supreme Court, *Furman v. Georgia,* 1972.
7. National Opinion Research Center s/s 1517.
8. Amnesty International USA *Newsletter,* Spring 1987, 4.
9. *San Francisco Chronicle* (Feb. 4, 1997), pp. 1, A7.
10. *San Francisco Examiner, Image* Magazine (Jan. 8, 1989): 19–23.
11. See Richard Brandt, *Ethical Theory* (Englewood Cliffs, NJ: Prentice-Hall, 1959).
12. Thomas Szasz, *The Myth of Mental Illness* (New York: Harper & Row, 1961).
13. *New York Times* (Feb. 26, 1995), p. E5.
14. U.S. Supreme Court, *Tison v. Arizona* (1987) and *McCleskey v. Kemp* (1989).
15. "Crime in the United States, 1994," p. 219, table 354.
16. See Hugh Bedau, "Capital Punishment and Retributive Justice," in *Matters of Life and Death,* Tom Regan (Ed.) (New York: Random House, 1980), 148–182.
17. It dropped from 3.09 people per 100,000 residents in 1975 to 2.74 per 100,000 in 1983. "Amnesty International and the Death Penalty," Amnesty International USA *Newsletter,* Spring 1987.
18. See H. Bedau, *The Death Penalty in America* (Chicago: Aldine, 1967), in particular Chapter 6, "The Question of Deterrence."
19. See Ernest van den Haag, "Deterrence and Uncertainty," *Journal of Criminal Law, Criminology and Police Science,* vol. 60, no. 2 (1969): 141–147.
20. I thank one of my reviewers, Wendy Lee-Lampshire of Bloomsburg University, for sharing this fact and calling this problem to my attention.

A World Without Punishment

Hugo Adam Bedau

Study Questions

1. Describe in your own words two of the "grievances" about the legal punishment system pointed out by Bedau.

2. Does Bedau believe that we could abolish the system of punishment without changing other things in our society? Explain.

3. Give the six basic claims that Bedau makes about the nature and justification of legal punishment.

4. Why does Bedau believe that we are not fully clear about the meaning or essence of punishment?

5. Why does Bedau believe that feeling pain is not the essence of punishment?

6. What is the difference that Bedau cites between the theory and practice of punishment regarding deprivations?

7. What are the three traditional justifications given for punishment? Explain the meaning of each.

8. What does Bedau believe is wrong with the justification of punishment as reformation or rehabilitation?

9. What does Bedau mean in saying that "conceptually, punishment is retributive"?

10. How does punishment as retributive differ from compensation and restitution?

11. How does Bedau explain the difference between deterrence and prevention?

12. What difference between special and general deterrence does he cite?

13. What five variables are supposed to play a role in deterrent efficacy?

14. What problems does Bedau have with the deterrence justification of punishment?

15. Does Bedau, then, think we should abolish legal punishment? Why or why not?

I.

Today, in contrast to whatever may have been true in earlier, more complacent times, current modes of punishment and the criminal justice system which prevails in our society have become the object of various familiar objections.[1]

1. Too many classes of acts (e.g., gambling) and conditions (e.g., public nudity or drunkenness) are punishable offenses; we suffer from an acute case of "overcriminalization."

2. Too few of those who are guilty of dangerous and harmful acts are caught, too few convicted, and too few punished.

3. Too many people are behind prison bars mainly on account of their class or status rather than as a result of their acts, e.g., they are blacks, or longhairs, or poor, or all three.

4. Too many people are sentenced to overly harsh punishments: harsh because severe, e.g., long term imprisonment for possession of marijuana; harsh because vague, e.g., indeterminate sentences for any offense.

5. Too many people are punished by imprisonment rather than being dealt with alternatively by the criminal justice system, e.g., conscientious draft resisters who during the 1960s were prosecuted and convicted as common criminals rather than treated non-punitively in light of their conscientious motives.

6. Too many punishments are imposed by statutes which rest on vague grounds of general deterrence and lack empirical evidence to show that such threats are likely to influence the conduct of large numbers of potential offenders.

7. Too many people suffer from harms and hardships which are not properly part of their punishment but which they cannot escape once they are at the mercy of those charged with the administration of punishment, e.g., the bail-or-jail system, overcrowded pre-trial detention facilities, abuses by the custodial staff in prison, victimization at the hands of other inmates.

8. Too many people are simply the victims of official lawlessness inflicted upon them by the corrupt and the vindictive, e.g., police brutality, judicial venality.

9. Too many people are being made worse by the prevailing system of punishment.

While particular grievances inspire such criticisms, they have led some to mount a radical challenge against the whole system. These grievances have inspired the vision of *a world without punishment,* a utopia long admired by anarchists and socialists, in which not only the whip and the gallows have disappeared, but in which shackles and bars, and all other devices whereby the state enlists coercive force against its own citizens in the name of "law and order," are abandoned. The combined effect of piecemeal objections to punishment can be the dream of a non-punitive, non-repressive society, a true community. This vision is interesting to contemplate if only because it raises some hard questions. Could we in fact entirely abolish all our punitive institutions and practices without utter chaos? What would be the result of such an anti-penal orientation in practice if

Hugo Adam Bedau, "A World Without Punishment?" *Punishment and Human Rights,* Milton Goldinger (Ed.) (Rochester, VT: Schenkman Books, Inc., 1974), pp. 141–162. Reprinted with permission.

we left everything else in society the same, e.g., did not simultaneously become hermits or saints, did not pursue radically different social and economic policies, did not confront acute limitations on natural resources? Would the result be a reasonable bargain for everyone, worth paying the costs of no punishment in order to get the advantages of no punishments? If the bargain seems a bad one (as it must to most people), and yet if the particular complaints aired against the prevailing system of punishment are nevertheless true, what modifications might we make either in our theory of punishment or in our penal practice so as to get a better system than we have at present?

The position I defend would answer some of these questions as follows. First, punishment necessarily has some features about it, viz., the deprivation of rights or the imposition of pain, which are bound to make it unattractive to decent persons and also to lend itself to abuses. Second, a fair assessment of current theory as to the nature and justification of punishment shows that the present system of punishment is unintelligible and indefensible. The resulting effects of this assessment upon the theory of punishment are as yet uncalculated. Third, except for fatal and mutilative punishments, whose direct effects are clear, we are not able to predict the total effect upon any given person of subjecting him to a given punishment for a given offense. This should make us extremely cautious about imposing some modes of punishment, e.g., long term detention, upon anyone who is expected subsequently to assume (or resume) a place in society as a normal individual. Fourth, the notorious harms imposed by the existing system of punishment justify immediate experimentation with radical alternatives wherever feasible. Even if abolition of the current penitentiary system of imprisonment is highly desirable, one should not suppose that this can be done without considerable costs and new incentives which may turn out to contradict essential features of our post-industrial society. Fifth, at the present time there is no general alternative available to us and acceptable by the public which is at once superior to punishment in avoiding its harms and abuses and not less effective in response to the genuine problem of criminal violence. Finally, whereas the grievances against the present system of punishment are genuine and legitimate, other consideration show that a world without punishment is both unattainable and undesirable.

It is not possible in brief compass to establish in detail the truth of all these claims, so far stated without even the semblance of argument. However, if we critically examine the current ideas among philosophers as to the nature and justification of punishment, we can see at least how the first three of the above half-dozen claims are correct, and, along the way, add some explanatory support for the other claims as well.

II.

During the past twenty years, philosophers in the English-speaking world have reached general agreement as to the nature of punishment. The roots of this conception are at least as old as Hobbes's *Leviathan*,[2] but not until fairly recently has the task been undertaken of giving an exact and formal definition of punishment. The task may at first seem quite easy ("Everyone understands what punishment is," says conventional wisdom), but it is not. A formal definition of any concept poses certain constraints. In addition, there are many things which are like or concurrent with punishment and thus difficult to distinguish from it, and this will confuse all but the most alert and skillful. For instance, in order to understand the idea of *punishing a person*, it is necessary to distinguish it from such related but different notions as controlling a person's conduct, revenge, intentionally harming another, unintentionally harming another, treatment, blaming, and shaming. Similarly, one must distinguish a person's being punished from a person's being taxed, feeling guilty, being blamed, being hurt. And one must be prepared to say whether God (if there is or were a God) could punish a person, whether a person can punish himself, whether the innocent can be punished, whether a dog can be punished, and so forth. It is out of the attempt to make these distinctions and answer these questions that the current consensus on the nature of punishment has emerged.[3] It can be expressed in the following statement:

A person, P, is punished by something, x, if and only if

(i) x is some pain or other consequence normally considered unpleasant,

(ii) x is intentionally imposed upon P by someone else, Q,

(iii) Q has the authority under the rules of the (legal or other) system to impose x upon P,

(iv) x is imposed on P by Q on account of an offense as defined by the (legal or other) rules,

(v) because P is authoritatively found to be the offender.

For our purposes, the emphasis upon *legal* rules in the above definition is unobjectionable, because in the present discussion, the idea of punishment and its attendant institutions are those of punishment within legal systems (in contrast to the punishment parents visit upon their children, school authorities upon students, etc.). Punishment, of course, is not confined to acts of government under law. Yet it is such punishments which pose the gravest social problem and which are primarily at issue whenever one seriously contemplates the idea of a world without punishment.

Now, if what one wants to do is to attack or criticize the very idea of punishment in order to eliminate the practice or institution of punishment from public life, theoretically the easiest way to do this would be to argue, on some ground or other, that one or more of the five conditions used in this definition has *no* proper application in human affairs. Consider in this light the complaint, mentioned earlier, that we suffer from an acute case of "overcriminalization."[4] The point of this complaint amounts to an attack under clause (iv) in the above definition; "overcriminalization" is the complaint that consensual conduct should not be made a criminal offense, and that we should repeal or nullify all statutes in the penal code which do so. The result would be a vast increase in the amount of conduct which is no longer criminal and therefore no longer punishable as such. In order to attack punishment by the route of pressing the objection of "overcriminalization," a further step must be taken. One must argue either that the conduct in question is not really harmful, or that although it is harmful it must be permitted because it cannot be prevented, or that its harmfulness can be controlled and regulated in non-punitive ways. In a similar manner, all the classic complaints against punishment can be understood and diagnosed by reference to this definition of punishment.

Before turning to a major objection to punishment as here defined, it is useful to consider first two relatively minor objections. Alternatives to punishment are almost invariably inspired by the feature of punishment identified in clause (i) of the above definition: the infliction of *pain*. Decent people are naturally repelled by the deliberate infliction of pain by one person upon another, except, perhaps, when a person has given his knowing consent to the suffering (as in earlier days, before the development of effective anesthesias, when a gangrenous limb had to be amputated to avoid death). It should be understood, however, that pain—the sensation or the feeling of physical or psychological pain—is neither a necessary nor a sufficient condition of punishment. That it is not a sufficient condition is shown, of course, by the presence of four other conditions in the standard definition of punishment. That it is not a necessary condition, however, is not so readily grasped. Yet consider the death penalty. It is hardly to be denied that killing persons is both a conceivable and an actual mode of punishment. But are we to suppose that it would cease to be a punishment if the sentence of death were carried out by administering (as, supposedly, happened to Socrates when he drank the hemlock) a lethal potion which is *entirely painless*? One might argue that such a painless execution is not as much of a punishment as an agonizingly painful execution; but this hardly matters. What does matter is that by executing a person, one has destroyed his capacity for any future experiences and conduct; one has *deprived* him of his life, something which, presumably, he values (most people do) and to which he has (absent his criminal conduct) a *right*. Accordingly, I would propose that the reference to pain in clause (i) of the standard definition of punishment be revised so as to refer instead to the deprivation of a person's rights.[5] A punishment, especially a punishment under law, always deprives a person of something to which he normally has a right, e.g., his life (the death penalty), his liberty (prison), or his property (fines). Whether or not he minds this, whether or not it also hurts him in some ordinary sense, is incidental. He has lost something of value, whatever he thinks or feels about it; and to do that to a person, in conformity with the other features of the concept of punishment outlined above, is to have punished him. Incidentally, it is just this feature of the revision of clause (i) above which helps us to see what it is about "enforced treatment," such as the regimen of "behavior modification" displayed in Anthony Burgess's *A Clockwork Orange*, which explains why one feels that the society therein depicted has not really abandoned punishment for therapy, but merely exchanged one mode of punishment for another. What remains constant in both cases, as the novel (and movie) show, is the deprivation of offenders' rights by duly constituted authority in consequence of the violation of the criminal code. And that is punishment, whatever else we may choose to call it.

The second preliminary objection is concerned with what we are to infer from our definition of punishment as to the *point* of punishing people. Even though, under this definition, punishing a person is an *intentional* undertaking, it is not clear *what* the intention is with which, in general, we punish people at all. To clarify the problem, consider what a judge should say to a typical burglar when sentencing him to three years in the penitentiary. If the judge is persuaded by our definition of punishment, he might say, "By the authority vested in me, I hereby sentence you to three years in the penitentiary *because* of your conviction on the offense as charged and the statutes providing such punishment for burglary." But what should the judge say if he begins in this way: "By the authority, etc., three years in the penitentiary *in order to . . .* ?" In order to *what?* In order to prevent him from any further burglary during the next three years? In order to make the burglar less inclined to further burglary after the next three years? In order to discourage other would-be burglars? In order to make the convict worse off, as cynics and the recidivism statistics would indicate? The definition of punishment under consideration gives no single answer to this question, and the issue before us is whether this is a merit or defect in the definition, or neither.

Why *must* there be any general intention with which society punishes its deviant and dangerous members? Why *must* there be some one thing (or, for that matter, some two or three things) which we do when we punish? A stray remark of Wittgenstein's anticipates these hesitations:

> "Why do we punish criminals? Is it from a desire for revenge? Is it in order to prevent a repetition of the crime?" And so on. The truth is there is no one reason. There is the institution of punishing criminals. Different people support this for different reasons, and for different reasons in different cases and at different times . . . and so punishments are carried out.[6]

Wittgenstein has not given an argument for the view that there is no single "in order to" about punishment. All he has done is help us to see that, in believing there is some one "in order to," we are ourselves in the grip of a certain picture about the institution of punishment under law, a picture for which we lack adequate evidence, a picture not necessary.

III.

Textbooks and treaties inform us that there are fundamentally three justifications of punishment: Retribution, Prevention (or Deterrence), and Reformation (or Rehabilitation).[7] Actually, the truly traditional justifications have been only the first two. Because I intend here to concentrate on them exclusively, it is best to say a brief word now about what is wrong with reformation or rehabilitation as the justification of punishment, which came into prominence only during the past century. Rarely has reformation or rehabilitation been held to be the *sole* or even the *primary* justification of punishment. Those who conceive of a world without punishment, and are thus ready to condemn all punishment for anyone no matter what the offender has done, do not have rehabilitation or reformation of offenders in mind when they do so. On the contrary, they often want to get rid of "punishment" in order to rehabilitate offenders. What they condemn is the abuse or neglect of the rehabilitative ideal. In other words, today, reformation or rehabilitation as the goal, aim, or justification of punishment has become progressively blurred with a *non-punitive alternative* to punishment, i.e., Treatment or Therapy.[8] This is but one result of viewing crime less as an example of individual wickedness and more as an instance of social sickness (as is neatly conveyed in the quip from *West Side Story,* "He's depraved on account of he's deprived"). For these reasons we can afford to omit any further canvass of punishment as rehabilitative in this discussion.

Let us turn now to the justification of punishment through appeal to retribution. Conceptually, punishment is retributive, as we have seen. There is general agreement that what we mean by punishment is the infliction of some deprivation on someone on account of his infraction of some rule. Retribution therefore enters into the very concept of punishment in a double sense. First, it is retribution which tells us *what* to do in order to punish: "Pay him back in the same coin." Punishment, unlike restitution and compensation to the victims of crime, leaves the person punished worse off than before because the coin in which he is paid back is a deprivation of his rights. Second, it is retribution which tells us *whom* to punish: "The guilty deserve to be punished" is a retributivist tautology. (This, by the way, shows us something peculiar about the very idea of punishing hostages in wartime. Punishment normally requires an identity between the person who is believed to be guilty of an offense and the person punished for it, whereas the practice of punishing hostages deliberately breaks this requirement. Perhaps the phrase, "punishing hostages" is a misnomer.) I see nothing wrong with these two retributivist features of punishment, and I cannot see anything in our institutions of punishment which would be improved by systematically abandoning either of these requirements. The fact that there may be more useful, non-retributive ways of handling criminals than punishing them is not an argument for a notion of non-retributive punishment.

Retribution is also often thought to give us possible, even if not necessary, answers to two other questions: Why in general ought we to punish anyone? What in general ought to be a person's punishment for a given offense? The familiar retributivist maxim, "Let the punishment fit the crime," is a partial answer to the second question, and (as is well known) is of little use to us except at the margins. Thus, this maxim assures us that a slap on the wrist for murder is an improper punishment, given the gravity of the offense and the triviality of the punishment. Likewise, death for overparking suffers from the converse flaw. The problem is to go beyond these margins, and the difficulty for the retributivist lies in showing us *how* we are to assess the relative gravity of other crimes, e.g., rape, kiting checks, and *what* constitutes proportionate severity in punishment for the gravity of each type of offense. But that is not all. Pure retributivism also requires us to be persuaded that no non-retributive considerations should enter into fitting punishments to crimes and to criminals, and that no non-retributive theory has any rational basis for apportioning the severity of punishments to the gravity of offenses. These are strong claims, and, because no version of pure retributivism has made them good, retributivism has been held for some years in low esteem.[9] As to why in general we ought to punish anyone, retributivism seems to be capable of nothing more than the unhelpful circular answer "Because people who commit crimes deserve to be punished." If we ask the retributivist, "Why, in general, do criminals deserve punishment?" either he gives us no answer at all, or he abandons pure retributivism by telling us about the *good on balance* which a system

of punishment produces. But this is an ill-disguised, quasi-Utilitarian account of the justification of punishment, and whereas it may be acceptable in its own right, it is not a type of justification open to the pure retributivist.

The only other alternative for the retributivist is to appeal to the idea that *justice* requires punishment of offenders, and that the good which punishment achieves is the good of justice. Sometimes it has even been claimed that punishment is in general *a good to those punished,* irrespective of the overall good to society of having offenders punished. If this is correct, and if this good cannot be obtained in any other way than by punishing offenders, then we have a very strong argument from the moral point of view (the only point of view worth considering on this issue) against a world without punishment.

We have seen how: (a) punishment involves depriving a person of some of his normal rights; (b) such a deprivation may be visited only upon the guilty (or those authoritatively found to be guilty); (c) the gravity of the offense must to some degree be reflected in the severity of the punishment; and (d) it is not proper to treat a person who deliberately chose to commit a crime as though he were a helpless infant, imbecile, or non-person. It is difficult to see how the institution of punishment could be improved (either in our understanding of it or in its function) by contradicting any of these four principles. Rather, the very reverse of humanization and liberation would result. To abandon these principles is either to make punishment more savage than it already is or to abandon punishment altogether in favor of some more savage alternative. To concede this much in no way requires endorsing any further retributivist principles, whatever they may be. Retributivism no doubt encompasses a variety of principles and notions, but there is no reason why we shouldn't pick and choose among them, retaining only those which fit together rationally with each other and with non-retributive considerations. To the degree to which this is done, the attack upon punishment because of its retributive features should diminish.

Let us turn now to deterrence. There is some confusion as to the nature of deterrence, and since deterrence is the aim or justification of punishment which has become most prominent in our civilization, it is important to clarify this concept at the start. Punishment is generally favored as a systematic way of dealing with offenders because it is believed that punishment prevents crime. But crime prevention as such and prevention by deterrence are two different things. Deterrence, as its etymology suggests, consists in control or influence over the behavior of someone by a *threat,* including the threat of penal sanction. Prevention, however, can be accomplished by any number of methods. For instance, crime can be prevented by manipulating the offender's external environment, e.g., through placing him in prison or stocks, or by banishment. It can be accomplished by alteration of his bodily capacities, through incapacitative and irreversible acts (death, mutilation), or by more subtle and temporary methods (drugs, chemotherapy). Theoretically, all of these are ways of preventing persons from behaving in certain ways and thus from committing criminal acts. *None involves deterrence at all.*

The idea of punishment as a deterrent is complex. Even if prevention is kept distinct from the narrower issue of deterrence, there still remains the further distinction between what is called *special* and what is called *general* deterrence. Special deterrence is usually defined as deterring person A from committing a crime by punishing him for some prior offense; general deterrence is usually defined as deterring persons, B, C, D . . . from committing a crime by punishing person A for some offense. Yet both of these definitions are ambiguous because they cut across a further distinction. Consider the situation of special deterrence. Theoretically, we could inflict on any given offender, A, who has committed a crime, *x,* a punishment, P, and obtain either or both of two deterrent effects: one could be the deterrence from another offense of the same sort, x^1, and another could be the deterrence from an altogether different offense, *y* (as when, after his ten years imprisonment for burglary, Smith is deterred not only from further burglary but also from assault). Let us call the former *primary* deterrence and the latter *secondary* deterrence. The same distinction applies within general deterrence. We have, then, four possible combinations of kinds of deterrence: special and general, primary and secondary. One would conjecture that the imposition of any given penalty would be most effective as a special, primary deterrent, and least effective as a general, secondary deterrent (that is, we would be far more likely to deter Smith from further burglary by punishing him for a prior act of burglary than we would be likely to deter Brown and Jones from assault by punishing Smith for burglary).

Since the time of Beccaria and Bentham, the deterrence efficacy of any given punishment has been understood to be a function of at least five presumably independent variables: severity, certainty, celerity, frequency, and publicity (degree of public perception of the liability to and imposition of the sanction). Subsequent analysis has shown that personality differences among potential offenders are also a relevant variable, and that each of the classic five variables is itself a complex of several factors. Crimes, too, vary in their nature, from the "expressive"—those which evince an inner drive or compulsion and in which prudential self-interest of the offender enters little or not at all—to the "instrumental."[10] It is easy to say, as one of the leading theoreticians of punitive deterrence has written, that "It is . . . a fundamental fact of social life that the risk of unpleasant consequences is a very strong motivational factor for most people in most situations."[11] It is another thing to verify quantitatively its many corollaries. What is the *degree of risk* that persons are willing to run of incurring the legally designated sanction? How *strong a motivational factor* is apprehension of this risk, and on what does its strength depend? How *large a role* does the legal sanction in the narrowest sense—the punishment meted out to an offender by a judge under a statute—play in these "unpleasant consequences"? The truth is, we have almost no reliable answers to these questions, for any given class of offenders, offenses, and sanctions.

Consider, as an example, the ongoing controversy over the relative effect of *severity* and *certainty* of sanctions in deterrence. Classic doctrine would maintain that these two factors are additive, but like much other conventional wisdom this assertion has been attacked. Some have argued that, at least where severe penalties are involved, the two are inversely related (the greater the severity of a sentence, the less certain its application, and conversely). Part of the problem is to determine which statistical model is the best to use in testing these hypotheses. Another part is conceptual: what is the best way to define "certainty" and "severity" in a punishment? Much of the problem lies in the available data on offenses, arrests, prison admissions, and release records. The most recent review of the whole set of issues leaves all of these questions essentially unanswered.[12] This ignorance should make us cautious in the face of the popular maxim, "The greater the severity of a punishment, the greater its deterrent efficacy." In the present state of our knowledge, we have little or no reason to believe that by increasing the severity of a punishment we can achieve a downturn in the crime index, or that by decreasing the severity we should expect an upsurge in crime. The folly of such ideas lies in the notion that we can leave everything else in society the same and control the rate of crime merely by alterations in sanction severity. It is difficult to think of a more naive approach to crime control.

I have stressed these conceptual complexities and empirical difficulties in our knowledge about deterrence because they affect the role it is reasonable to assign to deterrence in the theory of punishment and its justification. Philosophers of a Utilitarian persuasion, such as Bentham and Mill in the last century, tend to stress the importance of deterrence as the sole or the dominant justification of punishment. It is to be found also in the influential views of H.L.A. Hart, who defends the institution of punishment by appealing to its "beneficial consequences" when compared with alternative systematic ways of dealing with crimes and criminals.[13] The chief beneficial consequence of a system of punishment is in "preventing harmful crime."[14] Since incapacitation of convicted offenders plays only a small part in crime prevention, it is deterrence which emerges as the "General Justifying Aim" of punishment (in Hart's phrase).

We have seen how, in anything we could properly call an act or a system of punishment, several undeniably retributive features must be present. Can the same be said for deterrence? We have seen earlier how the very nature of punishment would be shaped by some who would build into it a preventative function, and we have also seen the difficulty in giving a retributive account of why anyone ought to be punished at all (i.e., why have a system of punishment?). In addition, we have seen how small a part in justifying punishment is played by appeal to the reform or rehabilitation of convicted offenders. What, then, is left, except an appeal to deterrence and prevention, "social defense" as some now fashionably call it? A dilemma, however, looms precisely at this point, and it is one perhaps better appreciated by the opponents of punishment (or, at any rate, the opponents of a purely deterrence justification of punishment) than by its advocates. The dilemma is that it is difficult to see how deterrence can justify punishment, when (a) we know so little about the deterrent effects, whether special or general, primary or secondary, and when (b) deterrence requires punishing (that is, inflicting

a rights-deprivation upon) a person *now* for something he did in the past in order to control someone's *future* conduct. Either we must justify both (a) and (b) or we cannot justify deterrence. But if one maintains that deterrence is a necessary justification of punishment, and if deterrence is unavailable to us in theory, then punishment cannot be justified as a system at all!

IV.

Some years ago John Rawls observed that most people regard punishment as "an acceptable institution. Only a few have rejected punishment entirely," he remarked, and as an afterthought added, "which is rather surprising when one considers all that can be said against it."[15] I have tried to show that the concept of punishment is something against which men naturally rebel, for punishment essentially involves a loss of freedom, of rights, and typically is painful and unpleasant for those who must suffer it. I have also tried to show how it is impossible to encompass under the concept of punishment many of the actual indignities and harms inflicted upon the persons who are punished by imprisonment. There is a considerable gap between what its theory of punishment (its conception and justification) can explain and what our practice reveals is in need of explanation.

Meanwhile, crime—not mere law-breaking, but dangerous and harmful conduct inflicted on persons without their consent—continues to be a prominent feature of our lives. There is no immediate prospect of its disappearance from our midst. So long as crime cannot be abolished, or at least diminished to a tolerable level (whatever that might be), there is no likelihood that the practice of punishment will disappear. To say this is not to defend the existing system of imprisonment. The prison system (jails, penitentiaries, prison farms, half-way houses, juvenile detention centers) touches the lives of more than a million offenders every year in this country. It was not built in a day, and it will not be dismantled in a day, not by administrative directive from above, nor by scholarly critique from outside, and not even by riot or rebellion from within. As a human institution, punishment has a disgraceful past; it probably does not have a glorious future. Still, punishment under law as a systematic way of dealing with dangerous and harmful conduct may be the least ugly, the least destructive institution available to us. Bad as it is, the alternatives are worse.

Notes

1. See, e.g., *Struggle for Justice,* A Report on Crime and Punishment Prepared for the American Friends Service Committee, New York, Hill and Wang, 1971.

2. Thomas Hobbes, *Leviathan* (1960), Chapter xxviii, reprinted in part in Gertrude Ezorsky, ed., *Philosophical Perspectives on Punishment,* Albany, State University of New York Press, 1972, pp. 3–5.

3. Writers who have contributed to this consensus include A.G.N. Flew, Stanley I. Benn, and H.L.A. Hart. See especially Hart, "Prolegomena to the Principles of Punishment," *Proceedings of the Aristotelian Society* (1959–60), reprinted in his *Punishment and Responsibility,* New York, Oxford University Press, 1968, pp. 1–27, especially pp. 4–5. My definition is adapted from Hart's with only minor changes.

4. For discussion, see Norval Morris and Gordon Hawkins, *The Honest Politician's Guide to Crime Control,* University of Chicago Press, 1970, Chapter i; and the forthcoming book by Godwin Schurs and myself on crimes without victims.

5. This revision is not original with me. It may be found already in John Rawls, "Two Concepts of Rules," *The Philosophical Review* (1955), reprinted in H.B. Acton, ed., *The Philosophy of Punishment,* London, Macmillan, 1969, at p. 111, where Rawls says that he proposes to "define" punishment in terms of a person's being "deprived of some of his normal rights."

6. Ludwig Wittgenstein, *Lectures and Conversations on Aesthetics, Psychology and Religious Belief* (ed. Cyril Barrett), Oxford, Basil Blackwell, 1966, p. 50.

7. See, e.g., Ted Honderich, *Punishment: The Supposed Justifications,* London, Hutchinson, 1969; Rudolph J. Gerber and Patrick D. McAnany, eds., *Contemporary Punishment,* University of Notre Dame Press, 1972; Stanley E. Grupp, ed., *Theories of Punishment,* Indiana University Press, 1971; Acton, ed., op. cit.; Packer, op. cit.; and Ezorsky, ed., op. cit.

8. See, e.g., Karl Menninger, *The Crime of Punishment,* New York, Viking Press, 1969; and Giles Playfair and Derrick Sington, *Crime, Punishment and Cure,* London, Secker & Warburg, 1965. Perhaps the classic modern source for this idea is the essay by George Bernard Shaw, *The Crime Imprisonment,* New York, Philosophical Library, 1946.

9. See H.L.A. Hart, *Punishment and Responsibility,* Oxford University Press, 1968, pp. 230 ff.

10. Franklin E. Zimring and Gordon J. Hawkins, *Deterrence: The Legal Threat to Crime Control,* University of Chicago Press, 1973, provides by far the best general discussion of all these issues.

11. Johannes Andenaes, "The Morality of Deterrence," *University of Chicago Law Review,* 37 (1970), pp. 649–664, at p. 664.

12. William C. Bailey and Ronald W. Smith, "Punishment: Its Severity and Certainty," *Journal of Criminal Law, Criminology and Police Science,* 63 (1972), pp. 530–539.

13. Hart, op. cit., pp. 8–9.

14. Hart, op. cit., pp. 235–236.

15. Rawls, op. cit., p. 106.

The Ultimate Punishment: A Defense

Ernest van den Haag

Study Questions

1. Why does van den Haag believe that maldistribution of punishment would not in itself make a punishment unjust?

2. What is his reason for holding that the punishment by death of some innocent persons would not in itself be a good reason to abolish the death penalty?

3. Does van den Haag believe that deterrence is the best reason to support the death penalty?

4. If we were not sure or could not prove that the death penalty was a better deterrent than life imprisonment, would that be a good reason to abolish it, according to van den Haag?

5. Does van den Haag believe that punishment is repayment for the victim's suffering and thus should be equal in kind?

6. What does he mean when he says that the lawbreaker "volunteers" for his punishment?

7. How does van den Haag respond to Justice Brennan's assertions that the death penalty is uncivilized, inhumane, and degrading?

In an average year about 20,000 homicides occur in the United States. Fewer than 300 convicted murderers are sentenced to death. But because no more than thirty murderers have been executed in any recent year, most convicts sentenced to death are likely to die of old age.[1] Nonetheless, the death penalty looms large in discussions: it raises important moral questions independent of the number of executions.

The death penalty is our harshest punishment.[2] It is irrevocable: it ends the existence of those punished, instead of temporarily imprisoning them. Further, although not intended to cause physical pain, execution is the only corporal punishment still applied to adults.[3] These singular characteristics contribute to the perennial, impassioned controversy about capital punishment.

I. Distribution

Consideration of the justice, morality, or usefulness of capital punishment is often conflated with objections to its alleged discriminatory or capricious distribution among the guilty. Wrongly so. If capital punishment is immoral *in se,* no distribution among the guilty could make it moral. If capital punishment is moral, no distribution would make it immoral. Improper distribution cannot affect the quality of what is distributed, be it punishments or rewards. Discriminatory or capricious distribution thus could not justify abolition of the death penalty. Further, maldistribution inheres no more in capital punishment than in any other punishment.

Maldistribution between the guilty and the innocent is, by definition, unjust. But the injustice does not lie in the nature of the punishment. Because of the finality of the death penalty, the most grievous maldistribution occurs when it is imposed upon the innocent. However, the frequent allegations of discrimination and capriciousness refer to maldistribution among the guilty and not to the punishment of the innocent.

Maldistribution of any punishment among those who deserve it is irrelevant to its justice or morality. Even if poor or black convicts guilty of capital offenses suffer capital punishment, and other convicts equally guilty of the same crimes do not, a more equal distribution, however desirable, would merely be more equal. It would not be more just to the convicts under sentence of death.

Punishments are imposed on persons, not on racial or economic groups. Guilt is personal. The only relevant question is: does the person to be executed deserve the punishment? Whether or not others who deserved the same punishment, whatever their economic or racial group, have avoided execution is irrelevant. If they have, the guilt of the executed convicts would not be diminished, nor would their punishment be less deserved. To put the issue starkly, if the death penalty were imposed on guilty blacks, but not on guilty whites, or, if it were imposed by a lottery among the guilty, this irrationally discriminatory or capricious distribution would neither make the penalty unjust, nor cause anyone to be unjustly punished, despite the undue impunity bestowed on others.[4]

Equality, in short, seems morally less important than justice. And justice is independent of distributional inequalities. The ideal of equal justice demands that justice be equally distributed, not that it be replaced by equality. Justice requires that as many of the guilty as possible be punished, regardless of whether others have avoided punishment. To let these others escape the deserved punishment does not do justice to them, or to society. But it is not unjust to those who could not escape.

These moral considerations are not meant to deny that irrational discrimination, or capriciousness, would be inconsistent with constitutional requirements. But I am satisfied that the Supreme Court has in fact provided for adherence to the constitutional requirement of equality as much as is possible. Some inequality is indeed unavoidable as a practical matter in any system.[5] But, *ultra posse nemo obligatur.* (Nobody is bound beyond ability.)

Recent data reveal little direct racial discrimination in the sentencing of those arrested and convicted of murder.[6] The abrogation of the death penalty for rape has eliminated a major source of racial discrimination. Concededly, some discrimination based on the race of murder victims may exist; yet, this discrimination affects criminal victimizers in an unex-

From *Harvard Law Review* 99 (1986). © 1986 by *Harvard Law Review.* Some footnotes have been deleted. Reprinted with permission.

pected way. Murderers of whites are thought more likely to be executed than murderers of blacks. Black victims, then, are less fully vindicated than white ones. However, because most black murderers kill blacks, black murderers are spared the death penalty more often than are white murderers. They fare better than most white murderers.[7] The motivation behind unequal distribution of the death penalty may well have been to discriminate against blacks, but the result has favored them. Maldistribution is thus a straw man for empirical as well as analytical reasons.

II. Miscarriages of Justice

In a recent survey Professors Hugo Adam Bedau and Michael Radelet found that 7,000 persons were executed in the United States between 1900 and 1985 and that 25 were innocent of capital crimes.[8] Among the innocents they list Sacco and Vanzetti as well as Ethel and Julius Rosenberg. Although their data may be questionable, I do not doubt that, over a long enough period, miscarriages of justice will occur even in capital cases.

Despite precautions, nearly all human activities, such as trucking, lighting, or construction, cost the lives of some innocent bystanders. We do not give up these activities, because the advantages, moral or material, outweigh the unintended losses. Analogously, for those who think the death penalty just, miscarriages of justice are offset by the moral benefits and the usefulness of doing justice. For those who think the death penalty unjust even when it does not miscarry, miscarriages can hardly be decisive.

III. Deterrence

Despite much recent work, there has been no conclusive statistical demonstration that the death penalty is a better deterrent than are alternative punishments.[9] However, deterrence is less than decisive for either side. Most abolitionists acknowledge that they would continue to favor abolition even if the death penalty were shown to deter more murders than alternatives could deter.[10] Abolitionists appear to value the life of a convicted murderer or, at least, his nonexecution, more highly than they value the lives of the innocent victims who might be spared by deterring prospective murderers.

Deterrence is not altogether decisive for me either. I would favor retention of the death penalty as retri-

bution even if it were shown that the threat of execution could not deter prospective murderers not already deterred by the threat of imprisonment.[11] Still, I believe the death penalty, because of its finality, is more feared than imprisonment, and deters some prospective murderers not deterred by the threat of imprisonment. Sparing the lives of even a few prospective victims by deterring their murderers is more important than preserving the lives of convicted murderers because of the possibility, or even the probability, that executing them would not deter others. Whereas the lives of the victims who might be saved are valuable, that of the murderer has only negative value, because of his crime. Surely the criminal law is meant to protect the lives of potential victims in preference to those of actual murderers.

Murder rates are determined by many factors; neither the severity nor the probability of the threatened sanction is always decisive. However, for the long run, I share the view of Sir James Fitzjames Stephen: "Some men, probably, abstain from murder because they fear that if they committed murder they would be hanged. Hundreds of thousands abstain from it because they regard it with horror. One great reason why they regard it with horror is that murderers are hanged."[12] Penal sanctions are useful in the long run for the formation of the internal restraints so necessary to control crime. The severity and finality of the death penalty is appropriate to the seriousness and the finality of murder.[13]

IV. Incidental Issues: Cost, Relative Suffering, Brutalization

Many nondecisive issues are associated with capital punishment. Some believe that the monetary cost of appealing a capital sentence is excessive.[14] Yet most comparisons of the cost of life imprisonment with the cost of execution, apart from their dubious relevance, are flawed at least by the implied assumption that life prisoners will generate no judicial costs during their imprisonment. At any rate, the actual monetary costs are trumped by the importance of doing justice.

Others insist that a person sentenced to death suffers more than his victim suffered, and that this (excess) suffering is undue according to the *lex talionis* (rule of retaliation).[15] We cannot know whether the murderer on death row suffers more than his victim suffered; however, unlike the murderer, the victim deserved none of the suffering inflicted. Further, the limitations of the lex talionis were meant to restrain private vengeance, not the social retribution that has taken its place. Punishment—regardless of the motivation—is not intended to revenge, offset, or compensate for the victim's suffering, or to be measured by it. Punishment is to vindicate the law and the social order undermined by the crime. This is why a kidnapper's penal confinement is not limited to the period for which he imprisoned his victim; nor is a burglar's confinement meant merely to offset the suffering or the harm he caused his victim; nor is it meant only to offset the advantage he gained.[16]

Another argument heard at least since Beccaria is that, by killing a murderer, we encourage, endorse, or legitimize unlawful killing. Yet, although all punishments are meant to be unpleasant, it is seldom argued that they legitimize the unlawful imposition of identical unpleasantness. Imprisonment is not thought to legitimize kidnapping; neither are fines thought to legitimize robbery. The difference between murder and execution, or between kidnapping and imprisonment, is that the first is unlawful and undeserved, the second a lawful and deserved punishment for an unlawful act. The physical similarities of the punishment to the crime are irrelevant. The relevant difference is not physical, but social.[17]

V. Justice, Excess, Degradation

We threaten punishments in order to deter crime. We impose them not only to make the threats credible but also as retribution (justice) for the crimes that were not deterred. Threats and punishments are necessary to deter and deterrence is a sufficient practical justification for them. Retribution is an independent moral justification.[18] Although penalties can be unwise, repulsive, or inappropriate, and those punished can be pitiable, in a sense the infliction of legal punishment on a guilty person cannot be unjust. By committing the crime, the criminal volunteered to assume the risk of receiving a legal punishment that he could have avoided by not committing the crime. The punishment he suffers is the punishment he voluntarily risked suffering and, therefore, it is no more unjust to him than any other event for which one knowingly volunteers to assume the risk. Thus, the death penalty cannot be unjust to the guilty criminal.[19]

There remain, however, two moral objections. The penalty may be regarded as always excessive as retribution and always morally degrading. To regard the death penalty as always excessive, one must believe that no crime—no matter how heinous—could possibly justify capital punishment. Such a belief can be neither corroborated nor refuted; it is an article of faith.

Alternatively, or concurrently, one may believe that everybody, the murderer no less than the victim, has an imprescriptible (natural?) right to life. The law therefore should not deprive anyone of life. I share Jeremy Bentham's view that any such "natural and imprescriptible rights" are "nonsense upon stilts."[20]

Justice Brennan has insisted that the death penalty is "uncivilized," "inhuman," inconsistent with "human dignity" and with "the sanctity of life,"[21] that it "treats members of the human race as nonhumans, as objects to be toyed with and discarded,"[22] that it is "uniquely degrading to human dignity"[23] and "by its very nature, [involves] a denial of the executed person's humanity."[24] Justice Brennan does not say why he thinks execution "uncivilized." Hitherto most civilizations have had the death penalty, although it has been discarded in Western Europe, where it is currently unfashionable probably because of its abuse by totalitarian regimes.

By "degrading," Justice Brennan seems to mean that execution degrades the executed convicts. Yet philosophers, such as Immanual Kant and G. W. F. Hegel, have insisted that, when deserved, execution, far from degrading the executed convict, affirms his humanity by affirming his rationality and his responsibility for his actions. They thought that execution, when deserved, is required for the sake of the convict's dignity. (Does not life imprisonment violate human dignity more than execution, by keeping alive a prisoner deprived of all autonomy?)[25]

Common sense indicates that it cannot be death—our common fate—that is inhuman. Therefore, Justice Brennan must mean that death degrades when it comes not as a natural or accidental event, but as a deliberate social imposition. The murderer learns through his punishment that his fellow men have found him unworthy of living; that because he has murdered, he is being expelled from the community of the living. This degradation is self-inflicted. By murdering, the murderer has so dehumanized himself that he cannot remain among the living. The social recognition of his self-degradation is the punitive essence of execution. To believe, as Justice Brennan appears to, that the degradation is inflicted by the execution reverses the direction of causality.

Execution of those who have committed heinous murders may deter only one murder per year. If it does, it seems quite warranted. It is also the only fitting retribution for murder I can think of.

Notes*

1. Death row as a semipermanent residence is cruel, because convicts are denied the normal amenities of prison life. Thus, unless death row residents are integrated into the prison population, the continuing accumulation of convicts on death row should lead us to accelerate either the rate of executions or the rate of commutations. I find little objection to integration.

2. Some writers, for example, Cesare Bonesana, Marchese di Beccaria, have thought that life imprisonment is more severe. See C. Beccaria, *Dei Delitti e Delle Pene* 62–70 (1764). More recently, Jacques Barzun has expressed this view. See Barzun, "In Favor of Capital Punishment," in *The Death Penalty in America* 154 (H. Bedau ed. 1964). However, the overwhelming majority of both abolitionists and of convicts under death sentence prefer life imprisonment to execution.

3. For a discussion of the sources of opposition to corporal punishment, see E. van den Haag, *Punishing Criminals* 196–206 (1975).

4. Justice Douglas, concurring in *Furman* v. *Georgia*, 408 U.S. 238 (1972), wrote that "a law which . . . reaches that [discriminatory] result in practice has no more sanctity than a law which in terms provides the same." Id. at 256 (Douglas, J., concurring). Indeed, a law legislating this result "in terms" would be inconsistent with the "equal protection of the laws" provided by the fourteenth amendment, as would the discriminatory result reached in practice. But that result could be changed by changing the distributional practice. Thus, Justice Douglas notwithstanding, a discriminatory result does not make the death penalty unconstitutional, unless the penalty ineluctably must produce that result to an unconstitutional degree.

5. The ideal of equality, unlike the ideal of retributive justice (which can be approximated separately in each instance), is clearly unattainable unless all guilty persons are apprehended, and thereafter tried, convicted and sentenced by the same court, at the same time. Unequal justice is the best we can do; it is still better than the injustice, equal or unequal, which occurs if, for the sake of equality, we deliberately allow some who could be punished to escape.

6. See Bureau of Justice Statistics, U.S. Department of Justice, Bulletin No. NCJ-98, 399, *Capital Punishment*

7. It barely need be said that any discrimination *against* (for example, black murderers of whites) must also be discrimination *for* (for example, black murderers of blacks).

8. Bedau & Radelet, *Miscarriages of Justice in Potentially Capital Cases* (1st draft, Oct. 1985) (on file at Harvard Law School Library).

9. For a sample of conflicting views on the subject, see Baldus & Cole, "A Comparison of the Work of Thorsten Sellin and Isaac Ehrlich on the Deterrent Effect of Capital Punishment," *Yale Law Journal*, 85 (1975), 170; Bowers & Pierce, "Deterrence or Brutalization: What Is the Effect of Executions?" 26 *Crime & Delinquency* (1980), 453; Bowers & Pierce, "The Illusion of Deterrence in Isaac Ehrlich's Research on Capital Punishment," *Yale Law Journal*, 85 (1975), 18; Ehrlich, "Fear of Deterrence: A Critical Evaluation of the 'Report of the Panel on Research on Deterrent and Incapacitative Effects,' " 6 (1977), 293; Ehrlich, "The Deterrent Effect of Capital Punishment: A Question of Life and Death," *American Economics Review,* 65 (1975), 397, 415–416; Ehrlich & Gibbons, "On the Measurement of the Deterrent Effect of Capital Punishment and the Theory of Deterrence," *Journal of Legal Studies,* 6 (1977), 35.

10. For most abolitionists, the discrimination argument . . . is similarly nondecisive: they would favor abolition even if there could be no racial discrimination.

11. If executions were shown to increase the murder rate in the long run, I would favor abolition. Sparing the innocent victims who would be spared, *ex hypothesi,* by the nonexecution of murderers would be more important to me than the execution, however just, of murderers. But although there is a lively discussion of the subject, no serious evidence exists to support the hypothesis that executions produce a higher murder rate. Cf. Phillips, "The Deterrent Effect of Capital Punishment: New Evidence on an Old Controversy," *American Journal of Sociology,* 86 (1980), 139 (arguing that murder rates drop immediately after executions of criminals).

12. H. Gross, *A Theory of Criminal Justice* (1979), 489 (attributing this passage to Sir James Fitzjames Stephen).

13. *Weems* v. *United States,* 217 U.S. 349 (1910), suggests that penalties be proportionate to the seriousness of the crime—a common theme of the criminal law. Murder, therefore, demands more than life imprisonment, if, as I believe, it is a more serious crime than other crimes punished by life imprisonment. In modern times, our sensibility requires that the range of punishments be narrower than the range of crimes—but not so narrow as to exclude the death penalty.

---

*Notes have been reordered and renumbered.

14. Cf. Kaplan, "Administering Capital Punishment," *University of Florida Law Review, 36* (1984), 177, 178, 190–191 (noting the high cost of appealing a capital sentence).

15. For an example of this view, see A. Camus, *Reflections on the Guillotine* (1959), 24–30. On the limitations allegedly imposed by the *lex talionis*, see Reiman, "Justice, Civilization, and the Death Penalty: Answering van den Haag," *Philosophy & Public Affairs, 14* (1985), 115, 119–134.

16. Thus restitution (a civil liability) cannot satisfy the punitive purpose of penal sanctions, whether the purpose be retributive or deterrent.

17. Some abolitionists challenge: if the death penalty is just and serves as a deterrent, why not televise executions? The answer is simple. The death even of a murderer, however well-deserved, should not serve as public entertainment. It so served in earlier centuries. But in this respect our sensibility has changed for the better, I believe. Further, television unavoidably would trivialize executions, edged in, as they would be, between game shows, situation comedies, and the like. Finally, because televised executions would focus on the physical aspects of the punishment, rather than the nature of the crime and the suffering of the victim, a televised execution would present the murderer as the victim of the state. Far from communicating the moral significance of the execution, television would shift the focus to the pitiable fear of the murderer. We no longer place in cages those sentenced to imprisonment to expose them to public view. Why should we so expose those sentenced to execution?

18. See van den Haag, "Punishment as a Device for Controlling the Crime Rate," *Rutgers Law Review, 33* (1981), 706, 719 (explaining why the desire for retribution, although independent, would have to be satisfied even if deterrence were the only purpose of punishment).

19. An explicit threat of punitive action is necessary to the justification of any legal punishment: *nulla poena sine lege* (no punishment without [preexisting] law). To be sufficiently justified, the threat must in turn have a rational and legitimate purpose. "Your money or your life" does not qualify; nor does the threat of an unjust law; nor, finally, does a threat that is altogether disproportionate to the importance of its purpose. In short, preannouncement legitimizes the threatened punishment only if the threat is warranted. But this leaves a very wide range of justified threats. Furthermore, the punished person is aware of the penalty for his actions and thus volunteers to take the risk even of an unjust punishment. His victim, however, did not volunteer to risk anything. The question whether any self-inflicted injury—such as a legal punishment—ever can be unjust to a person who knowingly risked it is a matter that requires more analysis than is possible here.

20. *The Works of Jeremy Bentham* 105 (J. Bowring ed. 1972). However, I would be more polite about prescriptible natural rights, which Bentham described as "simple nonsense." Id. (It does not matter whether natural rights are called "moral" or "human" rights as they currently are by most writers.)

21. *The Death Penalty in America*, 3d ed., H. Bedau (Ed.), (1982), 256–263, quoting *Furman* v. *Georgia*, 408 U.S. 238, 286, 305 (1972) (Brennan, J., concurring).

22. Id. at 272–73; see also *Gregg* v. *Georgia*, 428 U.S. 153, 230 (1976) (Brennan, J., dissenting).

23. *Furman* v. *Georgia*, 408 U.S. 238, 291 (1972) (Brennan, J., concurring)

24. Id. at 290.

25. See Barzun, supra, passim.

This Man Has Expired: Witness to an Execution

Robert Johnson

Study Questions

1. How was the execution of Gary Gilmore unlike most executions today?

2. In what ways do the death watch officers described by Johnson work as a team doing a job?

3. What attitude toward the prisoner about to die do the people on the death watch try to maintain? Why? How do they try to control him?

4. What is the effect of the shaving on the prisoner, according to Johnson? Why does he believe that most prisoners do not struggle or resist at the end?

5. What was the effect on Johnson of witnessing this execution?

The death penalty has made a comeback in recent years. In the late sixties and through most of the seventies, such a thing seemed impossible. There was a moratorium on executions in the U.S., backed by the authority of the Supreme Court. The hiatus lasted roughly a decade. Coming on the heels of a gradual but persistent decline in the use of the death penalty in the Western world, it appeared to some that executions would pass from the American scene [cf. *Commonweal*, January 15, 1988]. Nothing could have been further from the truth.

Beginning with the execution of Gary Gilmore in 1977, over 100 people have been put to death, most of them in the last few years. Some 2,200 prisoners are presently confined on death rows across the nation. The majority of these prisoners have lived under sentence of death for years, in some cases a decade or more, and are running out of legal appeals. It is fair to say that the death penalty is alive and well in America, and that executions will be with us for the foreseeable future.

Gilmore's execution marked the resurrection of the modern death penalty and was big news. It was commemorated in a best-selling tome by Norman Mailer, *The Executioner's Song*. The title was deceptive. Like others who have examined the death penalty, Mailer told us a great deal about the condemned but very little about the executioners. Indeed, if we dwell on Mailer's account, the executioner's story is not only unsung; it is distorted.

Gilmore's execution was quite atypical. His was an instance of state-assisted suicide accompanied by an element of romance and played out against a backdrop of media fanfare. Unrepentant and unafraid, Gilmore refused to appeal his conviction. He dared the state of Utah to take his life, and the media repeated the challenge until it became a taunt that may well have goaded officials to action. A failed suicide pact with his lover staged only days before the execution, using

From *Commonweal* (January 13, 1989): 9–15. © 1989 Commonweal Foundation. Reprinted with permission.

drugs she delivered to him in a visit marked by unusual intimacy, added a hint of melodrama to the proceedings. Gilmore's final words, "Let's do it," seemed to invite the lethal hail of bullets from the firing squad. The nonchalant phrase, at once fatalistic and brazenly rebellious, became Gilmore's epitaph. It clinched his outlaw-hero image, and found its way onto tee shirts that confirmed his celebrity status.

Befitting a celebrity, Gilmore was treated with unusual leniency by prison officials during his confinement on death row. He was, for example, allowed to hold a party the night before his execution, during which he was free to eat, drink, and make merry with his guests until the early morning hours. This is not entirely unprecedented. Notorious English convicts of centuries past would throw farewell balls in prison on the eve of their executions. News accounts of such affairs sometimes included a commentary on the richness of the table and the quality of the dancing. For the record, Gilmore served Tang, Kool-Aid, cookies, and coffee, later supplemented by contraband pizza and an unidentified liquor. Periodically, he gobbled drugs obligingly provided by the prison pharmacy. He played a modest arrangement of rock music albums but refrained from dancing.

Gilmore's execution generally, like his parting fete, was decidedly out of step with the tenor of the modern death penalty. Most condemned prisoners fight to save their lives, not to have them taken. They do not see their fate in romantic terms; there are no farewell parties. Nor are they given medication to ease their anxiety or win their compliance. The subjects of typical executions remain anonymous to the public and even to their keepers. They are very much alone at the end.

In contrast to Mailer's account, the focus of the research I have conducted is on the executioners themselves as they carry out typical executions. In my experience executioners—not unlike Mailer himself—can be quite voluble, and sometimes quite moving, in expressing themselves. I shall draw upon their words to describe the death work they carry out in our name.

Death Work and Death Workers

Executioners are not a popular subject of social research, let alone conversation at the dinner table or cocktail party. We simply don't give the subject much thought. When we think of executioners at all, the imagery runs to individual men of disreputable, or at least questionable, character who work stealthily behind the scenes to carry out their grim labors. We picture hooded men hiding in the shadow of the gallows, or anonymous figures lurking out of sight behind electric chairs, gas chambers, firing blinds, or, more recently, hospital gurneys. We wonder who would do such grisly work and how they sleep at night.

This image of the executioner as a sinister and often solitary character is today misleading. To be sure, a few states hire free-lance executioners and traffic in macabre theatrics. Executioners may be picked up under cover of darkness and some may still wear black hoods. But today, executions are generally the work of a highly disciplined and efficient team of correctional officers.

Broadly speaking, the execution process as it is now practiced starts with the prisoner's confinement on death row, an oppressive prison-within-a-prison where the condemned are housed, sometimes for years, awaiting execution. Death work gains momentum when an execution date draws near and the prisoner is moved to the death house, a short walk from the death chamber. Finally, the process culminates in the death watch, a twenty-four-hour period that ends when the prisoner has been executed.

This final period, the death watch, is generally undertaken by correctional officers who work as a team and report directly to the prison warden. The warden or his representative, in turn, must by law preside over the execution. In many states, it is a member of the death watch or execution team, acting under the warden's authority, who in fact plays the formal role of executioner. Though this officer may technically work alone, his teammates view the execution as a shared responsibility. As one officer on the death watch told me in no uncertain terms: "We all take part in it; we all play 100 percent in it, too. That takes the load off this one individual [who pulls the switch]." The formal executioner concurred. "Everyone on the team can do it, and nobody will tell you I did it. I know my team." I found nothing in my research to dispute these claims.

The officers of these death watch teams are our modern executioners. As part of a larger study of the death work process, I studied one such group. This team, comprised of nine seasoned officers of varying ranks, had carried out five electrocutions at the time I began my research. I interviewed each officer on the team after the fifth execution, then served as an official witness at a sixth electrocution. Later, I served as a behind-the-scenes observer during their seventh

execution. The results of this phase of my research form the substance of this essay.

The Death Watch Team

The death watch or execution team members refer to themselves, with evident pride, as simply "the team." This pride is shared by other correctional officials. The warden at the institution I was observing praised members of the team as solid citizens—in his words, country boys, These country boys, he assured me, could be counted on to do the job and do it well. As a fellow administrator put it, "an execution is something [that] needs to be done and good people, dedicated people who believe in the American system, should do it. And there's a certain amount of feeling, probably one to another, that they're part of that—that when they have to hang tough, they can do it, and they can do it right. And that it's just the right thing to do."

The official view is that an execution is a job that has to be done, and done right. The death penalty is, after all, the law of the land. In this context, the phrase "done right" means that an execution should be a proper, professional, dignified undertaking. In the words of a prison administrator, "We had to be sure that we did it properly, professionally, and [that] we gave as much dignity to the person as we possibly could in the process. . . . If you've gotta do it, it might just as well be done the way it's supposed to be done—without any sensation."

In the language of the prison officials, "proper" refers to the procedures that go off smoothly; "professional" means without personal feelings that intrude on the procedures in any way. The desire for executions that take place "without any sensation" no doubt refers to the absence of media sensationalism, particularly if there should be an embarrassing and undignified hitch in the procedures, for example, a prisoner who breaks down or becomes violent and must be forcibly placed in the electric chair as witnesses, some from the media, look on in horror. Still, I can't help but note that this may be a revealing slip of the tongue. For executions are indeed meant to go off without any human feeling, without any sensation. A profound absence of feeling would seem to capture the bureaucratic ideal embodied in the modern execution.

The view of executions held by the execution team members parallels that of correctional administrators but is somewhat more restrained. The officers of the team are closer to the killing and dying, and are less apt to wax abstract or eloquent in describing the process. Listen to one man's observations:

> It's a job. I don't take it personally. You know, I don't take it like I'm having a grudge against this person and this person has done something to me. I'm just carrying out a job, doing what I was asked to do. . . . This man has been sentenced to death in the courts. This is the law and he broke this law, and he has to suffer the consequences. And one of the consequences is to put him to death.

I found that few members of the execution team support the death penalty outright or without reservation. Having seen executions close up, many of them have lingering doubts about the justice or wisdom of this sanction. As one officer put it:

> I'm not sure the death penalty is the right way. I don't know if there is a right answer. So I look at it like this: if it's gotta be done, at least it can be done in a humane way, if there is such a word for it. . . . The only way it should be done, I feel, is the way we do it. It's done professionally; it's not no horseplaying. Everything is done by documentation. On time. By the book.

Arranging executions that occur "without any sensation" and that go "by the book" is no mean task, but it is a task that is undertaken in earnest by the execution team. The tone of the enterprise is set by the team leader, a man who takes a hard-boiled, no-nonsense approach to correctional work in general and death work in particular. "My style," he says, "is this: if it's a job to do, get it done. Do it and that's it." He seeks out kindred spirits, men who see killing condemned prisoners as a job—a dirty job one does reluctantly, perhaps, but above all a job one carries out dispassionately and in the line of duty.

To make sure that line of duty is a straight and accurate one, the death watch team has been carefully drilled by the team leader in the mechanics of execution. The process has been broken down into simple, discrete tasks and practiced repeatedly. The team leader describes the division of labor in the following exchange:

> The execution team is a nine-officer team and each one has certain things to do. When I would train you, maybe you'd buckle a belt, that might be all you'd have to do. . . . And you'd be expected to do one thing and that's all you'd be expected to do. And if everybody does what they were taught, or what they were

trained to do, at the end the man would be put in the chair and everything would be complete. It's all come together now.

So it's broken down into very small steps. . . .

Very small, yes. Each person has one thing to do.

I see. What's the purpose of breaking it down into such small steps?

So people won't get confused. I've learned it's kind of a tense time. When you're executin' a person, killing a person—you call it killin', executin', whatever you want—the man dies anyway. I find the less you got on your mind, why, the better you'll carry it out. So it's just very simple things. And so far, you know, it's all come together, we haven't had any problems.

This division of labor allows each man on the execution team to become a specialist, a technician with a sense of pride in his work. Said one man,

> My assignment is the leg piece. Right leg. I roll his pants leg up, place a piece [electrode] on his leg, strap his leg in. . . . I've got all the moves down pat. We train from different posts: I can do any of them. But that's my main post.

The implication is not that the officers are incapable of performing multiple or complex tasks, but simply that it is more efficient to focus each officer's efforts on one easy task.

An essential part of the training is practice. Practice is meant to produce a confident group, capable of fast and accurate performance under pressure. The rewards of practice are reaped in improved performance. Executions take place with increasing efficiency, and eventually occur with precision. "The first one was grisly," a team member confided to me. He explained that there was a certain amount of fumbling, which made the execution seem interminable. There were technical problems as well: The generator was set too high so the body was badly burned. But that is the past, the officer assured me. "The ones now, we know what we're doing. It's just like clockwork."

The Death Watch

The death watch team is deployed during the last twenty-four hours before an execution. In the state under study, the death watch starts at 11 o'clock the night before the execution and ends at 11 o'clock the next night when the execution takes place. At least two officers would be with the prisoner at any given time during that period. Their objective is to keep the prisoner alive and "on schedule." That is, to move him through a series of critical and cumulatively demoralizing junctures that begin with his last meal and end with his last walk. When the time comes, they must deliver the prisoner up for execution as quickly and unobtrusively as possible.

Broadly speaking, the job of the death watch officer, as one man put it, "is to sit and keep the inmate calm for the last twenty-four hours—and get the man ready to go." Keeping a condemned prisoner calm means, in part, serving his immediate needs. It seems paradoxical to think of the death watch officers as providing services to the condemned, but the logistics of the job make service a central obligation of the officers. Here's how one officer made this point:

> Well, you can't help but be involved with many of the things that he's involved with. Because if he wants to make a call to his family, well, you'll have to dial the number. And you keep records of whatever calls he makes. If he wants a cigarette, well he's not allowed to keep matches so you light it for him. You've got to pour his coffee, too. So you're aware what he's doing. It's not like you can just ignore him. You've gotta just be with him whether he wants it or not, and cater to his needs.

Officers cater to the condemned because contented inmates are easier to keep under control. To a man, the officers say this is so. But one can never trust even a contented, condemned prisoner.

The death watch officers see condemned prisoners as men with explosive personalities. "You don't know what, what a man's gonna do," noted one officer. "He's liable to snap, he's liable to pass out. We watch him all the time to prevent him from committing suicide. You've got to be ready—he's liable to do anything." The prisoner is never out of at least one officer's sight. Thus surveillance is constant, and control, for all intents and purposes, is total.

Relations between the officers and their charges during the death watch can be quite intense. Watching and being watched are central to this enterprise, and these are always engaging activities, particularly when the stakes are life and death. These relations are, nevertheless, utterly impersonal; there are no grudges but neither is there compassion or fellow-feeling. Officers are civil but cool; they keep an emotional distance from the men they are about to kill. To do otherwise, they maintain, would make it harder to execute condemned prisoners. The attitude of the officers is that the prisoners arrive as strangers and are easier to kill if they stay that way.

During the last five or six hours, two specific team officers are assigned to guard the prisoner. Unlike their more taciturn and aloof colleagues on earlier shifts, these officers make a conscious effort to talk with the prisoner. In one officer's words, "We keep them right there and keep talking to them—about anything except the chair." The point of these conversations is not merely to pass time; it is to keep tabs on the prisoner's state of mind, and to steer him away from subjects that might depress, anger, or otherwise upset him. Sociability, in other words, quite explicitly serves as a source of social control. Relationships, such as they are, serve purely manipulative ends. This is impersonality at its worst, masquerading as concern for the strangers one hopes to execute with as little trouble as possible.

Generally speaking, as the execution moves closer, the mood becomes more somber and subdued. There is a last meal. Prisoners can order pretty much what they want, but most eat little or nothing at all. At this point, the prisoners may steadfastly maintain that their executions will be stayed. Such bravado is belied by their loss of appetite. "You can see them going down," said one officer. "Food is the last thing they got on their minds."

Next the prisoners must box their meager worldly goods. These are inventoried by the staff, recorded on a one-page checklist form, and marked for disposition to family or friends. Prisoners are visibly saddened, even moved to tears, by this procedure, which at once summarizes their lives and highlights the imminence of death. At this point, said one of the officers, "I really get into him; I watch him real close." The execution schedule, the officer pointed out, is "picking up momentum, and we don't want to lose control of the situation."

This momentum is not lost on the condemned prisoner. Critical milestones have been passed. The prisoner moves in a limbo existence devoid of food or possessions; he has seen the last of such things, unless he receives a stay of execution and rejoins the living. His identity is expropriated as well. The critical juncture in this regard is the shaving of the man's head (including facial hair) and right leg. Hair is shaved to facilitate the electrocution; it reduces physical resistance to electricity and minimizes singeing and burning. But the process has obvious psychological significance as well, adding greatly to the momentum of the execution.

The shaving procedure is quite public and intimidating. The condemned man is taken from his cell and seated in the middle of the tier. His hands and feet are cuffed, and he is dressed only in undershorts. The entire death watch team is assembled around him. They stay at a discrete distance, but it is obvious that they are there to maintain control should he resist in any way or make any untoward move. As a rule, the man is overwhelmed. As one officer told me in blunt terms, "Come eight o'clock, we've got a dead man. Eight o'clock is when we shave the man. We take his identity; it goes with the hair." This taking of identity is indeed a collective process—the team makes a forceful "we," the prisoner their helpless object. The staff is confident that the prisoner's capacity to resist is now compromised. What is left of the man erodes gradually and, according to the officers, perceptibly over the remaining three hours before the execution.

After the prisoner has been shaved, he is then made to shower and don a fresh set of clothes for the execution. The clothes are unremarkable in appearance, except that velcro replaces buttons and zippers, to reduce the chance of burning the body. The main significance of the clothes is symbolic: they mark the prisoner as a man who is ready for execution. Now physically "prepped," to quote one team member, the prisoner is placed in an empty tomblike cell, the death cell. All that is left is the wait. During this fateful period, the prisoner is more like an object "without any sensation" than like a flesh-and-blood person on the threshold of death.

For condemned prisoners, like Gilmore, who come to accept and even to relish their impending deaths, a genuine calm seems to prevail. It is as if they can transcend the dehumanizing forces at work around them and go to their deaths in peace. For most condemned prisoners, however, numb resignation rather than peaceful acceptance is the norm. By the account of the death watch officers, these more typical prisoners are beaten men. Listen to the officers' accounts:

A lot of 'em die in their minds before they go to that chair. I've never known of one or heard of one putting up a fight. . . . By the time they walk to the chair,

they've completely faced it. Such a reality most people can't understand. Cause they don't fight it. They don't seem to have anything to say. It's just something like "Get it over with." They may be numb, sort of in a trance.

They go through stages. And, at this stage, they're real humble. Humblest bunch of people I ever seen. Most all of 'em is real, real weak. Most of the time you'd only need one or two people to carry out an execution, as weak and as humble as they are.

These men seem barely human and alive to their keepers. They wait meekly to be escorted to their deaths. The people who come for them are the warden and the remainder of the death watch team, flanked by high-ranking correctional officials. The warden reads the court order, known popularly as a death warrant. This is, as one officer said, "the real deal," and nobody misses its significance. The condemned prisoners then go to their deaths compliantly, captives of the inexorable, irresistible momentum of the situation. As one officer put it, "There's no struggle. . . .They just walk right on in there." So too, do the staff "just walk right on in there," following a routine they have come to know well. Both the condemned and the executioners, it would seem, find a relief of sorts in mindless mechanical conformity to the modern execution drill.

Witness to an Execution

As the team and administrators prepare to commence the good fight, as they might say, another group, the official witnesses, are also preparing themselves for their role in the execution. Numbering between six and twelve for any given execution, the official witnesses are disinterested citizens in good standing drawn from a cross-section of the state's population. If you will, they are every good or decent person, called upon to represent the community and use their good offices to testify to the propriety of the execution. I served as an official witness at the execution of an inmate.

At eight in the evening, about the time the prisoner is shaved in preparation for the execution, the witnesses are assembled. Eleven in all, we included three newspaper and two television reporters, a state trooper, two police officers, a magistrate, a businessman, and myself. We were picked up in the parking lot behind the main office of the corrections department. There was nothing unusual or even memorable about any of this. Gothic touches were notable by their absence. It wasn't a dark and stormy night; no one emerged from the shadows to lead us to the prison gates.

Mundane considerations prevailed. The van sent for us was missing a few rows of seats so there wasn't enough room for all of us. Obliging prison officials volunteered their cars. Our rather ordinary cavalcade reached the prison but only after getting lost. Once within the prison's walls, we were sequestered for some two hours in a bare and almost shabby administrative conference room. A public information officer was assigned to accompany us and answer our questions. We grilled this official about the prisoner and the execution procedure he would undergo shortly, but little information was to be had. The man confessed ignorance on the most basic points. Disgruntled at this and increasingly anxious, we made small talk and drank coffee.

At 10:40 P.M., roughly two-and-a-half hours after we were assembled and only twenty minutes before the execution was scheduled to occur, the witnesses were taken to the basement of the prison's administrative building, frisked, then led down an alleyway that ran along the exterior of the building. We entered a neighboring cell block and were admitted to a vestibule adjoining the death chamber. Each of us signed a log, and was then led off to the witness area. To our left, around a corner some thirty feet away, the prisoner sat in the condemned cell. He couldn't see us, but I'm quite certain he could hear us. It occurred to me that our arrival was a fateful reminder for the prisoner. The next group would be led by the warden, and it would be coming for him.

We entered the witness area, a room within the death chamber, and took our seats. A picture window covering the front wall of the witness room offered a clear view of the electric chair, which was about twelve feet away from us and well illuminated. The chair, a large, high-back solid oak structure with imposing black straps, dominated the death chamber. Behind it, on the back wall, was an open panel full of coils and lights. Peeling paint hung from the ceiling and walls; water stains from persistent leaks were everywhere in evidence.

Two officers, one a hulking figure weighing some 400 pounds, stood alongside the electric chair. Each had his hands crossed at the lap and wore a forbidding, blank expression on his face. The witnesses gazed at them and the chair, most of us scribbling

notes furiously. We did this, I suppose, as much to record the experience as to have a distraction from the growing tension. A correctional officer entered the witness room and announced that a trial run of the machinery would be undertaken. Seconds later, lights flashed on the control panel behind the chair indicating that the chair was in working order. A white curtain, opened for the test, separated the chair and the witness area. After the test, the curtain was drawn. More tests were performed behind the curtain. Afterwards, the curtain was reopened, and would be left open until the execution was over. Then it would be closed to allow the officers to remove the body.

A handful of high-level correctional officials were present in the death chamber, standing just outside the witness area. There were two regional administrators, the director of the Department of Corrections, and the prison warden. The prisoner's chaplain and lawyer were also present. Other than the chaplain's black religious garb, subdued grey pin-stripes and bland correctional uniforms prevailed. All parties were quite solemn.

At 10:58 the prisoner entered the death chamber. He was, I knew from my research, a man with a checkered, tragic past. He had been grossly abused as a child, and went on to become grossly abusive of others. I was told he could not describe his life, from childhood on, without talking about confrontations in defense of a precarious sense of self—at home, in school, on the streets, in the prison yard. Belittled by life and choking with rage, he was hungry to be noticed. Paradoxically, he had found his moment in the spotlight, but it was a dim and unflattering light cast before a small and unappreciative audience. "He'd pose for cameras in the chair—for the attention," his counselor had told me earlier in the day. But the truth was that the prisoner wasn't smiling, and there were no cameras.

The prisoner walked quickly and silently toward the chair, an escort of officers in tow. His eyes were turned downward, his expression a bit glazed. Like many before him, the prisoner had threatened to stage a last stand. But that was lifetimes ago, on death row. In the death house, he joined the humble bunch and kept to the executioner's schedule. He appeared to have given up on life before he died in the chair.

En route to the chair, the prisoner stumbled slightly, as if the momentum of the event had overtaken him. Were he not held securely by two officers, one at each elbow, he might have fallen. Were the routine to be broken in this or indeed any other way, the officers believe, the prisoner might faint or panic or become violent, and have to be forcibly placed in the chair. Perhaps as a precaution, when the prisoner reached the chair he did not turn on his own but rather was turned, firmly but without malice, by the officers in his escort. These included the two men at his elbows, and four others who followed behind him. Once the prisoner was seated, again with help, the officers strapped him into the chair.

The execution team worked with machine precision. Like a disciplined swarm, they enveloped him. Arms, legs, stomach, chest, and head were secured in a matter of seconds. Electrodes were attached to the cap holding his head and to the strap holding his exposed right leg. A leather mask was placed over his face. The last officer mopped the prisoner's brow, then touched his hand in a gesture of farewell.

During the brief procession to the electric chair, the prisoner was attended by a chaplain. As the execution team worked feverishly to secure the condemned man's body, the chaplain, who appeared to be upset, leaned over him and placed his forehead in contact with the prisoner's, whispering urgently. The priest might have been praying, but I had the impression he was consoling the man, perhaps assuring him that a forgiving God awaited him in the next life. If he heard the chaplain, I doubt the man comprehended his message. He didn't seem comforted. Rather, he looked stricken and appeared to be in shock. Perhaps the priest's urgent ministrations betrayed his doubts that the prisoner could hold himself together. The chaplain then withdrew at the warden's request, allowing the officers to affix the death mask.

The strapped and masked figure sat before us, utterly alone, waiting to be killed. The cap and mask dominated his face. The cap was nothing more than a sponge encased in a leather shell with a metal piece at the top to accept an electrode. It looked decrepit and resembled a cheap, ill-fitting toupee. The mask, made entirely of leather, appeared soiled and worn. It had two parts. The bottom part covered the chin and mouth, the top the eyes and lower forehead. Only the nose was exposed. The effect of a rigidly restrained body, together with the bizarre cap and the protruding nose, was nothing short of grotesque. A faceless man breathed before us in a tragicomic trance, waiting for a blast of electricity that would extinguish his life. Endless seconds passed. His last act was to swal-

low, nervously, pathetically, with his Adam's apple bobbing. I was struck by that simple movement then, and can't forget it even now. It told me, as nothing else did, that in the prisoner's restrained body, behind that mask, lurked a fellow human being who, at some level, however primitive, knew or sensed himself to be moments from death.

The condemned man sat perfectly still for what seemed an eternity but was in fact no more than thirty seconds. Finally the electricity hit him. His body stiffened spasmodically, though only briefly. A thin swirl of smoke trailed away from his head and then dissipated quickly. The body remained taut, with the right foot raised slightly at the heel, seemingly frozen there. A brief pause, then another minute of shock. When it was over, the body was flaccid and inert.

Three minutes passed while the officials let the body cool. (Immediately after the execution, I'm told, the body would be too hot to touch and would blister anyone who did.) All eyes were riveted to the chair; I felt trapped in my witness seat, at once transfixed and yet eager for release. I can't recall any clear thoughts from that moment. One of the death watch officers later volunteered that he shared this experience of staring blankly at the execution scene. Had the prisoner's mind been mercifully blank before the end? I hoped so.

An officer walked up to the body, opened the shirt at chest level, then continued on to get the physician from an adjoining room. The physician listened for a heartbeat. Hearing none, he turned to the warden and said, "This man has expired." The warden, speaking to the director, solemnly intoned: "Mr. Director, the court order has been fulfilled." The curtain was then drawn and the witnesses filed out.

The Morning After

As the team prepared the body for the morgue, the witnesses were led to the front door of the prison. On the way, we passed a number of cell blocks. We could hear the normal sounds of prison life, including the occasional catcall and lewd comment hurled at uninvited guests like ourselves. But no trouble came in the wake of the execution. Small protests were going on outside the walls, we were told, but we could not hear them. Soon the media would be gone; the protesters would disperse and head for their homes. The prisoners, already home, had been indifferent to the proceedings, as they always are unless the condemned prisoner had been a figure of some consequence in the convict community. Then there might be tension and maybe even a modest disturbance on a prison tier or two. But few convict luminaries are executed, and the dead man had not been one of them. Our escort officer offered a sad tribute to the prisoner: "The inmates, they didn't care about this guy."

I couldn't help but think they weren't alone in this. The executioners went home and set about their lives. Having taken life, they would savor a bit of life themselves. They showered, ate, made love, slept, then took a day or two off. For some, the prisoner's image would linger for that night. The men who strapped him in remembered what it was like to touch him; they showered as soon as they got home to wash off the feel and smell of death. One official sat up picturing how the prisoner looked at the end. (I had a few drinks myself that night with the same image for company.) There was some talk about delayed reactions to the stress of carrying out executions. Though such concerns seemed remote that evening, I learned later that problems would surface for some of the officers. But no one on the team, then or later, was haunted by the executed man's memory, nor would anyone grieve for him. "When I go home after one of these things," said one man, "I sleep like a rock." His may or may not be the sleep of the just, but one can only marvel at such a thing, and perhaps envy such a man.

Review Exercises

1. What essential characteristics of legal punishment distinguish it from other types of punishment?

2. What is the difference between the mechanisms of deterrence and prevention? Given their meanings, does the death penalty prevent murders? Deter would-be killers? How?

3. If legal punishment works as a deterrent, how does it work? For whom would it work? For whom would it not be likely to work?

4. Summarize the positive aspects of the deterrence view regarding the justification of legal punishment.

5. Explain two moral problems with the deterrence view, using an example comparable to the graffiti example in the text.

6. How does the retributivist view differ from the deterrence view?

7. What is the *lex talionis* version of this view? How does it differ from the proportional view?

8. Discuss the arguments for and against the identification of retributivism with revenge.

9. Why is the notion of responsibility critical to the retributivist view of legal punishment? How does the defense of insanity fit in here?

10. Discuss the use of deterrence arguments for the death penalty. Also summarize opponents' criticisms of these arguments.

11. Discuss the use of retributivist arguments for the death penalty. Summarize also opponents' criticisms of these arguments.

Discussion Cases

1. *Criminal Responsibility.* Consider the case of Robert Alton Harris described at the beginning of this chapter. Consider his crime and also his own life background.

Do you think that he should have been executed? Why or why not?

2. *Doctors and Execution.* When a person is executed, it is the practice that a medical doctor certify that the person executed is dead and when he or she has died. A state medical association has recently objected to the participation of doctors in executions. They assert that doctors take an oath to preserve life and should not be accessories to the taking of life. The state insisted that the doctors certifying death do not participate in the execution.

Should doctors be present at and certify the death of persons executed by the state? Why or why not?

3. *Death Penalty Cases.* Suppose that you were a member of a congressional or other committee that had as its mandate determining the type of

crime that could be considered to be punishable by death. What kinds of cases, if any, would you put on the list? Killing with sexual assault of a minor? Planned killing of a batterer by their spouse? Persons convicted of war crimes? Mob leaders or others who give an order to kill but who do not carry it out themselves? Killing of a police officer or public figure? Multiple murderers? Others?

Why would you pick out just those crimes on your list as appropriately punished by death, or as the worst crimes?

Selected Bibliography

Adenaes, Johannes. *Punishment and Deterrence*. Ann Arbor: University of Michigan Press, 1974.

Baird, Robert M., and Stuart E. Rosenbaum (Eds.). *The Philosophy of Punishment*. Buffalo, NY: Prometheus, 1988.

Bedau, Hugo Adam. *Death is Different: Studies in the Morality, Law, and Politics of Capital Punishment*. Boston: Northeastern University Press, 1987.

———. *The Death Penalty in America*. New York: Oxford University Press, 1982.

Berns, Walter. *For Capital Punishment*. New York: Basic Books, 1979.

Black, Charles L., Jr. *Capital Punishment: The Inevitability of Caprice and Mistake,* 2nd ed. New York: Norton, 1981.

Duff, Anthony (Ed.). *A Reader on Punishment*. New York: Oxford University Press, 1995.

Elliott, Carl. *The Rules of Insanity: Moral Responsibility and the Mentally Ill Offender*. Albany: State University of New York Press, 1996.

Erzorsky, Gertrude (Ed.). *Philosophical Perspectives on Punishment*. Albany: State University of New York Press, 1972.

Goldinger, Milton (Ed.). *Punishment and Human Rights*. Cambridge, MA: Schenkman, 1974.

Hart, H.L.A. *Punishment and Responsibility*. New York: Oxford University Press, 1968.

Montague, Phillip. *Punishment as Societal-Defense*. Lanham, MD: Rowman & Littlefield, 1995.

Murphy, Jeffrie G. *Punishment and Rehabilitation,* 2nd ed. Belmont, CA: Wadsworth, 1985.

Nathanson, Stephen. *An Eye for an Eye: The Morality of Punishing by Death*. Totowa, NJ: Rowman & Littlefield, 1987.

Sorell, Tom. *Moral Theory and Capital Punishment*. Oxford: Blackwell, 1988.

van den Haag, Ernest, and John P. Conrad. *The Death Penalty: A Debate*. New York: Plenum, 1983.

Walker, Nigel. *Why Punish?* New York: Oxford University Press, 1991.

❧ 14 ❧

Environmental Ethics

In December 1995, 2,000 people descended on a small California logging town and stormed the gates of its lumber mill. They were protesting the logging company's projected cutting of old-growth forests in the area. To block the bulldozers and logging trucks, the protesters even formed human chains across the roads. At the same time, a $3 million trial was taking place in San Francisco over whether the habitat of a sea-bird, the marbled murrelet, would be protected.[1] Both activities were concerned with a 3,000-acre grove of giant redwood trees in the Headwaters Forest in northern California. This area contains "the largest continuous grove of giant redwoods anywhere in the world." Some trees in this grove are 300 feet tall and 2,200 years old. Their trunks are so large that it would take six people holding hands to circle around them. Some of the trees were alive when Hannibal crossed the Alps and when the Great Wall of China was being built. The forest is the home for the furry weasel-like fisher, and coho salmon, and 160 other wildlife species.[2] It is also part of a lumbering community. It is owned by Pacific Lumber. To the community, the forest represents jobs, livelihood, and a way of life. One giant tree can bring $100,000 for its lumber. The value of the land and forest is estimated to be from $200 million to $800 million. Efforts have been under way for the U.S. government to obtain the land.

In December 1996, an agreement was reached by the owner of Pacific Lumber and members of the U.S. Congress to halt logging for ten months. Environmentalists were not pleased that the stay was only temporary and that it protected only 6,000 acres. By the time you read this, the case will have progressed to the next step.

Once upon a time, there were 2.1 million acres of these coastal redwoods in Oregon and California. Only 3.9 percent of this range now stands. In the entire world, only 86,000 acres of old-growth redwood forests remain; 6,000 of these are owned by Pacific Lumber, and the rest are in public preserves. It is not just old-growth redwoods that are at issue. The 10-million-acre North Woods region in northern Maine is also threatened by clear-cutting. These are spruce and fir forests that are so dense that Henry David Thoreau described them in his journals as "a standing night."[3] But why should we care whether these forests are preserved or cut for lumber? Arguments and feelings run strong on both sides of the issue. There is something wonderful about such large and old living things as these trees. On the other hand, we also value jobs and the things we make with lumber. How do we decide which takes precedence? In this case, what is the ethical thing to do?

This is just one of the many ethical problems that arise with regard to the environment.

Should we preserve wetlands or fill in the land and lease it for projects that will bring jobs to low-income areas? Should we dam a river for hydroelectric power and lessen the need for nuclear power, or shall we leave it wild? To resolve these conflicts of values, we need to do some comparative evaluation to determine what values ought to take precedence. However, more basic yet is the question of the very nature and source of *value.* What does it mean for something such as a job or a life or a plant to have value? How valuable is a life or an aesthetic experience of wilderness or wetland? One thing that ethics does is provide us with signposts that direct us toward key elements to consider when we make our ethical decisions. Ethics also can provide us with platforms from which to view an ethical debate. In this chapter we will examine some of the signposts and platforms from which we might make more intelligent decisions about environmental ethical issues. (The following chapter on animal rights overlaps this chapter in many regards, and we will note those places as we proceed.)

The Environment

Being clear about the terms we use in an ethical debate is one of the first things that can help us. We can start with the meaning of the term *environment.* The term comes from *environs,* which means "in circuit" or "turning around in" in Old French.[4] From this comes the common meaning of environment as surroundings and its spatial meaning as an area. However, we have also come to use the term to refer to what goes on in that space and to the climate and other factors that act on living organisms or individuals that inhabit that space. "The environment is what Nature becomes when we view it as a life-support system and as a collection of materials."[5] We can think of the system in a mechanistic fashion, as a collection of materials with various physical and chemical interactions. Or we can think of it in a more organic way, giving attention to the many ways in which the individuals are interde-

pendent in their very nature. From the latter viewpoint we cannot even think of an individual as an isolated atomic thing, for its environment is a very part of itself. From this point of view, the environment stands related to the beings within it not externally, but internally. As such, it takes on an even greater significance than from a mechanistic perspective.

Value

Most people realize the important impact that their environment has on them. The effect has a positive or negative value. Those things that produce benefit are good, and those that cause harm are bad. Growth is good, and poison is bad. But where does this goodness and badness, or positive or negative value, come from? Is it there in the poison or growth? This is a considerably difficult metaphysical and moral problem. (Refer to the discussion of moral realism in Chapter 2.) Does a thing have value in the same sense that it has hair or weight? This does not seem to be so, because a thing's value does not seem to be something it possesses. When we value something, we have a positive response toward it. However, it may not quite be as some philosophers have said, that things have value only in so far as we do happen to respond positively to them, that is, prefer or desire them. Rather, we want to know whether we should value them or value them highly. Is there something about the things that we value, some attributes that they have, for example, that are the legitimate basis for our valuing them? Although we will not go further into a discussion of the nature and basis of value here, we can be aware of the problems involved in trying to give an account of it. We should also be aware that the notion of value and its basis plays a key role in discussions of environmental ethics, as we shall see.

One distinction about value plays a particularly significant role in environmental ethics: the distinction between intrinsic and instrumental value. Things have *intrinsic value* or worth (sometimes referred to as *inherent* value) when they have value or worth in themselves for some reason. Pleasure, as we saw earlier in Chapter 4, is supposed to be intrinsically valuable: We value it for its own sake and not for what we can get with it. Something has *instrumental value* if it is valued because of its usefulness for some other purpose and for someone. Some environmentalists believe that trees, for example, have only instrumental and not intrinsic value. They think that trees are valuable because of their usefulness to us. Other environmentalists believe that plants and ecosystems have value in themselves in some sense, as we shall note later in this chapter.

Another term sometimes used in discussions in environmental ethics is *prima facie* value. The phrase literally means something like "at first glance." Something has prima facie value if it has the kind of value that can be overcome by other interests or values. For example, we might say that economic interests of one group are to be given weight and thus have prima facie value, but they may be overridden by stronger interests of another group or by greater values, such as human health.

These considerations regarding the nature and kinds of value play a key role in judging ethical matters relating to the environment. This is exemplified by two quite different perspectives in environmental ethics. One is anthropocentrism, and the other ecocentrism or biocentrism. We will consider each in turn here.

Anthropocentrism

As you may know, the terms *anthropocentrism* and *anthropocentric* refer to a human-centered perspective. A perspective is anthropocentric if it holds that humans alone have *intrinsic worth* or value. According to this perspective, those things are good that promote the interests of human beings. Thus, for example, some people believe that animals are valuable simply in so far as they promote the interests of humans or are useful to us in a variety of ways. (More discussion of this is found in the following chapter on animal rights.) Animals provide emotional, aes-

thetic, nutritional, clothing, entertainment, and medical benefits for us. Those people who hold an anthropocentric view may also believe that it is bad to cause animals needless pain, but if this is necessary to ensure some important human good, then it is justified. The same is true regarding preservation of wilderness. According to an anthropocentric perspective, the environment or nature has no value in itself. Its value is measured by how it affects human beings. Wilderness areas are instrumentally valuable to us as sources of recreation and relaxation and for providing for some of our physical needs such as lumber for building. Sometimes anthropocentric values conflict. For instance, we cannot both preserve the trees for their beauty or historical interest and yet also use them for lumber. Therefore, we need to think about the relative value of aesthetic experiences and historical appreciation as compared with cheaper housing and lumbering jobs. What is the value, for example, of being able to reflect on our history and our ancestors? Consider some 2,000-year-old trees. Touching one of these giants today is in some way touching the beginning of calendar time. We can think of all of the great moments and events of history that have occurred in the life of this tree and thus appreciate the reality of the events and their connection with us. How would the value of this experience compare with other values? Cost-benefit analyses present one method for making such comparisons.

Cost-Benefit Analysis

Because many environmental issues involve diverse values and competing interests, a technique known as cost-benefit analysis is and can be used to help us think about what is best to do. (See the brief discussion of this in Chapter 4.) If we have a choice between various actions or policies, we need to assess and compare the various harms or costs and benefits that each entails in order to know which is the better policy. Using this method we should choose that alternative having the greater net balance of benefits over harms or costs. It is basically a utilitarian form of reasoning. If we clean up the smoke stacks, then emissions are reduced and acid rain and global warming are curtailed—important *benefits*. However, this also creates *costs* for the company and its employees and those who buy its products or use its services. We want to know whether the benefits will be worth those costs. We also need to assess the relative costs and benefits of other alternatives.

Involved in such analyses are two distinct elements. One is an *assessment*—that is, a determination or description of these factual matters as far as they can be known. What exactly are the likely effects of doing this or that? The other is *evaluation*, the establishment of relative values. In cost-benefit evaluations, the value is generally a function of the usefulness to humans. The usual use of cost-benefit analysis is in the overall context of an anthropocentrism. Some things we find more useful or valuable to us than others. In addition, if we have a fixed amount of money or resources to expend on some environmental project, then we know that this money or these resources will not be available for work elsewhere or to buy other things. Thus, every expenditure will have a certain *opportunity cost*. In being willing to pay for the environmental project, then, we will have some sense of its importance in comparison with other things that we will not then be able to do or have. However, if we value something else just as much or more than a slight increase in cleaner air or water, for example, then we will not be willing to pay for the cleaner air or water.

In making such evaluations, we may know what monetary costs will be added to a particular forest product such as lumber if certain cutting were to be curtailed. However, we are less sure about how we should value the 2,000-year-old tree. How do we measure the historical appreciation or the aesthetic value of the tree or the animals that live in the tree? How do we measure the recreational value of the wilderness? What is beauty or a life worth? The value of these "intangibles" is difficult to measure, because measuring implies that we use a standard measure of value. Only if we have such a stan-

dard can we compare, say, the value of a breathtaking view to that of a dam about to be built on the site. However, we do sometimes use monetary valuations, even of such intangibles as human lives or life years. For example in insurance and other contexts, people attempt to give some measure of the value of a life.[6] Doing so is sometimes necessary, but obviously also problematic. (See Chapter 16 for further discussion of calculating the value of a life.)

Human Environmental Impact

Taking an anthropocentric instrumentalist point of view of the environment also means thinking about the various ways in which the environment impacts us. Consider, for example, just the following four environmental problems.

Global Warming First is the problem of *global warming*. Most scientists now admit that our modern industrial society has created a potentially deadly phenomenon known as the "greenhouse effect." This has resulted because many of our modern industries rely on the burning of fossil fuels. The gases given off are released into the atmosphere—gases such as carbon dioxide, methane, fluorocarbons, and nitrous oxide. Automobile exhaust contributes as well. The levels of these gases in the atmosphere have increased significantly from their preindustrial levels: 0.4 percent for carbon dioxide, 1 percent for methane, 5 percent for fluorocarbons, and 2 percent for nitrous oxide.[7] This increase may not seem dramatic, but the results may be. In the atmosphere these gases combine with water vapor and prevent the sun's infrared rays from radiating back into space. They are thus trapped and contribute to an increase in air temperature. The gases function much as the panes of a greenhouse. They will remain in the atmosphere for thirty to one hundred years, and the buildup has increased over time. Deforestation also contributes to the warming because as forests are destroyed they absorb less carbon dioxide. Just what climatic changes these two practices may cause is a matter of dispute among scientists. Scientists disagree on how much the earth will warm, how fast, and how different regions will be affected. Evidence is now accumulating for this effect, however, in receding glaciers and in the movement of plants and forests farther north and to higher altitudes. An increase or decrease in temperature and rainfall could play a role in droughts and famines and food production generally, as well as in floods and other unusual weather phenomena. What costs we would be willing to pay to prevent the various possible negative effects on us will depend on how bad we consider these effects to be. Those who calculate the costs and benefits involved in this area must also be able to factor in the uncertainties that are involved.

Ozone Depletion   A second environmental problem about which we have been concerned for some time is *ozone depletion*. In the past twenty years, scientists have detected holes or breaks in the layer of ozone at the upper reaches of the stratosphere. This layer of ozone protects us from the damaging effects of excessive ultraviolet radiation from the sun. Such radiation can cause skin cancer and cataracts. The breaks or holes in the ozone layer are caused by chlorine-bearing pollutants such as the chlorofluorocarbons used in fire extinguishers and as refrigerants, cleaning agents, and spray propellants. Carbon dioxide, which causes the greenhouse effect and global warming, has also been found to contribute to ozone depletion.[8] Currently, the largest hole is above Antarctica, where the ozone levels have declined by one-third in recent years. However, there are suspicions that it has migrated over Australia and led to increases in abnormalities there. Scientists had also been predicting openings over other areas in the northern hemisphere and recently had found a 9 percent to 14 percent decline in ozone levels there.[9] Now, however, there is some good news. According to a recent study, the buildup that causes ozone depletion is finally slowing. It is expected to peak around the turn of the century

and then begin a gradual recovery.[10] Among the reasons for this decline is an agreement signed by twenty-three countries in 1987 in Montreal to phase out the use of ozone-destroying chemicals. Is the cost to us to decrease or eliminate the causes of ozone depletion worth the savings in lives? Here again we come up against the issue of how to value human life. The greater its value, the more surely we ought to stop using these chemicals and the harder we ought to work to find alternatives.

Waste Disposal and Pollution   A third area of environmental impact upon us is *waste disposal and pollution*. No one wants the city dump located next to them, and yet the tons of garbage that we produce each year must be put somewhere. Industrial waste is washed into our rivers and lakes and blown into our air. Radioactive waste may be the greatest concern, partly because the long-term risks it poses are relatively unknown. We have more information about the short-term damage it can do. It is also of great concern because these dangerous materials must be contained for thousands of years. According to one estimate, "of the approximately 32,000 hazardous waste disposal sites in this country, from 1,200 to 2,000 . . . pose significant dangers to human health." This is all the more frightening because "about 600 of these sites have been abandoned by their owners."[11] Furthermore, military pollution may be the most extensive. According to a recent report from the group Physicians for Social Responsibility, more than 11,000 sites at more than 900 facilities are contaminated. The contaminants come from the production, testing, cleaning, and use of weapons, explosives, and rocket fuels, as well as from aircraft and electronic equipment. The cost for cleanup at these sites is estimated to be at least $150 billion.[12] Recycling programs aim to reduce the amount of aluminum, glass, paper, and plastics that we throw away each year. Again, we need to determine the economic value of health and life in order to determine what we ought to pay to eliminate or lessen the risks from these sources.

Wilderness Preservation The fourth environmental issue that concerns us here is *wilderness preservation*. The United States now has 671 federally designated wilderness areas, but these are being encroached upon by mining, mineral leasing, and road building, among other things.[13] The National Forest Service has responsibility for almost 200 million acres of land and the management of more than 150 national forests. Our forests and wilderness areas are valuable for many reasons. They provide habitats for wildlife, including some threatened species. They provide us with leisure and relaxation and with many possibilities for recreational opportunities such as white-water rafting, boating, fishing, hiking, and skiing. They also provide possibilities for aesthetic and religious experiences and simple communing with the wider world of nature. (See the reading in this chapter by Holmes Rolston III for other ways in which wilderness benefits us.) What is the extent of our obligation to preserve these forests and wilderness areas, especially in light of the fact that the preservation often has a negative effect on other human economic interests such as jobs? These conflicts leave us with many questions. However, from an anthropocentric perspective, we ought to determine what various things are worth to us and find ways to do comparative evaluations of their value so that we know what we ought to do. The fact that we differ in our evaluation is not a problem in itself for the anthropocentric position or for attempts to use cost-benefit analyses to aid our decision making. We discuss, argue, and change our minds. And sometimes we agree to disagree. Then we find political ways to negotiate these differences. We also sometimes face trade-offs. We cannot have all that we would like or all that would be desirable. Cost-benefit analyses play a role in letting us know the comparative value of doing one thing rather than another. Economists remind us that there are opportunity costs that come with our choices. And we must find some way to place a value on so-called intangibles such as life and beauty and even health in order to factor them into our decision making.

Ecocentrism

According to the anthropocentric perspective, environmental concerns ought to be directed to the betterment of people, who alone have intrinsic value. In contrast with this view is another that is generally called an *ecocentric* (or *biocentric*) perspective. It holds that it is not just humans that have intrinsic worth or value. There are variations within this perspective concerning what does have intrinsic worth. Some theorists hold that it is individual life forms that also have intrinsic worth, while others stress that it is whole systems or ecosystems that have such value. The ethical questions then become matters of determining what is in the best interests of these life forms or what furthers or contributes to, or is a satisfactory fit with, some ecosystem.

Ecocentrists are critical of anthropocentrists. Why, they ask, do only humans have intrinsic value and everything else only use value? Some fault the Judeo-Christian tradition for this view. In particular they single out the biblical mandate to "subdue" the earth and "have dominion over the fish of the sea and over the birds of the air and every living thing that moves upon the earth" as being responsible for this instrumentalist view of nature and other living things.[14] Others argue that anthropocentrism is reductionistic. All of nature, according to this view, is reduced to the level of "thinghood." The seventeenth-century French philosopher Rene Descartes is sometimes cited as a source of this reductionist point of view because of his belief that the essential element of humanity is the ability to think ("I think, therefore I am," etc.) and his belief that animals are mere machines.[15] Evolutionary accounts also depict humans at the pinnacle of evolution or the highest or last link in some great chain of being. We can ask ourselves whether we value too highly human beings and the human powers of reason and intelligence. "Knowledge is power" is a modern notion. One source of this view was the early modern philosopher Francis Bacon's *The New Organon*.[16] Ecocentrists criticize the view that we ought to seek to understand nature so that we can have power over it, because this view implies that our primary relation to nature is one of domination.

Ecocentrists hold that we ought rather to regard nature with admiration and respect, because of their view that nature and natural beings have intrinsic value. Let us return to our example of the 2,000-year-old trees. You may have seen or viewed pictures of trees large enough for tunnels to be cut through them for cars to drive through. In the 1880s such a tunnel was cut through one such tree, a giant sequoia, near Wawona on the south end of what is now Yosemite National Park. Tourists enjoyed driving through the tunnel. However, some claimed that this was a mutilation of and an insult to this majestic tree. They claimed that the tree itself had a kind of integrity, intrinsic value, and dignity that should not be invaded lightly. Another way to put it would be to say that the tree itself had moral standing.[17] What we do to the tree itself matters morally, they insisted.

On what account could trees be thought to have this kind of moral standing? All organisms, it might be argued, are self-maintaining systems:

> They grow and are irritable in response to stimuli. They reproduce. . . . They resist dying. They post a careful if also semipermeable boundary between themselves and the rest of nature; they assimilate environmental materials to their own needs. They gain and maintain internal order against the disordering tendencies of external nature. They keep winding up, recomposing themselves, while inanimate things run down, erode, and decompose.[18]

Because they are organized systems or integrated living wholes, they are thought to have intrinsic value and even moral standing. The value may be only prima facie, but nevertheless they have their own value in themselves and are not just to be valued in terms of their usefulness to people. The giant sequoias of Wawona should not just be thought of in terms of their tourist value. There are things that can be good and bad for the trees themselves. The tunnel in the Wawona tree, for example, eventually weakened the tree,

and it fell over in a snowstorm in 1968. Although trees are not *moral agents* who act responsibly for reasons, according to this general view they can still be thought of as moral patients. A *moral patient* is any being for which what we do to it matters in itself. A moral patient is any being toward whom we can have *direct duties* rather than simply *indirect duties*. We ought to behave in a certain way toward the tree for its sake and not just indirectly for the sake of how it will eventually affect us. There are things that are in their best interests, even if they take no conscious interest in them. (See further discussion of this in the treatment of "rights" in the following chapter.)

In addition to those ecocentrists who argue that all life forms have intrinsic value are others who stress the value of ecosystems. An *ecosystem* is a whole of interacting and interdependent parts within a circumscribed locale. "Ecosystems are a continuum of variation, a patchy mosaic with fuzzy edges. Some interactions are persistent, others occasional."[19] They are loosely structured wholes. The boundary changes and some members come and go. Sometimes there is competition within the whole. Sometimes there is symbiosis. The need to survive pushes various creatures to be creative in their struggle for an adaptive fit. There is a unity to the whole, but it is loose and decentralized. Why is this unity to be thought of as having value in itself? One answer is provided by Aldo Leopold. In the 1940s, he wrote in his famous essay "The Land Ethic" that we should think about the land as "a fountain of energy flowing through a circuit of soils, plants, and animals."[20] Look at any section of life on our planet and you will find a system of life, intricately interwoven and interdependent elements that function as a whole. It forms a *biotic pyramid* with myriad smaller organisms at the bottom and gradually fewer and more complex organisms at the top. Plants depend on the earth, insects depend on the plants, and other animals depend on the insects. Leopold did not think it amiss to speak about the whole system as being healthy and unhealthy. If the soil is washed away or abnormally flooded, the whole system suffers or is sick. In this system, individual organisms feed off one another. Some elements come and others go. It is the whole that continues. Leopold also believed that a particular type of ethics follows from this view of nature. It is a biocentric or ecocentric ethics. He believed that "a thing is right when it tends to preserve the integrity, stability, and beauty of the biotic community. It is wrong when it tends to do otherwise."[21] The system has a certain *integrity*, because it is a unity of interdependent elements that combine to make a whole with a unique character. It has a certain *stability*, not in that it does not change, but that it changes only gradually. Finally, it has a particular *beauty*. Here beauty is a matter of harmony, well-ordered form, or unity in diversity.[22] When envisioned on a larger scale, the entire earth system may then be regarded as one system with a certain integrity, stability, and beauty. Morality becomes a matter of preserving this system or doing only what fits it.

The kind of regard for nature that is manifest in biocentric views is not limited to contemporary philosophers. *Native American* views on nature provide a fertile source of biocentric thinking. Certain forms of *romanticism* have long regarded nature in a different way than that found in dominant Western perspectives. Such were the views of the transcendentalists, Ralph Waldo Emerson and Henry Thoreau. *Transcendentalism* was a movement of romantic idealism that arose in the United States in the mid-nineteenth century. Rather than regarding nature as foreign or alien, Emerson and Thoreau thought of it as a friend or kindred spirit. In fact, nature for them symbolized spirit. Thus, a rock is a sign of endurance and a snake of cunning. The rock and the snake can symbolize spirit because nature itself is full of spirit. As a result of this viewpoint, Thoreau went to Walden Pond to live life to its fullest and commune with nature. He wanted to know its moods and all its phenomena. While he and Emerson read the lessons of nature, they also read their Eastern texts. Some have characterized aspects of their nature theory

as idealism, the view that all is ideas or spirit, or as pantheism, the doctrine that holds that all is *god*.

John Muir, the prophet of Yosemite and founder of the Sierra Club, once urged Emerson to spend more time with him. He wrote to Emerson:

> I invite you to join me in a month's worship with Nature in the high temples of the great Sierra Crown beyond our holy Yosemite. It will cost you nothing save the time and very little of that for you will be mostly in eternity. . . . In the name of a hundred cascades that barbarous visitors never see . . . in the name of all the rocks and of this whole spiritual atmosphere.[23]

Such romantic idealistic views provide a stark contrast to anthropocentric views of a reductionist type. However, they also raise many questions. For example, we can ask the transcendentalist how nature can be spirit or god in more than a metaphorical sense. And we can ask followers of Aldo Leopold the following question. Why is the way things are or have become good? Nature can be cruel, at least from the point of view of certain animals and even from our own viewpoint as we suffer the damaging results of typhoons or volcanic eruptions. And, more abstractly, on what basis can we argue that whatever is is good?

Deep Ecology

Another variation within ecocentrism is the deep ecology movement. Members of this movement wish to distinguish themselves from establishment environmentalism which they call "shallow ecology" and which is basically anthropomorphic. The term *deep ecology* was first used by Arne Naess, the Norwegian philosopher and environmentalist.[24] Deep ecologists take a more holistic view of nature. In addition, they are characterized by their belief that we should look more deeply to find the *root causes* of environmental degradation. The idea is that our environmental problems are deeply rooted in the Western psyche, and that radical changes of viewpoint are necessary if we are to solve them.

Western *reductionism, individualism,* and *consumerism* are said to be the causes of environmental problems. The solution is to rethink and reformulate certain metaphysical beliefs about whether all reality is reducible to a kind of machine. It is also to rethink what it is to be an individual. Are individual beings as so many disparate independent atoms? Or are they interrelated parts of a whole? Solving our environmental problems also requires a change in our views about what is a good quality of life. The good life, they assert, is not one that stresses the possession of things and the satisfaction of wants and desires.

In addition to describing the radical changes in our basic outlook on life that we need to make, the deep ecologist platform also argues that any intrusion into nature to change it requires justification. If we intervene to change nature, then we must show that a vital need of ours is at stake.[25] We ought not lightly to intervene not only because we are not sure of the results of our action, which will be possibly far-reaching and harmful, but also because nature as it is is regarded as good and right and well-balanced. Their platform also includes the belief that the flourishing of nonhuman life requires a "substantial decrease in the human population."[26] (See the selection from Devall and Sessions included in this chapter.) The deep ecology movement has been quite politically active. Its creed contains the belief that people are responsible for the earth. Beliefs such as this often provide a basis for the tactics of groups such as Earth First! Its tactics have included various forms of ecosabotage—for example, spiking trees to prevent logging or cutting power lines.[27]

Both the tactics and the views underlying them have been criticized. The tactics have been labeled by some as "ecoterrorism."[28] The view that all incursions into nature must be justified by our vital needs seems to run counter to our intuitions, for the implication is that we must not build the golf course or the house patio because these would change the earth and vegetation, and the need to play golf or sit on a patio

are hardly vital. Others might have difficulty with the implied view that nature and other natural things have as much value as persons and thus persons' interests should not take precedence over the good of nature. The view that nature itself has a "good of its own" or that the whole system has value in itself is also problematic for many people. However, at the least, deep ecologists have provided a valuable service by calling our attention to the deep philosophical roots and causes of some of our environmental problems.

Ecofeminism

A new variant of ecological ethics has recently been developed by some feminists. It has come to be called *ecofeminism* or *ecological feminism*.[29] It may be seen as part of a broader movement that locates the source of environmental problems not in metaphysical or world views, as deep ecologists do, but in social practices. Social ecology, as this wider movement is called, holds that we should look to particular social patterns and structures to discover what is wrong with our relationship to the environment. Ecofeminists believe that the problem lies in a male-centered view of nature, that is, one of human domination over nature. According to Karen Warren, whose essay is included in this chapter, ecofeminism is "the position that there are important connections . . . between the domination of women and the domination of nature, an understanding of which is crucial to both feminism and environmental ethics."[30] Note here that deep ecologists and ecofeminists do not generally get along well with one another. The deep ecologists criticize ecofeminists for concentrating insufficiently on the environment, and ecofeminists accuse deep ecologists of the very male-centered view that they believe is the source of our environmental problems.[31] However, a variety of ecofeminist views are espoused by diverse groups of feminists.[32]

One version acknowledges the ways in which women differ from men and rejoices in it. This view is espoused by those who hold that because of their female experience or nature, women tend to value relationships and the concrete individual. (Refer to Chapter 7 and the ethics of care.) They stress caring and emotion, and they seek to replace conflict and assertion of rights with cooperation and community. These are traits that can and should carry over into our relationship to nature, they believe. Rather than using nature in an instrumentalist fashion, they urge a cooperation with nature. We should manifest a caring and benevolent regard for nature just as for other human beings. One version of this view would have us think of nature itself as in some way divine. Rather than think of god as a distant creator who transcends nature, these religiously oriented ecofeminists think of god as a being within nature. Some also refer to this god as Mother Nature or Gaia, after the name of the Greek goddess.[33]

Another version of ecofeminism rejects the dualism they find in the above position. They hold that this position promotes the devaluing and domination of both women and nature. Rather than dividing reality into two contrasting elements—the active and passive, the rational and emotional, the dominant and subservient—they encourage us to recognize the diversity within nature and among people. They would similarly support a variety of ways of relating to nature. Thus, they believe that even though science that proceeds from a male orientation of control over nature has made advances and continues to do so, its very orientation misses important aspects of nature. If instead we also have a feeling for nature and a listening attitude, then we might be able better to know what actually is there. They also believe that we humans should see ourselves as part of the community of nature, not a distinct nonnatural being functioning in a world that is thought to be alien to us.

It is sometimes difficult to know just what in particular are the practical upshots of ecocentrism, ecological feminism, and deep ecology. Yet the following sentiment is indicative of what might make a difference: "In behalf of the tiny beings that are yet to arrive on Earth, but whose genes are here now, let's try a little CPR for the Earth—conservation, protection and restoration. And a little tender loving care for the only bit of the universe we know to be blessed with life."[34]

As noted above, some anthropocentrists contend that they also believe in a wise use of nature, one that does not destroy the very nature that we value and on which we depend. On the other hand, it may well be that if we care for and about nature our treatment of it will be better in some important ways.

In the readings in this chapter, Holmes Rolston describes several ways in which we value the environment, Karen Warren discusses ecofeminism, and Bill Devall and George Sessions explain the key elements of deep ecology.

Notes

1. *San Francisco Examiner* (Dec. 17, 1995), p. A1.
2. Ibid.; also see the later reports in the Sept. 29, 1996 issue, pp. A1, A12.
3. Reported by Sara Rimer, "In Clear-Cutting Vote, Maine Will Define Itself," *New York Times* (Sept. 25, 1996), pp. A1, A14
4. Ernest Weekley, *An Etymological Dictionary of Modern English* (New York: Dover, 1967), pp. 516, 5183.
5. Mark Sagoff, "Population, Nature, and the Environment," *Report from the Institute for Philosophy and Public Policy*, vol. 13, no. 4 (Fall 1993), p. 10.
6. Safety regulation needs to make use of such monetary equivalencies, for how else do we decide how safe is safe enough? There is no such thing as perfect safety, for that would mean no risk. Thus, we end up judging that we ought to pay so much to make things just so much safer but no more. The implication is that the increased life years or value of the lives to be saved by stricter regulation is of so much but no more than this much of value. See Barbara MacKinnon, "Pricing Human Life," in *Science, Technology and Human Values* (Spring 1986), pp. 29–39.
7. "Science Times," *New York Times* (Feb. 7, 1989), p. B5. The data are from preindustrial to 1986 levels.
8. Ibid., "Science" (Nov. 24, 1992), p. B8.
9. *Science* (April 23, 1993), pp. 490–491.
10. *New York Times* (Aug. 26, 1993), p. A1.
11. Leonard G. Boonin, "Environmental Pollution and the Law," *Newsletter from the Center for Values and Social Policy at Boulder Colorado*, vol. XI, no. 2 (Fall 1992).

12. Reported in the *San Francisco Examiner,* May 16, 1993.

13. Joseph R. des Jardins, *Environmental Ethics* (Belmont, CA: Wadsworth, 1993), p. 48.

14. Genesis 1: 26–29. Others will cite St. Francis of Assisi as an example of the Christian with a respectful regard for nature.

15. Rene Descartes, *Meditations on First Philosophy.* However, it might be pointed out that for Descartes this was not so much a metaphysical point as an epistemological one; that is, he was concerned with finding some sure starting point for knowledge, and found at least that he was sure that he was thinking even when he was doubting the existence of everything else.

16. Francis Bacon, *Novum Organum,* Thomas Fowler (Ed.) (Oxford, 1889).

17. See Christopher Stone, *Do Trees Have Standing: Toward Legal Rights for Natural Objects* (Los Altos, CA: William Kaufmann, 1974).

18. Holmes Rolston III, *Environmental Ethics: Duties to and Values in the Natural World* (Philadelphia: Temple University Press, 1988), p. 97.

19. Ibid., p. 169.

20. Aldo Leopold, "The Land Ethic," in *Sand County Almanac* (New York: Oxford University Press, 1949).

21. Ibid., p. 262.

22. See John Hospers, *Understanding the Arts* (Englewood Cliffs, NJ: Prentice-Hall, 1982).

23. Quoted in the *San Francisco Examiner* (May 1, 1988), p. E5.

24. Arne Naess, *Ecology, Community, and Lifestyle,* David Rothenberg (Trans.) (Cambridge, UK: Cambridge University Press, 1989).

25. Paul Taylor, *Respect for Nature* (Princeton, NJ: Princeton University Press, 1986).

26. Naess, op. cit.

27. On the tactics of ecosabotage, see Bill Devall, *Simple in Means, Rich in Ends: Practicing Deep Ecology* (Layton, UT: Gibbs Smith, 1988).

28. See Michael Martin, "Ecosabotage and Civil Disobedience," *Environmental Ethics* 12 (Winter 1990), pp. 291–310.

29. According to Joseph des Jardins, the term *ecofeminism* was first used by Francoise d'Eaubonne in 1974 in her work *Le Feminisme ou la Mort* (Paris: Pierre Horay, 1974). See des Jardins, op. cit., p. 249.

30. Karen J. Warren, "The Power and Promise of Ecological Feminism," *Environmental Ethics* 9 (Spring 1987), pp. 3–20.

31. I thank an anonymous reviewer for this point.

32. See the distinctions made by Allison Jaggar between liberal (egalitarian) feminism, Marxist feminism, socialist feminism, and radical feminism in *Feminist Politics and Human Nature* (Totowa, NJ: Rowman & Allanheld, 1983).

33. See Carol Christ, *Laughter of Aphrodite: Reflections on a Journey to the Goddess* (San Francisco: Harper & Row, 1987).

34. David R. Brower, "Step Up the Battle on Earth's Behalf," *San Francisco Chronicle* (Aug. 18, 1993), p. A15.

Humans Valuing the Natural Environment

Holmes Rolston III

Study Questions

1. Why does Rolston believe there ought to be some ethics concerning the environment?

2. What kind of environmental ethics is secondary to human interests? How would this contrast with what Rolston calls an ethics in the primary sense?

3. What is the difference between an objective and a subjective value that nature may "carry"?

4. What does Rolston mean by the "life support value" of nature? What are some ways in which nature has this value for us?

5. In what sense does nature have economic value? What are some examples cited by Rolston?

6. What is the difference between the two kinds of recreational value that Rolston discusses—

nature as gymnasium and nature as theater? How can these sometimes provide for a conflict?

7. According to Rolston, is the scientific value of nature simply its use value? Explain.

8. How is the aesthetic value of nature different from its utility and life support value?

9. What does Rolston mean by nature's "genetic diversity" value? Give examples.

10. According to Rolston, what kinds of historical value does nature have?

11. How does nature have cultural-symbolization value? Give some examples.

12. How can nature build character, according to Rolston?

13. Why do we value both the diversity and unity of nature? Its stability and spontaneity?

14. What does Rolston mean by the "dialectical" value of nature? Give examples.

15. How does nature have life value and religious value, according to Rolston?

That there ought to be some ethic concerning the environment can be doubted only by those who believe in no ethics at all. For humans are evidently helped or hurt by the condition of their environment. Environmental quality is necessary, though not sufficient, for quality in human life. Humans dramatically rebuild their environment, in contrast to squirrels, which take the environment as they find it. But human life, filled with its artifacts, is still lived in a natural ecology where resources—soil, air, water, photosynthesis, climate—are matters of life and death. All that we have and are was grown in or gathered out of nature. Culture and nature have entwined destinies, similar to (and related to) the way minds are inseparable from bodies. So ethics needs to be applied to the environment.

Nevertheless, we are not here seeking simply to apply human ethics to environmental affairs. Environmental ethics is neither ultimately an ethics of

resource use; nor one of benefits, costs, and their just distribution; nor one of risks, pollution levels, rights and torts, needs of future generations, and the rest—although all these figure large within it. Taken alone, such issues enter an ethic where the environment is *secondary* to human interests. The environment is instrumental and auxiliary, though fundamental and necessary. Environmental ethics in the *primary,* naturalistic sense is reached only when humans ask questions not merely of prudential use but of appropriate respect and duty.[1]

That there ought be an environmental ethic in this deeper sense will be doubted by many, those entrenched in the anthropocentric, personalistic ethics now prevailing in the Western world. For them, humans can have no duties to rocks, rivers, or ecosystems, and almost none to birds or bears; humans have serious duties only to each other, with nature often instrumental in such duties. The environment is the wrong kind of primary target for an ethic. It is a means, not an end in itself. Nothing there counts morally. Nature has no intrinsic value.

Just this last claim—that nature has no intrinsic value—is what we will steadily be challenging. *Value* will therefore be a principal term in the arguments that follow. If this were an inquiry into human ethics, terms such as *rights, justice, beneficence and maleficence, social contracts, promises, benefits and costs, utility, altruism,* and *egoism* would be regularly used. These also play a part in environmental ethics, but the fundamental term that will most help to orient us is *value.* It will be out of *value* that we will derive *duty*.

One striking thing about humans in relation to the natural environment is the richness of their "uses" of it. We will begin with an account of humans valuing their environment. Every living thing exploits its environment for biological needs. Like squirrels, humans are hurt by poisons in groundwater, helped by a renewable food supply. But humans have a power to understand, appreciate, and enjoy nature far beyond their biological uses of it. Humans are helped by scenic vistas or scientific experiments conducted in the wilderness, but squirrels never use their environment in these ways. Humans dramatically study and rebuild their environments. Further, unlike animals, humans can take an interest in sectors remote from their immediate, pragmatic needs; they can espouse a view of the whole. . . . This means that nature carries for humans a vast array of values little shared by other species.

Holmes Rolston, III, "Humans Valuing the Natural Environment," in *Environmental Ethics: Duties to and Values in the Natural World* (Philadelphia: Temple University Press, 1988), pp. 1–25. Reprinted by permission.

To begin with an account of how humans value nature may seem to lead only to a secondary environmental ethics. But appearances are deceiving. Such a beginning will prove a strategic entry point into a primary environmental ethics, owing to the rich ways in which humans value nature. Even those who believe that we only need an ethic concerning the environment can start here and see what concerns develop, what gestalts change. Valuing nature may prove a route into doing what only humans can do, transcending what is immediately given and using it as a window into the universe. This trailhead is a good place to take off for points unknown.

Over the route that follows we will not always be able to travel using well-charted ethical arguments, for these do not exist in the wilderness. Ethicists have reflected upon human-to-human relationships for thousands of years, and although interhuman ethics remains frequently unsettled, there are well-worn tracks of debate. Environmental ethics is novel, at least in the classical and modern West; it lies on a frontier. This terrain is sufficiently unexplored to make discovery possible. We may also find ourselves deeper in the woods than we anticipated.

Values Carried by Nature

Asking about values *carried* by nature will let us make an inventory of how nature is valuable to humans, with the subtle advantage that the term *carry* lets us switch-hit on the question of objectivity and subjectivity. In the spectrum of values crossed here, some (the nutritional value in a potato) seem objectively there, while others (the eagle as a national symbol) are merely assigned. Either way, desired human experiences are tied in to the existence of something out there. As we uncover these valued "functions" of nature, we can begin to press the question whether and how far value intrinsic in nature enables humans to come to own these values. Notice too that things never have value generically, but rather have specific sorts of value. Some adjective needs to be filled into a blank before the noun: _____ value. Analogously, objects are not just colored *simpliciter* but are crimson or sky blue.

Life-Support Value

The ecological movement has made it clear that culture remains tethered to the biosystem and that the

options within built environments, however expanded, provide no release from nature. Humans depend on airflow, water cycles, sunshine, photosynthesis, nitrogen fixation, decomposition bacteria, fungi, the ozone layer, food chains, insect pollination, soils, earthworms, climates, oceans, and genetic materials. An ecology always lies in the background of culture, natural givens that support everything else. Some sort of inclusive environmental fitness is required of even the most advanced culture. Whatever their options, however their environments are rebuilt, humans remain residents in an ecosystem. Earlier ethics never paid much attention to ecosystems because humans had little knowledge of what was going on and even less power to affect these processes (though there was environmental degradation in ancient Mesopotamia). But lately, owing to human population increases, advancing technology, and escalating desires, we are drastically modifying our life-support system. Persons are helped and hurt by these alterations, and this raises ethical questions.

Economic Value

Though humans require natural givens, they do not take the environment ready to hand. They do not usually adapt themselves to wild nature; rather they labor over nature, rebuilding it to their cultural needs, owing to the remarkably flexible powers of the human hand and brain. Any living thing makes its environment into a resource. A squirrel hides a cache of acorns; a bird builds a nest. But these activities still involve ecologies, hardly yet economies, unless we choose to call all questions of efficient food and energy use economic. Achieving economic value, in the usual sense, involves the deliberate redoing of natural things, making them over from spontaneous nature, coupled with a commerce in such remade things. Animals do not exchange in markets; by contrast, markets are basic to every culture.

The price of petroleum proves that nature has economic value, but the sense in which it does can be contested, for human labor so dramatically adds to nature's raw value that an economist may here see valuing as a kind of adding-on of labor to what is initially valueless: "crude" oil has no value, but a petroleum engineer may "refine" it. The sense of the prefix *re-* in *resource* is that nature can be refitted, turned to use by human labor, and only the latter gives it value. Valuing is a kind of laboring. If this were entirely so, we should not say, strictly speaking, that nature *has* economic value, any more than we say that an empty glass has water in it. It only *carries* the value of labor. Marxists have often argued that natural resources should be unpriced, for resources as such have no economic value.[2] But a research scientist, mindful of the remarkable natural properties on which technology depends, may immediately add that human art has no independent powers of its own, and such a scientist may give a different valuation of this natural base.

There is a foundational sense in which human craft can never produce any unnatural chemical substances or energies. All humans can do is shift natural things around, taking their properties as givens. There is nothing unnatural about the properties of a computer or a rocket; as much as a warbling vireo or a wild strawberry, both are assemblages of completely natural things operating under natural laws. This sets aside essential differences between artifacts and spontaneous nature (which we examine later), but it does so to regain the insight that nature has economic value because it has an instrumental capacity—and this says something about the material on which the craftsmanship is expended. Nature has a rich utilitarian *pliability,* due both to the plurality of natural sorts and to their splendid, multifaceted powers. This is nature's economic value in a basic and etymological sense of something we can arrange so as to make a home out of it. Nature is a fertile field for human labor, but that agricultural metaphor (which applies as well to industry) praises not only the laborers but their surrounding environment. Nature is something recalcitrant yet often agreeable and useful, frequently enough to permit us to build our entire culture on it.

Despite the prefix, *resource* preserves the word *source* and recalls these generative qualities so profuse in their applications. It is sometimes thought that the more civilized humans become, the further we get *from* nature, released from dependency on the spontaneous natural course. This is true, but science and technology also take us further *into* nature. A pocket calculator is, in this perspective, not so much an exploitation of nature as it is a sophisticated appreciation of the intriguing, mathematical structure of matter-energy, properties enjoying an even more sophisticated natural use in the brain of the fabricator of the calculator.

Such economic value is a function of the state of science, but it is also a function of available natural properties, which often quite unpredictably mix with human ingenuity to assume value. *Penicillium* was a useless mold until 1928, when Alexander Fleming found (and much amplified) the natural antibacterial agency. The bread wheat, on which civilization is based, arose from the hybridization (probably accidental) of a mediocre natural wheat with a weed, goat grass. Who is to say where the miracle foods and medicines of the future will come from? Given the striking advances of technology, an endangered ecosystem is likely to contain some members of potential use. When humans conserve nature, we hope in the genius of the mind, but we also reveal our expectations regarding the as yet undiscovered wealth of natural properties that we may someday capture and convert into economic value.

In some respects, human ingenuity makes nature an infinite resource, because humans can always figure new ways to remake nature, find substitute resources, exploit new properties. By an increasingly competent use of natural resources, the human economy can grow forever. Over the centuries, especially in the last few, more and more of nature has been brought into the human orbit. But in some respects the West has been on an unprecedented growth trip, with Americans exploiting and filling up the New World, Europeans sucking prosperity from colonies, everyone mining nonrenewable resources. The recent economic boom may be atypical, only apparent or local. More persons are starving than ever before. The idea that nature is an inexhaustible resource may be a fantasy. Moral issues regarding the conservation and distribution of resources are becoming urgent, a principal concern in environmental ethics.

Recreational Value

It may seem frivolous to move from labor to play, from life support to recreation, but the question is a quite serious one: why do humans enjoy nature even when we no longer need it for economic or life-supportive reasons, when the sense of "enjoy" alters from beneficial use to pleasurable appreciation? For some, nature is instrumental to an active human performance; they want only terrain rough enough to test a jeep, or a granite cliff sound enough for pitons. Even so, it serves as a field for skill. For others, the natural qualities are crucial in contemplating an autonomous performance. They watch the fleecy cumulus building over the Great White Throne in Zion, listen for the bull elk to bugle, laud the aerial skills of the hummingbird at the bergamot, or laugh at the comic ostrich with its head in the sand. For the one group, nature is a place to *show what they can do;* for the other, values are reached as they are *let in on nature's show*—a difference surprisingly close to that between applied and pure science, to which we soon turn.

Recreational values can be found in sports and popular pastimes and can thus be humanistic, but they are not always so. People like to recreate in the great outdoors because they are surrounded by something greater than anything they find indoors. They touch base with something missing on baseball diamonds at the city park. The pleasures found to be satisfactory, recreating, re-creating there can be in sober sensitivity to objective natural characters. When persons enjoy watching wildlife and landscapes, though this may take considerable skill, the focus is on nature as a wonderland full of eventful drama and a bizarre repertory, a rich evolutionary ecosystem where truth is stranger than fiction. Persons come to own all these recreational values, but sometimes what they seem to be valuing is *creation* more than *recreation.*

These two sorts of recreational value—the gymnasium and the theater—can often be combined, as when a botanist enjoys the exertion of a hike up a peak and also pauses en route at the Parry's primrose by the waterfall. But the two often need to be compromised and are sometimes irreconcilable. It will strike a sportsman as ridiculous to say that snail darters and Furbish louseworts, threatened with extinction by the Tellico and Dickey and Lincoln dams, have more recreational value than will the reservoirs behind those dams, stocked with game fish. It will seem obscene to the naturalist to exterminate a rare life form in exchange for one more place to water-ski. The natural history values seem lately to be counting more. Every state wildlife magazine devotes more space to the nongame species than it did a decade ago, and every national park and wilderness area is much visited. And what if these values count still more in the next generation?

In choosing whether to log a wilderness, should policy favor the preferences of the young, whom surveys reveal to be more pronature, over those of older persons, who are more prodevelopment and less naturalistic? Should we favor the pronature preferences of the better educated over those of the less educated?[3] In social justice, politicians try to favor the disadvantaged and frequently think that seniority carries some weight, either in wisdom or in rights. But in environmental ethics, this view can weight the prejudices against wildlife and preservation, expressed by the less well-educated or older sectors of society, against another social ideal: a harmonious, caring relationship with wildlife and a desire for ample wilderness. This ideal, emerging in the better-educated and the younger generation, initially a minority view, may be more functional socially and in the long term result in a better balance between economic and recreational values.

Humans sometimes want the wild environment as an alternative to the built environment. Leisure, in contrast to work for pay; work (climbing, setting up camp) that isn't for pay; an environment with zest, in contrast to a boring or familiar job; the spartan contrasts with the citied comforts—all these meet otherwise unmet needs. Here humans value the wilderness or the park noneconomically for its unbuilt characteristics. Is this only some sort of escape value? Or is there some more positive characteristic in wildness that re-creates us?

Scientific Value

Science in its origins was a leisurely pursuit for intellectuals, and a good test still for unalloyed scientists is to ask whether they would continue their researches if they were independently wealthy and if these had no economic or life-supporting consequences. The alliance of pure science with naturalistic recreation is seldom noticed, but this only reveals how far recent science has sold its soul to the economists. Is being a naturalist a matter of recreation or of science? Does one do it for play or pay? Some ornithologists and mineralogists hardly ask; rather, whether avocationally or vocationally, they unite in valuing nature as an object worthwhile to be known in its own right, always caring for its fascinating characteristics.

Like music and the fine arts, natural science is an intrinsically worthwhile activity, but scientists find this difficult to say and, sometimes with much ingenuity, sell their study short by retreating to some utilitarian subterfuge. But natural science per se cannot be worthwhile unless its primary object, nature, is interesting enough to justify being known. To praise cognitive science is also to praise its object, for no study of a worthless thing can be intrinsically valuable. Filtering out all applied values, one reaches a residual scientific value in nature, an interest in both the natural stuff and this study of it which has enlisted the greatest human genius.

Natural science is our latest and perhaps most sophisticated cultural achievement, but we should not forget that its focus is primitive nature. Valuing science does not devalue nature; rather, we learn something about the absorbing complexity of the natural environment when we find that it can serve as the object of such noble studies. There is an intellectual adventure in discerning how the tunicates and the vertebrates are both so structured as to be included among the chordates, which are related to the echinoderms more closely than to the cephalopods; it is an accomplishment possible only because nature is a rich developmental system. Some say that we first understand things and afterward evaluate them, but if there is anyone for whom pure science has value, then nature contains at least the raw precursors of value.

The Jurassic fossil *Archaeopteryx,* linking the reptiles with the birds, has great scientific value but no economic or life-support value. The steaming pools of Yellowstone preserve an optimal thermal habitat for primitive anaerobic bacteria which, recent studies suggest, survive little changed from the time when life evolved under an oxygen-free atmosphere.[4] Odd, useless, and often rare things typically have high scientific values—like the finches on the Galápagos—for the clues they furnish to life's development and survival. Who is to say where tomorrow's scientific values may lie? A scientist might have been pardoned a generation back for thinking the Yellowstone microhabitats unimportant.

Science tells the natural tale: how things are, how they came to be. That story cannot be worthless, not only because human roots lie in it but because we find it a delightful intellectual pursuit. But scientists can be beguiled into severing values from nature at the same time that they find their principal entertainment in unraveling an account of the physical and biological saga. The older sciences (and many abstract ones still) fastened on morphology, structure, homeostatic processes. That itself was engaging, but now no natural science, whether astrophysics or ecology, escapes the evolutionary paradigm, and humankind is only beginning to understand what *natural history*—a sometimes despised term—is all about. That history has an epic quality, a certain wandering notwithstand-

ing, and it is surely a story worth telling—and valuing. This leads to the historical value in nature, which we presently specify.

Aesthetic Value

We value the Landscape Arch of the Canyonlands for the same reason that we value the "Winged Victory" of Samothrace: both have grace. Every admirer of the Tetons or of a columbine admits the aesthetic value carried by nature. A. F. Coimbra-Filho advocates saving three species of tiny, rare marmosets of the Atlantic rainforest because "the disappearance of any species represents a great esthetic loss for the entire world."[5] Yet justifying such value verbally is as difficult as is justifying the experience of pure science. The intrinsically valuable intellectual stimulation that the scientist defends is, in fact, a parallel to the aesthetic encounter that the aesthetician defends, for both demand a distance from everyday personal needs and yet a participatory experience that is nontransferable to the uninitiated. Sensitivities in both pure science and natural art help us see much further than is required by our pragmatic necessities. In both, one gets purity of vision.

In the discovery of such aesthetic value, it is crucial to separate this from both utility and life support, and only those who recognize this difference can value the desert or the tundra. The mist that floats about an alpine cliff, spitting out lacy snowflakes, tiny exquisite crystals, will increase the climber's aesthetic experience there even though the gathering storm may be dangerous. The glossy chestnut, half covered by the spined husk, is pretty as well as edible, and we lament its vanishing; but the head of a much too common weed, *Tragopogon,* is just as shapely. The distance that scientists cultivate, as well as the habit of looking closely, fits them to see the beauty that cold-blooded scientists are supposed to overlook. But beauty keeps turning up, and in unsuspected places, as in the stellate pubescence on the underside of a *Shepherdia* leaf or in a kaleidoscopic slide of diatoms. No one who knows the thrill of pure science can really be a philistine.

A prosaic scientist will complain that the admirer of nature overlooks as much as he or she sees: chestnuts aborted by the fungal blight, fractured snowflakes, imperfections everywhere. Contingencies sometimes add beauty, for a skein of geese is not less moving if one is out of line, nor is the cottonwood silhouetted against the wintry sky any less dramatic for the asymmetries within its symmetrical sweep.

Genetic-Diversity Value

Humans eat remarkably few plants in any volume (about 30 out of 300,000 species), and still remarkably fewer come from North America (one or two, pecans and cranberries). With the loss of fifteen cultivars, half the world would starve. Ten species provide 80 percent of the world's calories. Given increasing pressures within agriculture (monocultures, pesticides, herbicides, hybridized strains, groundwater pollution), given increased mutation rates from radioactivity, the nuclear threat, and imported exotic blights, it seems important to preserve the genetic reservoir naturally selected in wild organisms just in case, for instance, Americans need to crossbreed against such microorganisms as produced the corn blight of 1970, or to turn to food stocks adapted to the North American habitats.

It is prudent to preserve the foreign native habitats of the major food, fiber, and medicinal plants (if they now remain), and where such foreign preservation is impossible or unlikely, it becomes all the more important to protect domestic genetic diversity. Even today's poisons in wild plants, naturally evolved defenses, are likely sources of tomorrow's pesticides, herbicides, and medicines. Such resources, at present unknown, cannot be well protected *ex situ* (in zoos, seed depositories) but only *in situ,* by preserving natural ecosystems. Nor can laboratory genetic recombinations substitute for wildlands; natural diversity is required for the startpoint materials.

Historical Value

Wildlands provide historical value in two ways, cultural and natural. Americans (North, South, Canadian) have a recent heritage of self-development against a diverse and challenging environment, seen in pioneer, frontier, and cowboy motifs. New World cultures remain close to the memory of a primitive landscape. United States history goes back four hundred years; Greek history, four thousand years. The Americans' ancestral virtues were forged with the European invasion of a (so-called) empty continent, which it was their "manifest destiny" to develop. Even the Europeans have historical memories associated with nature: the British with the moors; the Germans with the Black Forest; the Russians with the steppes; the Greeks with the sea. Every culture remains resident in some environment.

Forests, prairies, and ranges ought to be preserved as souvenir places for each generation of Americans learning (however secondarily or critically) their forefathers' moods, regained there quite as much as in the Minuteman Historical Park. Such places provide a lingering echo of what Americans once were, of a way we once passed. It would be a pity not to have accessible to youth in every state some area big enough to force a camp in crossing it, to get lost in, to face the discomforts and hazards of, if for no other reason than to rouse the spine-tingling that braced our forebears. There is nothing like the howl of a wolf to resurrect the ghost of Jim Bridger. A wilderness trip mixes the romance and the reality of the past in present experience. Further, a vice in "white" history is to forget all the "red" years. Understanding the Indian experientially (so far as this is possible at all) requires wilderness to lift historical experience out of the books and recapture it on a vivid landscape.

On the stage of natural history, the human phenomenon is even more ephemeral than is American history on the stage of human history. At this range, wildlands provide the profoundest historical museum of all, a relic of the way the world was during 99.99 percent of past time. Humans are relics of that world, and that world, as a tangible relic in our midst, contributes to our sense of duration, antiquity, continuity, and identity. An immense stream of life has flowed over this continent Americans inhabit, over this Earth. The river of life is a billion years long, and humans have traveled a million years on it, recording their passage for several thousand years. If the length of the river of life were proportioned to stretch around the globe, the human journey would be halfway across a county, and humans would have kept a journal for only a few hundred feet. The individual's reach would be a couple of steps! On this scale, even the Greeks are recent, despite their ancient history, and people in every nation need nature as a museum of what the world was like for almost forever. . . .

Using nature as a museum of natural history, a teaching place, doubtless makes nature of instrumental value, but here the living museum and the historical reality are, although in small part, one and the same. When we treasure the living museum instrumentally, we may also come to recognize intrinsic value in the natural processes that still survive in remnant wild and rural areas.

Cultural-Symbolization Value

The bald eagle symbolizes American self-images and aspirations (freedom, strength, beauty), as does the bighorn ram, a "state animal" for Coloradoans. Flowering dogwood and the cardinal characterize Virginia. The pasqueflower is the state flower of South Dakota, the alligator a symbol for Florida, the moose for Maine, the maple leaf for Canada, the trillium for Ontario, the arbutus for Nova Scotia. The lion is a British symbol; the Russians have chosen the bear. Natural areas enter local cultural moods—Grandfather Mountain in western North Carolina, Natural Bridge and the Shendandoah River in central Virginia. Horsetooth Mountain, overlooking the city, provides the logo for Fort Collins, Colorado. Every homescape has its old and familiar haunts—swimming holes, water gaps, passes—which enter our sense of belongingness and identity. Culture commingles with landscape and wildlife in places named after geomorphic, faunal, or floral features: Tinkling Springs, Fox Hollow, Aspen, Crested Butte.

Character-Building Value

Wildlands are used by organizations that educate character—Boy and Girl Scouts, Outward Bound, and church camps. Similar growth occurs in individuals independently of formal organizations. The challenge of self-competence, in teamwork or alone, is valued, together with reflection over skills acquired and one's place in the world. Wildlands provide a place to sweat, to push oneself more than usual, perhaps to let the adrenalin flow. They provide a place to take calculated risks, to learn the luck of the weather, to lose and find one's way, to reminisce over success and failure. They teach one to care about his or her physical condition.

Wildlands provide a place to gain humility and a sense of proportion. Doing so partly recapitulates our historical experience; it anticipates the religious experience that we soon examine. What was earlier a recreational testing of what we can do is heightened into an achievement of self-identity. In a survey of 300 geniuses, Edith Cobb found evocative experiences in natural locales characteristic of their youth, a formative factor in their creativity.[6] Not only are youth affected so; several noted writers have reported how self-actualization was fostered in a wilderness setting.[7] Nature is a place to "know thyself."

Related to this is a therapeutic value in nature. An entirely normal use of wild and rural areas, reported by a majority, is for semitherapeutic recreation in a low-frustration environment. A minority use, less well explored, is as a setting to treat psychologically disturbed persons. For the mentally ill, the ambiguity and complexity in culture can be disorienting. It is hard to differentiate among friends, enemies, and the indifferent, hard to get resolve focused on what to do next or to predict the consequences of delay. But in the wilds or on the farm, supper has to be cooked; one needs firewood, and it is getting dark. There are probabilities in facing nature—maybe it won't rain when you forget your poncho—but there are no ambiguities. Exertion is demanded; visceral accomplishment is evident, again in a low-frustration environment. The self is starkly present, and the protocol is simpler. One really is on his own; or, one's friends are few, and she utterly depends on them. All this can mobilize the disturbed for recovery, perhaps using in basic form the same forces that create the character-building effect for us all.[8]

Diversity-Unity Values

We may next harness a pair of complementary values. The sciences describe much natural *diversity* and also much *unity*, terms which are descriptive and yet contain dimensions of value. [Biology has] traced every life form back to monophyletic or a few polyphyletic origins, while ecology has interwoven these myriad forms to connect them at present as fully as they have been related by paleontology. This macroscopic web is matched by the unity revealed by the electron microscope or the X-ray spectrometer. The natural pageant is a kind of symphony of motifs, each motif interesting, often orchestrated together, sometimes chaotic, and all spun from a few simple notes.

The story of science is the discovery of a bigger universe with more things in it, and the finding of laws and structures to explain their common composition and kinship. Humans value both the diversity and the unity.

Diversity is itself a diverse idea, sometimes requiring more exact specification, but we need here only the core focus on plurality, richness, variety, all unfolding from fundamental themes. Disparate sets of results are coordinated as spin-offs from simple processes; the world is simple in principles and rich in phenomena. The physical sciences have revealed the astronomical extent of matter coupled with its reduction into a few kinds of elements and particles, which dissolve into interradiating wave fields. The taxonomist has enlarged the array of natural kinds, while the biochemist has found only the materials of physics organized everywhere in parallel chemistries, such as glycolysis and the citric acid cycle or DNA and RNA at the core of life.

Stability and Spontaneity Values

A pair of complementary natural values rests on a mixture of ordered stability with what, rather evasively, we must call the appearance of spontaneity, counterparts that are not only descriptive but also valuational. That natural processes are regular—that gravity holds, rains come, oaks breed in kind, and succession is reset and repeated—yields laws and trends rooted in the causal principle; it means that nature is dependable, as well as being unified and intelligible. Every order is not a value, but some order supports value, and why is this natural dependability not a quite basic value? A requisite of any universe is that it be ordered, but we need not despise a necessary good, nor does such minimum essential order account for the ecological and biochemical constancy that supports life and mind, upon which all knowledge and security depend.

The polar value, really a sort of freedom, is hardly known to science by any such name; indeed, it is with some risk of offense and oversimplification that we here touch the long-debated issues surrounding determinism. Still, nature sometimes provides an "appearance" of contingency. Neither landscapes nor aspen leaves nor ecological successions are ever twice the same. In the laboratory, science abstracts out the regularly recurring components in nature to attain predictive control, while in the field nature always remains in part unique and particular, nonrepetitive. What happens there is always something of an adventure: the way the cottontail evades the coyote, or just when the last leaf is tossed from this maple and where the gusting wind lands it. We hardly know how to give a complete account of this. Rigorous determinists insist that nothing in nature (or in culture) can be either of chance or of choice, believing that to say otherwise is to destroy the fundamental axiom of all science. But others require a less rigidly closed system, finding that science still prospers when positing statistical laws, which need not specify every particular.

We are not sure whether *Australopithecus* had to develop in Africa or whether giraffes had to mutate so as to develop long necks, although both events may have been probable. Did the first ancestral birds storm-blown to the Galápagos Islands absolutely have to be finches? For the conservatives, it is safest to say theoretically that here we only reveal our ignorance of nature's detailed determinism, that nature's surprises are only apparent, though perhaps we cannot now or ever escape this appearance. For the liberals, it is bolder and more satisfying, as well as true to practical experience, to say that nature sometimes allows the real appearance of spontaneous novelty. What the Darwinian revolution did to the Newtonian view was to find nature sometimes a jungle and not a clock, and many have disliked the change. Contingencies do put a bit of chaos into the cosmos. But you can have a sort of adventure in Darwin's jungle that you cannot have in Newton's clock. Openness brings risk and often misfortune, but it sometimes adds excitement. Here nature's intelligibility, aesthetic beauty, dependability, and unity are checked by the presence of spontaneity, and this can be valued too.

Nor are these features of constancy and contingency in nature beyond our capacity to affect them. One of our fears is that technology with its manipulations and pollutants, including radioactive ones, will destabilize long-enduring ecosystems; another is that unabated human growth will transgress virtually the whole domain of spontaneous wildness; another is lest we should make the Earth a bit less autonomous by losing snail darters.

Dialectical Value

We humans are not really bounded by our skin; rather, life proceeds within an environmental theater across a surface of dialectic. The leg muscles are the largest in the body, and we need room to roam down by the river or along the seashore. The hands have evolved for grasping natural things, but so has the brain, and sentient experience underruns mental life. The crafting of an arrow point, a rifle, or a rocket is an environmental exchange. Society and artifacts are also requisite for mind, as is abstract thought, but nature is the most fundamental foil and foundation for mind, and this diffuses the human/natural and the value/fact line. Culture is carved out *against* nature but carved out *of* nature, and this fact is not simple to handle valuationally. Superficially, so far as nature is antagonistic and discomfiting, it has disvalue. Even here a subjectivist must take care lest nature gain objective value first on the negative side of the field, only later to require it positively. We cannot count the hurts in nature as objectively bad unless we are willing to count its helps as objectively good.

With deeper insight, we do not always count environmental conductance as good and environmental resistance as bad, but the currents of life flow in their interplay. An environment that was entirely hostile would slay us; life could never have appeared within it. An environment that was entirely irenic would stagnate us; human life could never have appeared there either. All our culture, in which our classical humanity consists, and all our science, in which our modern humanity consists, has originated in the face of oppositional nature. Nature insists that we work, and this laboring—even suffering—is its fundamental economic pressure. The pioneer, pilgrim, explorer, and settler loved the frontier for the challenge and discipline that put fiber into the American soul. One reason we lament the passing of wilderness is that we do not want entirely to tame this aboriginal element in which our genius was forged. We want some wildness remaining for its historical value and for its character-building value.

Life Value

Reverence for life is commended by every great religion, and even moralists who shy from religion accord life ethical value. John Muir would not let Gifford Pinchot kill a tarantula at the Grand Canyon, remarking that "it had as much right there as we did."[9] A thoroughgoing humanist may say that only personal life has value, making every other life form tributary to human interests, but a sensitive naturalist will suspect that this is a callous rationalization, anthropocentric selfishness calling itself objective hard science. The first lesson learned in evolution was perhaps one of conflict, but a subsequent one is of kinship, for the life we value in persons is advanced from but allied with the life in monkeys, perch, and louseworts. Mixed with other values, this Noah principle of preserving a breeding population is powerfully present in the Endangered Species Act. But if life generically is of value, then every specific individual in some degree instances this value, and this is why, without due cause, it is a sin to kill a mockingbird.

Religious Value

Nature generates poetry, philosophy, and religion not less than science, and at its deepest educational capacity we are awed and humbled by staring into the stormy surf or the midnight sky, or by peering down at the reversing protoplasmic stream in a creeping myxomycete plasmodium. Mountaintop experiences, sunsets, canyon strata, or a meadow of dog's-tooth violets can generate experiences of "a motion and a spirit that impels . . . and rolls through all things."[10] Wild nature thus becomes something like a sacred text. For wilderness purists intensely, and for most persons occasionally, wildlands provide a cathedral setting. There are memories of wilderness in the origins of monotheism (Mount Sinai, Jesus in the desert). Analogies with the natural world fill the Book of Job and Jesus' parables. The wilderness elicits cosmic questions, differently from town. Those thoughts struck in contemplation of nature are thoughts about who and where we are, about the life and death that nature hands us, and our appropriate conduct in this environment.

We might say, overworking the term, that nature is a religious "resource," as well as a scientific, recreational, aesthetic, or economic one. But, using a better word here, we want a wilderness "sanctuary" (and could we begin to think of wildlife sanctuaries in this way?) as a place to escape from the secular city, as a sacrosanct, holy place where we can get near to ultimacy. There is something Greater in the outdoors. Humans are programmed to ask why, and the natural dialectic is the cradle of our spirituality. The wilderness works on a traveler's soul as much as it does on his muscles.

Notes

1. See Holmes Rolston III, "Is There An Ecological Ethic?" *Ethics* 85 (1975): 93–109, reprinted in Rolston, *Philosophy Gone Wild* (Buffalo, NY: Prometheus Books, 1986), pp. 12–29.

2. Karl Marx, *Grundrisse* (New York: Random House, 1973), p. 366.

3. S. R. Kellert and J. K. Berry, *Knowledge, Affection and Basic Attitudes toward Animals in American Society,* Phase 3 of a U.S. Fish and Wildlife Service Study (Washington, D.C.: U.S. Government Printing Office, 1980).

4. T. D. Brock, "Life at High Temperatures," *Science* 158 (1967): 1012–1019.

5. A. F. Coimbra-Filho, A. Magnanini, and R. A. Mittermeier, "Vanishing Gold: Last Chance for Brazil's Lion Tamarins," *Animal Kingdom* 78, no. 6 (December 1975): 20–27, citation on p. 25.

6. Edith Cobb, "The Ecology of Imagination in Childhood, *Daedalus* 88 (1959): 537–548, a summary of *The Ecology of Imagination in Childhood* (New York: Columbia University Press, 1977).

7. N. R. Scott, "Toward a Psychology of Wilderness Experience," *Natural Resources Journal* 14 (1974): 231–237.

8. A. L. Turner, "The Therapeutic Value of Nature," *Journal of Operational Psychiatry* 7 (1976): 64–74.

9. N. Gifford Pinchot, *Breaking New Ground* (New York: Harcourt, Brace, 1947), p. 103.

10. William Wordsworth, "Lines Composed a Few Miles above Tintern Abbey" (1798).

The Power and the Promise of Ecological Feminism

Karen Warren

Study Questions

1. According to Warren, what is the promise and power of ecological feminism?

2. Why does Warren believe that treatment of the environment is a feminist issue?

3. What are the three features of what the author calls an oppressive conceptual framework?

4. To conclude that humans can rightly dominate nature, what two assumptions does Warren believe we must make?

5. Outline the argument that Warren gives to connect the domination of nature and women.

6. Why does the author then believe that ecofeminism is necessary to any feminist critique of patriarchy?

7. Why must feminism itself embrace ecological feminism, according to Warren?

8. What three reasons does Warren give for her position that feminism is essential for an adequate environmental ethic?

Ecological feminism is the position that there are important connections—historical, symbolic, theoretical—between the domination of women and the domination of nonhuman nature. I argue that because the conceptual connections between the dual dominations of women and nature are located in an oppressive patriarchal conceptual framework characterized by a logic of domination, (1) the logic of traditional feminism requires the expansion of feminism to include ecological feminism and (2) ecological feminism provides a framework for developing a distinctively feminist environmental ethic. I conclude that any feminist theory and any environmental ethic which fails to take seriously the interconnected dominations of women and nature is simply inadequate.

Introduction

Ecological feminism (ecofeminism) has begun to receive a fair amount of attention lately as an alternative feminism and environmental ethic.[1] Since Francoise d'Eaubonne introduced the term *ecofeminisme* in 1974 to bring attention to women's potential for bringing about an ecological revolution,[2] the term has been used in a variety of ways. As I use the term in this paper, ecological feminism is the position that there are important connections—historical, experiential, symbolic, theoretical—between the domination of women and the domination of nature, an understanding of which is crucial to both feminism and environmental ethics. I argue that the promise and power of ecological feminism is that *it provides a*

Karen Warren, "The Power and Promise of Ecological Feminism," *Environmental Ethics,* vol. 12, no. 2 (Summer 1990), pp. 125–146. Reprinted with permission.

distinctive framework both for reconceiving feminism and for developing an environmental ethic which takes seriously connections between the domination of women and the domination of nature. I do so by discussing the nature of a feminist ethic and the ways in which ecofeminism provides a feminist and environmental ethic. I conclude that any feminist theory *and* any environmental ethic which fails to take seriously the twin and interconnected dominations of women and nature is at best incomplete and at worst simply inadequate.

Feminism, Ecological Feminism, and Conceptual Frameworks

Whatever else it is, feminism is at least the movement to end sexist oppression. It involves the elimination of any and all factors that contribute to the continued and systematic domination or subordination of women. While feminists disagree about the nature of and solutions to the subordination of women, all feminists agree that sexist oppression exists, is wrong, and must be abolished.

A "feminist issue" is any issue that contributes in some way to understanding the oppression of women. Equal rights, comparable pay for comparable work, and food production are feminist issues wherever and whenever an understanding of them contributes to an understanding of the continued exploitation or subjugation of women. Carrying water and searching for firewood are feminist issues wherever and whenever women's primary responsibility for these tasks contributes to their lack of full participation in decision making, income producing, or high status positions engaged in by men. What counts as a feminist issue, then, depends largely on context, particularly the historical and material conditions of women's lives.

Environmental degradation and exploitation are feminist issues because an understanding of them contributes to an understanding of the oppression of women. In India, for example, both deforestation and reforestation through the introduction of a monoculture species tree (e.g., eucalyptus) intended for commercial production are feminist issues because the loss of indigenous forests and multiple species of trees has drastically affected rural Indian women's ability to maintain a subsistence household. Indigenous forests provide a variety of trees for food, fuel, fodder, household utensils, dyes, medi-

cines, and income-generating uses, while monoculture-species forests do not.[3] Although I do not argue for this claim here, a look at the global impact of environmental degradation on women's lives suggests important respects in which environmental degradation is a feminist issue.

Feminist philosophers claim that some of the most important feminist issues are *conceptual* ones: these issues concern how one conceptualizes such mainstay philosophical notions as reason and rationality, ethics, and what it is to be human. Ecofeminists extend this feminist philosophical concern to nature. They argue that, ultimately, some of the most important connections between the domination of women and the domination of nature are conceptual. To see this, consider the nature of conceptual frameworks.

A *conceptual framework* is a set of *basic* beliefs, values, attitudes, and assumptions which shape and reflect how one views oneself and one's world. It is a socially constructed lens through which we perceive ourselves and others. It is affected by such factors as gender, race, class, age, affectional orientation, nationality, and religious background.

Some conceptual frameworks are oppressive. An *oppressive conceptual framework* is one that explains, justifies, and maintains relationships of domination and subordination. When an oppressive conceptual framework is *patriarchal,* it explains, justifies, and maintains the subordination of women by men.

I have argued elsewhere that there are three significant features of oppressive conceptual frameworks: (1) value-hierarchical thinking, i.e., "up-down" thinking which places higher value, status, or prestige on what is "up" rather than on what is "down"; (2) value dualisms, i.e., disjunctive pairs in which the disjuncts are seen as oppositional (rather than as complementary) and exclusive (rather than as inclusive), and which place higher value (status, prestige) on one disjunct rather than the other (e.g., dualisms which give higher value or status to that which has historically been identified as "mind," "reason," and "male" than to that which has historically been identified as "body," "emotion," and "female"); and (3) logic of domination, i.e., a structure of argumentation which leads to a justification of subordination.[4]

The third feature of oppressive conceptual frameworks is the most significant. A logic of domination is not *just* a logical structure. It also involves a substantive value system, since an ethical premise is needed to permit or sanction the "just" subordination of that which is subordinate. This justification typically is given on grounds of some alleged characteristic (e.g., rationality) which the dominant (e.g., men) have and the subordinate (e.g., women) lack.

Contrary to what many feminists and ecofeminists have said or suggested, there may be nothing *inherently* problematic about "hierarchical thinking" or even "value-hierarchical thinking" in contexts other than contexts of oppression. Hierarchical thinking is important in daily living for classifying data, comparing information, and organizing material. Taxonomies (e.g., plant taxonomies) and biological nomenclature seem to require *some* form of "hierarchical thinking." Even "value-hierarchical thinking" may be quite acceptable in certain contexts. (The same may be said of "value dualisms" in non-oppressive contexts.) For example, suppose it is true that what is unique about humans is our conscious capacity to radically reshape our social environments (or "societies"), as Murray Bookchin suggests.[5] Then one could truthfully say that humans are better equipped to radically reshape their environments than are rocks or plants—a "value-hierarchical" way of speaking.

The problem is not simply *that* value-hierarchical thinking and value dualisms are used, but the *way* in which each has been used *in oppressive conceptual frameworks* to establish inferiority and to justify subordination.[6] It is the logic of domination, *coupled with* value-hierarchical thinking and value dualisms, which "justifies" subordination. What is explanatorily basic, then, about the nature of oppressive conceptual frameworks is the logic of domination.

For ecofeminism, that a logic of domination is explanatorily basic is important for at least three reasons. First, without a logic of domination, a description of similarities and differences would be just that—a description of similarities and differences. Consider the claim, "Humans are different from plants and rocks in that humans can (and plants and rocks cannot) consciously and radically reshape the communities in which they live; humans are similar to plants and rocks in that they are both members of an ecological community." Even if humans are "better" than plants and rocks with respect to the conscious ability of humans to radically transform communities, one does not *thereby* get any *morally* relevant distinction between humans and nonhumans, or an argument for the domination of plants and rocks by humans. To get *those* conclusions one needs to add at least two powerful assumptions, viz., (A2) and (A4) in argument A below:

(A1)   Humans do, and plants and rocks do not, have the capacity to consciously and radically change the community in which they live.

(A2)   Whatever has the capacity to consciously and radically change the community in which it lives is morally superior to whatever lacks this capacity.

(A3)   Thus, humans are morally superior to plants and rocks.

(A4)   For any X and Y, if X is morally superior to Y, then X is morally justified in subordinating Y.

(A5)   Thus, humans are morally justified in subordinating plants and rocks.

Without the two assumptions that *humans are morally superior* to (at least some) nonhumans, (A2), and that *superiority justifies subordination*, (A4), all one has is some difference between humans and some nonhumans. This is true *even if* that difference is given in terms of superiority. Thus, it is the logic of domination, (A4), which is the bottom line in ecofeminist discussions of oppression.

Second, ecofeminists argue that, at least in Western societies, the oppressive conceptual framework which sanctions the twin dominations of women and nature is a patriarchal one characterized by all three features of an oppressive conceptual framework. Many ecofeminists claim that, historically, within at least the dominant Western culture, a patriarchal conceptual framework has sanctioned the following argument B:

(B1)   Women are identified with nature and the realm of the physical; men are identified with the "human" and the realm of the mental.

(B2)   Whatever is identified with nature and the realm of the physical is inferior to ("below") whatever is identified with the "human" and the realm of the mental; or, conversely, the latter is superior to ("above") the former.

(B3)   Thus, women are inferior to ("below") men; or, conversely, men are superior to ("above") women.

(B4)   For any X and Y, if X is superior to Y, then X is justified in subordinating Y.

(B5) Thus, men are justified in subordinating women.

If sound, argument B establishes *patriarchy,* i.e., the conclusion given at (B5) that the systematic domination of women by men is justified. But according to ecofeminists, (B5) is justified by just those three features of an oppressive conceptual framework identified earlier: value-hierarchical thinking, the assumption at (B2); value dualisms, the assumed dualism of the mental and the physical at (B1) and the assumed inferiority of the physical vis-à-vis the mental at (B2); and a logic of domination, the assumption at (B4), the same as the previous premise (A4). Hence, according to ecofeminists, insofar as an oppressive patriarchal conceptual framework has functioned historically (within at least dominant Western culture) to sanction the twin dominations of women and nature (argument B), both argument B and the patriarchal conceptual framework, from whence it comes, ought to be rejected.

Of course, the preceding does not identify which premises of B are false. What is the status of premises (B1) and (B2)? Most, if not all, feminists claim that (B1), and many ecofeminists claim that (B2), have been assumed or asserted within the dominant Western philosophical and intellectual tradition.[7] As such, these feminists assert, as a matter of historical fact, that the dominant Western philosophical tradition has assumed the truth of (B1) and (B2). Ecofeminists, however, either deny (B2) or do not affirm (B2). Furthermore, because some ecofeminists are anxious to deny any ahistorical identification of women with nature, some ecofeminists deny (B1) when (B1) is used to support anything other than a strictly historical claim about what has been asserted or assumed to be true within patriarchal culture—e.g., when (B1) is used to assert that women properly are identified with the realm of nature and the physical.[8] Thus, from an ecofeminist perspective, (B1) and (B2) are properly viewed as problematic though historically sanctioned claims: they are problematic precisely because of the way they have functioned historically in a patriarchal conceptual framework and culture to sanction the dominations of women and nature.

What *all* ecofeminists agree about, then, is the way in which *the logic of domination* has functioned historically within patriarchy to sustain and justify the twin dominations of women and nature.[9] Since *all* feminists (and not just ecofeminists) oppose patriar-chy, the conclusion given at (B5), all feminists (including ecofeminists) must oppose at least the logic of domination, premise (B4), on which argument B rests—whatever the truth-value status of (B1) and (B2) *outside of* a patriarchal context.

That *all* feminists must oppose the logic of domination shows the breadth and depth of the ecofeminist critique of B: it is a critique not only of the three assumptions on which this argument for the domination of women and nature rests, viz., the assumptions at (B1), (B2), and (B4); it is also a critique of patriarchal conceptual frameworks generally, i.e., of those oppressive conceptual frameworks which put men "up" and women "down," allege some way in which women are morally inferior to men, and use that alleged difference to justify the subordination of women by men. Therefore, ecofeminism is necessary to *any* feminist critique of patriarchy, and, hence, necessary to feminism (a point I discuss again later).

Third, ecofeminism clarifies why the logic of domination, and any conceptual framework which gives rise to it, must be abolished in order both to make possible a meaningful notion of difference which does not breed domination and to prevent feminism from becoming a "support" movement based primarily on shared experiences. In contemporary society, there is no one "woman's voice," no *woman* (or *human*) *simpliciter:* every woman (or human) is a woman (or human) of some race, class, age, affectional orientation, marital status, regional or national background, and so forth. Because there are no "monolithic experiences" that all women share, feminism must be a "solidarity movement" based on shared beliefs and interests rather than a "unity in sameness" movement based on shared experiences and shared victimization.[10] In the words of Maria Lugones, "Unity—not to be confused with solidarity—is understood as conceptually tied to domination."[11]

Ecofeminists insist that the sort of logic of domination used to justify the domination of humans by gender, racial or ethnic, or class status is also used to justify the domination of nature. Because eliminating a logic of domination is part of a feminist critique—whether a critique of patriarchy, white supremacist culture, or imperialism—ecofeminists insist that *naturism* is properly viewed as an integral part of any feminist solidarity movement to end sexist oppression and the logic of domination which conceptually grounds it.

Ecofeminism Reconceives Feminism

The discussion so far has focused on some of the oppressive conceptual features of patriarchy. As I use the phrase, the "logic of traditional feminism" refers to the location of the conceptual roots of sexist oppression, at least in Western societies, in an oppressive patriarchal conceptual framework characterized by a logic of domination. Insofar as other systems of oppression (e.g., racism, classism, ageism, heterosexism) are also conceptually maintained by a logic of domination, appeal to the logic of traditional feminism ultimately locates the basic conceptual interconnections among *all* systems of oppression in the logic of domination. It thereby explains at a *conceptual* level why the eradication of sexist oppression requires the eradication of the other forms of oppression.[12] It is by clarifying this conceptual connection between systems of oppression that a movement to end sexist oppression—traditionally the special turf of feminist theory and practice—leads to a reconceiving of feminism *as a movement to end all forms of oppression*.

Suppose one agrees that the logic of traditional feminism requires the expansion of feminism to include other social systems of domination (e.g., racism and classism). What warrants the inclusion of nature in these "social systems of domination"? Why must the logic of traditional feminism include the abolition of "naturism" (i.e., the domination of oppression of nonhuman nature) among the "isms" feminism must confront? The conceptual justification for expanding feminism to include ecofeminism is twofold. One basis has already been suggested: by showing that the conceptual connections between the dual dominations of women and nature are located in an oppressive and, at least in Western societies, patriarchal conceptual framework characterized by a logic of domination, ecofeminism explains how and why feminism, conceived as a movement to end sexist oppression, must be expanded and reconceived as also a movement to end naturism. This is made explicit by the following argument C:

(C1) Feminism is a movement to end racism.

(C2) But Sexism is conceptually linked with naturism (through an oppressive conceptual framework characterized by a logic of domination).

(C3) Thus, Feminism is (also) a movement to end naturism.

Because, ultimately, these connections between sexism and naturism are conceptual—embedded in an oppressive conceptual framework—the logic of traditional feminism leads to the embrace of ecological feminism.[13]

The other justification for reconceiving feminism to include ecofeminism has to do with the concepts of gender and nature. Just as conceptions of gender are socially constructed, so are conceptions of nature. Of course, the claim that women and nature are social constructions does not require anyone to deny that there are actual humans and actual trees, rivers, and plants. It simply implies that *how* women and nature are conceived is a matter of historical and social reality. These conceptions vary cross-culturally and by historical time period. As a result, any discussion of the "oppression or domination of nature" involves reference to historically specific forms of social domination of nonhuman nature by humans, just as discussion of the "domination of women" refers to historically specific forms of social domination of women by men. Although I do not argue for it here, an ecofeminist defense of the historical connections between the dominations of women and of nature, claims (B1) and (B2) in argument B, involves showing that within patriarchy the feminization of nature and the naturalization of women have been crucial to the historically successful subordinations of both.[14]

If ecofeminism promises to reconceive traditional feminism in ways which include naturism as a legitimate feminist issue, does ecofeminism also promise to reconceive environmental ethics in ways which are feminist? I think so. This is the subject of the remainder of the paper.

Climbing from Ecofeminism to Environmental Ethics

Many feminists and some environmental ethicists have begun to explore the use of first-person narrative as a way of raising philosophically germane issues in ethics often lost or underplayed in mainstream philosophical ethics. Why is this so? What is it about narrative which makes it a significant resource for theory and practice in feminism and environmental ethics? Even if appeal to first-person narrative is a helpful literary device for describing ineffable experience or a legitimate social science methodology for documenting personal and social history, how is first-person narrative a valuable vehicle for argumentation for ethical decision making and theory building? One fruitful way to begin answering these questions is to ask them of a particular first-person narrative.

Consider the following first-person narrative about rock climbing:

> For my very first rock climbing experience, I chose a somewhat private spot, away from other climbers and on-lookers. After studying "the chimney," I focused all my energy on making it to the top. I climbed with intense determination, using whatever strength and skills I had to accomplish this challenging feat. By midway I was exhausted and anxious. I couldn't see what to do next—where to put my hands or feet. Growing increasingly more weary as I clung somewhat desperately to the rock, I made a move. It didn't work. I fell. There I was, dangling midair above the rocky ground below, frightened but terribly relieved that the belay rope had held me. I knew I was safe. I took a look up at the climb that remained. I was determined to make it to the top. With renewed confidence and concentration, I finished the climb to the top.
>
> On my second day of climbing, I rappelled down about 200 feet from the top of the Palisades at Lake Superior to just a few feet above the water level. I could see no one—not my belayer, not the other climbers, no one. I unhooked slowly from the rappel rope and took a deep cleansing breath. I looked all around me—really looked—and listened. I heard a cacophony of voices—birds, trickles of water on the rock before me, waves lapping against the rocks below. I closed my eyes and began to feel the rock with my hands—the cracks and crannies, the raised lichen and mosses, the almost imperceptible nubs that might provide a resting place for my fingers and toes when I began to climb. At that moment I was bathed in serenity. I began to talk to the rock in an almost inaudible, child-like way, as if the rock were my friend. I felt an overwhelming sense of gratitude for what it offered me—a chance to know myself and the rock differently, to appreciate unforeseen miracles like the tiny flowers growing in the even tinier cracks in the rock's surface, and to come to know a sense of *being in relationship* with the natural environment. It felt as if the rock and I were silent conversational partners in a long-standing friendship. I realized then that I had come to care about this cliff which was so different from me, so unmovable and invincible, independent and seemingly indifferent to my presence. I wanted to be with the rock as I climbed. Gone was the determination to conquer the rock, to forcefully impose my will on it; I wanted simply to work respectfully with the rock as I climbed. And as I climbed, that is what I felt. I felt myself *caring* for this rock and feeling thankful that climbing provided the opportunity for me to know it and myself in this new way.

There are at least four reasons why use of such a first-person narrative is important to feminism and environmental ethics. First, such a narrative gives voice to a felt sensitivity often lacking in traditional analytical ethical discourse, viz., a sensitivity to conceiving of oneself as fundamentally "in relationship with" others, including the nonhuman environment. It is a modality which *takes relationships themselves seriously*. It thereby stands in contrast to a strictly reductionist modality that takes relationships seriously only or primarily because of the nature of the *relators* or parties to those relationships (e.g., relators conceived as moral agents, right holders, interest carriers, or sentient beings). In the rock-climbing narrative above, it is the climber's relationships with the rock she climbs which takes on special significance—which is itself a locus of value—in addition to whatever moral status or moral considerability she or the rock or any other parties to the relationship may also have.[15]

Second, such a first-person narrative gives expression to a variety of ethical attitudes and behaviors often overlooked or underplayed in mainstream Western ethics, e.g., the difference in attitudes and behaviors toward a rock when one is "making it to the top" and when one thinks of oneself as "friends with" or "caring about" the rock one climbs.[16] These different attitudes and behaviors suggest an ethically germane contrast between two different types of relationship humans or climbers may have toward a rock: an imposed conqueror-type relationship, and an emergent caring-type relationship. This contrast grows out of, and is faithful to, felt, lived experience.

The difference between conquering and caring attitudes and behaviors in relation to the natural environment provides a third reason why the use of first-person narrative is important to feminism and environmental ethics: it provides a way of conceiving of ethics and ethical meaning *as emerging out of* particular situations moral agents find themselves in, rather than as being *imposed on* those situations (e.g., as a derivation or instantiation of some predetermined abstract principle or rule). This emergent feature of narrative centralizes the importance of *voice*. When a multiplicity of cross-cultural *voices* are centralized, narrative is able to give expression to a range of attitudes, values, beliefs, and behaviors which may be overlooked or silenced by imposed ethical meaning and theory. As a reflection of and on felt, lived experiences, the use of narrative in ethics provides a stance from which ethical discourse can be held accountable to the historical, material, and social realities in which moral subjects find themselves.

Lastly, and for our purposes perhaps most importantly, the use of narrative has argumentative significance. Jim Cheney calls attention to this feature of narrative when he claims, "To contextualize ethical deliberation is, in some sense, to provide a narrative or story, from which the solution to the ethical dilemma emerges as the fitting conclusion."[17] Narrative has argumentative force by suggesting *what counts* as an appropriate conclusion to an ethical situation. One ethical conclusion suggested by the climbing narrative is that what counts as a proper ethical attitude toward mountains and rocks is an attitude of respect and care (whatever that turns out to be or involve), not one of domination and conquest.

In an essay entitled "In and Out of Harm's Way: Arrogance and Love," feminist philosopher Marilyn Frye distinguishes between "arrogant" and "loving" perception as one way of getting at this difference in the ethical attitudes of care and conquest.[18] Frye writes:

> The loving eye is a contrary of the arrogant eye.
>
> The loving eye knows the independence of the other. It is the eye of a seer who knows that nature is indifferent. It is the eye of one who knows that to know the seen, one must consult something other than one's own will and interests and fears and imagination. One must look at the thing. One must look and listen and check and question.
>
> The loving eye is one that pays a certain sort of attention. This attention can require a discipline but *not* a self-denial. The discipline is one of self-knowledge, being able to tell one's own interests from those of others and of knowing where one's self leaves off and another begins. . . .
>
> The loving eye does not make the object of perception into something edible, does not try to assimilate it, does not reduce it to the size of the seer's desire, fear and imagination, and hence does not have to simplify. It knows the complexity of the other as something which will forever present new things to be known. The science of the loving eye would favor The Complexity Theory of Truth [in contrast to The Simplicity Theory of Truth] and presuppose The Endless Interestingness of the Universe.[19]

According to Frye, the loving eye is not an invasive, coercive eye which annexes others to itself, but one which "knows the complexity of the other as something which will forever present new things to be known."

When one climbs a rock as a conqueror, one climbs with an arrogant eye. When one climbs with a loving eye, one constantly "must look and listen and check and question." One recognizes the rock as something very different, something perhaps totally indifferent to one's own presence, and finds in that difference joyous occasion for celebration. One knows "the boundary of the self," where the self—the "I," the climber—leaves off and the rock begins. There is no fusion of two into one, but a complement of two entities *acknowledged* as separate, different, independent, yet *in relationship*; they are in relationship *if only* because the loving eye is perceiving it, responding to it, noticing it, attending to it.

An ecofeminist perspective about both women and nature involves this shift in attitude from "arrogant perception" to "loving perception" of the nonhuman world. Arrogant perception of nonhumans by humans presupposes and maintains *sameness* in such a way that it expands the moral community to those beings who are thought to resemble (be like, similar to, or the same as) humans in some morally significant way. Any environmental movement or ethic based on arrogant perception builds a moral hierarchy of beings and assumes some common denominator of moral considerability in virtue of which like beings deserve similar treatment or moral consideration and unlike beings do not. Such environmental ethics are or generate a "unity in sameness." In contrast, "loving perception" presupposes and maintains *difference*—a distinction between the self and other, between human and at least some nonhumans—in such a way that perception of the other as other *is* an expression of love for one who/which is recognized at the outset as independent, dissimilar, different. As Maria Lugones says, in loving perception, "Love is seen not as fusion and erasure of difference but as incompatible with them."[20] "Unity in sameness" alone is an *erasure of difference*.

"Loving perception" of the nonhuman natural world is an attempt to understand what it means *for humans* to care about the nonhuman world, a world *acknowledged* as being independent, different, perhaps even indifferent to humans. Humans *are* different from rocks in important ways, even if they are also both members of some ecological community. A moral community based on loving perception of oneself *in relationship with* a rock, or with the natural environment as a whole, is one which acknowledges and respects difference, whatever "sameness" also exists.[21] The limits of loving perception are determined only by the limits of one's (e.g., a person's, a community's) ability to respond lovingly (or with appropriate care, trust, or friendship)—whether it is to other humans or to the nonhuman world and elements of it.[22]

If what I have said so far is correct, then there are very different ways to climb a mountain and *how* one climbs it and *how* one narrates the experience of climbing it matter ethically. If one climbs with "arrogant perception," with an attitude of "conquer and control," one keeps intact the very sorts of thinking that characterize a logic of domination and an oppressive conceptual framework. Since the oppressive conceptual framework which sanctions the domination of nature is a patriarchal one, one also thereby keeps intact, even if unwittingly, a patriarchal conceptual framework. Because the dismantling of patriarchal conceptual frameworks is a feminist issue, *how* one climbs a mountain and *how* one narrates—or tells the story—about the experience of climbing also are *feminist issues.* In this way, ecofeminism makes visible why, at a conceptual level, environmental ethics is a feminist issue. I turn now to a consideration of ecofeminism as a distinctively feminist and environmental ethic.

Ecofeminism as a Feminist and Environmental Ethic

A feminist ethic involves a twofold commitment to critique male bias in ethics wherever it occurs, and to develop ethics which are not male-biased. Sometimes this involves articulation of values (e.g., values of care, appropriate trust, kinship, friendship) often lost or underplayed in mainstream ethics.[23] Sometimes it involves engaging in theory building by pioneering in new directions or by revamping old theories in gender sensitive ways. What makes the critiques of old theories or conceptualizations of new ones "feminist" is that they emerge out of sex-gender analyses and reflect whatever those analyses reveal about gendered experience and gendered social reality.

As I conceive feminist ethics in the pre-feminist present, it rejects attempts to conceive of ethical theory in terms of necessary and sufficient condi-

tions, because it assumes that there is no essence (in the sense of some transhistorical, universal, absolute abstraction) of feminist ethics. While attempts to formulate joint necessary and sufficient conditions of a feminist ethic are unfruitful, nonetheless, there are some necessary conditions, what I prefer to call "boundary conditions," of a feminist ethic. These boundary conditions clarify some of the minimal conditions of a feminist ethic without suggesting that feminist ethics has some ahistorical essence. They are like the boundaries of a quilt or collage. They delimit the territory of the piece without dictating what the interior, the design, the actual pattern of the piece looks like. Because the actual design of the quilt emerges from the multiplicity of voices of women in a cross-cultural context, the design will change over time. It is not something static.

What are some of the boundary conditions of a feminist ethic? First, nothing can become part of a feminist ethic—can be part of the quilt—that promotes sexism, racism, classism, or any other "isms" of social domination. Of course, people may disagree about what counts as a sexist act, racist attitude, classist behavior. What counts as sexism, racism, or classism may vary cross-culturally. Still, because a feminist ethic aims at eliminating sexism and sexist bias, and (as I have already shown) sexism is intimately connected in conceptualization and in practice to racism, classism, and naturism, a feminist ethic must be anti-sexist, anti-racist, anti-classist, anti-naturist and opposed to any "ism" which presupposes or advances a logic of domination.

Second, a feminist ethic is a *contextualist* ethic. A contextualist ethic is one which sees ethical discourse and practice as emerging from the voices of people located in different historical circumstances. A contextualist ethic is properly viewed as a *collage* or *mosaic,* a tapestry of voices that emerges out of felt experiences. Like any collage or mosaic, the point is not to have *one picture* based on a unity of voices, but a *pattern* which emerges out of the very different voices of people located in different circumstances. When a contextualist ethic is *feminist,* it gives central place to the voices of women.

Third, since a feminist ethic gives central significance to the diversity of women's voices, a feminist ethic must be structurally pluralistic rather than unitary or reductionistic. It rejects the assumption that there is "one voice" in terms of which ethical values, beliefs, attitudes, and conduct can be assessed.

Fourth, a feminist ethic reconceives ethical theory as theory in process which will change over time. Like all theory, a feminist ethic is based on some generalizations.[24] Nevertheless, the generalizations associated with it are themselves a pattern of voices within which the different voices emerging out of concrete and alternative descriptions of ethical situations have meaning. The coherence of a feminist theory so conceived is given within a historical and conceptual context, i.e., within a set of historical, socioeconomic circumstances (including circumstances of race, class, age, and affectional orientation) and within a set of basic beliefs, values, attitudes, and assumptions about the world.

Fifth, because a feminist ethic is contextualist, structurally pluralistic, and "in-process," one way to evaluate the claims of a feminist ethic is in terms of their *inclusiveness*: those claims (voices, patterns of voices) are morally and epistemologically favored (preferred, better, less partial, less biased) which are more inclusive of the felt experiences and perspectives of oppressed persons. The condition of inclusiveness requires and ensures that the diverse voices of women (as oppressed persons) will be given legitimacy in ethical theory building. It thereby helps to minimize empirical bias, e.g., bias rising from faulty or false generalizations based on stereotyping, too small a sample size, or a skewed sample. It does so by ensuring that any generalizations which are made about ethics and ethical decision making include—indeed cohere with—the patterned voices of women.[25]

Sixth, a feminist ethic makes no attempt to provide an "objective" point of view, since it assumes that in contemporary culture there really is no such point of view. As such, it does not claim to be "unbiased" in the sense of "value-neutral" or "objective." However, it does assume that whatever bias it has as an ethic centralizing the voices of oppressed persons is a *better bias*—"better" because it is more inclusive and therefore less partial—than those which exclude those voices.[26]

Seventh, a feminist ethic provides a central place for values typically unnoticed, underplayed, or misrepresented in traditional ethics, e.g., values of care, love, friendship, and appropriate trust.[27] Again, it need not do this at the exclusion of considerations of rights, rules, or utility. There may be many contexts in which talk of rights or of utility is useful or appropriate. For instance, in contracts or property relationships, talk of rights may be useful and appro-

priate. In deciding what is cost-effective or advantageous to the most people, talk of utility may be useful and appropriate. In a feminist *qua* contextualist ethic, whether or not such talk is useful or appropriate depends on the context; *other values* (e.g., values of care, trust, friendship) are *not* viewed as reducible to or captured solely in terms of such talk.[28]

Eighth, a feminist ethic also involves a reconception of what it is to be human and what it is for humans to engage in ethical decision making, since it rejects as either meaningless or currently untenable any gender-free or gender-neutral description of humans, ethics, and ethical decision making. It thereby rejects what Alison Jaggar calls "abstract individualism," i.e., the position that it is possible to identify a human essence or human nature that exists independently of any particular historical context.[29] Humans and human moral conduct are properly understood essentially (and not merely accidentally) in terms of networks or webs of historical and concrete relationships.

All of the props are now in place for seeing how ecofeminism provides the framework for a distinctively feminist and environmental ethic. It is a feminism that critiques male bias wherever it occurs in ethics (including environmental ethics) and aims at providing an ethic (including an environmental ethic) which is not male biased—and it does so in a way that satisfies the preliminary boundary conditions of a feminist ethic.

First, ecofeminism is quintessentially anti-naturist. Its anti-naturism consists in the rejection of any way of thinking about or acting toward nonhuman nature that reflects a logic, values, or attitude of domination. Its anti-naturist, anti-sexist, anti-racist, anti-classist (and so forth, for all other "isms" of social domination) stance forms the outer boundary of the quilt: nothing gets on the quilt which is naturist, sexist, racist, classist, and so forth.

Second, ecofeminism is a contextualist ethic. It involves a shift *from* a conception of ethics as primarily a matter of rights, rules, or principles predetermined and applied in specific cases to entities viewed as competitors in the contest of moral standing, *to a* conception of ethics as growing out of what Jim Cheney calls "defining relationships," i.e., relationships conceived in some sense as defining who one is.[30] As a contextualist ethic, it is not that rights, or rules, or principles are *not* relevant or important. Clearly they are in certain contexts and for certain purposes.[31] It is just that what *makes* them relevant or important is that those to whom they apply are entities *in relationship with* others.

Ecofeminism also involves an ethical shift *from* granting moral consideration to nonhumans *exclusively* on the grounds of some similarity they share with humans (e.g., rationality, interests, moral agency, sentiency, right-holder status) *to* "a highly contextual account to see clearly what a human being is and what the nonhuman world might be, morally speaking, *for* human beings."[32] For an ecofeminist, *how* a moral agent is in relationship to another becomes of central significance, not simply *that* a moral agent is a moral agent or is bound by rights, duties, virtue, or utility to act in a certain way.

Third, ecofeminism is structurally pluralistic in that it presupposes and maintains difference—difference among humans as well as between humans and at least some elements of nonhuman nature. Thus, while ecofeminism denies the "nature/culture" split, it affirms that humans are both members of an ecological community (in some respects) and different from it (in other respects). Ecofeminism's attention to relationships and community is not, therefore, an erasure of difference but a respectful acknowledgment of it.

Fourth, ecofeminism reconceives theory as theory in process. It focuses on patterns of meaning which emerge, for instance, from the storytelling and first-person narratives of women (and others) who deplore the twin dominations of women and nature. The use of narrative is one way to ensure that the content of the ethic—the pattern of the quilt—may/will change over time, as the historical and material realities of women's lives change and as more is learned about women-nature connections and the destruction of the nonhuman world.[33]

Fifth, ecofeminism is inclusivist. It emerges from the voices of women who experience the harmful domination of nature and the way that domination is tied to their domination as women. It emerges from listening to the voices of indigenous peoples such as Native Americans who have been dislocated from their land and have witnessed the attendant undermining of such values as appropriate reciprocity, sharing, and kinship that characterize traditional Indian culture. It emerges from listening to voices of those who, like Nathan Hare, critique traditional approaches to environmental ethics as white and bourgeois, and as failing to address issues of "black ecol-

ogy" and the "ecology" of the inner city and urban spaces.[34] It also emerges out of the voices of Chipko women who see the destruction of "earth, soil, and water" as intimately connected with their own inability to survive economically.[35] With its emphasis on inclusivity and difference, ecofeminism provides a framework for recognizing that what counts as ecology and what counts as appropriate conduct toward both human and nonhuman environments is largely a matter of context.

Sixth, as a feminism, ecofeminism makes no attempt to provide an "objective" point of view. It is a social ecology. It recognizes the twin dominations of women and nature as social problems rooted both in very concrete, historical, socioeconomic circumstances and in oppressive patriarchal conceptual frameworks which maintain and sanction these circumstances.

Seventh, ecofeminism makes a central place for values of care, love, friendship, trust, and appropriate reciprocity—values that presuppose that our relationships to others are central to our understanding of who we are.[36] It thereby gives voice to the sensitivity that in climbing a mountain, one is doing something in relationship with an "other," an "other" whom one can come to care about and treat respectfully.

Lastly, an ecofeminist ethic involves a reconception of what it means to be human, and in what human ethical behavior consists. Ecofeminism denies abstract individualism. Humans are who we are in large part by virtue of the historical and social contexts and the relationships we are in, including our relationships with nonhuman nature. Relationships are not something extrinsic to who we are, not an "add on" feature of human nature; they play an essential role in shaping what it is to be human. Relationships of humans to the nonhuman environment are, in part, constitutive of what it is to be a human.

By making visible the interconnections among the dominations of women and nature, ecofeminism shows that both are feminist issues and that explicit acknowledgment of both is vital to any responsible environmental ethic. Feminism *must* embrace ecological feminism if it is to end the domination of women because the domination of women is tied conceptually and historically to the domination of nature.

A responsible environmental ethic also *must* embrace feminism. Otherwise, even the seemingly most revolutionary, liberational, and holistic ecological ethic will fail to take seriously the interconnected dominations of nature and women that are so much a part of the historical legacy and conceptual framework that sanctions the exploitation of nonhuman nature. Failure to make visible these interconnected, twin dominations results in an inaccurate account of how it is that nature has been and continues to be dominated and exploited and produces an environmental ethic that lacks the depth necessary to be truly *inclusive* of the realities of persons who at least in dominant Western culture have been intimately tied with that exploitation, viz., women. Whatever else can be said in favor of such holistic ethics, a failure to make visible ecofeminist insights into the common denominators of the twin oppressions of women and nature is to perpetuate, rather than overcome, the source of that oppression.

This last point deserves further attention. It may be objected that as long as the end result is "the same"—the development of an environmental ethic which does not emerge out of or reinforce an oppressive conceptual framework—it does not matter whether that ethic (or the ethic endorsed in getting there) is feminist or not. Hence, it simply is *not* the case that any adequate environmental ethic must be feminist. My argument, in contrast, has been that it *does* matter, and for three important reasons. First, there is the scholarly issue of accurately representing historical reality, and that, ecofeminists claim, requires acknowledging the historical feminization of nature and naturalization of women as part of the exploitation of nature. Second, I have shown that the conceptual connections between the domination of women and the domination of nature are located in an oppressive and, at least in Western societies, patriarchal conceptual framework characterized by a logic of domination. Thus, I have shown that failure to notice the nature of this connection leaves at best an incomplete, inaccurate, and partial account of what is required of a conceptually adequate environmental ethic. An ethic which *does not* acknowledge this is simply *not* the same as one that does, whatever else the similarities between them. Third, the claim that, in contemporary culture, one can have an adequate environmental ethic which is *not* feminist assumes that, in contemporary culture, the label *feminist* does not add anything crucial to the nature or description of environmental ethics. I have shown that at least in contemporary culture this is false, for the word *feminist* currently helps to clarify just *how* the domination

of nature is conceptually linked to patriarchy and, hence, how the liberation of nature, is conceptually linked to the termination of patriarchy. Thus, because it has critical bite in contemporary culture, it serves as an important reminder that in contemporary sex-gendered, raced, classed, and naturist culture, an unlabeled position functions as a privileged and "unmarked" position. That is, without the addition of the word *feminist,* one presents environmental ethics as if it has no bias, including male-gender bias, which is just what ecofeminists deny: failure to notice the connections between the twin oppressions of women and nature *is* male-gender bias.

One of the goals of feminism is the eradication of all oppressive sex-gender (and related race, class, age, affectional preference) categories and the creation of a world in which *difference does not breed domination*—say, the world of 4001. If in 4001 an "adequate environmental ethic" is a "feminist environmental ethic," the word *feminist* may then be redundant and unnecessary. However, this is *not* 4001, and in terms of the current historical and conceptual reality the dominations of nature and of women are intimately connected. Failure to notice or make visible that connection in 1990 perpetuates the mistaken (and privileged) view that "environmental ethics" is *not* a feminist issue, and that *feminist* adds nothing to environmental ethics.[37]

Conclusion

I have argued in this paper that ecofeminism provides a framework for a distinctively feminist and environmental ethic. Ecofeminism grows out of the felt and theorized about connections between the domination of women and the domination of nature. As a contextualist ethic, ecofeminism refocuses environmental ethics on what nature might mean, morally speaking, *for* humans, and on how the relational attitudes of humans to others—humans as well as nonhumans—sculpt both what it is to be human and the nature and ground of human responsibilities to the nonhuman environment. Part of what this refocusing does is to take seriously the voices of women and other oppressed persons in the construction of that ethic.

A Sioux elder once told me a story about his son. He sent his seven-year-old son to live with the child's grandparents on a Sioux reservation so that he could "learn the Indian ways." Part of what the grandparents taught the son was how to hunt the four leggeds of the forest. As I heard the story, the boy was taught, "to shoot your four-legged brother in his hind area, slowing it down but not killing it. Then, take the four legged's head in your hands, and look into his eyes. The eyes are where all the suffering is. Look into your brother's eyes and feel his pain. Then, take your knife and cut the four-legged under his chin, here, on his neck, so that he dies quickly. And as you do, ask your brother, the four-legged, for forgiveness for what you do. Offer also a prayer of thanks to your four-legged kin for offering his body to you just now, when you need food to eat and clothing to wear. And promise the four-legged that you will put yourself back into the earth when you die, to become nourishment for the earth, and for the sister flowers, and for the brother deer. It is appropriate that you should offer this blessing for the four-legged and, in due time, reciprocate in turn with your body in this way, as the four-legged gives life to you for your survival." As I reflect upon that story, I am struck by the power of the environmental ethic that grows out of and takes seriously narrative, context, and such values and relational attitudes as care, loving perception, and appropriate reciprocity, and doing what is appropriate in a given situation—however that notion of appropriateness eventually gets filled out. I am also struck by what one is able to see, once one begins to explore some of the historical and conceptual connections between the dominations of women and of nature. A *re-conceiving and re-visioning* of both feminism and environmental ethics, is, I think, the power and promise of ecofeminism.

Notes

1. Explicit ecological feminist literature includes works from a variety of scholarly perspectives and sources. Some of these works are Leonie Caldecott and Stephanie Leland (Eds.), *Reclaim the Earth: Women Speak Out for Life on Earth* (London: The Women's Press, 1983); Jim Cheney, "Eco-Feminism and Deep Ecology," *Environmental Ethics* 9 (1987): 115–145; Andrée Collard with Joyce Contrucci, *Rape of the Wild: Man's Violence against Animals and the Earth* (Bloomington: Indiana University Press, 1988); Katherine Davies, "Historical Associations: Women and the Natural World," *Women & Environments* 9, no. 2 (Spring 1987): 4–6; Sharon Doubiago, "Deeper than Deep Ecology: Men Must Become Feminists," in *The New Catalyst Quarterly*, no. 10 (Winter 1987/88): 10–11; Brian Easlea, *Science and Sexual Oppression:* *Patriarchy's Confrontation with Women and Nature* (London: Weidenfeld & Nicholson, 1981); Elizabeth Dodson Gray, *Green Paradise Lost* (Wellesley, MA: Roundtable Press, 1979); Susan Griffin, *Women and Nature: The Roaring Inside Her* (San Francisco: Harper and Row, 1978); Joan L. Griscom, "On Healing the Nature/History Split in Feminist Thought," in *Heresies #13: Feminism and Ecology* 4, no. 1 (1981): 4–9; Ynestra King, "The Ecology of Feminism and the Feminism of Ecology," in *Healing Our Wounds: The Power of Ecological Feminism*, Judith Plant (Ed.) (Boston: New Society Publishers, 1989), pp. 18–28; "The Eco-feminist Imperative," in *Reclaim the Earth*, Caldecott and Leland (Eds.) (London: The Women's Press, 1983), pp. 12–16; "Feminism and the Revolt of Nature," in *Heresies #13: Feminism and Ecology* 4, no. 1 (1981): 12–16, and "What is Ecofeminism?" *The Nation*, 12 December 1987; Marti Kheel, "Animal Liberation Is a Feminist Issue," *The New Catalyst Quarterly*, no. 10 (Winter 1987–88): 8–9; Carolyn Merchant, *The Death of Nature: Women, Ecology and the Scientific Revolution* (San Francisco: Harper & Row, 1980); Patrick Murphy (Ed.), "Feminism, Ecology, and the Future of the Humanities," special issue of *Studies in the Humanities* 15, no. 2 (December 1988); Abby Peterson and Carolyn Merchant, "Peace with the Earth: Women and the Environmental Movement in Sweden," *Women's Studies International Forum* 9, no. 5–6 (1986): 465–479; Judith Plant, "Searching for Common Ground: Ecofeminism and Bioregionalism," in *The New Catalyst Quarterly*, no. 10 (Winter 1987/88): 6–7; Judith Plant (Ed.), *Healing Our Wounds: The Power of Ecological Feminism* (Boston: New Society Publishers, 1989); Val Plumwood, "Ecofeminism: An Overview and Discussion of Positions and Arguments," *Australasian Journal of Philosophy*, supplement to vol. 64 (June 1986): 120–137; Rosemary Radford Ruether, *New Woman/New Earth: Sexist Ideologies & Human Liberation* (New York: Seabury Press, 1975); Kirkpatrick Sale, "Ecofeminism—A New Perspective," *The Nation*, 26 September 1987): 302–305; Ariel Kay Salleh, "Deeper than Deep Ecology: The Eco-Feminist Connection," *Environmental Ethics* 6 (1984): 339–345, and "Epistemology and the Metaphors of Production: An Eco-Feminist Reading of Critical Theory," in *Studies in the Humanities* 15 (1988): 130–139; Vandana Shiva, *Staying Alive: Women, Ecology and Development* (London: Zed Books, 1988); Charlene Spretnak, "Ecofeminism: Our Roots and Flowering," *The Elmswood Newsletter*, Winter Solstice 1988; Karen J. Warren, "Feminism and Ecology: Making Connections," *Environmental Ethics* 9 (1987): 3–21; "Toward an Ecofeminist Ethic," *Studies in the Humanities* 15 (1988): 140–156; Miriam Wyman, "Explorations of Ecofeminism," *Women & Environments* (Spring 1987): 6–7; Iris Young, " 'Feminism and

Ecology' and 'Women and Life on Earth: Eco-Feminism in the 80's'," *Environmental Ethics* 5 (1983): 173–180; Michael Zimmerman, "Feminism, Deep Ecology, and Environmental Ethics," *Environmental Ethics* 9 (1987): 21–44.

2. Francoise d'Eaubonne, *Le Feminisme ou la Mort* (Paris: Pierre Horay, 1974), pp. 213–252.

3. I discuss this in my paper, "Toward an Ecofeminist Ethic."

4. The account offered here is a revision of the account given earlier in my paper "Feminism and Ecology: Making Connections." I have changed the account to be about "oppressive" rather than strictly "patriarchal" conceptual frameworks in order to leave open the possibility that there may be some patriarchal conceptual frameworks (e.g., in non-Western cultures) which are *not* properly characterized as based on value dualisms.

5. Murray Bookchin, "Social Ecology versus 'Deep Ecology'," in *Green Perspectives: Newsletter of the Green Program Project*, no. 4–5 (Summer 1987): 9.

6. It may be that in contemporary Western society, which is so thoroughly structured by categories of gender, race, class, age, and affectional orientation, that there simply is no meaningful notion of "value-hierarchical thinking" which does not function in an oppressive context. For purposes of this paper, I leave that question open.

7. Many feminists who argue for the historical point that claims (B1) and (B2) have been asserted or assume to be true within the dominant Western philosophical tradition do so by discussion of that tradition's conceptions of reason, rationality, and science. For a sampling of the sorts of claims made within that context, see "Reason, Rationality, and Gender," Nancy Tuana and Karen J. Warren (Eds.), a special issue of the American Philosophical Association's *Newsletter on Feminism and Philosophy* 88, no. 2 (March 1989): 17–71. Ecofeminists who claim that (B2) has been assumed to be true within the dominant Western philosophical tradition include: Gray, *Green Paradise Lost*; Griffin, *Woman and Nature: The Roaring Inside Her*; Merchant, *The Death of Nature*; Ruether, *New Woman/New Earth*. For a discussion of some of these ecofeminist historical accounts, see Plumwood, "Ecofeminism." While I agree that the historical connection between the domination of women and the domination of nature is a crucial one, I do not argue for that claim here.

8. Ecofeminists who deny (B1) when (B1) is offered as anything other than a true, descriptive, historical claim about patriarchal culture often do so on grounds that an objectionable sort of biological determinism, or at least harmful female sex-gender stereotypes, underlie (B1). For a discussion of this "split" among those ecofeminists ("nature feminists") who assert and those ecofeminists ("social feminists") who deny (B1) as anything other than a true historical claim about how women are described in patriarchal culture, see Griscom, "On Healing the Nature/History Split."

9. I make no attempt here to defend the historically sanctioned truth of these premises.

10. See, e.g., Bell Hooks, *Feminist Theory: From Margin to Center* (Boston: South End Press, 1984), pp. 51–52.

11. Maria Lugones, "Playfulness, 'World Travelling,' and Loving Perception," *Hypatia* 2, no. 2 (Summer 1987): 3.

12. At an *experiential* level, some women are "women of color," poor, old, lesbian, Jewish, and physically challenged. Thus, if feminism is going to liberate these women, it also needs to end the racism, classism, heterosexism, anti-Semitism, and discrimination against the handicapped that is constitutive of their oppression as black, or Latina, or poor, or older, or lesbian, or Jewish, or physically challenged women.

13. This same sort of reasoning shows that feminism is also a movement to end racism, classism, age-ism, heterosexism and other "isms," which are based on oppressive conceptual frameworks characterized by a logic of domination. However, there is an important caveat: ecofeminism is not compatible with all feminisms and all environmentalisms. For a discussion of this point, see my article, "Feminism and Ecology: Making Connections." What it *is* compatible with is the minimal condition characterization of feminism as a movement to end sexism that is accepted by all contemporary feminisms (liberal, traditional Marxist, radical, socialist, Blacks and non-Western).

14. See, e.g., Gray, *Green Paradise Lost*; Griffin, *Women and Nature*; Merchant, *The Death of Nature*; and Ruether, *New Woman/New Earth*.

15. Suppose, as I think is the case, that a necessary condition for the existence of a moral relationship is that at least one party to the relationship is a moral being (leaving open for our purposes what counts as a "moral being"). If this is so, then the Mona Lisa cannot properly be said to have or stand in a moral relationship with the wall on which she hangs, and a wolf cannot have or properly be said to have or stand in a moral relationship with a moose. Such a necessary-condition account leaves open the question whether *both* parties to the relationship must be moral beings. My point here is simply that however one resolves *that* question, recognition of the relationships themselves as a locus of value is a recognition of a source of value that is different from and not reducible to the values of the "moral beings" in those relationships.

16. It is interesting to note that the image of being friends with the Earth is one which cytogeneticist Barbara McClintock uses when she describes the importance

of having "a feeling for the organism," "listening to the material [in this case the corn plant]," in one's work as a scientist. See Evelyn Fox Keller, "Women, Science, and Popular Mythology," in *Machina Ex Dea: Feminist Perspectives on Technology,* Joan Rothschild (Ed.) (New York: Pergamon Press, 1983), and Evelyn Fox Keller, *A Feeling for the Organism: The Life and Work of Barbara McClintock* (San Francisco: W.H. Freeman, 1983).

17. Cheney, "Eco-Feminism and Deep Ecology," 144.

18. Marilyn Frye, "In and Out of Harm's Way: Arrogance and Love," *The Politics of Reality* (Trumansburg, NY: Crossing Press, 1983), pp. 66–72.

19. Ibid., pp. 75–76.

20. Maria Lugones, "Playfulness," p. 3.

21. Cheney makes a similar point in "Eco-Feminism and Deep Ecology," p. 140.

22. Ibid., p. 138.

23. This account of a feminist ethic draws on my paper, "Toward an Ecofeminist Ethic."

24. Marilyn Frye makes this point in her illuminating paper, "The Possibility of Feminist Theory," read at the American Philosophical Association Central Division Meetings in Chicago, 29 April–1 May 1986. My discussion of feminist theory is inspired largely by that paper and by Kathryn Addelson's paper "Moral Revolution," in *Women and Values: Reading in Recent Feminist Philosophy,* Marilyn Pearsall (Ed.) (Belmont, CA: Wadsworth Publishing Co., 1986) pp. 291–309.

25. Notice that the standard of inclusiveness does not exclude the voices of men. It is just that those voices must cohere with the voices of women.

26. For a more in-depth discussion of the notions of impartiality and bias, see my paper, "Critical Thinking and Feminism," *Informal Logic* 10, no. 1 (Winter 1988): 31–44.

27. The burgeoning literature on these values is noteworthy. See, e.g., Carol Gilligan, *In a Different Voice: Psychological Theories and Women's Development* (Cambridge, MA: Harvard University Press, 1982); *Mapping the Moral Domain: A Contribution of Women's Thinking to Psychological Theory and Education,* Carol Gilligan, Janie Victoria Ward, and Jill McLean Taylor (Eds.), with Betty Bardige (Cambridge, MA: Harvard University Press, 1988); Nel Noddings, *Caring: A Feminine Approach to Ethics and Moral Education* (Berkeley: University of California Press, 1984); Maria Lugones and Elizabeth V. Spelman, "Have We Got a Theory for You! Feminist Theory, Cultural Imperialism, and the Women's Voice," *Women's Studies International Forum* 6 (1983): 573–581; Maria Lugones, "Playfulness"; Annette C. Baier, "What Do Women Want in a Moral Theory?" *Nous* 19 (1985): 53–63.

28. Jim Cheney would claim that our fundamental relationships to one another as moral agents are not as moral agents to rights holders, and that whatever rights a person properly may be said to have are relationally defined rights, not rights possessed by atomistic individuals conceived as Robinson Crusoes who do not exist essentially in relation to others. On this view, even rights talk itself is properly conceived as growing out of a relational ethic, not vice versa.

29. Alison Jaggar, *Feminist Politics and Human Nature* (Totowa, NJ: Rowman & Allanheld, 1980), pp. 42–44.

30. Henry West has pointed out that the expression "defining relations" is ambiguous. According to West, "the 'defining' as Cheney uses it is an adjective, not a principle—it is not that ethics defines relationships; it is that ethics grows out of conceiving of the relationships that one is in as defining what the individual is."

31. For example, in relationships involving contracts or promises, those relationships might be correctly described as that of moral agent to rights holders. In relationships involving mere property, those relationships might be correctly described as that of moral agent to objects having only instrumental value, "relationships of instrumentality." In comments on an earlier draft of this paper, West suggested that possessive individualism, for instance, might be recast in such a way that an individual is defined by his or her property relationships.

32. Cheney, "Eco-Feminism and Deep Ecology," p. 144.

33. One might object that such permission for change opens the door for environmental exploitation. This is not the case. An ecofeminist ethic is anti-naturist. Hence, the unjust domination and exploitation of nature is a "boundary condition" of the ethic; no such actions are sanctioned or justified on ecofeminist grounds. What it *does* leave open is some leeway about what counts as domination and exploitation. This, I think, is a strength of the ethic, not a weakness, since it acknowledges that *that* issue cannot be resolved in any practical way in the abstract, independent of a historical and social context.

34. Nathan Hare, "Black Ecology," in *Environmental Ethics,* K. S. Shrader-Frechette (Ed.) (Pacific Grove, CA: Boxwood Press, 1981), pp. 229–236.

35. For an ecofeminist discussion of the Chipko movement, see my "Toward an Ecofeminist Ethic," and Shiva's *Staying Alive.*

36. See Cheney, "Eco-Feminism and Deep Ecology," p. 122.

37. I offer the same sort of reply to critics of ecofeminism such as Warwick Fox who suggest that for the sort of ecofeminism I defend, the word *feminist* does not add anything significant to environmental ethics and, consequently, that an ecofeminist like myself might as well call herself a deep ecologist. He asks: "Why doesn't she just call it [i.e., Warren's vision of a transformative

feminism] deep ecology? Why specifically attach the label *feminist* to it . . . ?" (Warwick Fox, "The Deep Ecology–Ecofeminism Debate and Its Parallels," *Environmental Ethics* 11 no. 1 [1989]: 14, n. 22). Whatever the important similarities between deep ecology and ecofeminism (or, specifically, my version of ecofeminism)—and, indeed, there are many—it is precisely my point here that the word *feminist* does add something significant to the conception of environmental ethics, and that any environmental ethic (including deep ecology) that fails to make explicit the different kinds of interconnections among the domination of nature and the domination of women will be, from a feminist (and ecofeminist) perspective such as mine, inadequate.

Deep Ecology

Bill Devall and George Sessions

Study Questions

1. How do the authors describe mainstream environmentalism?

2. How do Devall and Sessions describe the alternative presented by deep ecology?

3. What do they mean by the phrase "ecological consciousness"?

4. How is this exemplified in Taoism, according to the authors?

5. What was the origin of the phrase "deep ecology" and what are the two terms in it supposed to signify?

6. How do the authors contrast the view of deep ecology with what they describe as the dominant worldview?

7. Describe the two ultimate norms or intuitions that they believe characterize deep ecology.

8. Explain briefly each of the eight basic principles of the platform of the deep ecology movement.

I. Reform Environmentalism

Environmentalism is frequently seen as the attempt to work only within the confines of conventional political processes of industrialized nations to alleviate or mitigate some of the worst forms of air and

water pollution, destruction of indigenous wildlife, and some of the most short-sighted development schemes.

One scenario for the environmental movement is to continue with attempts at reforming some natural resource policies. For example, ecoactivists can appeal administrative decisions to lease massive areas of public domain lands in the United States for mineral development, or oil and gas development. They can comment on draft Environmental Impact Reports; appeal to politicians to protect the scenic values of the nation; and call attention to the massive problems of toxic wastes, air and water pollution, and soil erosion. These political and educational activities call to the need for healthy ecosystems.

However, environmentalism in this scenario tends to be very technical and oriented only to short-term public policy issues of resource allocation. Attempts are made to reform only some of the worst land use practices without challenging, questioning or changing the basic assumptions of economic growth and development. Environmentalists who follow this scenario will easily be labeled as "just another special issues group." In order to play the game of politics, they will be required to compromise on every piece of legislation in which they are interested.[1]

Generally, this business-as-usual scenario builds on legislative achievements such as the National Environmental Policy Act (NEPA) and the Endangered Species Act in the United States, and reform legislation on pollution and other environmental issues enacted in most industrialized nations.

Bill Devall and George Sessions, *Deep Ecology, Living as If Nature Mattered* (Salt Lake City: Peregrine, 1985), pp. 2, 7–11, 65–73. Reprinted with permission.

This work is valuable. The building of proposed dams, for example, can be stopped by using economic arguments to show their economic liabilities. However, this approach has certain costs. One perceptive critic of this approach, Peter Berg, directs an organization seeking decentralist, local approaches to environmental problems. He says this approach "is like running a battlefield aid station in a war against a killing machine that operates beyond reach and that shifts its ground after each seeming defeat."[2] Reformist activists often feel trapped in the very political system they criticize. If they don't use the language of resource economists—language which converts ecology into "input-output models," forests into "commodity production systems," and which uses the metaphor of human economy in referring to Nature—then they are labeled as sentimental, irrational, or unrealistic.

Murray Bookchin, author of *The Ecology of Freedom* (1982) and *Post-Scarcity Anarchism* (1970), says the choice is clear. The environmental/ecology movement can "become institutionalized as an appendage of the very system whose structure and methods it professes to oppose," or it can follow the minority tradition. The minority tradition focuses on personal growth within a small community and selects a path to cultivating ecological consciousness while protecting the ecological integrity of the place.[3]

II. Deep Ecology and Cultivating Ecological Consciousness

In contrast to the preceding scenarios, deep ecology presents a powerful alternative.

Deep ecology is emerging as a way of developing a new balance and harmony between individuals, communities and all of Nature. It can potentially satisfy our deepest yearnings: faith and trust in our most basic intuitions; courage to take direct action; joyous confidence to dance with the sensuous harmonies discovered through spontaneous, playful intercourse with the rhythms of our bodies, the rhythms of flowing water, changes in the weather and seasons, and the overall processes of life on Earth. We invite you to explore the vision that deep ecology offers.

The deep ecology movement involves working on ourselves, what poet-philosopher Gary Snyder calls "the real work," the work of really looking at ourselves, of becoming more real.

This is the work we call cultivating ecological consciousness. This process involves becoming more aware of the actuality of rocks, wolves, trees, and rivers—the cultivation of the insight that everything is connected. Cultivating ecological consciousness is a process of learning to appreciate silence and solitude and rediscovering how to listen. It is learning how to be more receptive, trusting, holistic in perception, and is grounded in a vision of nonexploitive science and technology.

This process involves being honest with ourselves and seeking clarity in our intuitions, then acting from clear principles. It results in taking charge of our actions, taking responsibility, practicing self-discipline and working honestly within our community. It is simple but not easy work. Henry David Thoreau, nineteenth-century naturalist and writer, admonishes us, "Let your life be a friction against the machine."

Cultivating ecological consciousness is correlated with the cultivation of conscience. Cultural historian Theodore Roszak suggests in *Person/Planet* (1978), "Conscience and consciousness, how instructive the overlapping similarity of those two words is. From the new consciousness we are gaining of ourselves as persons perhaps we will yet create a new conscience, one whose ethical sensitivity is at least tuned to a significant good, a significant evil."[4]

We believe that humans have a vital need to cultivate ecological consciousness and that this need is related to the needs of the planet. At the same time, humans need direct contact with untrammeled wilderness, places undomesticated for narrow human purposes.

Many people sense the needs of the planet and the need for wilderness preservation. But they often feel depressed or angry, impotent and under stress. They feel they must rely on "the other guy," the "experts." Even in the environmental movement, many people feel that only the professional staff of these organizations can make decisions because they are experts on some technical scientific matters or experts on the complex, convoluted political process. But we need not be technical experts in order to cultivate ecological consciousness. Cultivating ecological consciousness, as Thoreau said, requires that "we front up to the facts and determine to live our lives deliberately, or not at all." We believe that people can clarify their own intuitions, and act from deep principles.

Deep ecology is a process of ever-deeper questioning of ourselves, the assumptions of the dominant worldview in our culture, and the meaning and truth of our reality. We cannot change consciousness by only listening to others, we must involve ourselves. We must take direct action.

Organizations which work only in a conventional way on political issues and only in conventional politics will more or less unavoidably neglect the deepest philosophical-spiritual issues. But late industrial society is at a turning point, and the social and personal changes which are necessary may be aided by the flow of history.

One hopeful political movement with deep ecology as a base is the West German Green political party. They have as their slogan, "We are neither left nor right, we are in front." Green politics in West Germany, and to some extent in Great Britain, Belgium and Australia in the 1980s, goes beyond the conventional, liberal definition of a party, combining personal work (that is, work on clarifying one's own character) and political activism. In West Germany, especially, the Green party has sought a coalition with antinuclear weapons protesters, feminists, human rights advocates and environmentalists concerned with acid rain and other pollution in Europe.[5] Ecology is the first pillar of the German Greens' platform.

In Australia, the Greens are the most important political movement in the nation. In national and state elections in the early 1980s they were a deciding factor in electing Labor Party governments dedicated to some of the planks of the Green platform, including preserving wilderness national parks and rain forests.

The Greens present a promising political strategy because they encourage the cultivation of personal ecological consciousness as well as address issues of public policy. If the Greens propagate the biocentric perspective—the inherent worth of other species besides humans—then they can help change the current view which says we should use Nature only to serve narrow human interests. . . .

Alan Watts, who worked diligently to bring Eastern traditions to Western minds, used a very ancient image for this process, "invitation to the dance," and suggests that "the ways of liberation make it very clear that life is not going anywhere, because it is already *there*. In other words, it is playing, and those who do not play with it, have simply missed the point."[6]

Watts draws upon the Taoist sages, Sufi stories, Zen, and the psychology of Carl Jung to demonstrate the process of spontaneous understanding. It is recognized, however, that to say "you must be sponta-

neous" is to continue the massive double-bind that grips consciousness in the modern ethos.

The trick is to trick ourselves into reenchantment. As Watts says, "In the life of spontaneity, human consciousness shifts from the attitude of strained, willful attention to *koan,* the attitude of open attention or contemplation." This is a key element in developing ecological consciousness. This attitude forms the basis of a more "feminine" and receptive approach to love, an attitude which for that very reason is more considerate of women.[7]

In some Eastern traditions, the student is presented with a *koan,* a simple story or statement which may sound paradoxical or nonsensical on the surface but as the student turns and turns it in his or her mind, authentic understanding emerges. This direct action of turning and turning, seeing from different perspectives and from different depths, is required for the cultivation of consciousness. The *koan*-like phrase for deep ecology, suggested by prominent Norwegian philosopher Arne Naess, is: "simple in means, rich in ends."

Cultivating ecological consciousness based on this phrase requires the interior work of which we have been speaking, but also a radically different tempo of external actions, at least radically different from that experienced by millions and millions of people living "life in the fast lane" in contemporary metropolises. As Theodore Roszak concludes, "Things move slower; they stabilize at a simpler level. But none of this is experienced as a loss or a sacrifice. Instead, it is seen as a liberation from waste and busywork, from excessive appetite and anxious competition that allows one to get on with the essential business of life, which is to work out one's salvation with diligence."[8]

> But I believe nevertheless that you will not have to remain without a solution if you will hold to objects that are similar to those from which my eyes now draw refreshment. If you will cling to Nature, to the simple in Nature, to the little things that hardly anyone sees, and that can so unexpectedly become big and beyond measuring; if you have this love of inconsiderable things and seek quite simply, as one who serves, to win the confidence of what seems poor: then everything will become easier, more coherent and somehow more conciliatory for you, not in your intellect, perhaps, which lags marveling behind, but in your inmost consciousness, waking and cognizance. . . . Be patient toward all that is unsolved in your heart and to try to love the *questions themselves* like locked rooms and like books that are

written in a very foreign tongue. Do not now seek the answers, which cannot be given you because you would not be able to live them. And the point is, to live everything. *Live* the questions now. Perhaps you will then gradually, without noticing it, live along some distant day into the answer.

    —Ranier Maria Rilke, *Letters to a Young Poet* (1963)

Quiet people, those working on the "real work," quite literally turn down the volume of noise in their lives. Gary Snyder suggests that, "The real work is what we really do. And what our lives are. And if we can live the work we have to do, knowing that we are real, and that the world is real, then it becomes right. And that's the real work: to make the world as real as it is and to find ourselves as real as we are within it."[9]

Engaging in this process, Arne Naess concludes, people ". . . will necessarily come to the conclusion that it is not lack of energy consumption that makes them unhappy."[10]

One metaphor for what we are talking about is found in the Eastern Taoist image, the *organic self*. Taoism tells us there is a way of unfolding which is inherent in all things. In the natural social order, people refrain from dominating others. Indeed, the ironic truth is that the more one attempts to control other people and control nonhuman Nature, the more disorder results, and the greater the degree of chaos. For the Taoist, spontaneity is not the opposite of order but identical with it because it flows from the unfolding of the inherent order. Life is not narrow, mean, brutish, and destructive. People do not engage in the seemingly inevitable conflict over scarce material goods. People have fewer desires and simple pleasures. In Taoism, the law is not required for justice; rather, the community of persons working for universal self-realization follows the flow of energy.[11]

> To study the Way is to study the self.
> To study the self is to forget the self.
> To forget the self is to be enlightened by all things.
> To be enlightened by all things is to remove the barriers between one's self and others.
> —Dogen

As with many other Eastern traditions, the Taoist way of life is based on compassion, respect, and love for all things. This compassion arises from self-love, but self as part of the larger *Self,* not egotistical self-love.

Deep Ecology

The term *deep ecology* was coined by Arne Naess in his 1973 article, "The Shallow and the Deep, Long-Range Ecology Movements."[12] Naess was attempting to describe the deeper, more spiritual approach to Nature exemplified in the writings of Aldo Leopold and Rachel Carson. He thought that this deeper approach resulted from a more sensitive openness to ourselves and nonhuman life around us. The essence of deep ecology is to keep asking more searching questions about human life, society, and Nature as in the Western philosophical tradition of Socrates. As examples of this deep questioning, Naess points out "that we ask why and how, where others do not. For instance ecology as a science does not ask what kind of a society would be the best for maintaining a particular ecosystem—that is considered a question for value theory, for politics, for ethics." Thus deep ecology goes beyond the so-called factual scientific level to the level of self and Earth wisdom.

Deep ecology goes beyond a limited piecemeal shallow approach to environmental problems and attempts to articulate a comprehensive religious and philosophical worldview. The foundations of deep ecology are the basic intuitions and experiencing of ourselves and Nature which comprise ecological consciousness. Certain outlooks on politics and public policy flow naturally from this consciousness. And in the context of this book, we discuss the minority tradition as the type of community most conducive both to cultivating ecological consciousness and to asking the basic questions of values and ethics addressed in these pages.

Many of these questions are perennial philosophical and religious questions faced by humans in all cultures over the ages. What does it mean to be a unique human individual? How can the individual self maintain and increase its uniqueness while also being an inseparable aspect of the whole system wherein there are no sharp breaks between self and the *other?* An ecological perspective, in this deeper sense, results in what Theodore Roszak calls "an awakening of wholes greater than the sum of their parts. In spirit, the discipline is contemplative and therapeutic."[13]

Ecological consciousness and deep ecology are in sharp contrast with the dominant worldview of technocratic-industrial societies which regards humans as isolated and fundamentally separate from the rest of Nature, as superior to, and in charge of, the rest of creation. But the view of humans as separate and superior to the rest of Nature is only part of larger cultural patterns. For thousands of years, Western culture has become increasingly obsessed with the idea of *dominance:* with dominance of humans over nonhuman Nature, masculine over the feminine, wealthy and powerful over the poor, with the dominance of the West over non-Western cultures. Deep ecological consciousness allows us to see through these erroneous and dangerous illusions.

For deep ecology, the study of our place in the Earth household includes the study of ourselves as part of the organic whole. Going beyond a narrowly materialist scientific understanding of reality, the spiritual and the material aspects of reality fuse together. While the leading intellectuals of the dominant worldview have tended to view religion as "just superstition," and have looked upon ancient spiritual practice and enlightenment, such as found in Zen Buddhism, as essentially subjective, the search for deep ecological consciousness is the search for a more objective consciousness and state of being through an active deep questioning and meditative process and way of life.

Many people have asked these deeper questions and cultivated ecological consciousness within the context of different spiritual traditions—Christianity, Taoism, Buddhism, and Native American rituals, for example. While differing greatly in other regards, many in these traditions agree with the basic principles of deep ecology.

Warwick Fox, an Australian philosopher, has succinctly expressed the central intuition of deep ecology: "It is the idea that we can make no firm ontological divide in the field of existence: That there is no bifurcation in reality between the human and the non-human realms . . . to the extent that we perceive boundaries, we fall short of deep ecological consciousness."[14]

From this most basic insight or characteristic of deep ecological consciousness, Arne Naess has developed two *ultimate norms* or intuitions which are themselves not derivable from other principles or intuitions. They are arrived at by the deep questioning process and reveal the importance of moving to the philosophical and religious level of wisdom. They cannot be validated, of course, by the methodology of modern science based on its usual mechanistic assumptions and its very narrow definition of data. These ultimate norms are *self-realization* and *biocentric equality.*

I. Self-Realization

In keeping with the spiritual traditions of many of the world's religions, the deep ecology norm of self-realization goes beyond the modern Western *self* which is defined as an isolated ego striving primarily for hedonistic gratification or for a narrow sense of individual salvation in this life or the next. This socially programmed sense of the narrow self or social self dislocates us, and leaves us prey to whatever fad or fashion is prevalent in our society or social reference group. We are thus robbed of beginning the search for our unique spiritual/biological personhood. Spiritual growth, or unfolding, begins when we cease to understand or see ourselves as isolated and narrow competing egos and begin to identify with other humans from our family and friends to, eventually, our species. But the deep ecology sense of self requires a further maturity and growth, an identification which goes beyond humanity to include the nonhuman world. We must see beyond our narrow contemporary cultural assumptions and values, and the conventional wisdom of our time and place, and this is best achieved by the meditative deep questioning process. Only in this way can we hope to attain full mature personhood and uniqueness.

A nurturing nondominating society can help in the "real work" of becoming a whole person. The "real work" can be summarized symbolically as the realization of "self-in-Self" where "Self" stands for organic wholeness. This process of the full unfolding of the self can also be summarized by the phrase, "No one is saved until we are all saved," where the phrase "one" includes not only me, an individual human, but all humans, whales, grizzly bears, whole rain forest ecosystems, mountains and rivers, the tiniest microbes in the soil, and so on.

II. Biocentric Equality

The intuition of biocentric equality is that all things in the biosphere have an equal right to live and blossom and to reach their own individual forms of unfolding and self-realization within the larger Self-realization. This basic intuition is that all organisms and entities in the ecosphere, as parts of the interrelated whole, are equal in intrinsic worth. Naess suggests that biocentric equality as an intuition is true in principle, although in the process of living, all species use each other as food, shelter, etc. Mutual predation is a biological fact of life, and many of the world's religions have struggled with the spiritual implications of this. Some animal liberationists who attempt to side-step this problem by advocating vegetarianism are forced to say that the entire plant kingdom including rain forests have no right to their own existence. This evasion flies in the face of the basic intuition of equality.[15] Aldo Leopold expressed this intuition when he said humans are "plain citizens" of the biotic community, not lord and master over all other species.

Biocentric equality is intimately related to the all-inclusive Self-realization in the sense that if we harm the rest of Nature then we are harming ourselves. There are no boundaries and everything is interrelated. But insofar as we perceive things as individual organisms or entities, the insight draws us to respect all human and nonhuman individuals in their own right as parts of the whole without feeling the need to set up hierarchies of species with humans at the top.

The practical implications of this intuition or norm suggest that we should live with minimum rather than maximum impact on other species and on the Earth in general. Thus we see another aspect of our guiding principle: "simple in means, rich in ends." Further practical implications of these norms are discussed at length in chapters seven and eight.

A fuller discussion of the biocentric norm as it unfolds itself in practice begins with the realization that we, as individual humans, and as communities of humans, have vital needs which go beyond such basics as food, water, and shelter to include love, play, creative expression, intimate relationships with a particular landscape (or Nature taken in its entirety) as well as intimate relationships with other humans, and the vital need for spiritual growth, for becoming a mature human being.

Our vital material needs are probably more simple than many realize. In technocratic-industrial societies there is overwhelming propaganda and advertising which encourages false needs and destructive desires designed to foster increased production and consumption of goods. Most of this actually diverts us from facing reality in an objective way and from beginning the "real work" of spiritual growth and maturity.

Many people who do not see themselves as supporters of deep ecology nevertheless recognize an overriding vital human need for a healthy and high-quality natural environment for humans, if not for all life, with minimum intrusion of toxic waste, nuclear radiation from human enterprises, minimum acid rain and smog, and enough free flowing wilderness so humans can get in touch with their sources, the natural rhythms and the flow of time and place.

Drawing from the minority tradition and from the wisdom of many who have offered the insight of interconnectedness, we recognize that deep ecologists can offer suggestions for gaining maturity and encouraging the processes of harmony with Nature, but that there is no grand solution which is guaranteed to save us from ourselves.

The ultimate norms of deep ecology suggest a view of the nature of reality and our place as an individual (many in the one) in the larger scheme of things. They cannot be fully grasped intellectually but are ultimately experiential. We encourage readers to consider our further discussion of the psychological, social and ecological implications of these norms in later chapters.

As a brief summary of our position thus far, Figure 1 summarizes the contrast between the dominant worldview and deep ecology.

III. Basic Principles of Deep Ecology

In April 1984, during the advent of spring and John Muir's birthday, George Sessions and Arne Naess summarized fifteen years of thinking on the principles of deep ecology while camping in Death Valley, California. In this great and special place, they articulated these principles in a literal, somewhat neutral way, hoping that they would be understood and accepted by persons coming from different philosophical and religious positions.

Readers are encouraged to elaborate their own versions of deep ecology, clarify key concepts and think through the consequences of acting from these principles.

Basic Principles

1. The well-being and flourishing of human and nonhuman Life on Earth have value in themselves

Dominant Worldview	Deep Ecology
■ Dominance over Nature	■ Harmony with Nature
■ Natural environment as resource for humans	■ All nature has intrinsic worth/biospecies equality
■ Material/economic growth for growing human population	■ Elegantly simple material needs (material goals serving the larger goal of self-realization)
■ Belief in ample resource reserves	■ Earth "supplies" limited
■ High technological progress and solutions	■ Appropriate technology; nondominating science
■ Consumerism	■ Doing with enough/recycling
■ National/centralized community	■ Minority tradition/bioregion

Figure 1

(synonyms: intrinsic value, inherent value). These values are independent of the usefulness of the nonhuman world for human purposes.

2. Richness and diversity of life forms contribute to the realization of these values and are also values in themselves.

3. Humans have no right to reduce this richness and diversity except to satisfy *vital* needs.

4. The flourishing of human life and cultures is compatible with a substantial decrease of the human population. The flourishing of nonhuman life requires such a decrease.

5. Present human interference with the nonhuman world is excessive, and the situation is rapidly worsening.

6. Policies must therefore be changed. These policies affect basic economic, technological, and ideological structures. The resulting state of affairs will be deeply different from the present.

7. The ideological change is mainly that of appreciating *life quality* (dwelling in situations of inherent value) rather than adhering to an increasingly higher standard of living. There will be a profound awareness of the difference between big and great.

8. Those who subscribe to the foregoing points have an obligation directly or indirectly to try to implement the necessary changes.

Naess and Sessions Provide Comments on the Basic Principles

RE (1). This formulation refers to the biosphere, or more accurately, to the ecosphere as a whole. This includes individuals, species, populations, habitat, as well as human and nonhuman cultures. From our current knowledge of all-pervasive intimate relationships, this implies a fundamental deep concern and respect. Ecological processes of the planet should, on the whole, remain intact. "The world environment should remain 'natural'" (Gary Snyder).

The term "life" is used here in a more comprehensive nontechnical way to refer also to what biologists classify as "nonliving"; rivers (watersheds), landscapes, ecosystems. For supporters of deep ecology, slogans such as "Let the river live" illustrate this broader usage so common in most cultures.

Inherent value as used in (1) is common in deep ecology literature ("The presence of inherent value in a natural object is independent of any awareness, interest, or appreciation of it by a conscious being.").[16]

RE (2). More technically, this is a formulation concerning diversity and complexity. From an ecological standpoint, complexity and symbiosis are conditions for maximizing diversity. So-called simple, lower, or primitive species of plants and animals contribute essentially to the richness and diversity of life. They have value in themselves and are not merely steps toward the so-called higher or rational life forms. The second principle presupposes that life itself, as a process over evolutionary time, implies an increase of diversity and richness. The refusal to acknowledge that some life forms have greater or lesser intrinsic value than others (see points 1 and 2) runs counter to the formulations of some ecological philosophers and New Age writers.

Complexity, as referred to here, is different from complication. Urban life may be more complicated than life in a natural setting without being more complex in the sense of multifaceted quality.

RE (3). The term "vital need" is left deliberately vague to allow for considerable latitude in judgment. Differences in climate and related factors, together with differences in the structures of societies as they now exist, need to be considered (for some Eskimos, snowmobiles are necessary today to satisfy vital needs).

People in the materially richest countries cannot be expected to reduce their excessive interference with the nonhuman world to a moderate level overnight. The stabilization and reduction of the human population will take time. Interim strategies need to be developed. But this in no way excuses the present complacency—the extreme seriousness of our current situation must first be realized. But the longer we wait the more drastic will be the measures needed. Until deep changes are made, substantial decreases in richness and diversity are liable to occur: the rate of extinction of species will be ten to one hundred times greater than any other period of earth history.

RE (4). The United Nations Fund for Population Activities in their State of World Population Report (1984) said that high human population growth rates (over 2.0 percent annum) in many developing countries "were diminishing the quality of life for many millions of people." During the decade 1974–1984, the world population grew by nearly 800 million—more than the size of India. "And we will be adding about one Bangladesh (population 93 million) per annum between now and the year 2000."

The report noted that "The growth rate of the human population has declined for the first time in human history. But at the same time, the number of people being added to the human population is bigger than at any time in history because the population base is larger."

Most of the nations in the developing world (including India and China) have as their official government policy the goal of reducing the rate of human population increase, but there are debates over the types of measures to take (contraception, abortion, etc.) consistent with human rights and feasibility.

The report concludes that if all governments set specific population targets as public policy to help alleviate poverty and advance the quality of life, the current situation could be improved.

As many ecologists have pointed out, it is also absolutely crucial to curb population growth in the so-called developed (i.e., overdeveloped) industrial societies. Given the tremendous rate of consumption and waste production of individuals in these societies, they represent a much greater threat and impact on the biosphere per capita than individuals in Second and Third World countries.

RE (5). This formulation is mild. For a realistic assessment of the situation, see the unabbreviated version of the I.U.C.N.'s *World Conservation Strategy*. There are other works to be highly recommended, such as Gerald Barney's *Global 2000 Report to the President of the United States*.

The slogan of "noninterference" does not imply that humans should not modify some ecosystems as do other species. Humans have modified the earth and will probably continue to do so. At issue is the nature and extent of such interference.

The fight to preserve and extend areas of wilderness or near-wilderness should continue and should focus on the general ecological functions of these areas (one such function: large wilderness areas are required in the biosphere to allow for continued evolutionary speciation of animals and plants). Most present designated wilderness areas and game preserves are not large enough to allow for such speciation.

RE (6). Economic growth as conceived and implemented today by the industrial states is incompatible with (1)–(5). There is only a faint resemblance between ideal sustainable forms of economic growth and present policies of the industrial societies. And "sustainable" still means "sustainable in relation to humans."

Present ideology tends to value things because they are scarce and because they have a commodity value. There is prestige in vast consumption and waste (to mention only several relevant factors).

Whereas "self-determination," "local community," and "think globally, act locally," will remain key terms in the ecology of human societies, nevertheless the implementation of deep changes requires increasingly global action—action across borders.

Governments in Third World countries (with the exception of Costa Rica and a few others) are uninterested in deep ecological issues. When the governments of industrial societies try to promote ecological measures through Third World governments, practically nothing is accomplished (e.g., with problems of desertification). Given this situation, support for global action through nongovernmental international organizations becomes increasingly important. Many of these organizations are able to act globally "from grassroots to grassroots," thus avoiding negative governmental interference.

Cultural diversity today requires advanced technology, that is, techniques that advance the basic goals of each culture. So-called soft, intermediate, and alternative technologies are steps in this direction.

RE (7). Some economists criticize the term "quality of life" because it is supposed to be vague. But on closer inspection, what they consider to be vague is actually the nonquantitative nature of the term. One cannot quantify adequately what is important for the quality of life as discussed here, and there is no need to do so.

RE (8). There is ample room for different opinions about priorities: what should be done first, what next? What is most urgent? What is clearly necessary as opposed to what is highly desirable but not absolutely pressing?

Notes

1. The most informative recent book on reformist environmentalism in the context of British society is Philip Lowe and Jane Goyder's *Environmental Groups in Politics* (London: George Allen, 1983). Sociological explanations of the environmental movement in North America are found in Craig R. Humphrey and Frederick R. Butell's *Environment, Energy and Society* (Belmont, CA: Wadsworth, 1983); Allan Schnaiberg's *The Environment: From Surplus to Scarcity* (New York: Oxford, 1980); Lester Milbrath's *Environmentalists* (Albany: State University of New York Press, 1984); "Sociology of the Environment," *Sociological Inquiry* 53 (Spring 1983); Jonathon Porritt, *Green: The Politics of Ecology Explained* (New York: Basil Blackwell, 1985).

2. Peter Berg, editorial, *Raise the Stakes* (Fall 1983).

3. Murray Bookchin, "Open Letter to the Ecology Movement," *Rain* (April 1980), as well as other publications.

4. Theodore Roszak, *Person/Planet* (Garden City, NY: Doubleday, 1978), p. 99.

5. Fritjof Capra and Charlene Spretnak, *Green Politics* (New York: E.P. Dutton, 1984).

6. Alan Watts, *Psychotherapy East and West* (New York: Vintage, 1975), p. 184.

7. ———. *Nature, Man and Woman* (New York: Vintage, 1970), p. 178.

8. Roszak, p. 296.

9. Gary Snyder, *The Real Work* (New York: New Directions, 1980), p. 81.

10. Stephen Bodian, "Simple in Means, Rich in Ends: A Conversation with Arne Naess," *Ten Directions* (California: Institute for Transcultural Studies, Zen Center of Los Angeles, Summer/Fall 1982).

11. Po-Keung Ip, "Taosim and the Foundations of Environmental Ethics," *Environmental Ethics* 5 (Winter 1983), pp. 335–344.

12. Arne Naess, "The Shall and The Deep, Long-Range Ecology Movements: A Summary," *Inquiry* 16 (Oslo, 1973), pp. 95–100.

13. Theodore Roszak, *Where the Wasteland Ends* (New York: Anchor, 1972).

14. Warwick Fox, "Deep Ecology: A New Philosophy of Our Time?" *The Ecologist*, v. 14, 5–6, 1984, pp. 194–200. Arne Naess replies, "Intuition, Intrinsic Value and Deep Ecology," *The Ecologist*, v. 14, 5–6, 1984, pp. 201–204.

15. Tom Regan, *The Case for Animal Rights* (New York: Random House, 1983). For excellent critiques of the animal rights movement, see John Rodman, "The Liberation of Nature?" *Inquiry* 20 (Oslo, 1977). J. Baird Callicott, "Animal Liberation," *Environmental Ethics* 2, 4 (1980); see also John Rodman, "Four Forms of Ecological Consciousness Reconsidered" in T. Attig and D. Scherer (Eds.), *Ethics and the Environment* (Englewood Cliffs, NJ: Prentice-Hall, 1983).

16. Tom Regan, "The Nature and Possibility of an Environmental Ethic," *Environmental Ethics* 3 (1981), pp. 19–34.

Review Exercises

1. What is meant by the term *environment?*

2. Why is the notion of *value* problematic?

3. What is the difference between intrinsic, instrumental, and prima facie value? Give an example of each.

4. What is anthropocentrism? How is it different from ecocentrism?

5. How do cost-benefit analyses function in environmental arguments? Give an example of an environmental problem today and how a cost-benefit analysis would be used to analyze it.

6. Describe two different types of ecocentrism.

7. What is Aldo Leopold's basic principle for determining what is right and wrong in environmental matters?

8. What is deep ecology? According to this view, what are the root causes of our environmental problems?

9. Summarize the different ecofeminist views described in this chapter.

Discussion Cases

1. *The Greenhouse Effect.* Scientists disagree about the greenhouse effect. A minority believes that there is actually no warming trend occurring due to the release into the atmosphere of greenhouse gases. Others point out that there have been periods of warming and cooling throughout the history of the planet. Several bills are pending before Congress that will restrict the amount of greenhouse gases that may be released into the atmosphere. This will affect car manufacturers and coal-burning manufacturing plants, makers of aerosol sprays, cleaning solvents, and refrigerators.

As a member of Congress, would you vote for or against the bills? Why?

2. *Preserving the Trees.* XYZ Timber Company has been logging forests in the Northwest for decades. It has done moderately well in replanting where trees have been cut. However, the company has cut in areas where there are trees that are hundreds of years old. Now it plans to build roads into a similar area of the forest so as to cut down similar groups of trees. An environmental group, "Trees First," is determined to prevent this. Its members have blocked the roads that have been put in by the timber company. And they have also engaged in the practice known as "tree-spiking." In this practice, iron spikes are driven into trees. Loggers are outraged, for this makes cutting in areas where trees are spiked extremely dangerous to them. When their saws hit such a spike, they become uncontrollable, and in some cases loggers have been seriously injured. Forest rangers have been marking trees found to be spiked and noted that in some cases the spikes are in so far that they are not visible. They will be grown over and thus be an unknown danger for years to come. People from Trees First insist that this is the only to prevent short-sighted destruction of the forests.

Who is right? Why?

3. *Asphalt Yard:* Bill Homeowner has grown weary of keeping the vegetation on his property under control. Thus, he decides to simply pave over the whole of it.

Even if Bill had a legal right to do this to his property, would there be anything ethically objectionable about it? Why or why not?

Selected Bibliography

Armstrong, Susan J., and Richard G. Botzler (Eds.). *Environmental Ethics.* New York: McGraw-Hill, 1993.

Attfield, Robin, and Andrew Belsey (Eds.). *Philosophy and the Natural Environment.* New York: Cambridge University Press, 1994.

Bigwood, Carol. *Earth Muse* (Philadelphia: Temple University Press, 1993).

Blackstone, William (Ed.). *Philosophy and Environmental Crisis.* Athens: University of Georgia Press, 1974.

Bookchin, Murray. *The Philosophy of Social Ecology.* Montreal: Black Rose Books, 1990.

Callicott, J. Baird. *In Defense of the Land Ethic.* Albany: State University of New York Press, 1989.

Devall, Bill. *Simple in Means, Rich in Ends: Practicing Deep Ecology.* Layton, UT: Gibbs Smith, 1988.

Diamond, Irene, and Gloria Feman Orenstein (Eds.). *Reweaving the World.* San Francisco: Sierra Club Books, 1990.

Flader, Susan L. *Thinking Like a Mountain: Aldo Leopold and the Evolution of an Ecological Attitude Toward Deer, Wolves, and Forests.* Madison: University of Wisconsin Press, 1994.

Fox, Warwick. *Towards a Transpersonal Ecology.* Boston: Shambhala Press, 1990.

Fox-Keller, Evelyn. *Reflections on Gender and Science.* New Haven, CT: Yale University Press, 1985.

Gore, Albert. *Earth in the Balance.* New York: Houghton Mifflin, 1992.

Griffin, Susan. *Women and Nature: The Roaring Inside Her.* New York: Harper & Row, 1978.

Gruen, Lori, and Dale Jamieson (Eds.). *Reflecting on Nature: Readings in Environmental Philosophy.* New York: Oxford University Press, 1994.

Hargrove, Eugene. *Foundations of Environmental Ethics.* New York: Prentice-Hall, 1989.

Hill, John Lawrence. *The Case for Vegetarianism.* Lanham, MD: Rowman & Littlefield, 1995.

Leopold, Aldo. *Sand County Almanac.* New York: Oxford University Press, 1949.

Lovelock, James. *Gaia: A New Look at Life on Earth.* New York: Oxford University Press, 1981.

Marshall, Peter. *Nature's Web: Rethinking Our Place on Earth.* New York: Paragon House, 1995.

Merchant, Carolyn. *The Death of Nature: Women, Ecology, and the Scientific Revolution.* New York: Harper & Row, 1980.

Naess, Arne. *Ecology, Community, and Lifestyle.* David Rothenberg (Trans.). Cambridge, UK: Cambridge University Press, 1989.

Orlans, F. Barbara. *In the Name of Science: Issues in Responsible Animal Experimentation.* New York: Oxford University Press, 1993.

Passmore, John. *Man's Responsibility for Nature.* New York: Scribner's, 1974.

Piel, Jonathan (Ed.). *Energy for Planet Earth: Readings from Scientific American.* New York: Freeman, 1991.

Regan, Tom (Ed.). *Earthbound: New Introductory Essays in Environmental Ethics.* New York: Random House, 1984.

Reuther, Rosemary Radford. *New Woman/ New Earth.* New York: Seabury, 1975.

Rolston, Holmes, III. *Environmental Ethics: Duties to and Values in the Natural World.* Philadelphia: Temple University Press, 1988.

Sagoff, Mark. *The Economy of the Earth: Philosophy, Law, and the Environment.* Cambridge, UK: Cambridge University Press, 1988.

Shiva, Vandana, and Maria Miles. *Ecofeminism.* Atlantic Highlands, NJ: Zed Books, 1993.

Sikora, R. I., and Brian Barry (Eds.). *Obligations to Future Generations.* Philadelphia: Temple University Press, 1978.

Smith, Jane A., and Kenneth M. Boyd (Eds.). *Lives in the Balance: The Ethics of Using Animals in Biomedical Research.* New York: Oxford University Press, 1991.

Sterba, James P. (Ed.). *Earth Ethics: Environmental Ethics, Animal Rights, and Practical Applications.* Upper Saddle River, NJ: Prentice-Hall, 1995.

Stone, Christopher. *Do Trees Have Standing: Toward Legal Rights for Natural Objects.* Los Altos, CA: William Kaufmann, 1974.

———. *Earth and Other Ethics.* New York: Harper & Row, 1987.

Taylor, Paul. *Respect for Nature.* Princeton, NJ: Princeton University Press, 1986.

Thoreau, Henry David. "Maine Woods," in *The Writings of Henry David Thoreau.* Boston: Houghton Mifflin, 1894–95.

VanDeVeer, Donald, and Christine Pierce. *People, Penguins, and Plastic Trees.* Belmont, CA: Wadsworth, 1986.

Warren, Karen. *Ecological Feminism.* Boulder, CO: Westview, 1994.

● 15 ●

Animal Rights

Not long ago, astronauts aboard the space shuttle *Columbia* performed some unusual experiments. As part of their fourteen-day scientific mission, they used a "tiny guillotine" to decapitate six live rats and then performed various procedures on their bodies. They did not administer any anesthetic for the experiment. After the rats were dead, the scientists examined and dissected various organs, bones, and muscles of the rats as they appeared in space. When the shuttle returned to earth, NASA distributed tiny pieces of bone, muscle, brain tissue, and other body parts to scientists around the world. The purpose of the experiment was "to investigate countermeasures for the debilitating effects of weightlessness" according to one official. "Scientists hoped to discover how the rats changed with prolonged exposure to a lack of gravity." Among the problems astronauts have faced in space have been "severe cases of motion sickness and more subtle transformations that include anemia and a bone softening similar to osteoporosis." According to one scientist, the results of these studies were valuable because they might also be able to benefit the elderly and persons who were bedridden.[1]

Was this experiment ethically justifiable? Although we would like to do things to help our fellow humans, we also care about the proper treatment of animals. However, we are less sure about what this requires of us and why. We are uncertain because we are often unclear about our ultimate reasons for what we think we can rightly do to animals. We relate to and depend on our nonhuman counterparts in many ways. They are pets and provide some of us with companionship and comfort. Many people enjoy watching them in our zoos and circuses. Others find sport in the racing of animals or in the display of riding skills. Animals are used for work, for example, in herding sheep and cattle. Some people find pleasure and others economic interest or necessity in the hunting and trapping of nonhuman animals. Animals are sources of food (such as meat, fish, milk, eggs, and cheese) and clothing (leather, fur, and wool). Animals are used in experiments to test not only the safety and effectiveness of medical drugs and devices, but also the possible side effects of cosmetics. They provide us with medicinal aids such as hormones, blood-clotting factors, and treatments for diseases such as diabetes. They are also sources of wonderment because of their variety, beauty, and strength. However, nonhuman animals are also sentient creatures. They can feel pleasure and pain just as we do and can at times seem almost human in their perception and reactions to us. Thus, we can rightly ask whether we are justified in using them in all of the ways we do.

Sentience

In thinking about the ethical status of animals, we might look to the utilitarian Jeremy Bentham; he wrote that in order to know the ethical status of animals, we need not ask if they can speak, but only whether or not they can suffer.[2] Nonhuman animals are sentient just as we are. Besides feeling pleasure and pain, many higher animals probably also experience other types of emotions like fear and anger. Unlike Descartes (see the previous chapter), we do not think that animals are machines devoid of an inner sense or consciousness. Because of their sentience, we have laws that protect animals from cruelty. What counts as cruelty will be disputed. Whether caging certain animals, for example, is cruel is a matter about which many people will disagree.

People also disagree about the reasons why we ought not to be cruel to animals. Some believe that a major reason is the effects on those who are cruel. If one is cruel to a sentient animal, then will he or she not more likely be cruel to people as well? The effects on the character of the person who is cruel to animals will also be negative. Moreover, those who witness cruelty to animals will be affected by it. They will themselves feel bad at seeing an animal suffer. However, unless one believes that only human suffering can be bad, the reason most people would tend to give for the injunction to not be cruel to animals is because the suffering of the animals itself is bad for them. Whether or not something is cruel to an animal is the extent of the pain it causes it. Sometimes we speak of cruelty in terms of causing "unnecessary" pain. Not all pain is bad, even for us. It often tells us of some health problem that can be fixed. The badness of suffering may also be only prima facie bad. (See the discussion of this in the previous chapter.) The suffering may be worth it—that is, overcome by the good end to be achieved by it. Doing difficult things is sometimes painful, but we think it is sometimes worth the pain. In these cases, we experience not only the pain but also the benefit. In the case of animals, however, they would experience the pain of an experiment performed on them, for example, while we reap the benefit. Whether this is ever justified is a central question for those who are concerned with our treatment of animals. Although we address the issue of animal experimentation below, it is well to consider in the first place whether and why the paining of animals is in itself a bad thing. We will also have to acknowledge that animals have different capacities to feel pain. Those with more developed and complex nervous systems and brains will have more capacity to feel pain as well as pleasure of various sorts.

One further comment on the issue of pain and pleasure to animals is the following. In the wild it is a fact of life that animals feed on one another and in so doing cause pain. In the wild, predation is prevalent. Carnivores kill. The fawn is eaten by the cougar. Natural processes such as floods and volcanic eruptions also contribute to animal suffering and death in the wild. If animal suffering is so important, are we ethically obligated to lessen it in cases where we could do so, as in the many cases in the wild? For example, in 1986 the Hubbard Glacier in Alaska began to move and in a few weeks it had sealed off a particular fjord. Porpoises and harbor seals were trapped inside by the closure. Some people wanted to rescue the animals, while others held that this was a natural event that should be allowed to run its course.[3] We tend to think that we are generally more bound not to *cause pain* or harm than we are to relieve it. In special cases, admittedly, there may seem to be no difference where we are bound by some duty or relation *to relieve pain* or prevent the harm. A lifeguard may have an obligation to rescue a drowning swimmer that the ordinary bystander does not. A parent has more obligation to prevent harm to his or her child than a stranger does. In the case of nonhuman animals, would we say the same? Do we also feel constrained to prevent the pain and death to animals in the wild? In general, it would seem that while we may choose to do so out of sympathy, we may not be obligated to do so. At least the obligation to prevent the harm seems lesser in stringency than the obligation not to cause a similar harm. If we are less bound to relieve pain than not to cause it, we could not then argue that because we can allow the animals in the wild to die or suffer pain from natural processes, we may thus also cause a similar pain or harm to them. Furthermore, we may also be inclined to think that just because nature is cruel does not give *us* the right to be so.

Animal Rights

It is one thing to say that the suffering of a non-human animal, just as the suffering of us humans, is a *bad* thing in itself. It is another to say that we or the nonhuman animals have *a right* not to be caused to suffer or feel pain. To know what to say about the question of animal rights, we need to think a little about what a right is or what it means to have a right. A *right* (as opposed to something being right instead of wrong) is generally defined as a strong and *legitimate claim* that can be made by a claimant against someone. Thus, if I claim a right to freedom of speech, I am asserting my legitimate claim against anyone who would prevent me from speaking out. (See the further discussion of negative and positive rights in Chapter 12.) A person can claim a right to have or be given something as well as not to be prevented from doing something. I can claim the bicycle because it is mine. This would also mean that others have a duty not to take the bicycle from me. So also, if I have a right to health care, others may have a duty to provide it. Sometimes it is a contractual or other relation that is the reason why someone has a right to something. Thus, persons may come to have a right to care from a hospital because of a contractual relation they just have established, while a young child has a right to care from her parents because of the natural or legal relationship. Some of the rights we claim as *legal rights,* because they are claims that the law recognizes and enforces. However, we also hold that there are *moral rights*—in other

words, things we can rightly claim even if the law does nor give its support to the claim. (Recall the discussion of moral rights in Chapter 6.)

Just who can claim a moral right to something and on what grounds? One might think that in order to be the kind of being who can have rights one must *be able to claim* them. If this were so, then the cat who is left money in a will would not have a right to it. But then neither would the infant who inherits the money. We think we speak correctly when we say that the infant has a right to care from its parents even if the infant does not recognize this right and cannot claim it. *Future generations* do not even exist, and yet some believe that they have at least contingent rights (rights if they come to exist) that we not leave them a garbage-heap world depleted of natural resources.[4] Or one might think that only *moral agents* have rights. According to this view, only if one is a full member of the moral community with duties and responsibilities does one have rights. On the other hand it is not unreasonable to think that this is too stringent a requirement. Perhaps it is sufficient for one to be a *moral patient* in order to be the type of being who can have rights. In other words, if one is the kind of being to whom what we do matters morally in itself, then one is the kind of being who can have rights. If this is the case and if (as we considered in the previous chapter) some trees can be thought to be moral patients, then they would also be rightly said to have rights. If this does not seem to be correct, then what other reasons are possible for why a being might have rights?

We could argue that it is just because they can feel pain that sentient beings have a *right not to suffer,* or at least suffer needlessly. This would mean that others have a *duty* with regard to this claim. However, we may have duties not to cause pain needlessly to animals even if they had no right not to be treated in ways that cause them pain. We have many duties to do this or not do that which are not directly a matter of respecting anyone's rights. For example, I may have a duty not to destroy a famous building—but not because the building has a *right to exist.* Thus, to argue from the fact that we have duties to animals —for example, not to make them suffer needlessly—we cannot argue necessarily to the conclusion that they have rights. If we want to argue for this view, we would need to make a clearer connection between duties and rights or to show why some particular duties also imply rights. While the rights of someone seem to imply duties of others to protect or respect those rights, the existence of a duty to act in a certain way toward someone or something does not necessarily mean that they have a right to us acting in this way.

Some philosophers have pointed to the fact that animals have *interests* as a basis for asserting that they have rights. Having an interest in something is to have a consciousness of that thing and to want it. A being who has such a capacity is thus a being who can have rights, according to this position. Thus, Joel Feinberg says that it is because nonhuman animals have "conscious wishes, desires, and hopes; . . . urges and impulses" that they are the kind of beings who can have rights.[5] It is these psychological capacities that give these animals the status that makes them capable of having rights to certain treatment, according to this view. Tom Regan argues that the reason nonhuman animals have rights just as we do is because they are what he calls the "subject of a life."[6] The idea is similar to Feinberg's in that it is the fact that animals have an inner life, which includes conscious desires and wants, that is the basis for their status as rights possessors. Nonhuman animals differ among themselves in their capacity to have these various psychic experiences, and it probably parallels the development and complexity of their nervous system. A dog may be able to experience fear, but most probably the flea on its ear does not. This difference would be a problem for these writers only in practice where we would have to determine the character of a particular animal's inner life. The more serious challenge for them is to support the view itself that these inner psychic states are the basis for animal rights.

Peter Singer has made one of the stronger cases for the view that animals' interests are the basis for their having rights and rights that are equal to humans. (The article included in this chapter gives the essence of his argument.) Animals may have different interests than we do, but that does not mean that their interests are to be taken more lightly. According to Singer, not to respect the interests of animals is *speciesism*.[7] This is, he believes, an objectionable attitude similar to racism or sexism. It is objectionable because it treats animals badly simply because they are members of a different species and gives preference to members of our own species simply because we are human beings. But on what grounds is this objectionable? According to Singer, it is because of their ability to feel pleasure and pain that they are the type of being who can be said to have interests. Thus, they are different from plants in this regard. Plants have things that are *in their interest* even though they do not *have interests*. Because the interests of animals are similar to ours, they ought to be given equal weight, according to Singer. This does not mean that they have a right to whatever we have a right to. It would make no sense to say that a pig or horse has a right to vote, because it has no interest in voting. However, according to Singer, it would make sense to say that they had a right not to suffer or not to suffer needlessly or perhaps not to be used for no good purpose.

Others argue that animals need not be treated as equal to humans and that their interests ought not to be given equal weight with ours. It is because of the difference in species' *abilities* and *potentialities* that animals are a lesser form of being, according to this view. (See the article included here by Bonnie Steinbock for an example of this view.) This does not mean, however, that their interests ought to be disregarded. It may mean that peripheral interests of human being should not override more serious interests of animals. It is one thing to say that animals may be used if necessary for experiments that will save the lives of human beings and quite another to say that they may be harmed for the testing of cosmetics or even food or clothing that is not important for human life. Whether this would provide a sufficient basis for vegetarianism would then depend on the importance of animal protein, for example, and whether animals could be raised humanely for food.

Endangered Species

According to the World Wildlife Fund, "Without firing a shot, we may kill one-fifth of all species of life on this planet in the next [twenty] years."[8] We do this primarily by destroying their habitats. The *Global 2000 Report* asserts that within a few decades we will lose up to 20 percent of the species that now exist if nothing is done to change the current trend.[9] Other people contest these figures and projections. For example, they claim that these estimates are extreme and far exceed any known loss of species.[10] They also point out that species have been lost naturally without human intervention. However, throughout evolution the species that have been lost have been replaced at a higher rate than they have disappeared and thus we have the wondrous diversity that we now see. The rate of replacement now may not be able to keep up because the time scale of the loss has been speeded up.

Although we do need to get our facts straight about the loss of species, we also need to ask ourselves, why does the loss of species matter? In the first place, we should distinguish the position that holds that *individual animals* have rights or a particular moral status from that position that holds that it is *animal species* that we ought to protect, not individual animals. We generally believe that we have good *anthropocentric reasons* for preserving animal as well as plant species. We have aesthetic interests in the variety of different life forms. Bird watchers know the thrill of being able to observe some rare specimen. The unusual and the variety itself are objects of wonder. We also have nutritional and health interests in preserving species. They may now seem useless, but we do not know what unknown future threat may lead us to find in them the food or medicine we need. Loss of species leaves us genetically poorer and vulnerable. We

also have educational interests in preserving species. They tell us about ourselves, our history, and how our systems work or could work. "Destroying species is like tearing pages out of an unread book, written in a language humans hardly know how to read, about the place where they live."[11] If we destroy the mouse lemur, for example, we destroy the modern animal that is closest to the primates from which our own human line evolved.[12] From other species we can learn about the evolution of the senses of sight and hearing.

However, when we ask whether animal species have *moral standing* or *intrinsic value* or even *rights,* we run into matters that are puzzling. An animal species is not an individual. It is a collection and in itself cannot have the kind of interests or desires that may be the basis for rights or moral standing in individual animals. Thus, the philosopher Nicholas Rescher says, "moral obligation is . . . always interest-oriented. But only individuals can be said to have interests; one only has moral obligations to particular individuals or particular groups thereof."[13] If we can have duties to a group of individuals and a species as a group, we may have duties to species.

However, some people challenge the notion of a *species* as the *group* of the individuals that make it up. Consider just what we might mean by a "species." Is it not a *concept* constructed by us as a way of grouping and comparing organisms? Darwin had written, "I look at the term species, as one arbitrarily given for the sake of convenience to a set of individuals closely resembling each other."[14] If a species is but a term or *class* or *category,* then it does not actually exist. If it does not exist, then how could it be said to have rights? However, consider the following possibility suggested by Holmes Rolston. "A species is a living historical form (Latin *species*), propagated in individual organisms, that flows dynamically over generations."[15] As such, species are units of evolution that exist in time and in space. According to Rolston, "a species is a coherent, ongoing form of life expressed in organisms, encoded in gene flow, and shaped by the environment."[16] If we think of species in this way, it may be intelligible to speak of our having duties to an animal species. What it would amount to is our respecting "dynamic life forms preserved in historical lines, vital informational processes that persist generically over millions of years, overleaping short-lived individuals."[17] Our duties then would be to a dynamic continuum, a living environmental process, a "lifeline." According to this view, species are like stories and thus, "To kill a species is to shut down a unique story."[18] Or, finally, as Rolston writes, "A duty to a species is more like being responsible to a cause than to a person. It is commitment to an *idea* (Greek, *idea,* 'form,' sometimes a synonym for the Latin *species*)."[19] While his explanation of the nature of species and his arguments for the view that we have duties to them are often metaphorical ("story," "lifeline"), his reasoning is nevertheless intriguing. It also raises real metaphysical questions about the reality status of an idea. At the least, he gives us cause to rethink the view that only individuals are the kinds of beings toward whom we can have duties, and even possibly also the kinds of beings who can have rights.

Those who support animal rights as the rights of individual animals to certain treatment do not always agree in concrete cases with those who believe that it is species that ought to be protected and not individual animals. Suppose, for example, that a certain population of deer is threatened because their numbers have outstripped their food supply and they are starving to death. In some such cases, wildlife officials have sought to thin herds by selective killing or limited hunting. It is thought to be for the sake of the herd that some are killed. Animal rights activists are generally horrified at this policy and argue that ways should be found to save all of the deer. Those who seek to protect species of animals might not object if the practice of thinning will in fact serve that goal. We can see that these two groups might be at odds with one another.[20]

Animal Experimentation

We have considered various reasons that have been given for why we ought to treat animals in certain ways and not in others. One is their sentience. They can feel pleasure and pain. If pain is bad, then we ought not to cause it unless some greater good or duty pushes us to do so. Using this alone as a basis for treatment of animals would not show that we should never use animals for food or clothing or even as subjects of experimentation. In fact, some have pointed out that by growing animals for food and clothing, we allow animals that never would have been born to have a sentient life and feel pleasures. Unless the processes involve a greater amount of pain than pleasure, they argue, we have done them a favor by our animal farming practices. The same might be true of using animals in experimentation. If we actually grow certain animals to provide subjects for experimental laboratories, then they will have been given a life and experiences that they otherwise would not have had. However, there are several "ifs" in this scenario. One is whether the raising or use of the animals does in fact involve a great deal of pain, such that it would be better for them if they had not been born.

The practice of using nonhuman animals for research or experimental purposes has a history going back some 2,000 years. In the third century B.C. in Alexandria, Egypt, animals were used to study bodily function.[21] Aristotle cut open animals to learn about their structure and development. The Roman physician Galen used certain animals to show that veins do not carry air but blood. And in 1622, Harvey used animals to exhibit the circulation of the blood. They were used in 1846 to show the effects of anesthesia and in 1878 to demonstrate the relationship between bacteria and disease.[22] In the twentieth century, research with animals has made many advances in medicine possible, from cures for infectious diseases and development of immunization techniques and antibiotics to the development of surgical procedures. For example, in the development of a vaccine for polio, hundreds of primates were sacrificed. As a result of these experiments, polio is now almost eradicated. In 1952, there were 58,000 cases of this crippling disease, and in 1984 only four.[23] Now approximately 60 to 100 million experiments use nonhuman animals in the United States every year.[24]

Opposition to these practices dates from at least the nineteenth century and the antivivisectionists who campaigned against all use of animals in experimentation. Currently, the animal rights movement has gained prominence and strength. There seem to be three positions on the use of nonhuman animals in research. One opposes all use of animals. At the other end of the spectrum is the position that nonhuman animals have no rights or moral standing and thus can be used as we choose. In the middle is the belief that animals have some moral status and thus limits and restrictions should be placed on conducting research on these creatures. We have already discussed the problems regarding the basis for attributing moral status or rights to nonhuman animals, a matter that is crucial to determining what we want to say about animal experimentation. However, it is also useful to consider some of the other arguments used in this debate.

One issue is whether the use of animals was really *necessary* in order to effect the medical advances we have made. Without the use of animals, we would need to rely on research using only cell, tissue, and organ cultures or computer simulations. Those people who argue for the use of full animal subjects claim that these other methods are inadequate. They point out that the effects or reaction of a drug or procedure in the complex organism can be very different from that in these other contexts. If we went directly from these cell or computer studies to use in humans, we would put humans at risk. This was the case in the use of Thalidomide in the 1950s, a case in which insufficient animal studies resulted in deformation in many children born to women who used this drug to lessen nausea during their pregnancy. Whether using animals was necessary for various medical advances or whether other kinds

of studies could have been substituted is an empirical matter. We need to turn to the history of medicine to help us determine this.

A second concern about the use of nonhuman animals involves the extent to which *pain* is inflicted on these experimental subjects. "In 1984, the Department of Agriculture reported that 61% of research animals were not subjected to painful procedures and another 31% received anesthesia or pain-relieving drugs."[25] The rest did experience pain, but this was sometimes a necessary part of the experiment, such as in pain studies whose purpose is to find better ways to relieve pain in humans. Those who oppose animal research cite their own examples of cruelty to animal subjects. It is not just physical pain to which they point, but, for example, the psychological pain of being caged as in the case of primates. Because of their concern and political action, government restrictions and guidelines for animal research have been strengthened.[26]

Even those who support animal rights sometimes agree that the uses of animals in experimentation can be ethically supported if they "serve important and worthwhile purposes."[27] If they do, in fact, help us develop significant medical advances and if the information cannot be obtained in any other way, and if the experiments are conducted with as little pain caused to the animals as possible, then they may be justified. What we would want to say about other less vital purposes for using animals is still open. The use of nonhuman animals for food, entertainment, clothing, and the other purposes listed at the beginning of this chapter will probably need to be considered, each on its own terms. However, whatever we want to say about these practices, we will need to be as clear as we can about the other matters discussed in this chapter, matters about the nature and basis of moral standing and moral rights.

In the readings included in this chapter, Peter Singer and Bonnie Steinbock debate whether nonhuman animals ought to be treated equally in some way with humans.

Notes

1. As reported in the *New York Times* (Nov. 1, 1993), p. A7, and in the *San Francisco Examiner* (Oct. 31, 1993), p. A11.
2. Jeremy Bentham, *Introduction to the Principles of Morals and Legislation* (1789), Chapter 17.
3. Reported by Holmes Rolston III in *Environmental Ethics: Duties to and Values in the Natural World* (Philadelphia: Temple University Press, 1988), p. 50.
4. Joel Feinberg, "The Rights of Animals and Unborn Generations," *Philosophy and the Environmental Crisis,* William T. Blackstone (Ed.) (Athens: University of Georgia Press, 1974).
5. Ibid.
6. Tom Regan, *The Case for Animal Rights* (Berkeley: University of California Press, 1983).
7. Peter Singer, *Animal Liberation: A New Ethic for Our Treatment of Animals* (New York: Random House, 1975). Singer was not the first to use the term *speciesism*. R. Ryder also used it in his work *Victims of Science* (London: Davis-Poynter, 1975).
8. World Wildlife Fund paper, ca. 1992.
9. Council on Environmental Quality and the Department of State, *The Global 2000 Report to the President* (Washington, DC: U.S. Government Printing Office, 1980), vol. 1, p. 37; vol. 2, pp. 327–333.
10. See, for example, Julian L. Simon and Aaron Wildavsky, in "Facts, Not Species, are Periled," *New York Times* (May 13, 1993), p. A15.
11. Holmes Rolston III, op. cit., p. 129.
12. Ibid.
13. Nicholas Rescher, "Why Save Endangered Species?" in *Unpopular Essays on Technological Progress* (Pittsburgh: University of Pittsburgh Press, 1980), p. 83. A similar point is made by Tom Regan, *The Case for Animal Rights* (Berkeley: University of California Press, 1983), p. 359, and Joel Feinberg, "Rights of Animals and Unborn Generations," op. cit., pp. 55–56.
14. Charles Darwin, *The Origin of Species* (Baltimore, MD: Penguin, 1968), p. 108.
15. Holmes Rolston III, op. cit., p. 135.
16. Ibid., p. 136.
17. Ibid., p. 137.
18. Ibid., p. 145.
19. Ibid., p. 144.
20. In fact, one supporter of animal rights has referred to holistic views of the value of animals as "environmental fascism." Tom Regan, *The Case for Animal Rights* (Berkeley: University of California Press, 1983), pp. 361–362.
21. Jerod M. Loeb, William R. Hendee, Steven J. Smith, and M. Roy Schwarz, "Human vs. Animal Rights: In Defense of Animal Research," *Journal of the American Medical Association,* vol. 262, no. 19 (November 17, 1989), pp. 2716–2720.
22. Ibid.
23. Ibid.
24. This is a continuation of the estimate for 1980, as given by Peter Singer in "Animals and the Value of Life," in T. Regan (Ed.), *Matters of Life and Death: New Introductory Essays in Moral Philosophy,* 2nd ed. (New York: Random House, 1980, 1986), p. 339.
25. Ibid.
26. See, for example, the U.S. National Institute of Health's *Guide for the Care and Use of Laboratory Animals,* rev. ed. (1985).
27. Peter Singer, "Animals and the Value of Life," op. cit., p. 374.

All Animals Are Equal

Peter Singer

Study Questions

1. What argument against women's rights did Thomas Taylor give?
2. Why does Singer believe that the response to this argument, which stresses the similarity between women and men, does not go far enough?
3. Does equal consideration imply identical treatment? Why or why not, according to Singer?
4. Why does Singer believe it is wrong to tie equal treatment to the factual equality of those to be so treated? What principle does he propose instead?

5. What is *speciesism?* How does it parallel racism and sexism, according to Singer?

6. Why does Singer propose that all who can suffer, as Bentham said, ought to have their interests taken into consideration?

7. Why does Singer prefer the principle of equal consideration of interests to concerns about whether or not certain beings have rights?

8. Does Singer believe that there should be no experiments involving animals? Explain.

9. Why does Singer ask whether we would be willing to experiment on brain-damaged orphan children in order to save many other people? Does he believe that this would ever be justified?

Animal Liberation may sound more like a parody of other liberation movements than a serious objective. The idea of "The Rights of Animals" actually was once used to parody the case for women's rights. When Mary Wollstonecraft, a forerunner of today's feminists, published her *Vindication of the Rights of Woman* in 1792, her views were widely regarded as absurd, and before long an anonymous publication appeared entitled *A Vindication of the Rights of Brutes*. The author of this satirical work (now known to have been Thomas Taylor, a distinguished Cambridge philosopher) tried to refute Mary Wollstonecraft's arguments by showing that they could be carried one stage further. If the argument for equality was sound when applied to women, why should it not be applied to dogs, cats, and horses? The reasoning seemed to hold for these "brutes" too; yet to hold that brutes had rights was manifestly absurd. Therefore the reasoning by which this conclusion had been reached must be unsound, and if unsound when applied to brutes, it must also be unsound when applied to women, since the very same arguments had been used in each case.

In order to explain the basis of the case for the equality of animals, it will be helpful to start with an examination of the case for the equality of women. Let us assume that we wish to defend the case for women's rights against the attack by Thomas Taylor. How should we reply?

Peter Singer, "Animal Liberation," *New York Review,* 2nd edition 1990: 1–9, 36–37, 40, 81–83, 85–86. Reprinted with permission of the author.

One way in which we might reply is by saying that the case for equality between men and women cannot validly be extended to nonhuman animals. Women have a right to vote, for instance, because they are just as capable of making rational decisions about the future as men are; dogs, on the other hand, are incapable of understanding the significance of voting, so they cannot have the right to vote. There are many other obvious ways in which men and women resemble each other closely, while humans and animals differ greatly. So, it might be said, men and women are similar beings and should have similar rights, while humans and nonhumans are different and should not have equal rights.

The reasoning behind this reply to Taylor's analogy is correct up to a point, but it does not go far enough. There are obviously important differences between humans and other animals, and these differences must give rise to some differences in the rights that each have. Recognizing this evident fact, however, is no barrier to the case for extending the basic principle of equality to nonhuman animals. The differences that exist between men and women are equally undeniable, and the supporters of Women's Liberation are aware that these differences may give rise to different rights. Many feminists hold that women have the right to an abortion on request. It does not follow that since these same feminists are campaigning for equality between men and women they must support the right of men to have abortions too. Since a man cannot have an abortion, it is meaningless to talk of his right to have one. Since dogs can't vote, it is meaningless to talk of their right to vote. There is no reason why either Women's Liberation or Animal Liberation should get involved in such nonsense. The extension of the basic principle of equality from one group to another does not imply that we must treat both groups in exactly the same way, or grant exactly the same rights to both groups. Whether we should do so will depend on the nature of the members of the two groups. The basic principle of equality does not require equal or identical *treatment;* it requires equal consideration. Equal consideration for different beings may lead to different treatment and different rights.

So there is a different way of replying to Taylor's attempt to parody the case for women's rights, a way that does not deny the obvious differences between human beings and nonhumans but goes more deeply into the question of equality and concludes by finding nothing absurd in the idea that the basic principle of equality applies to so-called brutes. At this point such a conclusion may appear odd; but if we examine more deeply the basis on which our opposition to discrimination on grounds of race or sex ultimately rests, we will see that we would be on shaky ground if we were to demand equality for blacks, women, and other groups of oppressed humans while denying equal consideration to nonhumans. To make this clear we need to see, first, exactly why racism and sexism are wrong. When we say that all human beings, whatever their race, creed, or sex, are equal, what is it that we are asserting? Those who wish to defend hierarchical, inegalitarian societies have often pointed out that by whatever test we choose it simply is not true that all humans are equal. Like it or not we must face the fact that humans come in different shapes and sizes; they come with different moral capacities, different intellectual abilities, different amounts of benevolent feeling and sensitivity to the needs of others, different abilities to communicate effectively, and different capacities to experience pleasure and pain. In short, if the demand for equality were based on the actual equality of all human beings, we would have to stop demanding equality.

Still, one might cling to the view that the demand for equality among human beings is based on the actual equality of the different races and sexes. Although, it may be said, humans differ as individuals, there are no differences between the races and sexes as such. From the mere fact that a person is black or a woman we cannot infer anything about that person's intellectual or moral capacities. This, it may be said, is why racism and sexism are wrong. The white racist claims that whites are superior to blacks, but this is false; although there are differences among individuals, some blacks are superior to some whites in all of the capacities and abilities that could conceivably be relevant. The opponent of sexism would say the same: a person's sex is no guide to his or her abilities, and this is why it is unjustifiable to discriminate on the basis of sex.

The existence of individual variations that cut across the lines of race or sex, however, provides us with no defense at all against a more sophisticated opponent of equality, one who proposes that, say, the interests of all those with IQ scores below 100 be given less consideration than the interests of those with ratings over 100. Perhaps those scoring below the mark would, in this society, be made the slaves of those scoring higher. Would a hierarchical

society of this sort really be so much better than one based on race or sex? I think not. But if we tie the moral principle of equality to the factual equality of the different races or sexes, taken as a whole, our opposition to racism and sexism does not provide us with any basis for objecting to this kind of inegalitarianism.

There is a second important reason why we ought not to base our opposition to racism and sexism on any kind of factual equality, even the limited kind that asserts that variations in capacities and abilities are spread evenly among the different races and between the sexes: we can have no absolute guarantee that these capacities and abilities really are distributed evenly, without regard to race or sex, among human beings. So far as actual abilities are concerned there do seem to be certain measurable differences both among races and between sexes. These differences do not, of course, appear in every case, but only when averages are taken. More important still, we do not yet know how many of these differences are really due to the different genetic endowments of the different races and sexes, and how many are due to poor schools, poor housing, and other factors that are the result of past and continuing discrimination. Perhaps all of the important differences will eventually prove to be environmental rather than genetic. Anyone opposed to racism and sexism will certainly hope that this will be so, for it will make the task of ending discrimination a lot easier; nevertheless, it would be dangerous to rest the case against racism and sexism on the belief that all significant differences are environmental in origin. The opponent of, say, racism who takes this line will be unable to avoid conceding that if differences in ability did after all prove to have some genetic connection with race, racism would in some way be defensible.

Fortunately there is no need to pin the case for equality to one particular outcome of a scientific investigation. The appropriate response to those who claim to have found evidence of genetically based differences in ability among the races or between the sexes is not to stick to the belief that the genetic explanation must be wrong, whatever evidence to the contrary may turn up; instead we should make it quite clear that the claim to equality does not depend on intelligence, moral capacity, physical strength, or similar matters of fact. Equality is a moral idea, not an assertion of fact. There is no logically compelling reason for assuming that a factual difference in ability between two people justifies any difference in the amount of consideration we give to their needs and interests. *The principle of the equality of human beings is not a description of an alleged actual equality among humans: it is a prescription of how we should treat human beings.*

Jeremy Bentham, the founder of the reforming utilitarian school of moral philosophy, incorporated the essential basis of moral equality into his system of ethics by means of the formula: "Each to count for one and none for more than one." In other words, the interests of every being affected by an action are to be taken into account and given the same weight as the like interests of any other being. A later utilitarian, Henry Sidgwick, put the point in this way: "The good of any one individual is of no more importance, from the point of view (if I may say so) of the Universe, than the good of any other." More recently the leading figures in contemporary moral philosophy have shown a great deal of agreement in specifying as a fundamental pre-supposition of their moral theories some similar requirement that works to give everyone's interests equal consideration—although these writers generally cannot agree on how this requirement is best formulated.[1]

It is an implication of this principle of equality that our concern for others and our readiness to consider their interests ought not to depend on what they are like or on what abilities they may possess. Precisely what our concern or consideration requires us to do may vary according to the characteristics of those affected by what we do: concern for the well-being of children growing up in America would require that we teach them to read; concern for the well-being of pigs may require no more than that we leave them with other pigs in a place where there is adequate food and room to run freely. But the basic element—the taking into account of the interests of the being, whatever those interests may be—must, according to the principle of equality, be extended to all beings, black or white, masculine or feminine, human or nonhuman.

Thomas Jefferson, who was responsible for writing the principle of the equality of men into the American Declaration of Independence, saw this point. It led him to oppose slavery even though he was unable to free himself fully from his slaveholding background. He wrote in a letter to the author of a book that emphasized the notable intellectual achievements of Negroes in order to refute the then common view that they had limited intellectual capacities:

> Be assured that no person living wishes more sincerely than I do, to see a complete refutation of the doubts I myself have entertained and expressed on the grade of understanding allotted to them by nature, and to find that they are on a par with ourselves . . . but whatever be their degree of talent it is no measure of their rights. Because Sir Isaac Newton was superior to others in understanding, he was not therefore lord of the property or persons of others.[2]

Similarly, when in the 1850s the call for women's rights was raised in the United States, a remarkable black feminist named Sojourner Truth made the same point in more robust terms at a feminist convention:

> They talk about this thing in the head; what do they call it? ["Intellect," whispered someone nearby.] That's it. What's that got to do with women's rights or Negroes' rights? If my cup won't hold but a pint and yours holds a quart, wouldn't you be mean not to let me have my little half-measure full?[3]

It is on this basis that the case against racism and the case against sexism must both ultimately rest; and it is in accordance with this principle that the attitude that we may call "speciesism," by analogy with racism, must also be condemned. Speciesism—the word is not an attractive one, but I can think of no better term—is prejudice or attitude of bias in favor of the interests of members of one's own species and against those of members of other species. It should be obvious that the fundamental objections to racism and sexism made by Thomas Jefferson and Sojourner Truth apply equally to speciesism. If possessing a higher degree of intelligence does not entitle one human to use another for his or her own ends, how can it entitle humans to exploit nonhumans for the same purpose?[4]

Many philosophers and other writers have proposed the principle of equal consideration of interests, in some form or other, as a basic moral principle; but not many of them have recognized that this principle applies to members of other species as well as to our own. Jeremy Bentham was one of the few who did realize this. In a forward-looking passage written at a time when black slaves had been freed by the French but in the British dominions were still being treated in the way we now treat animals, Bentham wrote:

> The day *may* come when the rest of the animal creation may acquire those rights which never could

have been withholden from them but by the hand of tyranny. The French have already discovered that the blackness of the skin is no reason why a human being should be abandoned without redress to the caprice of a tormentor. It may one day come to be recognized that the number of the legs, the villosity of the skin, or the termination of the *os sacrum* are reasons equally insufficient for abandoning a sensitive being to the same fate. What else is it that should trace the insuperable line? Is it the faculty of reason, or perhaps the faculty of discourse? But a full-grown horse or dog is beyond comparison a more rational, as well as a more conversable animal, than an infant of a day or a week or even a month, old. But suppose they were otherwise, what would it avail? The question is not, Can they *reason?* nor Can they *talk?* but, Can they *suffer?*[5]

In this passage Bentham points to the capacity for suffering as the vital characteristic that gives a being the right to equal consideration. The capacity for suffering—or more strictly, for suffering and/or enjoyment or happiness—is not just another characteristic like the capacity for language or higher mathematics. Bentham is not saying that those who try to mark "the insuperable line" that determines whether the interests of a being should be considered happen to have chosen the wrong characteristic. By saying that we must consider the interests of all beings with the capacity for suffering or enjoyment Bentham does not arbitrarily exclude from consideration any interests at all—as those who draw the line with reference to the possession of reason or language do. The capacity for suffering and enjoyment is a *prerequisite for having interests at all,* a condition that must be satisfied before we can speak of interests in a meaningful way. It would be nonsense to say that it was not in the interests of a stone to be kicked along the road by a schoolboy. A stone does not have interests because it cannot suffer. Nothing that we can do to it could possibly make any difference to its welfare. The capacity for suffering and enjoyment is, however, not only necessary, but also sufficient for us to say that a being has interests—at an absolute minimum, an interest in not suffering. A mouse, for example, does have an interest in not being kicked along the road, because it will suffer if it is.

Although Bentham speaks of "rights" in the passage I have quoted, the argument is really about equality rather than about rights. Indeed, in a different passage, Bentham famously described "natural rights" as "nonsense" and "natural and imprescript-able rights" as "nonsense upon stilts." He talked of moral rights as a shorthand way of referring to protections that people and animals morally ought to have; but the real weight of the moral argument does not rest on the assertion of the existence of the right, for this in turn has to be justified on the basis of the possibilities for suffering and happiness. In this way we can argue for equality for animals without getting embroiled in philosophical controversies about the ultimate nature of rights.

In misguided attempts to refute the arguments of this book, some philosophers have gone to much trouble developing arguments to show that animals do not have rights.[6] They have claimed that to have rights a being must be autonomous, or must be a member of a community, or must have the ability to respect the rights of others, or must possess a sense of justice. These claims are irrelevant to the case for Animal Liberation. The language of rights is a convenient political shorthand. It is even more valuable in the era of thirty-second TV news clips than it was in Bentham's day; but in the argument for a radical change in our attitude to animals, it is in no way necessary.

If a being suffers there can be no moral justification for refusing to take that suffering into consideration. No matter what the nature of the being, the principle of equality requires that its suffering be counted equally with the like suffering—insofar as rough comparisons can be made—of any other being. If a being is not capable of suffering, or of experiencing enjoyment or happiness, there is nothing to be taken into account. So the limit of sentience (using the term as a convenient if not strictly accurate shorthand for the capacity to suffer and/or experience enjoyment) is the only defensible boundary of concern for the interests of others. To mark this boundary by some other characteristic like intelligence or rationality would be to mark it in an arbitrary manner. Why not choose some other characteristic, like skin color?

Racists violate the principle of equality by giving greater weight to the interests of members of their own race when there is a clash between their interests and the interests of those of another race. Sexists violate the principle of equality by favoring the interests of their own sex. Similarly, speciesists allow the interests of their own species to override the greater interests of members of other species. The pattern is identical in each case.

Animals and Research

Most human beings are speciesists. . . . Ordinary human beings—not a few exceptionally cruel or heartless humans, but the overwhelming majority of humans—take an active part in, acquiesce in, and allow their taxes to pay for practices that require the sacrifice of the most important interests of members of other species in order to promote the most trivial interests of our own species. . . .

The practice of experimenting on nonhuman animals as it exists today throughout the world reveals the consequences of speciesism. Many experiments inflict severe pain without the remotest prospect of significant benefits for human beings or any other animals. Such experiments are not isolated instances, but part of a major industry. In Britain, where experimenters are required to report the number of "scientific procedures" performed on animals, official government figures show that 3.5 million scientific procedures were performed on animals in 1988.[7] In the United States there are no figures of comparable accuracy. Under the Animal Welfare Act, the U.S. secretary of agriculture publishes a report listing the number of animals used by facilities registered with it, but this is incomplete in many ways. It does not include rats, mice, birds, reptiles, frogs, or domestic farm animals used in secondary schools; and it does not include experiments performed by facilities that do not transport animals interstate or receive grants or contracts from the federal government.

In 1986 the U.S. Congress Office of Technology Assessment (OTA) published a report entitled "Alternatives to Animal Use in Research, Testing and Education." The OTA researchers attempted to determine the number of animals used in experimentation in the U.S. and reported that "estimates of the animals used in the United States each year range from 10 million to upwards of 100 million." They concluded that the estimates were unreliable but their best guess was "at least 17 million to 22 million."[8]

This is an extremely conservative estimate. In testimony before Congress in 1966, the Laboratory Animal Breeders Association estimated that the number of mice, rats, guinea pigs, hamsters, and rabbits used for experimental purposes in 1965 was around 60 million.[9] In 1984 Dr. Andrew Rowan of Tufts University School of Veterinary Medicine estimated that approximately 71 million animals are used each year. In 1985 Rowan revised his estimates to distinguish between the number of animals produced, acquired, and actually used. This yielded an estimate of between 25 and 35 million animals used in experiments each year.[10] (This figure omits animals who die in shipping or are killed before the experiment begins.) A stock market analysis of just one major supplier of animals to laboratories, the Charles River Breeding Laboratory, stated that this company alone produced 22 million laboratory animals annually.[11]

The 1988 report issued by the Department of Agriculture listed 140,471 dogs, 42,271 cats, 51,641 primates, 431,254 rabbits, and 178,249 "wild animals": a total of 1,635,288 used in experimentation. Remember that this report does not bother to count rats and mice, and covers at most an estimated 10 percent of the total number of animals used. Of the nearly 1.6 million animals reported by the Department of Agriculture to have been used for experimental purposes, over 90,000 are reported to have experienced "unrelieved pain or distress." Again, this is probably at most 10 percent of the total number of animals suffering unrelieved pain and distress—and if experimenters are less concerned about causing unrelieved pain to rats and mice than they are to dogs, cats, and primates, it could be an even smaller proportion.

Other developed nations all use larger numbers of animals. In Japan, for example, a very incomplete survey published in 1988 produced a total in excess of eight million.[12] . . .

Among the tens of millions of experiments performed, only a few can possibly be regarded as contributing to important medical research. Huge numbers of animals are used in university departments such as forestry and psychology; many more are used for commercial purposes, to test new cosmetics, shampoos, food coloring agents, and other inessential items. All this can happen only because of our prejudice against taking seriously the suffering of a being who is not a member of our own species. Typically, defenders of experiments on animals do not deny that animals suffer. They cannot deny the animals' suffering, because they need to stress the similarities between humans and other animals in order to claim that their experiments may have some relevance for human purposes. The experimenter who forces rats to choose between starvation and electric shock to see if they develop ulcers (which they do) does so because the rat has a nervous system very similar to a human being's, and presumably feels an electric shock in a similar way.

There has been opposition to experimenting on animals for a long time. This opposition has made little headway because experimenters, backed by commercial firms that profit by supplying laboratory animals and equipment, have been able to convince legislators and the public that opposition comes from uninformed fanatics who consider the interests of animals more important than the interests of human beings. But to be opposed to what is going on now it is not necessary to insist that all animal experiments stop immediately. All we need to say is that experiments serving no direct and urgent purpose should stop immediately, and in the remaining fields of research, we should whenever possible, seek to replace experiments that involve animals with alternative methods that do not. . . .

When are experiments on animals justifiable? Upon learning of the nature of many of the experiments carried out, some people react by saying that all experiments on animals should be prohibited immediately. But if we make our demands absolute as this, the experimenters have a ready reply: Would we be prepared to let thousands of humans die if they could be saved by a single experiment on a single animal?

This question is, of course, purely hypothetical. There has never been and never could be a single experiment that saved thousands of lives. The way to reply to this hypothetical question is to pose another: Would the experimenters be prepared to carry out their experiment on a human orphan under six months old if that were the only way to save thousands of lives?

If the experimenters would not be prepared to use a human infant then their readiness to use nonhuman animals reveals an unjustifiable form of discrimination on the basis of species, since adult apes, monkeys, dogs, cats, rats, and other animals are more aware of what is happening to them, more self-directing, and, so far as we can tell, at least as sensitive to pain as a human infant. (I have specified that the human infant be an orphan, to avoid the complications of the feelings of parents. Specifying the case in this way is, if anything, overgenerous to those defending the use of nonhuman animals in experiments, since mammals intended for experimental use are usually separated from their mothers at an early age, when the separation causes distress for both mother and young.)

So far as we know, human infants possess no morally relevant characteristic to a higher degree than adult nonhuman animals, unless we are to count the infants' potential as a characteristic that makes it wrong to experiment on them. Whether this characteristic should count is controversial—if we count it, we shall have to condemn abortion along with the experiments on infants, since the potential of the infant and the fetus is the same. To avoid the complexities of this issue, however, we can alter our original question a little and assume that the infant is one with irreversible brain damage so severe as to rule out any mental development beyond the level of a six-month-old infant. There are, unfortunately, many such human beings, locked away in special wards throughout the country, some of them long since abandoned by their parents and other relatives, and, sadly, sometimes unloved by anyone else. Despite their mental deficiencies, the anatomy and physiology of these infants are in nearly all respects identical with those of normal humans. If, therefore, we were to force-feed them with large quantities of floor polish or drip concentrated solutions of cosmetics into their eyes [as has been done in experiments using animals], we would have a much more reliable indication of the safety of these products for humans than we now get by attempting to extrapolate the results of tests on a variety of other species. . . .

So whenever experimenters claim that their experiments are important enough to justify the use of animals, we should ask them whether they would be prepared to use a brain-damaged human being at a similar mental level to the animals they are planning to use. I cannot imagine that anyone would seriously propose carrying out the experiments described in this chapter on brain-damaged human beings. Occasionally it has become known that medical experiments have been performed on human beings without their consent; one case did concern institutionalized intellectually disabled children, who were given hepatitis. When such harmful experiments on human beings become known, they usually lead to an outcry against the experimenters, and rightly so. They are, very often, a further example of the arrogance of the research worker who justifies everything on the grounds of increasing knowledge. But if the experimenter claims that the experiment is important enough to justify inflicting suffering on animals, why is it not important enough to justify inflicting suffering on humans at the same mental level? What difference is there between the two? Only that one is a member of our species and the other is not? But to appeal to that difference is to reveal a bias no more defensible than racism or any other form of arbitrary discrimination. . . .

We have still not answered the question of when an experiment might be justifiable. It will not do to say "Never!" Putting morality in such black-and-white terms is appealing, because it eliminates the need to think about particular cases; but in extreme circumstances, such absolutist answers always break down. Torturing a human being is almost always wrong, but it is not absolutely wrong. If torture were the only way in which we could discover the location of a nuclear bomb hidden in a New York City basement and timed to go off within the hour, then torture would be justifiable. Similarly, if a single experiment could cure a disease like leukemia, that experiment would be justifiable. But in actual life the benefits are always more remote, and more often than not they are nonexistent. So how do we decide when an experiment is justifiable?

We have seen that experimenters reveal a bias in favor of their own species whenever they carry out experiments on nonhumans for purposes that they would not think justified them in using human beings, even brain-damaged ones. This principle gives us a guide toward an answer to our question. Since a speciesist bias, like a racist bias, is unjustifiable, an experiment cannot be justifiable unless the experiment is so important that the use of a brain-damaged human would also be justifiable.

This is not an absolutist principle. I do not believe that it could never be justifiable to experiment on a brain-damaged human. If it really were possible to save several lives by an experiment that would take just one life, and there were no other way those lives could be saved, it would be right to do the experiment. But this would be an extremely rare case. Admittedly, as with any dividing line, there would be a gray area where it was difficult to decide if an experiment could be justified. But we need not get distracted by such considerations now. . . . We are in the midst of an emergency in which appalling suffering is being inflicted on millions of animals for purposes that on any impartial view are obviously inadequate to justify the suffering. When we have ceased to carry out all those experiments, then there will be time enough to discuss what to do about the remaining ones which are claimed to be essential to save lives or prevent greater suffering. . . .

Notes

1. For Bentham's moral philosophy, see his *Introduction to the Principles of Morals and Legislation,* and for Sidgwick's see *The Methods of Ethics,* 1907 (the passage is quoted from the seventh edition; reprint, London: Macmillan, 1963), p. 382. As examples of leading contemporary moral philosophers who incorporate a requirement of equal consideration of interests, see R. M. Hare, *Freedom and Reason* (New York: Oxford University Press, 1963), and John Rawls, *A Theory of Justice* (Cambridge, MA: Harvard University Press, Belknap Press, 1972). For a brief account of the essential agreement on this issue between these and other positions, see R. M. Hare, "Rules of War and Moral Reasoning," *Philosophy and Public Affairs* 1 (2) (1972).

2. Letter to Henry Gregoire, February 25, 1809.

3. Reminiscences by Francis D. Gage, from Susan B. Anthony, *The History of Woman Suffrage,* vol. 1; the passage is to be found in the extract in Leslie Tanner (Ed.), *Voices From Women's Liberation* (New York: Signet, 1970).

4. I owe the term "speciesism" to Richard Ryder. It has become accepted in general use since the first edition of this book, and now appears in *The Oxford English Dictionary,* 2nd ed. (Oxford, UK: Clarendon Press, 1989).

5. *Introduction to the Principles of Morals and Legislation,* chapter 17.

6. See M. Levin, "Animal Rights Evaluated," *Humanist* 37, 1415 (July/August 1977); M. A. Fox, "Animal Liberation: A Critique," *Ethics* 88, 134–138 (1978); C. Perry and G. E. Jones, "On Animal Rights," *International Journal of Applied Philosophy* 1, 39–57 (1982).

7. *Statistics of Scientific Procedures on Living Animals,* Great Britain, 1988, Command Paper 743 (London: Her Majesty's Stationery Office, 1989).

8. U.S. Congress Office of Technology Assessment, *Alternatives to Animal Use in Research, Testing and Education* (Washington DC: Government Printing Office, 1986), p. 64.

9. *Hearings before the Subcommittee on Livestock and Feed Grains of the Committee on Agriculture,* U.S. House of Representatives, 1966, p. 63.

10. See A. Rowan, *Of Mice, Models and Men* (Albany: State University of New York Press, 1984), p. 71; his later revision is in a personal communication to the Office of Technology Assessment; see *Alternatives to Animal Use in Research, Testing and Education,* p. 56.

11. OTA, *Alternatives to Animal Use in Research, Testing and Education,* p. 56.

12. *Experimental Animals* 37, 105 (1988).

Speciesism and the Idea of Equality

Bonnie Steinbock

Study Questions

1. What is the basic question that the moral philosopher asks about how we treat members of species other than our own?

2. What is the difference between racism, sexism, and speciesism? Do they have any common characteristics?

3. Why does Bernard Williams believe that all persons should be treated equally? Is this similar to or different from the view of Wasserstrom?

4. Does Steinbock believe that the issue of equality depends on what we say about the rights of human beings or others? Explain.

5. What counterintuitive conclusions flow from treating the suffering or interests of humans and other animals equally? What is the value of our moral feelings on this issue?

6. What three aspects or characteristics of human beings give them special moral worth or a privileged position in the moral community?

7. Why is experimentation on animals that benefits humans justifiable?

8. Why do we regard human suffering as worse than comparable animal suffering?

9. What is the significance of the fact that we would be horrified to experiment on a severely mentally retarded human being in a way that we would not by using a more intelligent pig?

Most of us believe that we are entitled to treat members of other species in ways which would be considered wrong if inflicted on members of our own species. We kill them for food, keep them confined, use them in painful experiments. The moral philosopher has to ask what relevant difference justifies this difference in treatment. A look at this question will lead us to re-examine the distinctions which we have assumed make a moral difference.

It has been suggested by Peter Singer[1] that our current attitudes are "speciesist," a word intended to make one think of "racist" or "sexist." The idea is that membership in a species is in itself not relevant to moral treatment, and that much of our behavior and attitudes towards nonhuman animals is based simply on this irrelevant fact.

There is, however, an important difference between racism or sexism and "speciesism." We do not subject animals to different moral treatment simply because they have fur and feathers, but because they are in fact different from human beings in ways that could be morally relevant. It is false that women are incapable of being benefited by education, and therefore that claim cannot serve to justify preventing them from attending school. But this is not false of cows and dogs, even chimpanzees. Intelligence is thought to be a morally relevant capacity because of its relation to the capacity for moral responsibility.

What is Singer's response? He agrees that nonhuman animals lack certain capacities that human animals possess, and that this may justify different treatment. But it does not justify giving less consideration to their needs and interests. According to Singer, the moral mistake which the racist or sexist makes is not essentially the factual error of thinking that blacks or women are inferior to white men. For even if there were no factual error, even if it were true that blacks and women are less intelligent and responsible than whites and men, this would not justify giving less consideration to their needs and interests. It is important to note that the term "speciesism" is in one way like, and in another way unlike, the terms "racism" and "sexism." What the term "speciesism" has in common with these terms is the reference to focusing on a characteristic which is, in itself, irrelevant to moral treatment. And it is worth reminding us of this. But Singer's real aim is to bring us to a new understanding of the idea of equality. The question is, on what do claims to equality rest? The demand for human equality is a demand that the interests of all

From *Philosophy*, vol. 53, no. 204 (April 1978): 247–256. © 1978 Cambridge University Press. Reprinted by permission of the author and the publisher.

human beings be considered equally, unless there is a moral justification for not doing so. But why should the interests of all human beings be considered equally? In order to answer this question, we have to give some sense to the phrase, "All men (human beings) are created equal." Human beings are manifestly not equal, differing greatly in intelligence, virtue and capacities. In virtue of what can the claim to equality be made?

It is Singer's contention that claims to equality do not rest on factual equality. Not only do human beings differ in their capacities, but it might even turn out that intelligence, the capacity for virtue, etc., are not distributed evenly among the races and sexes:

> The appropriate response to those who claim to have found evidence of genetically based differences in ability between the races or sexes is not to stick to the belief that the genetic explanation must be wrong, whatever evidence to the contrary may turn up; instead we should make it quite clear that the claim to equality does not depend on intelligence, moral capacity, physical strength, or similar matters of fact. Equality is a moral ideal, not a simple assertion of fact. There is no logically compelling reason for assuming that a factual difference in ability between two people justifies any difference in the amount of consideration we give to satisfying their needs and interests. The principle of equality of human beings is not a description of an alleged actual equality among humans: it is a prescription of how we should treat humans.[2]

Insofar as the subject is human equality, Singer's view is supported by other philosophers. Bernard Williams, for example, is concerned to show that demands for equality cannot rest on factual equality among people, for no such equality exists.[3] The only respect in which all men are equal, according to Williams, is that they are all equally men. This seems to be a platitude, but Williams denies that it is trivial. Membership in the species Homo sapiens in itself has no special moral significance, but rather the fact that all men are human serves as a reminder that being human involves the possession of characteristics that are morally relevant. But on what characteristics does Williams focus? Aside from the desire for self-respect (which I will discuss later), Williams is not concerned with uniquely human capacities. Rather, he focuses on the capacity to feel pain and the capacity to feel affection. It is in virtue of these capacities, it seems, that the idea of equality is to be justified.

Apparently Richard Wasserstrom has the same idea as he sets out the racist's "logical and moral mistakes" in "Rights, Human Rights and Racial Discrimination."[4] The racist fails to acknowledge that the black person is as capable of suffering as the white person. According to Wasserstrom, the reason why a person is said to have a right not to be made to suffer acute physical pain is that we all do in fact value freedom from such pain. Therefore, if anyone has a right to be free from suffering acute physical pain, everyone has this right, for there is no possible basis of discrimination. Wasserstrom says, "For, if all persons do have equal capacities of these sorts and if the existence of these capacities is the reason for ascribing these rights to anyone, then all persons ought to have the right to claim equality of treatment in respect to the possession and exercise of these rights."[5] The basis of equality, for Wasserstrom as for Williams, lies not in some uniquely human capacity, but rather in the fact that all human beings are alike in their capacity to suffer. Writers on equality have focused on this capacity, I think, because it functions as some sort of lowest common denominator, so that whatever the other capacities of a human being, he is entitled to equal consideration because, like everyone else, he is capable of suffering.

If the capacity to suffer is the reason for ascribing a right to freedom from acute pain, or a right to well being, then it certainly looks as though these rights must be extended to animals as well. This is the conclusion Singer arrives at. The demand for human equality rests on the equal capacity of all human beings to suffer and to enjoy well being. But if this is the basis of the demand for equality, then this demand must include all beings which have an equal capacity to suffer and enjoy well being. That is why Singer places at the basis of the demand for equality, not intelligence or reason, but sentience. And equality will mean, not equality of treatment, but "equal consideration of interests." The equal consideration of interests will often mean quite different treatment, depending on the nature of the entity being considered. (It would be as absurd to talk of a dog's right to vote, Singer says, as to talk of a man's right to have an abortion.)

It might be thought that the issue of equality depends on a discussion of rights. According to this line of thought, animals do not merit equal consideration of interests because, unlike human beings, they do not, or cannot, have rights. But I am not going to discuss rights, important as the issue is. The fact that an entity does not have rights does not necessarily imply that its interests are going to count for less than the interests of entities which are right-bearers. According to the view of rights held by H. L. A. Hart and S. I. Benn, infants do not have rights, nor do the mentally defective, nor do the insane, in so far as they all lack certain minimal conceptual capabilities for having rights.[6] Yet it certainly does not seem that either Hart or Benn would agree that therefore their interests are to be counted for less, or that it is morally permissible to treat them in ways in which it would not be permissible to treat right-bearers. It seems to mean only that we must give different sorts of reasons for our obligations to take into consideration the interests of those who do not have rights.

We have reasons concerning the treatment of other people which are clearly independent of the notion of rights. We would say that it is wrong to punch someone because doing that infringes his rights. But we could also say that it is wrong because doing that hurts him, and that is, ordinarily, enough of a reason not to do it. Now this particular reason extends not only to human beings, but to all sentient creatures. One has a prima facie reason not to pull the cat's tail (whether or not the cat has rights) because it hurts the cat. And this is the only thing, normally, which is relevant in this case. The fact that the cat is not a "rational being," that it is not capable of moral responsibility, that it cannot make free choices or shape its life—all of these differences from us have nothing to do with the justifiability of pulling its tail. Does this show that rationality and the rest of it are irrelevant to moral treatment?

I hope to show that this is not the case. But first I want to point out that the issue is not one of cruelty to animals. We all agree that cruelty is wrong, whether perpetrated on a moral or nonmoral, rational or nonrational agent. Cruelty is defined as the infliction of unnecessary pain or suffering. What is to count as necessary or unnecessary is determined, in part, by the nature of the end pursued. Torturing an animal is cruel, because although the pain is logically necessary for the action to be torture, the end (deriving enjoyment from seeing the animal suffer) is monstrous. Allowing animals to suffer from neglect or for the sake of large profits may also be thought to be unnecessary and therefore cruel. But there may be some ends, which are very good (such as the advancement of medical knowledge), which can be accomplished by subjecting animals to pain in experiments. Although most people would agree that the pain inflicted on animals used in medical research ought to be kept to a minimum, they would consider pain that cannot be eliminated "necessary" and therefore not cruel. It would probably not be so regarded if the subjects were nonvoluntary human beings. Necessity, then, is defined in terms of human benefit, but this is just what is being called into question. The topic of cruelty to animals, while important from a practical viewpoint, because much of our present treatment of animals involves the infliction of suffering for no good reason, is not very interesting philosophically. What is philosophically interesting is whether we are justified in having different standards of necessity for human suffering and for animal suffering.

Singer says, quite rightly I think, "If a being suffers, there can be no moral justification for refusing to take that suffering into consideration."[7] But he thinks that the principle of equality requires that, no matter what the nature of the being, its suffering be counted equally with the like suffering of any other being. In other words sentience does not simply provide us with reasons for acting; it is the only relevant consideration for equal consideration of interests. It is this view that I wish to challenge.

I want to challenge it partly because it has such counter-intuitive results. It means, for example, that feeding starving children before feeding starving dogs is just like a Catholic charity's feeding hungry Catholics before feeding hungry non-Catholics. It is simply a matter of taking care of one's own, something which is usually morally permissible. But whereas we would admire the Catholic agency which did not discriminate, but fed all children, first come, first served, we would feel quite differently about someone who has this policy for dogs and children. Nor is this, it seems to me, simply a matter of sentimental preference for our own species. I might feel much more love for my dog than for a strange child—and yet I might feel morally obliged to feed the child before I fed my dog. If I gave in to the feelings of love and fed my dog and let the child go hungry, I would probably feel guilty. This is not to say that we can simply rely on such feelings. Huck Finn felt guilty at helping Jim escape, which he viewed as stealing from a woman who had never done him any harm. But while the existence of such feelings does not settle the morality of an issue, it is not clear to me that they can be explained away. In any event, their existence can serve as a motivation for trying to find a rational justification for considering human interests above nonhuman ones.

However, it does seem to me that this requires a justification. Until now, common sense (and academic philosophy) have been no such need. Benn says, "No one claims equal consideration for all mammals—human beings count, mice do not, though it would not be easy to say why not. . . . Although we hesitate to inflict unnecessary pain on sentient creatures, such as mice or dogs, we are quite sure that we do not need to show good reasons for putting human interests before theirs."[8]

I think we do have to justify counting our interests more heavily than those of animals. But how? Singer is right, I think, to point out that it will not do to refer vaguely to the greater value of human life, to human worth and dignity:

> Faced with a situation in which they see a need for some basis for the moral gulf that is commonly thought to separate humans and animals, but can find no concrete difference that will do this without undermining the equality of humans, philosophers tend to waffle. They resort to high-sounding phrases like 'the intrinsic dignity of the human individual.' They talk of 'the intrinsic worth of all men' as if men had some worth that other beings do not have or they say that human beings, and only human beings, are 'ends in themselves,' while 'everything other than a person can only have value for a person.' . . . Why should we not attribute 'intrinsic dignity' or 'intrinsic worth' to ourselves? Why should we not say that we are the only things in the universe that have intrinsic value? Our fellow human beings are unlikely to reject the accolades we so generously bestow upon them, and those to whom we deny the honor are unable to object.[9]

Singer is right to be skeptical of terms like "intrinsic dignity" and "intrinsic worth." These phrases are no substitute for a moral argument. But they may point to one. In trying to understand what is meant by these phrases, we may find a difference or differences between human beings and nonhuman animals that will justify different treatment while not undermining claims for human equality. While we are not compelled to discriminate among people because of different capacities, if we can find a significant difference in capacities between human and nonhuman animals, this could serve to justify regarding human interests as primary. It is not arbitrary or smug, I think, to maintain that human beings have a different

moral status from members of other species because of certain capacities which are characteristic of being human. We may not all be equal in these capacities, but all human beings possess them to some measure, and nonhuman animals do not. For example, human beings are normally held to be responsible for what they do. In recognizing that someone is responsible for his or her actions, you accord that person a respect which is reserved for those possessed of moral autonomy, or capable of achieving such autonomy. Secondly, human beings can be expected to reciprocate in a way that nonhuman animals cannot. Nonhuman animals cannot be motivated by altruistic or moral reasons; they cannot treat you fairly or unfairly. This does not rule out the possibility of an animal being motivated by sympathy or pity. It does rule out altruistic motivation in the sense of motivation due to the recognition that the needs and interests of others provide one with certain reasons for acting.[10] Human beings are capable of altruistic motivation in this sense. We are sometimes motivated simply by the recognition that someone else is in pain, and that pain is a bad thing, no matter who suffers it. It is this sort of reason that I claim cannot motivate an animal or any entity not possessed of fairly abstract concepts. (If some nonhuman animals do possess the requisite concepts—perhaps chimpanzees who have learned a language—they might well be capable of altruistic motivation.) This means that our moral dealings with animals are necessarily much more limited than our dealings with other human beings. If rats invade our houses, carrying disease and biting our children, we cannot reason with them, hoping to persuade them of the injustice they do us. We can only attempt to get rid of them. And it is this that makes it reasonable for us to accord them a separate and not equal moral status, even though their capacity to suffer provides us with some reason to kill them painlessly, if this can be done without too much sacrifice of human interests. Thirdly, as Williams points out, there is the "desire for self-respect": "a certain human desire to be identified with what one is doing, to be able to realize purposes of one's own, and not to be the instrument of another's will unless one has willingly accepted such a role."[11] Some animals may have some form of this desire, and to the extent that they do, we ought to consider their interest in freedom and self-determination. (Such considerations might affect our attitudes toward zoos and circuses.) But the desire for self-respect per se requires the intellectual capacities of human beings, and this desire provides us with special reasons not to treat human beings in certain ways. It is an affront to the dignity of a human being to be a slave (even if a well-treated one); this cannot be true for a horse or a cow. To point this out is of course only to say that the justification for the treatment of an entity will depend on the sort of entity in question. In our treatment of other entities, we must consider the desire for autonomy, dignity and respect, but only where such a desire exists. Recognition of different desires and interests will often require different treatment, a point Singer himself makes.

But is the issue simply one of different desires and interests justifying and requiring different treatment? I would like to make a stronger claim, namely, that certain capacities, which seem to be unique to human beings, entitle their possessors to a privileged position in the moral community. Both rats and human beings dislike pain, and so we have a prima facie reason not to inflict pain on either. But if we can free human beings from crippling diseases, pain and death through experimentation which involves making animals suffer, and if this is the only way to achieve such results, then I think that such experimentation is justified because human lives are more valuable than animals' lives. And this is because of certain capacities and abilities that normal human beings have which animals apparently do not, and which human beings cannot exercise if they are devastated by pain or disease.

My point is not that the lack of the sorts of capacities I have been discussing gives us a justification for treating animals just as we like, but rather that it is these differences between human beings and nonhuman animals which provide a rational basis for different moral treatment and consideration. Singer focuses on sentience alone as the basis of equality, but we can justify the belief that human beings have a moral worth that nonhuman animals do not, in virtue of specific capacities, and without resorting to "high-sounding phrases."

Singer thinks that intelligence, the capacity for moral responsibility, for virtue, etc., are irrelevant to equality, because we would not accept a hierarchy based on intelligence any more than one based on race. We do not think that those with greater capacities ought to have their interests weighed more heavily than those with lesser capacities, and this, he thinks, shows that differences in such capacities are irrelevant to equality. But it does not show this at all. Kevin Donaghy argues (rightly, I think) that what

entitles us human beings to a privileged position in the moral community is a certain minimal level of intelligence, which is a prerequisite for morally relevant capacities.[12] The fact that we would reject a hierarchical society based on degree of intelligence does not show that a minimal level of intelligence cannot be used as a cut-off point, justifying giving greater consideration to the interests of those entities which meet this standard.

Interestingly enough, Singer concedes the rationality of valuing the lives of normal human beings over the lives of nonhuman animals.[13] We are not required to value equally the life of a normal human being and the life of an animal, he thinks, but only their suffering. But I doubt that the value of an entity's life can be separated from the value of its suffering in this way. If we value the lives of human beings more than the lives of animals, this is because we value certain capacities that human beings have and animals do not. But freedom from suffering is, in general, a minimal condition for exercising these capacities, for living a fully human life. So, valuing human life more involves regarding human interests as counting for more. That is why we regard human suffering as more deplorable than comparable animal suffering.

But there is one point of Singer's which I have not yet met. Some human beings (if only a very few) are less intelligent than some nonhuman animals. Some have less capacity for moral choice and responsibility. What status in the moral community are these members of our species to occupy? Are their interests to be considered equally with ours? Is experimenting on them permissible where such experiments are painful or injurious, but somehow necessary for human well being? If it is certain of our capacities which entitle us to a privileged position, it looks as if those lacking those capacities are not entitled to a privileged position. To think it is justifiable to experiment on an adult chimpanzee but not on a severely mentally incapacitated human being seems to be focusing on membership in a species where that has no moral relevance. (It is being "speciesist" in a perfectly reasonable use of the word.) How are we to meet this challenge?

Donaghy is untroubled by this objection. He says that it is fully in accord with his intuitions, that he regards the killing of a normally intelligent human being as far more serious than the killing of a person so severely limited that he lacked the intellectual capacities of an adult pig. But this parry really misses the point. The question is whether Donaghy thinks that the killing of a human being so severely limited that he lacked the intellectual capacities of an adult pig would be less serious than the killing of that pig. If superior intelligence is what justifies privileged status in the moral community, then the pig who is smarter than a human being ought to have superior moral status. And I doubt that this is fully in accord with Donaghy's intuitions.

I doubt that anyone will be able to come up with a concrete and morally relevant difference that would justify, say, using a chimpanzee in an experiment rather than a human being with less capacity for reasoning, moral responsibility, etc. Should we then experiment on the severely retarded? Utilitarian considerations aside (the difficulty of comparing intelligence between species, for example), we feel a special obligation to care for the handicapped members of our own species, who cannot survive in this world without such care. Nonhuman animals manage very well, despite their "lower intelligence" and lesser capacities; most of them do not require special care from us. This does not, of course, justify experimenting on them. However, to subject to experimentation those people who depend on us seems even worse than subjecting members of other species to it. In addition, when we consider the severely retarded, we think, "That could be me." It makes sense to think that one might have been born retarded, but not to think that one might have been born a monkey. And so, although one can imagine oneself in the monkey's place, one feels a closer identification with the severely retarded human being. Here we are getting away from such things as "morally relevant differences" and are talking about something much more difficult to articulate, namely, the role of feelings and sentiment in moral thinking. We would be horrified by the use of the retarded in medical research. But what are we to make of this horror? Has it moral significance or is it "mere" sentiment, of no more import than the sentiment of whites against blacks? It is terribly difficult to know how to evaluate such feelings.[14] I am not going to say more about this, because I think that the treatment of severely incapacitated human beings does not pose an insurmountable objection to the privileged status principle. I am willing to admit that my horror at the thought of experiments being performed on severely mentally incapacitated human beings in cases in which I would find it justifiable and preferable to

perform the same experiments on nonhuman animals (capable of similar suffering) may not be a moral emotion. But it is certainly not wrong of us to extend special care to members of our own species, motivated by feelings of sympathy, protectiveness, etc. If this is speciesism, it is stripped of its tone of moral condemnation. It is not racist to provide special care to members of your own race; it is racist to fall below your moral obligation to a person because of his or her race. I have been arguing that we are morally obliged to consider the interests of all sentient creatures, but not to consider those interests equally with human interests. Nevertheless, even this recognition will mean some radical changes in our attitude toward and treatment of other species.[15]

Notes

1. Peter Singer, *Animal Liberation* (A New York Review Book, 1975).
2. Singer, 5.
3. Bernard Williams, "The Idea of Equality," *Philosophy, Politics and Society* (Second Series), Laslett and Runciman (Eds.) (Blackwell, 1962), 110–131, reprinted in *Moral Concepts*, Feinberg (Ed.) (Oxford, 1970), 153–171.
4. Richard Wasserstrom, "Rights, Human Rights, and Racial Discrimination," *Journal of Philosophy* 61, No. 20 (1964), reprinted in *Human Rights*, A. I. Melden (Ed.) (Wadsworth, 1970), 96–110.
5. Ibid., 106.
6. H. L. A. Hart, "Are There Any Natural Rights?," *Philosophical Review* 64 (1955), and S. I. Benn, "Abortion, Infanticide, and Respect for Persons," *The Problem of Abortion*, Feinberg (Ed.) (Wadsworth, 1973), 92–104.
7. Singer, 9.
8. Benn, "Equality, Moral and Social," *The Encyclopedia of Philosophy* 3, 40.
9. Singer, 266–267.
10. This conception of altruistic motivation comes from Thomas Nagel's *The Possibility of Altruism* (Oxford, 1970).
11. Williams, op. cit., 157.
12. Kevin Donaghy, "Singer on Speciesism," *Philosophic Exchange* (Summer 1974).
13. Singer, 22.
14. We run into the same problem when discussing abortion. Of what significance are our feelings toward the unborn when discussing its status? Is it relevant or irrelevant that it looks like a human being?
15. I would like to acknowledge the help of, and offer thanks to, Professor Richard Arneson of the University

of California, San Diego; Professor Sidney Gendin of Eastern Michigan University; and Professor Peter Singer of Monash University, all of whom read and commented on earlier drafts of this paper.

Review Exercises

1. List ten different ways in which we use non-human animals.
2. How is "cruelty" defined in terms of sentience?
3. How can the distinction between causing and allowing harm or pain be used to criticize the view that we can cause pain to animals because this is part of nature—that is, of what happens in the wild?
4. What is the meaning of the term *rights?*
5. For a being to be the kind of thing that can have rights, is it necessary that it be able to claim them? That it be a moral agent? Why or why not?
6. What do those who use the fact that animals have interests as a basis for their having rights mean by this?
7. Describe the issues involved in the debate over whether nonhuman animals' interests ought to be treated equally with those of humans.
8. List some anthropocentric reasons for preserving animal species.
9. What problems does the meaning of a "species" raise for deciding whether animal species have moral standing of some sort?
10. What reasons do supporters of the use of nonhuman animals in experimental research give? What reasons for opposing it do their opponents give? In particular, discuss the issues of pain and necessity.

Discussion Cases

1. *The Eye Test.* It has been standard industry practice to test the toxicity of consumer products on animals. In one test, rabbits are used to determine the effect on the eyes of shampoos and other cosmetics. Brian and Ayn are horrified as they read about the way this is done and how the rabbits must suffer. However, in one article the results of a survey about consumer products of this sort are reported. Most people, the survey found, do not want to use a product that has not first been adequately tested on animals.

Should animals be used in such testing of products? Why or why not?

2. *People Versus the Gorilla.* Of the approximately 250 remaining mountain gorillas, some 150 are located in the 30,000-acre Parc des Volcans in the small African country of Rwanda. Rwanda has the highest population density in Africa. Most people live on small farms. To this population, the park represents survival land for farming. Eliminating it could support 36,000 people on subsistence farms.

Should the park be maintained as a way of preserving the gorillas or should it be given to the people as a matter of their survival? Why?

3. *What Is a Panther Worth?* The Florida panther is an endangered species. Not long ago one of these animals was hit by a car and seriously injured. He was taken to the state university veterinary medical school where steel plates were inserted in both legs, his right foot was rebuilt, and he had other expensive treatment. The Florida legislature was considering a proposal to spend $27 million to build forty bridges that would allow the panther to move about without the threat of other car injuries and death. Those who support the measure point out that the Florida panther is unique and can survive only in swamp land near the Everglades.

Should the state spend this amount of money to save the Florida panther from extinction? Why or why not?

Selected Bibliography

Blackstone, William (Ed.). *Philosophy and Environmental Crisis.* Athens: University of Georgia Press, 1974.

Bostock, Stephen St. C. *Zoos and Animal Rights.* New York: Routledge, 1993.

Clark, Stephen. *The Moral Status of Animals.* Oxford, UK: Clarendon, 1977.

DeGrazia, David. *Taking Animals Seriously: Mental Life and Moral Status.* New York: Cambridge University Press, 1996.

Fox, Michael Allan. *The Case for Animal Experimentation.* Berkeley: University of California Press, 1986.

Frey, R. G. *Interests and Rights: The Case against Animals.* Oxford, UK: Clarendon, 1980.

Mason, Jim, and Peter Singer. *Animal Factories.* New York: Crown, 1980.

Midgley, Mary. *Animals and Why They Matter.* Harmondsworth, UK: Penguin, 1984.

Miller, Harlan B., and William H. Williams. *Ethics and Animals.* Clifton, NJ: Humana, 1983.

Norton, Bryan G. (Ed.). *Preservation of Species.* Princeton, NJ: Princeton University Press, 1986.

Orlans, F. Barbara. *In the Name of Science: Issues in Responsible Animal Experimentation.* New York: Oxford University Press, 1993.

Regan, Tom, and Peter Singer (Eds.). *Animal Rights and Human Obligations,* 2nd ed. Englewood Cliffs, NJ: Prentice-Hall, 1989.

Regan, Tom (Ed.). *Earthbound: New Introductory Essays in Environmental Ethics.* New York: Random House, 1984.

Regan, Tom. *The Case for Animal Rights.* Berkeley: University of California Press, 1983.

Rollin, Bernard E. *The Frankenstein Syndrome: Ethical and Social Issues in the Genetic Engineering of Animals.* New York: Cambridge University Press, 1995.

————. *The Unheeded Cry: Animal Consciousness, Animal Pain, and Science.* New York: Oxford University Press, 1989.

Rolston, Holmes, III. *Environmental Ethics: Duties to and Values in the Natural World.* Philadelphia: Temple University Press, 1988.

Russell, Burch. *The Principles of Humane Experimental Technique.* Springfield, IL: Charles C. Thomas, 1959.

Ryder, R. *Victims of Science.* London: Davis-Poynter, 1975.

Salt, Henry. *Animal Rights.* Fontwell, UK: Centaur, 1980.

Sikora, R. I., and Brian Barry (Eds.). *Obligations to Future Generations.* Philadelphia: Temple University Press, 1978.

Singer, Peter. *Animal Liberation,* 2nd ed. New York: New York Review of Books, 1990.

Smith, Jane A., and Kenneth M. Boyd (Eds.). *Lives in the Balance: The Ethics of Using Animals in Biomedical Research.* New York: Oxford University Press, 1991.

Sperlinger, David (Ed.). *Animals in Research: New Perspectives in Animal Experimentation.* New York: Wiley, 1981.

VanDeVeer, Donald, and Christine Pierce. *People, Penguins, and Plastic Trees.* Belmont, CA: Wadsworth, 1986.

❀ *16* ❀

Ethical Issues in Science and Technology

We begin our canvass of some of the ethical issues that arise in the use of science and technology with a case that involves scientific research in medicine. It is an example of a randomized clinical trial, a scientific research method that is an essential tool of modern medicine. This study seeks to determine the possible benefits of an experimental treatment for Parkinson's disease.[1] This frightening disease afflicts 1.5 million people in the United States and many others around the world. Its sufferers first experience weakness and then slurred speech, uncontrollable tremors, and eventually death. The cause of the disease is not entirely known and currently there is no cure. What is known is that the disease works by destroying a small section of the brain, the *substantia nigra,* that controls movement. One new hope for treatment of Parkinson's disease uses the transplanted brain cells from aborted six- to eight-week-old fetuses.[2] In the approximately two hundred cases of this experimental treatment worldwide, the results have been somewhat hopeful but mixed. One-third of participating patients have had their lives dramatically changed for the better, one-third show some improvement, while the remaining third seems not to have any long-lasting benefit from the treatment.

It is not clear that the benefits of this treatment result from the treatment itself and not from a placebo effect or from the disease's natural history. Because Parkinson's disease is so devastating and there is a real possibility that this particular treatment might provide hope for many sufferers, it may be incumbent upon us to find out whether this treatment is effective. In the United States, the National Institutes of Health are supporting two controlled clinical trials of this procedure through a $4.8 million grant for each trial. According to the trial protocols, participants are randomly assigned to one of two groups. One group is to receive the procedure, and the other is to receive a placebo. The study involves fitting the patient's head with a stereotaxic frame for precise measurement. It also involves drilling four holes a little smaller than the diameter of a pencil into each patient's skull. Finally, a physician inserts the fetal tissue through a tube into the proper site in the patient's brain. During the procedure the patient is kept awake so that the physicians know that there is no rupture of blood vessels that might cause a stroke. Only local anesthesia is given, and the anesthesiologist engages the patient in conversation throughout the surgery. To treat the placebo control group the same as the test group, every aspect of the procedure is the same except for the placement of the fetal tissue. Scientific method demands that neither the patients nor the researcher in charge of the study know which patients are in which group. This is to ensure that this knowledge does not influence the outcome.

Scientific Medicine

The design of this and other medical experiments using human subjects is guided by the demands of science. However, we can also ask whether this experiment, as an example of scientific medicine, is an ethical experiment. Since the Nuremberg trials and the resulting code for ethical experimentation, informed consent has been a requirement for the conduct of research involving human subjects. Are the patients in this trial, and others similar to it, likely to be able to give the requisite kind of informed consent to guarantee that the experiment is ethically acceptable? Consider the actual case. The potential participants already have experienced some symptoms of the disease. Here is a treatment that promises to help them. They are informed that the study is a randomized clinical trial and that if they agree to participate they may or may not get the experimental treatment. If they are randomized to the control group rather than the treatment group, then they will go through the same procedure including having holes drilled in their skull and tubes passed into their brain, but they will not actually be receiving anything that will benefit them. In fact, like those in the treatment group, they will be subject to the usual risk of brain damage and stroke that accompanies the procedure.

What kind of thought procedure would such persons be likely to undergo in the process of deciding whether to participate in this trial? Is informed and free consent likely? Would they really be informed of the various details of the procedure? Would they really understand what their chances were for being in the treatment group? Would they by the nature of their disease and great need be influenced, if not coerced, into joining the study? Would they also have to be willing to undergo this risky procedure solely for the sake of the knowledge that might be gained from the study and not for their own immediate benefit? In other

words, would they have to be willing to be used as guinea pigs? It is possible that the conditions of genuine informed and free consent would be met. However, it is also likely that these conditions could not be met, because the patients either would not understand what was involved or would be coerced into participation.

As in the testing of many new medical therapies, modern scientific methodology demands that studies be controlled and randomized or the information derived could be unreliable. However, to do this particular study we seem required to violate one of the demands for an ethical experiment using human subjects, namely, that the consent of the participants be informed and uncoerced. What we have here is an example of one of the many ethical dilemmas that we face today because we live in a world in which modern science and technology are pervasive. We use knowledge gained by science to help us, but we are also subject to the demands of science. Modern technologies provide us with many goods and opportunities, yet in giving us more choices they also present us with more difficult ethical decisions. The decisions have no easy answers. In fact, in many of our choices, such as the one people faced in conducting this experiment, we seem to have to violate one ethical demand or another no matter what we do. Those who analyze the ethics of research using human subjects continue to debate the issues surrounding the informed consent requirement. In the end, this requires that people not be used or not be used for goals and purposes to which they do not consent or make their own. You may recognize this as a requirement of Kant's moral philosophy and can refer to the discussion of its basis in Chapter 5. In this chapter, we will suggest ways to analyze a few other problems presented to us today by modern science and technology.

Science and Technology

In doing any ethical analysis, as you realize by now, it is always useful to begin with definitions.

For example, what is the meaning of the two key terms, *science* and *technology*? Philosophers of science have put much effort and thought into analyzing and describing science. We can put it in simple and broad terms and say that science is first of all a kind of knowing. The term *science* comes from the Latin "scientia," meaning to have knowledge. Today, however, science is characterized by a particular methodology, the hypothetico-deductive method. Observation and verification of hypotheses are essential to it. In itself, it is ethically neutral.[3] It is a means that we use to gain knowledge, and knowledge is a good. Science is valuable either because it is interesting and satisfies our curiosity or because of what good we can achieve by means of it.

The word *technology* comes from the Greek "techne," which means art or craft, and "logia," which means the systematic treatment of something. Thus, technology can be thought of as any systematic method or instrument for achieving some human purpose. Today we tend to think of technology as useful mechanisms or instrumentation. Knives are simple kinds of technology and computers more complicated forms. Just as science is either ethically neutral or good, so also and for the same reason is technology. The ethical problems come from the uses to which they are put. However, this does not mean that some technology could not become so powerful and appealing that we would find it difficult to resist certain problematic uses. Military weapons are just one example.

New or Old Ethical Issues?

It is not clear that modern technology presents us with any new ethical issues. Perhaps we simply are faced with old ethical issues with new applications. Issues of informed consent are not new, even if the kinds of experimentation involving human subjects are new. Issues relating to honesty in the conduct of scientific research have also been discussed since we began to wonder about what was good and right. Issues of harm and benefit are also traditional ethical matters that turn up as ethical issues in many of the technology-related ethical questions discussed today. However, the new applications sometimes give us new opportunities to examine the basis for values such as honesty and freedom. Just why are these valuable and how important are they? Answers to these questions take us back to the matters of ethical theory discussed in the first part of this text, and we will not pursue them again here, except to point out that they are important in this context as well as in more long-standing discussions.

In this chapter, we will consider a few modern scientific technologies and the uses to which they are put and some of the more unique ethical problems they present for us. However, we have already treated some ethical issues raised by modern technologies. In the chapter on euthanasia, for example, we saw how the various medical technologies have given us new control over the process of living and dying, from respirators to surgeries to drugs. The availability of these technologies gives us new ethical problems about whether and when to use them, as we saw in our discussion. In the remainder of this chapter we will focus on the ethical issues raised by new reproductive and genetic technologies, on privacy (which is an issue raised by various technologies), on problems of risk and risk evaluation in business and engineering-related areas, and on the ethical issues raised by new computer and information technologies.

Reproductive and Genetic Technologies

Many ethical issues are raised by the modern reproductive technologies as well as by genetic research and engineering. The following are just a few of them.

Reproduction

Technologies to control conception, pregnancy, and birth have raised ethical questions for some people about their use in abortion, for example.

But the new *reproductive technologies* also raise other ethical questions. There have been many debates about the ethical uses of the various modern reproductive techniques to combine sperm and egg in a dish and produce so-called test-tube babies. Among the ethical questions that have been raised are whether the whole artificiality or mechanization of these procedures makes them morally suspect. Answering this question would involve deciding whether the natural way of forming new humans was the only morally acceptable way. If so, one would have to decide whether one's conclusions should be based on something like a natural law argument or on utilitarian reasons, for example. Another major concern centers around the question of the moral status of the early embryo. In the United Kingdom recently, 3,000 embryos that had been frozen and stored for future implantations were thawed and allowed to die.[4] A British law limited the storage of these frozen embryos to five years. If they had not been claimed by then by their original donors, they were to be destroyed. Some people condemned the event as "prenatal massacre," while others held that even if these were early forms of human life we had no duty to keep them alive in a frozen limbo or to require their implantation in some womb.

The future possibility of *cloning* human beings—that is, making genetically duplicate copies of individuals—raises ethical questions not only about manipulation of human beings but also about personal identity. Genetically identical individuals can be made by replacing the nucleus of an egg with the DNA from another individual, either an adult of the species or an embryo. They also can be made by splitting an early embryo. Although such twinning also occurs naturally, it often presents difficulties as well as benefits for the twins. Do the difficulties outweigh the benefits such that we should not deliberately create twins? In addition, the source of the clone can be a generation older than the newly created individual. Are there good reasons for doing this? If one clones oneself for self-interested purposes, is this ethically acceptable? On

the other hand, if the clone is created to provide possible organ transplants for another, is this ethically acceptable? Other ethical issues raised by the use of *surrogate mothers* and *prenatal embryo transfer* are related to social matters such as the nature of parentage and to concerns about the dangers of commercialization and the buying and selling of babies.[5]

Genetics

Developments in modern genetics also have presented us with new ethical problems. One set is raised by the Human Genome Project. This is the effort undertaken at many laboratories around the world to locate the sites of the approximately 100,000 genes in the DNA of the human cell. Although each person's specific genetic makeup is unique, it is a variation of the basic human model. As of early 1996, some 6,300 of these genes had been identified.[6] The goal of the project is to "know the genome's finest details by the year 2005."[7] Many diseases are genetically based, including diabetes, cystic fibrosis, Huntington's disease, and cancer. At least 4,000 genetic diseases are known. The hope is that the knowledge gained by this project will contribute to the understanding and cure of these diseases. According to geneticist David Botstein, the impact of the Human Genome Project on medicine "should exceed that 100 years ago of X-rays, which gave doctors their first view inside the intact, living body."[8] However, the knowledge will also make it possible to detect predispositions to various diseases in the general population. This type of screening raises many ethical concerns. Its use for employment and for health and life insurance purposes is discussed below with regard to an ethical issue central to it, namely, the matter of privacy.

The possibility of gene therapy also presents us with new ethical problems. If it were possible to use these methods to "turn on," replace, or change malfunctioning genes, then this would be of great benefit for the many people who suffer from genetic disease. Using genetic techniques to provide the blood-clotting factor to hemophiliacs, cheaper insulin to diabetics, human growth hormone to those who need it, and better pain relievers is surely desirable and ethically defensible. However, use of the technology also raises ethical concerns. Among these questions are those related to the risks that exist for those who undergo experimental genetic therapies. We should also be concerned about the access to these procedures, so that it is not just those who are already well off who benefit from them. The biotechnology industry continues to grow. Should information and products of great medical benefit be able to be kept secret and patented by their developers? For example, the company Myriad Genetics recently announced that it had found a gene linked with breast cancer. The company also has attempted to patent the gene.[9] In another example, a newly developed technique allows the alteration of genes in sperm. These genes would affect not the individual himself but his offspring and would alter human lineage.[10] It is one thing to do this in the interest of preventing genetic disease in one's offspring, but it is quite another to add new genetically based capabilities to one's children or to the human race.

Although these are still somewhat remote possibilities only, they give us cause for some concern, not the least of which is whether we are wise enough to do more good than harm by these methods. In 1996 the White House appointed a new bioethics committee to study and advise it on some of these issues.[11] The National Bioethics Advisory Commission is composed of fifteen geneticists, ethicists, and others. This is the third such committee in recent years, all of which have been instrumental in policy formation. The current committee will have as its two major topics of discussion the rights of human research subjects and the use of genetic information. You can continue to follow news accounts of the new reproductive and genetic technologies as well as the reports of committees such as this one. As you do, you should be more aware of the variety of ethical issues that they involve or address. The issues are complex, but the first step in responding to them is to recognize them.

Privacy, Databases, and Screening Procedures

"In a typical five-day stay at a teaching hospital, as many as 150 people—from nursing staff to X-ray technicians to billing clerks—have legitimate access to a single patient's records."[12] Sixteen U.S. states do not now have any guarantees regarding the privacy of medical records.[13] Increasingly, more of the things that we used to take as guaranteed areas of privacy are no longer so. Thus, we need to consider whether this should be the case. We think that people generally have a right to privacy, but we are less sure what this means and what kinds of practices would violate privacy. Suppose, for example, that a technology existed that could read a person's mind and the condition of various parts of her body, could hear and see what goes on in one's home—his bedroom or bathroom—and could record all of these in a data bank that would be accessible to a variety of interested parties. What, if anything, would be wrong with this?[14] One of the things that we find problematic about others having access to this knowledge is that others would have access to matters that we would not want them to know. According to Thomas Scanlon, this is what the right to privacy is: a right "to be free from certain intrusions."[15] Some things, we say, are just none of other people's business.

The Value of Privacy

If this definition of privacy seems reasonable, then we can ask why we would not want certain intrusions as those in the hypothetical example. Many reasons have been suggested, and you may sympathize with some more than others. Four are provided here. The first concerns the kinds of feelings that one would have at certain things being known or observed—one's thoughts, bathroom behavior, or sexual fantasies, for example. It may well be that one should not feel emotions like shame or unease at such things being known. Perhaps we have these feelings simply as a result of social expectation. We may have these *negative feelings*, nevertheless.

A second reason why we might want certain things kept to ourselves is our desire to control information about us and to let it be known only to those to whom we choose to reveal it. Such control is part of our ability to own our own lives. We speak of it as a form of *autonomy* or self-rule. In fact, the loss of control over some of these more personal aspects of our lives is a threat to our very *selfhood,* some say. For example, in his study of what he calls "total institutions" such as prisons and mental hospitals, Erving Goffman described the way that depriving a person of privacy is a way of *mortifying* (literally killing) the self.[16] Having a zone of privacy around us that we control helps us define ourselves and mark us off from others and our environment. This reason for the value of privacy is related to both the third and fourth reasons.

Third, privacy helps in the formation and continuation of *personal relations.* We are more intimate with friends than strangers and more so with lovers than mere acquaintances. Those things about ourselves that we confide in with those closest to us are an essential part of those relationships. According to Charles Fried, "privacy is the necessary context for relationships which we would hardly be human if we had to do without—the relationships of love, friendship, and trust."[17] Sexual intimacies are thus appropriate in the context of a loving relationship because they are privacy sharings that help to establish and further that relationship.

Fourth, we want to keep certain things private because of the risk that the knowledge might be used against us to cause us harm. *Screening* procedures in particular come to mind here. Drug screening, AIDS virus testing, or genetic disease scans all make information available to others that could result in our social detriment. For example, we could be harmed in our employment or our ability to obtain insurance. The problem of *data banks* is also at issue here. Our medical records, records of psychiatric sessions, history of employment, and so forth, could be used legitimately by certain people. However, they may also be misused by those who have no business having access to them. In a particularly problematic recent case, the managed care company that was paying for the psychological counseling of one patient asked to inspect his confidential files. The psychologist, Dr. Arnold Holzman, was concerned. "The audit occurred, they rifled through my files," he said, and "made copies and went. But it changed things. He (the patient) became more concerned about what he was saying. . . . A few visits later he stopped coming."[18] Another case is also illustrative of the harm that can be caused by the invasion of privacy. When Nydia Vela was running for Congress in 1992 to represent New York, someone obtained a copy of her hospital records and sent them anonymously to the press. The *New York Post* published the material, including notes about her attempt to kill herself with sleeping pills and vodka. In spite of this, she won the election; still, she sued the hospital for invasion of privacy.[19]

Drug and Other Kinds of Screening

It is with this fourth reason in particular that the matter of possible *conflict of interest* arises. An employer may have a legitimate interest in having a drug-free workplace. It is an economic interest, for one's employees may not be able to do an effective job if they have drug-use problems. Passengers on public transportation may also have a legitimate interest in seeing that those who build and operate the bus, train, or plane are able to function well and safely. Airline passengers may have an interest in having other passengers and their bags scanned to prevent dangerous materials from being carried on board. It is not clear in whose interest is the drug screening of athletes. In professional athletics, it may be the economic interests of the owners, and in collegiate athletics and nonprofessional competitions such as the Olympics it may be for the sake of the fairness of the competition as well as the health of the athletes themselves.

In cases of conflicts of interest generally, and in the cases given here, we want to know on which side the interest is stronger. In the case of *drug testing* of airline pilots, the safety of the passengers seems clearly to outweigh any interest the pilots might have in retaining their privacy. In the case of employee drug use, it is not so clear that employers' economic interests outweigh the privacy interests of the employees. In these cases one might well argue that unless there is observable evidence of inefficiency, drug testing should not be done, especially mandatory random drug testing. In the case of *genetic screening* by life or health insurance providers, the answer also seems less clear. If a person has a genetic defect that will cause a disease that will affect his life expectancy, is his interest in keeping this information secret more important than the financial interests of the insurer knowing that information? A person's ability to obtain life insurance will affect payments to others on his or her death. In the case of health insurance coverage, where not socially mandated or funded, the weight might well be balanced in favor of the person because having access to health care plays such a major role in a person's health. In fact, some state legislatures are now moving to prevent health insurers from penalizing individuals who are "genetically predisposed to certain diseases."[20] As of mid-1996, twelve U.S. states had laws of this sort. In arguing for these laws, supporters insisted that they were designed to prevent "genetic discrimination." The phrase is apt in that it seeks to prevent people from being singled out and penalized for things that are not in their power to control—their genes.

In the case of *AIDS screening*, consequentialist arguments might make the most sense. We would thus ask whether mandatory testing would really produce more harm than good or more good than harm overall. Would mandatory screening lead fewer people to come forth voluntarily? What of the mandatory screening of physicians, dentists, and their patients? Some people argue that "mandatory testing of health workers for the AIDS virus . . . would be costly, disruptive, a violation of doctors' right to privacy, and the ruination of some careers."[21] The well-known case of a Florida dentist infecting a pa-

tient who later died caused quite a bit of alarm. However, in one study of patients of a surgeon who died of AIDS, 1,652 of his total of 1,896 patients were found and only one, an intravenous drug user, had AIDS.[22] The risk also goes the other way, with patients infecting health care workers. In 1990, the U.S. Centers for Disease Control reported that 5,819 of the 153,000 reported cases of AIDS, or 4 percent, involved health care workers. This included 637 physicians, 42 surgeons, 156 dentists and hygienists, and 1,199 nurses.[23] It is not known whether any of these had other risk factors, but it does raise serious concern for health care workers.

In the case of airport *security screening,* an interesting case was recently reported. A machine is under development that could see through a person's clothing so security personnel could determine better than with current metal detectors whether a person was carrying a concealed item that could pose a danger to others. Would people mind this invasion of their privacy? They would appear nude-like to the screeners. Or would the somewhat better detection achieved by this method not be worth the kind of invasion of privacy that was involved?

This as well as other screening procedures can be evaluated in several ways. However, one of the most reasonable is to compare the interests of the various parties involved in order to determine whether the interest in privacy on the part of the ones screened is stronger or more important morally than the interests of those who wish or need the information produced by the screening. Whether the privacy interest is stronger will depend on why privacy is important. You can determine this by considering some of the reasons why privacy is valuable as given above.

Risk and the Value of a Life
Almost everything we do involves some risk, but so also does not doing anything. We hope that the buildings we reside in are safe, but we know that they are not totally safe. The products that

we buy meet certain safety standards, we hope, but they may still pose some risk. The drugs that we use have gone through safety testing as well as that concerned with their efficacy. The transportation that we use also must meet certain socially acceptable safety standards. However, none of these pieces of modern technology is absolutely risk-free. Every once in a while when some tragic event occurs, a plane crash, for example, "our innocence about technology receives a jolt."[24] We then realize that all technologies carry risk with them. "Technologies switched on for our benefit do not carry a lifetime warranty of satisfaction."[25] At best these technologies involve risks that we are willing to take on—in other words, acceptable risk.[26] But how do we know what is acceptable risk?

To determine whether a certain risk is acceptable, some people have urged us to use a "willingness-to-pay" criterion.[27] The risks at issue here are risks to human life or health. The "willingness-to-pay" measure has two basic characteristics. First, it assumes that the measure to be used in valuing lives should be a function of the value that people place on their own lives. Second, it assumes that small increases (or decreases) of risk and the willingness of people to accept these in exchange for certain desired benefits (or costs) are the basis for interpreting this value. If many people (say 50) would each be willing to pay a certain amount (say $10,000) for a program that would save two of them from an untimely death, then the group would pay $500,000 to save two lives, or $250,000 for each. The "value of a life" to be used then would be $250,000.

We can make our highways and cars and buildings safer, but it will cost more. If we pay so much more we know that we will be able to save some number of lives. Should we pay that amount? That depends on our being able to give a dollar value to a life. At first glance, this seems to be quite wrong. Each human life is worth an infinite amount, we might want to say. Yet we would not be willing to pay even close to that amount. We would pay a certain amount but no

more. If so, it seems that we value the life at about that much. We buy cheaper smaller cars knowing that they present a greater risk. We do not take perfectly good care of our health. Then, some would argue, it seems reasonable that we as a society should also pay only so much to make things safer.

Many questions can be raised about this method of determining how safe we ought to make modern technologies. Not the least of the method's problems is that it relies on how much we *do* in fact value something, our lives, as a basis for determining how much we *ought* to value them. A second problem is that in making our choices we are often ignorant of how much risk is involved so that using peoples' choices about what risk they are willing to take on is not a reliable basis. The problem is amplified by the complexity of today's technologies. The more powerful the technology, the more ominous the side effects seem. "Life-support systems of transportation, communications, military security, biomedical enterprise, energy supply and banking become both more potent and more vulnerable." These technologies are part of complex systems, megasystems. We cannot opt out of them, and we are almost coerced into accepting the risks that they involve. "Failures are unprecedented in intensity of harm, geographical reach and speed of injection."[28] We need to be able to find some ways of calculating the risks as well as the benefits and to ask ourselves what we want or think we ought to pay to reduce those risks. This will depend first and foremost, however, on what we think about the value of a life and how we arrive at this value.

Information Systems and Computer Ethics

"Computers are the core technology of our times."[29] They provide the basis for a new way of communicating. *Information technology* is the name given to the joining of computers and communications systems. Through this technology an amazing amount of information can be stored and transmitted at amazingly fast speed. While the abacus is also a computing machine, advances in computer speed, memory, and size make today's computing machines entirely different. The technology now is pervasive and will become even more so. Almost everything we do is touched by this technology—from payrolls and banking to airline, hotel, concert, and sports reservations, from washing and cooking, to entertainment of all sorts. Everything is going digital. Instead of the analog mechanisms of LPs, we have compact disks. In place of traces of light on a film, cameras are moving to digital filmless imaging.[30]

Amazing as it is to the layperson, today's computers perform their feats through mazes of switches that are a multitude of yes's and no's, on's and off's. Yet the simplicity of this binary logic is having a powerful effect on society. Computer robots are taking the place of assembly workers. Two-year-old children know how to move around a screen scene with a mouse to play games and learn things that in the past they learned only when they went to school. More people are staying at home and telecommuting to work. Electronic mail whizzes us almost instantaneously to the desks of colleagues thousands of miles away. Students tap into library catalog systems and access sources of information on the Internet, an information superhighway. The future will bring even more marvelous things. There will be a paradigm shift in the way people communicate with one another. The personal computer, for example, will also be a phone. Voice, text, and video will come together in multimedia news and entertainment. CD-ROM–based multimedia will integrate audio, graphics, animation, and photographs in a variety of types of documents. One will be able to make personalized cards and letters complete with pictures and video of recent events. Imagine what the term papers of the future will be like as they make use of this confluence of technology! "As the fidelity of visual and audio elements improves, reality in all its aspects will be more closely simulated. This 'virtual reality,' or VR, will allow us to 'go' places and 'do' things we

never would be able to otherwise."[31] We will have PC wallets that we can use instead of tickets on airlines and at concerts. They will be able to tap into a global system that will allow us to find out where we are and how to get where we want to go. They will give us road and weather conditions and the menus at restaurants.[32] There are most surely even more wonderful things ahead.

Any technology, however, is also subject to errors, breakdowns, and misuse. The consequences of these mistakes and breakdowns when relying on computers can be enormous as entire systems of communication or transportation that depend on them can be shut down in an instant. (See the article by Forrester and Morrison in this chapter for examples of what can go wrong.) The technologies also raise ethical questions. The privacy issues that come with computerized data storage have already been discussed above. What to do about pornography on the Internet is a problem that has received considerable attention. Recall our discussion of pornography in Chapter 10, especially as it may relate to free speech issues. Issues of accountability and responsibility for computer technology errors are also among the matters that have both ethical and legal significance. In the remainder of this chapter we will focus on just three ethical issues that these technologies raise, acknowledging that there are others we cannot treat in the limited space here. (See the bibliography at the end of this chapter for sources of further discussion of computer and information technology ethics.)

One of the first things we notice in discussions of computer ethics is the overlap of the moral and the legal. As we have alluded before in this text (for example, in the discussions of pornography as well as euthanasia and abortion), there is a distinction between these two realms of morality and the law. Although many of our laws have a moral basis and cover things that are also moral matters, something does not have to be a legal matter to be a moral matter. Think of ordinary person-to-person lying or wishing in one's mind that harm comes to another. These are surely moral matters but not generally subject to the law. The three issues we focus on briefly here also have legal ramifications: theft, harm, and other social effects of computer and information technology. Our discussion here will focus primarily on the moral issues even when the general reference is to the law.

Computer Theft What counts as stealing or theft of computer-related material? If it is wrong, why is it wrong? One can gain access to computer files that one has no right to and "steal" the data in a way not dissimilar to the way that one takes material from a locked desk or file cabinet.[33] If one copies a computer program for one's own use, is this wrongful stealing? Whether something counts as stealing or theft depends on what counts as ownership. This depends on notions of property and property rights. On this matter, there continues to be something of a legal muddle. Sometimes ownership of software is claimed as a matter of intellectual property rights. These are rights to "the results of intellectual activity in the industrial, scientific, literary, or artistic fields."[34] Thus, some people claim rights to computer software using copyright law and practices. One cannot legally own an idea, but one can own its expression. It is not clear that this is also the case morally. If an idea is my own creative invention, it can be said to be mine, it would seem. This would be most difficult to legally enforce, however. Others see the software claims as best fitting patent law because they see software as a matter of making changes in computer hardware. Would this make sense morally? Though my changing of something is my way of exerting my influence on what I change, can I be said to own something that is there before I make changes in it? Still others believe that at least some computing ownership and theft matters ought to fall under contract law regarding trade secrets. In times past we could more easily distinguish print and mechanical inventions. Today these matters are no longer so simple.

One can notice, however, the extent to which these complex ownership matters rely on more philosophical notions about the nature and value of *property*. Just what does it mean to own something, what can I own, and why? One of the most well-known sources for views about the origins of property is the writing of John Locke. He holds that those who have put their *labor* into something have a *natural right* to the fruits of that labor.[35] Thus, if I plant seeds in ground that is owned in common, I have a natural right to keep and eat the vegetables that grow, according to Locke. According to later developments of this view, I do not have a right to the vegetables or other products themselves, especially if the resources are not my own, but merely to wages for the labor. According to a Marxist view, ideally one should not labor in order to possess its fruits or even wages. One should find fulfillment in the labor itself.[36] Thus, for Marx property is not so important: It is the labor itself that should be fulfilling. For his successor, Hegel, the fulfillment that comes from labor results from the fact that in laboring one finds a way to give concrete reality to one's inner self.[37] Thus, labor is a necessary stage in the process of self-development. Although these views are somewhat abstract, they may have some implications for what we say about property in the world of computers and information technology. What do we say is important about labor and property? Is it having the product possessed to keep and use for oneself? Is it the laboring itself that should ideally be its own reward? Or is it the ability to develop personally through expression of one's inner self? And furthermore, what kinds of things could one rightly be said to own if ownership is important?

Because the tradition of a natural rights basis for ownership raises so many problems, other philosophers have proposed a *social concept* of property. One such view is *utilitarian* in nature; that is the notion that we ought to allow people to own and transfer ownership of certain things in certain ways because this has good results overall. "Unless individuals and companies have some proprietary rights in what they create, they will not invest the time, energy, and resources needed to develop and market software," for example.[38] Whether some system of ownership is or is not a good one is thus an empirical question, namely, one about what particular system of ownership works the best. Does proprietary ownership of software, for example, prevent or stimulate creativity and development? Perhaps the general principle suggested by Deborah Johnson, who writes extensively about computer ethics, ought to be followed. According to her, we should design systems "so that software developers can own something of value but not something which will interfere, in the long run, with developments in the field."[39] Perhaps some combination of a natural rights and utilitarian view would be most reasonable. It does make some sense to say that it is appropriate for people to get something in return for contributing their efforts and creative ideas to some good project. This seems right not only because of the good that results from their contributions, but also because of the fairness principle involved.

Hackers, Viruses, and Computer Sabotage A second issue in computer ethics that has gained some notoriety in recent years involves the harm that results from deliberate destructive activities.[40] Computer hacking involves breaking into a computer system. In some cases, the purpose is simple curiosity or the challenge of cracking a security system. In these cases, one can ask whether any harm is done. If there is none, is there anything wrong with it? Is it or is it not similar to asking whether there is any wrong done if someone breaks into your home and just looks around? One difference might be the fear that is instilled in the homeowner who knows this has happened. However, if no one knows, then what would we say? On the other hand, if the hacker not only breaks in but also does some damage by way of planting bothersome or harmful viruses and worms, then this is another matter. Breaking in to steal money or to change grades or data also causes harm. Some would argue that if the hacker breaks in to do some good, then the hacking is justified. If, for example, the hacker seeks to test some security system and the result is that the system is tightened, then the hacker could be said to perform a valuable service. If one is judging on utilitarian grounds and if the good results overall outweigh the bad ones, then the break-in is justified, according to this view. Some forms of hacking may be likened to engaging in civil disobedience. If the break-in is to protest something they view as an injustice—say, capitalist financial systems or the military-industrial complex—then in this view their sabotage is justified. To decide whether this is so, one would need to consider whether breaking the law is ever justified for purposes of civil disobedience and also whether what is being protested is, in fact, an evil.

Social Effects of Information Technology Although we can cite many advantages of these new technologies, there are also social effects that are somewhat worrisome. One is the effect of the technology on jobs and work. Sometimes the results are harmful to the health of the workers, as in the case of the repetitive strain injuries caused by work at video display terminals. This problem, however, is no different from other technologies that pose a risk to human health. Ways ought to be found to manage or overcome the risks. Where this cannot be done or it is costly, questions can be raised from a cost-benefit analysis perspective. Is the prevention of health problems and disability of workers worth a certain payment? The same problems discussed earlier about the value of a quality of life arise in this context.

Another problem is the replacement of workers by robots and other electronic devices. Just because telephone operators are now replaced by automatic switches, we do not conclude that we ought to return to the human operators. However, we can surely ask whether society has not some responsibility for worker displacement, when society is the beneficiary of the new way of doing things. Is it not a form of "payback" in the sense that we should not get the new benefit without paying for it, including paying those who are out of a job because of it?

A more difficult philosophical problem posed by the development of information technology is the problem of centralization of power. Those who have the more powerful tools will have the greater power. If these tools are centralized either in government or in private organizations, then we may rightly have some cause for concern. On the one hand, centralization brings with it a certain amount of increased efficiency. It avoids duplication, for example. On the other hand, we value our freedom and our privacy. To the extent that the centralization of computer technology threatens these, they are problematic, and ways ought to be found to lessen their control over our lives or to give us more control in the form of vetoes or consent requirements or privacy regulations, for example.

Finally, the fact that those who have the more powerful tools will have greater freedom and opportunity raises questions about access to this technology. If only those who are already socially advantaged have access to the educational opportunities that involve training in these computer and information-technology skills, then the gap between the haves and have-nots will grow even wider than now. If there is an inherent unfairness in the fact that children born into disadvantaged circumstances will be handicapped from the start, then means must be found to make computer education as widely available as possible. This is in the interest of not only greater benefit to all, but also justice.

In the readings in this chapter, Robert Sinsheimer focuses on ethical issues involved in genetic technology, and Tom Forrester and Perry Morrison address privacy issues raised by the new information technologies.

Notes

1. See Barbara MacKinnon, "How Important Is Consent for Controlled Clinical Trials?" *Cambridge Quarterly of Healthcare Ethics,* vol. 5, no. 2 (Spring 1996), pp. 221–227.

2. We will bracket the issue of using aborted fetuses in research for the purpose of focusing on the other aspects of this study.

3. This would not be the case if it included the belief that only what was observable and verifiable was real or valuable.

4. The story was covered by various newspapers for August 1, 1996. See, for example, *The Vancouver Sun* (Aug. 1, 1996), p. A8.

5. The procedure known as "embryo transfer" involves flushing the embryo out of the uterus and implanting it in the uterus of another female. Sometimes this is done when a wife is able to carry a fetus but not able to conceive because of damaged or missing ovaries. Her husband can provide the sperm for artificial insemination of a surrogate. The procedure then transfers the fetus to her uterus, and she undergoes a normal pregnancy and birth.

6. *New York Times* (Jan. 5, 1996), p. A11.

7. "A Map for an Incredible Journey," *San Francisco Chronicle* (Aug. 18, 1996), "Sunday Interview," p. 3.

8. Ibid.

9. Reported in *New York Times* (May 21, 1996).

10. *New York Times* (Nov. 22, 1994), p. A1

11. *Science,* vol. 273 (Aug. 2, 1996), p. 583.

12. Who's Looking at Your Files?" *Time* (May 6, 1996), pp. 60–62.

13. Ibid.

14. This is modeled after a "thought experiment" by Richard Wasserstrom in "Privacy," *Today's Moral Problems,* 2nd ed. (New York: Macmillan, 1979), pp. 392–408.

15. Thomas Scanlon, "Thomson on Privacy," in *Philosophy and Public Affairs,* vol. 4, no. 4 (Summer 1975), pp. 295–333. This volume also contains other essays on privacy, including one by Judith Jarvis Thomson on which this article comments. W. A. Parent offers another definition of privacy as "the condition of not having undocumented personal knowledge about one possessed by others." W. A. Parent, "Privacy, Morality, and the Law," *Philosophy and Public Affairs,* vol. 12, no. 4 (Fall 1983), pp. 269–288.

16. Erving Goffman, *Asylums* (Garden City, NY: Anchor Books, 1961).

17. Charles Fried, *An Anatomy of Values: Problems of Personal and Social Choice* (Cambridge, MA: Harvard University Press, 1970), p. 142.

18. "Questions of Privacy Roil Arena of Psychotherapy," *New York Times* (May 22, 1996), p. A1.

19. "Who's Looking at Your Files?" op. cit.

20. "Bill in New Jersey Would Limit Use of Genetic Tests by Insurers," *New York Times* (June 18, 1996), p. A1.

21. *New York Times* (Dec. 27, 1990), pp. A1, A15.
22. Ibid.
23. Ibid.
24. "TWA Crash Raises Technology Issues," in *Seattle Post Intelligence* (Aug. 7, 1996), p. A9.
25. Ibid.
26. See discussion of the phrase in Guido Calebresi and Philip Bobbitt, *Tragic Choices* (New York: W. W. Norton, 1978). Also see Baruch Fischhoff, Sarah Lichtenstein, Paul Slovic, S. L. Derby, and Ralph L. Keeney, *Acceptable Risk* (Cambridge: Cambridge University Press, 1981); Baruch Fischhoff et al., "How Safe Is Safe Enough? A Psychometric Study of Attitudes Toward Technological Risks and Benefits," *Decision Research Report* (Eugene, OR: 1976), pp. 76–79; and Barbara MacKinnon, "Pricing Human Life," *Science, Technology, and Human Values*, vol. 11, no. 2 (Spring 1986), pp. 29–39.
27. See Barbara MacKinnon, "Pricing Human Life," in *Science, Technology, and Human Values*, vol. 11, no. 2 (Spring 1986), pp. 29–39. Also see J.G.U. Adams, " . . . and How Much for Your Grandmother?" in Steven E. Rhoads (Ed.), *Valuing Life: Public Policy Dilemmas* (Boulder, CO: Westview, 1980), pp. 146ff; and M. W. Jones-Lee, *The Value of a Life* (Chicago: University of Chicago Press, 1976).
28. "TWA Crash Raises Technology Issues," op. cit.
29. Tom Forrester and Perry Morrison, *Computer Ethics: Cautionary Tales and Ethical Dilemmas in Computing* (Cambridge, MA: MIT Press, 1990), p. 1.
30. See, for example, "Konica Plans Electronic Camera," *San Francisco Chronicle* (Aug. 17, 1996), p. D8.
31. Bill Gates, *The Road Ahead* (New York: Viking Press, 1995), p. 130.
32. Ibid., pp. 74–78.
33. An interesting discussion of the use of such analogies in ethical analyses of computer ethics can be found in Deborah G. Johnson, *Computer Ethics*, 2nd ed. (Englewood Cliffs, NJ: Prentice-Hall, 1994), pp. 11–14.
34. Ibid., p. 31.
35. See John Locke, *Two Treatises of Government* (1690). Also note the discussion of the relevance of this view to computer-related property in Johnson, op. cit., pp. 70–75.
36. Karl Marx, "Economic and Philosophical Manuscripts," T. B. Bottomore (Ed.), in *Karl Marx: Early Writings* (London, 1963).
37. G.W.F. Hegel, *Hegel's Philosophy of Right*, translated with notes by T. M. Knox (Oxford, 1942).
38. Johnson, op. cit., p. 73.
39. Ibid., p. 74.
40. See Forrester and Morrison, op. cit., pp. 40–67, and Johnson, op. cit., pp. 103–123.

Genetic Engineering: Life as a Plaything

Robert L. Sinsheimer

Study Questions

1. According to Sinsheimer, how will the old ways of evolution be changed by current genetic-engineering techniques?

2. Describe three ways in which the new techniques of genetic control might be realized.

3. What three questions does Sinsheimer think we ought to ask about these possibilities? Explain each.

4. What problems does Sinsheimer raise regarding the possibility of our using genetic engineering to take over the control from nature of our own selves?

5. How does Sinsheimer use the analogy of a card game to explain one of his concerns?

6. Describe the problems he raises about university research in this area.

7. In particular, how does Sinsheimer believe this type of genetic control poses risks to a sense of human dignity?

In a process almost as old as the earth, a huge panoply of organisms has evolved. The process has been one of chance and selection, and the star player has been the gene. For 3 billion years, natural changes in the number, structure, and organization of genes have determined the course of evolution.

We have now come to the end of that familiar pathway. Genetics—the science of heredity—has unlocked the code book of life, and the long-hidden strategies of evolution are revealing themselves. We now possess the ability to manipulate genes, and we can direct the future course of evolution. We can reassemble old genes and devise new ones. We can plan, and with computer simulation ultimately anticipate, the future forms and paths of life. Mutation and natural selection will continue, of course. But henceforth, the old ways of evolution will be dwarfed by the role of purposeful human intelligence. In the hands of the genetic engineer, life forms could become extraordinary Tinkertoys and life itself just another design problem.

Genetic engineering is a whole new technology. To view it as merely another technological development may make sense for those who invest in its commercial exploitation. But such a view is myopic for anyone concerned with the future of humanity. I want to consider three major areas of concern that will surely arise from this new technology. The first is the transformation of the science of biology itself. The development of molecular genetics is a transition as profound for biology as the development of quantum theory was for physics and chemistry. Until recently, biology was essentially an analytical science, in which researchers undertook the dissection of Nature as observed. Genetic engineering now furnishes us with the ability to design and invent living organisms as well as to observe and analyze their function. If we consider the significance of synthesis to the science of chemistry, we can perhaps envision the importance of this development for the science of biology.

A New Biology

The new techniques open the door to a detailed understanding of the form and organization of genetic structures in higher organisms, of the control of gene expression, and of the processes of cellular differentiation. Out of such knowledge will come a new biology that gives us the means to intervene in life processes at the most basic possible level.

Robert L. Sinsheimer, "Genetic Engineering: Life as a Plaything," *Technology Review* (April 1983), pp. 14, 15, 70. Reprinted with permission.

The impact of this new biology on the practical and technical arts—the second area of development—will be profound. With this technology, human ingenuity could design agricultural crops that thrive in arid zones or brackish waters, that provide better human nutrition, that resist disease and pests. Human-designed crops, adapted to the needs of efficient agricultural technology, could leap ahead of their natural parasites and predators.

In chemistry, microorganisms could be programmed to carry out the complex organic synthesis of new pharmaceuticals, pesticides, and chemical catalysts. Other organisms could be programmed to degrade chemical compounds and reduce environmental pollution. In animal husbandry, the prospects seem equally bright for designing disease-resistant, fast-growing, nutritious animal forms. In medicine, we envision the synthesis of antibiotics, hormones, vaccines, and other complex pharmaceuticals. But these achievements, almost certainly feasible, will pale before the potential latent in the deeper understanding of biology.

Control over gene expression will provide a whole new array of therapies for genetic disorders. And that introduces the third domain of consequence and the most profound. With the decline of infectious diseases, genetic disorders are now increasingly the source of ill health. Diabetes, cystic fibrosis, sickle-cell anemia, and Tay-Sachs disease all stem from well-recognized genetic defects. The possibilities of human gene therapy—replacing the "bad" gene with the "good"—are extraordinary.

The Darker Side

It is not hard to sense the excitement, the challenge, the promise in all these ventures. But is there a catch? Is there a darker side to this vision as we have come to see it in other new technologies? Some of us believe there may be—that life is not just another design problem, that life is different from nonlife. Just as nature stumbled upon life some 3 billion years ago and unwittingly began the whole pageant of evolution, so too the new creators may find that living organisms have a destiny of their own. They may find that genetic engineering has consequences far beyond those of conventional engineering.

As we become increasingly confident that this technology can, in fact, be achieved, there are a few major questions to be asked: Is it safe, is it wise, is it moral?

First, is it safe? If we can keep the developments open to public scrutiny, then I believe in the short term it probably is. We can monitor the hazards of any new product we introduce into the biosphere and can probably cope with any immediate, untoward consequence.

For the long term, however, I am considerably less sure. Life has evolved on this planet in a delicately balanced, intricate, self-sustaining network. Maintaining this network involves many interactions and equilibria that we understand only dimly. I would suggest that we must take great care, as we replace the creatures and vegetation of earth with human-designed forms, as we reshape the animate world to conform to human will, that we not forget our origins and inadvertently collapse the ecological system in which we have found our niche.

Through intensive study, we have learned of the different pathogens that prey on humans, animals, and major crops. But we have a very limited understanding of the evolutionary factors that led to their existence. We have limited knowledge about the reservoir of potential pathogens—organisms that could be converted by one or two or five mutations from harmless bugs into serious menaces. And thus we cannot really predict whether our genetic tinkering might unwittingly lead to novel and unexpected hazards.

More broadly, is it wise for us to assume responsibility for the structure and cohesion of the animate world? Do we want to engineer the planet so that its function requires the continuous input of human intelligence? Do we want to convert Earth into a giant Skylab?

Life as Our Plaything

What happens to the reverence for life when life is our creation, our plaything? Will we have species with planned obsolescence? Will we have genetic olympics for homing pigeons or racing dogs? Will we have a zoo of reconstructed vanished species—dinosaurs or sabre-toothed tigers—or as-yet unimagined species? Genetic engineering will inevitably change our sense of kinship with all our fellow creatures.

Will the extinction of species mean much when we can create new ones at will? Until now, we have all been the children of nature, the progeny of evolution. But from now on the flora and fauna of Earth will increasingly be our creations, our designs, and

thus our responsibility. What will happen to our nature in such a world?

The most profound consequence of this technology is its application to humankind. The impetus to employ genetic engineering on the human race will come, I believe, out of our humanitarian tradition. Genetic engineering will be seen as just another branch of surgery, albeit at the most delicate level. Since we now know that many sources of human misery are genetic in origin, the urge to remedy these defects and even eliminate their transmission to succeeding generations will be irresistible. Thus, these changes will become part of the human genetic inheritance—for better or worse.

Having acquired the technology to provide genetic therapy, will we then be able to draw a line and restrict human genetic experimentation? How will we define a "defect"? And how will we argue against genetic "improvement"? Or should we? Will we even stop to consider the morality of what's being done?

The extent to which our more specifically human qualities—our emotions and intellects, our compassion and conscience—are genetically determined is not yet known. But geneticists cannot escape the dark suspicion that more is written in our genes than we like to think.

What will happen if we tamper with our physical or mental traits, given the complexity of human development and behavior? Such banal qualities as height and weight can surely affect one's identity, and good health has its own concomitants. How many of our greatest artistic works have been produced by the afflicted or the neurotic?

I suspect human genetic engineering is repugnant to many people because they think its purpose is to impose an identity upon a descendant, to replace the sport of Nature with models of human fancy.

In some sense, education is an attempt to impose an identity. An educational system demands adherence to values of attention, concentration, delayed gratification, and so on. Mere literacy, while enlarging freedom by opening new worlds of knowledge, destroys the freedom of innocence. Yet clearly we have long decided that the virtues of literacy outweigh any drawbacks. University literacy is regarded as good and mandated in most societies. Might there be similar genetic characteristics that we would come to regard as a universal good?

Cloning can be seen as an extreme effort to impose a particular identity—upon a descendant. But all human genetic engineering will move us toward that extreme.

Genetic Lottery

Genetic engineering is the ultimate technology, for it makes plastic the very user and creator of that technology. This new tool makes conceivable a vast number of alternative evolutionary paths. We may even be able to adapt humankind to varied technological regimes.

Will we try, for instance, to breed—or mutate— people fit to work in special environments? Miniature people to travel in space or live on our overpopulated Earth? Will we create people resistant to carcinogens, radiation, and pesticides to work in chemical factories, nuclear plants, and farms? Or, alternatively, will we breed people who are better able to tolerate cytotoxic drugs should they contract cancer? What intellectual abilities, psychological strengths and life spans would we choose?

I hope it is clear that the whole character of human life is at issue. To use a simile: Life has been a game, like cards, where each of us seeks to make the best of the hands (or genes) dealt to us. Shall it become a game like football, a collective strategy in which people play assigned roles in a coordinated plan? Or might it become more like a card game with a rigged deck, with more aces and fewer treys. If so, who designates the aces?

How will people react when they realize that their very genes are the product of a social decision? Will they rebel against such predestination? Will they become sullen and passive? Or will our descendants be proud they were each "planned," not the product of a genetic lottery but the recipient of the best inheritance our culture could devise at the time? How will they then react should a better model become available during their teens?

To what extent should we consciously leave a place for the element of chance in human affairs?

I suspect there is no turning back from the use of this awesome knowledge. Given the nature of our society, which embraces and applies any new technology, it appears that there is no means, short of unwanted catastrophe, to prevent the development of genetic engineering. It will proceed. But this time, perhaps we can seek to anticipate and guide its consequences.

Taking the Larger View

I believe the university is the place to address and analyze the social consequences of technological innovation. Yet even in academia, pressures for immediate results distract researchers from the quest for deeper understanding. Indeed, a salient characteristic of our increasingly secular society is its emphasis on the short-term payoff. We must try to avoid this myopia in developing this new technology. We must seek to protect the larger view.

Among other things, we must insist that university research continue to be available for public scrutiny in the open scientific literature, that it not be secreted as proprietary information and industrial know-how. We must also insist that private funding directed toward patentable and profitable inventions does not grossly exceed public funding directed toward the general increase of knowledge, including an understanding of possible hazards.

I would suggest that what we sorely need now is a new group of trained professionals to mediate between scientists and engineers on the one hand and citizenry on the other. Such professionals should be practicing scientists more broadly educated in our humanistic traditions. They would be trained to understand the potential implicit in this new technology, able to balance the ethos of environmentalists with the concerns of those who cherish civil liberty, able to perceive the imperatives of a technological society and still bear in mind that technology exists to serve. They would remember that the human species is very diverse, that it encompasses both a Mahatma Gandhi and an Adolf Hitler.

Ecclesiastes tells us that "he that increaseth knowledge increaseth sorrow." The modern version might be "he that increaseth knowledge increaseth power." Western society has become, in a sense, an extraordinary machine for converting knowledge into power.

Human beings, of course, are sprung from the same DNA and built of the same molecules as all other living things. But if we begin to regard ourselves as just another crop to be engineered, just another breed to be perfected, we will lose our awe of humanity and undermine all sense of human dignity.

The Invasion of Privacy

Tom Forrester and Perry Morrison

Study Questions

1. What is the example of the three young French men supposed to show, according to Forrester and Morrison?

2. How else can things go wrong with computer-based record keeping?

3. What examples of computer-based government surveillance practices do the authors cite?

4. What do Forrester and Morrison believe is the basic conflict of interests that such surveillance practices exemplify?

5. What examples of what they believe is justifiable surveillance do the authors give?

6. According to the authors, what two basic processes exemplify how democracy functions? What kind of balance ought they ideally achieve?

7. How are surveillance techniques sometimes used by private companies?

8. What benefits and dangers do Forrester and Morrison cite regarding such use?

9. How does this area of computer use again exemplify the kind of balance the authors discuss?

On Friday 9 November 1979, three young Frenchmen filled their car with petrol at a service station in Etampes, a small town near Paris. The owner of the service station noticed that the license plate was patched together with pieces of tape and became suspicious, especially after the cheque they offered had a scrawled signature on its face. He took a note of the license number and contacted police after the men had left. A routine interrogation of their database revealed to police that the car had been stolen and a patrol car was dispatched to intercept. The police caught up with the young men who had stopped at traffic lights. Two officers in plain clothes jumped out

Tom Forrester and Perry Morrison, *The Invasion of Privacy* (Cambridge, MA: MIT Press, 1990), pp. 88–90, 96–98, 99–103. Reprinted with permission.

of the patrol car, one holding a machine gun, the other a .357 magnum revolver. The only uniformed officer remained in the car. Although the precise sequence of the subsequent events is still not clear, it is known that the officer with the magnum revolver opened fire on the trio. A bullet pierced the windscreen and hit one of the young men just under the nose. The other two men were then informed that their assailants were police (not gangsters) and they were handcuffed while an ambulance came to assist their injured friend.

Later investigations placed the whole matter in a quite different light. One of the three men had purchased the car, quite legally, ten days before. It was true that the car had once been stolen, but that was in 1976 and it had been recovered by the insurance company which then sold it to the firm from which the man later legally bought it. The primary cause of this incident therefore was a failure to update the computer file covering the vehicle so that changes in status and ownership were accurately represented. Unfortunately, at the time of interrogation, police records still labeled the vehicle as stolen and police reacted as if they were dealing with potentially dangerous criminals.[1]

This example shows the impact that databases and computer-based information of all kinds can have on the quality of our lives. It also demonstrates the considerable faith we place in computer-based records—a faith that may be unjustified—and shows some of the dangers for individuals when such records are inadequate for the purposes for which they were designed. . . .

What we must bear in mind from the outset is that the hallmark of any truly democratic society is a balance of power between limits that are acceptable to the majority of its citizens. This is much easier to say than to achieve, since conflicts exist between the needs and expectations of the individual and the obligations and roles of the organizations and agencies that serve key functions in any complex, technological society. Therefore, this chapter is really about balance and how it is (and isn't) maintained in the kind of society that the Western democracies have constructed. It is through this lens that the fundamental ethical issues associated with privacy, surveillance and democracy will be viewed.

Database Disasters

Although the following cases were isolated incidents, they are nevertheless starkly illustrative of the way things can go wrong with computer-based record keeping and surveillance.

Houston schoolteacher Darlene Alexander believed that she had a respectable credit record—that is until she applied for a $75,000 mortgage and the lender informed her that she had accumulated too much debt to be considered. Her records showed outstanding accounts for American Express, Master-Card and Visa, and a $22,800 loan for a Chevrolet Camaro. None of the accounts were really hers—and she owned outright a 1983 Datsun. Ms. Alexander had become a victim of the so-called "credit doctors"—people who steal good credit histories and then sell them to those who have accumulated atrocious credit histories. An impostor had opened accounts in her name and had taken out loans, the net result being that Ms. Alexander is now stuck with a poor lending history and has little chance of gaining credit for a home purchase or other important purposes.

In many ways the *modus operandi* of credit doctors is very similar to that of the most malicious kinds of hackers. Generally, credit doctors work by bribing credit agency employees to reveal the passwords to their systems. Then, logging in with a personal computer, they search for someone with the same name as their client—someone who also happens to have a good credit history. Having found this, the credit doctor copies the information associated with this person (including the all-important social security number) and supplies it to their client. Hey Presto! The client now has instant, easy credit. But what makes credit doctoring even more attractive is that generally the offense will not be discovered until the real owner of the identity happens to make an inquiry—mostly as a result of too much debt being accumulated. But by that time the credit doctor will have already supplied them with another illicitly gained line of credit.[2]

In another interesting incident, American Express contacted one of its members because of concern that he may not be able to pay his account. American Express had actually accessed this person's current account to discover that the member had less money than they were owed, causing the company to "deactivate" his card. However, it appears that the fine print of the American Express application form reserves the right to access members' accounts in order to determine if the member has the capacity to actually pay. Some might argue that we vilify used car dealers for less than this![3]

A further example of a database dust-up severely affected the life of Michael DuCross, a Canadian-born Indian living in Huntington Beach, California. At around 9:00 p.m. on 24 March 1980, DuCross drove to a local supermarket and was stopped by a police patrol car after he had made an illegal left-hand turn. The policeman took down DuCross's name and driving license number and asked for a check of identity using his two-way radio. The request went to Sacramento, the state's capital and then was sent 3,000 miles east to the FBI's National Crime Information Center in Washington. These records indicated that DuCross was wanted by the Federal government for going AWOL from the Marine Corps at Christmas, 1969. Based on that information and despite his protestations of innocence, DuCross was taken to the brig at Camp Pendleton, California. *Five months later,* the charges were dropped after it was discovered that DuCross had never gone AWOL—he had left the Marine Corps voluntarily in 1969 under a special discharge program for resident aliens. Again, the faith placed in the accuracy of computer-based records appears to have been totally misplaced: the victim, Michael DuCross, lost five months of his life because of blatant database mismanagement.[4]

Another example of misplaced trust in the adequacy of computer-based records is provided by the experience of a US citizen whose wallet was stolen by a criminal who subsequently adopted his identity. The thief was later involved in a robbery involving murder and through the circumstances of the case, his adopted identity became known to the Los Angeles Police Department. This information was duly stored in their database and when the legitimate owner of the identity was stopped for a routine traffic violation, the computer indicated that he was a prime murder suspect and he was immediately arrested. As might be expected, he spent a few days in jail until the full details were revealed. Now, at first sight this incident might be regarded as a tolerable error. However, even after the confusion of identities had been discovered, this individual was arrested *five times in fourteen months* on the basis of the same incorrect data records. After extensive frustration, he managed to obtain a letter from the local chief of police indicating that he was *not* a real murder suspect and that the database records were wrong. Yet, although the letter was sufficient for his local area, experience soon showed that it held little weight when he traveled in other states. Only after a protracted court battle was the record finally expunged.[5]

Of course the vast majority of database errors are not as devastating as this—mostly they just produce hardship and frustration. Yet the frequency with which such hardship and frustration occurs is increasing, given the rapid penetration of database services into more domestic areas of our lives. For example, in 1977, Harvey Saltz, a former Los Angeles district attorney, formed UD Registry Inc., which provides landlords with information about prospective tenants. Saltz's company takes information from legal suits filed by landlords against tenants and 1,900 landlords (at the last count) pay him an annual fee to identify potential tenants who have been sued by landlords in the past.

On the face of it, this seems like a reasonable precaution for landlords to take. However, anyone who has ever attempted to find rented accommodation and been puzzled by rejection could gain some insight from the case of Barbara Ward, a resident of Los Angeles. In 1972, she rented an apartment and found that it was infested with cockroaches and rodents. When her landlord refused to deal with the infestation, Ward gave him 30 days notice and he countered with an eviction notice. Ward went to court with documentary evidence in the form of county health records, but the landlord failed to show. The case was dropped, but a few years later, Ward was refused accommodation by several landlords because her listing in Harvey Saltz's UD Registry computer showed that she had once been served with an eviction notice. Unfortunately for Ward, she was not aware of UD Registry's existence, let alone the fact that it had generated and was perpetuating incomplete information about her tenancy history.[6]

Perhaps the most extensive case study in the public domain on the effects of surveillance can be found in *The File,* by Peter Kimball, a former professor of journalism at Columbia University.[7] When released under the Freedom of Information Act, Kimball's personal file at the FBI revealed that for more than 30 years he had been classified as an undesirable citizen and a communist sympathizer—one who was "too clever" to be found holding a party card. This classification resulted from the combination and embellishment of two incidents early in his life. . . .

Big Brother Is Watching You

For many civil liberties' campaigners, the US National Security Agency (NSA) is the very epitome of what we have most to fear in terms of the invasion of individuals' privacy and the covert control of peoples' lives. The responsibilities and limitations of the NSA have never been clearly defined by the US Congress and since its establishment by President Truman in 1952, it has operated solely on the basis of a series of White House directives. This agency has a budget that is some five to six times that of the CIA and is reputed to have the most sophisticated and awesome computing capability of any single existing organization— enough to intercept and analyze perhaps 70 per cent of all telephone, telex, data and radio transmissions generated on earth. In 1971, the agency decided it needed a high-temperature incinerator to dispose of the masses of printouts and secret documents that it generated every day in the course of its activities. The specification required that the unit be capable of destroying at least six tons an hour and not less than 36 tons in any eight-hour shift, such is the size and extent of the agency's activities.[8]

Of course, the NSA was not created in some political or social vacuum. Like a number of other intelligence agencies in the United States, it emerged as a response to perceived threats and social circumstances that alarmed governments of the day. For example, during the Kennedy administration, far-reaching efforts were initiated to keep track of civil rights' activists such as Martin Luther King, members of Congress such as Abner Mikva and members civil liberties' organizations like the American Civil Liberties Union, the American Friends Services Committee and the National Association for the Advancement of Colored Peoples (NAACP). During the Johnson administration, concern about race riots, civil rights demonstrations and anti-war protests prompted the President to order the army to increase its surveillance activities, thereby creating files on about 100,000 individuals and a vast number of organizations. Richard Nixon was accused of having violated the law by obtaining the computerized tax files of his political enemies—but he was unsuccessful in his attempts to require all television sets sold in the United States to be equipped with a device that would allow them to be turned on from a central location![9]

In 1967, the FBI established the National Crime Information Center to maintain computer-based files on missing persons, warrants, stolen property, securities, criminal histories and registered property (guns, vehicles, etc.). With an annual operating budget of approximately $6 million, NCIC houses some 8 million individual dossiers (that is, on one in every 30 Americans) and this is expected to grow to encompass records on 90 per cent of all US residents with arrest records—or as many as 35 million people, approximately 40 per cent of the US labor force. About 64,000 federal, state and local police agencies have authority to access NCIC data via one of the 17,000 terminals now linked to the Center.[10]

Once more, this illustrates the classic tug-of-war between the perceived role of the state in preserving law and order and its own national security, versus the rights of individuals to fundamental democratic freedoms. A good example of the instability of this democratic tightrope is the NSA's involvement with the establishment of encryption standards. Encryption—or more properly cryptography—is the science of codes and code-breaking. Because of the sensitivity of many financial transactions and other data communications, encryption is becoming an increasingly favored precaution. With encryption, even if a transmission is tapped or illicitly recorded, decoding the message is so computationally demanding that only the most skilled of individuals with the best of computing facilities could hope to achieve it within a reasonable period of time.

During the establishment of the Data Encryption Standard (DES)—a set of universally acceptable conventions for encryption—the NSA lobbied strongly inside ANSI (the US representative within the International Standards Organization (ISO)) to have the DES disapproved. The most popular interpretation of this act is that wide standardization of encryption and its concomitant routine use would make it substantially more difficult for the NSA to monitor overseas voice and data communications. Similarly, in the early 1980s several major banks and financial institutions in the US met to determine characteristics of encryption keys (the number sequences used to decode encrypted messages) that were of prodigious length (some 50–100 digits long). Once more, the

NSA successfully exerted enormous pressure on these bodies to drop the proposal and again for very obvious practical reasons. The facts are that encryption keys of this length would have possibly meant that messages would have taken 3–4 days to break using the existing facilities of the NSA and obviously this would have placed the agency in extreme difficulties if it wished to monitor such transactions. Even worse, it would have become a nightmare for the organization if such practices caught on and became commonplace.[11]

Despite these alarming developments, we must also bear in mind that in many circumstances the need for surveillance appears patently obvious and totally warranted. For example, in the war against drugs and terrorism, the application of sophisticated technology would appear to be an appropriate and much-needed source of countermeasures. In accordance with this, the US Defense Advanced Research Projects Agency (DARPA) is now involved in a multi-million dollar program to apply artificial intelligence and parallel processing techniques to the detection and elimination of drug-related criminal activities. These initiatives will involve tracking currency, cargo shipments and telephone usage so that subtle, but telltale, patterns are revealed to investigating authorities. By tracing serial numbers of cash and monitoring the movements of container shipments, DARPA also hopes that almost real-time control and detection of narcotics activities can be provided.[12]

Yet while almost all of us would want to see the drug trade and its social destructiveness ended, we might not appreciate such technologies being applied to our everyday lives—and this is the practical implication behind such moves. After all, what distinguishes your telephone from that used by a drug dealer? What differentiates your bank account from the slush fund of a narcotics racket? Given these problems, several pertinent questions come to mind. Are the costs to privacy greater than the benefits of squeezing drug trafficking out of existence? Is the damage visible on the streets preferable to the kind of invisible, secret damage that surveillance could bring to society and its freedoms? Might we expect that the drug rackets—just like the oldest profession—can never be eliminated? Instead, their collective response might be to counter with high technology foils of their own—scramblers, encryption devices, etc. After all, drug syndicates already use some of the best and most sophisticated equipment—a brand-new wrecked aircraft or two is a negligible business cost, given the incredible profits that can be made from narcotics trading. Furthermore, with huge amounts of money on offer, what defense can high technology offer to the ancient art of bribery and corruption? What point is there in creating elaborate technological surveillance systems if their locks, keys and blueprints have already been sold? And if this is the most we can hope for from high technology in combating the drug problem, why should we accept the destruction of privacy that its possibly ineffectual application may bring?

The Surveillance Society

. . . A useful model of democratic societies is one which depicts their functioning as a constant dialogue involving two basic processes—conflict and consensus. Indeed, anyone who has ever witnessed a natural disaster and observed the ease with which law and order and "normal" civilization can break down, can strongly testify to the fact that society is a finely balanced construction of obligations and expectations that is negotiated within the bounds of these processes. Clearly, this balance is frighteningly easy to tip (in any direction) and one of the most important "weights" we must consider concerns the rights and obligations of the individual versus the rights and obligations of the group. In particular, we must be concerned with those groups who hold enormous power and influence over the effective management of society—our governments, judiciaries, police, security agencies and so on.

Rather like a delicate tightrope act, we can expect that the powers accorded to these groups will teeter and sway to some extent, but hopefully the processes of public debate, information released by the press and that released by informants or ethically troubled members of such groups ("whistle-blowers") can help to preserve a rough semblance of balance, both in terms of increasing and diminishing the power they are accorded. We should also bear in mind that "overbalancing" (in all directions) of the democratic balancing act, emerges not simply from blatant attempts to marshal greater power (although this can happen, too), but more often from attempts to fulfill a particular role and to maximize effectiveness in that role. That is, organizations and groups of all kinds possess a rationality that is attuned to their objectives. The police, for example, see their role as the preven-

tion of crime and the apprehension of law-breakers. The maximization of this function is of supreme interest to them and the costs associated with invasion of privacy, wrongful arrest, forced confessions and even fabrication of evidence, can often be considered to be acceptable so long as the primary role of the police in the prevention and apprehension of criminal elements is achieved. Hence, like most organizations faced with a demanding organizational mission, their rationality is concentrated upon fulfillment of this mission or role, perhaps with serious disregard to the costs that may accrue in consequence. This is not to say that the individuals who comprise such organizations (not just the police) do not have misgivings about the methods used. But collectively, for any large organization an organizational rationality prevails which is maintained by peer pressure, selection, socialization and training of an organization's recruits, as well as by reward structures and overt and covert penalties for failure to demonstrate loyalty.

Again, we need to question whether our democratic tightrope act is not becoming dangerously unbalanced when we learn of the already mentioned incidents and the statistics on surveillance. For example, the US Office of Technology Assessment (OTA) has recently found that of 142 domestic federal agencies surveyed, 35 already used or planned to use electronic surveillance methods including concealed microphones. The OTA also found that 36 of these agencies (not counting those in intelligence) used a total of 85 computerized record systems for investigative purposes and maintained 288 million files on 114 million people. In addition, OTA found that 35 agencies in Justice, Treasury and Defense departments already used or planned to use:

- Closed-circuit television (29 agencies)
- Night vision systems (22)
- Miniature transmitters (21)
- Telephone taps, recorders, and pen registers (these show the telephone number dialed) (14)
- Electronic beepers and sensors (15)
- Computer usage monitoring (6)
- Electronic mail monitoring (6)
- Cellular radio intercepts (5)
- Satellite interceptions (4)

As for the 85 computer-based record systems, none of the operators provided statistics requested by the

OTA on record completeness or accuracy. (Note that the OTA study did not include the CIA, NSA or Defense Intelligence Agency.)[13]

Just When You Thought No One was Listening

It is a mistake to believe that the only threat to privacy lies in the databases of super-secret intelligence agencies, police or other authorities. Developments in surveillance technologies are also available to those with sufficient need and sufficient funds to purchase them. For example, microphone transmitters these days are almost the size of a pin head and can be embedded almost anywhere. Some do not need wires to transmit—they send out microwave signals that can be read by equipment outside the building. They can be turned on and off by remote control, or set to be activated by heat, radiation, the vibrations of a voice, body movement or pressure. A bug located in a chair, for example, can be programmed to turn itself on whenever someone sits down. Bugs can also be hidden in typewriters and computer keyboards, picking up and transmitting the electronic signals given off by each key—effectively allowing the eavesdropper to watch as the message is keyed in.

One way to make bugs harder to detect is to design them so that they transmit along frequencies that are very close to those used by standard radio or TV broadcasts. Another method is called "frequency hopping." With this technique, the bug transmits using a preset sequence of frequencies—often for only a few milliseconds on each frequency—and a "frequency agile" receiver also attuned to this sequence, picks up the transmissions in a perfectly synchronized fashion. Yet the hardest bugs to detect are those that do not transmit through the air. Instead, they transmit using any available metallic medium: a power cable, an air-conditioning vent or even metallic paint. A listening post somewhere outside the building then "plugs in" and monitors whatever the bug relays. Finally, the "Hollywood" countermeasure we all know—turning on the shower, radio and taps to provide a noisy background to defeat bugs—is a thing of the past. Sophisticated electronic filters can now remove almost all extraneous noise and produce a clear, untainted voice signal.

More exotic methods of surveillance allow eavesdroppers to monitor computers as they work. The electromagnetic transmissions emitted by chips and CRTs—a phenomenon known as "tempest"—can be recorded some distance away from the machine for later analysis. The only known precaution against this kind of interception (and the exploitation of tempest itself is still in its infancy) is the use of specially designed and prohibitively expensive shielding. Another exotic surveillance technique uses laser beams that are aimed against a window or any surface that can vibrate slightly from the impact of sound waves. The laser beam is affected by the minute vibrations caused by voices and these can be decoded by appropriate ancillary equipment.[14]

However, we don't need to look for industrial espionage, cloak-and-dagger experts and switched-on private eyes in order to find evidence of high-technology surveillance. Although we might immediately associate surveillance with bugging devices and sophisticated electronics, it appears that our own employers, with the very computer systems we are familiar with, are involved in surveillance of their own employees. At Pacific South West Airlines offices in San Diego and Reno, the main computer recorded exactly how long each of their 400 reservation clerks spent on every call and how much time passed before they picked up their next one. Workers earned negative points for such infractions as repeatedly spending more than the average 109 seconds handling a call and taking more than 12 minutes in bathroom trips beyond the total one hour allocation they have for lunch and coffee breaks. If employees accrued more than 37 points in any single year, they could have lost their jobs. One employee of 14 years' standing, Judy Alexander, took disability leave after compiling 24 demerit points and complaining that "I'm a nervous wreck. The stress is incredible." PSA defended the system by arguing that it was a productivity booster and that it was no more severe than the monitoring that occurs in other airlines.[15]

As part of this general defense, supporters of computer monitoring argue that it is also used to provide incentives for employees and effectively rewards individuals for true merit and effort. They also point out that what is being measured is factual and hard, and that workers tend to favor such systems—they've seen too many cases of the wrong people being promoted for the wrong reasons. With the facts that the computer gathers, diligent workers can legitimately argue a case for better pay and conditions and this case does not rely upon personal opinions or personalities. Furthermore, these systems can help eliminate rampant waste—employees calling long-distance for private purposes, a team carrying the load for an unproductive team member, identifying the theft of materials by matching the stock used with the amount processed by line workers (and discovering discrepancies). Finally, monitoring on a computer network can assist in troubleshooting and fine-tuning of a system,[16] as well as streamlining job design and fairly apportioning workloads.

However, there is also the danger of turning workers into better-paid battery hens—denying them job satisfaction and eliminating the human element from their work. For example, although reservation clerks may be given an incentive to process more calls when they are being monitored, it may also eliminate any human spontaneity or friendliness in their communication. Surely this is as big a factor in return business as prompt and efficient handling? Similarly, workers may become sufficiently aggravated to devise ways to beat the system—as workers in one particular factory did by leaving their machine tools running while they had their coffee breaks. Unfortunately for them, the computer detected differences in the amount of power used and managers twigged the scam. However, the point surely is that such adversarial circumstances are best avoided and that a constant contest between the employees and the system is, in the long run, mutually disadvantageous.

Once again it seems, we are faced with a question of balance between the rights and expectations of the individual versus the obligations and objectives of the group—the group this time being our employers. Clearly, profits are important to the continued functioning of capitalist societies and profit itself is dependent upon competitiveness. However, just how far we are willing to proceed in the pursuit of competitiveness and profitability is a matter of judgment. For example, the use of cheap child labor was once regarded as a sensible business strategy, but now our ethical sense and labor protection laws prohibit this practice. It remains to be seen in which direction our ethical intuitions will take us in determining the nature of future employment—whether we can all expect to be monitored in the interest of profit and accountability, or whether we shall see a renewed interest in designing jobs for people.

In addition, we need to ask what kind of precedent computer-based monitoring of employees will set for other invasive practices. For example, similar arguments can be marshaled for compulsory drug testing of key personnel such as pilots, train drivers, plant operators and so on.[17] If these people have the potential to kill thousands by accident, then do we not have the right to ensure that they are in a fit state to work? On the other hand, why not also monitor the alcohol purchases of convicted drunk drivers? And after that . . . ? Perhaps this is the most contentious aspect of any form of computer-based monitoring: it is not so much the harm it may currently be causing, but what it represents—a yawning Pandora's box of things to come.

Notes

1. Jacques Vallee, *The Network Revolution: Confessions of a Computer Scientist* (Berkeley, CA: And/Or Press, 1982).

2. Larry Reibstein and Lisa Drew, "Clean Credit for Sale: A Growing Illegal Racket," *Newsweek,* Sept. 12, 1988, p. 49.

3. Sundar Iyengar, "American Express Is Watching . . . ," *Forum on Risks to the Public in Computer Systems,* May 4, 1986, vol. 8, no. 66. See also Jeffrey Rothfeder et al., "Is Nothing Private?" *Business Week,* Sept. 4, 1989.

4. David Burnham, "Tales of a Computer State," *The Nation,* April 1983.

5. D. Dyer, "The Human Element," *Forum on Risks to the Public in Computer Systems,* Oct. 16, 1985, vol. 1, no. 22.

6. David Burnham, "Tales of a Computer State."

7. Peter Kimball, *The File* (San Diego, CA: Harcourt Brace Jovanovitch, 1983).

8. Perry Morrison, "Limits to Technocratic Consciousness: Information Technology and Terrorism as Example," *Science, Technology and Human Values,* 1986, vol. 11, no. 4, pp. 4–16; David Burnham, *The Rise of the Computer State* (New York: Random House, 1983).

9. Morrison, "Limits to Technocratic Consciousness."

10. Charles Bruno, "The Electronic Cops," *Datamation,* June 15, 1984, pp. 115–124. For a more up-to-date account of the NCIC see Evelyn Richards, "Proposed FBI Crime Computer System Raises Questions on Accuracy, Privacy—Report Warns of Potential Risk Data Bank Poses to Civil Liberties," *Washington Post,* Feb. 13, 1989.

11. Curtis Jackson, "NSA and Encryption Algorithms," *Forum on Risks to the Public in Computer Systems,* March 2, 1986, vol. 2, no. 20; Dave Platt, "Data Encryption Standard," *Forum on Risks to the Public in Computer Systems,* Feb. 28, 1986, vol. 2, no. 17.

12. Gary H. Anthes, "DARPA Program to Battle War on Drugs, Terrorism," *Federal Computer Week,* April 24, 1989, vol. 3, no. 17, pp. 1 and 53; Gary T. Marx, *Undercover: Police Surveillance in America* (Berkeley, CA: University of California Press, 1988).

13. Lee Byrd, "Americans' Privacy Exposed by New Technology, Congress Told," *ARPANET Telecom Digest,* vol. 5, no. 155, Oct. 24, 1985. See also *Criminal Justice, New Technologies and the Constitution* (Washington, DC: OTA, US Congress, 1988), and David H. Flaherty, "The Emergence of Surveillance Societies in the Western World: Toward the Year 2000," *Government Information Quarterly,* vol. 5, no. 4, 1988, pp. 377–387.

14. Gary T. Marx and Sanford Sherizen, "Monitoring on the Job," in Tom Forrester (Ed.), *Computers in the Human Context* (Cambridge, MA: MIT Press, 1989), reprinted from *Technology Review,* Nov.–Dec. 1986; and George J. Church, "The Art of High-Tech Snooping," *Time,* April 20, 1987, pp. 19–21.

15. Stephen Koepp, "The Boss that Never Blinks," *Time,* July 28, 1986, pp. 38–39.

16. Geoffrey S. Goodfellow, "Electronic Surveillance," *Forum on Risks to the Public in Computer Systems,* Oct. 16, 1985, vol. 5, no. 22.

Review Exercises

1. Why does the randomized clinical trial for Parkinson's disease create problems for informed consent?

2. What do we mean by *science* and *technology*? Are they ethically neutral? Why or why not?

3. How do modern science and technology raise both old and new ethical issues?

4. Give examples of modern reproductive technologies. What ethical issues do they raise?

5. What is the Human Genome Project and its purpose? Describe one ethical issue it raises.

6. What is *privacy*? What are two reasons why we ought to value privacy?

7. Discuss and give examples of the kinds of conflicts of interest involved in various screening procedures.

8. How does the value of a life play a role in decisions about how safe is safe enough?

9. What is the willingness-to-pay model for determining the value of a life? What are some problems with it?

10. Describe some of the contemporary uses of computer and information technology.

11. How do we know whether an activity is a case of computer theft?

12. Contrast the views of Locke, Marx, and Hegel on the matter of property.

13. Describe a utilitarian position on whether we ought to have stringent property-rights laws.

14. Describe three different views on whether computer hackers are justified in what they do.

15. Describe two social ethical concerns raised by the new developments in computer and information technology.

Discussion Cases

1. *Health Records and Privacy.* The Health Services Department of country X is attempting to update and computerize its records. It wants the ability to gather health data from every hospital and clinic in the country. This would provide a centralized source of information for health care workers. Thus, if a particular person moves in from out of town and joins the local HMO, his records can be transferred from the centralized health record source. Having access to this information would also help in emergencies by providing information on a person's allergies and drugs being taken so that nothing that would react with these drugs would be given. Care is being taken that no unauthorized persons have access to the system.

Should the Health Services Department set up such a system?

2. *University Break-In.* Student B found a way past the university security system and gained access to student records. She was able to check on the grades of friends, enemies, and classmates. She did not change the grades and told no one about them.

Was there anything wrong with this student simply looking at the records? Should she also report the break-in, letting the administration know that its security system was weak?

3. *Cloning Oneself.* Mr. and Mrs. Q have a young daughter who has health problems. One of these requires tissue donations from a compatible do-

nor on a regular basis. If she does not get these treatments, she will likely die by age 40. A new technology has come along in which their daughter can be cloned. Some of her cells can be taken and implanted in an embryo that Mrs. Q will carry to term. The new child would be the genetic twin (although younger) of their other daughter. This new child would be able to provide the needed donation for the other daughter.

Should the parents go ahead and clone their daughter to provide a source for treatment of her disease?

Selected Bibliography

Ethical Issues in Reproductive Technology and Genetics

Alpern, Kenneth D. (Ed.). *The Ethics of Reproductive Technology.* New York: Oxford University Press, 1992.

Bayertz, Kurt. *GenEthics: Technological Intervention in Human Reproduction as a Philosophical Problem.* New York: Cambridge University Press, 1994.

Bayles, Michael D. *Reproductive Ethics.* Englewood Cliffs, NJ: Prentice-Hall, 1984.

Buckley, John J., Jr. (Ed.). *Genetics Now: Ethical Issues in Genetic Research.* Washington, DC: University Press of America, 1978.

Callahan, Joan C. (Ed.). *Reproduction, Ethics, and the Law.* Bloomington: Indiana University Press, 1996.

Drlica, Karl. *Double-Edged Sword: The Promises and Risks of the Genetic Revolution.* Reading, MA: Addison-Wesley, 1994.

Goodfield, June. *Playing God: Genetic Engineering and the Manipulation of Life.* New York: Random House, 1977.

Hull, Richard T. (Ed.). *Ethical Issues in the New Reproductive Technologies.* Belmont, CA: Wadsworth, 1990.

Keane, Noel P., and Dennis L. Breo. *The Surrogate Mother.* New York: Everest House, 1981.

Nichols, Eve K. *Human Gene Therapy.* Cambridge, MA: Harvard University Press, 1988.

Paul, Diane B. *Controlling Human Heredity, 1865 to the Present.* Atlantic Highlands, NJ: Humanities Press, 1995.

President's Commission for the Study of Ethical Problems in Medicine and Biomedical and Behavioral Research. Washington, DC: President's Commission, 1983.

Shiva, Vandana, and Ingunn Moser (Eds.). *Biopolitics: A Feminist and Ecological Reader on Biotechnology.* Atlantic Highlands, NJ: Zed Books, 1995.

Singer, Peter, and Deane Wells. *Making Babies: The New Science and Ethics of Conception.* New York: Scribner's, 1985.

Smith, George Patrick. *Bioethics and the Law: Medical, Socio-Legal and Philosophical Directions for a Brave New World.* Lanham, MD: University Press of America, 1993.

Snowden, R., G. D. Mitchell, and E. M. Snowden. *Artificial Reproduction: A Social Investigation.* Winchester, MA: Allen & Unwin, 1983.

Stanworth, Michelle (Ed.). *Reproductive Technologies: Gender, Motherhood and Medicine.* Minneapolis: University of Minnesota Press, 1987.

Suzuki, David T. *Genethics: The Clash Between the New Genetics and Human Values.* Cambridge, MA: Harvard University Press, 1989.

Walters, William, and Peter Singer (Eds.). *Test-Tube Babies.* New York: Oxford University Press, 1982.

Warnock, Mary. *A Question of Life: The Warnock Report on Human Fertility and Embryology.* New York: Blackwell, 1985.

Privacy

Brandeis, Louis D., and Charles Warren, "The Right to Privacy." *Harvard Law Review,* vol. IV (Dec. 15, 1890), pp. 193–220.

Burnham, David. *The Rise of the Computer State.* New York: Random House, 1983.

Flaherty, David. *Protecting Privacy in Surveillance Societies.* Chapel Hill: University of North Carolina Press, 1989.

Freedman, Warren. *The Right of Privacy in the Computer Age.* New York: Quorum, 1987.

Fried, Charles. *An Anatomy of Values: Problems of Personal and Social Choice.* Cambridge, MA: Harvard University Press, 1970.

Hoffman, L. J. (Ed.). *Computers and Privacy in the Next Decade.* New York: Academic Press, 1980.

Inness, Julie. *Privacy, Intimacy, and Isolation.* New York: Oxford University Press, 1992.

McLean, Deckle. *Privacy and Its Invasion.* Westport, CT: Praeger, 1995.

Pennock, J. Roland, and John Chapmann (Eds.). *Privacy.* New York: Atherton, 1971.

Pierce, Christine, and Donald VanDeVeer (Eds.). *AIDS: Ethics and Public Policy.* Belmont, CA: Wadsworth, 1987.

Schoeman, Ferdinand David. *Philosophical Dimensions of Privacy: An Anthology.* Cambridge, UK: Cambridge University Press, 1984.

———. *Privacy and Social Freedom.* New York: Cambridge University Press, 1992.

Thomson, Judith Jarvis. "The Right to Privacy." *Philosophy and Public Affairs,* vol. 4, no. 4 (Summer 1975), pp. 295–333.

Wachs, Raymond. *Personal Information: Privacy and the Law.* Oxford: Clarendon, 1989.

Risk Evaluation and the Value of a Life

Calebresi, Guido, and Philip Bobbitt. *Tragic Choices*. New York: W. W. Norton, 1978.

Dorman, Peter. *Markets and Mortality: Economics, Dangerous Work, and the Value of Human Life*. New York: Cambridge University Press, 1996.

Fischhoff, Baruch. *Acceptable Risk*. Cambridge, UK: Cambridge University Press, 1981.

Gould, Leroy C. *Perception of Technological Risks and Benefits*. New York: Russell Sage Foundation, 1988.

Imperato, Pascal James. *Acceptable Risks*. New York: Viking, 1985.

Jones-Lee, M. W. *The Value of a Life*. Chicago: University of Chicago Press, 1976.

Kleinig, John. *Valuing Life*. Princeton, NJ: Princeton University Press, 1991.

Lewis, H. W. *Technological Risk*. New York: W. W. Norton, 1992.

Rhoads, Steven E. (Ed.). *Valuing Life: Public Policy Dilemmas*. Boulder, CO: Westview, 1980.

Ethical Issues in Information Technology

Brown, Geoffrey. *The Information Game: Ethical Issues in the Microchip World*. Atlantic Highlands, NJ: Humanities Press International, 1990.

Buckle, Stephen. *Natural Law and the Theory of Property*. New York: Oxford University Press, 1991.

Bynum, Terrell E. (Ed.). *Computers and Ethics*. New York: Blackwell, 1985.

Denning, P. J. (Ed.). *Computers Under Attack: Intruders, Worms, and Viruses*. Reading, MA: ACM Books/Addison-Wesley, 1991.

Dunlop, Charles, and Rob Kling (Eds.). *Computerization and Controversy Value Conflicts and Social Choices*. Orlando, FL: Academic Press, 1991.

Ermann, David M., Mary B. Williams, and Claudio Gutierrez (Eds.). *Computers, Ethics, and Society*. New York: Oxford University Press, 1990.

Feenberg, Andrew. *Critical Theory of Technology*. New York: Oxford University Press, 1991.

Forrester, Tom, and Perry Morrison. *Computer Ethics: Cautionary Tales and Ethical Dilemmas in Computing*. Cambridge, MA: MIT Press, 1990.

Forrester, Tom (Ed.). *Computers in the Human Context: Information Technology, Productivity, and People*. Cambridge, MA: MIT Press, 1989.

Gates, Bill. *The Road Ahead*. New York: Viking, 1995.

Johnson, Deborah G., and Helen F. Nissenbaum (Eds.). *Computers, Ethics, and Social Values*. Englewood Cliffs, NJ: Prentice-Hall, 1995.

Johnson, Deborah. *Computer Ethics*, 2nd ed. Englewood Cliffs, NJ: Prentice-Hall, 1994.

Kullman, Ernest A. *Ethical Decision Making and Information Technology*. New York: Mitchell McGraw-Hill, 1993.

Parker, Donn B., Susan Swope, and Bob Baker. *Ethical Conflicts in Information and Computer Science, Technology, and Business*. Wellesley, MA: QED Information Sciences, 1990.

Paul, Ellen Frankel, Fred D. Miller, and Jeffrey Paul (Eds.). *Property Rights*. New York: Cambridge University Press, 1994.

Shrader-Frechette, Kristin. *Ethics of Scientific Research*. Lanham, MD: Rowman & Littlefield, 1994.

Spinello, Richard A. *Ethical Aspects of Information Technology*. Englewood Cliffs, NJ: Prentice-Hall, 1995.

U.S. Congress, Office of Technology Assessment. *Finding a Balance: Computer Software, Intellectual Property, and the Challenge of Technological Change*. OTA-TCT-527. Washington, DC: U.S. Government Printing Office, 1992.

❀ 17 ❀

Global Issues

One of the most hauntingly sad images of the recent war in Bosnia-Herzegovina was that of a pair of young lovers lying together dead in a section of no-man's land in Sarajevo. She was Bosnian, and he was of Serbian ancestry, yet this did not matter to them. They thought they could flee together, but they were gunned down by snipers. He was shot first and died instantly. Before she died, she crawled to him. How many times over the years have such scenarios been played out, have families been torn apart, have relationships been shattered, and have homes and neighborhoods been destroyed? We would like to think that, in an ideal world, the tragic destruction, divisions, and suffering caused by war would not occur. Nor would people waste away and die in famine and starvation. Some tragedies are from natural causes, but many are human-made. Wars, ethnic divisions, and mass migrations of people driven from their homes are only some of the many man-made tragedies that people around the globe suffer. We wonder if anything will ever change. We may also ask what business is this of ours, even if we could do something about it.

Among the many problems that face the peoples of the world today are those that arise from the nature of modern technological developments. For example, modern communication technologies make possible global interactions on a scale never known before. However, as the information age continues its amazing march forward, the poorest nations are being left behind. At an international meeting in Geneva, Switzerland, in 1995, telecommunications industry representatives pointed out that some regions of the world are falling farther and farther behind as investors hesitate to fund communication infrastructure development because of political instability.[1] Other technological changes also present challenges to development. Automation diminishes the significance of manual labor. Genetic engineering decreases the importance of raw materials such as hemp and weakens nations that depend economically on them for export. In addition, global financial markets and multinational corporations have an increasing impact on national economies. International trade agreements such as GATT (General Agreement on Tariffs and Trade) also play a role in nations' economic progress. Satellite communication technologies also make it clear to the poor across the globe how people in the richer nations live. The economic gap between those nations that have invested in education and technology and those that have been unable to develop in these ways will likely widen. As it does, problems of migration and immigration and citizenship are likely to become even more significant than at present.

Furthermore, worldwide economic problems are closely interrelated with problems of violence and war and peace. For example, not long ago "one in five Egyptian workers [was] jobless, as [was] one in four Algerian workers."[2] This is a recipe for restlessness, resentment, and possibly violence. Mass urban migration in poor countries creates crowded city environments that create scarcity in potable water, housing, and jobs. This creates discontent and political instability. Political instability in one nation or area of the world can no longer be confined to that area. Thus, such conditions do and will continue to affect us all. Moreover, poverty can have devastating effects on the environment. It is unreal and perhaps also unfair to ask those who are living at subsistence levels to preserve forests or soils or ecosystems when to do so threatens their own survival.

In this final chapter, we will first consider a few issues of economic development: the gulf between rich and poor nations, poverty and famine, trade and debt, and population growth. Then we will attend to global environmental issues, the problem of human rights, and the notion of "sustainable development." Following this brief descriptive survey, we will examine how ethics should address these issues. Finally, we will treat problems of violence, military intervention, and world peace. Obviously, we cannot adequately address all of these issues in the space here. Yet the hope is that by raising these issues our perspective will be expanded. We will be encouraged to realize that ethical issues apply not only to personal or national matters, but also to international and global matters.

Global Economic Problems

We have become accustomed to categorizing nations in terms of their economic status and level of development as rich and poor, more affluent and less affluent, developed and developing, and first, second, third, and possibly fourth world nations. Whichever classification system we use, a tremendous gap clearly exists between the level of economic development of those nations at the top and those at the bottom. According to Gustav Speth of the human development program of the United Nations, "an emerging global elite, mostly urban-based and interconnected in a variety of ways, is amassing great wealth and power, while more than half of humanity is left out."[3] More than half of the people of the world (that is, more than 3 billion people) live on incomes less than $2 per day. Yet there are also 358 billionaires in the world who control assets larger than the combined annual incomes of those countries that have 45 percent of the world's population.[4] Mexico is among the countries with the largest gap between the rich and poor—in this case, generally between the industrialized north with its Spanish-speaking Mexicans and the rural south with its 10 million Indians.[5]

It is also clear that the status of nations can change, and that the rate of change of nations varies. Some improve, some remain the same, and some fall backward. And some do so faster than others. According to the 1996 *Human Development Report,* 89 countries are "worse off economically than they were a decade or more ago." In addition, "70 developing countries [have] incomes lower than they were in the 1960s or 1970s." Among these are Ghana, Haiti, Liberia, Nicaragua, Rwanda, and Venezuela.[6] In the 1980s, the economies of East Asia grew at a rate of 7.4 percent, and Latin America and sub-Saharan Africa at rates of 1.8 percent and 1.7 percent.[7] Forty years ago, some of the nations of Latin America and sub-Saharan Africa were similar in level of development with East Asian nations such as Korea. Now the four nations known as the East Asian "Tigers" or "Dragons"—Korea, Taiwan, Hong Kong, and Singapore–have far outstripped these other countries. They now have higher gross national products (GNPs) than Russia, Eastern European nations, and even Portugal.[8]

The causes of these differences in rate and direction of development are political and geographic, climatic and economic. However, according to one analyst, there are four reasons for the success of these four newly industrialized

East Asia economies: They have concentrated on educational improvements, they have high saving and investment rates, they have strong political systems, and they have followed a policy of manufacturing for export.[9] Whatever the complex of causes, it is clear that nations will continue to vary widely in their levels of economic development.

Other points are also worth noting. In 1984, the world added 80 million people to its population. In 1994, it added approximately 100 million people.[10] This population increase has been more typical in third and fourth world countries and has a more devastating effect there. It is not just the increasing numbers of people in specific parts of the world that are the problem, some argue, but the fact that their national resources do not match their numbers. Nevertheless, in poorer countries population increases often wipe out whatever economic progress they might have been able to achieve. Africa's population growth rate is the highest in the world. From 1960 to 1990, for example, Kenya's population quadrupled. Tragically, the only thing keeping the population under control in Africa now is the AIDS epidemic. In some African countries—Uganda, for example—the incidence of this disease is now decreasing, though it is increasing in other countries such as India where more than 3 million out of its 1996 population of 950 million were infected with the virus.[11] Other diseases and health problems also sap the economic well-being of citizens and nations. Recently, UNICEF reported that 585,000 women die each year in pregnancy and childbirth. In sub-Saharan Africa, the number is 1 in 13 women, and in South Asia 1 in 35. (This compares with 1 in 3,300 in the United States and 1 in 7,300 in Canada.) The overall total of childbirth deaths is 20 percent higher than had previously been thought. Possibly 18 million more women suffer debilitating illnesses or injuries from pregnancy and childbirth-related causes.[12]

Although the countries of Latin America differ from one another in culture, fertility rates, life expectancy, and climate zone, average economic growth is lower than what was expected decades earlier. In both sub-Saharan Africa and Latin America, slow growth rates have also been blamed on the countries' continued reliance on the export of raw materials. In the 1970s, commodity prices fell dramatically while oil prices quadrupled. The printing of money to pay for imports caused high inflation, and borrowing caused high debt levels. Foreign protectionism also contributed to economic decline. Furthermore, the countries were unable or unwilling to continue investing in education. For example, an elementary school teacher in Argentina with ten years' experience could recently expect to make $110 a month, a university professor $37, and a doctor $120.[13]

In the Arab and Muslim world of North Africa and the Middle East, the situation is different. In medieval times these peoples possessed a highly developed science, medicine, and literature. Now, according to some analysts, "Much of the Arab and Muslim world appears to have difficulty in coming to terms with the nineteenth century, with its composite legacy of secularization, democracy, laissez-faire economics, industrial and commercial linkages among different nations, social change, and intellectual questioning."[14] These nations, however, vary significantly in their political structure and religious orientation.

Human Rights

In February 1996, the leaders of twenty-five Asian and European nations held a meeting on trade and economics in Bangkok, Thailand. One of the most contentious issues they addressed, more behind the scenes than in public discussions, was the issue of human rights.[15] The discussions focused on the role of human rights in economic development. According to some Westerners, political freedoms, civil rights, and labor standards are not separable from economic progress. They stress that "child labor, women's rights, deforestation, pollution, intellectual property rights, a free press (and) civil liberties" are essential to any secure development.[16] Some

Asians at this meeting responded that this was not their way, and that the welfare of society and economic development ought to come first before human rights. They insisted that human rights should temporarily be put on hold for the sake of economic growth. Thus, it would be better, they say, to give a starving person a loaf of bread than a crate on which to stand and speak his mind. But according to Alex Magno, a political scientist at the University of the Philippines, it is not so much an "Asian way" that gives human rights a back seat, but political self-interest on the part of rulers who are spurred on by a growing middle class. The middle class is "not an Islamic or Buddhist or Catholic middle class," but one that "is intoxicated with growth, whose own personal fortunes depend on the G.N.P. rate."[17] Moreover, a group from Forum Asia insisted that the notion of human rights is not strictly a Western import but also their own concern. It points out that the real Western imports are the economic practices of "consumerism, capitalism, investment, (and) industrialization."[18] This debate raises the following ethical question, How important are human political and civil rights in comparison with the economic development of a society? You might recall some of the discussions on natural rights from Chapter 6 and the discussions of utilitarianism in Chapter 4 to help clarify the issue for yourself.

Sustainable Development

Many people who work for the development of poor nations view the environmentalist movement as an example of Western elitism.[19] For example, only such environmental elitists, they suggest, can afford to preserve unchanged an environment or wilderness that the poor need to use and change in order to survive. Yet others see the two concerns, development and environment, as closely intertwined and capable of moving forward together. What is needed, they say, is not development that ignores environmental concerns, but "sustainable development." For example, Gus Speth, president of World Resources Institute, writes, "It is . . . clear that develop-

ment and economic reforms will have no lasting success unless they are suffused with concern for ecological stability and wise management of resources."[20] The idea is that if the forests in an area are depleted, or the land is ruined by unwise or short-sighted overuse, then the people living there will not have what they need to continue to develop; that is, development will not be sustainable. Rapid population growth has been said by some critics to be a significant cause of environmental degradation.[21] However, others point out that the situation is more complex. Certainly poverty causes environmental problems as people destroy forests for fuel, for example. Pricing policies as well as weak agrarian reforms and mismanagement and intergroup conflict are among the other factors that contribute to "the vicious downward spiral of poverty and environmental degradation. The poor have been exploited, shifted, and marginalized to the extent that they often have no choice but to participate in the denigration of resources, with full knowledge that they are mortgaging their own future."[22] On the contrary, Jessica Tuchman Mathews suggests that we can have development without environmental destruction, but we need to "change the means of production, developing technologies that will enable us to meet human needs without destroying the earth."[23] In June 1992, the U.N. Conference on Environment and Development held in Rio de Janeiro produced two documents, "The Earth Charter" and "Agenda 21." To ensure that the environmental goals contained in these documents were realized, those who attended the conference called on the United Nations to set up a group to monitor and work toward the goals. Thus, in late 1992, the 47th U.N. General Assembly created the Commission on Sustainable Development. The commission has representatives from fifty-three U.N. member states and meets annually.

Ethical Issues

It should be clear from this brief survey of global economic and environmental issues that any ethical analysis of these problems is bound to be incomplete. The primary reason is that determining what is better or worse and where our obligations lie will depend heavily on complex and often contested empirical assessments of causes and events. Therefore, in this text we can only indicate some guideposts, if you will, for ethical analysis. What kinds of ethical questions can arise in these discussions? What ethical notions are relevant?

Among the notions that are relevant are *obligation* and *responsibility*. When thinking about problems elsewhere in the world, we often hear the question, "What business is that of ours?" Some of the basic ethical questions that we can address are: Should we be concerned about what happens to people far distant from us? To what degree are we responsible for this? Why should we be responsible for these problems? The easiest and often most convincing answer for these questions is a self-interested one; that is, the problem may seem to be far distant from us and thus one that doesn't affect us, but if we look at the issues more closely and consider what history tells us, we will see that problems there are likely to affect us here. The argument about whether we have any responsibility for what happens far off will then be turned into one about how what happens there might affect us and how likely this would be. We then listen to what the experts tell us and make our judgments accordingly. But the main reason given for our concern is *self-interest*. A more basic question that we can address is whether self-interest is the best ethical stance. It may be true that many people are more likely to be moved by considerations of self-interest. Yet we can ask whether ethics requires anything else of us than to act in our own self-interest. This is a problem that we addressed in Chapter 3 on egoism.

In the first place, we might consider whether *charity* or altruistic concern for the plight of others ought to play a role in our view of ourselves in relation to far distant peoples. Charity is certainly an ethically important notion. However, a more difficult consideration is whether we have any obligation to help those in need in faraway

places. Charity, in some sense, is optional. But if we are obligated to help others, then this is not an optional matter. As Kant reminded us, although we may decide not to do what we ought to do, we do not thereby escape the obligation. It is still there. But are we under any obligation to help those faraway persons in need, and why or why not?

In one reading in this chapter, Peter Singer comments on the distinction between charity and obligation or duty. According to him, giving to victims of famines, for example, is not charity but duty. In fact, he believes that we have an obligation to help those less well off than ourselves to the extent that helping them does not make us less well off than they are, or require us to sacrifice something of comparable value. This is an ethically demanding position. It implies that I must always justify spending money on myself or my family or friends. Whether I am justified in doing so, in this view, depends on whether anything I do for myself or others is of comparable moral importance to the lives of others who are perhaps starving and lacking in basic necessities.

Singer's position is a consequentialist or *utilitarian* one. So is that of Garrett Hardin. Hardin believes that we have no such obligation to give because to do so will do no good.[24] For example, famine relief only postpones the inevitable death and suffering. According to Hardin, this is because overpopulation produced by famine relief will again lead to more famine and death. However, whether his prediction is correct is an empirical matter. In other words, it needs to be verified or supported by observation and historical evidence. For example, will all forms of famine relief, especially when combined with other aid, necessarily do more harm than good as Hardin predicts? His position needs to respond to questions such as this.

Another basis for obligation to aid those in distant lands may be found in past behavior. As noted in our discussion of affirmative action in Chapter 11, the principle of *compensatory justice* requires that we make amends for our wrongful or harmful past action. If I have caused your injury, then I ought to do what will undo it or at least minimize its effects. Historians can point to examples in which nations or institutions of nations have done things that have helped to cause the low economic status of other nations. Trade or investment policies, for example, could be cited, as well as harmful colonial practices. Some have argued that Western corporations or banks have played a role in preventing other nations from becoming more self-sufficient. Among other things, they have given financial incentives to invest in what is eventually not helpful to these nations. Other analysts point out that "the developed world's consumption and capital are often more responsible for resource depletion in the poorer countries than are the growing populations of those countries."[25] The argument from compensatory justice is that the corporations or countries that have contributed to the unfortunate situation of poorer third world nations owe them something in return for past harms done to them.

Still another basis for obligation to poorer nations on the part of richer nations may be found in considerations of *distributive justice*. Is it fair, it may be asked, that some people or nations are so rich and others so poor? As we noted in Chapter 12, various answers can be given to this question. Egalitarians will argue that the gap between rich and poor is something wrong in itself, because we are all members of the same human family and share the same planet. On the one hand, some argue that it is morally permissible for some to have more and others less if the difference is a function of something like the greater effort or contributions of the richer nations. Thus, they might point to the sacrifice and investment and savings practices of the newly industrialized East Asian nations as justifying their having more. They sacrificed and saved while others did not. On the other hand, if the wealth of some and poverty of others results instead from luck and fortune, then it does not seem fair that the lucky have so much and the unlucky so little. Is it not luck that one nation has oil and another next to it does not? On the other hand,

again, more libertarian-minded thinkers will likely argue that unless the richer nations gained their riches by wrongful means, the resulting unequal distribution of wealth is not wrong nor unjust. Unless they took it from other nations, for instance, it is rightly theirs. Another fairness concern could be mentioned. Developing countries have more than 75 percent of the world's population and in 1991 accounted for 30 percent of the world's energy use.[26] We could ask whether this represents a fair share. However, this would seem to imply that there was only a set amount of energy and that each nation should withdraw from it only a fair share based on its population. That there is a fixed amount might be true of nonrenewable energy resources such as fossil fuels, but not necessarily true of all energy sources.

Thus, while many of these ethical questions depend for adequate answers on a knowledge of historical and empirical factors, they also depend for answers on basic ethical notions and evaluations. These are issues of charity and obligation, fairness and justice. Different ethical issues arise when considering other interrelated global issues, such as those coming under the general heading of war and peace.

War and Peace

The twentieth century has had two great or world wars. Fear of even greater destruction has probably deterred a third such war. Still, there are many examples throughout the world of continuing civil strife both between and within nations. We have witnessed such strife in republics of the former Soviet Union, Afghanistan, Bosnia-Herzegovina, Rwanda, northern Iraq, and elsewhere. Hostilities are sometimes grounded in long-standing ethnic and religious hatreds. In some cases, colonial or war powers have drawn national boundaries that do not match ethnic or tribal groupings. Terrorist groups with a sense of mission or just cause are active around the globe. Countries are being threatened by religious fundamentalist groups within them who disagree with the very notion of a secularized state and who stir up resentment fueled by poverty, scarcity, crowded environments, and new depersonalized state structures. In Algeria, for example, the urban percentage of the population rose from 15 percent in 1958 to more than 50 percent at the time of fundamentalist Islamic uprisings in 1992.[27] Moreover, in some countries, the torture of political prisoners and political dissidents continues despite international condemnation.

The simple availability of weapons of destruction on the small and large scale also provides a temptation to use them to settle problems. Of the total of $76 billion spent by various countries on weapons from 1991 to 1993, $32 billion in sales came from the United States, with the United Kingdom as the second highest supplier with $13 billion.[28] These weapons were sold around the world, with Asia and Europe receiving the most. However, the Middle East "probably contains more soldiers, aircraft, missiles, and other weapons than anywhere else in the world."[29] For the most part, these arms are purchased by and sold to recognized countries. However, there is also a global black market in weapons, such that any group with enough financial support has access to them. In fact, possession of nuclear weapons by more nations or groups may become a reality, a particularly frightening prospect. These are weapons of a totally different kind. Their use by the United States during World War II was their first and only use so far. Nations have tried for some time to limit their possession and testing. Treaties to do so have been extremely difficult to devise and sell.

Poverty, economic instability, and a sense that it is injustice that has caused it can also cause military conflicts. Thus, ethical discussions of war and military intervention are not entirely independent of issues of economics and development. Consider, for example, the problem of water. "Out of 200 of the world's major river basins, 148 are shared by two countries and 52 are shared by three to ten countries."[30] With the importance of fresh water to an economy, issues of past behavior and ownership rights can provide a basis for conflict.

Another factor leading to instability and violence is demographics. Population demographics show population rates highest among the poorest nations. City populations are growing the fastest. "Already, in most Arab countries at least four out of every ten people are under the age of fifteen—the classic recipe for subsequent social unrest and political revolution."[31] Put this together with global communications that reveal how rich nations live, an interpretation of history that breeds resentment, and dwindling resources, and military conflict may be all but inevitable. Between 1950 and 1990, "there was a fivefold increase in the number of urban residents in third-world countries. Almost 40 percent of their citizens now live in cities. In 2025, two out of every three inhabitants of poor countries will be urban dwellers—4.4 billion people." These figures come from a report presented at Habitat II, a U.N.-sponsored conference on cities that was held in Istanbul in June 1996.[32]

Are there any ethical principles that can be of use in judging issues of war and peace? People have debated these issues ever since they began to reason ethically. Many of the principles of justified military intervention and conduct of war have been developed over the centuries, from the medieval era to the present. Some of these principles are still used in discussions on the subject. While some do not apply easily to present-day conditions, some of their elements may. We will summarize the traditional contrasting perspectives of pacifism and militarism first, and then address the issues of military intervention and world peace. In the process, conclusions for what moral assessments we may make about other types of war and strife may emerge.

Pacifism Versus Militarism

If we were to define pacifism as the view that the use of force, including lethal force, is never justified, we would probably define a position that has had few supporters. We would have similar difficulties finding a hearing for militarism—which we might define as the view that the use of force, especially military force, is always noble and just. However, some aspects of a form of militarism are not without supporters. In his essay, "The Moral Equivalent of War," the American pragmatist philosopher William James called for a substitute for war, something that could develop the sense of loyalty and self-sacrifice called forth in war. He envisioned something like today's California Conservation Corps, in which groups of people work to clear brush and clean up the environment. Furthermore, not all pacifists oppose the use of all types of force. After all, there are nonphysical means that are forceful, and many pacifists also support the use of physical and even lethal physical force when it is necessary, such as to defend oneself. The question is whether such lethal means are ever justified to defend others or by a nation to defend itself.

The reasons given in support of pacifism vary. Some people believe that nonviolent means to achieve some good end are preferable to violent means because they work better. Violence does more harm than good, they argue, for violence only begets violence. How can we determine whether or not this is true? We can look to see if historical examples support the generalization. We can also inquire whether this may result from something in human nature. Our judgments will then depend on adequate factual assessments. However, nonconsequentialist reasons are also given in support of pacifism—for example, that to kill another is wrong in itself. The reasons for this must be presented, and any exceptions to the rule must be discussed. Pacifists must address the criticism that it seems inconsistent to hold that life is of the highest value and yet not be willing to use force to defend it.

Intermediate between the more extreme versions of some forms of pacifism and militarism is a range of positions according to which the use of force, including military force, is sometimes justified. The problem is to circumscribe when it is and when it is not morally permissible to use force. Even some people who have been long known for their opposition to war have relented when faced with a Somalia or a Bosnia. "Moral isolation is simply not a defensible position for those opposed to war," according to longtime pacifist William Sloane Coffin, Jr.[33] Massive famine caused by civil war and "ethnic cleansing" are likely candidates for military intervention if this is the only way to eliminate them, some argue. Nevertheless, national boundaries and the national right to self-determination also cannot be ignored, so that not every seeming injustice is rightly a candidate for military intervention. Political philosopher Michael Walzer puts it this way: "I think of this in terms of the old international law doctrine of humanitarian intervention. . . . It was always held that in cases of massacre on the other side of the border, you have a right, and maybe an obligation, to go in and stop it if you can."[34] People have certain fundamental rights that states may not override. To what extent, and when, are others obligated to protect these rights?

In a speech to the U.S. Military Academy at West Point on January 5, 1992, President George Bush put forth the following criteria: "Using military force makes sense as a policy where the stakes warrant, where and when force can be effective, where its application can be limited in scope and time, and where the potential benefits justify the potential costs and sacrifice."[35] These criteria are not new. They have traditionally been part of international law. They are also part of what is known as "just war theory." Because these principles are still used in the discussions and debates about justified military intervention, it would be well to briefly summarize them here. Some people have preferred the use of the phrase "justified war" instead of "just war" because they believe that in just war theory there is a presumption against the use of military force that must be overcome.

Just War Theory

Just war theory has a long history. Its origins can be traced to the writings of St. Augustine, the Bishop of Hippo in North Africa, in about 400 A.D. Augustine was concerned about how to reconcile traditional Christian views about the immorality of violence with the necessity of defending the Roman Empire from invading forces.[36] He asked what one should do in case one sees an individual attacking an innocent, defenseless victim. His response was that one should intervene and do whatever is necessary (but only so much as was necessary) to protect the victim, even up to the point of killing the aggressor. Further developments of the theory were provided by Thomas Aquinas, the practices of medieval chivalry, and jurists such as Grotius. In modern times, the theory was given additional detail by the Hague and Geneva conventions.

There is general agreement that just war theory includes two basic areas: principles that would have to be satisfied for a nation to be justified in using military force, or initiating a war, and principles governing the conduct of the military action or war itself. These have been given the Latin names of *jus ad bellum* (the justness of going to war) and *jus in bello* (justness in war).

Jus ad Bellum

Just Cause The first principle that provides a condition for going to war is the *just cause principle*. To use force against another nation, there must be a serious reason to justify it. In the previous Bush quotation, the phrase is "when the stakes warrant it." Examples traditionally given by just war theorists have included to respond to aggression and to restore rights unjustly denied. However, this principle does not provide a definitive list of just causes. Instead, it gives guidelines for what types of issues need to be addressed.

Proportionality Not only must the cause be just, according to the theory, but the probable good to be produced by the intervention must outweigh the likely evil that the war or use of force will cause. This is the second principle, the *proportionality principle*. It requires that before engaging in such action the probable costs and benefits be considered, and that they be compared with the probable costs and benefits of doing something else or of doing nothing. Involved in this utilitarian calculation are two elements: One assesses the likely costs and benefits, and the other weighs their relative value. The first requires historical and empirical information, while the second involves ethical evaluations. In making such evaluations, we might well compare lives likely to be saved with lives lost, for example. But how do we compare the value of freedom and self-determination, or a way of life with the value of a life itself? (Refer to the discussion of cost-benefit analysis in Chapters 4 and 16.)

Last Resort A third requirement for justly initiating a war or military intervention is the *last resort principle*. The idea is that military interventions are extremely costly in terms of suffering, loss of life, and other destruction. Thus, other means must be considered first. They need not all be tried first, for some will be judged useless beforehand. However, this principle may well require that some other means be attempted, means that are judged to have a chance of achieving the goal that the just cause specifies. Negotiations, threats, and boycotts are such means. When is enough enough? When have these measures been given sufficient trial? There is always something more that could be tried. This is a matter of prudential judgment and is therefore always uncertain.[37]

Right Intention A fourth principle in the jus ad bellum part of the just war theory is the *right intention principle*. It requires that the intervention be always directed to the goal set by the cause and to the eventual goal of peace. Thus, wars fought to satisfy hatreds or to punish others are unjustified. However, this principle also requires that what is done during the conduct of the war is necessary and that it not unnecessarily make peace harder to attain. There should be no gratuitous cruelty, for example. This moves us into discussion of the conduct of a war, the second area covered by the just war theory principles.[38]

Jus in Bello

Proportionality Even if a war were fought for a just cause, with the prospect of achieving more good than harm, as a last resort only, and with the proper intention, it still would not be fully just if it were not conducted justly or in accordance with certain principles or moral guidelines. The jus in bello part of the just war theory consists of two principles. The first is a principle of *proportionality*. In the conduct of the conflict, this principle requires that for the various limited objectives, no more force than necessary be used, and that the force or means used be proportionate to the importance of the particular objective for the cause as a whole.

Discrimination   The second principle is the principle of *discrimination*. This prohibits direct intentional attacks on noncombatants and non-military targets. The principle has two basic elements. One directs us to focus on the issue of what are and are not military targets, and who is and is not a combatant. Are roads and bridges and hospitals that are used in the war effort of the other side to be considered military targets? The general consensus is that the roads and bridges are targets if they contribute directly and in significant ways to the military effort, but that hospitals are not legitimate targets. The principle to be used in making this distinction is the same for the people as for the things. Those people who contribute directly are combatants, and those who do not are not combatants. Obviously, there are gray areas in the middle. One writer puts it this way: Those people who are engaged in doing what they do for persons as persons are noncombatants, and those who are doing what they do specifically for the war effort are combatants.[39] Thus, those who grow and provide food would be noncombatants, while those who make or transport the military equipment would be combatants.

Note, too, that although we also hear the term *innocent civilians* in such discussions, it is noncombatants who are supposed to be out of the fight and not people who are judged on some grounds to be innocent. Soldiers fighting unwillingly might be thought to be innocent but are nevertheless combatants. Those behind the lines spending time verbally supporting the

cause are not totally innocent, yet they are noncombatants. The danger of using the term *innocents* in place of *noncombatants* is that it also allows some to say that no one living in a certain country is immune because they are all supporters of their country and so not innocent. However, this is contrary to the traditional understanding of the principle of discrimination.

The reason that the terms *combatant* and *noncombatant* are preferable is also related to the second aspect of the principle of discrimination, namely, that noncombatants not be the subject of direct attack. The reason why combatants are not immune is because they are a threat. Thus, when someone is not or is no longer a threat, as when they have surrendered or are incapacitated by injury, then they are not to be regarded as legitimate targets. This principle does not require that for a war to be conducted justly no noncombatants be injured or killed, but that they not be the direct targets of attack. While directly targeting and killing civilians may have a positive effect on a desired outcome, this would nevertheless not be justified according to this principle. It is not a consequentialist principle. The end does not justify use of this type of means. This principle may be grounded in the more basic *principle of double effect,* which we discussed in Chapter 8. If this is true, then the other aspect of the principle of double effect would be relevant; that is, not only must the civilians not be directly targeted, but also the number of them likely to be injured when a target is attacked must not be disproportionately great compared to the significance of the target.

According to just war theory, then, for a war or military intervention to be justified, certain conditions for going to war must be satisfied, and the conduct in the war must follow certain principles or moral guidelines. We could say that if any of the principles are violated, that a war is unjust, or we could say that it was unjust in this regard, but not in some other aspects. Some of just war theory has become part of national and international law, including the U.S. Army Rules for Land Warfare and the U.N. Charter. However, some of its principles also appeal to common human reason. As such you, too, can judge whether these are valid or reasonable qualifications and whether they can play a useful role in debates about justified use of military force.

We have not made nuclear weapons a focus here. Obviously, they represent a uniquely devastating kind of power. Moreover, they not only kill and destroy, but also harm in other ways, such as through radiation effects and resulting genetic changes. Some nuclear weapons are more controllable in their effects than others. Stockpiling and disposal of these weapons and their nuclear fuel components also represent significant risks. Some of the principles of just war theory would surely apply to the use of nuclear weapons. Could they be used in a way that was proportional? Would the harm they cause ever be outweighed by the good of a particular cause? Could be used in a way that would pass muster with the principle of discrimination? It is not just nuclear weapons, however, that would find difficulty with the principle of discrimination, but also chemical and biological weapons. The principles of traditional just war theory thus may serve a useful function in evaluating the use not only of conventional weapons in war or military actions, but also any kind of method of mass destruction. Whether possessing these weapons merely as a threat to achieve some good end is justifiable is another difficult ethical question. It involves, among other things, questions about the inherent risks of doing so, and problems with the very idea of using something as a threat without the intention or the willingness to actually use it.

Terrorism

In today's changing world order, another use of force or violence as a means of achieving national or individual goals has gained prominence. That is the use of terrorism or terror tactics. It is not clear what counts as *terrorism*. The term has been used to refer to the violent acts of those with whom we disagree. If we ourselves use force or military means, it is not counted as

terrorism! However, there is a more neutral definition that we can give to this term, which is the destruction of property that is not directly involved, or the harming of people not directly involved, in the matters being protested. An example, then, is bombing people at airports or bombing those going about their business in buildings or on the street. The supporters of such bombings and killings might argue that these actions are justified as means necessary to achieve a good end. They might also argue that other means will not work, and that the end is sufficiently good to justify the use of extreme means. These are consequentialist arguments.

Arguments against such tactics on consequentialist grounds might point out that these means will not have the desired effect, or that the end is not good and thus does not outweigh the harm done. In contrast, nonconsequentialist arguments also can be advanced. These may also appeal to something like the principle of discrimination in the just war theory, namely, that these are innocent civilians or people who are not part of some fight and thus should not be directly targeted and harmed.

World Peace

Given the growing gap between richer and poorer nations, the potential for environmental destruction, the number of people supporting new nations and independence, the volatility and depth of ethnic animosities of the people living in new nations, and the proliferation of weapons (including nuclear weapons), what hope can there be for anything like world peace? Perhaps the threat is as much to order as to peace. As the 1980 Report of the Brandt Commission on International Development Issues puts it: "War is often thought of in terms of military conflict, or even annihilation. But there is a growing awareness that an equal danger might be chaos—as a result of mass hunger, economic disaster, environmental catastrophes, and terrorism, so we should not think only of reducing the traditional threats to peace, but also of the need for change from chaos to order."[40]

Whether for the sake of world peace or order, especially in this post-Cold War age, concerted efforts internationally may be the best hope. According to Michael Renner, perhaps the problem is that we have put too much emphasis on the motto "If you want peace, prepare for war." Instead, he suggests that we should prepare for peace, if we want peace.[41] However, to prepare for peace may necessitate a much greater emphasis on the role of the United Nations and its peacekeeping duties. The United Nations celebrated its fiftieth birthday in 1995. According to one news editorial, the United Nations "suddenly finds itself in the grip of a midlife crisis: a struggle between its grand ambitions for peace and the humbling realities of a world uncertain of its shared responsibilities."[42] The need for its peacekeeping and conflict-prevention capacities will certainly continue to increase. However, nations have not been willing to give this effort much financial support. The United States currently owes $1.5 billion for the United Nation's peacekeeping missions. The 1991 U.N. assessments were only $1 for every $2,016 the United States spent on its own defense department.[43]

The hope for world peace depends on several more factors, one being global reduction in military armaments. Such reduction involves the difficult work of establishing treaties to control biological, chemical, nuclear, and conventional weapons. Hope for world peace also depends on efforts to control the international arms trade as well as on finding ways to resolve the inevitable conflicts without resorting to force. In addition, development in poorer nations and a sense of fairness and good will between nations will also be essential to world peace. And, finally, whether peace can be realized depends on the ability of nations to consider not only their own self-interest but also their place in and responsibility for the world community. We may ask what role the individual could possibly have in this effort. As citizens of the world, we have at least the duty to keep informed and to realize that our ethical concern should not be limited to personal matters or even matters within our own community. This is also a big order, but one that can be filled.

In this chapter's readings, Peter Singer and Onora O'Neill raise questions about our responsibilities to relieve famine, Jodi Jacobson points out the significance of gender bias in efforts to promote development in Third World countries, and Barbara Harff discusses international responsibilities and principles of intervention.

Notes

1. *New York Times* (Oct. 9, 1995), p. C4. In particular, "the rate of growth of telephone lines in African countries like Chad, Zaire, and Niger badly lags behind the growth even in other developing countries like China, Egypt, and India." However, Worldtel, a fund to help such countries build telephone networks, hoped to raise $500 million for this purpose.
2. Paul Kennedy, "Preparing for the 21st Century: Winners and Losers," *The New York Review of Books,* vol. XL, no. 4 (Feb. 11, 1993): 42. This discussion can also be found in Paul Kennedy, *Preparing for the 21st Century* (New York: Random House, 1993). See also Robert D. Kaplan, "Cities of Despair," *New York Times* (June 6, 1996).
3. Quoted by Barbara Crosette in "U.N. Survey Finds World Rich-Poor Gap Widening," *New York Times* (July 15, 1996), p. A3.
4. Ibid.
5. Anthony DePalma, "Mexico's Serious Divisions Getting Wider and Deeper," *New York Times* (July 20, 1996), p. A8.
6. "U.N. Survey."
7. Kennedy, 33–34.
8. Ibid., 34.
9. Ibid.
10. Lester R. Brown, *State of the World 1993* (Washington, DC: Worldwatch Institute, 1993), p. xvi.
11. Lawrence K. Altman, "India Quickly Leads in HIV Cases," in *New York Times International* (July 8, 1996).
12. Barbara Crosette, "New Tally of World Tragedy: Women Who Die Giving Life," *New York Times International* (June 11, 1996), p. A1.
13. Brown, *State of the World 1993*.
14. Kennedy, "Preparing for the 21st Century," p. 39. Kennedy also notes that in the "centuries before the Reformation, Islam led the world in mathematics, cartography, medicine, and many other aspects of science and industry; and contained libraries, universities, and observatories, when Japan and America possessed none and Europe only a few" (p. 38).

15. Seth Mydans, "Do Rights Come First? Asia and Europe Clash," *New York Times International* (March 1, 1996), p. A6.

16. Ibid.

17. Ibid.

18. Ibid.

19. See Ramachandra Guha, "Radical American Environmentalism and Wilderness Preservation: A Third World Critique," in *Environmental Ethics* 11 (Spring 1989): 71–83.

20. James Gustave Speth, "Resources and Security: Perspectives from the Global 2000 Report," *World Future Society Bulletin* (1981).

21. Paul Ehrlich is noted for this view. See his *The Population Bomb* (New York: Ballantine, 1968).

22. R. Paul Shaw, World Bank official, as quoted in Mark Sagoff, "Population, Nature, and the Environment," *Report from the Institute for Philosophy and Public Policy,* vol. 13, no. 4 (Fall 1993), p. 8.

23. As quoted in Sagoff, "Population, Nature, and the Environment," p. 9; from Jessica Tuchman Mathews, "Redefining Security." *Foreign Affairs* (Spring 1989).

24. Garrett Hardin, "Living on a Lifeboat," *Bioscience* (October 1974).

25. Mark Sagoff, "Population, Nature, and the Environment," p. 8.

26. Nicholas Lenssen, "Providing Energy in Developing Countries," in Brown, *State,* 102.

27. Kaplan, "Cities of Despair."

28. *Statistical Abstracts of the United States, 1995.* U.S. Department of Commerce, Bureau of the Census. U.S. Government Printing Office, pp. 360–361, tables 557, 560.

29. Kennedy, "Preparing for the 21st Century," 38.

30. Speth, "Resources and Security."

31. Kennedy, "Preparing," 42.

32. *New York Times* (June 6, 1996).

33. Quoted in *New York Times* (Dec. 21, 1992), A1.

34. Ibid.

35. *New York Times* (Jan. 6, 1993), A5.

36. Robert W. Tucker, *The Just War* (Baltimore: Johns Hopkins Press, 1960), 1.

37. We might consider this particular principle as what is called a "regulative" rather than a "substantive" principle. Instead of telling us when is enough or the last thing we should try, it can be used to prod us to go somewhat further than we otherwise would.

38. Some versions of the just war theory also note that for a war to be just it must be declared by a competent authority. This was to distinguish not only just wars from battles between individuals, but also civil wars and insurrections. These would need to be argued for on other grounds. This principle also would direct the discussion of the justness of a war of nations to whether the proper national authorities had declared the war, with all of the constitutional issues, for example, that this raises.

39. James Childress, "Just-War Theories," *Theological Studies* (1978): 427–445.

40. In Speth, "Resources and Security."

41. Michael Renner, "Preparing for Peace," in *State of the World 1993,* Lester R. Brown (Ed.) (New York: Norton, 1993), 139.

42. Editorial, *San Francisco Chronicle* (May 23, 1993).

43. Ibid.

Famine, Affluence, and Morality

Peter Singer

Study Questions

1. How does Singer use the situation in Bengal in 1971 to exemplify the moral problem he wants to address?

2. With what assumption or moral principle does Singer begin his discussion?

3. Explain what he means by his second principle. Does it require us to do good or prevent harm?

How far does it require that we go to prevent the harm?

4. Why does he believe that this second principle is quite controversial?

5. Should it make any difference to our moral obligation that others could help those in need and do not?

6. Does Singer believe, then, that there is a significant moral difference between "duty" and "charity"?

7. How does Singer respond to the views of Sidgwick and Urmson that morality must not demand too much of us?

8. What is his response to the criticism that following his principle is impractical? How does he respond to the idea that governments rather than individuals should be the source of relief for the distant poor and starving?

9. What contrast does he make between a strong and a moderate version of how much we ought morally to give to these others in need?

10. What does he conclude about the consumer society and philosophers and philosophy?

As I write this, in November 1971, people are dying in East Bengal from lack of food, shelter, and medical care. The suffering and death that are occurring there now are not inevitable, not unavoidable in any fatalistic sense of the term. Constant poverty, a cyclone, and a civil war have turned at least nine million people into destitute refugees; nevertheless, it is not beyond the capacity of the richer nations to give enough assistance to reduce any further suffering to very small proportions. The decisions and actions of human beings can prevent this kind of suffering. Unfortunately, human beings have not made the necessary decisions. At the individual level, people have, with very few exceptions, not responded to the situation in any significant way. Generally speaking, people have not given large sums to relief funds; they have not written to their parliamentary representatives demanding increased government assistance; they have not demonstrated in the streets, held symbolic fasts, or done anything else directed toward providing the refugees with the means to satisfy their essential needs. At the government level, no government has given the sort of massive aid that would enable the refugees to survive for more than a few days. Britain, for instance, has given rather more than

most countries. It has, to date, given £14,750,000. For comparative purposes, Britain's share of the nonrecoverable development costs of the Anglo–French Concorde project is already in excess of £275,000,000, and on present estimates will reach £440,000,000. The implication is that the British government values a supersonic transport more than thirty times as highly as it values the lives of the nine million refugees. Australia is another country which, on a per capita basis, is well up in the "aid to Bengal" table. Australia's aid, however, amounts to less than one-twelfth of the cost of Sydney's new opera house. The total amount given, from all sources, now stands at about £65,000,000. The estimated cost of keeping the refugees alive for one year is £464,000,000. Most of the refugees have now been in the camps for more than six months. The World Bank has said that India needs a minimum of £300,000,000 in assistance from other countries before the end of the year. It seems obvious that assistance on this scale is not forthcoming. India will be forced to choose between letting the refugees starve or diverting funds from her own development program, which will mean that more of her own people will starve in the future.[1]

These are the essential facts about the present situation in Bengal. So far as it concerns us here, there is nothing unique about this situation except its magnitude. The Bengal emergency is just the latest and most acute of a series of major emergencies in various parts of the world, arising both from natural and from man-made causes. There are also many parts of the world in which people die from malnutrition and lack of food independent of any special emergency. I take Bengal as my example only because it is the present concern, and because the size of the problem has ensured that it has been given adequate publicity. Neither individuals nor governments can claim to be unaware of what is happening there.

What are the moral implications of a situation like this? In what follows, I shall argue that the way people in relatively affluent countries react to a situation like that in Bengal cannot be justified; indeed, the whole way we look at moral issues—our moral conceptual scheme—needs to be altered, and with it, the way of life that has come to be taken for granted in our society.

In arguing for this conclusion I will not, of course, claim to be morally neutral. I shall, however, try to argue for the moral position that I take, so that anyone

From *Philosophy & Public Affairs*, vol. 1, no. 3 (Spring 1972); 229–243. © 1972 by Princeton University Press. Reprinted with permission of Princeton University Press.

who accepts certain assumptions, to be made explicit, will, I hope, accept my conclusion.

I begin with the assumption that suffering and death from lack of food, shelter, and medical care are bad. I think most people will agree about this, although one may reach the same view by different routes. I shall not argue for this view. People can hold all sorts of eccentric positions, and perhaps from some of them it would not follow that death by starvation is in itself bad. It is difficult, perhaps impossible, to refute such positions, and so for brevity I will henceforth take this assumption as accepted. Those who disagree need read no further.

My next point is this: if it is in our power to prevent something bad from happening, without thereby sacrificing anything of comparable moral importance, we ought, morally, to do it. By "without sacrificing anything of comparable moral importance" I mean without causing anything else comparably bad to happen, or doing something that is wrong in itself, or failing to promote some moral good, comparable in significance to the bad thing that we can prevent. This principle seems almost as uncontroversial as the last one. It requires us only to prevent what is bad, and not to promote what is good, and it requires this of us only when we can do it without sacrificing anything that is, from the moral point of view, comparably important. I could even, as far as the application of my argument to the Bengal emergency is concerned, qualify the point so as to make it: if it is in our power to prevent something very bad from happening, without thereby sacrificing anything morally significant, we ought, morally, to do it. An application of this principle would be as follows: if I am walking past a shallow pond and see a child drowning in it, I ought to wade in and pull the child out. This will mean getting my clothes muddy, but this is insignificant, while the death of the child would presumably be a very bad thing.

The uncontroversial appearance of the principle just stated is deceptive. If it were acted upon, even in its qualified form, our lives, our society, and our world would be fundamentally changed. For the principle takes, firstly, no account of proximity or distance. It makes no moral difference whether the person I can help is a neighbor's child ten yards from me or a Bengali whose name I shall never know, ten thousand miles away. Secondly, the principle makes no distinction between cases in which I am the only person who could possibly do anything and cases in which I am just one among millions in the same position.

I do not think I need to say much in defense of the refusal to take proximity and distance into account. The fact that a person is physically near to us, so that we have personal contact with him, may make it more likely that we *shall* assist him, but this does not show that we *ought* to help him rather than another who happens to be further away. If we accept any principle of impartiality, universalizability, equality, or whatever, we cannot discriminate against someone merely because he is far away from us (or we are far away from him). Admittedly, it is possible that we are in a better position to judge what needs to be done to help a person near to us than one far away, and perhaps also to provide the assistance we judge to be necessary. If this were the case, it would be a reason for helping those near to us first. This may once have been a justification for being more concerned with the poor in one's own town than with famine victims in India. Unfortunately for those who like to keep their moral responsibilities limited, instant communication and swift transportation have changed the situation. From the moral point of view, the development of the world into a "global village" has made an important, though still unrecognized, difference to our moral situation.

Expert observers and supervisors, sent out by famine relief organizations or permanently stationed in famine-prone areas, can direct our aid to a refugee in Bengal almost as effectively as we could get it to someone in our own block. There would seem, therefore, to be no possible justification for discriminating on geographical grounds.

There may be a greater need to defend the second implication of my principle—that the fact that there are millions of other people in the same position, in respect to the Bengali refugees, as I am, does not make the situation significantly different from a situation in which I am the only person who can prevent something very bad from occurring. Again, of course, I admit that there is a psychological difference between the cases; one feels less guilty about doing nothing if one can point to others, similarly placed, who have also done nothing. Yet this can make no real difference to our moral obligations.[2] Should I consider that I am less obliged to pull the drowning child out of the pond if on looking around I see other people, no further away than I am, who have also noticed the child but are doing nothing? One has only to ask this question to see the absurdity of the view that numbers lessen obligation. It is a view that is an ideal excuse for inactivity; unfortunately most of the major evils—poverty, overpopulation, pollution—are problems in which everyone is almost equally involved.

The view that numbers do make a difference can be made plausible if stated in this way: if everyone in circumstances like mine gave £5 to the Bengal Relief Fund, there would be enough to provide food, shelter, and medical care for the refugees; there is no reason why I should give more than anyone else in the same circumstances as I am; therefore I have no obligation to give more than £5. Each premise in this argument is true, and the argument looks sound. It may convince us, unless we notice that it is based on a hypothetical premise, although the conclusion is not stated hypothetically. The argument would be sound if the conclusion were: if everyone in circumstances like mine were to give £5, I would have no obligation to give more than £5. If the conclusion were so stated, however, it would be obvious that the argument has no bearing on a situation in which it is not the case that everyone else gives £5. This, of course, is the actual situation. It is more or less certain that not everyone in circumstances like mine will give £5. So there will not be enough to provide the needed food, shelter, and medical care. Therefore by giving more than £5 I will prevent more suffering than I would if I gave just £5.

It might be thought that this argument has an absurd consequence. Since the situation appears to be that very few people are likely to give substantial amounts, it follows that I and everyone else in similar circumstances ought to give as much as possible, that is, at least up to the point at which by giving more one would begin to cause serious suffering for oneself and one's dependents—perhaps even beyond this point to the point of marginal utility, at which by giving more one would cause oneself and one's dependents as much suffering as one would prevent in Bengal. If everyone does this, however, there will be more than can be used for the benefit of the refugees, and some of the sacrifice will have been unnecessary. Thus, if everyone does what he ought to do, the result will not be as good as it would be if everyone did a little less than he ought to do, or if only some do all that they ought to do.

The paradox here arises only if we assume that the actions in question—sending money to the relief funds—are performed more or less simultaneously, and are also unexpected. For if it is to be expected that everyone is going to contribute something, then clearly each is not obliged to give as much as he would have been obliged to had others not been giving too. And if everyone is not acting more or less simultaneously, then those giving later will know how much more is needed, and will have no obligation to give more than is necessary to reach this amount. To say this is not to deny the principle that people in the same circumstances have the same obligations, but to point out that the fact that others have given, or may be expected to give, is a relevant circumstance: those giving after it has become known that many others are giving and those giving before are not in the same circumstances. So the seemingly absurd consequence of the principle I have put forward can occur only if people are in error about the actual circumstances—that is, if they think they are giving when others are not, but in fact they are giving when others are. The result of everyone doing what he really ought to do cannot be worse than the result of everyone doing less than he ought to do, although the result of everyone doing what he reasonably believes he ought to do could be.

If my argument so far has been sound, neither our distance from a preventable evil nor the number of other people who, in respect to that evil, are in the same situation as we are, lessens our obligation to mitigate or prevent that evil. I shall therefore take as established the principle I asserted earlier. As I have already said, I need to assert it only in its qualified form: if it is in our power to prevent something very bad from happening, without thereby sacrificing anything else morally significant, we ought, morally, to do it.

The outcome of this argument is that our traditional moral categories are upset. The traditional distinction between duty and charity cannot be drawn, or at least, not in the place we normally draw it. Giving money to the Bengal Relief Fund is regarded as an act of charity in our society. The bodies which collect money are known as "charities." These organizations see themselves in this way—if you send them a check, you will be thanked for your "generosity." Because giving money is regarded as an act of charity, it is not thought that there is anything wrong with not giving. The charitable man may be praised, but the man who is not charitable is not condemned. People do not feel in any way ashamed or guilty about spending money on new clothes or a new car instead of giving it to famine relief. (Indeed, the alternative does not occur to them.) This way of looking at the matter cannot be justified. When we buy new clothes not to keep ourselves warm but to look "well-dressed" we are not providing for any important need. We would not be sacrificing anything significant if we were to continue to wear our old clothes, and give the money to famine relief. By doing so, we would be preventing another person from starving. It follows from what I have said earlier that we ought to give money away, rather than spend it on clothes which we do not need to keep us warm. To do so is not charitable, or generous. Nor is it the kind of act which philosophers and theologians have called "supererogatory"—an act which it would be good to do, but not wrong not to do. On the contrary, we ought to give the money away, and it is wrong not to do so.

I am not maintaining that there are no acts which are charitable, or that there are no acts which it would be good to do but not wrong not to do. It may be possible to redraw the distinction between duty and charity in some other place. All I am arguing here is that the present way of drawing the distinction, which makes it an act of charity for a man living at the level of affluence which most people in the "developed nations" enjoy to give money to save someone else from starvation, cannot be supported. It is beyond the scope of my argument to consider whether the distinction should be redrawn or abolished altogether. There would be many other possible ways of drawing the distinction—for instance, one might decide that it is good to make other people as happy as possible, but not wrong not to do so.

Despite the limited nature of the revision in our moral conceptual scheme which I am proposing, the revision would, given the extent of both affluence and famine in the world today, have radical implications. These implications may lead to further objections, distinct from those I have already considered. I shall discuss two of these.

One objection to the position I have taken might be simply that it is too drastic a revision of our moral scheme. People do not ordinarily judge in the way I have suggested they should. Most people reserve their moral condemnation for those who violate some moral norm, such as the norm against taking another person's property. They do not condemn those who indulge in luxury instead of giving to famine relief. But given that I did not set out to present a morally neutral description of the way people make moral judgments, the way people do in fact judge has nothing to do with the validity of my conclusion. My conclusion follows from the principle which I advanced earlier, and unless that principle is rejected, or the arguments shown to be unsound, I think the conclusion must stand, however strange it appears.

It might, nevertheless, be interesting to consider why our society, and most other societies, do judge differently from the way I have suggested they should. In a well-known article, J. O. Urmson suggests that the imperatives of duty, which tell us what we must do, as distinct from what it would be good to do but not wrong not to do, function so as to prohibit behavior that is intolerable if men are to live together in society.[3] This may explain the origin and continued existence of the present division between acts of duty and acts of charity. Moral attitudes are shaped by the needs of society, and no doubt society needs people who will observe the rules that make social existence tolerable. From the point of view of a particular society, it is essential to prevent violations of norms against killing, stealing, and so on. It is quite inessential, however, to help people outside one's own society.

If this is an explanation of our common distinction between duty and supererogation, however, it is not a justification of it. The moral point of view requires us to look beyond the interests of our own society. Previously, as I have already mentioned, this may hardly have been feasible, but it is quite feasible now. From the moral point of view, the prevention of the starvation of millions of people outside our society must be considered at least as pressing as the upholding of property norms within our society.

It has been argued by some writers, among them Sidgwick and Urmson, that we need to have a basic moral code which is not too far beyond the capacities of the ordinary man, for otherwise there will be a general breakdown of compliance with the moral code. Crudely stated, this argument suggests that if we tell people that they ought to refrain from murder and give everything they do not really need to famine relief, they will do neither, whereas if we tell them that they ought to refrain from murder and that it is good to give to famine relief but not wrong not to do so, they will at least refrain from murder. The issue here is: Where should we draw the line between conduct that is required and conduct that is good although not required, so as to get the best possible result? This would seem to be an empirical question, although a very difficult one. One objection to the Sidgwick–Urmson line of argument is that it takes insufficient account of the effect that moral standards can have on the decisions we make. Given a society in which a wealthy man who gives five percent of his income to famine relief is regarded as most generous, it is not surprising that a proposal that we all ought to give away half our incomes will be thought to be absurdly unrealistic. In a society which held that no man should have more than enough while others have less than they need, such a proposal might seem narrow-minded. What it is possible for a man to do and what he is likely to do are both, I think, very greatly influenced by what people around him are doing and expecting him to do. In any case, the possibility that by spreading the idea that we ought to be doing very much more than we are to relieve famine we shall bring about a general breakdown of moral behavior seems remote. If the stakes are an end to widespread starvation, it is worth the risk. Finally, it should be emphasized that these considerations are relevant only to the issue of what we should require from others, and not to what we ourselves ought to do.

The second objection to my attack on the present distinction between duty and charity is one which has from time to time been made against utilitarianism. It follows from some forms of utilitarian theory that we all ought, morally, to be working full time to increase the balance of happiness over misery. The position I have taken here would not lead to this conclusion in all circumstances, for if there were no bad occurrences that we could prevent without sacrificing something of comparable moral importance, my argument would have no application. Given the present conditions in many parts of the world, however, it does follow from my argument that we ought, morally, to be working full time to relieve great suffering of the sort that occurs as a result of famine or other disasters. Of course, mitigating circumstances can be adduced—for instance, that if we wear ourselves out through overwork, we shall be less effective than we would otherwise have been. Nevertheless, when all considerations of this sort have been taken into account, the conclusion remains: we ought to be preventing as much suffering as we can without sacrificing something else of comparable moral importance. This conclusion is one which we may be reluctant to face. I cannot see, though, why it should

be regarded as a criticism of the position for which I have argued, rather than a criticism of our ordinary standards of behavior. Since most people are self-interested to some degree, very few of us are likely to do everything that we ought to do. It would, however, hardly be honest to take this as evidence that it is not the case that we ought to do it.

It may still be thought that my conclusions are so wildly out of line with what everyone else thinks and has always thought that there must be something wrong with the argument somewhere. In order to show that my conclusions, while certainly contrary to contemporary Western moral standards, would not have seemed so extraordinary at other times and in other places, I would like to quote a passage from a writer not normally thought of as a way-out radical, Thomas Aquinas.

> Now, according to the natural order instituted by divine providence, material goods are provided for the satisfaction of human needs. Therefore the division and appropriation of property, which proceeds from human law, must not hinder the satisfaction of man's necessity from such goods. Equally, whatever a man has in superabundance is owed, of natural right, to the poor for their sustenance. So Ambrosius says, and it is also to be found in the *Decretum Gratiani*: "The bread which you withhold belongs to the hungry; the clothing you shut away, to the naked; and the money you bury in the earth is the redemption and freedom of the penniless."[4]

I now want to consider a number of points, more practical than philosophical, which are relevant to the application of the moral conclusion we have reached. These points challenge not the idea that we ought to be doing all we can to prevent starvation, but the idea that giving away a great deal of money is the best means to this end.

It is sometimes said that overseas aid should be a government responsibility, and that therefore one ought not to give to privately run charities. Giving privately, it is said, allows the government and the noncontributing members of society to escape their responsibilities.

This argument seems to assume that the more people there are who give to privately organized famine relief funds, the less likely it is that the government will take over full responsibility for such aid. This assumption is unsupported, and does not strike me as at all plausible. The opposite view—that if no one gives voluntarily, a government will assume that its citizens are uninterested in famine relief and would not wish to be forced into giving aid—seems more plausible. In any case, unless there were a definite probability that by refusing to give one would be helping to bring about massive government assistance, people who do refuse to make voluntary contributions are refusing to prevent a certain amount of suffering without being able to point to any tangible beneficial consequence of their refusal. So the onus of showing how their refusal will bring about government action is on those who refuse to give.

I do not, of course, want to dispute the contention that governments of affluent nations should be giving many times the amount of genuine, no-strings-attached aid that they are giving now. I agree, too, that giving privately is not enough, and that we ought to be campaigning actively for entirely new standards for both public and private contributions to famine relief. Indeed, I would sympathize with someone who thought that campaigning was more important than giving oneself, although I doubt whether preaching what one does not practice would be very effective. Unfortunately, for many people the idea that "it's the government's responsibility" is a reason for not giving which does not appear to entail any political action either.

Another, more serious reason for not giving to famine relief funds is that until there is effective population control, relieving famine merely postpones starvation. If we save the Bengal refugees now, others, perhaps the children of these refugees, will face starvation in a few years' time. In support of this, one may cite the now well-known facts about the population explosion and the relatively limited scope for expanded production.

This point, like the previous one, is an argument against relieving suffering that is happening now, because of a belief about what might happen in the future; it is unlike the previous point in that very good evidence can be adduced in support of this belief about the future. I will not go into the evidence here. I accept that the earth cannot support indefinitely a population rising at the present rate. This certainly poses a problem for anyone who thinks it important to prevent famine. Again, however, one could accept the argument without drawing the conclusion that it absolves one from any obligation to do anything to prevent famine. The conclusion that should be drawn is that the best means of preventing famine, in the long run, is population control. It would then follow from the position reached earlier that one ought to be doing all one can to promote population control (unless one held that all forms of population control were wrong in themselves, or would have significantly bad consequences). Since there are organizations working specifically for population control, one would then support them rather than more orthodox methods of preventing famine.

A third point raised by the conclusion reached earlier relates to the question of just how much we all ought to be giving away. One possibility, which has already been mentioned, is that we ought to give until we reach the level of marginal utility—that is, the level at which, by giving more, I would cause as much suffering to myself or my dependents as I would relieve by my gift. This would mean, of course, that one would reduce oneself to very near the material circumstances of the Bengali refugee. It will be recalled that earlier I put forward both a strong and a moderate version of the principle of preventing bad occurrences. The strong version, which required us to prevent bad things from happening unless in doing so we would be sacrificing something of comparable moral significance, does seem to require reducing ourselves to the level of marginal utility. I should also say that the strong version seems to me to be the correct one. I proposed the more moderate version—that we should prevent bad occurrences unless, to do so, we have to sacrifice something morally significant—only in order to show that even on this surely undeniable principle a great change in our way of life is required. On the more moderate principle, it may not follow that we ought to reduce ourselves to the level of marginal utility, for one might hold that to reduce oneself and one's family to this level is to cause something significantly bad to happen. Whether this is so I shall not discuss, since, as I have said, I can see no good reason for holding the moderate version of the principle rather than the strong version. Even if we accepted the principle only in its moderate form, however, it should be clear that we would have to give away enough to ensure that the consumer society, dependent as it is on people spending on trivia rather than giving to famine relief, would slow down and perhaps disappear entirely. There are several reasons why this would be desirable in itself. The value and necessity of economic growth are now being questioned not only by conservationists, but by economists as well.[5] There is no doubt, too, that the consumer society has had a distorting effect on the goals and purposes of its members. Yet looking at the matter purely from the point of view of overseas aid, there must be a limit to the extent to which we should deliberately slow down our economy; for it might be the case that if we gave away, say, forty percent of our Gross National Product, we would slow down the economy so much that in absolute terms we would be giving less than if we gave twenty-five percent of the much larger GNP than we would have if we limited our contribution to this smaller percentage.

I mention this only as an indication of the sort of factor that one would have to take into account in working out an ideal. Since Western societies generally consider one percent of the GNP an acceptable level for overseas aid, the matter is entirely academic. Nor does it affect the question of how much an individual should give in a society in which very few are giving substantial amounts.

It is sometimes said, though less often now than it used to be, that philosophers have no special role to play in public affairs, since most public issues depend primarily on an assessment of facts. On questions of fact, it is said, philosophers as such have no special expertise, and so it has been possible to engage in philosophy without committing oneself to any position on major public issues. No doubt there are some issues of social policy and foreign policy about which it can truly be said that a really expert assessment of the facts is required before taking sides or acting, but the issue of famine is surely not one of these. The facts about the existence of suffering are beyond dispute. Nor, I think, is it disputed that we can do something about it, either through orthodox methods of famine relief or through population control or both. This is therefore an issue on which philosophers are competent to take a position. The issue is one which faces everyone who has more money than he needs to support himself and his dependents, or who is in a position to take some sort of political action. These categories must include practically every teacher and student of philosophy in the universities of the Western world. If philosophy is to deal with matters that are relevant to both teachers and students, this is an issue that philosophers should discuss.

Discussion, though, is not enough. What is the point of relating philosophy to public (and personal) affairs if we do not take our conclusions seriously? In this instance, taking our conclusion seriously means acting upon it. The philosopher will not find it any easier than anyone else to alter his attitudes and way of life to the extent that, if I am right, is involved in doing everything that we ought to be doing. At the very least, though, one can make a start. The philosopher who does so will have to sacrifice some of the benefits of the consumer society, but he can find compensation in the satisfaction of a way of life in which theory and practice, if not yet in harmony, are at least coming together.

Notes

1. There was also a third possibility: that India would go to war to enable the refugees to return to their lands. Since I wrote this paper, India has taken this way out. The situation is no longer that described above, but this does not affect my argument, as the next paragraph indicates.

2. In view of the special sense philosophers often give to the term, I should say that I use "obligation" simply as the abstract noun derived from "ought," so that "I have an obligation to" means no more, and no less, than "I ought to." This usage is in accordance with the definition of "ought" given by the *Shorter Oxford English Dictionary*: "the general verb to express duty or obligation." I do not think any issue of substance hangs on the way the term is used; sentences in which I use "obligation" could all be rewritten, although somewhat clumsily, as sentences in which a clause containing "ought" replaces the term "obligation."

3. J. O. Urmson, "Saints and Heroes," in *Essays in Moral Philosophy*, Abraham I. Melden (Ed.) (Seattle and London, 1958), p. 214. For a related but significantly different view see also Henry Sidgwick, *The Methods of Ethics*, 7th ed. (London, 1907), pp. 220–221, 492–493.

4. Summa Theologica II–II. Question 66, Article 7, in Aquinas, *Selected Political Writings*, A. P. d'Entreves (Ed.), J. G. Dawson (Trans.) (Oxford, 1948), p. 171.

5. See, for instance, John Kenneth Galbraith, *The New Industrial State* (Boston, 1967); and E. J. Mishan, *The Costs of Economic Growth* (London, 1967).

Kantian Approaches to Some Famine Problems

Onora O'Neill

Study Questions

1. How is the moral problem about famine different today than in ages past, according to O'Neill?

2. According to O'Neill, how are moral theories supposed to help us with problems such as this?

3. Does Kant give us a precise set of rules for answering specific moral questions?

4. What are some maxims that might be used to guide action in contexts where famine is an issue?

5. In Kant's view, how are we to decide whether some policy is morally required? How does this differ from a utilitarian way of judging?

6. What is the difference between using someone as a means and using someone as a mere means?

7. How is the person who is deceived (as in the case of false promises or other lying) or coerced (as in the case of the debtor described here) used as a mere means?

8. How else may we fail to treat persons as ends in themselves?

9. What is the difference between the requirements of justice and of beneficence in Kantian ethics, according to O'Neill?

10. What are some ways in which the hungry and destitute may be vulnerable to deception and coercion?

11. What is the basis in Kantian thought, according to O'Neill, for beneficence?

12. In what way is Kant's moral theory less ambitious than utilitarian moral theory?

Are Famine and World Hunger New Moral Problems?

Moral problems aren't usually new. Most of the questions that give us pause or sleepless nights have been faced by others ever since (no doubt also before) the beginnings of systematic reflection about what we do. We know very well, for example, that we are not the first to be tempted to put career before everything else. If the temptation persists, we may want to consult our predecessors or other authorities. We may find ourselves thinking about Macbeth's vaulting ambition, perhaps comforted by the thought that, unlike him, we do not put career above everything—no murder for advancement, for example,

But when we wonder what we or others should do about global famine there are fewer familiar literary or religious traditions or philosophical discussions to which to turn. This is not because famine is new but because there is today far more that we (or others) can do—or refrain from doing—that will affect the risk and course of famine. Through history millions have died of sheer starvation and of malnutrition or from illnesses that they might have survived with better food. Whenever there were such deaths, nearby survivors may have realized that they could help prevent some deaths and may have done so, or wondered whether to do so. But nobody sought to prevent faraway deaths. Distance made an important difference; with few exceptions there was nothing to be done for the victims of faraway famines.

In a global economy things are different. Food from areas with agricultural surplus (nowadays mainly North America, Australia, and western Europe) can be distributed to the starving in Bangladesh or Somalia. Longer-term policies that affect economic development, fertility levels, and agricultural productivity may hasten or postpone far-off famines or make them more or less severe. Consequently we can now ask whether we ought to do some of these newly possible actions. Ought we (or others) to try to distribute food or aid, to control fertility, or to further economic development? Who should foot the bills and suffer the other costs? To whom (if anyone) should aid be given and to whom should it be denied?

Onora O'Neill, "Kantian Approaches to Some Famine Problems," in *Matters of Life and Death,* 3rd ed., Tom Regan (Ed.) (New York: McGraw-Hill, 1993), pp. 294–297, 319–328. Reprinted by permission of the publisher.

How much hardship or sacrifice, if any, is demanded of those who have the means to help? . . .

Moral Theories
and Morally Acceptable Theories

Moral theories typically include a number of rather general principles that enjoin or forbid, commend or condemn some types of action. Examples of such general principles of action include the Good Samaritan principle and principles like "Injure nobody" or "Do whatever will produce the best results for everybody," or "Do as you would be done by." Many moral theories consist of more than one such principle, and when there is more than one, the theory usually explains their relationship. For example, a moral theory that includes the principle "Always do what produces the best results for everybody" will probably include a principle for settling what sorts of things count as good or bad results.

This minimal account of moral theories accepts that there can be many different moral theories. Some may be incompatible with others. For example, one moral theory might include the principle "Always do the act likely to have the best total results," and another the principle "Do what appeals to you most, even when it will produce less good total results than you could achieve by suiting yourself less well."

If we want moral theories to help us decide about difficult moral problems, then we need to choose one of these theories. If we do not, we would face various theories that enjoin or forbid, commend or condemn incompatible actions and so cannot give us guidance. In making this choice, we want to pick not just *any* moral theory, but one that is *morally acceptable*. . . .

The Facts of Famine

An enormous amount is known about the numbers of people now living and about the resources they have to live on. There are also many careful and scrupulous studies of the likely rate of growth of population and resources in various regions and countries. It may then seem easy to discover whether the world either is or will be overpopulated, whether there will be famines, and when and where they are most likely to occur. But it turns out that this is not easy, indeed, that the experts disagree passionately. They don't, on the whole, disagree with passion about the particular figures (which all accept as being no more than careful estimates). They often do disagree about the import of these figures. But some matters are not controversial, and I shall sketch these briefly. . . .

The Look of Famine

Famine is a hidden killer, a dark horse. In the Book of Revelation, other killers are symbolized by highly visible horses and horsemen: the white horse of Conquest, the red horse of War, and the pale horse of Death itself. But Famine is symbolized by a black horse and horseman. And so it is in human experience. When famine strikes, relatively few people die "of hunger." They die for the most part of illnesses they would easily have survived if hunger had not weakened them. They die of flu and of intestinal troubles, and disproportionately many of those who die are very young or old. When there is famine, the survivors too are affected in hidden ways. Children may suffer brain damage as a result of early malnutrition; whole populations may be listless and lethargic, unable to muster the energy needed for economic advance, still living but permanently weakened.

We have all seen pictures of starving, skeletal children in the appeals of famine-relief charities. But such emaciation is only the visible and publicizable fraction of the damage the black horse can do. When we wonder whether famine is likely, we must remember that most of the impact of hunger is less dramatic. Whenever death rates are higher than they would be with adequate nutrition, hunger is *already* taking its toll. Perhaps there will be future famines that are far more visible than today's hunger, large-scale versions of the disastrous famines that have recently occurred in the southern Sahara, in Bangladesh, and in Ethiopia. Perhaps there will be nothing so dramatic but rather many lives of unrelenting hunger and premature death, without mass migration in search of food or any of the other horrors of extreme famine. If we remember that most of the impact of hunger is of this sort, then we can see that famine is not some unknown evil that might strike human populations in the future, but a more virulent case of evil suffered by many now living. The question that divides the experts is less whether there will be future, dramatic episodes of famine than whether the endemic hunger and malnutrition that millions now live with can be ended or will become more intense and severe as time goes on.

Hunger does not have to produce dramatic and catastrophic episodes of famine to inflict acute suffering. Hunger destroys lives in two senses: it literally kills—destroys—the biological basis of life, and it also destroys the lives persons lead, their biographical lives, even when it leaves the biological organism functioning. The survivors of famines and near famine suffer the biological deaths of those they love, and their own biographical lives are often shattered by hunger and the destruction of ways of life.

The Extent of Famine

To get a feel for the extent of these miseries, it helps to have a few figures. The population of the world is around 4½ billion—and rising very fast. If we project present rates of growth, we can imagine a world whose human population doubles and redoubles every few decades. But a *projection* of exiting trends is not *prediction*. There is no point in projecting this sort of figure and entertaining the fantasy of a world without resources but weighed down by or literally covered with living humans. Long before this point is reached, the availability of resources will limit the population that can remain alive.

The history of the last two centuries is one of rapid increases in available resources, which have permitted a corresponding growth in human population. Two centuries ago there were only 800 million human beings alive. We do not know how many there will be in another two centuries. But however few or many there are, there will not be more alive than there are resources to sustain them. (There may be fewer, since some or all persons may live at a higher-than-subsistence standard.) Sustained overpopulation is impossible: as soon as there are more people than there are resources, some people die. When populations expand beyond resources available to them, they are pruned by famine. But we do not have to be at the mercy of famines. Populations can control their own rates of growth and ensure that they don't grow faster than the resources available to them. A population that succeeds in this task (and some have) need not suffer or risk famine. It can be free not only of the spectacular miseries of catastrophic famines but also of the slower, hidden famine that shows itself in premature deaths, lack of resistance to illness, and lack of energy. On these matters the experts do not disagree.

Controversies About Avoiding Famines

When we ask *how* famine and hunger can best be ended and whether it is at all likely that they will be ended, there is great controversy. All agree that the task of ending famine is at best enormous and daunting. But even experts disagree about what is possible. Some awareness of these disagreements is helpful in considering moral problems raised by famine.

Some experts—often spoken of as neo-Malthusians—think that the only secure way to end famine is by limiting population growth. In the long run no increase in available food could match population increase. Other experts—often called developmentalists—think that the first aim must be economic growth, which is a prerequisite of lowering population growth.

Developmentalists themselves disagree whether the most important changes are economic or political. They debate whether economic policies available within current political structures, such as foreign aid and international loans and investment by transnational corporations, provide an adequate framework to develop the now underdeveloped world. Are there—as some political economists believe—features of the present structures of aid and trade that prevent such policies from transforming the economic prospects of underdeveloped regions but which might be changed by political transformations? Is it even possible that the main obstacle to economic growth in the poorest regions lies in the present international economic order, despite its ostensible commitment to the goal of development?

These debates are ethically important because social inquiry itself is no matter of ethically neutral "facts." The debates between different experts often show that their disputes are *already* moral disagreements. There is no way in which those who want to do something about world hunger and poverty can hope that experts will present "the facts," and equally no way in which those who take action can shirk making informed judgments about what is possible. . . .

A Simplified Account of Kant's Ethics

Kant's theory is frequently and misleadingly assimilated to theories of human rights. It is, in fact, a theory of human obligations; therefore it is wider in scope than a theory of human rights. (Not all obligations generate corresponding rights.) Kant does not, however, try to generate a set of precise rules defining human obligations in all possible circumstances; instead, he attempts to provide a set of *principles of obligation* that can be used as the starting points for moral reasoning in actual contexts of action. The primary focus of Kantian ethics is, then, on *action* rather than either *results,* as in utilitarian thinking, or *entitlements,* as in theories that make human rights their fundamental category. Morality requires action of certain sorts. But to know *what* sort of action is required (or forbidden) in which circumstances, we should not look just at the expected results of action or at others' supposed entitlements but, in the first instance, at the nature of the proposed actions themselves.

When we engage in moral reasoning, we often need go no further than to refer to some quite specific principle or tradition. We may say to one another, or to ourselves, things like "It would be hypocritical to pretend that our good fortune is achieved without harm to the Third World," or "Redistributive taxation shouldn't cross national boundaries." But when these specific claims are challenged, we may find ourselves pushed to justify or reject or modify them. Such moral debate, on Kant's account, rests on appeals to what he calls the *Supreme Principle of Morality,* which can (he thinks) be used to work out more specific principles of obligation. This principle, the famous Categorical Imperative, plays the same role in Kantian thinking that the Greatest Happiness Principle plays in utilitarian thought.

A second reason why Kant's moral thought often appears difficult is that he offers a number of different versions of this principle, that he claims are equivalent, but which look very different. A straightforward way in which to simplify Kantian moral thought is to concentrate on just one of these formulations of the Categorical Imperative. For present purposes I shall choose the version to which he gives the sonorous name of *The Formula of the End in Itself.*

The Formula of the End in Itself

The "Formula of the End in Itself" runs as follows:

> Act in such a way that you always treat humanity, whether in your own person or in the person of any other, never simply as a means but always at the same time as an end.

To understand this principle we need in the first place to understand what Kant means by the term *maxim.* The maxim of an act or policy or activity is the *underlying principle* of the act, policy or activity, by which other, more superficial aspects of action are guided. Very often interpretations of Kant have supposed that maxims can only be the (underlying) intentions of individual human agents. If that were the case it would limit the usefulness of Kantian modes of moral thought in dealing with world hunger and famine problems. For it is clear enough that individual action (while often important) cannot deal with all the problems of Third World poverty. A moral theory that addresses *only* individual actors does not have adequate scope for discussing famine problems.

It is helpful to think of some examples of maxims that might be used to guide action in contexts where poverty and the risk of famine are issues. Somebody who contributes to famine-relief work or advocates development might have an underlying principle such as, "Try to help reduce the risk or severity of world hunger." This commitment might be reflected in varied surface action in varied situations. In one context a gift of money might be relevant; in another some political activity such as lobbying for or against certain types of aid and trade might express the same underlying commitment. Sometimes superficial aspects of action may seem at variance with the underlying maxim they in fact express. For example, if there is reason to think that indiscriminate food aid damages the agricultural economy of the area to which food is given, then the maxim of seeking to relieve famine might be expressed in action aimed at limiting the extent of food aid. More lavish use of food aid might *seem* to treat the needy more generously, but if in fact it will damage their medium- or long-term economic prospects, then it is not (contrary to superficial appearances) aimed at improving and securing their access to subsistence. On a Kantian theory, the basis for judging action should be its *fundamental* principle or policy, and superficially similar acts may be judged morally very different. Regulating food aid in order to drive up prices and profit from them is one matter; regulating food aid in order to enable local farmers to sell their crops and to stay in the business of growing food quite another.

When we want to work out whether a proposed act or policy is morally required we should not, on Kant's view, try to find out whether it would produce more happiness than other available acts. Rather we should see whether the act or policy is required by, or ruled out by, or merely compatible with maxims that avoid using others as mere means and maxims that treat others as ends in themselves. These two aspects of Kantian duty can each be spelled out and shown to have determinate implications for acts and policies that may affect the risk and course of famines.

Using Others as Mere Means

We use others as *mere means* if what we do reflects some maxim *to which they could not in principle consent*. Kant does not suggest that there is anything wrong about using someone as a means. Evidently every cooperative scheme of action does this. A government that agrees to provide free or subsidized food to famine-relief agencies both uses and is used by the agencies; a peasant who sells food in a local market both uses and is used by those who buy it. In such examples each party to the transaction can and does consent to take part in that transaction. Kant would say that the parties to such transactions use one another but do not use one another as *mere* means. Each party assumes that the other has its own maxims of action and is not just a thing or prop to be used or manipulated.

But there are other cases where one party to an arrangement or transaction not only uses the other but does so in ways that could only be done on the basis of a fundamental principle or maxim to which the other could not in principle consent. If a false promise is given, the party that accepts the promise is not just used but used as a mere means, because it is *impossible* for consent to be given to the fundamental principle or project of deception that must guide every false promise, whatever its surface character. Those who accept false promises *must* be kept ignorant of the underlying principle or maxim on which the "undertaking" is based. If this isn't kept concealed, the attempted promise will either be rejected or will not be a *false* promise at all. In false promising the deceived party becomes, as it were, a prop or tool—a *mere* means—in the false promisor's scheme. Action based on any such maxim of deception would be wrong in Kantian terms, whether it is a matter of a breach of treaty obligations, of contractual undertakings, or of accepted and relied upon modes of interaction. Maxims of deception *standardly* use others as mere means, and acts that could only be based on such maxims are unjust.

Another standard way of using others as mere means is by coercing them. Coercers, like deceivers, standardly don't give others the possibility of dissenting from what they propose to do. In deception, "consent" is spurious because it is given to a principle that couldn't be the underlying principle of *that* act at all; but the principle governing coercion may be brutally plain. Here any "consent" given is spurious because there was no option *but* to consent. If a rich or powerful landowner or nation threatens a poorer or more vulnerable person, group, or nation with some intolerable difficulty unless a concession is made, the more vulnerable party is denied a genuine choice between consent and dissent. While the boundary that divides coercion from mere bargaining and negotiation varies and is therefore often hard to discern, we have no doubt about the clearer cases. Maxims of coercion may threaten physical force, seizure of possessions, destruction of opportunities, or any other harm that the coerced party is thought to be unable to absorb without grave injury or danger. A moneylender in a Third World village who threatens not to make or renew an indispensable loan, without which survival until the next harvest would be impossible, uses the peasant as mere means. The peasant does not have the possibility of genuinely consenting to the "offer he can't refuse." The outward form of some coercive transactions may *look* like ordinary commercial dealings: but we know very well that some action that is superficially of this sort is based on maxims of coercion. To avoid coercion, action must be governed by maxims that the other party can choose to refuse and is not bound to accept. The more vulnerable the other party in any transaction or negotiation, the less their scope for refusal, and the more demanding it is likely to be to ensure that action is noncoercive.

In Kant's view, acts done on maxims that coerce or deceive others, so therefore cannot in principle have the consent of those others, are wrong. When individuals or institutions, or nation states act in ways that can only be based on such maxims they fail in their duty. They treat the parties who are either deceived or coerced unjustly. To avoid unjust action it is not enough to observe the outward forms of free agreement and cooperation; it is also essential to see that the weaker party to any arrangement has a genuine option to refuse the fundamental character of the proposal.

Treating Others as Ends in Themselves

For Kant, as for utilitarians, justice is only one part of duty. We may fail in our duty, even when we don't use anyone as mere means (by deception or coercion), if we fail to treat others as "ends in themselves." To treat others as "Ends in Themselves" we must not only avoid using them as mere means but also treat them as rational and autonomous beings with their own maxims. If human beings were *wholly* rational and autonomous then, on a Kantian view, duty would require only that they not use one another as mere means. But, as Kant repeatedly stressed, but later Kantians have often forgotten, human beings are *finite* rational beings. They are finite in several ways.

First, human beings are not ideal rational calculators. We *standardly* have neither a complete list of the actions possible in a given situation nor more than a partial view of their likely consequences. In addition, abilities to assess and to use available information are usually quite limited.

Second, these cognitive limitations are *standardly* complemented by limited autonomy. Human action is limited not only by various sorts of physical barrier and inability but by further sorts of (mutual or asymmetrical) dependence. To treat one another as ends in themselves such beings have to base their action on principles that do not undermine but rather sustain and extend one another's capacities for autonomous action. A central requirement for doing so is to share and support one another's ends and activities at least to some extent. Since finite rational beings cannot generally achieve their aims without some help and support from others, a general refusal of help and support amounts to failure to treat others as rational and autonomous beings, that is as ends in themselves. Hence Kantian principles require us not only to act justly, that is in accordance with maxims that don't coerce or deceive others, but also to avoid manipulation and to lend some support to others' plans and activities. Since famine, great poverty and powerlessness all undercut the possibility of autonomous action, and the requirement of treating others as ends in themselves demands that Kantians standardly act to support the possibility of autonomous action where it is most vulnerable, Kantians are required to do what they can to avert, reduce, and remedy famine. On a Kantian view, beneficence is as indispensable as justice in human lives.

Justice and Beneficence in Kant's Thought

Kant is often thought to hold that justice is morally required, but beneficence is morally less important. He does indeed, like Mill, speak of justice as a *perfect duty* and of beneficence as an *imperfect duty*. But he does not mean by this that beneficence is any less a duty; rather, he holds that it has (unlike justice) to be selective. We cannot share or even support *all* others' maxims *all* of the time. Hence support for others' autonomy is always selective. By contrast we can

make all action and institutions conform fundamentally to standards of nondeception and noncoercion. Kant's understanding of the distinction between perfect and imperfect duties differs from Mill's. In a Kantian perspective justice isn't a matter of the core requirements for beneficence, as in Mill's theory, and beneficence isn't just an attractive but optional moral embellishment of just arrangements (as tends to be assumed in most theories that take human rights as fundamental).

Justice to the Vulnerable in Kantian Thinking

For Kantians, justice requires action that conforms (at least outwardly) to what could be done in a given situation while acting on maxims neither of deception nor of coercion. Since anyone hungry or destitute is more than usually vulnerable to deception and coercion, the possibilities and temptations to injustice are then especially strong.

Examples are easily suggested. I shall begin with some situations that might arise for somebody who happened to be part of a famine-stricken population. Where shortage of food is being dealt with by a reasonably fair rationing scheme, any mode of cheating to get more than one's allocated share involves using some others and is unjust. Equally, taking advantage of others' desperation to profiteer—for example, selling food at colossal prices or making loans on the security of others' future livelihood, when these are "offers they can't refuse"—constitutes coercion and so uses others as mere means and is unjust. Transactions that have the outward form of normal commercial dealing may be coercive when one party is desperate. Equally, forms of corruption that work by deception—such as bribing officials to gain special benefits from development schemes, or deceiving others about their entitlements—use others unjustly. Such requirements are far from trivial and frequently violated in hard times; acting justly in such conditions may involve risking one's own life and livelihood and require the greatest courage.

It is not so immediately obvious what justice, Kantianly conceived, requires of agents and agencies who are remote from destitution. Might it not be sufficient to argue that those of us fortunate enough to live in the developed world are far from famine and destitution, so if we do nothing but go about our usual business will successfully avoid injustice to the destitute? This conclusion has often been reached by those who take an abstract view of rationality and forget the limits of human rationality and autonomy. In such perspectives it can seem that there is nothing more to just action than meeting the formal requirements of nondeception and noncoercion in our dealings with one another. But once we remember the limitations of human rationality and autonomy, and the particular ways in which they are limited for those living close to the margins of subsistence, we can see that mere conformity to ordinary standards of commercial honesty and political bargaining is not enough for justice toward the destitute. If international agreements themselves can constitute "offers that cannot be refused" by the government of a poor country, or if the concessions required for investment by a transnational corporation or a development project reflect the desperation of recipients rather than an appropriate contribution to the project, then (however benevolent the motives of some parties) the weaker party to such agreements is used by the stronger.

In the earlier days of European colonial penetration of the now underdeveloped world it was evident enough that some of the ways in which "agreements" were made with native peoples were in fact deceptive or coercive or both. "Sales" of land by those who had no grasp of market practices and "cession of sovereignty" by those whose forms of life were prepolitical constitute only spurious consent to the agreements struck. But it is not only in these original forms of bargaining between powerful and powerless that injustice is frequent. There are many contemporary examples. For example, if capital investment (private or governmental) in a poorer country requires the receiving country to contribute disproportionately to the maintenance of a developed, urban "enclave" economy that offers little local employment but lavish standards of life for a small number of (possibly expatriate) "experts," while guaranteeing long-term exemption from local taxation for the investors, then we may doubt that the agreement could have been struck without the element of coercion provided by the desperation of the weaker party. Or if a trade agreement extracts political advantages (such as military bases) that are incompatible with the fundamental political interests of the country concerned, we may judge that at least some leaders of that country have been "bought" in a sense that is not consonant with ordinary commercial practice.

Even when the actions of those who are party to an agreement don't reflect a fundamental principle of coercion or deception, the agreement may alter the life circumstances and prospects of third parties in ways to which they patently could not have not consented. For example, a system of food aid and imports agreed upon by the government of a Third World country and certain developed countries or international agencies may give the elite of that Third World country access to subsidized grain. If that grain is then used to control the urban population and also produces destitution among peasants (who used to grow food for that urban population), then those who are newly destitute probably have not been offered any opening or possibility of refusing their new and worsened conditions of life. If a policy is imposed, those affected *cannot* have been given a chance to refuse it: had the chance been there, they would either have assented (and so the policy would not have been *imposed*) or refused (and so proceeding with the policy would have been evidently coercive).

Beneficence to the Vulnerable in Kantian Thinking

In Kantian moral reasoning, the basis for beneficent action is that we cannot, without it, treat others of limited rationality and autonomy as ends in themselves. This is not to say that Kantian beneficence won't make others happier, for it will do so whenever they would be happier if (more) capable of autonomous action, but that happiness secured by purely paternalistic means, or at the cost (for example) of manipulating others' desires, will not count as beneficent in the Kantian picture. Clearly the vulnerable position of those who lack the very means of life, and their severely curtailed possibilities for autonomous action, offer many different ways in which it might be possible for others to act beneficently. Where the means of life are meager, almost any material or organizational advance may help extend possibilities for autonomy. Individual or institutional action that aims to advance economic or social development can proceed on many routes. The provision of clean water, of improved agricultural techniques, of better grain storage systems, or of adequate means of local transport may all help transform material prospects. Equally, help in the development of new forms of social organization—whether peasant self-help groups, urban cooperatives, medical and contraceptive services, or improvements in education or in the position of women—may help to extend possibilities for autonomous action. Kantian thinking does not provide a means by which all possible projects of this sort could be listed and ranked. But where some activity helps secure possibilities for autonomous action for more people, or is likely to achieve a permanent improvement in the position of the most vulnerable, or is one that can be done with more reliable success, this provides reason for furthering that project rather than alternatives.

Closing the Gender Gap in Development

Jodi L. Jacobson

Study Questions

1. Why do international agencies seem oblivious to the dilemma of subsistence farmers in the third world?

2. How is gender bias a primary cause of poverty?

3. What three assumptions about development does Jacobson describe, and how do they involve beliefs about gender? Are these assumptions true or false? Explain.

4. How do women and men function in providing subsistence and welfare?

5. How does not giving full value to women's work cripple development goals?

6. How do the economic status and circumstances of women affect population rise or decline? What is meant by the "population trap"?

7. How does population growth affect the environment?

8. How would sustainable development gain by considering women's roles in these economies?

9. What kinds of development programs are suggested?

The women of Sikandernagar, a village in the Indian state of Andhra Pradesh, work three shifts per day. Waking at 4:00 a.m., they light fires, milk buffaloes, sweep floors, fetch water, and feed their families. From 8:00 a.m. until 5:00 p.m., they weed crops for a meager wage. In the early evening they forage for branches, twigs, and leaves to fuel their cooking fires, for wild vegetables to nourish their children, and for grass to feed the buffaloes. Finally, they return home to cook dinner and do evening chores. These women spend twice as many hours per week working to support their families as do the men in their village. But they do not own the land on which they labor, and every year, for all their effort, they find themselves poorer and less able to provide what their families need to survive.[1]

As the twentieth century draws to a close, some 3 billion people—more than half the earth's population—live in the subsistence economies of the Third World. The majority of them find themselves trapped in the same downward spiral as the women of Sikandernagar.[2]

In the not-so-distant past, subsistence farmers and forest dwellers were models of ecologically sustainable living, balancing available resources against their numbers. Today, however, the access of subsistence producers to the resources on which they depend for survival is eroding rapidly. As their circumstances grow more and more tenuous, pressures on the forest and croplands that remain within their grasp grow increasingly acute. Yet in an era when sustainable development has become a global rallying cry, most governments and international development agencies seem oblivious to this dilemma.

The reason is brutally simple: women perform the lion's share of work in subsistence economies, toiling

---

Jodi L. Jacobson, "Closing the Gender Gap in Development" is reprinted from *State of the World 1993: A Worldwatch Institute Report on Progress Toward a Sustainable Society*, edited by Lester R. Brown et al. with the permission of W. W. Norton & Company, Inc. Copyright © 1993 by Worldwatch Institute.

longer hours and contributing more to family income than men do. Yet in a world where economic value is computed in monetary terms alone, women's work is not counted as economically productive when no money changes hands.

Women are viewed as "unproductive" by government statisticians, economists, development experts, and even their husbands. A huge proportion of the world's real productivity therefore remains undervalued, and women's essential contributions to the welfare of families and nations remain unrecognized. So while the growing scarcity of resources within subsistence economies increases the burden on women and erodes their productivity, little is being done to reverse the cycle.

Ironically, by failing to address the pervasive gender bias that discounts the contributions of women, development policies and programs intended to alleviate impoverishment—and the environmental degradation that usually follows—actually are making the problem worse.

Gender bias is a worldwide phenomenon, afflicting every social institution from individual families to international development organizations. But it is especially pernicious in the Third World, where most of women's activity takes place in the nonwage economy for the purpose of household consumption. In Sikandernagar, for example, women earn less than half the amount men do for the same work. Because their cash income is not enough to buy adequate supplies of food and other necessities (which they are responsible for obtaining one way or another), they work additional hours to produce these goods from the surrounding countryside.[3]

In most societies, gender bias compounds—or is compounded by—discrimination based on class, caste, or race. It is especially pervasive in the poorest areas of Africa, Asia, and Latin America, where it ranges from the exclusion of women from development programs to wage discrimination and systemic violence against females. In its most generic form, this prejudice boils down to grossly unequal allocation of resources—whether of food, credit, education, jobs, information, or training.

Gender bias is thus a primary cause of poverty, because in its various forms it prevents hundreds of millions of women from obtaining the education, training, health services, child care, and legal status needed to escape from poverty. It prevents women from transforming their increasingly unstable subsis-

tence economy into one not forced to cannibalize its own declining assets.

And it is also the single most important cause of rapid population growth. Where women have little access to productive resources and little control over family income, they depend on children for social status and economic security. The greater competition for fewer resources among growing numbers of poor people accelerates environmental degradation. Increased pressure on women's time and labor in turn raises the value of children—as a ready labor force and hedge against an uncertain future. The ensuing high rates of population growth become part of a vicious cycle of more people, fewer resources, and increasing poverty. A necessary step in reducing births voluntarily, then, is to increase women's productivity and their control over resources.

The Dimensions of Gender Bias

Implicit in the theory and practice of conventional economic development are three assumptions that are influenced by sex differences—and that reinforce the biases. One assumption is that within a society, both men and women will benefit equally from economic growth. The second is that raising men's income will improve the welfare of the whole family. The third is that within households, the burdens and benefits of poverty and wealth will be distributed equally regardless of sex. Unfortunately, none of these assumptions holds true.

The first assumption—that economic growth is gender-blind—is rarely challenged. But as economies develop, existing gender gaps in the distribution of wealth and in access to resources usually persist, and in many cases grow worse. From the fifties through the early eighties, for example, worldwide standards of living as measured by widely used basic indicators—including life expectancy, per capita income, and primary school enrollment—rose dramatically. Yet women never achieved parity with men, even in industrial countries.

According to the Human Development Index prepared by the United Nations Development Programme, which gauges the access people have to the resources needed to attain a decent standard of living, women lagged behind men in every country for which data were available. The differences were least pronounced in Sweden, Finland, and France, where measures of women's level of access as a share of men's passed 90 percent. They were most pronounced in Swaziland, South Korea, and Kenya, where women had less than 70 percent the access that men did.[4]

Not only do women not automatically benefit from economic growth; they may even fall further behind. Unless specific steps are taken to redress inequity, gender gaps often increase over time—especially where access to resources is already highly skewed. This has happened, for example, with literacy. In 1985, 60 percent of the adult population worldwide was able to read, compared with about 46 percent in 1970—clearly a significant improvement. Literacy rose faster among men than among women, however, so the existing gender gap actually widened. Between 1970 and 1985, the number of women unable to read rose by 54 million (to 597 million), while that of men increased by only 4 million (to 352 million). These numbers reflect females' much lower access to education in developing countries.[5]

The second assumption—that social strategies to raise men's income by increasing their access to productive resources will lead directly to improvements in total family welfare—is also not supported by the evidence. It may seem reasonable to assume that each dollar of income earned by a poor man in Bangladesh, Bolivia, or Botswana would go toward bettering the lot of his wife and children. Indeed, development programs have been built on the premise that what is good for men is good for the family. But in many areas this is patently not the case, because it is women who effectively meet the largest share of the family's basic needs, and because men often use their income to purchase alcohol, tobacco, or other consumer products.

Generally speaking, men in subsistence economies have fewer responsibilities than women to produce food and other goods solely for household consumption. While a woman labors to produce food for her children and family, her husband may focus his energies on developing a business or pursuing interests that do not include his wife and children.

In much of sub-Saharan Africa, for instance, both men and women plant crops, but they do so with different goals. Husbands and wives maintain separate managerial and financial control over the production, storage, and sale of their crops. Men grow cash crops and keep the income from them—even though their wives still do the weeding and hoeing. Women, by contrast, use their land primarily for subsistence crops to feed their families. They are also expected to provide shelter, clothing, school fees, and medical care for themselves and their children, and so must earn income to cover what they cannot produce or collect from the village commons land. Given adequate acreage, high yields, or both, women do plant and market surplus crops to earn cash. When land is scarce or the soil poor, they sell their labor or put more time into other income-producing activities.[6]

Because responsibilities for securing the goods needed for household consumption often fall to the woman, even an increase in the income of a male within a household may not mean an increase in total consumption by family members. As subsistence economies become increasingly commercialized, for example, men whose families are below the poverty line often spend any additional cash income to raise the productivity of their own crops, and sometimes to increase their personal consumption. In Africa, according to one World Bank report, "it is not uncommon for children's nutrition to deteriorate while wrist watches, radios, and bicycles are acquired by the adult male household members." The connection between malnutrition and the diversion of income by males to personal consumption has also been found in Belize, Guatemala, Mexico, and throughout the Indian subcontinent.[7]

In fact, contrary to conventional assumptions, women are the main breadwinners in a large share of families throughout the Third World. They contribute proportionately more of their cash income to family welfare than men do, holding back less for personal consumption. A study in Mexico found that wives accounted for 40 percent or more of the total household income, although their wage rates were far lower than their husbands'. The women contributed 100 percent of their earnings to the family budget, while husbands contributed at most 75 percent of theirs. Similar discrepancies in the amount of money contributed have been found to be virtually universal throughout the developing world.[8]

Moreover, studies in every region of the Third World confirm that it is the mother's rather than the father's income or food production—and the degree of control she maintains over that income—that determines the relative nutrition of children. In Guatemala, for example, the children of women earning independent incomes had better diets than those of women who were not earning their own money or who had little control over how their husbands' earnings were spent. Women who retain control over income and expenditures spend more not only on food but also on health care, school expenses, and clothing for their children. Similar patterns have been found in studies from the Dominican Republic, Ghana, India, Kenya, Peru, and the Philippines.[9]

Differences in the responsibilities and workloads of men and women within subsistence economies can also affect family welfare. A project in the Indian state of West Bengal, for example, gave villagers conditional access to trees on private land. The "lops and tops" of trees were to be reserved for women's needs, while men were to harvest the timber for cash on a sustainable basis. In response to offers from a contractor, however, the men sold the trees for a lump sum. Women obtained little fuel.[10]

The third assumption—that within poor households resources will be distributed equally regardless of sex—may seem so obvious as to be beyond question. But even when a man's income is used to improve his family's, it may improve the welfare of males at the expense of females. In many cultures, a family's resources are distributed according to the status of household members, rather than according to their need. Men and boys fare far better than women and girls. In India, for instance, studies show that in many states sons consistently receive more and better food and health care than their sisters. Consequently, far more girls than boys die in the critical period between infancy and age five. And with the exception of girls aged 10 to 14, Indian females die from preventable causes at far higher rates than males do through age 35.[11]

Basic indicators of caloric intake and life expectancy measured by the Indian government's 1991 census reveal a growing gender gap in several states since 1980. In fact, contrary to sex ratios found in most countries, the ratio of women to men in India has actually been declining since the early part of the century. There are now only 929 women for every 1,000 men, compared with 972 in 1901. Dr. Veena Mazumdar, director of the Delhi-based Centre for Women's Development Studies, notes that "the declining sex ratio is the final indicator that registers [that] women are losing out on all fronts—on the job market, in health and nutrition and economic prosperity."[12]

Evidence of similar patterns of discrimination in the allocation of household resources has been found in Bangladesh, Nepal, Pakistan, throughout the Middle East and North Africa, and in parts of sub-Saharan Africa. Harvard economist and philosopher Amartya Sen calculates that 100 million women in the developing world are "missing," having died prematurely from the consequences of such gender bias.[13]

Because of these patterns, argues Bina Agarwal, professor of agricultural economics at the Institute of Economic Growth in Delhi, "existing poverty estimates need revision." The current practice is to first identify poor households by specified criteria and then calculate the total numbers, the assumption being that all members are equally poor. However, Agarwal argues, this reveals little about the relative poverty of men and women. The differences in the distribution of resources within households mean there are poor women in households with cash incomes or consumption levels above the poverty line. Conversely, there are nonpoor men in households below the poverty line.[14]

Globally, much of this discrimination against females in families and societies stems from another form of gender gap—the huge disparity between the real economic and social benefits of women's work and the social perception of women as unproductive.

In every society, women provide critical economic support to their families, alone or in conjunction with spouses and partners, by earning income—in cash or in kind—in agriculture, in formal and informal labor markets, and in emerging international industries, such as the manufacture of semiconductors. U.N. data indicate that, on average, women work longer hours than men in every country except Australia, Canada, and the United States. Hours worked earning wages or producing subsistence goods are rarely offset by a reduction of duties at home. Time allocation studies confirm that women throughout the world maintain almost exclusive responsibility for child care and housework. Moreover, disparities in total hours worked are greatest among the poor: in developing countries, women work an average of 12–18 hours a day—producing food, managing and harvesting resources, and working at a variety of paid and unpaid activities—compared with 8–12 hours on average for men.[15]

In subsistence economies, measuring work in terms of the value of goods produced and time spent shows that women usually contribute as much as or more than men to family welfare. The number of female-headed households is growing. But "even where there is a male earner," notes World Bank consultant Lynn Bennett, "women's earnings form a major part of the income of poor households."[16]

The low valuation of women's work begins with the fact that in developing countries, most of women's activity takes place in the nonwage economy for the purpose of household consumption—producing food crops, collecting firewood, gathering fodder, and so on. "Income generation" of this type is critically important; indeed, the poorer the family, the more vital is the contribution of women and girls to the essential goods that families are unable to buy with cash. But in the increasingly market-oriented economies of the Third World, work that does not produce cash directly is heavily discounted.[17]

Low valuation is further reinforced by women's institutionally enforced lack of control over physical resources. In most subsistence economies, females have few legal rights regarding land tenure, marital relations, income, or social security. In a world where control over land confers power, the value of wives' and mothers' contributions in subsistence economies also is discounted because these are directed mainly at day-to-day sustenance and do not yield such visible assets.

The "invisible" nature of women's contributions feeds into the social perception that they are "dependents" rather than "producers." Indeed, the tendency at every level of society seems to be to play down the importance of female contributions to family income, which anthropologist Joke Schrijvers, cofounder of the Research and Documentation Centre on Women and Autonomy in the Netherlands, attributes to the "ideology of the male breadwinner."[18]

The ideology appears to be universal. And rather than combatting the idea that women's work has low economic value, governments and international development agencies have tacitly condoned it. Thus despite overwhelming evidence to the contrary, these institutions persist in counting women as part of the dependent or "nonproductive" portion of the population.

This bias is then perpetuated by government recordkeeping practices: official definitions of what constitutes "work" often fail to capture a large share of women's labor. In India, conventional measures based on wage labor showed that only 34 percent of Indian females are in the labor force, as opposed to 63 percent of males. But a survey of work patterns by occupational categories including household production and domestic work revealed that 75 percent

of females over age five are working, compared with 64 percent of males. In a study of Nepalese villages, estimates of household income based only on wages earned put the value of female contributions at 20 percent. Taking account of subsistence production, however, brought this contribution to 53 percent. And in a study of women in the Philippines, "full income" contributions were found to be twice as high as marketed income.[19]

Given such distorted pictures of their national economies, it is not surprising that policymakers in virtually every country invest far less in female workers than in males. Moreover, international development assistance agencies, staffed mostly by men with a decidedly western view of the world, have based their decisions on the erroneous premise that what is good for men is good for the family. And because most strategists neither integrate women into their schemes nor create projects that truly address women's economic needs, development efforts aimed at raising productivity and income often bypass women altogether.

Ignoring the full value of women's economic contributions cripples efforts to achieve broad development goals. Lack of investment results in lower female productivity. Coupled with persistent occupational and wage discrimination, this prevents women from achieving parity with men in terms of jobs and income, and leads to further devaluation of their work. The omnipresence of this bias is a sign that virtually every country is operating far below its real economic potential.

Current measures of economic development tell little about how the benefits of that development will be distributed. Higher aggregate levels of agricultural production, for example, do not necessarily imply lower levels of malnutrition. A rising gross national product does not always produce a decline in the incidence of poverty or an improvement in equity. And a real increase in the health budget of a country does not automatically lead to better access to primary health care among those most in need of it. . . .

Female Poverty and the Population Trap

From food production to control over income, indications are that the position of women within subsistence economies is growing increasingly insecure. As women's access to resources continues to dwindle in subsistence economies, their responsibilities—and the demands on their time and physical energy—increase. They are less likely to see the utility of having fewer children, even though population densities in the little land left for subsistence families are rapidly increasing.

These trends extend from rural areas into urban ones. Environmental degradation and impoverishment have driven millions of people into the slums and shantytowns of Third World cities. In these urban subsistence economies, women maintain their heavy burden of labor and responsibility for the production of subsistence goods. And urban women are also discriminated against in the access to resources they require to support their families. "When urban authorities refuse to provide water supply, sanitation, and refuse collection to low-income urban areas," writes Diana Lee-Smith and Catalina Hinchey Trujillo of the Women's Shelter Network, "it is the women who have to make up for the lack of such services . . . who have to work out ways of finding and transporting water and fuel and keeping their homes reasonably clean, [all] with inadequate support from urban laws and institutions which usually completely fail to comprehend their situation.[20]

The growing time constraints imposed on women by the longer hours they must work to make ends meet simultaneously lower women's status and keep birth rates high. When they can no longer increase their own labor burdens, women lean more heavily on the contributions of their children—especially girls. In fact, the increasing tendency in many areas of keeping girls out of school to help with their mothers' work virtually ensures that another generation of females will grow up with poorer prospects than their brothers. In Africa, for example, "more and more girls are dropping out of both primary and secondary school or just missing school altogether due to increasing poverty," states Phoebe Asiyo of the United Nations Fund for Women.[21]

Rapid population growth within subsistence economies, in turn, compounds the environmental degradation—the unsustainable escalation of soil erosion, depletion, and deforestation—first put in motion by the increasing separation of poor farmers from the assets that once sustained them. The health of women and girls, most affected by environmental degradation because of the roles they play, declines further. The cycle accelerates.

This is the population trap: many of the policies and programs carried out in the name of development actually increase women's dependence on children as a source of status and security. Moreover, environmental degradation triggered by misguided government policies is itself causing rapid population growth, in part as a result of women's economically rational response to increasing demands on their time caused by resource scarcity. Unless governments move quickly to change the conditions confronting women in subsistence economies, rapid population growth will continue unabated.

The objective of reducing population growth is critical to reversing the deterioration of both human and environmental health. But the myopic divorcing of demographic goals from other development efforts has serious human rights implications for the hundreds of millions of women who lack access to adequate nutrition, education, legal rights, income-earning opportunities, and the promise of increasing personal autonomy.

Toward a New Framework for Development

In the post-Earth Summit era, sustainable development has become a slogan of governments everywhere. But given the abysmal record of conventional development strategies in the realms of equity, poverty, and the environment, it is imperative to ask, Development *for whom?* With input *from whom?*

Failing to ask these questions is a failure in the fundamental purpose of development itself. If women in subsistence economies are the major suppliers of food, fuel, and water for their families, and yet their access to productive resources is declining, then more people will suffer from hunger, malnutrition, illness, and loss of productivity. If women have learned ecologically sustainable methods of agriculture and acquired extensive knowledge about genetic diversity—as millions have—yet are denied partnership in development, then this wisdom will be lost.

Without addressing issues of equity and justice, then, development goals that are ostensibly universal—such as the alleviation of poverty, the protection of ecosystems, and the creation of a balance between human activities and environmental resources—simply cannot be achieved.

In short, development strategies that limit the ability of women to achieve their real human potential are also strategies that limit the potential of communities and nations. Only when such strategies recognize and are geared toward reducing gender bias and its consequences can we begin to solve many of those economic and environmental problems that otherwise promise to spin out of control.

Improving the status of women, and thereby the prospects for humanity, will require a complete reorientation of development efforts away from the current overemphasis on limiting women's reproduction. Instead, the focus needs to be on establishing an environment in which women and men together can prosper. This means creating mainstream development programs that seek to expand women's control over income and household resources, improve their productivity, establish their legal and social rights, and increase the social and economic choices they are able to make.

Notes*

1. Information on women in Sikandernagar from Maria Mies, *Indian Women in Subsistence and Agricultural Labour,* Women, Work and Development Paper 12 (Geneva: International Labour Organization (ILO), 1986).

2. Some 1.2 billion people live in "absolute poverty," and more than 2 billion others—including the land-poor, sharecroppers, wage laborers, village artisans, and street hawkers—have cash incomes insufficient to meet more than their most immediate needs. Urban or rural, all are subsistence producers because they must rely wholly or in part on their own labor to produce, gather, or scavenge goods they cannot purchase. Number of poor worldwide from Alan B. Durning, *Poverty and the Environment: Reversing the Downward Spiral,* Worldwatch Paper 92 (Washington, DC: Worldwatch Institute, November 1989), and from U.N. Development Programme (UNDP), *Human Development Report* (1991).

3. Mies, *Indian Women.*

4. UNDP, *Human Development Report 1991.*

5. United Nations Department of International Economic and Social Affairs (UNDIESA), *The World's Women: Trends and Statistics 1970–1990* (New York: United Nations, 1991).

6. See, for example, Kevin Cleaver and Gotz Schreiber, *The Population, Agriculture, and Environment Nexus in Sub-Saharan Africa* (Washington, DC: World Bank, 1992), Jean Davison (Ed.), *Agriculture, Women, and Land: The African Experience* (Boulder, CO: Westview, 1988), and ILO, *Rural Development and Women in Africa* (Geneva: 1984).

7. Cleaver and Schreiber, *The Population, Agriculture, and Environment Nexus in Sub-Saharan Africa;* Marilyn Carr, "Technologies for Rural Women: Impact and Dissemination," in Iftikhar Ahmed (Ed.), *Technology and Rural Women: Conceptual and Empirical Issues* (London: George Allen & Unwin, 1985); Rae Lesser Blumberg, "Gender Matters: Involving Women in Development in Latin America and the Caribbean," prepared for the Agency for International Development Bureau for Latin America and the Caribbean, Washington, DC, November 1990; George Acsadi and Gwendolyn Johnson-Acsadi, "Safe Motherhood in South Asia: Sociocultural and Demographic Aspects of Maternal Health," background paper prepared for the Safe Motherhood Conference, Pakistan, 1987.

8. Blumberg, "Gender Matters."

9. Ibid.; Bina Agarwal et al., *Engendering Adjustment for the 1990s: Report of a Commonwealth Expert Group on Women and Structural Adjustment* (London: Commonwealth Secretariat, 1990); Acsadi and Johnson-Acsadi, "Safe Motherhood in South Asia."

10. Augusta Molnar and Gotz Schreiber, "Women and Forestry: Operational Issues," *Women in Development Working Papers,* World Bank, May 1989.

11. Meera Chatterjee, *Indian Women: Their Health and Productivity* (Washington, DC: World Bank, 1991); Arun Ghosh, "Eighth Plan: Challenges and Opportunities—XII, Health, Maternity and Child Care: Key to Restraining Population Growth," *Economic and Political Weekly,* April 20, 1991.

12. Chatterjee, *Indian Women: Their Health and Productivity;* Government of India, Census Commissioner, Registrar General, Census of India, *Provisional Population Totals,* Paper One of 1991 (New Delhi: 1991); Mazumdar quoted in Aisha Ram, "Women's Health: The Cost of Development in India," status report from Rajasthan to Panos Institute, Washington, DC, 1991.

13. Acsadi and Johnson-Acsadi, "Safe Motherhood in South Asia"; Jodi L. Jacobson, *Challenge of Survival: Safe Motherhood in the SADCC Region* (New York: Family Care International, 1991); Amartya Sen, "More Than 100 Million Women Are Missing," *New York Review of Books,* Dec. 20, 1990.

14. Bina Agarwal, "Neither Sustenance Nor Sustainability: Agricultural Strategies, Ecological Degradation and Indian Women in Poverty," in Bina Agarwal (Ed.), *Structures of Patriarchy: State, Community, and Household in Modernising Asia* (London: Zed Books, 1988)

15. UNDIESA, *The World's Women;* Agarwal et al., *Engendering Adjustment for the 1990s.*

16. Lynn Bennett, "Gender and Poverty in India: Issues and Opportunities Concerning Women in the Indian Economy," World Bank internal document, 1989.

*Some notes have been deleted and the remaining ones renumbered.—ED.

17. Ibid.; Agarwal et al., *Engendering Adjustment for the 1990s*; Acsadi and Johnson-Acsadi, "Safe Motherhood in South Asia."

18. Joke Schrijvers, "Blueprint for Undernourishment: The Mahaweli River Development Scheme in Sri Lanka," in Agarwal, *Structures of Patriarchy*.

19. Bennett, "Gender and Poverty in India"; Chatterjee, *Indian Women: Their Health and Productivity*; Nepal and Philippines from UNDIESA, *The World's Women*.

20. Diana Lee-Smith and Catalina Hinchey Trujillo, "The Struggle to Legitimize Subsistence Women and Sustainable Development," *Environment and Urbanization*, April 1992.

21. Phoebe Asiyo, "What We Want: Voices from the South," presented at Women's Health: *The Action Agenda for the Nineties*, 18th Annual National Council on International Health Conference, Arlington, VA, June 23–26, 1991.

Strategic, Legal, and Moral Dimensions of Humanitarian Intervention

Barbara Harff

Study Questions

1. What does Harff suggest as a sensible way to determine whether to intervene militarily in cases like Bosnia?

2. According to Harff, what are the risks of a failure to intervene in some situations?

3. What international standards of human rights do the statements of the Genocide Convention, the U.N. Universal Declaration of Human Rights, and the U.N. Charter provide?

4. According to Harff, what has been the nature, incidence, and results of ethnic conflict worldwide since 1945?

5. How does the author describe the cases of Bosnia, Somalia, Liberia, and the Kurds?

6. What four kinds of responses to threats to international security are given in the *Agenda for Peace*?

7. Describe some of the actions that the international community has at its disposal for responding to such threats.

8. Does Harff believe that individual states should even act unilaterally? Under what conditions?

9. What provides the justification for intervention in international law and the principles on which the United Nations was founded?

Many legal scholars favor intervention against states that perpetrate massive human rights violations; their arguments are based upon moral principles and international standards of justice. But at present, policymakers and government leaders often allow their political interests to outweigh these other considerations. In affirming respect for the sovereignty of states, they fail to acknowledge that sovereignty is not necessarily absolute, and they ignore other provisions of international law that in some situations should be given priority. This short-sighted position has prevented the United States and Western Europe from mounting an effective cooperative effort to deal with the Bosnian conflict.

A number of newspaper columnists have contributed to the paralysis. Aware that the crisis in Bosnia has reached a point where a military commitment would be required to end the campaign of ethnic cleansing, they evoke the image of young Americans dying for the sake of nebulous policy objectives. But the sensible way to meet this concern is not to rule

Barbara Harff, "Bosnia and Somalia: Strategic, Legal, and Moral Dimensions of Humanitarian Intervention," *Report from the Institute for Philosophy and Public Policy*, vol. 12, no. 3/4 (Summer/Fall 1992), pp. 1–7. Reprinted with permission.

out intervention, but rather to insist that it combine precise policy goals, clear strategic objectives, and tactics that are suited to the desired end-state of the military involvement. It is illogical to conclude on the basis of an extreme case of requiring an extensive military commitment that all forms of intervention are misguided in principle or are someone else's responsibility. If a coherent strategy for intervention had been in place from the beginning, the Bosnian crisis might never have assumed the proportions of genocide.

A multitude of ethnic conflicts may develop in the former Soviet Union and elsewhere in the next decade. Responses to these conflicts will, in turn, set the stage for the twenty-first century. In the early phases of ethnic conflict, will global leaders stand idly by while would-be dictators fight to expand their power base by killing their citizens, crossing internationally recognized boundaries, inflaming irredentist passions, and implementing ideologies of ethnic superiority?

It may prove to be a costly mistake if the last superpower and its friends (and sometimes allies) become isolationist paper tigers once again. Explosions of ethnic passion rarely remain internal affairs. From a strategic perspective, it is clear that a future diffusion of ethnic passion, hatred, and rebellion will eventually call for much greater military measures than a maximum collective show of force with a minimum use of weapons in Bosnia. Failure to exert our capabilities may mean that we will lose our chance to build a world free from the forces that create global instability. From a cost-benefit perspective—as abhorrent as that may seem, when we consider the loss of lives in Bosnia and similar theaters—early warning measures, a clear policy position, and a strategy with civil and military components are the best guarantees to forestall adventurers of the caliber of Saddam Hussein and Radovan Karadzic. From an American perspective, to be able to intervene with the knowledge that the U.S. is proceeding on a clearly plotted course that is strategically sound, morally correct, legally justified and internationally supported makes the task easier for the young men and women who have joined the military in order to fight for their country's just cause. Indeed, the more clearly designed the policy and tactical objectives are, the greater the likelihood that few if any American lives will be lost—provided action is taken swiftly in response to early signs of impending disaster.

The Legal Foundations of Humanitarian Intervention

Hersch Lauterpacht, one of the great scholars of international law, once asked whether law can promote the "realization of socially obtainable justice." My own answer is a qualified yes. We can achieve minimum standards of justice by affirming such essential goods as the right to live, and by enforcing sanctions against those who deprive people of those essential goods. Mass murder is unacceptable in all national legal systems and, in principle, states should apply their domestic laws to their own and others' external behavior. In other words, foreign policy should reflect the standards of national morality defined by domestic law.

In accordance with this principle, the Genocide Convention forbids governments to take steps to destroy any distinct national, ethnic, or religious group. Article 3 of the Universal Declaration of Human Rights asserts that "everyone has the right to life, liberty, and security of person." The large number of signatories to the human rights and genocide conventions attests to the fact that international morality in regard to the protection of fundamental human rights coincides with national moralities. These treaties constitute, as Lauterpacht writes, "a recognition of fundamental rights superior to the law of the sovereign State."

Thus, when basic rights are violated to the degree we see at present in Somalia and Bosnia, international responses should follow, under the leadership of a United Nations that asserts and, ideally, enforces codified standards of morality. The most common argument against such action is based on Article 2, paragraph 7 of the U.N. Charter, which prohibits intervention in matters that are within the domestic jurisdiction of any state. In contrast, Article 34 identifies a competing principle by empowering the Security Council to investigate disputes that cause international friction, while Article 51 and Chapter VIII of the Charter offer regional organizations the legal justification for collective intervention.

The Bosnian situation is illustrative. If one accepts Bosnia's claim to being an independent state (as the U.N. did when it granted Bosnia a seat in the General Assembly), then under Article 51, the Bosnians have the right of self-defense, including the right to ask for outside help and to invite intervention by individual states, regional organizations, or the U.N. If one denies that Bosnia is an independent state (as does what remains of the federal Yugoslav government), then the situation is one of civil war between a state and a secessionist region. In this circumstance, the Security Council is empowered to execute collective measures, on the grounds that the situation is causing widespread abuse of human rights and international friction. Accordingly, in response to Serbian atrocities in Bosnia and Croatia, the first act of the General Assembly in the fall 1992 session was to deny membership to Serbia/Montenegro as the successor state to Yugoslavia.

Once it is established that international standards of human rights are being violated, the right to impose such standards should prevail over assertions of national sovereignty. But the path that leads from recognizing that a crime against humanity is being committed to the prescription of appropriate responses and sanctions is fraught with political difficulties. In principle, the U.N., as a collective body representing the great majority of states, is the entity that should delegate authority for any kind of intervention to willing and capable member states. Ideally, all full members would bear both the responsibility and the costs of the actions undertaken, even if the burden of action fell to the United States as perhaps the only country presently able to take a strong stand on such matters. Specific actions to be taken would be decided by the Security Council with the assistance of the Military Staff Committee (see Article 46).

The targets of international sanctions can be expected to complain that they are being victimized by a new brand of imperialism under the guise of the new world order. Given the archaic structure of the Security Council, in which the former imperial powers play a larger role than other states, such claims may have some *prima facie* plausibility. But such a claim by weaker states at no time and in no place mitigates the crimes of mass political murder, ethnic cleansing, or complicity in mass starvation of ethnic rivals.

What has been lacking, time and time again, on the part of states with the capacity to act is the political will to take a strong stand and accept the consequences of boldness. Standards of international morality and order are not achieved through timidity; precedent is never set through inaction. Violent ethnic conflicts in the Third World have steadily increased in frequency and intensity since the 1960s, as Ted Robert Gurr has demonstrated in a study tracking some 200 minorities during the entire postwar period. The disintegration of the Soviet, Yugoslav, and Ethiopian states has released the evil genies of nationalist xenophobia and ethnic hatred in vast new areas. Genocides—directed against people on the basis of their ethnic, racial, or social identity—and politicides—directed against people on the basis of their political beliefs—often follow war and revolution in poor countries. In my own work, I have identified more than forty such episodes since 1945 and have shown that they caused greater loss of life than all the wars fought *between* states during that period. For this reason, it is essential to demonstrate that building states on mass graves violates the moral standards of global society, and must lead with some certainty to sanctions proportional to the crimes.

In the absence of a formal international authority to monitor and police the human rights performances of states, communal and nationalist contenders seeking territory or autonomy often press their claims by force. Intimidation of opposing forces within states and assaults on less powerful neighbors are becoming more common, most acutely so in Eastern Europe. Yugoslavia in particular has regressed to a nineteenth-century mentality. Myths and memories of old injustices are invoked to mobilize young Serbs and Croats for war against one another, and together against Muslims. The territorial ambitions of the contenders take no account of Yugoslavia's carefully balanced heterogeneity; a resurgent nationalism calls instead for the creation of fictive homelands, purified of "alien peoples." The claims being made by the most militant of Serbs are reminiscent of Nazi ideology, and one can well imagine that in the future, nationalist Serbs, if unchecked, will assert their racial and cultural superiority over competing ethnic groups in a greater Serbia extending from Macedonia to Austria.

Civil Wars, Rebellion, Repression

Bosnia, Somalia, and Iraqi Kurdistan exemplify three distinct types of crimes against humanity in which the international community has a legal and moral imperative to intervene. Bosnia is a case that combines elements of civil and international war. On the civil side, Bosnia-Hercegovina's declaration of independence provoked uprisings by Bosnian Serbs concerned with their status in the new state. On the international side, they were armed by and acted as agents of "greater Serbian" nationalists. Recent events offer clear evidence of direct Serbian military support through air strikes and artillery barrages. The states of the European Community face a double responsibility, first because they helped precipitate the civil war by granting what many observers thought was premature recognition of Bosnian independence, and second because they have ample capacity to act. Yet EC leaders have largely behaved like bystanders, offering verbal condemnation and sending inadequate relief. It is clear that most European leaders find it politically more acceptable to condemn the participants and to talk about eventual war-crimes trials than to risk military casualties by trying to stop the war while it is still in progress.

Meanwhile, new civil wars and acts of aggression tragically similar to events in Bosnia are already under way or imminent in Macedonia, Moldova, the Caucasus, and some of the new republics of Central Asia. The international community has a compelling legal right and obligation to defend the civilian victims of such conflicts, not merely to provide them with minimal humanitarian assistance. The situation in Bosnia is all the more urgent because actions there will send a message to ambitious and potentially ruthless nationalists in all the states of the former Soviet bloc and elsewhere.

In Somalia, mass starvation is the result of the complete disintegration of political order. The process began in 1988 with a north-south civil war and massacres of northern civilians that attracted virtually no international attention. Since then, feuding clan leaders and warlords have made most of the country into a deadly wasteland in which humanitarian assistance, belatedly supplied, is seized at gunpoint. International pressure and diplomacy might have forestalled the crisis at an early stage. The immediate task must be to protect civilians against mass starvation, followed by restoration of critical elements of the transport infrastructure and preparation of the groundwork for an interim government. None of these tasks can be accomplished unless peacekeeping forces are authorized to use force. Somalia is a member of two regional organizations with the potential, in theory, to respond more forcefully: the Organization of African Unity and the Islamic Conference. Neither has acted decisively.

A similar situation existed in Lebanon and has now emerged in Liberia. The Liberian case is instructive: a West African peacekeeping force, operating under international auspices, temporarily stabilized the country and facilitated negotiations among the principal factions. The West African precedent for international intervention has been marred by the recent renewal of fighting in Liberia, but the peacekeeping effort undertaken so far appears preferable to the belated and inadequate international response to the Somali conflict. Other weak African states are at risk of similar crises.

Iraq exemplifies a more common kind of humanitarian crisis. Since the 1960s the Ba'athist regime in Baghdad has repeatedly used deadly force, including poison gas, against civilian Kurds suspected of rebellion. In the aftermath of the Gulf War, the Kurds revolted again and the Allies eventually responded with humanitarian aid in a Kurdish zone protected by Allied air cover. But for many Kurds, the response came too late. Allied leaders did not act until they were pressured by domestic and regional political considerations. Media coverage of atrocities mobilized public outrage in Western countries, and the Turkish government expressed its concern about the destabilizing effect of a flood of Kurdish refugees on its own Kurdish minority.

The main precedents for humanitarian intervention to end gross human rights violations like those in Iraq are unilateral ones: India in East Pakistan, now Bangladesh, in 1971; Vietnam in Cambodia, in 1978; and Tanzania in Uganda, in 1979. The intervenors' motives in these cases were politically suspect, but, on balance, unilateral action in each instance was better than inaction: it helped to end the killings and, except in Uganda, led to the establishment of regimes with greater respect for human rights. The establishment of a security zone in Iraq was more easily achieved because it was done under international auspices in a pariah state that had lost credibility and clout in the Arab world; two previous decades of Iraqi abuse of Kurdish villagers had no significant international consequences.

Many future conflicts are likely to require international responses of the kind offered in Iraq. Chronic warfare and repression persist in Sudan and Myanmar (Burma); Ethiopia is at serious risk of renewed warfare that could be forestalled by international action. More distant crises can also be anticipated in such large Third World countries as Nigeria and Pakistan, where there are deep regional cleavages.

An Agenda for Peace:
Responding to International Crises

The need for a more active role by the U.N. in such conflicts has been explicitly recognized by the new Secretary General, Boutros Boutros-Ghali. His *Agenda for Peace,* issued on June 17, 1992, focuses attention on threats to international security arising from "ethnic, religious, social, cultural or linguistic strife." The Agenda outlines four kinds of responses: preventive diplomacy, peacemaking, peacekeeping, and post-conflict peace-building. "Peace-building" refers to policies that address the root causes of conflict: "economic despair, social injustice and political oppression." The case of the Iraqi Kurds highlights the need to organize such responses to gross human rights violations at an early stage rather than wait for news of atrocities to create political pressures for action. The more quickly the U.N. acts, the less devastation communal conflicts will cause, whereas the longer that effective responses are delayed, the more difficult and costly peacekeeping and peace-building will be.

Let me conclude by examining the kinds of actions that the international community has at its disposal for responding to civil wars, repression, and anarchy that threaten the human rights and lives of large numbers of people. All have been used selectively to remedy past violations. The first are lowest in cost, and pose the least challenge to sovereignty. The last constitutes the revocation of a state's sovereignty. Military occupation and trusteeship are, or should be, the ultimate sanctions for states and local leaders that will not desist from mass killings.

1) Issue early-warning assessments of impending or escalating conflicts; send fact-finding missions and widely publicize their results. Establish a U.N.-sponsored news bureau with instant access to satellite telecommunications to assure global distribution of news and reports (a CNN for peace). These policies are particularly appropriate to civil wars and repression in their early stages. Fact-finding reports issued after six months of deadly and widely publicized conflict, as in Bosnia now, are little more than empty gestures.

2) Call on governments and their opponents to seek accommodation, provide international mediation and arbitration, offer political and material incentives to encourage contenders to reach agreements. These actions are well-suited for the early and middle stages of civil wars.

3) Condemn putative violations of international law, issue formal warnings of impending sanctions, set deadlines for corrective action by the perpetrators. Such responses may help restrain states from gross human rights abuses. They are less likely to influence contenders in civil wars, especially those (like the Bosnian Serbs) whose moral and political ties to the international community are weak. More important, these symbolic acts help set the legal and political stage for more forceful international action.

4) Withdraw diplomatic recognition, apply sanctions, embargo military goods, energy supplies, and commodities that prolong fighting. These actions can be applied to all armed contenders in civil wars, and against state perpetrators of gross human rights violations. Of these options, embargoes are the most likely to be effective but are also the most difficult to enforce consistently. Implementing them is likely to require higher-order responses.

5) Use limited shows of force such as overflights by military aircraft, the stationing of warships offshore, and the introduction of moderately armed peacekeeping forces with sufficient firepower to defend themselves if attacked. These actions convey strong messages to belligerents and position international forces to respond more forcefully if warnings are not heeded.

6) Begin selective applications of force such as interdiction of military movements, air strikes on strategic targets, and the capture and disarming of combatants (individually or in small units). These actions require the international community to "take sides," which is politically feasible when one state or party is clearly the aggressor or perpetrator, as in Bosnia, but which may be impossible in other civil war situations. Selective use of force also poses risks of escalation that may worsen and prolong conflict.

7) Use collective military intervention with the objectives of separating forces, disarming contenders, protecting neutral areas, and establishing secure procedures and zones for delivering and distributing humanitarian aid. This is the most decisive and costly form of international response, and seems to be the only one that might remedy the current situations in Bosnia and Somalia. The key is to use all means necessary to establish secure and defensible zones in which civilians can be supplied and protected. This is an interim strategy that must be complemented by diplomatic and political initiatives aimed at bringing

about a political settlement. There is no denying the high-risk nature of such undertakings, but the consequences of inaction will ultimately lead to far greater cost and injustice.

8) Establish interim, internationally sponsored trusteeships, rebuild civil administration and basic services, provide material and technical assistance, supervise free elections. This form of wholesale intervention is equivalent to Allied policies in occupied Germany after 1945 and current U.N. actions in Cambodia, and is appropriate to Somalia's situation today. It requires a costly long-term commitment. Peacekeeping units must remain in place and be authorized to use force until authority can be transferred to elected local leadership.

Collective Responsibility

The international community has a wide range of options for responding to emerging communal conflicts and humanitarian crises. The choices are not restricted to passivity on the one hand and total war on the other. There are diverse and graduated responses that can be tailored to fit specific circumstances. Many of these responses have had demonstrably constructive effects in the recent past: belligerents have been separated by peacekeeping forces, abusive governments have been discouraged or prevented from continuing gross human rights abuses, humanitarian assistance has been delivered to victims of ongoing civil wars.

The central issue for timely and effective response is political will. The responses can be carried out under the direct auspices of the U.N. itself or under the authority of regional organizations. If international organizations default on their legal obligations to respond because of political paralysis, and if regional organizations are unable to act, then a strong argument can be made that individual states have the right to act unilaterally. But unilateral military intervention should not be used unless and until all collective remedies are exhausted. The intervenor must prove necessity and proportionality: military intervention has to be shown to be imperative and should remain the last resort.

International law provides the justification for all such actions. The U.N. was not founded so that it could impede progress by doggedly clinging to standards of absolute sovereignty. Instead, it was founded to limit the arbitrary rule of "sovereigns" and to

imbue the world's citizens with a sense of collective responsibility for one another and for the survival of the species. The official *History of the United Nations War Crimes Commission* includes an appendix which is as compelling today as it was in 1948. After observing that "the idea of sovereignty paralyses the moral sense of humanity," the author points out that periods of growth in international law coincide with world upheavals. "The pressure of necessity stimulates the impact of natural law and of moral ideas and converts them into rules of law deliberately and overtly recognized by the consensus of civilized mankind." The humanitarian crises of the post-Cold War world point to the compelling necessity of translating international consensus into prompt and effective collective action.

Review Exercises

1. Discuss three elements likely to contribute to the growing gap between rich and poor nations.

2. What is meant by "sustainable development"?

3. How does self-interest play a role in the question of whether we ought to intervene to aid other nations?

4. What is the difference between charity and obligation, and how are they relevant to the problem of rich and poor nations?

5. How would considerations of compensatory justice arise in discussions of the problem of responsibility of richer to poorer nations?

6. Discuss three different positions on what constitutes distributive justice and how they would be applied to the issue of rich versus poor nations.

7. What is pacifism? Are there different versions of it? Explain.

8. Give a consequentialist argument and a nonconsequentialist argument for and against some form of pacifism.

9. List and explain the four basic principles of the *jus ad bellum* part of just war theory.

10. Explain the two basic elements of the principle of discrimination.

Discussion Cases

1. *Military Intervention.* Amy and June are arguing with each other about what to do about the situation in Mosnia. A civil war there has civilians being killed routinely. The country's beautiful cities are being shelled and destroyed. It seems clear to most outsiders which group is in the wrong. Still Amy says that this is their war and their problem and we have no right or responsibility to intervene. Anyway, she argues, it is so complicated and the animosities between these people are so deep-seated that we would only get mired down for years if we intervened. June, on the other hand, urges that the international community does have a moral responsibility to intervene when the rights of innocent people of an independent nation are violated. We cannot just do nothing, she says.

Who is right? Why?

2. *Controlling Global Environmental Threats.* Consider the threats to civilization as we know it caused by global warming and the creation of gaps in the protective ozone layer. Consider also the various nations and what they each contribute to the threats. Suppose that there are no strong international curbs. Each nation, then, must determine what its responsibility is for lessening the threats. However, if nation X does lessen its own contribution by means of controls on emissions and use of other damaging chemicals, it will be put at a disadvantage economically in comparison with similarly developed nations who do not so discipline themselves. It is the problem of the "free rider"; that is, when others do their share, I benefit most by not contributing.

Does nation X have a responsibility to do its share when other nations do not do theirs? Why or why not?

3. *Nations Rich and Poor.* Nations X and Y share a border. Nation X is among the richest nations in the world. Nation Y is relatively poor, and would probably be considered a third world nation. Many people from nation Y travel illegally to nation X to work. This builds resentment among some of the people in nation X, who pay for their health care and accept their children who are born there as citizens. There are trade barriers between the two nations. If these were lowered, nation Y would benefit, for companies from nation X would be likely to open branches there and there would be many new jobs. However, many workers from nation X fear that they would lose their jobs to the cheaper labor in nation Y.

Should the trade barriers between these two nations be lowered? Should the only question at issue for members of nation X be whether this was in their own best interest? Why or why not?

Selected Bibliography

Aiken, William, and Hugh LaFollette. *World Hunger and Morality*, 2nd ed. Upper Saddle River, NJ: Prentice-Hall, 1996.

Alonso, Harriet Hyman. *Peace as a Woman's Issue: A History of the U.S. Movement for World Peace and Women's Rights.* Syracuse, NY: Syracuse University Press, 1993.

Bauer, P. T. *Equality, the Third World and Economic Delusion.* Cambridge, MA: Harvard University Press, 1981.

Bayles, Michael D. *Morality and Population Policy.* Birmingham: University of Alabama Press, 1980.

Beitz, Charles R. *Political Theory and International Relations.* Princeton, NJ: Princeton University Press, 1979.

Borman, William. *Gandhi and Non-Violence.* Albany: State University of New York Press, 1986.

Commoner, Barry. *Making Peace With the Planet.* New York: Pantheon, 1990.

Durch, William J., and Barry M. Blechman. *Keeping the Peace: The United Nations in the Emerging World Order.* Washington, DC: Henry L. Stimson Center, 1992.

Elkington, John, and Julia Hailes. *The Green Consumer Guide.* London: Victor Golzncz, 1988.

Falk, Richard A., and Samuel S. Kim (Eds.). *The War System: An Interdisciplinary Approach.* Boulder, CO: Westview, 1980.

Foster, Mary LeCron, and Robert A. Rubinstein. *Peace and War: Cross Cultural Perspectives.* New Brunswick, NJ: Transaction Books, 1986.

Frost, Mervyn. *Ethics in International Relations.* New York: Cambridge University Press, 1996.

Guinan, Edward. *Peace and Non-Violence: Basic Writings.* New York: Paulist Press, 1975.

Hardin, Garrett. *Promethean Ethics.* Seattle: University of Washington Press, 1980.

Harris, Adrienne, and Ynestra King. *Rocking the Ship of State: Toward a Feminist Peace Politics.* Boulder, CO: Westview, 1989.

Kegley, Charles W., Jr. *The Long Postwar Peace. Contending Explanations and Projections.* New York: HarperCollins, 1991.

Kennedy, Paul. *Preparing for the 21st Century.* New York: Random House, 1993.

Lappé, Frances Moore. *World Hunger: Twelve Myths.* New York: Grove, 1986.

Lee, Steven P. *Morality, Prudence, and Nuclear Weapons.* New York: Cambridge University Press, 1996.

Luper-Foy, Steven (Ed.). *Problems of International Justice.* Boulder, CO: Westview, 1988.

McAllister, Pam (Ed.). *Reweaving the Web of Life: Feminism and Nonviolence.* Philadelphia: New Society, 1982.

Nardin, Terry (Ed.). *The Ethics of War and Peace.* Princeton, NJ: Princeton University Press, 1996.

Postel, Sandra. *Last Oasis: Facing Water Scarcity.* New York: W.W. Norton, 1992.

Ramsey, Paul. *The Just War: Force and Political Responsibility.* New York: Scribner's, 1968.

Rapoport, D., and Y. Alexander. *The Morality of Terrorism.* New York: Pergamon, 1982.

Reich, Robert B. *The Work of Nations: Preparing Ourselves for 21st Century Capitalism.* New York:. Knopf, 1991.

Shiva, Vandana. *Close to Home: Women Reconnect Ecology, Health and Development Worldwide.* Atlantic Highlands, NJ: Zed Books, 1994.

Teichman, Jenny. *Pacifism and the Just War: A Study in Applied Philosophy.* Oxford: Blackwell, 1986.

Turner, Stansfield. *Terrorism and Democracy.* Boston: Houghton-Mifflin, 1991.

Walzer, Michael. *Just and Unjust Wars.* New York: Basic Books, 1977.

Wardlaw, Grant. *Political Terrorism.* Cambridge, UK: Cambridge University Press, 1982.

Wasserstrom, Richard A. *War and Morality.* Belmont, CA: Wadsworth, 1970.

Weigel, George. *Peace and Freedom: The Christian Faith, Democracy and the Problem of War.* Washington DC: Institute of Religion and Democracy, 1983.

Westra, Laura, and Peter S. Wenz (Eds.). *Faces of Environmental Racism: Confronting Issues of Global Justice.* Lanham, MD: Rowman & Littlefield, 1995.

Wheeler, Charlene Eldridge, and Peggy Chin. *Peace and Power: A Handbook of Feminist Process.* New York: National League for Nursing, 1989.

Wilkinson, Paul. *Political Terrorism.* London: Macmillan, 1974.

Wortman, Sterling, and Ralph Cummings, Jr. *To Feed This World.* Baltimore: Johns Hopkins Press, 1978.

Appendix

How to Write an Ethics Paper

Writing a paper does not have to be difficult. It can at least be made easier by following certain procedures. Moreover, you want to do more than write a paper, you want to write a *good* paper. You can do several things to improve your paper, changing it from a thing of rags and patches to a paper of which you can be proud. If it is a good paper, then you will also have learned something from producing it. You will have improved your abilities to understand and communicate, and you will have come to appreciate the matters about which you have written.

In what follows, I will review general procedures for writing papers and then outline elements that are particularly important for writing ethics papers. By following the suggestions given here, you should be able to produce a good ethics paper.

Writing a Paper

Several elements are basic to any paper. Among these are its content, the content's structure and format, and the correct usage of grammar, spelling, and gender-neutral pronouns.

Content

The subject matter of your paper is partly determined by the course for which it is assigned. Sometimes the topic will be chosen for you. At other times you will choose it yourself from a list or some general area. You can select something in which you are particularly interested or something that you would like to explore. It may be a topic you know something about or one about which you know little but would like to know more. Sometimes you can begin with a tentative list that is the result of brainstorming. Just write down ideas as they come into your head. Sometimes you will have to do exploratory reading or library research to find and decide on your topic. In any case, choosing a topic is the first order of business in writing a paper. This is true of papers in general and ethics papers in particular. (See the section "Types of Ethics Papers" for more details on ethics topics.)

Structure

I still recall the good advice of a teacher I had in graduate school. It was two simple bits of advice, but this did not make it less valuable.

1. A paper should have a beginning, a middle, and an end.
2. First you should tell what you are going to do. Then you should do it. Finally, you should tell what you have said or done.

This may seem overly simplistic. However, you would be surprised how papers suffer from not including the first or last of these elements. Over the years of writing papers in school and beyond, I have found this simple advice extraordinarily helpful.

You can develop the structure of your paper with an outline. Here is a sample outline using the advice just described.

1. *Beginning paragraph(s).* Tell what you are going to do or say. Explain what the problem or issue is and how you plan to address it. You should make your reader want to go on. One way to do this is by showing why there is a problem. This can be done by giving contrasting views on something, for example. This is a particularly good way to begin an ethics paper.
2. *Middle paragraph(s).* Do what you said you were going to do. This is the bulk of the paper. It will have a few divisions, depending on how you handle your subject matter. (A more detailed outline of an ethics paper is given at the end of this appendix.)
3. *End paragraph(s).* Tell what you have done or said or concluded. More often than not, students end their papers without really ending them. Perhaps they are glad to have finished the main part of the paper and then forget to put an ending to it. Sometimes they really have not come to any conclusion and thus feel unable to write one. The conclusion can be tentative. It can tell what you have learned, for example, or it can tell what questions your study has raised for you.

Some word-processing programs provide an outlining function. These are helpful because they provide ways in which to set your main points first and then fill in the details. Parts can be expanded, moved, and reoriented. You can look at your paper as you progress with just the main headings or with as much detail as you like and have. In this way you can keep your focus on the logic of your presentation. If your word processor provides such a program, you should get acquainted with and use it.

Format

How you arrange your ideas is also important. Among the matters dealing with such arrangement are the following.

Size This is most often the first, and perhaps the most significant, question asked by students when a paper is assigned: "How long does it have to be?" To pose the question of length in this way may suggest that the student will do no more than the minimum required. Although an excellent paper of the minimum length may fetch a top grade, it is probably a good idea to aim at more than the minimum length. It is also not enough just to know how many pages within a range are expected. If I type with a large print (font), then I will write much less in five pages than if I use a small one. A word-count estimate is more definite. For example, one could be told that the paper should be between eight and ten pages with approximately 250 typed words per page. In some cases, professors have been very specific, for instance, expecting ten pages of Times style font, size 12, with one-inch margins all around! You should have definite information as to what is expected in this regard.

Footnotes Does the instructor expect footnotes? If so, must they be at the bottom of the page or is it permissible to place them at the end of the paper? Is there a specific format that must be followed for these? (Suggestions for this are found at the end of this appendix.) Footnotes have three basic purposes.

The first purpose of a footnote is to give the source of a direct quotation. This is to give proper credit for ideas and statements of other authors. You use quotations to back up or give examples of what you have said. You should always introduce or comment on the quotations that you use. You can introduce the quotation with something like:

```
One example of this position is that
of Jack Sprat, who writes in his
book, Why One Should Eat No Fat,
that " . . . ."[1]
```

Sometimes you will want to follow a quote with your own interpretation of it, such as: "I believe that this means . . . ." In other words, you should always put the quotation in a context.

The second purpose is to give credit for ideas that you have used but summarized or put into your own words. Sometimes students think that the instructor will be less pleased if they are using others' ideas and are tempted to treat them as their own without giving a footnote reference. Actually, these attempts are often suspicious. Thus, the student who says that "Nowhere in his writings does Descartes mention x, y, or z" is obviously suspicious; it is unlikely that the student will have read all of the works of Descartes or know this on his or her own. It is a sign of a good paper that one gives credit for such indirect references. It shows that the student has read the source that is cited and has made an attempt to put it into his or her own words. This is a plus for the paper.

The third purpose of footnotes is to give some further information or clarification. For example, you might want to say that you mean just this in the paper and not that. You might also want to say something further about a point in the paper but you don't want to markedly interrupt the current line of thought.

Title Page and Bibliography You will also want to know whether the instructor expects a title page, a bibliography, and so forth. Even if they are not expected, a title page and a folder are nice touches. A bibliography will be fitting for certain types of papers, namely, research papers, and unnecessary for others. A paper in which you are mainly arguing for a point and developing ideas of your own may not require a bibliography. If a bibliography *is* required, then just how extensive it should be will depend on the purpose or type of paper and its length.

Grammar and Spelling

In many cases your paper will be graded not only on its content but also on its mechanics, such as grammar and spelling. It is always advisable to check your paper for grammar before the final version. For example, make sure all of your sentences are complete sentences. In the initial writing or revision a sentence may lose its verb,

or the subject and predicate may no longer match, and so forth. You should review the paper to correct such mistakes.

Misspelling often is a sign of carelessness. We know how to spell the words, but we do not take care to do so. Sometimes we are uncertain and do not take the time to look up the word in a dictionary. In using a word processor, the checking of spelling is made much simpler. However, even here some spelling mistakes can be missed. For example, a spell checker cannot tell that you mean to say "to" instead of "too" or that you wanted to write "he" rather than "hell."

Gender

Today we are much more conscious of gender issues and gender bias than in times past. In writing your ethics paper, you should be careful to avoid gender or sexist bias. For example, you should avoid such terms as *mailman* and *policeman*. Acceptable substitutes are *mail carrier* and *police officer*. You can also avoid gender bias by not using traditional gender roles. You might, for instance, speak of the business executive as a "she" and the nurse as a "he."

In times past it may also have been acceptable to use the pronoun *he* throughout a paper. Today this is often less acceptable or not acceptable at all. It is not always easy to remedy the situation, however, even when one wants to be fair and nondiscriminatory. If one is referring to a particular male or female, then the proper pronoun is easy. But if the reference can be either male or female, then what should one do with the pronouns? One can say "she" or "he" or "he or she." You can also alternate pronouns throughout the paper, sometimes using "he" and sometimes "she." As I have done in this paragraph, you can also use the gender-neutral "you," "one," or "they" when possible.

Types of Ethics Papers

There are several basic types of ethics papers that can be described. You should be clear from the beginning which type you have been assigned or which you intend to pursue if you have a choice. The following sections describe three types of ethics papers. Short versions of each can be found at the end of this appendix.

A Historical Approach

If you have already covered at least part of the beginning of this text, you will have some background in the history of ethics. Writings on ethics go back to the time of Plato in the West and earlier in other cultures. Other major figures in the history of ethics are Aristotle, Augustine, Aquinas, Locke, Hume, Kant, Marx, Mill, Nietzsche, Kierkegaard, and Sartre. And innumerable philosophers in the twentieth century have written and are writing on matters of ethics. If you are interested in exploring the ethical views of one of these philosophers, you can start with a general overview of their philosophy as given in some more general historical commentary on their philosophy. The *Encyclopedia of Philosophy* might be an initial starting point for you. From this you can determine whether a philosopher's views interest you, and you can see in general what type of ethical theory he or she espouses.

The main point of a historical exposition is to summarize or analyze the views of a philosopher. It involves learning and writing down in some structured way your own understanding of those views. Your own views and interpretive comments can be added either as you go along or in some final paragraphs. You can also add your own critical or evaluative comments (positive or negative or both), possibly saving them for the end of the paper. Alternatively, you might make the paper entirely exposition, without adding your own views or critical comments.

A Problem in Ethical Theory

Another type of ethics paper is one that examines some particular issue in ethical theory. Part I of this text addresses several of these. Among these problems are:

- The Nature of Ethical Reasoning
- An Ethics of Rights Versus an Ethics of Care
- Ethical Relativism

- Moral Realism
- Moral Pluralism
- Ethical Egoism
- Why Be Moral?
- The Nature of a Right
- Charity Versus Obligation
- What Is Justice?
- What Is Virtue?

The point of a paper that treats a matter of ethical theory is to examine the problem itself. One approach is to start with a particular view on the issue, either in general or from some philosopher's point of view, and then develop it using your own ideas. Another approach is to contrast two views on the issue, and then try to show which view seems more reasonable in your opinion. For example, you could give two views on the nature of justice. One view might hold that justice requires some kind of equality. Thus, a just punishment is one that fits the crime, or a just distribution of wealth is one that is equal. Then contrast this with another view and follow that one with your own comments. For another approach, one might do a general presentation that simply tries to state the gist of the issue or problem.

A Contemporary Moral Issue

A third type of ethics paper focuses on some practical moral issue that is debated today. Part II of this text presents a selection of such issues. However, in each chapter in Part II, there are several issues from which you could choose. You might, for example, just focus on the issue of active euthanasia or physician-assisted suicide. You might write about the ethical issues that arise in our treatment of endangered species. Both issues are treated as part of chapters in this text. You might want instead to address some ethical issue that is not treated in this text. One example is gun control. However, on this topic as well as the others just mentioned, you should be certain to focus on the ethical issues involved if you are to make this an ethics paper.

Is It an Ethics Paper?

An ethical problem can be approached in different ways. Not all of them are ethical approaches or would make the basis of an ethics paper. Take the problem of violence in this country. Many people believe that this society is too violent. One approach to examining the problem is to focus on questions about the causes of violence. Is it something in our history or our psyche? Does the media cause violence or reflect it or both? To make either issue the focus of one's paper is not to do ethics or an ethics paper. It is, rather, to do a sociological analysis or to give a descriptive account of the situation.

An ethics paper requires that one take a normative approach and ask about what is better or worse, right or wrong, good or bad, just or unjust, and so on. Therefore, regarding violence, an ethics paper might begin with a clarification of what is meant by violence and a description of the different kinds of violence. Next it should become a discussion of what kinds of violence are justified or unjustified, for example. It might address the question of whether social or legal force is justified to diminish violence. This latter discussion could raise issues of the morality of legal force or the importance of individual liberty. In such discussions one would be doing ethics, because one would be addressing the ethical issues about just and unjust behavior or the moral justification of some practice or the moral value of liberty.

To be sure that your presentation is one that strictly addresses an ethical issue *as* an ethical problem, you should make sure you do not appeal primarily to authorities who are not authorities on ethical matters. For instance, if you are addressing the issue of gun control, you should not appeal to legal sources, such as the U.S. Constitution, to back up your ideas. You may appeal to ethical values that are part of the Constitution, such as the value of life or freedom of speech, but then you are using them as ethical values apart from whether or not the law values them. If you are considering whether the law ought to permit active euthanasia or physician-assisted suicide, you may consider whether having such a law would or would not promote certain ethical values. This would be an approach that could be used in an ethics paper.

Structuring or Analyzing an Ethical Argument

Most ethics papers either present or analyze ethical arguments, so you should consider some of the elements and types of ethical arguments. Among these are the following.

Reasons and Conclusions

It is important to notice or be clear about what follows from what. Sometimes key words indicate this. For example, consider this statement: "Since X has better results than its alternative Y, we ought thus to adopt X." In this statement the conclusion is that we ought to adopt some practice. The reason for this is that it has better results than its alternative. The key to knowing what follows from what in this example are the words *thus* and *since*. Being clear about this distinction enables you to make a better argument, for you can then back up your conclusion with other reasons and fill in the conclusions with more details.

Types and Sources of Evidence

As just noted, if you are to make an ethical argument, strictly speaking, you cannot appeal simply to legal sources as such in order to make your case. You also cannot appeal to scientific sources for the ethical values or principles that you want to stress. For instance, although physicians are experts in diagnoses and prognoses, this medical expertise does not make them experts in knowing what kind of life is worthwhile or valuable, or how important are rights or autonomy. So, also, natural scientists can give us valuable information about the results of certain environmental practices, but this information and knowledge does not determine just how important or valuable wilderness or endangered species are. Sometimes religious sources or authorities can be used in ethical arguments.

When this is acceptable in an ethics or moral philosophy paper, however, it is usually because the values supported by the religious sources are ethical values. For example, respect for one's parents might be promoted by a religion, but it can also be reasoned about by those who are not members of that religion.

Types of Reasons

As noted throughout this text, one primary distinction in the types of reason given in ethical arguments is the one between the appeal to consequences of some action or practice, and judging acts as right or wrong regardless of the consequences. It is important to be clear about which type of reason you or your source uses or critically evaluates.

Consequentialist Reasoning Your argument or the argument that you are summarizing or evaluating may be one that appeals to consequences. For example, you or the argument may assert that if we do such and such it will produce certain bad results. The argument can document this from some scientific source. The argument must also show why these results are bad, such as they may result in loss of life or produce great suffering.

Nonconsequentialist Reasoning The argument appeals to some basic moral value or what is alleged to be a moral right. For example, it might be based on the idea that we ought to be honest no matter the consequences. It may appeal to certain basic rights that ought to be protected whatever the consequences. To complete the argument or our evaluation of it, we should show or ask what the basis is for this type of assertion. For example, we might want to ask why autonomy is said to be a value or why liberty of action is a moral right.

Other Types of Reasons These are not the only types of reasons that can be given. One might say that something is just or unjust because all persons, when they think about it in the proper light, would agree that this is just. This is an appeal to something like common moral rationality or a common moral sense. Although this is problematic, the appeals to other types of reasons are also not without their critics.

Some people believe that persons of good character or virtue or of caring temperaments will best be able to judge what is right. To give a moral reason appealing to this sort of belief will also need explanation. But it will be a start to notice this is the type of reason that is being given.

Top-to-Bottom or Bottom-to-Top Reasoning?

Another way to construct or analyze ethical arguments is to decide whether the reasoning moves from top to bottom or bottom to top. In the first approach, we start with a concrete case or situation and our judgment about it, and then ask what moral value or principle leads us to make this judgment about it.

Top to Bottom The top-to-bottom argument starts with a particular moral principle or moral value, and then applies it to some situation. For example, one might do the following:

1. Start with the assertion that happiness is the most important value, or the principle that we always ought to do whatever promotes the greatest amount of happiness (the utilitarian moral principle).
2. Then we would ask which alternative among those that we are analyzing would promote the most happiness.

Bottom to Top The bottom-to-top argument starts with a situation in which we intuitively feel that a certain course of action is right. For example, one might take the following approach:

1. Start with a case in which we believe that if someone is in great danger of drowning and we can save them, then we ought to do so.
2. Then we proceed to ask why we believe that this is so. What value does it promote or what rights or principles? We ask why we be-

lieve that we ought to do so. We might conclude that it flows from a moral principle that says that we always ought to help others in great need when we can do so without much cost to ourselves, and that this is a matter of obligation rather than of charity.

Although one can do a paper using one or the other of these types of reasoning, actual moral reasoning often does both. Thus, your ethics paper could also incorporate both types.

Using Analogies

Many writings in ethics today use real or imaginary examples in their arguments. Among the more famous ones are the violinist analogy of Judith Thomson (described in Chapter 9 on abortion) and the tub example of James Rachels (in the Chapter 8 reading on euthanasia). There are also innumerable lifeboat examples. The method of arguing by analogy is as follows: If I start with some case and reach a certain moral conclusion about it, and if there is another case that is like it in the relevant respects, then I should conclude the same about it. Consider this example:

> If we are dividing a pie and one person is hungrier than another, then that person should get the bigger piece. This is only fair. So, also, then we should say that in society at large the fair distribution of wealth is one in which those people who have greater needs should have a greater share of the wealth.

We can critically evaluate an analogy by considering whether the analogy fits. We ask whether the two situations or scenarios are similar in the relevant respects. Thus, in the previous example we might ask whether being hungrier than another is the same as having greater needs. We might also wonder whether there is anything crucially different between what is fair among individuals in sharing some good and what is fair in society with regard to sharing a nation's wealth. We might say that nothing else matters so much in the pie-sharing situation, but that additional things do matter in the situation of sharing a nation's wealth.

Many other considerations go into making an ethical argument a strong argument. However, these few given here should help you construct and critically analyze ethical arguments, which are the heart of an ethics paper.

Sample Ethics Papers

Here are three shortened versions or outlines of the three types of ethics papers described. The first gives an outline of a historical ethics paper. The other two give examples of papers addressing issues in ethical theory and practice. Although there are a few endnotes here as examples, other examples of endnotes can be found throughout this text. You can also use the end-of-chapter bibliographies found in this text for examples of one type of bibliographical format.

Historical Approach

Kant's Theory of the Good Will

I. The Problem: Is it always good to do what you yourself think is right? Sometimes people seem to act out of conscience and we like to praise this. However, sometimes they then do things that turn out to hurt others. How can we praise such behavior? Is it enough to have a good intention or a good will? In this paper I plan to consider this issue from the perspective of the modern philosopher, Immanuel Kant, who is known for his views on the importance of motive in ethics. I will look briefly at who Kant was and then proceed to examine his views on the good will. Finally, I will see whether his views help me to answer the question I have posed in this paper.

II. Kant's Theory of the Good Will

   A. Who was Kant?

   B. What Kant holds on the good will

      1. It is always good

      2. To act with a good will is to act out of duty

      3. To act with a good will is to act out of respect for the moral law

   C. How this position relates to the initial problem

III. In this paper I have described Kant's views on the good will. I have found that, according to Kant, it is always good because the person who acts with a good will acts with the motive to do what morality requires. I then returned to the original questions that I posed to see how Kant answered them. Finally, in my view Kant does (not) give a reasonable answer to my question, because . . .

A Problem in Ethical Theory

Moral Relativism

Many people today seem to be moral relativists. We tend to believe that what is good for some people is not necessarily also good for others. In some circumstances it seems that it is permissible to lie, and at other times it seems that we ought to tell the truth. On the other hand, we also argue with one another all the time about what actually is right and wrong. We do not seem to always accept the view that there is no better way. Are we then moral relativists or not? What is moral relativism? This paper will address these questions. It will begin with an attempt to determine what ethical relativism is. Then it will look at some of the arguments about whether it is true. Finally it will draw some conclusions about whether we actually do believe in ethical relativism.

What Ethical Relativism Is

According to the philosopher, Richard Grace, ethical relativism is a theory which holds that " . . . ."[1] He goes on to explain that. . . . As I understand it, this would mean. . .

Two Views of Ethical Relativism

Professor Grace believes that what ethical relativism asserts is not correct. The reasons he gives for his view are. . . .[2]

References as Footnotes

---

1. Richard Grace, "What Relativism Is," <u>Journal of Philosophy</u>, vol. 3, no. 2 (June 1987): 5-6.

2. Ibid., 6.

A contrasting view is held by the philosopher Eleanor Brown. She writes that " . . . . ."[3] The reasons that Professor Brown believes that ethical relativism is a valid theory are. . . .

My Views

I believe that Professor Grace has given reasonable arguments against ethical relativism. In particular I agree with his argument that. . . . My reason for this is that this is true to my experience. For example. . . .

My Conclusions

In this paper I have looked at two views on ethical relativism, one critical of it and one supporting it. Now that I have become clearer about what relativism is and have looked at opposing views on it, I conclude that it is (not) a reasonable view. Additionally, I believe that if we understand relativism in the way that these philosophers have explained it, we generally do not behave as though we were ethical relativists. For example. . . . On the other hand, there are some things that are still questions in my mind about ethical relativism. Among these are. . . . I look forward sometime to finishing my inquiry into this difficult problem.

References as Endnotes

Endnotes

1. Richard Grace, "What Relativism Is," Journal of Philosophy, vol. 3, no. 2 (June 1987): 5-6.

2. Ibid., 6.

3. Eleanor Brown, Relativism (Cambridge, Mass: Harvard University Press, 1988), 35.

A Contemporary Ethical Issue

The Ethics of Cloning

Just the other day in the newspaper there was a report of a case of the cloning of a human being.[1] According to this report, while we have cloned vegetables and some small animals in the past, there has never before been a published report of a case of a human being being cloned. This case has raised quite a stir. In particular many people have raised ethical questions about this case. There is a diversity of opinion about whether such a practice is right or wrong. In this paper I will examine the ethical debate over the cloning of human beings. I will begin with a description of the process and this case. Next I will summarize the arguments for and against this practice. Finally I will present my own conclusions about the ethics of cloning human beings.

What Is Cloning?

There are two types of cloning.[2] One is. . . . The other is. . . . In this case the second type was used. What these scientists did was. . . .

The Case against Cloning

Many people wonder about the ethics of cloning human beings. Some express fears that it would be abused. For example, Professor . . . is quoted in the news article saying that. . . .[3] The idea seems to be that many people might have themselves cloned so that they could use this clone for organ transplants. Others worry that. . . . The arguments of Professor . . . seem reasonable. I especially agree with him that. . . .

The Case in Favor of Cloning

On the other hand, Doctor . . . and others argue that with the right kinds of safeguards the cloning of humans would be just as ethically acceptable as the cloning of carrots. Among the safeguards that they list are. . . .[4] One of the problems that I see with this position is. . . .

My Conclusions

In this paper I have found that the project to clone human beings consists of a process of. . . . I have looked at ethical arguments in support of and critical of this procedure when applied to humans. I conclude that while there may be some advantages to be gained from this method of producing babies, what worries me about cloning humans is. . . . I will continue to follow this issue as it develops, for I'm sure that this is not the last time we will hear of the cloning of humans nor the last of the debate about its ethical implications.

Endnotes

1. The Sue City Daily News, January 17, 1993, C7.

2. Jane Gray, Modern Genetics (New York: The American Press, 1988), 5-10.

3. The Sue City Daily News, C7.

4. See Chapter 4 in Martin Sheen and Sam Spade, Cloning (San Francisco: The Free Press, 1991), 200-248.

Index